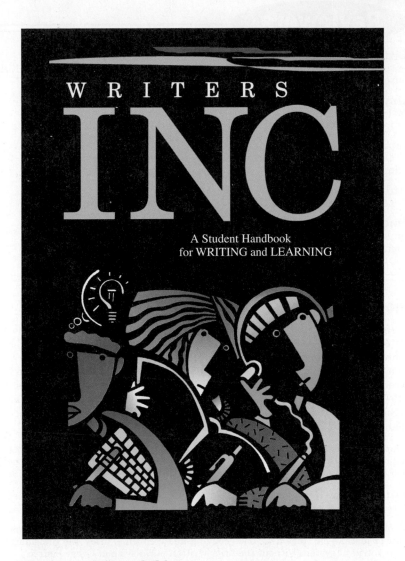

WRITERS INC

A Student Handbook
for WRITING and LEARNING

Written and Compiled by

Patrick Sebranek, Dave Kemper, and Verne Meyer

Illustrated by **Chris Krenzke**

WRITE SOURCE®

GREAT SOURCE EDUCATION GROUP
a Houghton Mifflin Company
Wilmington, Massachusetts

Reviewers

Britta Carns
Renton School District
Renton, Washington

Edmund Desmond
Hofstra University
Hempstead, New York

Susan Dinges
Mt. Olive Township Public Schools
Budd Lake, New Jersey

Paula Denise Findley
White Hall, Arkansas

Timothy R. Hart, Ed. D.
Cincinnati Public Schools
Cincinnati, Ohio

Stephanie Anne Izabal
Huntington Beach Unified High
  School District
Huntington Beach, California

Harriet Maher
Lafayette Parish School System
Lafayette, Louisiana

Jenny R. May
Mason City Schools
Mason, Ohio

Constance McGee
Pembroke Pines, Florida

Marie T. Raduazzo
Arlington Public Schools
Arlington, Massachusetts

Acknowledgements

Writers INC is a reality because of the help and advice of our team of students, educators, writers, editors, and designers: Laura Bachman, Ron Bachman, William Baughn, Amy Bauman, Heather Bazata, Colleen Belmont, Chris Erickson, Hillary Gammons, Mariellen Hanrahan, Tammy Hintz, Mary Anne Hoff, Lois Krenzke, Joseph Lee, Joyce Becker Lee, Ellen Leitheusser, Douglas Niles, Kelly King, Rob King, Pamela Reigel, Christine Rieker, Steven Schend, Janae Sebranek, Lester Smith, Vicki Spandel, Julie Spicuzza, Stephen D. Sullivan, Randy VanderMey, John Van Rys, Jean Varley, and Claire Ziffer.

Printed in the United States of America

International Standard Book Number: 978-0-669-52994-4 (hardcover)

5 6 7 8 9 10 - 1083 - 11 10

International Standard Book Number: 978-0-669-52995-1 (softcover)

6 7 8 9 10 - 1083 - 11 10

4500238603

Using the Handbook

Your *Writers INC* handbook provides concise, easy-to-use guidelines, models, and strategies to help you with all of your writing. If that's not enough, you can also refer to our Web site **www.thewritesource.com** for more information. Here are some of the writing aids you will find on the Web site:

- links to publishing sites;
- additional writing samples, including an APA research paper;
- MLA and APA documentation updates; and
- a sample multimedia report.

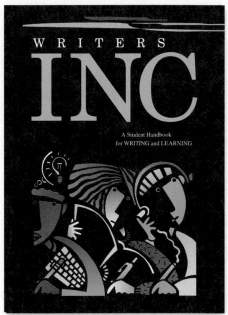

Writers INC will also help you with your other learning skills, including critical reading, test taking, note taking, and Internet searches.

In addition, the "Student Almanac" in the back of the handbook contains tables, lists, maps, terms, and charts covering everything from science to history.

Your handbook guide . . .

The **Table of Contents** (starting on the next page) lists the five major sections of the handbook and the chapters found in each. Use the table of contents when you're looking for a *general* topic.

The **Index** (starting on page 620) provides a thorough listing of the information covered in *Writers INC*. Use the index when you're looking for a *specific* topic.

The **Color Coding** used for the "Proofreader's Guide" (the yellow pages) makes this important section easy to find. The guide covers punctuation, capitalization, spelling, usage, grammar, and more.

The **Cross-References** throughout the handbook tell you where to turn for more information about a topic. Some of these references are within the text. *Example:* (See page 5). Other cross-references are set off from the text because of their importance. (See *example* below.)

[HOT LINK] See "Assessment Rubric," page 138, for a helpful revising and editing guide.

Table of **Contents**

The Process of Writing

UNDERSTANDING THE WRITING PROCESS

Why Write? 1
Writing as a Process 3
One Writer's Process 9
Traits of Effective Writing 21
Writing with a Computer 27
Publishing Your Writing 33

USING THE WRITING PROCESS

A Guide to Prewriting 41
A Guide to Drafting 53
A Guide to Revising 59
A Guide to Group Advising 73
A Guide to Editing and Proofreading 79

BASIC ELEMENTS OF WRITING

Writing Sentences 85
Writing Paragraphs 99

THE ART OF WRITING

Writing with Style 111
Writer's Resource 121

The Forms of Writing

PERSONAL WRITING

Journal Writing   **131**
Descriptive Writing   **135**
Narrative Writing   **139**

CREATIVE WRITING

Writing Stories and Plays   **151**
Writing Poetry   **163**
  Poetry Terms   **170**

ACADEMIC WRITING

Writing Expository Essays   **173**
Other Forms of Expository Writing   **183**
  Process Essay   **184**
  Essay of Definition   **186**
  Cause-Effect Essay   **188**
  Comparison-Contrast Essay   **191**
  Essay of Opposing Ideas   **194**
Writing Persuasive Essays   **197**
Other Forms of Persuasive Writing   **207**
  Pet Peeve Essay   **208**
  Editorial   **210**
  Personal Commentary   **212**
  Problem-Solution Essay   **214**
  Essay of Argumentation   **217**
Writing a Position Paper   **221**

The Forms of Writing

RESPONDING TO LITERATURE

Personal Responses to Literature **233**
Writing a Book Review **239**
Writing a Literary Analysis **245**
  Literary Terms **253**

RESEARCH WRITING

Writing the Research Paper **263**
Writing Responsibly **273**
MLA Documentation Style **281**
Sample MLA Research Paper **299**
APA Documentation Style **309**

WORKPLACE WRITING

Writing Business Letters **321**
Special Forms of Workplace Writing **329**
  Memos **330**
  E-Mail Messages **332**
  Brochures **334**
  Résumés **336**

The Tools of Writing

SEARCHING FOR INFORMATION

Types of Information   339

Using the Internet   347

Using the Library   353

READING SKILLS

Reading Graphics   367

Critical Reading Skills   373

Improving Vocabulary Skills   385

STUDY SKILLS

Improving Classroom Skills   401

Listening and Note-Taking Skills   407

Writing to Learn   415

Test-Taking Skills   423

Taking Exit and Entrance Exams   437

SPEAKING, THINKING, AND VIEWING SKILLS

Speech Skills   453

Multimedia Reports   465

Thinking Skills   469

Viewing Skills   479

Proofreader's Guide

MARKING PUNCTUATION

Period **487**

Question Mark **488**

Exclamation Point **488**

Comma **489**

Semicolon **493**

Colon **494**

Hyphen **495**

Apostrophe **498**

Quotation Marks **500**

Italics (Underlining) **502**

Parentheses **503**

Dash **504**

Ellipsis **505**

Brackets **506**

CHECKING MECHANICS

Capitalization **507**

Plurals **510**

Numbers **512**

Abbreviations **513**

Acronyms and Initialisms **515**

Commonly Misspelled Words **517**

USING THE RIGHT WORD **523**

PARTS OF SPEECH

Noun **533**

Pronoun **535**

Verb **539**

Adjective **545**

Adverb **546**

Preposition **547**

Conjunction **548**

Interjection **548**

USING THE LANGUAGE

Constructing Sentences **550**

Using Phrases **552**

Using Clauses **553**

Using Sentence Variety **554**

Diagramming Sentences **556**

Getting Sentence Parts to Agree **558**

Using Fair Language **561**

Student Almanac

LANGUAGE

Manual Alphabet   **565**
The History of the English Language   **566**
Traffic Signs   **568**
Common Parliamentary Procedures   **569**
Six-Year Calendar   **570**

SCIENCE

Weights and Measures   **571**
The Metric System   **573**
Handy Conversion Factors   **574**
Periodic Table of the Elements   **575**
Our Solar System   **576**
Computer and Internet Terms   **577**

MATHEMATICS

Math Symbols   **581**
Math Tables   **582**
Math Terms   **583**

GEOGRAPHY

Using the Maps   **589**
World Maps   **591**
Index to World Maps   **601**

GOVERNMENT

Branches of the U.S. Federal Government   **603**
The U.S. Constitution   **604**
U.S. Presidents and Vice Presidents   **607**
Order of Presidential Succession   **608**

HISTORY

Historical Time Line   **609**

INDEX   620

Understanding the Writing
PROCESS

Why Write?   1

Writing as a Process   3

One Writer's Process   9

Traits of Effective Writing   21

Writing with a Computer   27

Publishing Your Writing   33

> "Writing allows you to penetrate your life
> and learn to trust your own mind."
>
> —Natalie Goldberg

WHY Write?

Writing requires practice—a lot of it. You wouldn't expect to pick up a guitar and play it with ease and skill, unless you practiced a lot. Well, the same is true of writing. You shouldn't expect to write well, unless you practice. We may be stating the obvious here—but this point is so important that it can't be emphasized enough. You will never appreciate the best that writing has to offer unless you regularly put pen to paper (or fingers to the keyboard).

Writing regularly—as in every day—will help you develop writing fluency, which essentially means feeling comfortable with the act of writing. Writer Dan Kirby and his coauthors make this statement in their book, *Inside Out*: "Fluency is the first consideration. It is the basis for all that follows." Once you feel at ease with writing, many good things will begin to happen. (See the next page.)

Tip If you aren't already writing in a journal or notebook, start as soon as possible. No other activity can help you as much as journaling can to become fluent as a writer.

Preview

- **Reasons to Write**
- ***Writers INC* and You**

Reasons to Write

To Develop a Personal Voice

You may have heard your teachers talk about the importance of voice in writing. Writer Donald Graves explains voice in this way: "Voice is the imprint of ourselves in our writing. Take the voice away . . . and there's no writing, just words following words." Voice is the writer's unique personality that comes through in his or her writing.

If you are an infrequent writer, there's little chance that your writing voice will develop. On the other hand, if you are a frequent and fluent writer, your writing should speak with a great deal of personality and appeal.

Remember: Write to discover your personal voice.

To Become More Reflective

You probably lead a busy life. As a result, you may have little time to relax and reflect on things. This is where writing can help. By its very nature, writing is perfectly suited to examining daily happenings.

Writer Ray Bradbury once said, "Writing lets the world burn through you." If you write regularly in a journal, you know exactly what he means. In a typical entry, you will consider the events in your life, and in the process, ask questions, make decisions, and set goals. In short, you can reflect—or "let the world burn through you."

Remember: Write to reflect on your life.

To Become More Analytical

Writing is often called thinking on paper because it forces you to concentrate all of your attention on the words in front of you. As writer Paul J. Meyer states, "Writing crystallizes thought," helping you see things more clearly and logically.

With practice, you will become more analytical in your writing, intent on finding the patterns and relationships between ideas. Before you know it, you'll be making many interesting connections and comparisons. Reaching this level of maturity should be one of your primary goals as a writer.

Remember: Write to think more analytically.

Writers INC and You

Writers INC is a portable resource of valuable information. What you won't find are exercises or assignments—not one. Note the subtitle on the cover: *A Student Handbook for Writing and Learning. Writers INC* is a guide for your own writing and learning. Now and for years to come, it will help you make writing an important part of your life.

"When I write, I am always struck at how magical and unexpected the process turns out to be."

—Ralph Fletcher

Writing as a
PROCESS

At the start of her career, author Annie Dillard thought that all you really needed was "paper, pen, and a lap" to write something. But before too long, she discovered that "in order to write so much as a sonnet [a 14-line poem], I needed a warehouse." Of course, the author is exaggerating, but only to make a point. Dillard soon learned that she had to spend a lot of time—and write numerous drafts—to produce effective finished products.

You may know from experience what Dillard is talking about. Think of your best essays, reports, and stories. You probably put forth a great deal of effort (enough to fill a warehouse?) to produce each one, changing some parts many times from draft to draft. You may also know that writing really becomes satisfying when it reflects your best efforts. If you work hard at your writing, you—and your readers—will almost always be pleased with the results.

Preview

- **Writing Is Discovering**
- **The Writing Process in Action**
- **A Closer Look at the Process**
- **Advice from the Pros**

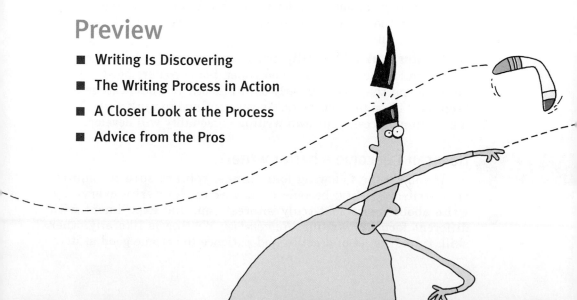

Writing Is Discovering

Writing is not trying to figure out everything you want to say *before* you put pen to paper or fingers to the keyboard. Working in this way will result in having very little to say, or worse yet, having nothing to say at all. (Ever hear of writer's block?) Writing almost always works best when it springs from the discoveries you make *during* the writing process.

Take NOTE The five steps in the writing process discussed in this handbook are **prewriting, writing the first draft, revising, editing and proofreading,** and **publishing.**

Setting the Stage

Before you use the writing process, it's important that you understand the following points about writing:

- **Experience shapes writing.** Each of your experiences becomes part of what you know, what you think, and what you have to say in your writing. Writing is the process of capturing those thoughts and experiences in words.

- **Writing never follows a straight path.** Writing is a backward as well as a forward activity, so don't expect to move neatly through the steps in the writing process. Writing by its very nature includes detours, wrong turns, and repeat visits.

- **Each assignment presents special challenges.** For one assignment, you might search high and low for a topic. For another one, you might do a lot of prewriting and planning. For still another, you might be ready to write your first draft almost immediately.

- **Each writer works differently.** Some writers work more in their heads, while others work more on paper. Some writers need to talk about their writing early on, while others would rather keep their ideas to themselves. As you continue to work with the writing process, your own writing personality will develop.

FAQ **How can I become a better writer?**

If you do the following four things, you are sure to improve your writing ability: become a regular reader, write every day, write about topics that truly interest you, and experiment with different forms of writing. *Remember:* Writing is like any other skill. It takes a lot of practice and patience to become good at it.

The **Writing Process** in Action

The next two pages provide a basic look at the writing process in action. Use this information as a general guide whenever you write.

■ PREWRITING

Choosing a Topic and Gathering Details

1. Search for a meaningful writing idea—one that truly interests you and meets the requirements of the assignment.

2. Use a selecting strategy (listing, clustering, freewriting, and so on) to identify possible topics. (See pages 43–45.)

3. Learn as much as you can about your topic. (See pages 46–49.)

4. Decide on an interesting or important part of the topic—your focus— to develop. Express your focus in a sentence to help map out your writing.

5. Think about an overall plan or design for organizing your writing. This plan can be anything from a brief list to a detailed outline. (See page 52.)

■ WRITING THE FIRST DRAFT

Connecting Your Ideas

1. Write the first draft while your prewriting is still fresh in your mind.

2. Set the right tone by giving your opening paragraph special attention. (See page 55.)

3. Refer to your plan for the main part of your writing but be flexible. A more interesting route may unfold as you write.

4. Don't worry about getting everything right at this point; just concentrate on developing your ideas.

┌HELP FILE────────────────

Experienced writers often view the drafting process as a stimulating release, especially if they have spent a lot of time researching a topic and have a lot of ideas percolating in their minds. Approach your own drafting with the same kind of energy and enthusiasm, and you'll do your best work.

■ **REVISING**

Improving Your Writing

1. Review your first draft, checking the ideas, organization, voice, word choice, and sentence fluency of your writing. (See pages 65–72.)

2. Ask at least one classmate to react to your work.

3. Add, cut, reword, or rearrange ideas as necessary. (You may have to change some parts several times before they say what you want them to say.)

4. Carefully assess the effectiveness of your opening and closing paragraphs.

5. Look for special opportunities to make your writing as meaningful and interesting as possible. (See page 64.)

■ **EDITING AND PROOFREADING**

Checking for Accuracy

1. Edit your revised writing for conventions.

2. Have a dictionary, thesaurus, and your *Writers INC* handbook close at hand as you work.

3. Ask a reliable editor—a friend, a classmate, a parent, or a teacher—to check your writing for errors you may have missed.

4. Prepare a neat final copy of your writing.

5. Proofread the final draft for errors before submitting it.

■ **PUBLISHING**

Sharing Your Work

1. Share the finished product with your teacher, writing peers, friends, and family members.

2. Decide if you will include the writing in your portfolio. (See page 35.)

3. Post your writing on your personal or class Web site or elsewhere online. (See pages 38–39.)

4. Consider submitting your work to a school, a local, or a national publication. (Ask your teacher for recommendations for places to publish.) Make sure to follow the requirements for submitting manuscripts. (See pages 36–37.)

A Closer Look at the Process

Keep the following tips in mind whenever you write. They will help make each of your writing projects satisfying and meaningful.

Keep time on your side. Effective writing requires a lot of searching, planning, writing, reflecting, and revising. In order to do all of these things, you must give yourself plenty of time. If your teacher provides you with a timetable for your writing, make sure to follow it. Otherwise, create your own. (Always reserve plenty of time for revising.) As you probably know, waiting until the last minute takes all of the fun out of writing.

   Remember: Good writing takes time.

Limit your topic. It would be almost impossible to write an effective essay or report about a general subject such as photography. You wouldn't know where to begin or end. But if you limited this subject to a specific topic—let's say, the use of photography by investigative reporters—then you would find it much easier to manage your writing.

   Remember: Good writing has a focus, meaning that it stems from and is built around a limited topic.

Work from a position of authority. The more you know about your topic, the easier it is to write about it. So collect as much information as you can during prewriting—tapping into your own thoughts, asking other people for their ideas, consulting print material, surfing the Net, and so on.

   Remember: Good writing requires good information.

Pace yourself when you revise. Many of the pros believe that the real writing takes place when they add, cut, rearrange, and rewrite different parts of their first drafts. They do not rush these changes or make them all at once. Instead, they pace themselves, working very patiently and methodically at times, making revisions until all of the parts seem clear and complete.

   Remember: Good writing usually requires a series of changes before it says exactly what you want it to say.

Take some risks. Don't be afraid to experiment in your writing. For example, you might share a personal story in an essay or develop an interview report in a question-and-answer format, much like you would find in many magazine articles. Then again, you might change the sequence of events in a narrative to add suspense. If one experiment doesn't work out, you can always try something else.

   Remember: Good writing is a process of discovery.

Advice from the Pros

Keep the following thoughts in mind as you develop your writing. They come from experienced authors who appreciate writing as a process of discovery.

"I don't pick subjects so much as they pick me."

—Andy Rooney

"When I speak to students about writing, I hold myself up as an example of that ancient axiom—write about what you know."

—Robert Cormier

"The inspiration comes while you write."

—Madeleine L'Engle

"Writing comes more easily if you have something to say."

—Sholem Asch

"I think one is constantly startled by the things that appear before you on the page while you write."

—Shirley Hazzard

"By the time I reach a fifth version, my writing begins to have its own voice."

—Ashley Bryan

"Half of my life is an act of revision."

—John Irving

"I am an obsessive rewriter, doing one draft and then another and another, usually five. In a way, I have nothing to say but a great deal to add."

—Gore Vidal

"I believe in impulse and naturalness, but followed by discipline in the cutting."

—Anaïs Nin

"Write visually, write clearly, and make every word count."

—Gloria D. Miklowitz

> "Writing is really rewriting—making the story better, clearer, truer."
>
> —Robert Lipsyte

ONE WRITER'S Process

When you install new computer software, the instructions guide you through the setup process one step at a time. In a similar way, the writing process helps you produce effective essays, narratives, and reports—one step at a time. To become a skilled and confident writer, you must gain a working knowledge of these steps: prewriting, writing, revising, editing and proofreading, and publishing. *Remember:* Developing a piece of writing can be a complex undertaking; breaking it down into steps keeps you on track and helps you do your best work.

This chapter shows how student writer Todd Michaels developed an expository essay using the steps in the writing process. As you follow his work, you'll see how he shaped his initial idea into an effective finished piece of writing.

Preview

- Prewriting: Selecting and Gathering
- Writing the First Draft: Connecting the Ideas
- Revising: Improving the Writing
- Revising: Checking for Style
- Editing: Checking for Accuracy
- Publishing: Sharing the Final Copy

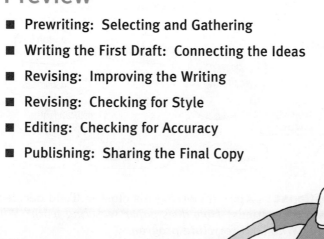

■ **PREWRITING**

Selecting and Gathering

In an environmental science class, Todd Michaels' teacher gave the following assignment:

> **In an expository essay, examine one example of the reduce-reuse-recycle principle in action.**

On the next two pages, you'll see how Todd selected a topic, gathered information about it, and focused his thoughts for writing.

1. **Selecting a Topic . . .** Todd freely listed possible topics—glass recycling, secondhand stores, paper recycling, e-mail versus paper mail, new automotive technology, and so on. After discussing his list with a classmate, he selected paper recycling as his topic.

2. **Exploring First Thoughts . . .** To collect his initial thoughts about his topic, Todd wrote freely for 10 minutes about paper recycling. Here is one passage from this writing.

> I must have delivered thousands of newspapers when I had a paper route. I wonder how many pounds I carried? A lot of that paper came from recycled stuff, and lots of people recycled their newspapers and other paper scraps. Today, we're still recycling, but how's it going? Is America still dumping a lot of paper in landfills? Are we wasting less paper because of e-mail and recycling . . . ?

3. **Gathering Details . . .** To explore his subject further, Todd completed a "paper-recycling" cluster. (See page 43.)

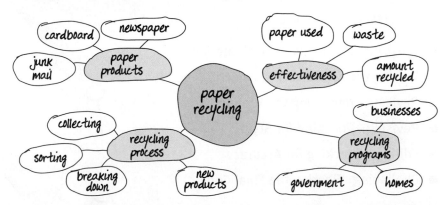

4. **Generating Questions . . .** After reviewing his cluster, Todd decided to explore the following questions: *How does paper recycling work? What paper gets recycled? Who uses recycling programs?*

5. **Carrying Out Research . . .** With these questions in mind, Todd read articles, searched Web sites, and visited a recycling plant. He took notes that included facts, analysis, quotations, and paraphrases. Here are some of his notes:

Paper Recycling

"Municipal Solid Waste." Environmental Protection Agency.
  (April 27, 2004) www.epa.gov
- recycling has risen from 34 million tons in 1990 to
  68 million tons in 2001
- 45% of paper is now recycled
- paper accounted for largest source of trash in landfills,
  so recycling paper has had greatest impact

Beck, R. W. "U. S. Recycling Economic Information Study." (July 2001).
- in 2001, recycling businesses employed 1.1 million people, with
  payroll of $37 billion and gross revenues of $236 billion
- largest part of these businesses is paper recycling

Case, Clifford. Testimony before the U. S. Senate. (July 1, 2002).
- "Recycling makes environmental and economic sense."
- (Case is founder of the National Recycling Coalition)

---

6. **Forming a Thesis . . .** To guide his writing, Todd needed to write a thesis statement. (See page 51.) Based on his thinking and research, he came up with the following statement:

> Paper recycling is such a success that it should encourage the United States to reuse even more materials.

NOTE As Todd's essay evolves, he may need to revise this statement.

7. **Planning the First Draft . . .** After forming his thesis, Todd created a writing plan by listing the main ideas he wanted to cover in his essay.

Writing Plan
1. Extent of paper recycling
2. Businesses that recycle paper
3. How paper recycling works
4. Problems with paper recycling

■ **WRITING THE FIRST DRAFT**

Connecting the Ideas

Todd wrote his first draft freely, using his writing plan and notes as a general guide. His goal was to get his ideas on paper without worrying about every word and comma being right.

Paper Recycling

The opening paragraph leads up to the thesis statement.

From the home to large paper chutes at the office, paper recycling has become an everyday occurrence. Americans have stopped there throwaway attitudes with a committment to recycle. Recycling has risen from 34 million tons in 1990 to 98 million tons in 2001. Paper recycling is very important to America and the environment. Paper recycling is such a success that it should encourage the United States to reuse even more materials.

The writer develops each main point with details.

Paper recycling has indeed become a big deal, and a big business. Clifford Case testified before the senate in 2002, "Recycling makes environmental and economic sense." Americans they through away more paper (38 percent of the total waste) than anything else so recycling means big gains. Businesses save lots of paper just by using e-mail to communicate with each other and the Internet to advertise. For example, Fort Howard Corp. at Green Bay uses recycled paper for all its bathroom tissue, it recycles enough paper to cover 100 acres 18 ft deep. The U.S. Postal Service recycles more than a million tons of material and buys $160 million worth of recycled paper each year. Foreign countries are buying our paper waste. If you see a MADE IN TAIWAN tag, it probably was a newspaper in America.

The recycling process is explained.

Paper recycling works by first getting paper collected and sorted. Recyclable paper includes computer printouts, newspaper, scrap paper, and cardboard boxes. The paper is turned into pulp which is dried and the new paper is formed on cylinders. A large spinning blade mixes the paper to a pulp. This new paper is used to make newspapers, cereal and shoe boxes, toilet tissue, egg cartons, and even in building insulation and cow bedding!

Each paragraph covers a different aspect of recycling.

But not all types of paper can be recycled. Carbon paper, glossy paper, photographs, or paper with tape, glue or staples. The Recycling equipment can't take that stuff out. Changes are being made that might make it possible to work with these items. Equipment is currently under development to remove ink from glossy magazines and catalogs.

The writer concludes by restating his main point.

Although landfills are still filling up with more than 2/3 of our recyclable waste, paper recycling has become a success story. While only 18 percent of metal cans and 2 percent of plastics are recycled, 40 percent of white paper is too. In 2001, recycling was a $220 billion business. It could be much larger. Big business is very involved. Recycling fever hasn't been this high in the U.S. since World War II when people felt it was there duty to recycle. Americans are recycling paper on a daily basis so they can save the environment and there future.

■ **REVISING**

Improving the Writing

Todd took a break after finishing his first draft. When he was ready to review his work, he looked carefully at the ideas he had developed. He wrote brief notes in the margin, identifying parts that needed to be changed. (Todd used the "Editing and Proofreading Marks" found inside the back cover.)

Todd's comments

Paper Recycling

curbside collection
From the home ∧to large paper chutes at the office, paper

recycling has become an everyday occurrence. Americans
replaced
have ~~stopped~~ there throwaway attitudes with a committment
and they are recycling in record numbers
to recycle ∧ Recycling has risen from 34 million tons in 1990
with paper being the largest part of that amount
to 98 million tons in 2001, ∧ ~~Paper recycling is very important~~

~~to America and the enviroment.~~ Paper recycling is such a

success that it should encourage the United States to reuse

even more materials.

> **Cut sentence; doesn't add anything new.**

Paper recycling has indeed become a big deal, and a big
, the founder of the National Recycling Coalition,
business. Clifford Case ∧ testified before the senate in 2002,

"Recycling makes environmental and economic sense."

Americans they through away more paper (38 percent of
there is much to be
the total waste) than anything else so, ∧ ~~recycling means big~~
gained by recycling paper.
~~gains. Businesses save lots of paper just by using e-mail to~~

~~communicate with each other and the Internet to advertise.~~

For example, Fort Howard Corp. at Green Bay uses recycled
each year
paper for all its bathroom tissue, it recycles enough paper ∧ to

cover 100 acres 18 ft deep. The U.S. Postal Service recycles

more than a million tons of material and buys $160 million
and it won the 1999 Environmental Mailer of the Year Award.
worth of recycled paper each year ∧ Foreign countries are
on a manufactured paper product
buying our paper waste. If you see a MADE IN TAIWAN tag ∧

it probably was a newspaper in America.

> **Identify the speaker.**

> **Cut unnecessary idea.**

> **Tell how often.**

> **Add information about the award.**

Include a topic sentence.

 # The process of paper recycling is simple. First paper is
~~Paper recycling works by first getting paper~~ collected
and sorted. Recyclable paper includes computer printouts,
newspaper, scrap paper, and cardboard boxes. The ~~paper is~~
paper
~~turned into~~ pulp ~~which~~ is dried and the new paper is formed
on cylinders. *A large spinning blade mixes the paper to a*
pulp. This new paper is used to make newspapers, cereal

Reorder these items.

and shoe boxes, toilet tissue, egg cartons, and even in
building insulation and cow bedding!
                    Recycling equipment cannot handle
        But not all types of paper can be recycled. Carbon
paper, glossy paper, photographs, or paper with tape, glue or
These types of paper must be sorted out.
staples. ~~The recycling equipment can't take that stuff out.~~

Clarify this idea.

Advancements
~~Changes~~ are being made that might make it possible to
work with these items. Equipment is currently under
development to remove ink from glossy magazines and
catalogs.

        Although landfills are still filling up with more than 2/3
of our recyclable waste, paper recycling has become a
success story. While only 18 percent of metal cans and 2
percent of plastics are recycled, 40 percent of white paper is
in fact, recycled.
~~too.~~ In 2001, recycling was a $220 billion business. It could
                has discovered the advantages of paper recycling.
be much larger. Big business ~~is very involved.~~ Recycling
fever hasn't been this high in the U.S. since World War II
when people felt it was there duty to recycle. ~~Americans~~
Perhaps people today feel that although it is there
~~are recycling paper on a daily basis so they can save the~~
environmental duty to recycle there are economic rewards as well.
~~environment and there future.~~

Be more specific here.

Rework the closing sentence so it has more impact.

■ REVISING

Checking for Style

After revising his draft for large-scale issues, Todd was ready to revise it for style. He read his work aloud, checking for sentence smoothness and strong nouns, verbs, and modifiers. He made his changes on a printout of his first revision.

Paper Recycling

Phrasing is clarified.

From ~~the~~ home curbside collection to large *scrap* paper chutes *at* at the office, paper recycling has become an everyday occurrence. Americans have replaced there throwaway attitudes with a committment to recycle and they are recycling in record numbers. Recycling has risen from 34 million tons in 1990 to 68 million tons in 2001, with paper

Word choice is improved.

being the largest part of that ~~amount.~~ *increase.* Paper recycling is such a success that it should encourage the United States to reuse even more materials.

Paper recycling has indeed become a big deal, and a big business. Clifford Case, the founder of the National Recycling Coalition, testified before the *U.S.* senate in 2002, "Recycling makes environmental and economic sense." Americans they through away more paper (38 percent of the total waste) than anything else so there is much to be gained by recycling paper. For example, Fort Howard Corp. at Green Bay uses recycled paper for all its bathroom tissue, it recycles enough

A specific noun is used.

paper each year to cover 100 acres 18 ft deep. The U.S. Postal Service recycles more than a million tons of ~~material~~ *scrap paper* and

A rambling sentence is fixed.

buys $160 million worth of recycled paper each year ~~and~~ it won the 1999 Environmental Mailer of the Year Award. Foreign countries are *even* buying our paper waste. If you see a MADE IN TAIWAN tag on a manufactured paper product, *in another life* it probably was a newspaper in America.

The process of paper recycling is simple. First paper is collected and sorted. Recyclable paper includes computer printouts, newspapers, scrap paper, and cardboard boxes. A large spinning blade mixes the paper to a pulp. The pulp is dried *on screens* and the new paper is formed on cylinders. This new paper is used to make newspapers, cereal and shoe boxes, toilet tissue, egg cartons, ~~and even in~~ building insulation and *livestock* ~~cow~~ bedding!

~~But~~ not all types of paper can be recycled. Recycling equipment cannot handle carbon paper, glossy paper, photographs, or paper with tape, glue or staples. These types of papers must be sorted out. *However, new technologies may* ~~Advancements are being made that might~~ make it possible to work with these items. *For example* Equipment is currently under development to remove ink from glossy magazines and catalogs.

Although landfills are still filling up with more than 2/3 of our recyclable waste, paper recycling has become a success story. While only 18 percent of metal cans and 2 percent of plastics are recycled, 40 percent of white paper is in fact, recycled. In 2001, recycling was a $220 billion business. *but* It could be much larger. Big business has discovered the advantages of paper recycling. Recycling fever hasn't been this high in the U.S. since World War II when people felt it was there duty to recycle. Perhaps people today *realize* ~~feel~~ that although it is there environmental duty to recycle, there are economic rewards as well.

Modifying phrase is added.

Ideas are made parallel.

A specific subject is used; passive verb phrase "are being made" is cut.

Transitional words are used.

Two sentences are combined.

A stronger verb is used.

■ **EDITING**

Checking for Accuracy

Having revised his essay for style, Todd turned his attention to the accuracy of his writing. He checked for spelling, grammar, usage, and punctuation errors. He also added the sources he used for outside information. (Some sources are in parentheses.)

A hyphen is added to a compound adjective.

Usage and spelling errors are corrected.

A source is added.

The double subject "they" is deleted; a usage error is corrected.

A comma splice is corrected; an abbreviation is spelled out.

Paper Recycling

From curbside collection at home to large scrap-paper chutes at the office, paper recycling has become an everyday occurrence. Americans have replaced ~~there~~ *their* throwaway attitudes with a ~~committment~~ *commitment* to recycle, and they are recycling in record numbers. Recycling has risen from 34 million tons in 1990 to 68 million tons in 2001, with paper being the largest part of that increase. *(Municipal)* Paper recycling is such a success that it should encourage the United States to reuse even more materials.

Paper recycling has indeed become a big deal, and a big business. Clifford Case, the founder of the National Recycling Coalition, testified before the U. S. senate in 2002, "Recycling makes environmental and economic sense." Americans ~~they~~ *threw* ~~through~~ away more paper (38 percent of the total waste) than anything else so there is much to be gained by recycling paper. For example, Fort Howard ~~Corp.~~ *Corporation* at Green Bay uses recycled paper for all its bathroom tissue, it recycles enough paper each year to cover 100 acres 18 ~~ft~~ *feet* deep. *(Howard 230)* The U.S. Postal Service recycles more than a million tons of scrap paper and buys $160 million worth of recycled paper each year. It won the 1999 Environmental Mailer of the Year Award. Foreign countries are even buying our paper waste. If you see a

MADE IN TAIWAN tag on a manufactured paper product, in another life it probably was a newspaper in America.

The process of paper recycling is simple. First paper is collected and sorted. Recyclable paper includes computer printouts, newspapers, scrap paper, and cardboard boxes. A large spinning blade mixes the paper to a pulp. The pulp is dried on screens and the new paper is formed on cylinders. This new paper is used to make newspapers, cereal and shoe boxes, toilet tissue, egg cartons, building insulation, and livestock bedding.

Not all types of paper can be recycled. Recycling equipment cannot handle carbon paper, glossy paper, photographs, or paper with tape, glue or staples. These types of papers must be sorted out. However, new technologies may make it possible to work with these items. For example, equipment is currently under development to remove ink from glossy magazines and catalogs.

Although landfills are still filling up with more than two-thirds 2/3 of our recyclable waste, paper recycling has become a success story. While only 18 percent of metal cans and 2 percent of plastics are recycled, 45 40 percent of white paper is in fact, recycled. In 2001, recycling was a $236 $220 billion business, but it could be much larger. (Beck) Recycling fever hasn't been this high in the United States U.S. since World War II when people felt it was their there duty to recycle. Perhaps people today realize that, although it is their there environmental duty to recycle, there are economic rewards as well.

A comma is added to a compound sentence; end punctuation is changed.

A comma is added to a series.

A fraction is spelled out.

Numbers are changed for accuracy.

Usage errors are corrected; a comma is added.

■ **PUBLISHING**

Sharing the Final Copy

Todd produced a neat final copy of his essay. He proofread this copy for errors before sharing it with his classmates. Here is a portion of Todd's first page.

Follow your teacher's directions for placement of name, class, and so on.

Todd Michaels

Ms. Herman

Environmental Science

January 20, 2010

Paper Recycling

From curbside collection at home to large scrap-paper chutes at the office, paper recycling has become an everyday occurrence. Americans have replaced their throwaway attitudes with a commitment to recycle, and they are recycling in record numbers. Recycling has risen from 34 million tons in 1990 to 118 million tons in 2008, with paper being the largest part of that increase (Municipal). Paper recycling is such a success that it should encourage the United States to reuse even more materials.

Points to Remember

■ **Do the necessary prewriting.** Todd gathered a great deal of information about his subject before he started writing. Thorough prewriting makes the rest of the writing process go more smoothly.

■ **Write with confidence.** Because of his thorough preparation, Todd was able to get all his thoughts on paper effectively.

■ **Expect to make many changes.** Todd wasn't satisfied with just making a few changes. He wanted to make all of his ideas as clear and complete as possible. Remember: No writer, not even the most accomplished author, ever gets it right the first or the second time.

"Good writing excites me and makes life worth living."

—Harold Pinter

Traits of
EFFECTIVE Writing

When you think of creative writing, you probably think of stories, poems, and plays—forms of writing that require a lot of imagination. This is creative writing in the traditional sense: an inventive, sometimes playful form of writing. And when you think of academic writing, you probably think of essays and research papers—forms of writing that require a lot of information and analysis, but not a lot of imagination.

However, it shouldn't be that way. In their own way, essays and research papers can be creative, too. Simply put, an essay that is informative *and* creative exhibits the basic traits found in all good writing: stimulating ideas, clear organization, engaging voice, and so on.

Learning about the traits of writing—and putting them into practice—will help you write better in all your classes.

Preview

- **Quick Guide**
- **The Traits in Action**
- **Checklist for Effective Writing**

"The greatest courtesy of all is to make [your writing] interesting."

—Scott Rice

Quick Guide

The **six traits** listed below identify the main features found in effective essays, stories, and articles. If you write with these traits in mind, you will most likely be pleased with the results.

IDEAS: Effective writing presents interesting and vital information about a specific topic. It has a clear purpose or focus, or as writer Donald Murray states, "It has a controlling vision, which orders what is being said." The ideas are thoroughly elaborated and analyzed and hold the reader's attention from start to finish.

ORGANIZATION: In terms of basic structure, good writing has a clearly developed beginning, middle, and ending. Within the text, transitions are used to show relationships between ideas. The overall arrangement of ideas unifies the writing and makes the writer's purpose clear.

VOICE: In the best writing, you can hear the writer's voice—her or his special way of expressing ideas and emotions. Voice gives writing personality: it shows that the writer sincerely cares about her or his topic and audience.

WORD CHOICE: In good writing, the nouns and verbs are specific. The modifiers are colorful (and used somewhat sparingly). The overall level of language helps to communicate the message and set an appropriate tone. In short, all the right words are in all the right places.

SENTENCE FLUENCY: Effective writing flows from sentence to sentence. But it isn't, by any means, predictable. Sentences vary in length, and they don't all begin in the same way. Sentence fluency gives rhythm to writing, which makes the writing enjoyable to read.

CONVENTIONS: Good writing follows the accepted standards of punctuation, mechanics, usage, and spelling. It is edited with care to ensure that the work is accurate and easy to follow.

The Traits in Action

On the next three pages, writing samples exhibit each of the traits of writing. These samples show quality writing in action.

Ideas

The following paragraph focuses on an interesting topic (two space rovers) and provides many engaging details that elaborate on that topic.

> **Vision and Opportunity are the most sophisticated robots ever designed by humans. Following several less-than-successful missions to Mars, these two rovers were launched in 2003. After a seven-month journey to the Red Planet, the rovers landed on opposite sides of Mars in January 2004. They went to work immediately, and a year later, the robots were still roving up hills and into craters, sending pictures and chemical and mineral analyses back to Earth. Each solar-powered rover photographed everything from the dirt underneath the vehicle's six tires to vast panoramas of the Martian landscape. Their drills bored holes in rocks while sensitive instruments analyzed the makeup of the planet. Together, the two rovers have provided the most detailed close-up of an alien world we have ever had.**

■ Explanations, descriptions, and facts provide the reader with a wealth of information about the topic.

Organization

In this paragraph, a student writer outlines the three main innovations of Dr. Maria Montessori. The details are organized by order of importance.

> **A hundred years ago, the Italian doctor Maria Montessori developed a revolutionary teaching method. The most innovative part of her approach was making students responsible for their own learning. Dr. Montessori urged teachers "to cease handing out the ordinary prizes and punishments" so that students had to rely on internal motivations to learn. That meant no grades and no detentions. Dr. Montessori also changed the structure of the classroom. She removed desks and seating charts to encourage students to move about freely in the classroom and select their own projects. This shift allowed each learner to set his or her own pace. Finally, Dr. Montessori mixed different ages and levels of students. Older students thus could help younger students, and both benefited. Over the last hundred years, Dr. Montessori's approach has become a popular alternative across the globe.**

■ Transitions such as *most innovative, also,* and *finally* guide the reader through the main points of the paragraph.

Voice

In the following closing paragraph, the writer reaffirms his argument that bilingual education promotes quality language learning. Notice how the writer's appealing, knowledgeable voice connects with his audience—his classmates.

> **The United States welcomes immigrants with the promise of opportunity, equality, freedom, and a better life. Bilingual education is the best way to fulfill that promise for immigrant students. It validates and celebrates the newcomers' cultures while teaching them the skills they'll need to be successful in this country. At the same time, mainstream students in this country have the chance to attain highly valued bilingual skills, right from the source. Bilingual education teaches newcomers not only English but also the language of freedom and equality for all. That's a language everyone can understand.**

- From sentence to sentence, the writer's sincere interest in the topic comes through: "The United States welcomes immigrants . . . ," "It validates and celebrates the newcomers' cultures . . . ," "That's a language everyone can understand."

Word Choice

In this passage, the writer shares information about the people that Christopher Columbus first met in the Americas. The writer chooses his words very carefully to help readers appreciate these people.

> **The word *Taino* means "men of the good," and from most indications the Taino were very good. Living on tropical islands in the Caribbean, the indigenous people of "La Taina" developed gentle personalities. And by all accounts, generosity and kindness directed daily life at the time of Taino contact with the Spanish. To understand the Taino world, picture South Pacific islands, lush and inviting. The people dwelled in small, spotless villages of neatly appointed thatch huts along inland rivers and coastal waters. These handsome people had no need of clothing for warmth. They bathed often, which prompted a curious royal law forbidding the practice. The Spanish obviously did not appreciate the benefits of regular bathing.**

- Notice the specific verbs such as *developed, directed, picture, bathed,* and *prompted,* and the colorful adjectives such as *tropical, indigenous, gentle, lush, inviting,* and *spotless.* These words help create the image of an untroubled, idyllic lifestyle.

Sentence Fluency

This paragraph is part of an analysis of two literary characters, Bigger in *Native Son* and Alan in *Equus*. Notice how the student writer varies the length and structure of her sentences.

> Bigger must struggle with the pressure and anxiety of his first job. Because of this family's desperate financial situation, he is forced to take the one job he is offered. Bigger works as a chauffeur for Mr. Dalton's wealthy suburban family. But the young man cannot relate to them. He sees himself as a foreigner, forced to live and work among the privileged. The Daltons tell him where, when, and even how to drive. Like Alan, Bigger cannot deal with the extreme discomfort he is feeling. After only two days on the job, he quits. Unlike Alan, however, Bigger does not have the option of getting a job that interests him.

- ■ Note that the sentences vary in length from 8 words to 18 words, and only two sentences begin the same way. This variety helps create a smooth flow of ideas.

Conventions

The following brief biographical paragraph shows mastery of conventions.

> Amelia Earhart is the most famous aviatrix in history. Much of her fame is due to her accomplishments in life, but some springs from the unsolved mystery surrounding her disappearance and death. This famous aviation pioneer never flew in an airplane until 1920, but by 1922, she had already set the woman's altitude record at 14,000 feet! In 1932, Earhart became the second person to fly solo across the Atlantic, exactly five years after Charles Lindbergh's historic flight. She followed this in 1935 with a daring flight from Hawaii to California. Two years later, Earhart accepted her greatest challenge: flying around the world. She flew more than 22,000 miles—from California to Florida; through South America, Africa and Asia; and then out across the Pacific. She departed from New Guinea on July 2. A few hours later, after a last cryptic radio message, Earhart and her airplane disappeared into the trackless waters. She lives on in the pages of history and in the hearts of young aviators everywhere.

- ■ Notice how the commas and semicolons direct the progression of events within different sentences. They help establish an effective, smooth rhythm in the passage.

Checklist for Effective Writing

If a piece of writing meets the following standards, it exhibits the traits of effective writing. Check your work using these standards.

Ideas

The writing . . .

_____ maintains a clear, specific focus or purpose.

_____ presents information that elaborates on the focus.

_____ holds the reader's attention (and answers his or her questions about the topic).

Organization

_____ includes a clear beginning, middle, and ending.

_____ contains specific details—arranged in the best order—to support the main ideas.

Voice

_____ speaks in a sincere, natural way.

_____ shows that the writer really cares about the topic.

Word Choice

_____ contains specific, clear nouns and verbs.

_____ presents an appropriate level of formality or informality.

Sentence Fluency

_____ flows smoothly from sentence to sentence.

_____ displays varied sentence beginnings and lengths.

Conventions

_____ adheres to the rules of grammar, spelling, and punctuation.

_____ follows established guidelines for presentation.

"For me, it [the computer] was obviously the perfect new toy. I began playing on page 1 . . . and have been on a rewriting high ever since."

—William Zinsser

Writing with a
COMPUTER

Pens, pencils, notebooks, and folders—all of these will prove useful during a writing project. However, no writing tool is more valuable than the personal computer. When you write with a computer, you stay at a piece of writing longer, take more risks, and get more feedback from your writing peers.

Writing with a computer may be most helpful when you revise. First drafts that are written longhand often contain crossed-out lines, squeezed-in words, and arrows connecting different parts. They're usually a mess and are hard to work with. By contrast, revising with a computer is a much easier process. You can add, delete, and rearrange copy right on the screen—or on a clean printed copy of your work. And you can continue to make changes until your writing says exactly what you want it to say.

Preview

- **A Guide to the Process**
- **Designing Your Writing**
- **Effective Design in Action**

A Guide to the Process

■ PREWRITING

The Upside

- Using a computer allows you to gather your thoughts and feelings without worrying about sloppy handwriting.
- Using a computer allows you to get more ideas on paper in less time—especially if you can type well.
- Using a computer can spark your inventiveness and creativity.
- Using a computer can be quite helpful during freewriting. You can fill the screen and keep going, without so much as having to flip over a sheet of paper.

The Downside

- Because you may not be able to use certain prewriting techniques like clustering, you may do less prewriting and planning with a computer.
- Because it's so easy to revise on a computer, you may be tempted to go back and change your writing, disrupting the free flow of your thoughts.

Best Advice: Try both methods. Find out whether prewriting on a screen or prewriting on paper is better for you. It's your choice.

■ WRITING THE FIRST DRAFT

The Upside

- Using a computer may help you stay with a piece of writing longer and develop it more thoroughly.
- Computers allow you to concentrate on ideas rather than on the appearance of your writing.
- Writing on a computer makes it easier for you to share early drafts. You can simply print out a copy for others to read. By sharing your work, you also become more aware of a real audience.

The Downside

- Deleting whole sections of copy on a computer is very tempting. But most experts agree that it is important to save all of your ideas in early drafts.

Best Advice: Do your drafting on a computer; then save, print out, share, and keep paper copies of what you've written.

■ REVISING

The Upside

- Using a computer saves you time and toil during each step in the revising process, especially for longer writing assignments.
- Using a computer allows you to move, delete, and add large chunks of information by using a few simple commands. As a result, you have more time to improve your writing.
- Using a computer makes group advising sessions easier because everyone gets a clean printout to read and react to.

The Downside

- Some people find it difficult to reread and evaluate writing on a screen. *Solution:* Simply print out the document, make the changes on paper, and then input them.

> **Best Advice: Use your computer for revising. Take advantage of the speed and ease a computer offers, but slow down long enough to reflect on your writing. (If you print out a copy of your work first, and then revise on screen, you can easily undo any hasty revising later.)**

■ EDITING AND PROOFREADING

The Upside

- Use the spell- and grammar-checkers and the search-and-replace capabilities (available in most word-processing programs) to help you prepare your writing for publication.
- Use the formatting features (if provided) to create the table of contents, outline, and graphics for a research paper.

The Downside

- You may not see errors such as missing words or misplaced commas as easily on a screen as on paper.
- You may also come to rely too much on your spell- and grammar-checkers. These checkers aren't foolproof. For example, a spell-checker won't be able to distinguish between words that sound the same but are spelled differently (*hole* and *whole*). *Solution:* Use these programs; then do a careful final read yourself.

> **Best Advice: Do your editing and proofreading on a computer. Clearly, the computer is valuable in this final step of preparing a paper for publication. But also carefully check for errors yourself.**

Designing Your Writing

The test of good page design is that your writing is clear and easy to follow. Consider these tips for creating clean, attractive essays and articles.

Typography

■ **Use an easy-to-read serif font for the main text.** (Serif type, like this type, has tails at the tops and bottoms of the letters.) For most types of writing, use a 10- or 12-point type size.

■ **Make titles and headings short and to the point.** Headings of equal importance should be stated in the same way. Follow the basic rules for capitalizing titles and headings. (See page 508.6.)

■ **Consider using a sans serif font for the title and headings.** (Sans serif type, like this type, does not have tails.) Use larger type, perhaps 18-point, for your title and 14-point type for any headings. (Use **boldface** for headings if they seem to get lost on the page.)

Take NOTE On screen, most people find a sans serif font easier to read. So for writing that you publish online, consider a **sans serif font** for the body and a **serif font** for the title and any headings.

Spacing and Margins

■ **Maintain a one-inch margin around each page** (top, bottom, left, and right).

■ **Hit the tab key to indent the first line of each paragraph.** This key should be set at five spaces.

■ **Leave only one space after each sentence** to make your writing easier to read.

■ **Avoid placing headings, hyphenated words, and starts of new paragraphs at the bottom of a page.** Also avoid single words at the bottom of a page or carried over to the top of the next page.

Graphic Devices

■ **Create bulleted lists to highlight important points.** Be selective; you don't want too many lists in your writing. (See page 32.)

■ **Include charts or other graphics.** Graphics should not be so small that they get lost nor so large that they overpower the page. You can also put graphics on separate pages. (See page 32.)

Effective Design in Action

The following two pages (page 1 and page 5) from a student essay show effective design elements.

McGinn 1

Kendall McGinn
Mr. Gilding
Social Studies
Feb. 25, 2006

The title is 18-point sans serif type.

The Return of the Buffalo

At one point in the early twentieth century, it seemed that the American buffalo would continue to exist only in pictures or on the buffalo nickel. Its population of 100 million in 1700 had been reduced to 1,000 by 1889. In recent years, that number has increased to nearly 400,000 (Hodgson 71). The buffalo, once endangered, has returned.

Before the Europeans came to North America, the native people of the North American plains and the buffalo were one *Pte Oyate*, or Buffalo Nation. The big bull *tantanka* was life itself. These Native Americans followed the herds and used the buffalo for food, clothing, shelter, religious ceremonies, and medicine. A Lakota leader summed up this unity between human and animal: "When the Creator made the buffalo, he put power in them. When you eat the meat, that power goes into you, heals the body and spirit" (qtd. in Hodgson 69).

The main text is 10-point serif type.

Open Season on Buffalo

During the expansion of the United States, a cultural clash occurred, and the Europeans practically destroyed the buffalo. By the year 1800, it was reported that there were only about 30 million buffalo left in the United States.

The heading is 14-point sans serif.

McGinn 5

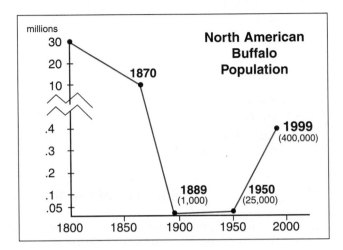

The buffalo is "returning" to North America in ever-increasing numbers. Cable Network News owner Ted Turner raises almost 10,000 buffalo on his Montana and New Mexico ranches. "I guess I've gone buffalo batty," Turner says. He supports the raising of buffalo as an excellent source of low-fat meat and as a way to help save this once endangered species (Hodgson 75).

Buffalo ranchers are, in fact, learning that raising buffalo has many benefits. Raising buffalo is more cost-effective and more environmentally safe than raising cattle. Here are four main benefits:

- Buffalo don't overeat.
- Their sharp hooves loosen hard soil.
- Buffalo improve grass crops.
- They adapt to any climate.

Buffalo living in Florida seem just as happy as those living in Alaska. In Hawaii, they even survived a hurricane. Hawaiian rancher Bill Mowry recalls how the buffalo "loved every minute of it" (qtd. in Allen 105).

"Writing becomes real when it
has an audience."

—Tom Liner

PUBLISHING
Your Writing

Publishing is the driving force behind writing. It makes all of your prewriting, drafting, and revising worth the effort. Publishing is to a writer what a live performance is to a musician or an exhibit is to an artist. It is why you have worked so hard in the first place—to share a finished piece of writing that effectively expresses your thoughts and feelings.

The easiest and by far the most helpful form of publishing is sharing a finished project with your classmates. As writer Tom Liner states, "You learn ways to improve your writing by seeing its effect on others."

You can also select a piece of writing for your classroom portfolio or submit something to your school newspaper or literary magazine. If you're really adventurous, you may even want to submit your writing outside of school, perhaps to a national literary magazine. This chapter will help you with all your publishing needs.

Preview

- **Publishing Ideas**
- **Preparing a Portfolio**
- **Sending Your Writing Out**
- **Places to Publish**
- **Publishing Online**
- **Creating Your Own Web Site**

Publishing Ideas

As you will see in the ideas listed below, publishing covers a great deal of territory. Some of these ideas are easy to carry out, like sharing your writing with your classmates. Others are more challenging and take more time and effort, such as entering a favorite piece in a writing contest.

Performing
Sharing with Classmates
Reading to Other Audiences
Producing a Video
Performing on Stage

Displaying
Bulletin Boards / Display Cases
Libraries
Business Windows
Clinic Waiting Rooms
Literary/Art Fairs

Self-Publishing
Family Newsletter
Greeting/Special-
   Occasion Cards
Booklets
Personal Web Sites
   (See page 39.)

Submitting (In School)
School Newspaper
Literary Magazine
Classroom Collection
Class-Project Display
Writing Portfolio (See page 35.)

Submitting (Outside of School)
City Newspaper
Area Historical Society
Local Arts Council
Church Publications
Young Writers' Conferences
Magazines/Contests
   (See page 37.)
Online Publications
   (See page 38.)

Publishing Tips

These tips will help you prepare your writing for publication.

■ Work with your writing until you feel good about it from start to finish.

■ Ask for input and advice throughout the writing process.

■ Save all drafts of your writing for reference.

■ Carefully edit your work for correctness.

■ Present your final copy cleanly and neatly.
(See pages 30–32 and 79–83.)

■ Know your publishing options.

■ Follow the necessary publication guidelines.
(See pages 36 and 38.)

Preparing a Portfolio

A **writing portfolio** is a collection of your work that shows your skill as a writer. It is different from a writing folder that contains writing in various stages of completion. In most cases, you will be asked to compile a *showcase portfolio*—a collection of your best writing for a school term, such as a quarter or semester. Compiling a showcase portfolio allows you to participate in the assessment process. You decide which writing and samples to include; you reflect upon your writing progress; you make sure that all the right pieces are in all the right places. You are in control.

What You Should Include

Most showcase portfolios contain the following basic components. Check with your teacher for the specific requirements.

- **A table of contents** listing the pieces included in your portfolio
- **An opening essay or letter** detailing the story behind your portfolio (how you compiled it, what it means to you, etc.)
- **A specified number of finished pieces** representing your best writing in the class (Your teacher may require you to include all of your prewriting, drafting, and revising work for some pieces.)
- **A best "other" piece** related to your work in another content area
- **A cover sheet** attached to each piece of writing, discussing the reason for its selection, the work that went into it, and so on
- **Evaluation sheets or checklists** charting the basic skills you have mastered as well as the skills you still need to work on (Your teacher will supply these sheets.)

How You Should Work

1. Keep track of all your writing (including planning notes and drafts). This way, when it comes to compiling your portfolio, you will have all the pieces to work with.

2. Make sure that you understand all of the requirements for your portfolio.

3. Use an expandable folder for your portfolio to avoid dog-eared or ripped pages. Keep your papers in a "safe environment."

4. Maintain a regular writing/compiling schedule. It will be impossible to produce an effective portfolio if you approach it as a last-minute project.

5. Develop a feeling of pride in your portfolio. Make sure that it reflects a positive image of yourself. Look your best!

Sending Your Writing Out

Q. What types of writing can I submit?

A. There are markets for all types of writing—essays, articles, stories, plays, and poems. Newspapers are most interested in essays and articles. With magazines, it depends. Some magazines publish essays, articles, stories, and poetry; others accept only essays.

HELP FILE

Check the *Writer's Market* or the *Writer's Market: The Electronic Edition* (CD-ROM or online download) to find out who publishes what. If your school library doesn't have either of these resources, your public library will.

Q. Where should I submit my writing?

A. You will probably have better success if you try to publish your work locally. Consider area newspapers and publications put out by local organizations. If you're interested in submitting something to a national publication, turn again to the *Writer's Market*. It includes a special section devoted to teen and young-adult publications. (Also see page 37 in this handbook for additional ideas.)

Q. How should I submit my work?

A. Check the publication's masthead for submission guidelines. (The masthead is the small print on one of the opening pages identifying the publisher and editors of the publication, subscription rates, the mailing address, and so on.) You can also call the publication or go to its Web site. Most publications expect you to include . . .

- **a brief cover letter** (to a specific editor) identifying the title and form of your writing and the word count;
- **a neatly printed copy of your work** with your name on each page—double-spaced and paper-clipped; and
- **a SASE** (self-addressed stamped envelope) large enough to hold your manuscript so that it can be returned after it has been read.

Q. What should I expect?

A. First, you should expect to wait a long time for a reply. (It may take up to two months in some cases.) Second, you should not be surprised or disappointed if your writing is not accepted for publication at the first place you send it. Consider it a learning experience and keep submitting.

Places to Publish

Listed below are five well-respected publications that accept student submissions and three writing contests to enter. (Refer to the *Writer's Market*—found in most libraries—for more places to publish.)

PUBLICATIONS

Teen Ink (Grades 6–12)
FORMS: Articles, art, photos, reviews, poems, fiction
SEND TO: P.O. Box 30
        Newton, MA 02461

The High School Writer
    (Grades 9–12)
FORMS: Fiction, poetry, nonfiction
SEND TO: Writer Publications
        P.O. Box 718
        Grand Rapids, MN 55744

Skipping Stones: A Multicultural Children's Magazine (Ages 8–16)
FORMS: Art, stories, photos and articles in any language
SEND TO: P.O. Box 3939
        Eugene, OR 97403

WRITING CONTESTS

Read *Writing Contests*
    (Grades 9–12)
FORMS: Short stories, personal essays
SEND TO: *Read Essay Contest*
        Weekly Reader Corporation
        200 First Stamford Place
        P.O. Box 120023
        Stamford, CT 06912-0023

The American Library of Poetry: Student Poetry Contest
    (Grades 8–9 and 10–12)
FORMS: One poem of no more than 20 lines on any subject, and in any form
SEND TO: Review Committee
        The American Library of Poetry
        P.O. Box 978
        Houlton, ME 04730

The Poetry Zone: Teen Scene
    (Ages 13–18)
FORM: Poems
SEND TO: poems@pzone.freeserve.co.uk in an email
        (no attachments)

Take NOTE   Always check with the contest or publication and with your teacher about guidelines for submitting your writing. Include a self-addressed stamped envelope with any inquiry.

Publishing Online

The Internet offers many publishing opportunities. There are online magazines, writing contests, and other sites that accept submissions. The questions and answers below will help you publish your writing on the Net.

Q. What should I do first?

A. Begin by checking with your teachers to see if your school has its own Internet site where students can post their work. If not, suggest that one be started. Also ask your teachers about Web sites they know of that accept student submissions.

Q. How should I begin my Web search?

A. Use a search engine to find places to publish. (See pages 348–350.) Here's one starting point: Refer to the search engine's index of topics, and look for an "education" topic; then click on the "K–12" subheading to see what develops. You can also enter "student, publish" as a search phrase, and go from there.

Q. Does the Write Source have a Web site?

A. Yes, you can visit our Web site at www.thewritesource.com. Follow the "Publish It" link for a list of other Web sites that accept student submissions.

Q. How should I submit my work?

A. Before you do anything, make sure that you understand the publishing conditions related to a particular site and share this information with your parents. Then follow these guidelines:

- Include a message explaining why you are contacting the site. Most publishers receive many messages each day, so keep your message brief and make your purpose clear.

- Send your work in an appropriate format. Some sites have online forms into which you can paste a text. Others list the electronic file formats they prefer to receive.

- Provide the publisher with correct information for contacting you. E-mail addresses sometimes change, so a site may ask for other information. (However, don't give personal information unless your parents approve.)

Q. What should I expect?

A. Within a week or so of your submission, you should receive a note from the publisher verifying that your work has been received. However, it may take many weeks for the publisher to make a decision about publishing your work. If one site doesn't publish your work, you can always submit it to another one.

Creating Your Own Web Site

To create a Web site on your home computer, check with your Internet service provider to find out how to get started. If you are using a school computer, ask your teacher for help. Then start designing your site. Use the questions and answers below as a starting point.

Q. **How do I plan my site?**

A. Think about the number of pages you want on your Web site. Should you put everything on one page, or would you like to have a number of pages (perhaps a home page, a page of poetry, a page of short stories, a page of favorite links, and so forth)? Check out other student sites for ideas. Then plan your pages by sketching them out. Note how the pages will be linked by marking the hot spots on your sketches.

Q. **How do I make the pages?**

A. Start each page as a separate file. Many word-processing programs let you save a file as a Web page. If yours doesn't, you will have to add hypertext markup language (HTML) codes to format the text and make links to graphics and other pages. Your teacher may be able to explain how to do this. Otherwise, you can find instructions about HTML on the Net. (See the "Web Design" page on our Web site at www.thewritesource.com for help.)

Q. **How do I know whether my pages work?**

A. You should always test your pages. Using your browser, open your first page. Then follow the links to make sure they work correctly and that all the pages look right.

Q. **How do I get my pages on the Net?**

A. You must upload your finished pages to your Internet provider's computer. Ask your provider how to do this. (If you're working on your home computer, make sure to get your parents' approval first. If you're using the school's equipment, work with your teacher.) Your provider will also tell you how you can access the pages later, in case you want to make changes. After you upload a page, visit your site to make sure it still works.

HELP FILE

Once your site is up and working, e-mail your friends and tell them to visit it. Ask visitors to your site to spread the word to other people they know. In addition, mention your page in chat rooms and post announcements on electronic bulletin boards. Ask your provider for tips on how to advertise your page to the rest of the Net.

Using the Writing
PROCESS

A Guide to Prewriting 41

A Guide to Drafting 53

A Guide to Revising 59

A Guide to Group Advising 73

A Guide to Editing and Proofreading 79

"As soon as you connect with your true subject, you will write."

—Joyce Carol Oates

A Guide to
PREWRITING

Author Barry Lane says writers "continually move back and forth between the sea and the mountain" during a writing project. As Lane explains it, writing begins in the "sea of experience," which contains the memories, experiences, and information that writers work with. When they actually write, writers begin to climb the "mountain of perception," forming new understandings, linking ideas, and drawing conclusions. If they need more details, they head back to the sea.

Prewriting refers to the beginning of a writing project—when you're still at sea—selecting a topic, gathering information about it, and so on. Prewriting also refers to trips back to the sea—when you need to carry out additional research and planning in the middle of a writing project. If you give prewriting the proper attention, you've laid a solid foundation for all of the other steps in the writing process.

Preview

- Quick Guide
- Using Selecting Strategies
- Freewriting Tips
- Using Collecting Strategies
- Using Graphic Organizers
- A Closer Look at Prewriting

Quick Guide

PURPOSE: The main purpose of prewriting is to select and develop specific topics for writing. It deals with all of the brainstorming, discussing, collecting, and planning you do before you write.

✱ You may also do some prewriting activities later in the writing process. For example, once you review your first draft, you may decide to gather some additional information about your topic. (Writing is a recursive process, meaning that a writer may repeat or revisit steps during the writing process.)

STARTING POINT: During prewriting, you do the following:
- select a specific topic that truly interests you,
- collect information about it,
- focus on a specific part of the topic for writing, and
- plan how to use the supporting information.

Tip: When you are assigned a topic, always try to make a personal connection with it.

FOCUS: Prewriting can be carried out in a variety of ways. You may start by making a list or a cluster of possible topics. This activity may prompt you to write freely about some item from that list or cluster. Then you may do some research before focusing on a specific way to write about the topic. Once you've established a focus, or thesis, you may arrange your supporting information with an outline or some other graphic organizer.

THE BIG PICTURE: When prewriting, pay special attention to three key traits of writing: ideas, organization, and voice.

Ideas ● Collect as much information as you can. The more you know about your topic, the easier it will be to write about it.

Organization ● Decide on the best arrangement of the facts and details you have collected. Create a master plan that holds all of the information together. (See page 52.)

Voice ● To write with voice, you must have a sincere interest in your writing idea. You must also consider your intended audience and the purpose of your writing.

Using Selecting Strategies

The following strategies will help you select a specific topic for your writing. The key is to learn which strategies work best for you.

1. **Journal Writing** . . . Write in a journal on a regular basis. Explore your personal feelings, develop your thoughts, and record events and happenings of each day. Underline thoughts in your journal writing that you would like to explore further. (See pages 132–134.)

   Journal Writing Ideas
   - **I was shocked when . . .**
   - **"Sometimes you have to go out on a limb."**
   - **Putting my foot in my mouth**

2. **Freewriting** . . . Write nonstop for 5–10 minutes to discover possible writing ideas. Begin writing with a particular focus in mind—one that is somehow related to your assignment. (See page 45 for tips.)

3. **Clustering** . . . Begin a cluster with a nucleus word related to your writing topic or assignment. Then cluster ideas around the nucleus word. Circle each idea you write and draw a line connecting it to the closest related idea. (See the sample below.)

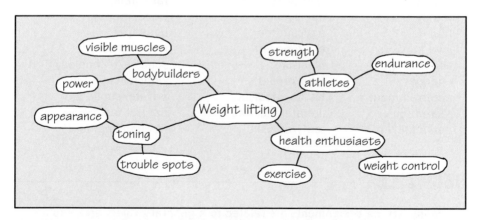

   ✱ After 3 or 4 minutes of clustering, scan your cluster for an idea to explore in a freewriting. (A specific writing topic should begin to emerge during this freewriting.)

4. **Listing** . . . Begin with a thought or a key word related to your assignment and simply start listing words and ideas. Listing ideas with a group of friends or classmates (brainstorming) is also an effective way to search for writing ideas.

5. **Reflecting, Participating, and Listening** ... Think about possible writing ideas as you read, as you ride to school, and as you wait in the cafeteria line. Be alert for potential topics as you visit with friends, or as you shop, work, or travel. Participate in activities related to your writing assignment. Also, talk to other people who are knowledgeable about your possible writing idea.

6. **Using the "Essentials of Life" Checklist** ... Below you will find a checklist of the essential elements in our lives. The checklist provides an endless variety of topic possibilities. Consider the third category, food. It could lead to the following writing ideas:

   - sensible eating habits
   - fast-food overload
   - a favorite type of food
   - truth in labeling on food packages

ESSENTIALS OF LIFE CHECKLIST

clothing	communication	exercise/training
housing	purpose/goals	community
food	measurement	arts/music
education	machines	faith/religion
family	intelligence	trade/money
friends	agriculture	heat/fuel
love	environment	rules/laws
senses	plant life	science/technology
energy	land/property	work/occupation
entertainment	health/medicine	private/public life
recreation	literature/books	natural resources
personality	tools/utensils	freedom/rights

HELP FILE

Many writing assignments are related to a general subject area you are studying. Let's say, for example, you were asked to write an essay about exercise and training, or about opportunities in education. Your first task would be to focus on a specific aspect of that subject:

General Subject Area: **Exercise and Training**
Specific Writing Topic: **Aerobic Spinning**

General Subject Area: **Opportunities in Education**
Specific Writing Topic: **Internships for High School Students**

Freewriting TIPS

The Process . . .

- Write nonstop and record whatever comes into your head. Write for at least 5–10 minutes if possible.

- Begin writing about an assigned subject. Otherwise, pick anything that comes to mind and begin writing.

- Don't stop to judge, edit, or correct your writing. Freewriting is exploratory writing, nothing more.

- Keep writing even when you seem to be drawing a blank. If necessary, switch to another topic, or write "I'm drawing a blank" until a new idea comes to mind.

- When a certain topic seems to be working, stick with it as long as you can. Record as many details about it as possible.

  ✱ Keep a small notebook close at hand and write freely in it whenever you have an idea you don't want to forget, or write in it just for something to do. These freewritings will help you become a better writer.

The Result . . .

- Review your writing and underline ideas you like. These ideas may serve as starting points for writing assignments.

- Share your writing with your peers. You can learn a great deal by reading and reacting to the freewriting of your fellow writers.

- Continue freewriting about ideas you want to explore further. (You could approach this focused freewriting as a first draft.)

Some Reminders . . .

- Thoughts are constantly passing through your head; you always have *something* on your mind.

- Freewriting helps you get these thoughts on paper.

- Freewriting helps you develop your thoughts by exploring, connecting, and making meaning out of them.

- Freewriting may seem difficult when you first try it; just stick with it and don't become discouraged.

Using Collecting Strategies

Once you've selected a topic, you need to gather details for writing. The activities and strategies that follow should help you do this. If you need to explore your writing ideas in great detail, and if time permits, use two or more of these strategies.

Gathering Your Thoughts

Freewriting ■ At this point, you can approach freewriting in two ways. (1) You can do a focused freewriting, exploring your topic from a number of different angles. (2) You can approach your freewriting as if it were a quick version of the actual paper. A quick version will give you a good feel for your topic and will also tell you how much you know about it or need to find out.

Clustering ■ Try clustering again, this time with your topic as the nucleus word. This clustering will naturally be more focused or structured than an initial clustering because you now have a specific topic in mind.

5 W's of Writing ■ Answer the 5 W's—*Who? What? When? Where?* and *Why?*—to identify basic information about your topic. (Add *How?* to the list for even better coverage.)

Directed Writing ■ Write whatever comes to mind about your topic, using the questions listed below. (Repeat the process as often as you need to, selecting a different mode each time.)

Describe it.	What do you see, hear, feel, smell, or taste?
Compare it.	What is it similar to? What is it different from?
Apply it.	What can you do with it? How can you use it?
Associate it.	What connections between this and something else come to mind?
Analyze it.	What parts does it have? How do they work together?
Argue for or against it.	What do you like about it? What don't you like about it? What are its strengths and its weaknesses?

Directed Dialoguing ■ Create a dialogue between two people in which your specific topic is the focus of the conversation. This writing will help you explore differing opinions about the topic.

Audience Appeal ■ Select a specific audience to address in an exploratory writing. Consider a group of parents, a live television audience, or the readers of a popular teen magazine. This writing will help you see your topic from a different point of view.

Questioning ■ Ask questions to gather information about your topic. You can use the questions in the chart below if your topic falls into any of these three different categories: **problems** (peer pressure), **policies** (grading), or **concepts** (student internships).

	Description	Function	History	Value
PROBLEMS	What is the problem? What are the signs of the problem?	Who or what is affected by it? What new problems may it cause in the future?	What is the current status of the problem? What or who caused it?	What is the significance? Why is it more (or less) important than other problems?
POLICIES	What type of policy is it? What are its most important features?	What is the policy designed to do? What is needed to make it work?	What brought this policy about? What are the alternatives to this policy?	Is the policy working? What are its advantages and disadvantages?
CONCEPTS	What type of concept is it? Who or what is related to it?	Who has been influenced by this concept? Why is it important?	When did it originate? How has it changed over the years?	What practical value does it hold? What is its social worth?

Focusing Your Research

Reading ■ Use different sources—books, magazines, newspapers, the Internet—to gather information about your topic. Read with a critical eye, always evaluating the quality and purpose of the information.

Taking Notes ■ Write down important facts, opinions, and quotations. Keep track of any information you will need for citations and works-cited pages. (See page 268.)

Talking to Others

Interviewing ■ Interview an expert about your topic. Meet the expert in person, communicate by phone, or send questions to be answered. (See page 346 for more information on interviewing.)

Discussing ■ Talk with your classmates, teachers, or other people to find out what they know about your subject. Take notes to help you remember the important things they say.

Using Graphic **Organizers**

Graphic organizers can help you gather and organize your details for writing. Clustering is one method (see page 43); these next two pages list other useful organizers. Re-create the organizer on your own paper to do your gathering.

Cause/Effect Organizer

Use to collect and organize details for cause/effect essays.

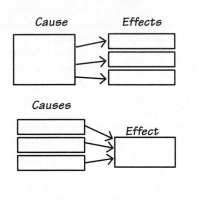

Problem/Solution Web

Use to map out problem/ solution essays.

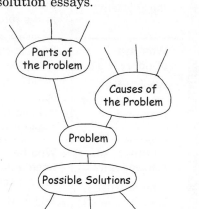

Time Line

Use for personal narratives to list actions or events in the order they occurred.

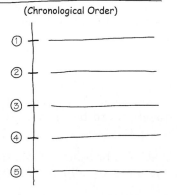

Evaluation Collection Grid

Use to collect supporting details for essays of evaluation.

Subject: _____

Points to Evaluate	Supporting Details
1.	
2.	
3.	
4.	

Venn Diagram

Use to collect details to compare and contrast two topics.

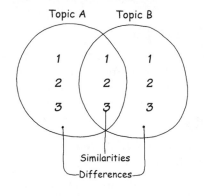

Line Diagram

Use to collect and organize details for academic essays.

Process (Cycle) Diagram

Use to collect details for science-related writing, such as how a process or cycle works.

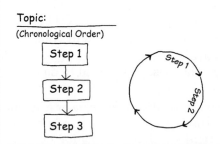

5 W's Chart

Use to collect the *Who? What? When? Where?* and *Why?* details for personal narratives and news stories.

Subject: _____

Who?	What?	When?	Where?	Why?

Definition Diagram

Use to gather information for extended definition essays.

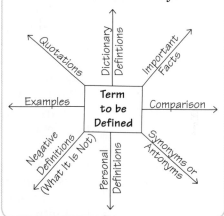

Sensory Chart

Use to collect details for descriptive essays and observation reports.

Subject: _____

Sights	Sounds	Smells	Tastes	Textures

"Good writing is formed partly through plan
and partly through accident."

—Ken Macrorie

A **Closer Look** at Prewriting

What should you do after you've gathered information about your writing idea? Well, you can either plan and write your first draft, or you can consider how well you match up with your topic before you go any further.

Taking Inventory of Your Thoughts

After carefully considering the questions that follow, you will be ready to (1) move ahead with your writing or (2) change your topic.

Purpose: Does my topic meet the assignment requirements? Am I writing to analyze, describe, persuade, entertain, or retell?

Self: How do I feel about the topic? Have I made a personal connection with it?
Do I have enough time to develop it?

Topic: How much more do I need to know about this topic? Has my research changed my thinking about it? What part of the topic will I focus on?

Audience: Who are my readers?
How much do they already know about this subject? How can I get them interested in my ideas?

Form and Style: How should I present my ideas—in a narrative, an essay, a report, or a multimedia presentation? Can I think of an interesting way to begin or lead into my paper?

FAQ

What kinds of information should I collect before I write my first draft?

That depends on the type of writing you are doing. If you are developing a personal narrative, your information will come from your own experiences. But if you are writing an expository essay on a complex subject like learning disabilities, you'll need to do a great deal of research.

In the case of argumentative writing like persuasive or academic essays, your research will go beyond simply seeking information; you will be reading with a critical eye, searching for opposing viewpoints on your topic.

Forming Your Thesis Statement

After you have completed enough exploring and collecting, you should begin to develop a more focused interest in your topic. If all goes well, this interest will become the thesis of your writing. **A thesis statement identifies the focus for your academic essays.** It usually highlights a special condition or feature of the topic, expresses a specific feeling, or takes a stand.

State your thesis in a sentence that effectively expresses what you want to explore in your essay. Write as many versions as it takes to come up with a sentence that sets the right tone and direction for your writing. Use the following formula to write a thesis statement.

FORMULA

A specific topic
+ a particular feature, feeling, or stand
= an effective thesis statement.

Thesis Statement: **Young children exposed to low levels of lead** *(specific topic)* **may face health problems later in life.** *(particular feature)*

SAMPLE THESIS STATEMENTS

Writing Assignment: Essay about opportunities in education
Specific Subject: High school internships
Thesis Statement: **Internship programs** *(specific topic)* **give students real-world experiences** *(particular feature)*.

Writing Assignment: Essay on the Civil War
Specific Subject: General George McClellan
Thesis Statement: **General George McClellan's overcautious tactics** *(specific topic)* **prolonged the war** *(particular feeling)*.

Writing Assignment: Essay about an outdoor activity
Specific Subject: Use of barbed hooks for fishing
Thesis Statement: **Barbed hooks** *(specific topic)* **should be banned from fishing** *(particular stand)*.

HELP FILE

If you try to cover too much ground, your essay will go on and on and be hard to follow. That is why it is so important to establish a specific thesis for your writing assignments. A strong thesis statement clearly lets the reader know what the essay will be about.

Organizing Your Details

With a clear thesis in mind, you may need to design a writing plan before you start your first draft. Your plan can be anything from a brief list of ideas to a detailed sentence outline. (See page 177.) Use the guidelines that follow to help organize your details for writing.

1. **Study your thesis statement.** It may suggest a logical method of organization.

2. **Review the details you have gathered.** Make sure they support your thesis. Also see if a plan of organization begins to emerge.

3. **Consider the methods of organization listed below.**

METHODS OF ORGANIZATION

- **Chronological order** *(time)* is effective for sharing personal narratives, summarizing steps, and explaining events in the order in which they occurred. (See page 106.)

- **Order of location** *(spatial)* is useful for many types of descriptions. Details can be described from left to right, from right to left, from top to bottom, from edge to center, and so on. (See page 105.)

- **Illustration** *(deductive)* is a method of arrangement in which you first state a general idea (thesis statement) and follow with specific reasons, examples, and facts. (See page 107.)

- **Climax** *(inductive)* is a method of arrangement in which you present specific details followed by a general statement or a conclusion. (See page 107.)

- **Compare-contrast** is a method of arrangement in which you show how one topic is different from and similar to another topic. (See page 108.)

- **Cause-effect** is a type of arrangement that helps you make connections between a result and the events that came before it. Usually, you begin with the cause of something, and then you discuss a number of specific effects. (See page 108.)

- **Problem-solution** is a type of arrangement in which you state a problem and explore possible solutions.

- **Classification** is a type of arrangement that can be used to explain a term or a concept (a machine, a theory, a game, and so on). Begin by placing the topic in the appropriate *class*, and then provide details that show how your subject is different from and similar to others in the same class. (See page 105.)

"Every time I sit down and write,
I know it's going well when it sort of
takes over and I get out of the picture."

—Sandra Belton

A Guide to
DRAFTING

This is it—your first draft, your first complete look at a writing idea. All of your searching and planning have led up to this point. Write as much of your first draft as possible in the first sitting while all of your prewriting is still fresh in your mind. Think of drafting as the process of connecting all of the ideas that you have collected about your topic. Refer to your planning notes as you write but be open to new ideas as they emerge. Keep these additional points in mind as you write:

- Concentrate on developing your ideas, not on producing a final copy. Do, however, strive for quality.
- Include as much detail as possible.
- Continue writing until you make all of your main points or until you come to a logical stopping point.

Preview

- **Quick Guide**
- **Writing an Opening Paragraph**
- **Developing the Middle**
- **Writing a Closing Paragraph**

"The only true creative aspect of writing is the first draft. That's when it's coming straight from your head and your heart."

—Evan Hunter

Quick Guide

PURPOSE: Drafting is your first attempt at developing your writing idea. It allows you to get your thoughts about a topic on paper.

STARTING POINT: You're ready to write a first draft once you . . .

- collect enough information about your topic,
- establish a thesis (focus) for your writing, and
- organize your supporting ideas.

Some writers pay special attention to the specific wording in their opening paragraph before they dive headfirst into their first draft. Once the beginning part is set, they find it much easier to carry out the rest of their writing. Other writers are more interested in getting all of their thoughts on paper right away. Author John Steinbeck supports the second approach: "Write freely and as rapidly as possible and throw the whole thing on paper."

FORM: When drafting with pen and paper, write on every other line, and use only one side of the paper. Double-space when using a computer. This will make revising by hand much easier.

Remember: Write your first draft freely, without being too concerned about neatness and correctness. This is why a first draft is often called a *rough draft*. Just make sure that your writing is legible.

THE BIG PICTURE: When writing a first draft, give special attention to these traits of effective writing: ideas, organization, and voice.

Ideas ● Develop all the relevant thoughts and ideas you have collected and consider new ideas as they come to mind. (A first draft is your first look at a developing writing idea.)

Organization ● Use your prewriting and planning as a general guide when you write. Try to work logically through your draft from the opening to the closing paragraph.

Voice ● Speak honestly and naturally so the real you comes through in your writing.

Writing an Opening Paragraph

For almost all of your academic writing—essays, reviews, and research papers—you need to plan an opening or lead paragraph. Your opening should help clarify your thinking about your topic and accomplish three things: (1) *introduce your topic*, (2) *gain your reader's attention*, and (3) *identify your thesis*.

The opening paragraph is one of the most important elements in any composition because it sets the tone and establishes the basic organization for your writing. There are many ways to begin an opening paragraph. Several possible starting points are listed below:

- Share some thought-provoking details about the subject.
- Ask your reader a challenging question.
- Begin with an informative quotation.
- Provide a dramatic, eye-opening statement.
- Open with some thoughtful dialogue or an engaging story.
- Identify the main points you plan to cover.

HELP FILE

Your opening affects the direction and style of your entire piece of writing. If you don't like how the first or second draft of your opening sounds, keep trying. You'll know when you hit the right version because it will help you visualize the rest of your draft.

Sample Opening Paragraph

The writer of the opening paragraph below introduces the topic and provides the thesis of the essay. The essay focuses on Dr. Martin Luther King Jr.'s "I Have a Dream" speech, and the opening paragraph establishes a serious, academic tone.

> On August 28, 1963, Dr. Martin Luther King Jr. stood in the shadow of the Lincoln Memorial and spoke words that have resonated down through the decades: "I have a dream. . . ." His speech turned out to be one of the most influential orations of all time. The "I Have a Dream" speech neatly summed up Dr. King's nonviolent call for deep social change and became a road map for the civil rights movement in the United States and around the world.

Developing the Middle

The middle paragraphs in your draft should support your thesis. Make sure to use your planning notes (outline, list, cluster) as a general guide for your writing. Here are some ways to support your thesis:

Explain: Provide important facts, details, and examples.

Narrate: Share a brief story (anecdote) or re-create an experience to illustrate or clarify an idea.

Describe: Tell how someone appears or how something works.

Summarize: Present only the most important ideas.

Define: Identify or clarify the meaning of a specific term or idea.

Argue: Use logic and evidence to prove something is true.

Compare: Show how two things are alike or different.

Analyze: Examine the parts of something to better understand the whole.

Reflect: Express your thoughts or feelings about something.

FAQ ❓ **How many different methods of support should I use?**

For most essays and other longer compositions, you should use at least two or three of these methods to develop your thesis. For example, in an essay of definition, you might provide one or two dictionary definitions, compare your subject to something similar, and share a brief story about it.

Supporting Your Thesis

The paragraphs in the middle part of an essay contain the main points and supporting details that develop your thesis. In most cases, you should develop each main point in a separate paragraph. Remember that specific details add meaning to your writing and make it worth reading. Writing that lacks effective detail gives an incomplete picture.

A well-written supporting paragraph often contains three levels of detail:

Level 1: **Controlling sentences name the topic:**
Dr. King used a powerful rhetorical structure to get his point across.

Level 2: **Clarifying sentences support the main point:**
He began by evoking the image of Lincoln, the Great Emancipator, who "five score years ago" freed the slaves.

Level 3: **Completing sentences add details to complete the point:**
Dr. King put that fact in perspective by pointing out that, one hundred years later, people of color were still not free.

Sample Middle Paragraphs

The first middle paragraph *explains* Dr. King's speech and *summarizes* his vision of a brighter future. By providing background information, the writer prepares the reader for a closer analysis in later paragraphs.

> **Dr. King's speech was aimed at motivating and guiding a civil rights movement that required direction. The speech contained a general, idealistic outline of the rights and privileges that civil rights activists deemed inalienable to everyone. Dr. King's rhetoric showed what a world might look like in which skin color and ethnicity were nothing more than superficial characteristics. He broadly described a world where, for example, children of all races and ethnicities could live together as equals, and people would be judged based on their ability and character instead of the color of their skin (Harrison and Gilbert).**

The next paragraph *analyzes* the speech by breaking it down into its parts and showing how the parts worked together.

> **Dr. King used a powerful rhetorical structure to get his point across. He began by evoking the image of Lincoln, the Great Emancipator, who "five score years ago" freed the slaves. Dr. King put that fact in perspective by pointing out that, one hundred years later, people of color were still not free. Next, Dr. King called his people to action. He said his people could not be satisfied as long as discrimination and segregation continued, but at the same time, he told his followers, "We must not allow our creative protest to degenerate into physical violence" ("Dream"). After this, Dr. King delivered the famous "I Have a Dream" section of the speech, in which he laid out his vision of an ideal world in which these changes have been completed. By beginning in history, marching through the present, and looking to the future, Dr. King created a road map to civil rights that people still follow today.**

In this paragraph, the author *compares* and *contrasts* Dr. King's approach to the strategies advocated by Malcolm X.

> **Dr. King's road map may seem obvious now, but it was controversial even among civil rights leaders. For example, though Malcolm X attended King's March on Washington, he decried it as a "Farce on Washington" (Jenkins 371). While Dr. King spoke about the importance of integration, Malcolm X advocated "racial separation"—for blacks to willfully remove themselves from the systems of white oppression and colonialism that had enslaved them. Dr. King's nonviolent approach also did not sit well with Malcolm X, who advocated change "by any means necessary" and said that African Americans had to fight against those who fought against them (Jenkins 546–547).**

Using Quotations

In this paragraph, the writer *summarizes* information from the speech in order to lead up to a *quotation* of Dr. King's exact words. (Quotations are best used when the exact words of the source are succinct and powerful.)

> In the end, Dr. King's approach won out due to the timelessness of his ideas. He borrowed much of his language from ideas familiar to most Americans, quoting the Constitution, the Bible, and hymns and spirituals. Dr. King reinterpreted all of these familiar concepts but then moved on to create a new vision. One of his most enduring ideas came near the end of the speech: "I have a dream that my four little children will one day live in a nation where they will not be judged by the color of their skin but by the content of their character" (Harrison and Gilbert 96). By referring to his children, Dr. King told his audience that he was working to improve life for the next generation. Now, more than 30 years after he spoke these words, we are the grandchildren who have inherited the freedoms Dr. King helped to win.

Writing a Closing Paragraph

The closing paragraph allows you to tie up your essay neatly. You can refer to your thesis, review your main supporting points, answer any unresolved questions, or connect with the reader's experience.

Sample Closing Paragraph

Here the writer *reflects* on Dr. King's speech, describing the personal effect of the speech.

> Dr. King's speech exemplifies the bravery of all the men and women who endeavor to change the world for the better. His candor and brilliant description of the problems with equality in the United States are extremely admirable. Reformers like Dr. King have the power to reach back into the terrible past, reshape the stormy present, and create a better future for everyone.

FAQ **?** **How can I make my drafts sound natural and sincere?**

Your writing will sound natural and honest if you remember one thing: The writer is never alone. Think of your writing as one-half of a conversation with a reader you invent. Talk to your silent partner. In addition, relax when you write rather than nervously bouncing around. Think about what you've already said, and let that help you decide what you should say next.

> "I tend to do as much revising
> as editors will let me do."
>
> —Tom Wolfe

A Guide to
REVISING

In most cases, experienced writers have one important advantage over you when it comes to developing a piece of writing. They have time—time to step away from a completed first draft before they do any revising, and time to shape and reshape their writing into an effective finished product. They also have another advantage—an extensive working knowledge of the revising process. More specifically, with a first draft in hand, they know just how much work is ahead of them.

In basic terms, revising deals with making changes in your writing until it says what you want it to say. Author Ernest Hemingway rewrote one of his endings 27 times before he felt satisfied with it. Now, you may have neither the time nor the desire to rework any part of your writing 27 times, but you should always make as many improvements as possible before turning in your paper. You owe it to yourself and to your readers.

Preview

- Quick Guide
- Using Basic Revising Guidelines
- Revising in Action
- A Closer Look at Revising
- Revising for the Traits
- Revising Checklist

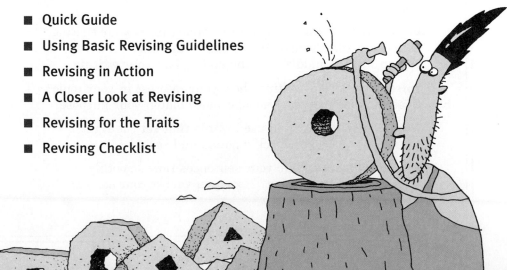

Quick Guide

PURPOSE: Revising is the process of improving the details that carry the message in your writing. It consists of adding new information, rewriting or rearranging parts, and cutting unnecessary ideas.

✱ Don't pay undue attention to conventions too early in the process; otherwise, you may overlook ways to improve the content of your writing.

STARTING POINT: You're ready to revise once you . . .
■ complete a first draft,
■ set it aside for a day or two (if possible), and
■ closely review your writing.

   Concentrate first on the big picture—the focus and organization of your writing. Then examine how specific parts support the thesis.

FORM: If you're writing with pen and paper, make your changes on your first draft. Then recopy your work if necessary. If you're using a computer, make your changes by hand on a printed copy before you enter the changes on the computer.

✱ No matter how you revise, always save an original copy of your work. You may want to add something back in later.

THE BIG PICTURE: When revising, address these traits of writing: ideas, organization, voice, word choice, and sentence fluency.

Ideas ● Make sure you have included enough information to support or develop your focus. And have you answered your readers' most pressing questions? This is called elaboration.

Organization ● Check the overall structure of your writing. Also check the effectiveness of each main part—the beginning, the middle, and the ending—in your writing.

Voice ● Does your writing show your interest in your topic? Does the tone (polite, serious, casual) match your purpose?

Word Choice ● Have you used words that set the right tone? Have you used specific nouns and verbs?

Sentence Fluency ● Do your sentences flow smoothly from one idea to the next? Have you varied your sentence beginnings and lengths?

"In the writing process, the more a thing cooks, the better."

—Doris Lessing

Using Basic Revising Guidelines

No writer gets it right the first time. Few writers even get it right the second time. In fact, professional writers almost always carry out many revisions before they are satisfied with their work. Don't be surprised if you have to do the same. To help you make the best revising moves, follow the guidelines listed below:

- **Set your writing aside.** Get it out of your mind for awhile. This will help you see your first draft more clearly when you're ready to revise.

- **Carefully review your draft when you're ready.** Read it at least two times: once silently and once aloud. It also helps to have at least one other person react to your writing—someone whose opinion you trust.

- **Look at the big picture.** Decide if you've effectively developed your focus (thesis). If your thinking about the topic has changed, change your focus.

- **Look at specific chunks of information.** Rewrite any parts that aren't as clear or effective as you would like them to be. Also cut information that doesn't support your focus and add ideas if you feel your readers need more information.

- **Evaluate your opening and closing paragraphs.** Make sure that they effectively introduce and wrap up your writing.

Revising Timed Writings

Writer Peter Elbow recommends "cut-and-paste revising" when you have little time to make changes in your writing. For example, let's say you are working on an in-class, timed writing assignment, and you have only 15 minutes to revise your writing. The five steps that follow describe this quick revising technique:

1. Don't add any new information to your writing.
2. Remove unnecessary facts and details.
3. Find the best possible information and go with it.
4. Put the pieces in the best possible order.
5. Do what rewriting is necessary.

"If you haven't revised, you're not finished."
—Patricia T. O'Conner

Revising in Action

When you revise a first draft, focus on making improvements to the paper as a whole. You can make these improvements in four basic ways: adding, deleting, moving, or reworking information. (See the next page for examples.)

Adding Information

Add information to your writing if you need . . .

- to spell out key details for making a point,
- to clarify or complete an interesting idea, or
- to link sentences or paragraphs and improve sentence flow.

Deleting Information

Delete material from your draft if it . . .

- doesn't support your focus or thesis or
- seems redundant or repetitious.

Reordering Material

Move material in your writing if it . . .

- does not help to create a clear flow of ideas,
- seems out of order, or
- would have more impact in a different position.

Reworking Material

Rewrite material in your writing if it . . .

- seems confusing or unclear,
- doesn't maintain the proper voice, or
- is too complex and needs to be simplified.

Take NOTE Learn to think like a reader when you revise and ask yourself these types of questions: *Does this passage make sense? Does my essay begin and end effectively? Is this the right voice? Do any sentences sound confusing?*

Sample Revision

The writer of the paper below made major improvements by moving, adding, deleting, and reworking sections of his paper. (See the editing and proofreading marks inside the back cover.)

The Sky's Not the Limit

Ever since movies began, filmmakers have tried to put imaginary things on film. Still, the effects never seemed real enough. People used model building, hand-drawn cartoons, or stop-motion animation. In the last 20 years, however, computer-generated imagery (CGI) has made it possible to create *Anything that can be imagined can be put on-screen and look real.* believable special effects in movies. CGI allows filmmakers to show things realistically onscreen that people could only imagine before.

CGI can create totally imaginary characters that look real. An early example is a knight leaping out of a stained-glass window in *Young Sherlock Holmes* (1985). ~~Dinosaurs are the most popular creatures for special effects over the years, starting with the stop-motion puppets of The Lost World (1925).~~ Later on, CGI showed us believable dinosaurs in *Jurassic Park* (1993). More recently, CGI and the voice and acting of Andy Serkis created the incredible character of Gollum (*Lord of* *Today, CGI even replaces older special effects technologies like the* the *Rings: The Two Towers*, 2002). ~~Even though I loved and~~ *Yoda puppet from* The Empire Strikes Back *(1980).* ~~believed in Yoda as a puppet in The Empire Strikes Back (1980), the technology is outmoded and too limited.~~ Many of the aliens in the newer *Star Wars* films are all CGI creations (*Revenge of the Sith*, 2005). Now, even the most fantastic creatures from folklore to science fiction can seem real on-screen.

A sentence is moved for clarity.

An interesting detail is added.

An unnecessary detail is deleted.

An important idea is reworded for appropriate voice.

A **Closer Look** at Revising

Knowing Your **Purpose and Audience**

Always know why you are writing—your purpose. Are you sharing information, arguing for or against something, analyzing a process? When you have a clear purpose, it is much easier to know what to change in your writing. Also consider your readers—your audience. How much do they know about your topic? Lastly, make sure that your writing voice matches the intended audience and purpose.

Escaping the "Badlands"

The later stage of revising is one of the most important in the whole composing process. Why? Because here you can escape the "badlands" of writing—those stretches of uninspired ideas that can make an essay seem boring. Use these questions as a guide to check for these "badlands."

- **Is your topic worn-out?** An essay entitled "Lead Poisoning" sounds like a real yawner. With a new twist, you can revive it: "Get the Lead Out!"

- **Is your approach stale?** If you have been writing primarily to please a teacher or to get a good grade, start again. Try writing to learn something or to trigger a particular emotion in your readers.

- **Is your voice predictable or fake?** If it is ("A good time was had by all"), start again. This time, be honest. Be real.

- **Does your draft sound boring?** Maybe it's boring because it pays an equal amount of attention to everything. Try skimming through the less significant parts by "telling" what happened; then focus on the more important parts by "showing" what happened. (See page 113.)

- **Does your essay follow the formula too closely?** For example, the basic structure of an essay provides you with an organizing frame to build on. However, if a frame is followed too closely, it may get in the way. Read your draft again, and if your inner voice says "formula," change the structure in some way.

Take NOTE

Think of revising as an opportunity to try a number of new and different ways to energize your writing. If you need to refuel your thinking at any point during the revising process, consider using one of the prewriting activities in the handbook. (See pages 43–49.)

Revising for Ideas

Use these next two pages as a guide to revising the information, or ideas, in your writing.

Check for Depth (Level of Detail)

Let's say you are writing a technical essay explaining how the healing process works, and you realize that a certain passage needs more support. To improve the passage, you add more details.

Original Passage (Too general)

As soon as you receive a minor cut, the body's healing process begins to work. Blood from tiny vessels fills the wound and begins to clot. In less than 24 hours, a scab forms.

Revised Version (More specific)

As soon as you receive a minor cut, the body's healing process begins to work. In a simple wound, the first and second layers of skin are severed along with tiny blood vessels called capillaries. As these vessels bleed into the wound, disklike structures called platelets help stop the bleeding by sticking to the edges of the cut and to one another, forming a plug. The platelets then release chemicals that react with certain proteins in the blood to form a clot. The blood clot, with its fiber network, begins to join the edges of the wound together. As the clot dries out, a scab forms, usually in less than 24 hours.

Check the Overall Focus

After reviewing your essay about teen magazines, you notice that your opening paragraph lacks a specific focus. You revise the opening so that it builds to a main point about your topic.

Opening Paragraph (Lacks focus or direction)

Teen magazines are popular with young girls. These magazines contain a lot of how-to articles about self-image, fashion, and boy-girl relationships. Girls read these magazines for advice on how to act and how to look. There are many popular magazines to choose from, and girls who don't really know what they want are the most eager readers.

Revised Version (Builds to a specific focus)

Adolescent girls often see teen magazines as handbooks on how to be teenagers. These magazines influence the way they act and look. For girls who are unsure of themselves, these magazines can exert an enormous amount of influence. Unfortunately, the advice these magazines give about self-image, fashion, and boys may do more harm than good.

Check the Focus of Each Supporting Paragraph

Suppose you are developing an expository essay about paper recycling, and you discover that one of the paragraphs lacks focus. You change it and narrow the discussion to just one aspect of paper recycling.

Original Paragraph (Not focused on one main point)

Paper recycling has indeed become big business. Since Americans throw away more paper than anything else, there is much to be gained by recycling paper. For example, Fort Howard Corporation of Green Bay, Wisconsin, uses recycled paper to produce bathroom tissue. Recycling equipment at this time cannot handle certain types of paper, including paper with staples, glossy paper, envelopes, and so on. Five thousand community programs exist nationwide for the recycling of paper products.

Revised Version (One main point developed in detail)

Paper recycling has indeed become big business. Manufacturers use recycled paper to make cardboard, paper napkins, printing paper, and toweling, as well as insulation and animal bedding. The demand for recycled products of all kinds is increasing daily. To help meet the demand, U.S. papermakers have invested $10 billion in new recycling capacity in the past 10 years. As a result, the use of recycled paper has grown more than four times faster than the overall growth in paper consumption. Recycled paper now provides more than 37 percent of the raw material fiber used at U.S. mills. This percentage should continue to grow well into the 21st century.

Check for Clarity and Completeness

Let's say a classmate has a few questions about a paragraph in your narrative. She doesn't know who Mai is or what blue and pink costumes you are talking about. In your revision, you elaborate on these ideas.

Original Paragraph (Confusing ideas)

Mai and I played make-believe a lot. She was my constant companion in our long dresses or in our ballerina costumes. They were blue and pink and also itchy. We wore them when we played house and a lot of other things, including riding our tricycles.

Revised Version (A clear, more unified paragraph)

My days of make-believe sometimes included my sister Mai, who was my constant companion. We played in long dresses or dressed up in our ballerina costumes. Her costume was blue and mine was pink. They itched worse than poison ivy, but we'd wear them for hours. We wore them when we played house and store and restaurant . . . and even when we rode our tricycles down the driveway.

Revising for Organization

Good writing has structure. It leads readers logically and clearly from one point to the next. You can have great ideas in your writing, but if they aren't organized effectively, readers won't be able to follow them. There are four general areas to consider when revising: the overall plan, the opening, the flow of ideas, and the closing.

Check the Overall Plan of Your Writing

Let's say you've shared a position paper in a response group. Everyone likes your topic, but they get lost in the middle. Some paragraphs are hard to follow. What's the next step? Tackle organization with a fresh look at what the paper absolutely must do—support your thesis. To get started, you check your essay against these questions.

1. Is my thesis strong, clearly focused, and supportable?

2. Are my main supporting points expressed in clear topic sentences?

3. Do all my paragraphs have enough details?

4. Is any information unnecessary or distracting?

5. Does the order of details support my topic sentences and the overall focus or thesis?

6. Are there any gaps in my thinking?

Check Your Opening

Suppose the opening paragraph in your persuasive essay doesn't effectively build to the specific focus of your writing. In the revised version, you add a series of questions and a thought-provoking thesis to lead the readers into the rest of the essay.

Original Opening (Lacks interest and purpose)

The lack of student motivation is a common subject in the news. Educators want to know how to get students to learn. Today's higher standards mean that students will be expected to learn even more. Another problem in urban areas is that large numbers of students are dropping out. How to interest students is a challenge.

Revised Version (Effectively leads readers into the essay)

How can we motivate students to learn? How can we get them to meet today's rising standards of excellence? How can we keep students in school long enough to learn? The answer to these problems is quite simple. Give them money. <u>**Pay students to study and learn and stay in school.**</u>

Check for Flow of Ideas

Let's say a classmate cannot follow your descriptive essay about a home in the country because you haven't connected your thoughts well enough. In the revision, you add transitional phrases to make it easier for your reader to follow your ideas spatially, or by location.

Original First Words in the Four Middle Paragraphs

There was a huge, steep hill . . .

Buffalo Creek ran . . .

A dense "jungle" covered . . .

Within walking distance from my house . . .

Revised Version (Phrases connect ideas)

Behind the house, there was a huge, steep hill . . .

Across the road from the house, Buffalo Creek ran . . .

On the far side of the creek bank was a dense "jungle" covered . . .

Up the road, within walking distance from my house . . .

FAQ

How do I know how to organize my essay?

There is a specific method of organization that is best suited for each type of writing you do. For example, narratives are usually organized by time; descriptive essays are often organized by location; persuasive essays, by order of importance. Of course, you may also customize or combine these methods to suit your particular essay. (See pages 52 and 105–108 for more information.)

Check Your Closing

Suppose that the closing for your book review is too general and flat. It doesn't effectively summarize the main points in the review, nor does it provide any final thought-provoking ideas. In your revision, you help readers understand the importance of the book by summarizing your main points and by adding a strong recommendation.

Original Closing (Sketchy and uninteresting)

Native Son deals with a young man's struggle against racism. It shows the effects of prejudice. Everyone should read this book.

Revised Version (More specific and relevant)

Native Son deals with a young man's struggle in a racist society, but it deals with so much more. It shows how prejudice affects people, how it closes in on them, and what some people will do to find a way out. Anyone who wants to better understand racism in America should read this book.

*"Once you begin to hear your own voice,
it's easier to find it again and to sustain it longer."*

—Vicki Spandel

Revising for Voice

Author William Zinsser advises young writers to "be yourself" in your writing. Let your voice come through in your essays and reports. Writing that has voice sounds genuine, and it holds your reader's attention.

Check Your Purpose

After reviewing the first draft of your feature article, you realize that it lacks personality. This is a definite problem since the purpose of your writing is to share a personal experience. To make a personal connection with your readers, you rewrite your draft in the first-person point of view. (See page 259.)

Original Passage (Lacks personality)

Cemeteries can teach us a lot about history. They make history seem more real. There is an old grave of a Revolutionary War veteran in the Union Grove Cemetery. . . .

Revised Version (Connects with the readers)

I've always had a special feeling for cemeteries. It's hard to explain any further than that, except to say history never seems quite as real as it does when I walk between rows of old gravestones. One day I discovered the grave of a Revolutionary War veteran. . . .

Check Your Enthusiasm

While reviewing your biographical sketch, a classmate notes that the writing doesn't express any strong feelings. To take care of this problem, you inject more energy and genuine feeling into your writing.

Original Version (Lacks feeling and energy)

She turned to me. My grandmother was 86 years old. Her skin was wrinkled, but she had youthful blue eyes. She placed her gnarled hand upon mine and squeezed it.

Revised Version (Expresses real feelings)

She turned to me. My grandmother was 86 years old, and she was beautiful. Her wrinkled skin was an intricate map of wisdom and hard times, but the spark in her blue eyes hinted at eternal youth and vibrancy. In a soothing expression of tenderness, she placed her gnarled hand upon mine and squeezed it gently.

Revising for Word Choice

The best words add to the meaning, tone, and sound of your writing. Here are some things to look for when revising for word choice.

Locate Problems with Word Choice

Let's say a writing lab tutor has just checked the first draft of your narrative. She has noted three problems with word choice: *redundancy, repetition,* and *jargon.*

Redundancy ■ Words or phrases that are used together but mean the same thing.

Original Version: I helped Carlos paint his car <u>cherry red in color</u>.

Revised Version: I helped Carlos paint his car cherry red.

Repetition ■ Words or phrases that are unnecessarily repeated.

Original Version: I knew <u>the car</u> belonged to Carlos since he waved at me from the front seat of <u>the car</u>.

Revised Version: I knew the car belonged to Carlos since he waved at me from the front seat.

Jargon ■ Specialized words or phrases that are not adequately explained.

Original Version: The spoiler improved the car's stability.

Revised Version: The spoiler—an air deflector on the trunk—improved the car's driving stability.

Use the Right Level of Language

Suppose your teacher has just read the first part of your persuasive essay, and she noticed that your overall level of language seems too informal for the assignment. To make sure that you understand what she means, you review the characteristics of informal and formal English.

Informal English is characterized by a personal tone, the occasional use of popular expressions *(forget it)*, contractions, shorter sentences, and so on. Informal English sounds like one person talking to another person in a relaxed setting.

Formal English is characterized by a serious tone, a careful attention to appropriate word choice, and longer sentences. Formal English, such as you are reading in this sentence, is carefully worded so that it can withstand repeated readings without sounding trite or stale.

✱ After reviewing these explanations, check your essay to determine how you can make each part sound more formal.

Revising for Effective Sentence Fluency

Author E. B. White advises writers to "approach sentence style by way of simplicity, plainness, orderliness, and sincerity." That's good advice from someone who knows style. The following information will help you know what to look for when revising your sentences for style and smoothness.

Avoid Sentence Problems

After reading over your news story, you realize that certain passages sound short and choppy. To solve this problem, you combine the sentences to make them read more smoothly.

Original Passage: Many houses were destroyed. Some just lost their shutters or their windows. Others lost parts of their roofs.

Revised Version: **While many houses were completely destroyed, some lost only their shutters, their windows, or parts of their roofs.**

You also noted that a few of your sentences contained misplaced modifiers and dangling modifiers. (See page 90.) You corrected these problems, too.

Original Sentence: I saw a flipped-over car driving to school.
(misplaced modifier)

Revised Version: **Driving to school, I saw a flipped-over car.**

Original Sentence: Meowing pitifully, we found an injured cat.
(dangling modifier)

Revised Version: **We found an injured cat meowing pitifully.**

FAQ

How can I tell if my sentences read smoothly?

Read your writing out loud, paying special attention to the flow of your ideas. Then have someone else read it aloud as you listen carefully for anything that causes the reader to stumble. Edit your writing until all of your sentences read smoothly.

HELP FILE

Use the following strategy to add variety to your sentences:

- In one column on a piece of paper, list the opening words in each of your sentences. Then decide if you need to vary some beginnings.

- In another column, list the verbs in each sentence. Then decide if you need to replace any overused "be" verbs (*is, are, was, were*) with more vivid ones (*snap, stare, stir*).

- In a third column, identify the number of words in each sentence. Then decide if you need to change the length of some of your sentences.

Revising Checklist

Use this checklist as a guide when you revise your writing. **Remember:** When you revise, you improve the information that carries your message.

Ideas

_____ Is my topic important and relevant?

_____ Have I developed a specific focus or thesis statement?

_____ Does each paragraph support my main point?

_____ Have I included enough details to make my ideas clear?

Organization

_____ Does my writing follow a clear pattern of organization?

_____ Have I developed effective beginning, middle, and closing parts?

_____ Do I need to reorder any parts?

Voice

_____ Does my voice fit the purpose of my writing?

_____ Do I sound interested in, and knowledgeable about, my topic?

Word Choice

_____ Have I used an appropriate level of formality or informality?

_____ Do I use specific nouns and vivid verbs?

_____ Do I avoid unneeded repetition and redundancies?

Sentence Fluency

_____ Are my sentences complete and clearly written?

_____ Do my sentences flow smoothly?

_____ Have I varied my sentence beginnings and lengths?

"The first rule in listening to comments about your work is 'Never defend yourself' — unless you can tell that your critic has misunderstood something."

—Ken Macrorie

A Guide to
GROUP Advising

All writers can benefit from an interested audience, especially one that offers helpful advice. And who could make a better audience than your fellow writers? Those of you who work in writing groups already know the value of writers sharing their drafts. The rest of you should try it as soon as possible—no matter how nerve-racking it may seem to let your peers read your writing. You can handle it.

Exactly how can a writing group help you? Well, your fellow writers can tell you what they view as the strengths and potential trouble spots in your writing. This feedback is valuable throughout the writing process, but it is especially helpful during the early stages of revising when you are evaluating your first draft. Some experts go so far as to say that talking about your work will help you more than anything else you do during the writing process.

Preview

- Using Writing-Group Guidelines
- A Closer Look at Responding
- Group-Advising Strategies
- Peer Response Sheet

Using Writing-Group Guidelines

The guidelines below will help you conduct effective group-advising sessions. (If you're just starting out, work in small groups of three or four classmates.)

Role of the Writer-Reader

- **Come prepared with a meaningful piece of writing.** Make a copy for each group member (if this is what the group usually does).

- **Introduce your writing.** However, don't say too much; let your writing do the talking.

- **Read your copy out loud.** Don't stop to comment on your writing; just read it as clearly as you can.

- **Listen and take notes as the group reacts to your writing.** Don't be defensive about your writing since this will stop some members from commenting honestly. Answer all of their questions.

- **Share your concerns with your fellow writers.** If, for example, you're not sure about your ending, ask your listeners to pay special attention to it. Asking for specific advice may help your peers open up.

Role of the Listener-Responders

- **Listen carefully and take notes as the writer reads.** Keep your notes brief so you don't miss any part of the reading. (Afterward, read the text silently if the writer has supplied individual copies.)

- **Imagine yourself as the intended audience.** If, for example, the writing was meant for younger readers, a business, or the writer's peers, react to it with that audience in mind.

- **Keep your comments positive and constructive.** Instead of saying, "Great job," make more meaningful comments: "Sharing the personal story in the opening really grabbed my attention."

- **Focus your comments on specific things you observe.** An observation such as "I notice that many of your sentences start in the same way" is more helpful than "Add style to your writing."

- **Ask questions of the author.** "What do you mean when you say . . . ?" "Where did you get your facts about . . . ?"

- **Listen to other comments and add to them.** In this way, you help one another become better writers and better group advisors.

A Closer Look at Responding

Remember that the goal of group-advising sessions is to help each writer develop her or his writing into an effective finished product. The information on this page will help group members achieve this goal.

Making Your Responses Count

As a listener-responder, you will make two general types of responses: descriptions and assessments.

1. **Describing What You've Heard or Read . . .** A writer may simply want responders to say what they think the writing is about. (*Can you follow my main points?*) As a responder, you listen attentively and describe what you've heard without making any comments about the effectiveness of the writing. A writer may, however, ask you to identify parts that are not clearly stated.

2. **Assessing the Writing . . .** At other times, a writer may want responders to evaluate a piece of writing. (*What are the strengths and weaknesses in my writing? Does the opening work for you? What changes should I make?*) As a responder, you should note specific things you like or have questions about, and you should make specific suggestions for revisions. (See pages 26 and 78.)

Asking the Writer Questions

Writer and teacher Nancie Atwell suggests that listener-responders ask the following types of questions while reviewing a piece of writing.

To help writers reflect on their purpose and audience . . .
Why are you writing this?
Who will read this, and what do they need to know?

To help writers focus their thoughts . . .
What message are you trying to get across?
Do you have more than one main point?
What are the most important examples?

To help writers think about their information . . .
What do you know about the topic?
Does this part say enough?
Does your writing cover all of the basics
(*Who? What? Where? When? Why?* and *How?*)?

To help writers with their openings and closings . . .
What are you trying to say in the opening?
How else could you start your writing?
How do you want your readers to feel at the end?

Group-Advising Strategies

These next two pages provide four different strategies that you can use in group-advising sessions.

Critiquing a Paper

Use the following checklist as a basic guide when you assess a piece of writing in progress.

___ **Purpose:** Is it clear what the writer is trying to do—entertain, inform, persuade, describe? Explain.

___ **Audience:** Does the writing address a specific audience? Will the readers understand and appreciate this subject? Why?

___ **Ideas:** Does the writer develop the subject with enough information?

___ **Organization:** Are the ideas arranged in the best way, making the main points clear to the readers?

___ **Voice:** Does the writing sound sincere and honest? Does the writer speak to his or her audience? Explain.

___ **Word Choice:** Does the writer include any technical terms? Are these terms defined? Does the level of language fit the audience and topic?

___ **Sentence Fluency:** Do the sentences read smoothly from start to finish? Are the sentences varied in length and structure?

___ **Purpose Again:** Does the writing succeed in making you smile, nod, or react in some other way? What is especially good about the writing?

Reacting to Writing

Peter Elbow, in *Writing Without Teachers,* offers four types of reactions group members might have to a piece of writing:

- **Pointing** refers to a reaction in which a group member "points out" words, phrases, or ideas that impress her or him.

- **Summarizing** refers to a reader's general reaction to the writing—a list of main ideas or a single sentence that sums up the work.

- **Telling** refers to readers describing what happens in a piece of writing: first this happens, then this happens, later this happens, and so on.

- **Showing** refers to feelings expressed about the piece. Elbow suggests that readers express these feelings metaphorically. A reader might, for example, refer to something in the writing as if it were a voice quality, a color, a shape, a piece of clothing, and so on. ("Your writing has a neat, tailored quality.")

Appreciating Good Writing

What makes for good writing? The "Checklist for Effective Writing" on page 26 in this handbook lists the traits that show up in effective essays, stories, and articles. The list below approaches the qualities of good writing in a somewhat different way. Use either list as a guide during group-advising sessions. Good writing is . . .

- **original** (the topic or the approach is lively and energized),
- **organized** (the ideas are presented in a sensible or effective order),
- **detailed** (the details are specific and colorful),
- **clear** (the sentences clearly and smoothly move the writing forward),
- **correct** (the final product is clean and correct), and
- **effective** (the writing is engaging and informative).

Feeling Your OAQS

Here's a simple and effective four-step scheme that can be used when discussing early drafts during group-advising sessions.

Observe
Appreciate
Question
Suggest

Observe means to notice what another person's essay is designed to do, and to say something about the design or purpose. For example, you might say, "Even though you are writing about your boyfriend, it appears that you are trying to get a message across to your parents."

Appreciate means to identify something in the writing that impresses or pleases you. You can find something to appreciate in any piece of writing. For example, you might say, "You make a very convincing point" or "With your description, I can actually see his broken tooth."

Question means to ask whatever you want to know after you have read the essay. You might ask for background information, a definition, an interpretation, or an explanation. For example, you might say, "Why didn't you tell us what happened when you got to the emergency room?"

Suggest means to give helpful advice about possible changes. Offer this advice honestly and courteously. Be specific and be positive. For example, you might say, "With a little more physical detail—especially more sounds and smells—your third paragraph could be the highlight of the whole essay. What do you think?"

Peer Response Sheet

Use a response sheet like the one below to make comments about another person's writing. (Sample comments are included.)

Response Sheet

Responder's Name: Amber Hayward

Writer's Name: Jack O'Neill

Title: McKinley's Mighty Eleven

What I liked about your work:

• You use a lot of sensory details and descriptions, so now I know what it feels like to play soccer.

• You're obviously knowledgeable about your topic.

• It was really exciting the way you described, moment by moment, the final goal of the last game.

• Your metaphors were great! "Trevor made a jailbreak with the ball . . ." "Alex moved like quicksilver through the opposition . . ."

Changes I would suggest:

• There's too much here—describing the team, the season, and the last game. What if you just focus on the last game?

• While the play-by-play is exciting, I had trouble following parts of it.

• In the middle, your writing voice became more informational than storylike. Can you give us the info. in the same tone as the rest of the piece?

• You use some soccer terms — "wingback," "sweeper," and a "Metodo defense"—that confused me.

HELP FILE

Carefully review the feedback that you receive during peer-response sessions; then plan your revising accordingly. You may or may not agree with all of the suggestions that are made.

"In writing, punctuation plays the role of body language. It helps readers hear you the way you want to be heard."

—Russell Baker

A Guide to EDITING and PROOFREADING

There comes a point in any writing project (like a fast-approaching due date) when you must prepare your work for publication. You've worked on your writing's content and style in depth—prewriting through revising. All the right words and ideas are in place. Now you must edit and proofread your writing for "surface errors," the problems with conventions that keep a reader from understanding or enjoying your message. You should check your writing for errors in punctuation, mechanics (specifically spelling and capitalization), and grammar.

Student writer Katie Pingle knows how important this step is in the writing process. In fact, one of the essential things she has learned about writing is the need to edit again and again. As she states, "There is nothing worse than reading a final piece of work with a lot of errors. It's so frustrating."

Preview

- **Quick Guide**

- **10 Common Errors to Watch For**

- **Editing in Action**

- **Checklist for Editing and Proofreading**

"I can't write five words but that I change seven."

—Dorothy Parker

Quick Guide

PURPOSE: Editing and proofreading deal with the line-by-line changes you make to improve the readability and accuracy of your writing. More specifically, when you edit, you make sure that the sentences in your revised writing are clear and correct. When you proofread, you make sure your writing is free of errors.

STARTING POINT: You're ready to edit once you . . .

■ complete your major revisions—adding, cutting, rewriting, or rearranging the ideas in your writing;

■ make a clean copy of your revised writing; and

■ set your writing aside for a day or two (if time permits).

When you edit your writing, try to focus on one type of potential error at a time. This will help you edit more carefully and more thoroughly. (See page 83 for a checklist.)

Remember: Have a someone else check your work as well. You're too close to your writing to spot everything that needs to be changed.

FORM: If you're working with pen and paper, do your editing on a neat copy of your revised writing. (Try to use a different color ink for your editing.) Then complete a final copy of your work.

If you're working on a computer, do your editing on a printed copy of your writing. Then enter the changes on the computer. Save the edited copy so you have a record of your changes.

THE BIG PICTURE: When you edit and proofread, focus your attention on the conventions of writing. Make sure your writing is free of errors in punctuation, mechanics, and grammar.

Punctuation ● Review your work for all forms of punctuation; however, the most common errors involve commas and apostrophes. (See pages 489–493 and 498–499.)

Mechanics ● Check your work for spelling and capitalization. (See pages 507–509 and 516–522.)

Grammar ● Review your work for grammar errors. Pay special attention to subject-verb agreement, pronoun-antecedent agreement, and usage errors. (See pages 81, 83, and 558–560.)

10 Common Errors to Watch For

1. **Missing Comma After Long Introductory Phrases** ■ Place a comma after a long introductory phrase.

    Because of the terrible thunderstorm‸our school bus was late.

2. **Confusing Pronoun Reference** ■ Make sure the reader knows whom your pronoun refers to. (See page 89.)   Mr. Wilson

    When Bob talked with Mr. Wilson, ~~he~~ offered him a scholarship.

3. **Missing Comma in a Compound Sentence** ■ Use a comma between two independent clauses joined by a coordinating conjunction—*and, but, or, nor, so, for,* or *yet.* (See 489.1.)

    I don't know what to say‸but I have to deliver a speech.

4. **Missing Comma(s) with a Nonrestrictive Phrase** ■ Use commas to set off a phrase that is not needed to understand the sentence. (See 491.2.)

    Rob spoke with Lester‸who is a new student.

5. **Comma Splices** ■ Do not use a comma to separate clauses that could stand alone as sentences. (See page 88.)

    I made the varsity baseball team⨀I will be a starting pitcher.

6. **Subject-Verb Agreement Errors** ■ Verbs must agree in number with their subjects. Singular subjects take singular verbs, and plural subjects take plural verbs. (See pages 542 and 558.)

    has

    A list of new band members ~~have~~ been posted in the band room.

7. **Missing Comma in a Series** ■ Use commas to separate individual words, phrases, or clauses in a series. (See 490.3.)

    Chuck played football with Jamal, Paul, Steve‸and Chul.

8. **Pronoun-Antecedent Agreement Errors** ■ A pronoun must agree in number with the word that the pronoun refers to. (See page 560.1.)

    her

    Either Sally or Maria dropped ~~their~~ books in the puddle.

9. **Missing Apostrophe to Show Ownership** ■ Use an apostrophe after a noun to show possession. (See 498.3–498.4.)

    Carry that carton out to the principal's car.

10. **Misusing *Its* and *It's*** ■ *Its* is a possessive pronoun meaning "belonging to it." *It's* is a contraction of "it is" or "it has."

    It's a fact that a minnow has teeth in its throat.

Editing in Action

Note the editing changes made in these paragraphs from an essay on computer-generated graphics (CG).

A capitalization error is corrected.

A usage error is corrected.

A comma splice is corrected.

Apostrophes are added to show possession.

Pronoun-antecedent agreement is corrected.

A comma is added to a compound sentence.

CG lets filmmakers create dangerous effects, such as a rampaging forest fire or even a tidal wave hitting New York city (*Deep Impact*, 1998). Nobody gets hurt, and nothing gets damaged, since it's all in the computer. CG can even create a realistic army on the battlefield from only a few figures (*Lord of the Rings: Return of the King*, 2003). Filmmakers save millions of dollars by not having to hire thousands of extras. In short, CG can show stories that were too dangerous (or impossible) to shoot before.

While it has many favorable effects on moviemaking, CG can also shortchange an audience's imagination. Some of the best movies have relied on the viewers' minds to complete what they don't see. In the movie *Jaws* (1975), the excitement comes from rarely seeing the shark. Director Steven Spielberg admits, "The shark would be fully CG today, and it wouldn't be a better movie. I would have used the shark too much" (Westbrook, 8). If CG shows everything on screen, nothing is left to the imagination. That can ruin a movie.

Checklist for Editing and Proofreading

Use this checklist as a guide when you edit and proofread your writing. Also refer to "10 Common Errors to Watch For" on page 81. *Remember:* **Edit your writing only after you have revised it**.

Conventions

Look at Punctuation . . . (See pages 487–506.)

_____ Do my sentences end with the proper punctuation?

_____ Do I use commas correctly in compound sentences?

_____ Do I use commas correctly in a series and after long introductory phrases or clauses?

_____ Do I use apostrophes correctly?

_____ Do I punctuate dialogue correctly?

Look at Mechanics . . . (See pages 507–509 and 516–522.)

_____ Do I start my sentences with capital letters?

_____ Do I capitalize proper nouns?

_____ Have I checked for spelling errors (including those the spell-checker may have missed)?

Look at Grammar . . . (See pages 550–563.)

_____ Do the subjects and verbs agree in my sentences?

_____ Do my sentences use correct and consistent verb tenses?

_____ Do my pronouns agree with their antecedents?

_____ Have I avoided any other usage errors?

Check for Presentation . . . (See pages 27–32.)

_____ Does the title effectively lead into the writing?

_____ Are sources of information properly presented and documented?

_____ Does my writing meet the requirements for final presentation?

BASIC ELEMENTS
of Writing

Writing Sentences   85

Writing Paragraphs   99

> "Whatever sentence will bear to be read twice,
> we may be sure was thought twice."
>
> —Henry David Thoreau

Writing
SENTENCES

Sentences are basic to written communication. A well-chosen phrase may communicate an important idea, but a well-written sentence is still the most effective way to get a point across. This is true in e-mail messages, writing assignments, business letters, notes to friends, job applications, and so on.

You can learn the most about writing effective sentences by reading them—in books, magazines, and newspapers, and on the Internet. Then you have to practice by writing regularly in a variety of forms (not all of them formal). This chapter provides guidelines for writing effective sentences that are clear, complete, and sophisticated. (See pages 550–560 for more on sentences.)

Preview

- **Understanding the Basics**
- **Writing Complete and Clear Sentences**
- **Writing Natural and Acceptable Sentences**
- **Combining Sentences**
- **Modeling Sentences**
- **Expanding Sentences**
- **Sentence-Writing Tips**

Understanding the Basics

Simple sentences in the English language follow five basic patterns. (See pages 524–525 for more information.)

1. Subject + Verb

┌─S─┐ ┌─V─┐
Naomie winked.

Some verbs like *winked* are intransitive. Intransitive verbs *do not* need a direct object to express a complete thought. (See 539.3)

2. Subject + Verb + Direct Object

┌─S─┐ ┌─V─┐ ┌─DO─┐
Harris grinds his teeth.

Some verbs like *grinds* are transitive. Transitive verbs *do* need a direct object to express a complete thought. (See 540.1.)

3. Subject + Verb + Indirect Object + Direct Object

┌─S─┐ ┌─V─┐ ┌──IO──┐ ┌──DO──┐
Elena offered her friend an anchovy.

The direct object names who or what receives the action; the indirect object names to whom or for whom the action was done.

4. Subject + Verb + Direct Object + Object Complement

┌───S───┐ ┌─V─┐ DO ┌──────OC──────┐
Room 222 named Ravi the class webmaster.

The object complement renames or describes the direct object.

5. Subject + Linking Verb + Predicate Noun (or Predicate Adjective)

┌─S─┐LV┌──PN──┐   ┌─S─┐LV┌────PA────┐
Paula is a math whiz.   **Paula is very intelligent.**

A linking verb connects the subject of the sentence to the predicate noun or predicate adjective. The predicate noun renames the subject; the predicate adjective describes the subject.

Inverted Order

In the sentence patterns above, the subject comes before the verb. In a few types of sentences, such as the two below, the subject comes *after* the verb.

LV┌─S─┐ ┌─PN─┐
Is Larisa a poet? (A question)

LV ┌──S──┐
There was a meeting. (A sentence beginning with "there")

"To err is human, but when the eraser wears out ahead of the pencil, you're overdoing it." —J. Jenkins

Writing Complete Sentences

By definition, a complete sentence expresses a complete thought and contains both a subject and a predicate. Several ideas, not just one, may make up this complete thought. The trick is getting those ideas to work together in a clear, interesting sentence that expresses your exact meaning.

The most common sentence errors are *fragments, comma splices, rambling sentences,* and *run-ons.*

Fragment ■ A fragment is a group of words used as a sentence. It is not a sentence, though, because it lacks a subject, a verb, or some other essential part. Because of the missing part, the thought is incomplete.

Fragment: **Spaghetti all over the table.** (This fragment lacks a verb.)

Sentence: **Spaghetti flew all over the table.**

Fragment: **When Aneko opened the box.** (This fragment has a subject and verb, but it does not convey a complete thought. We need to know what happened "when Aneko opened the box.")

Sentence: **When Aneko opened the box, spaghetti flew all over the table.**

Fragment: **Laughing and scooping up a pile of spaghetti. Kate remarked, "Now, that's what I call a spaghetti mess!"** (The fragment is followed by a complete sentence. This fragment, a participial phrase, can be combined with the sentence to form a complete thought.)

Sentence: **Laughing and scooping up a pile of spaghetti, Kate remarked, "Now, that's what I call a spaghetti mess!"**

FAQ ## Is it ever acceptable to use fragments?

Yes, when you have good reason. For example, single words or phrases set off as sentences can have a dramatic effect. In one of her articles, writer Anna Quindlan uses the following three fragments to dramatize the problems facing urban youths:

> **"Teenage mothers. Child abuse. Crowded schools."**

✱ You can also use fragments when you write dialogue because people often use incomplete thoughts when they talk.

> **"Hey, Rico. My house?"**
> **"Yeah, right. On Tuesday afternoon."**
> **"Whatever."**

Comma Splice ■ A comma splice results when two independent clauses are connected ("spliced") with only a comma. The comma is not enough: a period, a semicolon, or a conjunction is needed. (*Note:* An independent clause presents a complete thought and can stand alone as a sentence.)

Splice: The concertgoers had been waiting in the hot sun for two hours, many were beginning to show their impatience by chanting and clapping.

Corrected: The concertgoers had been waiting in the hot sun for two hours, and many were beginning to show their impatience by chanting and clapping. (A coordinating conjunction has been added.)

Corrected: The concertgoers had been waiting in the hot sun for two hours; many were beginning to show their impatience by chanting and clapping. (The comma has been changed to a semicolon.)

Rambling Sentence ■ A rambling sentence seems to go on and on in a monotonous fashion (often because of too many *and*'s.) To correct this error, remove some of the *and*'s, fix the punctuation, and reword different parts if it results in a better passage.

Rambling: The intruder entered through the window and tiptoed down the hall and stood under the stairwell and waited in the shadows.

Corrected: The intruder entered through the window. He tiptoed down the hall and stood under the stairwell, waiting in the shadows.

Corrected: The intruder, who had entered through the window, tiptoed down the hall. He stood under the stairwell and waited in the shadows.

Run-On Sentence ■ A run-on is two (or more) sentences joined without adequate punctuation or a connecting word.

Run-on: I thought the ride would never end my eyes were crossed, and my fingers were numb.

Corrected: I thought the ride would never end. My eyes were crossed, and my fingers were numb.

"If any man wishes to write in a clear style, let him first be clear in his thoughts." —Johann Wolfgang von Goethe

Writing **Clear** Sentences

Nothing is more frustrating for readers than writing that has to be reread just to understand its basic meaning. Look carefully at the common errors that follow. If you recognize any of them as errors you sometimes make in your own writing, use this section as a checklist when you revise. Avoiding these errors will help to make your sentences clear and readable.

Incomplete Comparison ■ An incomplete comparison is the result of leaving out a word or words that are necessary to show exactly what is being compared to what.

Incomplete: **I get along with Rosa better than my sister.**
(Do you mean that you get along with Rosa better than you get along with your sister . . . or that you get along with Rosa better than your sister does?)

Clear: **I get along with Rosa better than my sister does.**

Ambiguous Wording ■ Ambiguous wording is wording that is unclear because it has two or more possible meanings.

Ambiguous: **Mike decided to take his new convertible to the drive-in movie, which turned out to be a real horror story.**
(What turned out to be a real horror story—Mike's taking his new convertible to the drive-in or the movie?)

Clear: **Mike decided to take his new convertible to the drive-in movie, a decision that turned out to be a real horror story.**

Indefinite Reference ■ An indefinite reference is a problem caused by careless use of pronouns. As a result, readers are not sure who or what the pronoun(s) is referring to.

Indefinite: **In *To Kill a Mockingbird*, she describes the problems faced by Atticus Finch and his family.** (Who is *she*?)

Clear: **In *To Kill a Mockingbird*, the author, Harper Lee, describes the problems faced by Atticus Finch and his family.**

Indefinite: **As he pulled his car up to the service window, it made a strange rattling sound.** (Which rattled, the car or the window?)

Clear: **His car made a strange rattling sound as he pulled up to the service window.**

Misplaced Modifiers ■ Misplaced modifiers are modifiers that have been placed incorrectly; therefore, the meaning of the sentence is not clear. (Modifiers should be placed as close as possible to the word they modify.)

Misplaced: **We have an assortment of combs for physically active people with unbreakable teeth.** (People with unbreakable teeth?)

Corrected: **For physically active people, we have an assortment of combs with unbreakable teeth.** (Corrected by rearranging the sentence.)

We have an assortment of combs for physically active people with unbreakable teeth.

Dangling Modifiers ■ Dangling modifiers are modifiers that appear to modify the wrong word or a word that isn't in the sentence.

Dangling: **Trying desperately to get under the fence, Chan's mother called her.**
(The phrase *trying desperately to get under the fence* appears to modify *Chan's mother.*)

Corrected: **Trying desperately to get under the fence, Chan heard her mother call her.**
(Corrected by rewording and adding *Chan,* the person being referred to by the modifier.)

Dangling: **After standing in line for five hours, the manager announced that all the tickets had been sold.**
(In this sentence, it appears as if the manager had been *standing in line for five hours.*)

Corrected: **After I stood in line for five hours, the manager announced that all the tickets had been sold.**
(Corrected by rewording the sentence.)

"Don't worry about writing the perfect sentence, or you'll never get past the first line."

—Jan Greenbough

Writing Natural Sentences

One of the greatest temptations facing writers is to use big words, clever words, and fancy words. For some reason, we get the idea into our heads that writing *simply* is not writing effectively. Nothing could be further from the truth.

The best writing is honest and natural, not fancy or artificial. That's why it is so important to master the art of freewriting. It is your best chance at developing a sincere, simple style. The samples that follow demonstrate wordy and artificial writing; rewrite any passages in your own work that sound like these sentences.

Deadwood ■ Deadwood is wording that fills up lots of space but does not add anything important or new to the overall meaning.

> **Wordy:** At this point in time, I feel the study needs additional work before the subcommittee can recommend it be resubmitted for further consideration.
>
> **Concise:** The study needs more work.

Flowery Language ■ Flowery language is writing that uses more or bigger words than needed. It is writing that often contains too many adjectives or adverbs.

> **Flowery:** The cool, fresh breeze, which came like a storm in the night, lifted me to the exhilarating heights from which I had been previously suppressed by the incandescent cloud in the learning center.
>
> **Concise:** The cool breeze was a refreshing change from the muggy classroom air.

Trite Expression ■ A trite expression is one that is overused and stale; as a result, it sounds neither sincere nor natural.

> **Trite:** It gives all of us a great deal of pleasure to present to you this plaque as a token of our appreciation.
>
> **Natural:** Please accept this plaque with our heartfelt thanks.

Jargon ■ Jargon is language used in a certain profession or by a certain group of people. It is usually very technical and not at all natural.

> **Jargon:** I'm having conceptual difficulty with these employee mandates.
>
> **Natural:** I don't understand these work rules.

Euphemism ■ A euphemism is a word or a phrase that is substituted for another because it is considered a less offensive way of saying something.

Euphemism: I am so exasperated that I could expectorate.

Natural: I am so mad I could spit.

Wordiness ■ Wordiness occurs when extra words are used in a sentence, such as when a word, phrase, or synonym is repeated unnecessarily.

Redundant: He had a way of keeping my attention by raising and lowering his voice all the time throughout his whole speech.

Concise: He kept my attention by raising and lowering his voice when he spoke.

Double Subject: Some people they don't use their voices as well as they could. (Drop *they; people* is the only subject needed.)

Concise: Some people don't use their voices as well as they could.

Tautology: repeat again, descend down, audible to the ear, refer back, unite together (Each word group says the same thing twice.)

Cliche ■ A cliche is an overused word or phrase that springs quickly to mind but just as quickly bores the user and the audience. A cliche gives the reader nothing new or original to think about.

Cliche: Her face was as red as a beet.

Natural: Her face turned a deep shade of red.

CLICHES TO AVOID

after all is said and done	food for thought
beat around the bush	grin and bear it
believe it or not	in a nutshell
best foot forward	in one ear and out the other
better late than never	in the nick of time
calm before the storm	last but not least
cart before the horse	lesser of two evils
chalk up a victory	more than meets the eye
come through with flying colors	no time like the present
crying shame	put your foot in your mouth
don't rock the boat	quiet enough to hear a pin drop
drop in the bucket	raining cats and dogs
easier said than done	see eye to eye
face the music	shot in the arm
fish out of water	sink or swim

"You can be a little ungrammatical if you come from the right part of the country."

—Robert Frost

Writing Acceptable Sentences

What Robert Frost says is certainly true. Much of the color and charm of literature comes from the everyday habits and customs—and especially the speech—of its characters. Keep that in mind when you write fiction of any kind. However, when you write essays, reports, and most other assignments, keep in mind that it's just as important to use language that is correct, appropriate, and therefore acceptable.

Nonstandard Language ■ Nonstandard language is often acceptable in everyday conversation, but seldom in formal writing.

Colloquial: Avoid the use of colloquial language such as *go with, wait up*.

Hey, wait up! Cam wants to go with. (Nonstandard)

Hey, wait! Cam wants to go with us. (Acceptable)

Double Preposition: Avoid the use of certain double prepositions: *off of, off to, in on*.

Reggie went off to the movies. (Nonstandard)

Reggie went to the movies. (Acceptable)

Substitution: Avoid substituting *and* for *to* in formal writing.

Try and get here on time. (Nonstandard)

Try to get here on time. (Acceptable)

Avoid substituting *of* or *have* when combining with *could, would, should,* or *might*.

I should of studied for that test. (Nonstandard)

I should have studied for that test. (Acceptable)

Slang: Avoid the use of slang or any other "in" words.

The museum trip was way cool. (Nonstandard)

The museum trip was memorable. (Acceptable)

Double Negative ■ A double negative is the improper use of two negative words to perform the same function in a sentence. In standard English, use only one negative word in a sentence.

Awkward: **I haven't got no money.**

Corrected: **I haven't got any money. / I have no money.**

✱ Using the words *hardly, barely,* or *scarcely* with the words *no* or *not* also results in a double negative.

Shifts in Construction ■ A shift in construction is a change in the structure or style midway through a sentence. (See page 558.)

Shift in Number:	When a person has the flu, they ought to stay at home.
Corrected:	When people have the flu, they ought to stay at home.
Shift in Person:	When you are well again, you can do all the things a person loves to do.
Corrected:	When you are well again, you can do all the things you love to do.
Shift in Voice:	Marcia is playing soccer again, and many new skills are being learned by her. (The shift is from *active* to *passive voice.* See 541.1.)
Corrected:	Marcia is playing soccer again and learning many new skills. (Both verbs are in the *active voice.*)
Shift in Tense:	Marcia drinks juice and got plenty of rest.
Corrected:	Marcia drinks juice and gets plenty of rest.

✱ A tense shift is acceptable in a sentence that states one action as happening before another action.

> **I think** (present tense) **he completed** (past tense) **his assignment last night.**

Unparallel Construction ■ Unparallel construction occurs when the kind of words or phrases being used changes in the middle of a sentence. (See page 115.)

Unparallel:	In my hometown, folks pass the time shooting pool, pitching horseshoes, and at softball games. (The sentence switches from the *-ing* words—*shooting* and *pitching*—to the prepositional phrase *at softball games.*)
Parallel:	In my hometown, folks pass the time shooting pool, pitching horseshoes, and playing softball. (Now all three activities are *-ing* words—they are consistent, or parallel.)
Unparallel:	For the open house, teachers prepare handouts for parents and are organizing the students' work for display. (In this sentence, the verbs *prepare* and *organizing* are unparallel—not stated in the same way.)
Parallel:	For the open house, teachers prepare handouts for parents and organize the students' work for display. (Now both verbs are stated in the same way.)

Combining Sentences

If you were to write a sentence about a tornado that struck a small town without warning, causing a great deal of damage, a number of serious injuries, and several deaths, you would have six different ideas:

1. **There was a tornado.**
2. **The tornado struck a small town.**
3. **The tornado struck without warning.**
4. **The tornado caused a great deal of damage.**
5. **The tornado caused a number of serious injuries.**
6. **The tornado caused several deaths.**

Of course, you wouldn't express each idea separately like this. Instead, you would combine the ideas into longer, more detailed sentences. Sentence combining, which can be done in a variety of ways (see below), is one of the most effective writing techniques you can practice.

- Use a series to combine three or more similar ideas.
  The tornado struck the small town without warning, causing **extensive damage, numerous injuries,** and **several deaths.**

- Use a relative pronoun *(who, whose, that, which)* to introduce the subordinate (less important) ideas.
  The tornado, **which was completely unexpected,** swept through the small town, causing extensive damage, numerous injuries, and several deaths.

- Use an introductory phrase or clause for the less important ideas.
  Because the tornado was completely unexpected, it caused extensive damage, numerous injuries, and several deaths.

- Use a participial phrase *(-ing, -ed)* to begin or end a sentence.
  The tornado swept through the small town without warning, **leaving a trail of death and destruction.**

- Use a semicolon. (Also use a **conjunctive adverb** if appropriate.)
  The tornado struck the town without warning; **therefore,** it caused extensive damage, numerous injuries, and several deaths.

- Repeat a key word or phrase to emphasize an idea.
  The unexpected tornado left a permanent **scar** on the small town, a **scar** of destruction, injury, and death.

- Use correlative conjunctions *(not only, but also; either, or)* to compare or contrast two ideas in a sentence.
  The unexpected tornado inflicted **not only** immense property damage **but also** immeasurable human suffering.

- Use an appositive (or an appositive phrase) for emphasis.
  A single incident, **a tornado that came without warning,** changed the face of the small town forever.

Modeling Sentences

Study the writing of your favorite authors, and you may find sentences that seem to flow on forever, sentences that are direct and to the point, and "sentences" that aren't by definition complete thoughts. (Authors do occasionally break the rules.)

Take NOTE   Generally speaking, most popular authors write in a relaxed, engaging style. This style is characterized by sentences with a lot of personality, rhythm, balance, and variety.

The Modeling Process

Imitating certain sentences because you like the way they sound or the way they make a point is called *sentence modeling*. Here's the process:

- **Reserve** a special section in your notebook to list effective sentences you come across—those that flow smoothly, use effective descriptive words, and contain original figures of speech such as metaphors, similes, and personifications. (See pages 124–126.)

- **Copy** the well-made sentences (or short passages) into your notebook.

- **Study** each sentence so you know how it is put together. Read it out loud. Look for phrases and clauses set off by commas. Also focus on word endings (*-ing, -ed*) and on the location of articles (*a, an, the*) and prepositions (*to, by, of*).

- **Write** your own version of the sentence, imitating it part by part. Try to use the same word endings, articles, and prepositions, but work in your own nouns, verbs, and modifiers.

- **Continue** imitating a number of different sentences in order to fine-tune your sense of sentence style.

THE PROCESS IN ACTION

Study the following sentence:

> **He has a thin face with sharp features and a couple of eyes burning with truth oil.** —Tom Wolfe

Now look carefully at the sentence below. Compare it part by part to the original sentence. Can you see how the modeling was done?

> **He has an athletic body with a sinewy contour and a couple of arms bulging with weight-room dedication.**

Expanding Sentences

Details seem to spill out of accomplished writers' minds naturally. Readers marvel at how effectively these authors can expand a basic idea with engaging details. Maybe you envy good writers because of this special ability and wish you could write in the same way. The truth is you can. All it takes is a little practice.

Cumulative Sentences

Above all other types of sentences, the *cumulative sentence* marks an accomplished writer. What you normally find in a cumulative sentence is a main idea that is expanded by modifying words, phrases, or clauses. (See page 555.1 for more information.) Here's a sample cumulative sentence with the expanding modifiers coming *after* the main clause (in purple).

> **Maly was studying at the kitchen table, memorizing a list of vocabulary words, completely focused, intent on acing tomorrow's Spanish quiz.**

Discussion: Notice how each new modifier adds another level of meaning to the sentence. Three modifying phrases have been added. Here's another cumulative sentence with expanding modifiers coming *before* and *after* the main clause (in purple).

> **Before every practice, Kesha Sims and Tonya Harper work on free throws, taking 50 shots each.**

Discussion: In this case, a prepositional phrase (**Before every practice**) and a participial phrase (**taking 50 shots each**) add important details to the main clause.

Expanding with Details

When you practice expanding sentences on your own, remember that there are five basic ways to expand upon an idea:

Individual words: José prepared his breakfast *quickly.*

Prepositional phrases: José ate *with his cat on his lap.*

Participial (-*ing* or -*ed*) phrases: *Looking at the clock,* José gobbled his first piece of toast.

Subordinate clauses: José was still eating *when his mother left for work.*

Relative clauses: The cat, *who loves leftovers,* purred for a treat.

```
┌─HELP FILE─────────────────────────────────────────────
│   To write stylistic sentences, you need to practice sentence modeling and
│ sentence expanding. You also need to become a regular and attentive reader,
│ noticing the style as well as the content of what you read.
└───────────────────────────────────────────────────────
```

Sentence-Writing Tips

How can you make sure that your sentences are effective? Keep these important points in mind:

1. **Vary the pattern of your sentences.**
   Your writing will be interesting if you use a variety of sentence patterns. (See page 86.)

2. **Express complete thoughts.**
   Your writing will be easy to follow if it has no sentence errors such as fragments and comma splices. (See pages 87–88.)

3. **Be clear in your thinking.**
   Your writing will be clear if it is free of ambiguous wording and incomplete comparisons. (See page 89.)

4. **Speak honestly and naturally.**
   Your writing will sound natural if you avoid flowery language, jargon or technical language, deadwood, wordiness, euphemisms, and cliches. (See pages 91–92.)

5. **Follow the rules of standard English.**
   Your writing will reflect favorably on you if it is free of nonstandard language, double negatives, or shifts in construction. (See pages 93–94.)

6. **Combine short, choppy sentences.**
   Your writing will read smoothly if you avoid using too many short, choppy sentences. (See page 95.)

7. **Imitate stylistic sentences.**
   Your writing will have style if you pay special attention to the sound and rhythm of your sentences. (See page 96.)

8. **Practice expanding basic ideas.**
   Your writing will also have style if you pay special attention to the ways in which you add specific details to your sentence. (See page 97.)

"The paragraph [is] a mini-essay;
it is also a maxi-sentence."   —Donald Hall

Writing
PARAGRAPHS

In the real world of literature, the paragraph is not considered a form of writing. You wouldn't, for example, head to the local bookstore to buy a book of paragraphs. Nor would you pursue a writing career because you want to write award-winning paragraphs.

However, paragraphs are very important as building blocks for other kinds of writing. When you write an essay, for instance, you develop paragraphs to organize your thoughts into manageable units. The paragraphs work together to build a clear, convincing essay. Learning how to write effective paragraphs will give you control of all your academic writing—from essays to articles to research papers.

Preview

- **The Parts of a Paragraph**
- **Types of Paragraphs**
- **Understanding Details**
- **Arranging Your Details**
- **Connecting Your Details**

"Constructing a paragraph requires a clear, logical manner of thinking." —Jonathan Snyder

The Parts of a Paragraph

Most paragraphs begin with a topic sentence, identifying the topic of the writing. The sentences in the body of the paragraph support or explain the topic, while the closing sentence brings the paragraph to a logical stopping point. (See the expository paragraph on page 101.)

The Topic Sentence ■ The topic sentence tells your readers what your paragraph is about. Here is a formula for topic sentences:

FORMULA	**A specific topic**
	+ a particular feeling or feature about the topic
	= an effective topic sentence.

Topic Sentence **The average cost of a Hollywood film** (*specific topic*) **runs between 30 and 50 million dollars** (*particular feature*).

FAQ **Is a topic sentence always the first sentence?**

No, you can position a topic sentence anywhere in a paragraph, just as long as it works. For example, you can present details that build up to an important summary statement (topic sentence). This strategy is especially effective in persuasive writing.

The Body ■ The body is the main part of the paragraph. This is where you place all of the information readers need to understand the topic. The sentences in the body should contain details that clearly support the topic sentence. Arrange these details in the best possible order.

Body Sentence **The salary of a top star such as Johnny Depp or Angelina Jolie can add $20 million to the cost of a major film.**

[HOT LINK] Turn to "Arranging Your Details," pages 105–108, when you have questions about how to organize the details in a paragraph.

The Closing ■ The closing (clincher) sentence comes after all the details have been included in the body of the paragraph. This sentence may (1) remind readers of the topic, (2) summarize the paragraph, or (3) link the paragraph to the next one.

Closing Sentence **Anyone who has bought a movie ticket recently knows that the consumer pays for these extravagant productions.**

Types of Paragraphs

There are four types of paragraphs: expository, descriptive, narrative, and persuasive. (Notice how the details support each topic sentence.)

Expository

An **expository paragraph** presents facts, gives directions, defines terms, and so on. It should clearly inform readers about a specific subject.

> The average cost of a Hollywood film runs between 30 and 50 million dollars. There are many reasons for this outlandish expense. The currently popular action-adventure productions are filled with special effects that cost huge amounts of money. In addition, most producers think in terms of blockbuster films. Instead of making a number of smaller, less-expensive films, they focus on big, elaborate films that could be smash hits. Of course, blockbuster films require big stars, which adds significantly to the production costs. The salary of a top star such as Johnny Depp or Angelina Jolie can add $20 million to the cost of a major film. Then the nonstop, full-throttle promotion of a film adds another enormous expense. All of these factors have contributed to the inflated costs of making movies. Anyone who has bought a movie ticket recently knows that the consumer pays for these extravagant productions.

Descriptive

A **descriptive paragraph** presents a single clear picture of a person, a place, a thing, or an idea. It should contain plenty of sensory details—specific sights, sounds, and smells.

> When I told my grandfather I was reading *Tom Sawyer* for school, he showed me his favorite copy of the book—a first edition his grandfather gave to him when Grandpa graduated from college in 1960. It was a hardcover book squarer in shape than modern books. Its cover was bright blue, and the texture of the cloth binding still felt like a new book, except where other shelved books had rubbed it smooth. The spine and the front cover showed the title—*The Adventures of Tom Sawyer*—in gold letters raised a little from the cover. The cover also held other fancy black and gold designs. I flipped a few pages, and the paper felt heavier and thicker than normal. Grandpa told me that it was rag paper, made out of cloth and fabric instead of wood pulp. The pages were a little yellowed, and they had that sharp smell of mildew that you sometimes find in old books. Considering that the book was printed 130 years ago, it was really in good shape. Just holding this copy of *Tom Sawyer* felt like history.

Narrative

A **narrative paragraph** tells a story. It should include details that answer the 5 W's *(Who? What? When? Where?* and *Why?)* about the experience.

In first grade, I learned some of the harsh realities of life. I found out that circuses aren't all they're supposed to be. We were going to the circus for our class trip, and I was really excited about it. Our class worked for weeks on a circus train made of shoe boxes. The day of the trip finally came, and the circus I dreamed of turned out to be nothing but one disappointment after another. First, I couldn't see much of anything. I could just barely make out some tiny figures scurrying around in the three rings. After the first half hour, all I wanted to do was buy a soda and a monkey-on-a-stick and get out of there. Of course, nothing in life is that easy. We weren't allowed to buy anything, so I couldn't have my souvenir; and instead of a cold soda to quench my thirst, I had lukewarm milk that the room mothers had so thoughtfully brought along. I returned to school tired and a little wiser. I remember looking at our little circus train on the window ledge and thinking that I'd rather sit and watch it do nothing than go to another circus.

Persuasive

A **persuasive paragraph** expresses an opinion and tries to convince the reader that the opinion is valid. It should contain supporting points that help solidify your argument.

Capital punishment should be abolished for three major reasons. First of all, common sense tells me that two wrongs don't make a right. To kill someone convicted of murder contradicts the reasoning behind the law that taking another's life is wrong. The state, however, is committing the same violent, dehumanizing act it is condemning. In addition, the death penalty is not an effective deterrent. Numerous studies show that murder is usually the result of complex psychological and sociological problems and that most murderers do not contemplate the consequences of their acts; or, if they do, any penalty is seen as a far-off possibility. The offense, on the other hand, brings immediate gratification. Most importantly, everyone must realize that death is final and cannot be altered. Errors in deciding guilt or innocence will always be present in our system of trial by jury. There is too great a risk that innocent people will be put to death. Official records show that it has happened in the past. For these reasons, I feel capital punishment should be replaced with a system that puts all doubt on the side of life—not death.

Understanding Details

There are many types of details you can include in paragraphs (and longer forms of writing.). Your reason for writing determines which details are most important to your work. The key types of details are explained below and on the next page.

- **Facts** are details that can be proven. Facts remain constant, regardless of the type of paragraph you write.

  > Originally built in 1797 and restored in 1925, the USS *Constitution* is the oldest commissioned ship in the United States Navy.

  > To help build muscles, the body produces creatine naturally.

- **Statistics** present significant numerical information about a chosen topic.

  > By their junior year, 20 percent of Jefferson High students have cars.

  > A regular one-ounce bag of chips contains 10 grams of fat.

- **Examples** are individual samples that illustrate a main point.

  > People have greater responsibilities when they live in smaller communities. In our town, Mrs. Schultz is both the mayor and the only letter carrier. Many of our teachers, such as Mr. Smith, Mr. Walker, and Miss Araebo, are volunteer firefighters.

- **Anecdotes** are brief stories or "slices of life" that help you make your point. They can illustrate a point more personally than a matter-of-fact listing of details.

  > People who lived during the Great Depression always worried about having enough food, even long after such problems were a thing of the past. Marc Damis was a millionaire many times over, but his relatives found thousands of sugar and ketchup packets from local restaurants in his house after he died.

  ✱ Make sure that an anecdote makes a point and really fits with your specific topic.

- **Quotations** are words from another person that you repeat exactly in your writing. Quotations can provide powerful supporting evidence.

  > Vivid description allows the reader to see the writer's topic. Artist Pablo Picasso put it this way: "Often while reading a book, one feels that the author would have preferred to paint rather than write: one can sense the pleasure he derives from describing a landscape or a person" (Charlton 80). In this sense, descriptive writing, so often dismissed, is the opportunity for a writer to act as an artist.

■ **Definitions** provide the meanings of unfamiliar terms. Definitions may add some clarity to your writing.

> That painting has a lot of texture since it is a fresco—a painting applied directly onto wet plaster.

> While some people have heard of this as the title of a stage play, the Mikado is actually another name for the emperor of Japan.

■ **Reasons** justify ideas or actions, expand motives, and answer the "Why?" question.

> Nordhoff and Hall's novel *Mutiny on the Bounty* should be taught without focusing solely on the mutiny and its repercussions. Its first-person account reveals the good and bad of life in the British Navy of the eighteenth century. It shows us the politics and economics behind British colonial policies. It also presents life in Tahiti and the South Seas before its culture became forever altered by British and French colonialism.

■ **Explanations** make things clearer and answer the "How?" question. Explanations clarify an idea or a deed.

> People can solve the problem of rising gas prices in many ways. The simplest methods include carpooling and the use of public transportation. Additional solutions include the use of hybrid cars or even biodiesel cars, which use cooking oil for fuel.

■ **Summaries** give a shorter version of something said, written, or done.

> On March 23, 1775, Patrick Henry gave a speech to the Virginia Convention. He noted his reasons for rebelling against the British Crown—his love for his country, his distrust of British governors, and his hope for others to stand up against oppression. Most remember only his closing remark that summed up his argument—"Give me liberty, or give me death!"

■ **Comparisons** show how two topics are similar and/or different.

> The Eiffel Tower and the Statue of Liberty are both great examples of nineteenth-century French architecture and design.

> Mahatma Gandhi's approach to social change differed greatly from that of his Russian contemporary, Vladimir Ilyich Lenin.

■ **Analyses** break down a complex whole into its major parts.

> American government thrives due to the balance of powers among its three branches of leadership—the executive (the president), which enforces laws; the legislative (the Congress), which makes laws; and the judicial (the Supreme Court), which interprets laws.

Arranging Your Details

On the next four pages, you will find sample paragraphs following seven basic methods of organization. Review these samples when you have questions about arranging the details in your own writing.

Classification

Classification is an effective method for explaining a complex term or concept. To classify, you break a topic down into categories and subcategories to help readers better understand it. The following paragraph classifies the main groups of people that make up the population of Canada.

> Canada's 29–30 million people can be divided into three main groups: founding people, descendants of Europeans, and more recent immigrants. Founding people, about 2 percent of the population, are those who came across the Bering Strait from Asia thousands of years ago. This group includes Inuit (northern aboriginal people) and Métis (people of mixed heritage). The second group, those with European heritage, make up about 85 percent of the population. Most of this group are descended from British and French colonists, although almost all other European countries are represented. The third group, recent immigrants, makes up the rest of the population and adds more diversity to the mix. These immigrants come from all over the world, including Vietnam, China, Haiti, and Jamaica. All three groups help give Canada a rich and interesting culture.

Order of Location

Order of location is effective for organizing a description. It provides unity by arranging details in a logical way—left to right, right to left, top to bottom, and so on. In the sample paragraph, a student describes the statue of Shakespeare in Westminster Abbey.

> An impressive statue of William Shakespeare in Westminster Abbey commemorates the famous poet and playwright. Above the statue is an inscription saying "William Shakespeare 124 years after death by public esteem." (Shakespeare died in 1616 and the statue was erected in 1740.) The statue itself is of white marble and is a life-sized depiction of the Bard of Avon in fashionable garb. His familiar bearded face leans against his right hand; his right elbow rests on a carved pile of books, none of which are titled. Shakespeare's body leans toward the pillar of books, and his legs are crossed in a very informal way. Shakespeare's left hand points to a scroll set on a pedestal in front of him. Painted on the scroll is a quote from *The Tempest*, though some letters have been rubbed off. Carved heads on the rest of the pedestal are the faces of Queen Elizabeth I, King Henry V, and King Richard III.

"First, work hard to master the tools.
Simplify, prune, and strive for order." —William Zinsser

Chronological Order

SHARING A STORY

Chronological (time) **order** is effective for sharing a story or explaining a process. Information is organized according to what happens first, second, third, and so on. The paragraph below uses chronological order to tell about a morning in the life of Michael Dayne.

> When Michael heard the alarm at 5:30 a.m., his legs automatically swung to the floor. Groggy but awake, he pulled on his work clothes, stumbled downstairs, laced up his boots, and hurried across the farmyard. His first stop was the chicken house, where he scooped ground oats into the metal feeders and cleaned the water trays. Then it was off to the barn to pump water for the horses and fill their feed boxes with hay. From there, he hurried to the hog house, poked ground corn down into the self-feeders, and checked the automatic floats in the water troughs. His chores finished, Michael jogged back to the house, washed up, changed clothes, and ate his own breakfast. He then grabbed his book bag, trotted out to the road, and hopped on the school bus. Settling into the back seat, Michael checked his watch. "It's 6:45," he thought, "and the 'townies' are just waking up."

EXPLAINING A PROCESS

Chronological order is also useful when explaining a process or series of steps. The writer introduces the topic and then describes the process step by step.

> Did you ever wonder what makes your hair grow? To understand the process, you first have to look at your scalp—just common skin. About 100,000 tiny holes, called follicles, poke through the top layer of skin (epidermis) and into the bottom layer (dermis). At the bottom of each follicle lies a seedlike pocket called a papilla. A small blood vessel carries food into the papilla, which works like a little factory, using the food to build hair cells. The cells form a strand that grows up through the dermis and past an oil gland that provides a coating to keep the hair soft and moist. The strand continues to grow through the epidermis and into the air above. Now and then, each papilla pauses, rests, and then goes back to work again. However, if all your papillae stop working for good, you've reached that stage in your life called baldness.

Illustration

Illustration (general to specific) is a method of organization in which a general idea (the topic sentence) is stated and followed with specific details, facts, and examples that clarify or support the idea. The paragraph below opens with a main point about humpback whales and follows with an explanation of the current research on the subject.

It's hard to say how humpback whales find their way. They may rely on their excellent sense of hearing to pick up low-frequency sound waves that bounce off common ocean features such as rock and coral. Scientists also believe that they may look for familiar landforms. Two researchers recently detected a small amount of magnetic material in humpbacks, which may allow them to migrate by sensing the earth's magnetic field. This may explain why whales get stranded. Some researchers think it's because they are drawn to coasts with low magnetic forces, thinking they are clear waterways. This would also explain how they could follow such precise migration paths.

Climax

Climax (specific to general) is a method of organization in which the specific details lead up to an important summary statement. (If a topic sentence is used, it is placed at the end.) The following paragraph shows the excitement building as the writer waits for a concert to begin.

As the lights dimmed in the amphitheater, multicolored spotlights began to circle overhead, bouncing off the ceiling and swirling over the heads of the crowd. The sound began to build. At first, it sounded like thunder rumbling in the distance, but soon it grew to a deafening roar. People all around were stamping their feet, clapping their hands, and whistling through their fingers to show that they were ready for the show to begin. The crowd noise was soon drowned out by a blast of bass guitar and drums that seemed to come out of nowhere. Behind a blinding flash of light and a shower of glittering sparks, the band appeared on stage and began to play. At last, the concert had begun.

HELP FILE

When you organize a paragraph from general to specific, you are working **deductively**. Most scientific and informative writing requires deductive reasoning because it helps make complicated material easy to understand. When you organize from specific to general, you are working **inductively**. Inductive reasoning is often used in personal essays and short stories.

Cause and Effect

Cause-and-effect organization helps show the relationship between events and their results. A piece organized this way can begin with a general statement about the *effect* and follow with specific *causes*, or it can begin with the cause and follow with specific effects. The paragraph below defines hypothermia, explains its cause, and discusses its effects.

Hypothermia means that a person's body temperature has dropped below the normal 98.6° F. This condition usually results from prolonged exposure to cold. As hypothermia sets in, it causes all bodily functions to slow. At first, the dropping temperature affects blood flow and breathing. Heart rate and blood pressure decrease, and breathing becomes slower and shallower. As body temperature drops further, these effects become even more dramatic until somewhere between 86° and 82° F, the person lapses into unconsciousness. When body temperature reaches between 65° and 59° F, heart action, blood flow, and electrical brain activity stop. You would think that at this point the body would give out, but that does not necessarily happen. As the body cools down, the need for oxygen also slows. A person can be in a deep hypothermic state for an hour or longer and still be revived without serious long-term effects or complications.

Comparison

Organizing by comparison helps show the similarities or differences between two subjects. Often, you will end up showing both the similarities and differences. (See pages 191–193 for more information.) The paragraph below compares writing for the stage with screenwriting and emphasizes the difference between the two forms of writing.

Though stage writing and screenwriting might seem similar, they are very different art forms. Since the time of Sophocles and Aeschylus 2,500 years ago, stage plays have had to work within the limits of sets, lighting, costumes, and a handful of special effects. As a result, stage plays have always focused on dialogue to tell their stories. Screenwriting, a much younger art form, has always deemphasized dialogue. For the first three decades of filmmaking, films were silent. The only dialogue appeared on "cards" to be read between shots. Screenwriters therefore focused on action, quick cuts, and special effects to tell their stories. This difference remains true today. A successful film such as *The Lion King* has to be completely rewritten to work onstage, and even the masterworks of Shakespeare are often reworked for screen. Though screenwriting and stage writing are related art forms, they use two very different approaches to storytelling.

Connecting Your Details

Once you've arranged all the details in your writing, you need to tie them together so they read smoothly. The transitional words and phrases below can help.

SHOW LOCATION

above	away from	beyond	into	over
across	behind	by	near	throughout
against	below	down	off	to the right
along	beneath	in back of	on top of	under
among	beside	in front of	onto	
around	between	inside	outside	

SHOW TIME

about	before	later	second	today
after	during	meanwhile	soon	tomorrow
afterward	finally	next	then	until
as soon as	first	next week	third	when
at	immediately	now	till	yesterday

COMPARE THINGS (show similarities)

also	likewise	in the same way
as	similarly	like

CONTRAST THINGS (show differences)

although	even though	still	on the other hand
but	however	yet	otherwise

EMPHASIZE A POINT

in fact	truly	to emphasize
especially	to repeat	for this reason

CONCLUDE or SUMMARIZE

all in all	therefore	finally	put simply	in summary
as a result	to sum up	last	to conclude	in conclusion

ADD INFORMATION

additionally	for example	also	as well	likewise
again	for instance	and	besides	moreover
along with	in addition	another	finally	next

CLARIFY

that is	in other words	for instance	put another way

The Art of
WRITING

Writing with Style   111

Writer's Resource   121

> "When I write, I read everything out loud to get the right rhythm."
>
> —Fran Lebowitz

Writing with
STYLE

Think about your hair. This morning when you first yawned into the mirror, you had to make some choices: Should I wash my hair? Should I blow it dry or just comb it? Should I use mousse, gel, or spritz? Should I try something new—braid it, rubber-band it, slick it, tease it—or just leave it? Do I want my jersey number shaved in back, or should I get a Mohawk? Whatever you do—or don't do—that is your style.

Your writing style, similarly, comes from the choices you make. It is *your* words, *your* sentences, *your* paragraphs—nobody else's. Fortunately, you don't have to change your style every month to be in fashion. *Your writing will always be in style if you make sure that it sounds like you, an honest and interested writer.*

Preview

- **Key Stylistic Reminders**
- **Using Anecdotes**
- **Using Metaphors**
- **Using Repetition**
- **Using Strong, Colorful Words**
- **Breaking the Mold**
- **Avoiding the Ailments of Style**

> "Have something to say and say it as clearly
> as you can. That is the only secret of style."
>
> —Matthew Arnold

Key Stylistic Reminders

What really makes a good writing style? Not much. As odd as it may sound, the less you try to add style to your writing, the more stylistic it will probably be. Style is not using flowery language, nor is it trying to sound as if you are the supreme authority on your subject.

Your writing will always be in style if you follow three simple rules: (1) Be purposeful. (2) Be clear. (3) Be sincere. (See page 26 for another guide to good writing.)

1. **Be purposeful.** Writer Kurt Vonnegut states, "It is the genuine caring [about a topic], and not your games with language, which will be the most compelling and seductive element in your style." The bottom line is this: If you expect to produce effective writing, select topics that interest you.

2. **Be clear.** Keep things simple, orderly, and direct in your writing. Many of our best writers, including Mark Twain and Rachel Carson, have been plain talkers, speaking directly and clearly to their readers. Stylistic writing doesn't play games with readers, making them try to figure things out. Instead, it is easy to understand, and follow, from start to finish.

3. **Be sincere.** Writing works best when it sounds like one person (you) sincerely communicating with another person. It doesn't sound uncertain, phony, or pushy. Nor does it try to impress readers with a lot of ten-dollar words. It's honest and heartfelt and rings true for the reader.

FAQ ? **Why is it important to write with style?**

"Do so as a mark of respect for your readers," says Kurt Vonnegut. If your writing is dull, your readers will think that you don't care about your topic or about them. They, in turn, will show little interest in your writing. On the other hand, if you speak honestly in your writing and engage your readers' interest, they will appreciate what you have to say.

Using Anecdotes

Anecdote is the more technical term for brief "slices of life." *The American Heritage College Dictionary* (4th edition) defines an anecdote as "a short account of an interesting or humorous event."

These brief slices of life add a spark to your writing. They allow you to **show** your readers something in a lively and interesting manner rather than just to **tell** them matter-of-factly.

Showing ■ In the following anecdote, student writer Jared Jenkins shows that he can be a sensitive and understanding big brother.

> Last week, my little brother Eddy found out about Santa Claus. A kid in his class broke the news, and Eddy moped around all day, avoiding everybody. Finally that night, he came into the living room and flopped down on the couch next to me and said, "Jared, you know all that stuff about Santa, right?"
>
> "Yeah, buddy," I said. "Tough break, huh?"
>
> "Yeah. And anyway . . . I'm wondering if it's maybe like that for leprechauns, too."
>
> I just looked at him, not sure what to say.
>
> He must have seen the truth on my face. "Yeah, that's what I thought," Eddy said, blinking back tears. He got up to leave.
>
> I wished I could somehow put Santa back on the North Pole and put leprechauns back in clover, but all I could say was, "Hey, Eddy, you want to shoot some hoops?"
>
> Eddy turned and smiled. It was the right thing to say.

Telling: This brief anecdote is much more effective that simply telling the reader, "I understood how my little brother felt."

Showing ■ In the following anecdote, student writer Anya Dbrovnek helps the reader see a special part of her neighborhood library.

> Slivers of rain flick against the large library windows, but inside by the reading corner, everything is dry and warm. A small cluster of children gathers among bright pillows and stuffed animals, gazing up at the librarian as she reads. Mouths hang open as the children listen in silence. Thunder rumbles outside, and a little boy sidles up next to the reader, who stretches out an arm and draws him near.

Telling: Note how much more effective this *showing* anecdote is than a *telling* statement such as, "Children enjoy the reading corner in the library."

"Metaphors create tension and excitement by producing new connections and, in doing so, reveal a truth about the world we had not previously recognized."

—Gabriele Rico

Using Metaphors

A metaphor compares an idea or an image in your writing to something new and brings your basic ideas to life for your readers.

To Create a Picture ■ In the examples that follow, note how the basic ideas become a powerful picture when they are stated metaphorically.

Basic idea:	**My performance was a real disappointment.**
Metaphor:	**My performance was a real choke sandwich, all peanut butter and no jelly.**
Basic idea:	**The sunset changed the color of our rivers.**
Metaphor:	**Our rivers were red and purple streaks of sunset.**

To Expand an Idea ■ Because a metaphor can unify ideas in a series of sentences, extending a metaphor can help you to expand and clarify your ideas. Note how the metaphor (comparing family relationships to fabric) is extended in the following passage.

Metaphor:	**My family is a rich tapestry of personalities bound together by affection and respect.**
Extended:	**My family is a rich tapestry of personalities bound together by affection and respect. But my family was at loose ends last summer, at least until the reunion in August. Whatever feelings had been torn over my brother's divorce, whatever emotions had frayed over my grandmother's lingering illness, they were mended at the county park under a grove of red oak trees.**

* Be careful with this technique. Your writing will sound unnatural or forced if you use too many extended metaphors.

HELP FILE

Make sure your metaphors are original and clear. Be especially careful not to mix your metaphors. For example, the reporter who wrote "In the final debate, Senator Jones fielded each of his opponent's accusations and eventually scored the winning shot" has created a mixed metaphor. He carelessly shifts from baseball to basketball.

Using Repetition

There's a good chance that your writing will have style if you use repetition for the purpose of rhythm, emphasis, or unity. Just remember to keep the repeated words or ideas *parallel*, or stated in the same way. (The examples below show parallelism in action. Also see page 464.) As with any stylistic technique, repetition is effective only when used selectively.

For Rhythm and Balance ■ Notice how the patterns of words or phrases flow smoothly from one to the next in the following sentences:

> **At one time or another, the Austrians, the Russians, and the British fought against Napoleon's army.**
>
> **That scrumptious sandwich contains tender ham, crisp lettuce, and juicy tomatoes.**
>
> **Jumal wants to graduate from college, become a volunteer medic, and work in the African sub-Sahara.**

For Emphasis and Effect ■ Notice the intensity created by repetition of a basic sentence structure in the following passages:

> **Mom and Dad danced in the rain. They waltzed cheek to cheek; they schottisched side by side; they do-si-doed arm in arm. Because the drought had broken, the wheat would grow.**
>
> **—Mary Anne Hoff**
>
> **We shall fight on the beaches, we shall fight on the landing grounds, we shall fight in the fields and in the streets, we shall fight in the hills; we shall never surrender.**
>
> **—Winston Churchill**

For Unity and Organization ■ Notice how the repeated pattern at the beginning of each paragraph creates a poetic effect in this description of a man, a business, and his family.

> **I see Grandfather Aurelio in the wrinkled black-and-white photo, his eyes young and sharp like mine as he looks beyond the volcanic hills of Sicily, and beyond the Mediterranean toward America.**
>
> **I see Grandfather Aurelio in the folded napkins that bear his name, in the checkered tablecloths and the wooden chairs, in the tin ceiling that he painted gold, and in the whole storefront of his Brooklyn restaurant.**
>
> **I see Grandfather Aurelio in my father's face, the keen eyes and granite jaw, the care lines carved by 50 years of dishes and ovens, the look of love and understanding, as I search beyond these walls for distant shores.**
>
> **—Joseph Aurelio**

Using Strong, Colorful Words

Suppose, at a basketball game, you see a soaring power forward slam home a dunk shot. Then suppose you write "The player scored a basket." How effectively do you think you have communicated the event? Obviously, not very well. By using specific, colorful words, you can create clear and colorful word pictures for your reader.

Specific Nouns ■ Some nouns are **general** (*vegetable, pants, computer*) and give the reader a vague, uninteresting picture. Other nouns are more **specific** (*okra, corduroys, laptop*) and give the reader a much clearer, more detailed picture.

In the chart that follows, the italicized word at the top of each column is a general noun. The second word in each column is more specific. The third term is more specific yet. Finally, the word at the bottom of each column is a very specific noun. These last nouns are the type that can make a big difference in your writing.

person	*place*	*thing*	*idea*
woman	landmark	drink	belief
scientist	national landmark	coffee	strong belief
Marie Curie	Mount Rushmore	cappuccino	conviction

Vivid Verbs ■ Like nouns, verbs can be too general to create a vivid word picture. For example, the verb *looked* does not say the same thing as *stared, glared, glanced, peeked,* or *inspected.* The statement "Ms. Shaw *glared* at the two goof-offs" is much more vivid and interesting than "Ms. Shaw *looked* at the two goof-offs."

■ Whenever possible, use a verb that is strong enough to stand alone without the help of an adverb.

    A verb and an adverb: Hashim sat quickly on the couch.
    A vivid verb: Hashim plopped on the couch.

■ Avoid overusing the "be" verbs (*is, are, was, were* . . .). Often a better verb can be made from another word in the same sentence.

    A "be" verb: Yolanda is someone who plans for the future.
    A stronger verb: Yolanda plans for the future.

■ Use active rather than passive verbs. (See page 541.)

    A passive verb: Another deep pass was launched by Gerald.
    An active verb: Gerald launched another deep pass.

■ Use verbs that show rather than tell.

    A verb that tells: Greta is very tall.
    A verb that shows: Greta towers over her teammates.

Specific Adjectives ■ Use precise adjectives to describe the nouns in your writing. Strong adjectives can help make the nouns you choose even clearer and more interesting to the reader. For example, describing your uncle's new car as a *"sleek, red* convertible" offers your reader a definite mental image of the car.

■ Avoid using adjectives that carry little meaning: *neat, big, pretty, small, cute, fun, bad, nice, good, great, funny,* and so on.

Overused adjective:	The big house on the square belongs to an architect.
Specific adjective:	The Victorian house on the square belongs to an architect.

■ Use adjectives selectively. If your writing contains too many adjectives, they will simply get in the way and lose their effectiveness.

Too many adjectives:	A tall, shocking column of thick, yellow smoke marked the exact spot where the unexpected explosion had occurred.
Selective use:	A column of thick, yellow smoke marked the spot where the explosion had occurred.

Specific Adverbs ■ Use adverbs when you think they can add detail or color to a sentence. For example, the statement "Mayor Meyer *reluctantly* agreed to meet the protesters" presents a clearer picture than "Mayor Meyer agreed to meet the protesters." Don't, however, use a verb and an adverb when a single vivid verb would be better. (See page 116.)

The "Right Words" ■ The words in your writing should be specific and colorful and should have the right connotation. The *connotation* of a word is the meaning or feeling it suggests beyond its dictionary definition. (The *denotation* of a word is its direct dictionary meaning.) Note how the underlined words in the passage below suggest negative, almost pathetic feelings about the subject, an abandoned building.

The small factory had been <u>abandoned</u> long ago, each year <u>losing</u> <u>strength</u> until the roof <u>sagged</u> and the walls bowed with <u>fatigue.</u> Years had darkened the bricks to the color of <u>dried blood,</u> as though the life of the building had <u>seeped</u> out through its walls. The windows were <u>cracked</u> or <u>broken,</u> and a <u>weathered</u> piece of plywood <u>barred</u> the door. On that whole building, only one thing was new: a sign that read, "<u>Condemned.</u>"

—Lee Becker

Breaking the Mold

You've heard the old expression "Rules were made to be broken." The rules of sentences, paragraphs, and essays are no exception. Once you have mastered these rules, you can sometimes break them (or at least bend them) to create special stylistic effects in your writing.

Sentence Strategies

Using Different Kinds of Sentences ■ Most academic essays rely on declarative sentences—sentences that make statements. By occasionally breaking out of the declarative mold, you can make the reader take notice.

- **Interrogative sentences** ask a question.

  What would be a better name for the "No Child Left Behind" Act?

- **Imperative sentences** make commands or requests.

  Consider what Stephen Hawking thinks about "string theory."

- **Exclamatory sentences** communicate strong emotion.

  Water levels have dropped as much as 200 feet!

- **Conditional sentences** express statements contrary to fact.

  Even if the tornado had destroyed the whole school, Grover High would remain because there would still be teachers and students.

Using Long and Short Sentences ■ The sentences in academic essays tend to be of the same basic length. Incorporating a few very long and very short sentences can draw attention to key points.

- **A very long sentence** can effectively *package* important information.

  Considering all that was stacked against Lincoln's address at Gettysburg—the fact that he composed it on the train trip and in his boarding room, that he spoke for five minutes after another person's two-hour speech, and that he believed that "the world will little note nor long remember what we say here"—this speech should have simply slipped into obscurity.

- **A very short sentence** makes a strong point.

  It did not.

Using Juxtaposition ■ Juxtaposition simply means putting contrasting ideas together. Use juxtaposition to catch the reader's attention.

  For short-term muscle gain, some high school athletes risk a lifetime of health problems.

Paragraph Strategies

Varying the Position of the Topic Sentence ■ Place your topic sentence where it works best. Below, the topic sentence comes last.

> As a favor to the mayor, some city council members support the education referendum. Others block it out of antagonism. Meanwhile, the centrists on the council are loading the referendum with more riders than an elephant with a howdah (seat) full of preschoolers. No one seems to be considering the education referendum on its own terms.

Using Lists ■ Present your details in an effective way, perhaps in a bulleted or numbered list. Use numbers if the details have a natural sequence; otherwise, use bullets.

> The education referendum features three main measures meant to improve the quality of facilities in North Haven:
>
> - the building of a new middle school,
> - moving grade school students to the current middle school building, and
> - closing Dingham and Dodge grade schools.
>
> Each measure has merit, yet each one impacts the quality of education in North Haven.

Essay Strategies

Follow Your Feelings ■ Let your personal thoughts and feelings about the topic guide your writing, and see what develops. As you proceed, you may discover an effective line of thought to follow for your essay.

Concentrate on Your Questions ■ Focus your writing on the questions or uncertainties you have about a topic. Let mystery shape your writing the way that it shapes an investigation.

Use a Published Essay as a Guide ■ Model your own writing after a published essay that you admire. Follow the author's pattern of ideas as much as you can, but don't worry if your essay begins to take on a shape of its own.

Create a Multigenre Paper ■ Rethink the traditional approach to essay writing—as either narrative, expository, or persuasive. Instead, use different combination of ideas. For example, you might start by explaining an issue, continue by arguing for a key point, follow with an account of the issue's impact in your own life, and so on.

Avoiding the Ailments of Style

When you revise your writing, watch closely for these stylistic ailments, or trouble spots.

Primer Style ■ If your writing contains many short sentences, one right after another, it may sound like a grade school textbook:

> **Our policy for makeup assignments is unfair. The teachers go strictly by the rules. They don't care about the amount of work we have. They don't care about our other activities.**

The Cure: The main cure is to combine some of your ideas into longer, smoother-reading sentences. (See page 95.) Here's the revised passage:

> **When it comes to makeup assignments, our teachers go strictly by the rules. They don't care about the amount of work we have or about our other activities.**

Passive Style ■ If your writing seems slow-moving and impersonal, you may have used too many passive verbs. With passive verbs, the subject of the sentence receives the action. Here's an example written in the passive voice:

> **Our biology teacher was loved by us. She was often asked for extra help, which was always given. She was visited by her students before and after school and was often at the center of some lively discussions.**

The Cure: Flip the sentence. Make the subject give or do the action, not receive it. Here's the same passage written in the active voice:

> **We loved our biology teacher. We were always asking for extra help, and she was always willing to give it. Students often dropped in before and after school to visit and share in some lively discussions.**

Insecurity ■ Does your writing contain many qualifiers (*to be perfectly honest, it seems to me, maybe*) or intensifiers (*really, truly, totally*)? These words and phrases suggest that you lack confidence in your ideas.

> **I totally and completely agree with Mr. Grim about changing the school's dress code, but that's only my opinion.**

The Cure: Visualize yourself standing before an audience and say exactly what you mean. Here is the revised version:

> **I agree with Mr. Grim about changing our school's dress code.**

[HOT LINK] For other ailments of style, see "Flowery Language," "Jargon," "Wordiness," and "Cliche." (See pages 91–92.)

"You always feel that you could have put more into [your writing]."

—Emily Carr

Writer's
RESOURCE

Are you a free spirit, ready to write on just about any topic, at any time? Or are you more systematic, a clock puncher, interested in keeping track of each writing move as you go along? Then again, are you a detail person, always asking yourself, "What is my *purpose*? Who is my *audience*? Should I add a *modifier*?" Or are you a visionary, a dreamer, always looking for different forms of writing to experiment with?

In all probability, you don't fit just one of these writing personalities. Maybe you're a free-spirited visionary, or a free-spirited detail person. (Is that possible?) No matter how you approach writing, you'll find valuable information in this chapter.

Preview

- **Thinking and Writing Moves**
- **Writing Topics**
- **Writing Techniques**
- **Writing Terms**
- **A Survey of Writing Forms**

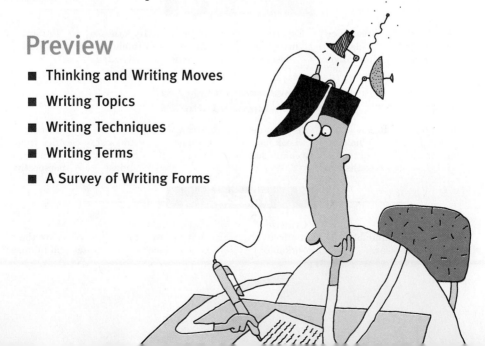

Thinking and Writing Moves

Writing is really thinking on paper. For example, you start a writing project by *gathering* information. Soon after, you focus and organize your thoughts, and so on. Use this chart as a basic thinking guide whenever you write essays, reports, and research papers.

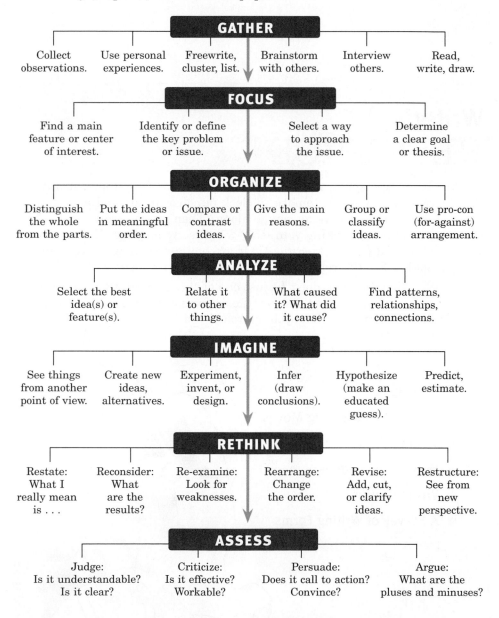

GATHER

| Collect observations. | Use personal experiences. | Freewrite, cluster, list. | Brainstorm with others. | Interview others. | Read, write, draw. |

FOCUS

| Find a main feature or center of interest. | Identify or define the key problem or issue. | Select a way to approach the issue. | Determine a clear goal or thesis. |

ORGANIZE

| Distinguish the whole from the parts. | Put the ideas in meaningful order. | Compare or contrast ideas. | Give the main reasons. | Group or classify ideas. | Use pro-con (for-against) arrangement. |

ANALYZE

| Select the best idea(s) or feature(s). | Relate it to other things. | What caused it? What did it cause? | Find patterns, relationships, connections. |

IMAGINE

| See things from another point of view. | Create new ideas, alternatives. | Experiment, invent, or design. | Infer (draw conclusions). | Hypothesize (make an educated guess). | Predict, estimate. |

RETHINK

| Restate: What I really mean is . . . | Reconsider: What are the results? | Re-examine: Look for weaknesses. | Rearrange: Change the order. | Revise: Add, cut, or clarify ideas. | Restructure: See from new perspective. |

ASSESS

| Judge: Is it understandable? Is it clear? | Criticize: Is it effective? Workable? | Persuade: Does it call to action? Convince? | Argue: What are the pluses and minuses? |

Writing Topics

Whenever you need a writing topic for a narrative or an essay, review these lists for ideas. Tip: Compile your own list of possible writing ideas in a notebook. (See pages 43–45.)

Descriptive

Person: friend, teacher, relative, classmate, religious leader, coworker, neighbor, teammate, coach, entertainer, politician, sister, brother, bus driver, an older person, a younger person, someone who spends time with you, someone you wish you were like

Place: school, neighborhood, the beach, the park, a hangout, the bus stop, your room, the locker room, a restaurant, the library, a church, a stadium, the cafeteria, the hallway

Thing: a billboard, a photograph, a poster, a computer, a musical instrument, a tool, a pet, a bus, a boat, a book, a car, a cat, a dog, a drawing, a collection, a junk drawer

Narrative

During school: first memories, lunch hour, stage fright, learning to drive, odd field trips, asking for help, the big game, the school play, a school project

After school: just last week, on the bus, learning a lesson, a kind act, homesick, a big mistake, a reunion, getting lost, being late, Friday night, an embarrassing moment, staying overnight, getting hurt, success, a practical joke, being a friend, a family visit, on your own, moving, building a ____, the first day of ____, the last day of ____, a miserable time, cleaning up

Expository

How to . . . surf the Net, make spaghetti sauce, get a job, entertain a child, get in shape, study for a test, conserve energy, take a good picture

How to operate . . . control . . . run . . .
How to choose . . . select . . . pick . . .
How to build . . . grow . . . create . . .
How to fix . . . clean . . . wash . . .
How to protect . . . warn . . . save . . .

The causes of . . . global warming, snoring, inflation, shin splints, tornadoes, urban sprawl, poor grades, overpopulation

Kinds of . . . music, crowds, friends, teachers, love, rules, compliments, commercials, dreams, happiness, neighbors, pollution, taxes, heroes, vacations, pain, communication

Definition of . . . best friend, poverty, generation gap, greed, the metric system, loyalty, a newsgroup, bioengineering, a team, literature, humor, courage, pressure, faith, personality, entertainment

Persuasive

For-Against . . . study halls, donating organs, capital punishment, the current speed limit, gun control, courtroom television, current graduation requirements, final exams, a career in the armed forces, teen centers, open lunch hours, girls on the football team, limited work hours for teens during the school year, curfews

Writing Techniques

Experiment with some of these techniques in your own stories and essays.

Allusion ■ A reference to a familiar person, place, thing, or event.

I have feet that put Steven Spielberg's E.T. to shame. They are a tangle of toes held together by bunions.

Analogy ■ A comparison of ideas or objects that are completely different but that are alike in one important way.

Benjamin Franklin witnessed the first successful balloon flight. When asked what good such an invention was, Franklin answered, "What good is a newborn baby?"

Anecdote ■ A brief story used to illustrate or make a point. (See page 113.)

In a passenger train compartment, a lady lit a cigarette, saying to Sir Thomas Beecham, a famous orchestra conductor, "I'm sure you don't object."

"Not at all," replied Beecham, "provided you don't mind if I'm sick."

"I don't think you know who I am," the lady pointed out. "I'm one of the railroad directors' wives."

"Madam," said the conductor, "if you were the director's only wife, I should still be sick." (The story makes a point about the unpleasantness of secondhand smoke.)

Antithesis ■ Using opposite ideas to emphasize a point. (See page 463.)

There was no possibility of being hired at the town's cotton gin or lumber mill, but maybe there was a way to make the two factories work for her.

—Maya Angelou, *Wouldn't Take Nothing for My Journey Now*

Colloquialism ■ A common word or phrase suitable for ordinary, everyday conversation but not for formal speech or writing.

y'all listen up   run this by her   no way

Exaggeration ■ An overstatement or stretching of the truth to emphasize a point. (*See hyperbole and overstatement.*)

The Danes are so full of *joie de vivre* [joy of life] that they practically sweat it.   —Bill Bryson, *Neither Here nor There*

Flashback ■ A technique in which a writer interrupts a story to go back and explain an earlier time or event for the purpose of making something in the present more clear.

In *The Outsiders*, readers first meet Ponyboy as he leaves a movie theater and is jumped by gang members. Later, the author goes back and explains what led up to the conflict.

Foreshadowing ■ Hints or clues about what will happen next in a story.

> Dulcie walked down the school steps and looked at the boiling sky. A voice inside her said, "Go back." She didn't, but two blocks later, she wished she had. Rain suddenly roared down ferociously from the swirling clouds, and the heavy drops pelted Dulcie as she ran. Then the rain stopped, and the air became deathly calm. "Get home," the voice said. "This is only the beginning." Then the voice went silent.

> **NOTE** Later in the story, this foreshadowing is borne out when a tornado descends on Dulcie's hometown.

Hyperbole ■ (hi-púr-bə-lē) Exaggeration used to emphasize a point.

> We didn't need to [read] because my father has read everything . . . and people in town have said that talking to him about anything is better than reading three books. —Cynthia Marshall Rich

Irony ■ An expression in which the author says one thing but means just the opposite. (See page 257.)

> But then I was lucky enough to come down with the disease of the moment in the Hamptons, which was Lyme disease. —Kurt Vonnegut

Juxtaposition ■ Putting two words or ideas close together to create a contrasting of ideas or an ironic meaning.

> Just remember, we're all in this alone. —Lily Tomlin

Local Color ■ The use of details that are common in a certain place. (The following passage lists foods common to small-town Southern life.)

> Folks had already brought over more cakes and pies, and platters of fried chicken and ham, and their good china bowls full of string beans, butterbeans, okra, and tomatoes. —Olive Ann Burns, *Cold Sassy Tree*

Metaphor ■ A figure of speech that compares two things without using the words *like* or *as*.

> Perfectionism is the voice of the oppressor, the enemy of the people.
> —Anne Lamott, *Bird by Bird*

Overstatement ■ An exaggeration or a stretching of the truth. (See *exaggeration* and *hyperbole*.)

> I bet you could set off dynamite in an A & P and the people would by and large keep reaching and checking oatmeal off their lists and muttering "Let me see, there was a third thing, began with an A, asparagus, no, ah, yes, applesauce!"
> —John Updike, "A & P"

Oxymoron ■ Connecting two words with opposite meanings.

> war for peace black light controlled chaos

Paradox ■ A true statement that says two opposite things.

The miniature, metal toy cars of the 1960s are no longer playthings.

Parallelism ■ Repeating similar grammatical structures (words, phrases, or sentences) to give writing rhythm.

All this waste happens before any lid is popped, any can is opened, or any seal is broken.

—Allison Rozendaal, student writer

Personification ■ A figure of speech in which a nonhuman thing is given human characteristics.

And what I remember next is how the moon, the pale moon with its one yellow eye . . . stared through the pink plastic curtains.

—Sandra Cisneros, "One Holy Night"

Pun ■ A phrase that uses words that sound the same in a way that gives them a funny effect.

I have come to believe that opposing gravity is something not be taken—uh, lightly.

—Daniel Pinkwater, "Why I Don't Fly"

Sensory Details ■ Details that are experienced through the senses. They help readers to see, feel, smell, taste, and hear what is being described.

I stood backstage, surrounded by giggles and rustling tulle. The smell of talcum powder, hairspray, and rosin rolled in from the stage. A familiar, acrid taste filled my mouth. The music rose, and the dancers swept onto the stage in a frothy swirl of pink and blue.

Simile ■ A figure of speech that compares two things using *like* or *as*.

They [the old men] had hands like claws, and their knees were twisted like the old thorn trees.

—William Butler Yeats

Slang ■ Informal words or phrases used by a particular group of people.

dis   ain't   chill out

Symbol ■ A concrete object used to represent an idea. (See page 261.)

hourglass = time passing   dove = peace

Synecdoche ■ Using part of something to represent the whole.

Idle hands are the devil's playground. (*Hands* represent the person.)

Understatement ■ The opposite of exaggeration. By using very calm language, an author can bring special attention to an object or an idea.

He [our new dog] turned out to be a good traveler, and except for an interruption caused by my wife's falling out of the car, the journey went very well.

—E. B. White, "A Report in Spring"

Writing Terms

On the next two pages you will find a glossary of terms used to describe different aspects of the writing process.

Argumentation: Writing or speaking in which a point of view is debated.

Arrangement: The order in which details are placed in a piece of writing.

Audience: Those people who read or hear what you have written.

Balance: The arranging of words or phrases so they are parallel—stated in the same way.

Body: The main part of a piece of writing, supporting or developing the thesis statement.

Brainstorming: Collecting ideas by thinking freely about all the possibilities; used most often with groups.

Case study: The in-depth story of one individual whose experiences speak for the experiences of a larger group.

Central idea: The main point of a piece of writing, often stated in a thesis statement or a topic sentence.

Closing sentence: The sentence that summarizes the point being made in a paragraph.

Coherence: The logical arrangement of ideas in writing.

Deductive reasoning: A logical presentation of information in which a main idea is stated early in a piece of writing and supporting details follow.

Description: Writing that paints a colorful picture of a topic.

Details: Words used to describe a person, convince an audience, explain a process, and so on; to be effective, details should appeal to the senses.

Editing: Checking your writing for the correct use of conventions. (See pages 79–83.)

Emphasis: Placing greater stress on the most important idea in a piece of writing.

Essay: A multiparagraph composition in which ideas on a special topic are presented, explained, argued for, or described in an interesting way.

Expository writing: Writing that explains. (See page 255.)

Extended definition: Writing that offers an in-depth examination of a concept, including personal definitions, negative definitions (what it is not), uses of the concept, and so on.

Figurative language: Language that goes beyond the normal meaning of the words used.

Focus: Concentrating on a specific aspect of a subject in writing. (Often called the *thesis*.)

Freewriting: Writing freely and rapidly, without strict structure; focused freewriting is writing rapidly on a specific topic or angle.

Generalization: An idea emphasizing the general characteristics rather than the specific details of a subject.

Grammar: The system of rules of a language for generating sentences; the system of inflections, syntax, and word formation of a language.

Idiom: A phrase or an expression that means something different from what the words actually say (using *over his head* for *didn't understand*).

Illustration: Using an experience to make a point or clarify an idea.

Inductive reasoning: A logical presentation of information in which specific examples and details lead up to the main concluding idea.

Inverted sentence: A sentence in which the normal word order is reversed or switched; usually the verb comes before the subject.

Journal: Personal exploratory writing that often contains impressions and reflections; a journal is often a source of ideas for writing.

Limiting the subject: Narrowing a general subject to a specific topic that is suitable for a writing assignment.

Literal: The actual, dictionary meaning of a word; language that means what it appears to mean.

Loaded words: Words that are slanted for or against the subject.

Logic: Correct reasoning; correctly using facts, examples, and reasons to support your point.

Modifier: A word, a phrase, or a clause that limits or describes another word or group of words.

Narration: Writing that tells a story or recounts an event.

Objective: Relating information in an impersonal manner without feelings or opinions. (See *subjective*.)

Observation: Paying close attention to people, places, things, and events to collect details for later use.

Overview: A general idea of what is or will be covered in a piece of writing.

Personal narrative: Writing that covers an event in the writer's life.

Persuasion: Writing that is meant to change a reader's thinking or action.

Poetic license: The freedom a writer has to bend the rules of writing to achieve a certain effect.

Point of view: The position or angle from which a story is told. (See page 259.)

Premise: A statement or central idea that serves as the basis of a discussion or a debate.

Process: A method of doing something that involves several steps or stages.

Profile: Writing that reveals an individual or re-creates a time period, using interviews and research.

Proofreading: A final check for errors. (See pages 79–83.)

Prose: Writing in the usual sentence form. Prose becomes poetry when it takes on rhyme and rhythm.

Purpose: The specific reason a person has for writing; the goal of writing.

Reminiscence (*Memoir*): Writing that focuses on a memorable past experience.

Report: A multiparagraph form of writing that results from gathering and organizing facts on a topic.

Revision: Changing a piece of writing to improve the content (ideas).

Subjective: Thinking or writing that includes personal feelings, attitudes, and opinions. (See *objective*).

Syntax: The order and relationship of words in a sentence.

Theme: The message in a piece of writing (lengthy writings may have several themes). (See page 261.)

Thesis statement: A statement of the purpose, intent, or main idea of an essay.

Tone: The writer's attitude toward her or his subject; a writer's tone can be serious, sarcastic, solemn, and so on.

Topic: The specific subject for a writing assignment.

Transitions: Words or phrases that tie ideas together. (See page 109.)

Unity: A sense of oneness in writing in which each sentence helps to develop the main idea.

Universal: A topic or an idea that applies to everyone.

Usage: The way in which words or phrases are used in a language; language is generally considered to be standard (formal and informal) or nonstandard.

Vivid details: Details that appeal to the senses and help the reader see, feel, smell, taste, or hear a writing idea.

Voice: A writer's distinct, personal manner of expression.

A Survey of Writing Forms

The following chart classifies the forms of writing covered in this handbook. You can learn a great deal about writing by experimenting with a variety of forms.

NARRATIVE WRITING	(See pages 139–149.)
Remembering & Sharing (*Exploring Experiences*) Promotes writing fluency.	Journals • Diaries • Logs • Notebooks Personal Narratives and Essays • Memoirs Descriptive Essays • Freewriting • Listing

EXPOSITORY WRITING	(See pages 173–196 and 263–319.)
Informing & Analyzing (*Sharing Information*) Develops organizing skills.	Expository Essays • Process Essays Essays of Definition • Cause-Effect Essays Comparison-Contrast Essays • Summaries Essays of Opposing Ideas • Research Papers

PERSUASIVE WRITING	(See pages 197–231.)
Arguing & Evaluating (*Judging the Worth of Something*) Reinforces critical thinking.	Persuasive Essays • Pet Peeves Editorials • Personal Commentaries Problem-Solution Essays • Position Papers Essays of Argumentation

WRITING ABOUT LITERATURE	(See pages 233–261.)
Understanding & Interpreting (*Reacting to Texts*) Fosters critical reading.	Journal Entries • Letters to the Author Book Reviews • Mini-Reviews Literary Analyses • Dialogues

CREATIVE WRITING	(See pages 151–171.)
Inventing & Imitating (*Reshaping Ideas*) Encourages creativity.	Stories • Patterned Fiction Free Verse Poetry • Traditional Poetry Plays • Dialogues • Monologues

WORKPLACE WRITING	(See pages 321–337.)
Questioning & Answering (*Writing to Get a Job Done*) Builds real-world writing skills.	Request Letters • Complaint Letters Letters of Application • Memos E-Mail Messages • Brochures • Résumés

Personal
WRITING

Journal Writing   131

Descriptive Writing   135

Narrative Writing   139

> "Writing is not apart from living.
>   Writing is a kind of double living."
>   —Catherine Drinker Bowen

JOURNAL Writing

Pick up a school yearbook and flip through the pages. Some photos show crowded halls; some show actors in the school musical; and some others show championship teams. Highlights of a whole year can be captured in a single book.

When you write in a journal, you create your own yearbook in words. A *personal journal* lets you keep track of your day-to-day experiences, thoughts, and feelings. A *reader-response journal* helps you reflect on the books you read, and a *learning log* helps you think about the classes you take. Whatever the journal, every entry is a snapshot of your life, of your feelings, and of the world you live in.

If you become a regular journal writer, you'll begin to enter the world of your inner thoughts; and in time, you'll feel a little sharper, as if your senses have been fine-turned. A squeaky car door will no longer go unnoticed. You'll begin to wonder, "How long has it been squeaky, why hasn't anyone fixed it, and what else is squeaky in my life?"

Preview

- Journal Writing
- Types of Journals
- Great Beginnings

Journal Writing

It doesn't take much to keep a journal: a notebook, a handy supply of your favorite pens or pencils (or a computer), and a promise on your part to write regularly. The last point is the key. Journal writing works best when it is done on a regular basis.

Make sure to find an appropriate time and place to do your journal writing. Choose the time of day that is best for you. Do you like to write in the morning when you feel refreshed or right before bed when you can relax and reflect on your day? Pick a favorite spot where you feel comfortable and can write without distractions. Then start writing. It's that simple.

Diary and Journal

When you think of a diary, you may picture a small locked book with a key that you keep hidden from your brothers or sisters. Diaries and journals are both meant to record your experiences, but journal writing reflects more deeply on those experiences. Here is a typical diary entry about a first prom:

> **Carlos came to my house to pick me up for the prom. My parents took lots of pictures. We went to a fancy restaurant with all of our friends. We were a little late to the dance, but we stayed until the very last song was over.**

The following text is a journal entry about the same event:

> **My first prom! A day full of manicures, pedicures, and make-up couldn't calm the millions of butterflies in my stomach. Would Carlos like my dress and my hair? All those butterflies disappeared when I floated down the stairs and saw the look on his face. His eyes lit up. "Wow! You look amazing." For the rest of the night, he made me feel like a princess. I didn't open one door, and he pulled out my chair for me at dinner. He was so sweet, and I loved it! I really feel like I'm growing up. I mean, at the restaurant with all our friends, we felt like adults because we took care of everything ourselves.**

> **NOTE** Notice how the journal entry goes beyond simply recording events; it shows what the writer felt and thought as well.

HELP FILE

In the best of all worlds, journal writing will become a very important part of your life, as important as good food and regular exercise. Even if you don't reach that level of commitment, your journal writing will help you feel more comfortable with the physical act of writing—and feel more confident in your ability to express yourself.

Journal-Writing Tips

Journal writers gain many benefits. They develop *fluency*, which means they learn to write quickly, freely, and easily. They sort out their thoughts and feelings and experiment with their writing voice. They also accumulate a storehouse of ideas for essay topics and stories. The following tips can help you get all these benefits.

- **Be yourself.** Focus on expressing your thoughts and feelings freely. No one is going to grade your work. Just carry on as honestly and sincerely as you can.

- **Be descriptive.** Don't simply state "this happened, and then that happened." Instead, include enough details to recapture a particular time and place.

- **Date your entries.** Also review your entries from time to time to see how far you've come.

- **Focus on ideas.** If you need help to get started, ask yourself a question like, "What am I feeling today?" or "What's on my mind?" (See "Great Beginnings" on page 134 for more ideas.)

- **Experiment with your writing.** Write an entire entry as a poem or as song lyrics. Write another entry in the style of your favorite author. Write an entry as if you were your cat, reporting on his day. Write according to your own rules.

Types of Journals

Journals can also help you get the most out of special events, trips, books, and classes. Try some of these types of journals.

Learning Log ■ Writing in a learning log, or class journal, gets you more actively involved in your course work. It helps you make important facts and ideas part of your own thinking. (See pages 416–417 for more.)

Response Journal ■ Writing in a reader-response journal enriches each of your reading experiences—whether you are reading the newest title by your favorite author, an article in a magazine, or a chapter in a class text.

Dialogue Journal ■ In a dialogue journal, you and a partner carry on a conversation (first one person writes, then the other) about experiences you have had, books you have read, and issues that concern you.

Travel Log ■ In a travel log or special-events journal, you record your experiences on a special trip, such as a family vacation or a forensics competition. Sometimes when you are tightly packed in a car or bus, a journal can give you your own private space.

Great Beginnings

Most of the ideas for your journal writing will come from your personal experiences. However, when nothing personal moves you to write, use the experiences of a friend or a family member to get you started, or page through a newspaper or magazine for ideas. On those occasions when you still draw a blank, consider the following starting points.

Open-Ended Sentences ■ Complete one of the following open-ended sentences and write about the idea from as many angles as possible.

I wonder . . .

I wish I could tell someone about . . .

One thing I've learned is . . .

The best part of the day was . . .

The worst part of the day was . . .

If I could change one thing about today, it would be . . .

Tomorrow, I plan to . . .

I was once . . . , but now I am . . .

I feel fortunate to have . . .

I need help with . . .

My life would be completely different if . . .

I'm afraid of . . .

I know I can . . .

Everyone says . . . , but I think . . .

Unsent Letters ■ Write a letter to anyone (a friend, a family member, a famous person) to see what develops. Share recent experiences, ask questions, reflect on the news, and so on.

Story Starters ■ Write a quick rough draft of a story based on something you see, hear, feel, smell, taste, or think. Perhaps your growling stomach gets you thinking about lunch, so write a story that starts in the cafeteria.

"Essentials of Life" List ■ Consider the "Essentials of Life" list on page 44 of your handbook. *Entertainment* is one category in the list. You could write an entertainment-related journal entry about . . .

your favorite thing to do on a Friday night,

the last movie you saw,

the things that make you laugh, or

the kind of music that relaxes you or gets you pumped up.

"Don't tell me the moon is shining;
show me the glint of light on broken glass."
—Anton Chekhov

DESCRIPTIVE Writing

Descriptive writing can be very powerful when it effectively captures the sights, sounds, smells, and tastes related to a topic. Imagine a weeping willow shaking its shaggy head in a strong wind. Now imagine a row of pine trees sighing in a light breeze. Each description creates a specific image and mood, and each one transports the reader to a different time and place.

Since descriptive writing requires careful observation and reflection, you are sure to learn some new and valuable things about your topic during the writing process. Interestingly, descriptive writing plays an important role in most forms of writing, from stories and poems to narratives and essays. So you can apply the insights that you gain in this chapter to just about any type of writing.

Preview

- **Writing Guidelines**
- **Sample Descriptive Writing**
- **Assessment Rubric**

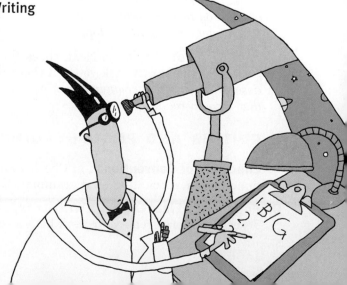

Writing Guidelines

In a good description, you write from a position of authority. Either you already know your topic well, or you must closely observe the person, place, or thing you are describing. Use vivid sensory and memory details to bring your topic to life and make it clear why the topic is important to you.

■ PREWRITING

1. **Selecting a Topic . . .** Choose a worthy topic, such as people (*individuals you admire*), places (*favorite spots*), or things (*special gifts*).

   ✱ If you choose a person, get his or her permission before you start, and use good judgment in your description.

2. **Gathering Details . . .** Imagine that you are planning a painting of your topic; jot down every shape, color, texture, or feature that comes to mind. Also record details firsthand as you observe your topic. Include sensory details—sights, sounds, smells, tastes, and so on.

3. **Focusing Your Thoughts . . .** Review your collecting and decide which idea or feeling would work best as the focus of your writing. Plan your description to support this focus. Also, choose a pattern of organization, perhaps following order of location. (See pages 105–108).

■ WRITING AND REVISING

4. **Connecting Your Ideas . . .** Write your first draft freely, working in sensory and memory details according to your prewriting.

5. **Improving Your Writing . . .** Review your first draft, paying special attention to *ideas, organization,* and *voice.* Ask yourself these questions: *Have I included enough sensory details? Have I used order of location or some other clear pattern to organize my details? Does the tone of my writing fit my topic, and do I create an effective mood?*

6. **Improving Your Style . . .** Next, check the *word choice* and *sentence fluency* of your draft. Ask yourself these questions: *Do the words in my description create a clear image of my topic? Are my sentences varied and smooth reading?*

■ EDITING AND PROOFREADING

7. **Checking for Conventions . . .** Check your work for errors in punctuation, mechanics, and grammar. Use the rubric on page 138.

8. **Preparing a Final Copy . . .** Write or type a neat final copy of your description; proofread your work before sharing it.

Sample Descriptive Essay

In this essay, student writer Roel Zinkstok describes one of his favorite settings: the garden behind his house. The garden serves as a pleasurable meeting place for his family.

Leaving the Garden

The opening shows readers the garden during the day.

Usually, our back garden is not very special. Most of it is laid with terra-cotta orange and dark gray stones. Our house rises three stories on the west side of it; the garage borders on the south end and is thickly covered with dark green ivy. Along the north side grows a hedge with tiny leaves that turn rusty red in the fall. A row of low yews runs parallel to the house, and towering over them are two tall birches and a huge conifer, some 45 feet tall. A few flower beds strive to brighten the garden's edges.

This garden changes magically on a warm summer's evening. As the sun sets, the garden seems to slowly shrink into the darkness. When it gets too dark to see, my mother puts a table lamp or candles on an old, paint-chipped table. This lamp creates a small bubble of golden light in the center of the garden and casts grotesque shadows along the borders, making our seats around the table feel even more cozy. Over our heads, the starry dome of night makes it seem as though we are sitting on the brink of the universe.

The details in the body focus on the garden's nighttime mystique.

Throughout the years, we have all sat there together—my father, my mother, my twin brother, and my two older sisters—talking, reading, or just sharing the silence. Here my father and I have discussed religion and faith, literature and science, or simply the day just passed. Here I have read great books, following their stories in my imagination from my garden chair. At times, soft music wafts toward us from the nearby house of a concert pianist, forming wonderful melodies that dance through the trees. Here my family has sat till far past midnight in the halo of light—with the music and the bugs.

In closing, the writer discusses the garden's importance in his life.

In recent years, my sisters have left home to study in Amsterdam. Now it is my turn to leave, my turn to become independent. That means letting go of the guiding hand of my parents. But I know that they will always be sitting there in the garden, leaving a chair vacant for me and my siblings, as the Jews at Pesach leave a chair for Elijah. When I return next summer, I will find my father and mother waiting in the garden with the lamp on the old table . . . and we will talk together for the rest of the night—and, in a way, forever. ■

Assessment Rubric

Use this rubric as a checklist to evaluate your descriptive writing. The rubric is arranged according to the traits of writing described in your handbook. (See pages 21–26.)

Ideas

The writing . . .

_____ focuses on an interesting or important topic.

_____ includes sensory and memory details.

_____ shows the topic in a fresh light.

Organization

_____ starts by capturing the reader's attention.

_____ follows a clear pattern of organization (perhaps order of location).

_____ ends by reflecting on the importance of the topic.

Voice

_____ shows the author's feelings about the topic (*tone*).

_____ creates a specific feeling in the reader (*mood*).

Word Choice

_____ uses specific, concrete nouns to create a precise picture.

_____ uses modifiers that make the image clear.

Sentence Style

_____ flows smoothly from one sentence to the next.

_____ varies the types and kinds of sentences.

Conventions

_____ correctly applies the basic rules of spelling and grammar.

_____ follows the standard guidelines for presentation.

"Be surprised by the crazy, wonderful
events that will come dancing out of your
past when you stir up the pot of memory."
— William Zinsser

NARRATIVE Writing

A personal narrative re-creates a specific experience or event in your life. The narrative can focus on a funny situation, a frightening experience, or a life-changing encounter. Whatever the focus, a narrative uses sensory details, specific action, and revealing dialogue to bring the experience to life.

Your personal narratives should invite the reader to share in your experiences, to feel the same things that you felt. You'll know your writing is a success when you can say, "That's just how it felt to lose the championship game," or "That's what life was really like with my friend Mia." As you write, be prepared to learn something new about the events, about others, and even about yourself. That's what writing personal narratives can do.

Preview

- ■ Writing Guidelines
- ■ Sample Personal Narrative
- ■ Sample Extended Personal Narrative
- ■ Sample Personal Essay
- ■ Assessment Rubric

Writing Guidelines
Personal Narrative

In a personal narrative, you re-create an incident that happened to you over a short period of time. This incident could be an uplifting event, a frightening encounter, a humorous occurrence, or some other type of memorable experience. Be sure to include enough specific details to make the incident come alive for your readers. Even if you can't recall everything, fill in the gaps with details that seem to fit. (The pros do it all the time.)

■ PREWRITING

1. **Selecting a Topic . . .** Think of a specific incident in your life that you think is worth sharing. (See page 123 for ideas.)

2. **Gathering Ideas . . .** Imagine that you are sharing this event with a friend. What details would you include? Think about the specific actions related to the event. If any parts seem fuzzy, ask others who were involved what they remember. Focus on the following types of details:

   ■ **Sensory details:** what you saw, heard, smelled, tasted, or touched

   ■ **Reflective details:** what you thought and felt about the experience

   ■ **Actions:** what people did or experienced

   ■ **Dialogue:** what people said to each other

3. **Organizing Your Narrative . . .** Since narratives are usually told in chronological order, you can use a time line to organize your details. Below is the first part of an example time line. At the top, the writer listed each key action, with the corresponding mood in parentheses. Beneath the line, the writer listed details related to the action.

Time Line

Pregame (Anticipation)	On the field (Excitement)	Start of Game (Energy)
soft rain	harder rain	kickoff
teammates by me	cheering fans	run toward offense
jog out to a roar	game plan yelled	find my man

■ WRITING

4. **Hooking Your Reader . . .** Start your narrative right in the action. Doing so will immediately get your reader's attention. (See the sample on page 143.)

5. **Keeping the Reader Interested . . .** Let the reader feel as if the experience is unfolding right before him or her. You can do this by showing the reader the experience rather than telling him or her about it.

   ■ **Use sensory details.** Sensory details allow your reader to see, hear, smell, taste, and touch the same things you did.

TELLING	SHOWING
We ate a delicious Thanksgiving dinner.	The skin of the turkey crackled as Uncle Bill carved it, and steam rose, curling out above mounds of sage dressing.

   ■ **Use specific action.** Describe exactly what happens. Special details help the reader visualize the action.

TELLING	SHOWING
Our car went out of control and went into a ditch.	Our car hit ice and fishtailed. Dad wrenched the wheel toward the skid, but it was too late. The sedan slid sideways, tipped, and rolled over into the ditch.

   ■ **Use dialogue.** Let the people in your narrative speak for themselves. Use words that reveal their unique voices.

TELLING	SHOWING
My friends Jana and Ella couldn't agree on what kind of pizza to order.	"Anchovies?" Jana said. "You gotta be crazy. Who eats anchovies?"
	"I do," Ella replied. "But I could also go for a ham and pineapple."
	"Ham and pineapple!"

■ REVISING

6. **Improving Your Writing . . .** Read over your first draft (silently and aloud) to check for its overall effectiveness. Use the six traits of writing as a revising guide.

   ■ **Ideas:** *Do I focus on a specific event or experience? Do I use details and dialogue to show instead of tell? Does my narrative make the reader want to know what happens next?*

   ■ **Organization:** *Do I hook the reader's attention in the beginning? Does my narrative flow smoothly as if I were sharing it with a friend? Do I include events in the order that they occurred? Is there a satisfying resolution or ending?*

   ■ **Voice:** *Does my narrative have a tone that fits the topic? Does my personality come through in my writing?*

   ■ **Word Choice:** *Do I use specific, concrete nouns to make a clear image? Do I use active verbs to tell what happens? Have I used words that have the right feeling (connotation)?*

   ■ **Sentence Fluency:** *Do I begin sentences in a variety of ways? Do I use sentences of different lengths?*

■ EDITING

7. **Checking for Conventions . . .** Once you have finished revising your narrative, make sure your work adheres to the rules of English.

   ■ **Conventions:** *Have I checked for punctuation, mechanics, and grammar errors? Have I cited my sources correctly? Have I used the rubric on page 149 as a final check of my revising and editing?*

■ PROOFREADING

8. **Preparing a Final Copy . . .** Write or type a neat final copy of your narrative. Proofread your copy before sharing it.

HELP FILE

The most effective personal narratives usually follow the classic plot line of fictional stories. People (**characters**) in a specific place and time (**setting**) deal with a problem (**conflict**). A series of events or actions (**plot**) leads to a moment of truth (**climax**), which tells whether the people succeed or fail. The ending (**resolution**) tells how the event affected the person. For more about this story structure, see the sample fictional story on pages 154-156.

Sample **Personal Narrative**

In this personal narrative, student writer Matt Vice focuses on a recent memorable event in his life: the last football game of the season. Matt uses strong sensory details to bring the narrative to life and place the readers right in the action.

The Game

The narrative starts right in the middle of the action.

The rain hit my helmet lightly, like a soft tapping on a door. I pulled my chin strap tightly around my face and snapped it on the other side. Forty-three teammates standing beside me started to jog, workhorses on the move, the clip-clop of our spikes the only sound.

As we approached the field, the rain picked up. I looked at my teammates after hearing the cheers from our fans. I said to myself, "This is why I play football; this is what it's all about." As we burst through the gate, the roar of the crowd engulfed us. Our coach gathered us together on the sidelines and barked the game plan to us. Forty-four sets of eyes locked on him as if we were hypnotized. We broke the huddle, and the receiving team trotted out onto the field.

The ball was kicked. It soared high above our heads as the two teams ran full charge at each other. I found my man and fixed on him like a missile locking on to its target. The return man was hit hard and brought down around the 50-yard line.

> "I said to myself, 'This is why I play football; this is what it's all about.'"

The crowd was yelling; the cheerleaders were pumped. I heard the chanting fade into the background as the game progressed. Two quarters passed, then three. Hard-hitting crunches and cracks could be heard play after play. Each team traded scores.

This paragraph serves as a transition between two parts of the game.

With less than a minute left in the game, we had a 24-to-17 lead. The rain was running down my helmet like an overflowing gutter. With time running out, the opposing quarterback dropped back. The crowd went silent as he passed to an open receiver in the end zone. Everything seemed to go into slow motion as the ball dropped securely into his hands. I stood openmouthed, dumbfounded, and barely breathing. They made the extra point, so the score was tied, which meant overtime.

The opposing team won the coin toss and went first. The official put the ball on the 10-yard line. In three short plays, they scored again, putting them ahead by six. I felt like I was in a bad dream. After the extra point, it was our turn. Our first two plays were stopped cold by their tenacious defense. On third down, our quarterback dropped back and connected with the tailback a yard short of the end zone. I snapped my helmet, anticipating heading out onto the field for the extra point.

> "Fourth down in overtime . . . this is the stuff dreams are made of. "

Fourth down in overtime . . . this is the stuff dreams are made of. A quarterback sneak was our money play, a play we had executed to perfection at least 30 times throughout the season. How could it go wrong?

Specific details re-create the final play for readers.

Eleven men broke the huddle and slowly walked to the line. The center placed his hands on the ball, keeping the laces up for luck. The quarterback barked his cadence like a general shouting orders. Eyes were locked; the crowd was silent. At the snap of the ball, their linemen charged us, trying to crack the wall. Our quarterback took a hit and fumbled before he could cross the line. The game was over. We lost by inches.

I went still and fell to my knees. Our quarterback sat in the end zone, alone. I could hear sobs from the crowd. Tears ran down my face, or maybe it was just the rain. I couldn't tell. Some teammates were consoled by their families or hugged by their friends. Our last game was not supposed to end in this way.

The closing is neatly tied to the opening.

Heads down, our team walked slowly back to the locker room, the once thunderous footsteps now silent. For the first time that night, I felt the cold. ■

Sample Extended Personal Narrative

Some important experiences occur over an extended period of time. In this sample, student writer Natalie Garcia focuses on her search to find her father, a search that spanned a number of years. Note the "I remember . . ." details she includes.

Finding My Family

The opening provides important background information.

When I was four years old, I saw my dad all of the time. Although my parents were divorced, he used to drive all the way from Michigan just to see me. Sometimes he'd pick me up in his old blue pickup truck, and I'd travel back to his house, bumping along the potholed streets, listening to the radio.

I remember always waking up early in the morning, running into his room, and jumping on his bed to wake him. Soon after, I would smell homemade tortillas and eggs. Sometimes he even made breakfast burritos for a special treat. On other days, I just ate cereal.

I remember the sound of music from the ice-cream truck that would cruise through his neighborhood. We would run out of the house, and my dad would pick me up and hold me while I chose what I wanted. Sometimes I'd choose an orange push-up, but most of the time, I picked the green ice-cream frog on a stick with gum-ball eyes. It was my favorite.

My dad worked as a truck driver, and he'd often bring crates of produce home—bushels of bumpy brown potatoes, bright green peppers, and juicy orange-red tomatoes. I loved to eat the tomatoes whole, sprinkled with salt. I still do that now.

The writer shares deep feelings and concerns.

All of a sudden, my dad stopped visiting, and I was devastated. I wrote to him as many times as I could, but he never answered my letters. I thought that he didn't love me anymore. I asked my mom over and over why he didn't write to me. She said he probably didn't have the time. But how could someone not have enough time for his own child?

About a year ago, I finally received a return letter from my dad. There was a phone number on the letter, so I called. I asked about all of the letters he never answered, and he said, "I never got them." I didn't believe that, but I didn't care. I now had him back in my life, and that's all I wanted.

Then last year I came home from school and found an unexpected letter. When I read it, I found out that I had an older half-sister, which really shocked me. (My family was suddenly growing.) She told me the real reason that my dad had never answered my letters: His English skills weren't very good. That, I understood, and I cried with joy after reading the letter.

> **"Then last year I came home from school and found an unexpected letter."**

I called my dad. During our conversation, for the first time since I was four years old, I heard him

In the final paragraph, the writer shares the resolution to the problem.

say, "I love you." I now know that I have family—here with Mom, of course, but now there's also Dad and a half-sister. My family may be scattered over three states, but knowing that everyone is out there is the best feeling in the world. It makes me feel like a hole in my heart has been filled. ■

Narrative-Writing Tips

The following activities will help you find additional writing ideas for personal narratives:

- **Page through** family photo albums.

- **Talk** to your grandparents.

- **Complete** a series of "I remember . . ." statements.

- **Draw** a winding highway on your paper, representing a map of your life. Note memorable experiences on the map.

- **Collect** possible writing ideas related to different categories: early childhood, elementary school, holidays, and so on.

Writing Guidelines Personal Essay

A personal essay shares the details of a specific event or time in your life, emphasizing what you learned from the experience. In this way, a personal essay is part recollection and part reflection.

■ PREWRITING

1. **Selecting a Topic . . .** Review your journal entries for possible topics, or list ideas that come to mind as you read the sample essay on the next page.

2. **Gathering Details . . .** Write freely about your topic for at least 5–10 minutes. Use one of the following open-ended sentences as a starting point:

   - ■ **(The topic) makes me feel . . .**
   - ■ **(The topic) causes me to . . .**
   - ■ **(The topic) concerns me because . . .**

3. **Focusing Your Thoughts . . .** Think about the tone of your personal essay. How do you want your reader to feel? What details express this feeling best? What order of events would create the strongest impression?

■ WRITING AND REVISING

4. **Connecting Your Ideas . . .** As you write your first draft, let your personality and voice come through. (Write what you are thinking and feeling.) Your opening should grab the reader's attention, the middle should re-create the experience, and the ending should reflect on it.

5. **Improving Your Writing . . .** As you review your first draft, ask yourself the following questions: *Does my essay reveal the importance of the experience? Have I organized the details in an effective way? Does my tone fit my topic? Then make the necessary changes.*

6. **Improving Your Style . . .** Check the *word choice* and *sentence fluency* of your work, making sure your writing reads smoothly and clearly.

■ EDITING AND PROOFREADING

7. **Checking for Conventions . . .** Check for spelling, grammar, and punctuation errors. Use the rubric on page 149 as a final check.

8. **Preparing a Final Copy . . .** Write or type a neat final copy of your essay. Proofread your copy carefully before sharing it.

Sample **Personal Essay**

In this personal essay, Kylee Simpson writes about a moment when her life changed forever. She spends most of the essay reflecting on the meaning of that one moment and telling what it taught her about her life.

At Least I Know

Everybody has to grow up, and for most people the change from childhood to adulthood is a gradual one. Not for me. I remember the moment my childhood ended. It was right after a big basketball game—Panthers 28, Bulldogs 25—and the whole gymnasium stirred with excitement. The parking lot lights shone brightly through the dark sky as my friend Jenna and I headed home. Suddenly, Jenna's cell phone rang.

"I gotta get this," she said, pausing on the sidewalk. She answered and listened, nodding solemnly. Even in the darkness, I could see her face go gray. After what seemed like forever, she hung up. Her eyes were fixed in a blank stare.

"Jen? Jenna? What's wrong?" My stomach twisted.

"It's Mia. She was in a car accident. . . . Mia's dead."

I felt like I'd been hit in the chest with a brick, and I had to fight to take a breath. I'd seen Mia in seventh hour. She had been making faces, cracking me up. Mia was the one girl in our group I shared my deepest secrets with . . . and now . . . now she was gone. Jenna collapsed into my arms, and we sobbed tears of disbelief.

The next few days were a blur. The school provided grief counselors, but I felt like I had to work through everything myself. During seventh hour, I just stared at Mia's empty desk and tried to imagine her there. I don't remember a word the teacher said, or a word that anybody else said. Just a week before, my life was all about clothes and hair, basketball games and tests. Now Mia was gone, and my old life was gone, too.

Why didn't I ever tell Mia how I felt about her? The answer was simple. I didn't know how much she meant to me until it was too late. Still, I had to try. Maybe I couldn't tell her face to face, but I could share my feelings in writing. For months, my journal was full of Mia—poems, stories, and drawings. I don't know whether she saw what I was writing or knew what she meant to me, but at least I knew.

My life is different today. Since Mia died, I've learned to take each day as a blessing and to cherish my friends and family. You never know how long someone will be around. Now I take every opportunity to express my feelings to the people I care about. It's even okay if they don't say anything back. At least they know how I feel about them—at least I know. ■

Assessment Rubric

Use this rubric as a checklist to evaluate your narrative writing. The rubric is arranged according to the traits of writing described in your handbook. (See pages 21–26.)

Ideas

The writing . . .

_____ focuses on a specific experience or time in the writer's life.

_____ presents an appealing picture of the action and the people.

_____ uses dialogue and sensory details.

_____ makes the reader want to know what happens next.

Organization

_____ begins by pulling the reader into the narrative.

_____ gives events in an order that is easy to follow.

_____ uses transition words and phrases to connect ideas.

Voice

_____ creates a tone and mood that fit the topic.

_____ shows the writer's personality.

Word Choice

_____ contains specific nouns, vivid verbs, and colorful modifiers.

Sentence Fluency

_____ flows smoothly from one idea to the next.

_____ uses a variety of sentence lengths and structures.

Conventions

_____ applies the basic rules of writing.

_____ uses the format provided by the teacher or another effective design. (See pages 30–32.)

Creative
WRITING

Writing Stories and Plays   151

Writing Poetry   163

> "Fact and fiction, fiction and fact.
> Shape-shifting into one another . . ."
>
> —Gail Godwin

Writing
STORIES AND PLAYS

Imagine writing a story that stems from real life experience—maybe a high school girl who has to move. Also consider that this person may have a special friend that she soon won't see anymore. You could use this set of circumstances to develop an effective short story about saying good-bye or about breaking up.

This example illustrates how creative writing works—"fact and fiction, fiction and fact," blending together to form imaginative pieces of writing. A memory may develop into a poem, an image (like a special gift) may inspire a story, and a recent experience may be portrayed in a play.

Remember: Creative writing is the process of inventing, the process of making something new and different—something made-up. But it also has solid roots in the real-world experiences and memories of the writer—fact and fiction, blending together. This chapter includes guidelines and samples for several types of creative writing.

Preview

- **Story Writing**
- **Playwriting**
- **Assessment Rubric**

Writing Guidelines Story Writing

Story writing often begins with a question: "What can I create out of this image, memory, or feeling?" The image of a rickety old tree house can grow into a story about the builders. The memory of a former classmate can evolve into a story about losing a friend. Build your story with a few interesting characters, realistic dialogue, and believable action.

■ PREWRITING

1. **Getting Started . . .** All you're looking for is a seed, a starting point for your story. Let's say that you had spent a lot of time by a river when you were young. That river could be the setting for a story. And let's also say you recall that both good and bad things had happened there. Those happenings could spark ideas for the story line or plot.

   ✱ If no ideas come to mind, review your journal entries, freewrite about your experiences, or refer to the information on the next page.

2. **Focusing Your Thoughts . . .** Organize your thoughts for writing. In most stories, there are people (*characters*) in a place (*setting*) doing something (*plot*) about a problem (*conflict*) and, in the process, gaining a new understanding about life (*theme*).

■ WRITING AND REVISING

3. **Connecting Your Ideas . . .** Write your first draft freely, using your planning and prewriting as a guide. Start right in the middle of the action and let your characters tell the story by what they say and do. (See the sample story beginning on page 154.)

4. **Improving Your Writing . . .** Make sure you have created interesting characters and situations. Also, make sure that as the characters deal with the conflict, the plot builds to a climax. Focus also on the way your narrator sounds.

5. **Improving Your Style . . .** Check your *word choice* and *sentence fluency* to make sure that they fit your story and help you create a strong mood.

■ EDITING AND PROOFREADING

6. **Checking for Conventions . . .** Edit your revised writing for punctuation, mechanics, and grammar. Use the rubric on page 162 as a final check of your revising and editing.

7. **Preparing a Final Copy . . .** Proofread your copy before sharing it.

Patterns of Fiction

The following patterns of fiction are not based on any hard-and-fast rules that must be followed during the story-writing process. Think of them more as general approaches to story writing. After reviewing these patterns, you may think of many good ideas for stories.

The Quest (Return) ■ In a quest, the main character sets out in search of something, experiences various adventures, and finally returns—either triumphant or wiser. (A freshman sets out to make the basketball team and succeeds against significant odds.)

Sample Stories

"How Much Land Does a Man Need?" by Leo Tolstoy

"A Worn Path" by Eudora Welty

"By the Waters of Babylon" by Stephen Vincent Benet

The Initiation ■ A main character (usually a young person) is faced with a new situation that tests his or her abilities or beliefs. How the character deals with the situation determines the direction of his or her life. (A young boy loses a dog that he loves and learns something about life in the process.)

Sample Stories

"The Widow and the Parrot" by Virginia Woolf

"Araby" by James Joyce

"A Sunrise on the Veldt" by Doris Lessing

The Union ■ In this pattern, two people grow fond of each other, but their parents or some other authority figure or circumstance comes between them. The couple usually gets together in the end after overcoming various obstacles. (The son of a farmer and the daughter of a migrant worker meet secretly in spite of their parents' objections.)

Sample Stories

"Hoods I Have Known" by Sondra Spatt

"Horsetrader's Daughter" by D. H. Lawrence

(Any romantic stories)

The Choice ■ The main character is faced with a difficult decision near the end of this type of story. Making this decision is the high point of the plot. (An out-of-work laborer must decide if he should work for someone he dislikes.)

Sample Stories

"A Problem" by Anton Chekhov

"The Monkey's Paw" by W. W. Jacobs

"The Gift of the Magi" by O. Henry

Sample Short Story

In the following short story, student writer Jacob Emory creates a modern-day quest. The story follows one young man through a tumultuous day on his search for the perfect gift.

Just Perfect

"I can't just get her any old thing for Valentine's Day. I have to find the perfect gift!" Jeremy Jones earnestly explained to his best friend, Giff. They were sitting on a bench outside of school, the last bell having rung a few minutes before.

"You've got, like, almost two hours before you're supposed to go over to her place," Giff replied helpfully, looking at his watch.

"I know. But I don't have a clue!"

"Flowers? Candy? Something like that?"

Jeremy shook his head. "Those are way too predictable. No, it has to be something unique—something with lots of meaning."

"Well, let's see. Andrea's into swimming, right? Maybe you could get her some fins? Or a snorkel and a nice face mask?"

Jeremy looked at his friend, shaking his head. "Are you crazy? Those are about as impersonal as you can get!"

"Well, what about a swimming suit then?"

"Hmm. . ." Jeremy thought about that. The idea of a cute swimming suit had a certain appeal.

"You are not serious. Are you?" Veronica Sanchez asked, surprising the boys as she came up behind their bench.

"Well, it kind of seemed like a good idea," Jeremy admitted.

"Why don't you just buy yourself a T-shirt that says 'Male Chauvinist Pig'? That would have about the same effect," she offered.

Veronica, one of his friends since grade school, had introduced Jeremy to Andrea last fall, so he was inclined to put some stock in her opinion. "A swimming suit is a bad idea, you think?"

She snorted in amusement. "Like, hopeless, is all."

"Well, what do you suggest?" he demanded, growing exasperated.

"You're right about one thing—she's big into swimming. What about a cool beach towel? You know, a big fluffy one, maybe with something romantic on it, like a sunset?"

Even Giff was nodding in agreement. "Okay, that's a good idea," acknowledged Jeremy, turning to his buddy. "Now, can you give me a ride to the mall?"

"You really planned this out ahead of time, didn't you?" Giff said sarcastically. "But, I don't have to be at work until 6:00. Let's go."

"Good luck!" Veronica called after them as they headed out to the parking lot.

The dashboard clock read "4:23" as they rolled onto Main Street. "Let's see, I can buy the towel, be home by 5:15, shower and clean up and still get to Andrea's by 6:00. This is working out!" Jeremy declared.

A series of unexpected events builds suspense.

The loud "pop" from the left side of the car destroyed his optimism as thoroughly as it blew out the tire. Giff swerved the vehicle onto the shoulder and came to a stop.

"Oh, great," Giff said. "Help me dig out the spare."

"Why do these things keep happening to me?" Jeremy demanded.

"Hey, I don't see you shelling out for a new tire," Giff said sourly.

Forty-five minutes later, grimy and sweating, the boys were back in the car and moving. "Step on it!" urged Jeremy, keenly aware of time slipping away.

"I'm going as fast as I—" Giff was interrupted by the wail of a police siren. Grimacing in frustration, he pulled over again. They waited in silence as a young police officer came up and asked Giff for his license, then went back to her car to check it out.

"At least she didn't give you a ticket," Jeremy said twenty minutes later, watching the police car's flashing red lights fade as they finally pulled away.

"No thanks to you," Giff replied. "Now, I'm going to be late for work—I'll drop you off at your place!"

"But the mall!"

"No time," declared Giff.

A transitional paragraph moves the story ahead.

It was almost quarter to six as Jeremy trudged toward his front door, empty-handed. He glanced next door, toward his grandmother's house, as he was turning the knob. That's when he thought of his grandmother's greenhouse, the little glassed-in porch where she grew plants all year long. "Maybe flowers aren't such a bad idea after all," Jeremy told himself. He had fifteen minutes before he was supposed to go over to Andrea's.

He slipped in the side door, heard the blare of TV from the main room, and figured he could just get into the porch, snip a few roses—or tulips, or whatever—and still be in time for his date.

"Oh, Jeremy!" his grandmother said, surprising him in the kitchen. "I'm so glad you're here—could you help me for a minute?"

"Uh, sure, Gram," he said, trying not to be obvious as he looked at the clock. Thirteen minutes left.

Sixteen minutes later, he had moved a dozen heavy boxes for his grandmother and decided that it was time to be frank. After all his help, she owed him a few flowers anyway.

"Um, Gram—I have a date for Valentine's Day. Could I take some flowers from your greenhouse?"

"Oh, I'm so sorry, Jeremy," she replied. "Of course, you'd be welcome to them—if I had any. But I cleaned out the greenhouse this past weekend so I could plant some spring herbs."

Jeremy tried not to show his disappointment. He ended up a half hour late getting to Andrea's, still sweaty from moving his grandmother's boxes. Even after washing his hands twice, he hadn't been able to get the tire-grime out from under his fingernails.

And he had nothing to give her for Valentine's Day.

Even so, she seemed glad to see him.

"I . . . I'm sorry about not having a gift," he explained. "But maybe I could entertain you with the story of what just happened to me?"

To his surprise, she agreed. After hearing about the flat tire, the police officer, and his grandmother's chores, she surprised him by laughing.

"You know," she said, "I don't think anyone's ever gone to so much trouble to give me a present before! Jeremy, I'm truly touched." ■

> **A brief interchange adds intensity to the story.**

> **The closing scene provides a satisfying ending.**

HELP FILE

Make sure your story has a strong ending. Here are some strategies:

- **Resolve the conflict.** Show how the character lives after confronting the central problem.

- **Tie the ending back to the beginning.** Return to a specific setting, symbol, or idea from the start of the story.

- **Show character change.** Show how the events of the story have changed your character. Remember, not all endings have to be happy ones.

- **Use a quotation.** Search online or in books for quotations that match the theme of your story. Work the quotation into the ending of your story.

Sample Fictionalized Journal Entry

For an astronomy assignment, Carter Williams wrote a fictional journal entry about his stay on the moon. Obviously, he has spent time researching his topic.

A Journal from Luna One

September 03, 2024, 0300 hours, Greenwich Mean Time: Captain Dale and Lieutenant Speckman just took off after six weeks on the moon. They'll send a signal when they dock with the orbiter overhead. It'll take three more days before they reach Cape Canaveral and a week before their bodies adjust to Earth's gravity.

Meanwhile, I'm here, alone in the lunar night—just me and the robots. When the sun comes up, we'll get to work. I'll have one of the robots stack the supplies in the empty module while the other two help me build the second habitation module. I like building on the moon, lifting a 500-pound water-recycling unit as if it were a bale of hay. It makes me feel like a superhero. When we're done, *Luna One* will be able to handle a crew of six people, and that's not counting the 'bots.

After that, our next big job will be to construct the helium-3 mining plant. It's about two miles from here. Right now, the site is just a barren crater dotted by cargo sleds, but soon it'll be filled with helium derricks like a twentieth-century oilfield. If that crater contains as much helium-3 as the scientists think, it'll supply every fusion reactor in North America. Of course, the mining plant will be fully automated, including its weapon systems. When I think of all the crazy wars fought over oil in the last century, I get chills worrying about the space wars that'll be fought over all that helium-3.

Dawn is approaching. On Earth, sunrise brings rosy skies, a blur of brightness in the east slowly spreading across the heavens. That's not the way it is here on the moon. Since there's no atmosphere, the sky overhead remains pitch black even after the sun crests the horizon. There'll be no blue, no clouds—just star-speckled blackness and the staring sun.

There it is now, a harsh bright light spilling in the viewport, almost as if someone flipped a switch. It's going to be a long day—literally. The sun'll be overhead for two weeks of Earth time; when it sets, cold night will close in for another two weeks.

We've got to work while the sun shines. Already, I hear the solar cells humming to life. The rover will be fully charged in a few hours. In the meantime, my robot buddies and I have work to do. It's time to power them up and get them going, time to continue building a new world here on the moon. ∎

Interesting details draw readers into the entry.

The writer smoothly works in factual information.

Writing Guidelines Playwriting

A play script explores a conflict in the lives of two or more characters. In a play, the characters do almost all of the work—from revealing their personalities to advancing the plot, from identifying the setting to dealing with the theme. As your script develops, so should your characters, to a point where you know them well. (See pages 160–161 for a sample script.)

■ PREWRITING

1. **Getting Started . . .** To start out, think of an actual situation or conflict to build a script around: You and a family member may argue about your future. Someone you know may be headed for big trouble. If you can't "find" an idea, invent one: A girl competes in a diving competition. An elderly gentleman can't remember where he lives.

2. **Focusing Your Efforts . . .** Once you have a situation in mind, identify your main characters and consider how this situation complicates their lives. Then decide how your play will start (who will be doing what and where).

■ WRITING AND REVISING

3. **Connecting Your Ideas . . .** Write your first draft freely, using your planning and prewriting as a general guide. After introducing the main characters and their problem, let the rest of the play work itself out as you listen to and imagine your characters' interactions. Include stage directions as necessary. (See page 159 for additional tips.)

4. **Improving Your Writing . . .** Read your first draft silently and aloud, paying special attention to the characters, plot, and sound of your play. Ask yourself the following questions: *Are my characters believable? Does the problem complicate the characters' lives? Does the dialogue sound natural for each character? Why or why not?*

5. **Improving Your Style . . .** Focus next on your *word choice* and *sentence fluency,* with these two questions in mind: *Do the words fit each speaker's personality and the situation? Do the sentences sound realistic—like people actually speaking?*

■ EDITING AND PROOFREADING

6. **Checking for Conventions . . .** Edit your revised writing, watching for errors in punctuation, mechanics, and grammar. Use the rubric on page 162 as a final check of your revising and editing.

7. **Preparing a Final Copy . . .** Write a clean final copy and proofread it.

Playwriting Tips

Pay special attention to each of the following elements as you write your play scripts.

Dialogue ■ How the characters speak should reveal something about their identity. (Clues to voice or delivery can be included in stage directions as well as in word choice.) Write the dialogue as speakers actually speak. People often interrupt each other and, at times, talk past or ignore one another.

Conflict ■ Build your play around a believable situation or problem, one that makes sense in the lives of the characters. (The conflict should make life increasingly difficult for the main characters until the play reaches a turning point.)

Stage Directions ■ In the stage directions, indicate the time and place of the action, entrances and exits, and so on. Your directions may also indicate what each of the characters is doing on stage. However, don't complicate your play with too many directions.

Form ■ Follow the accepted format for a script, beginning with the title and following with a list of characters and an explanation of the setting *before* the first words are spoken.

Related Forms

If you enjoy writing scripts, here are two more forms to try:

Monologue ■ Have a character carry on a one-way conversation. The main challenge of this type of writing is to have your character reveal something important about his or her personality during the monologue. You often find monologues in longer pieces of writing—plays, novels, or short stories. A monologue within a play is called a *soliloquy*.

Ad Script ■ Create a television (or radio) ad script for a real or imagined product. To get started, determine what your product can do, how it can do it better than similar products, and what kind of story would best sell this idea to your audience. Tell a very brief story, one that covers either 30 or 60 seconds.

✱ There are special stage directions to consider for ad scripts:
Add graphic, Add music, Cut to, Fade in, Insert, and so on.

Sample Play

This brief one-act play by Kimi Yoshida dramatizes what it is like to be a high school junior.

Being Me

Characters: **Kimi**, a high school junior
Dad, Kimi's father
Ms. Kick, the vice principal
Erin, Kimi's best friend
Tony, a senior Kimi likes

The initial stage directions establish the setting.

Kimi stands downstage center, illuminated by a spotlight. The other characters are in partial shadow, spaced apart upstage. Each is in a separate setting: Dad reads a paper in an easy chair; Ms. Kick sits at a desk; Erin perches on a stool and holds a cell phone; and Tony lounges on a park bench listening to music. The other characters are illuminated only when they are speaking.

Kimi: (*to audience*) Nobody knows what it's like . . . being me. Oh, lots of people think they know, but they don't. They drop in on my life now and then, but none of them sees the whole picture.

Dad rustles his newspaper, and the light goes up on him.

Dad: Kimi!
Kimi: Yeah, Dad?
Dad: The Burger Bungalo is hiring.
Kimi: I need a car to have a job.
Dad: You need a job to have a car. Gas costs money. And insurance—imagine my rates!
Kimi: I don't need a great car, just something that runs.

Dad is reading his paper again. His light fades.
Ms. Kick begins marking attendance records, and the light goes up on her.

The dialogue reveals something about each character.

Ms. Kick: Kimi! Where were you first hour? I have an attendance slip reporting you absent.
Kimi: I was there—just two minutes late, was all. I dropped my folder in the commons and had to chase my papers around—
Ms. Kick: That will be a detention, young lady.
Kimi: But that's not fair! If I have detention, I miss the bus, and my dad has to leave work to pick me up.

Ms. Kick continues to mark her records, and her light fades.

Erin punches a number into a cell phone. Her light goes up.

Erin: You got a detention? Just don't show up.

Kimi: Geez, Erin. Do you want to get me in even more trouble? With my luck, I'd end up suspended—and then I would never get a car.

Erin: Come on; ditch detention and come with me to the mall. You can't be scared all the time, you know.

Kimi: I'm not scared—it just sounds like a stupid idea.

Erin: Another call. Got to go!

Erin takes another call on her cell phone. Her light fades.

Kimi: (*to audience*) Well, maybe that's not quite true—I feel like I am scared all the time. I get pulled every which way, and no one will let me . . . just be me.

Tony pulls earphones from his ears. His light goes up.

Tony: Yo, Kimi.

Kimi: Hi, Tony. What's up?

Tony: Nothin'. Hey, wanna go out this Friday? There's a party down at Craggy's. Should be pretty decent.

Kimi: I'd love to! But Friday. I . . . I have to baby-sit.

Tony drags his earphones back into place. His light fades.

Kimi: Why is it so hard—being me?

Dad: (*light goes up*) Kimi! What time will you be home?

Ms. Kick: (*light goes up*) Kimi! Get in here and be quiet.

Erin: (*light goes up*) Kimi! Come on.

Tony: (*light goes up*) Kimi! It's gonna be a great party.

All four supporting characters ad lib, increasing in frenzy. Kimi claps her hands to her ears, and the four fall silent—though they continue their harangue in pantomime. Kimi takes a step downstage and drops her hands; lights fade on other characters.

Kimi: (*to audience*) Sometimes when I shut out all the voices and hold really still and listen really hard, I hear something else—a still, small voice speaking deep inside me. I listen, and it grows louder. And if I am very patient, I can hear what that voice is saying, and I know who that voice is. It's me. (*She turns, looks at the shadowy characters one by one, faces the audience, and shrugs.*) As long as I hear that voice, I know I can make it . . . and keep being me.

She strolls offstage. ∎

Each new conversation builds tension.

The ending ties everything together.

Assessment Rubric

Use this checklist to evaluate your fiction and script writing. This rubric is arranged according to the traits of writing described in your handbook. (See pages 21–26.)

Ideas

The writing . . .

_____ contains an engaging setting, story line, and theme.

_____ brings the action alive with dialogue and details.

_____ develops interesting characters.

Organization

_____ follows a basic plot line, building effectively to a climax, or high point of interest. (See page 259.)

_____ progresses in a storylike way. (Explanations or stage directions are kept to a minimum.)

Voice

_____ uses an effective storytelling voice.

_____ sounds realistic in terms of the characters' dialogue.

_____ maintains a consistent voice for each character.

Word Choice

_____ contains specific nouns, vivid verbs, and colorful modifiers.

_____ employs a level of language appropriate to each character.

Sentence Fluency

_____ flows smoothly from one idea (or line) to the next.

Conventions

_____ follows the rules of punctuation, mechanics, and grammar.

_____ uses appropriate formatting guidelines for final copies.

"Poetry is when an emotion
has found its thought and the
thought has found words."

—Robert Frost

Writing POETRY

Before there were books, there were poems. Early cultures passed their most treasured tales from generation to generation in poems. Even today, poetry plays an important role in our culture. Children chant nursery rhymes as they play. Poetry is in the song lyrics we hear every day. And public speakers often recite poems to illustrate, summarize, or add impact to an idea. We are surrounded by poetry.

Poetry arises from life itself. An experience causes a feeling; that feeling gives rise to a thought; the thought is captured in expressive language; and a poem results. You can write poetry, too. The contents of this chapter will guide you to your own poems.

Preview

- **Writing Guidelines**
- **Sample Free-Verse Poem**
- **Sample Prose Poem**
- **Sample Tanka**
- **Sample Tercet**
- **Sample Rap Poem**
- **Poetry Terms**

Writing Guidelines

The writing process for poetry is similar to that for any other type of writing. It involves choosing a topic, gathering details, writing a first draft, revising, editing, proofreading, and publishing.

■ PREWRITING

1. **Choosing a Topic . . .** Inspiration often comes out of the blue, which is why poets carry writing journals. Sometimes, however, you need an idea for a particular occasion: a holiday, a friend's birthday, or a class assignment. If you can't find the right subject in your journal, try one of the following strategies.

   - **Read poems.** Good poetry often inspires more poetry. You can find collections of poetry at your library or online. (A great place to start is www.Poets.org.)

   - **Use the "Essentials of Life" checklist.** Any of the subjects in that list can launch a poem. ("Your House," on page 167, sprang from the subject "housing.")

   - **Make a list of memories.** A memorable event from your own life can be an excellent subject for a poem.

   - **Write about your mood.** Lots of poems are written to capture a specific feeling.

2. **Gathering Details . . .** To gather details for your poem, try one or both of the following:

   - **Write a list of details.** Jot down whatever comes to mind about your topic. Keep going until you run out of ideas. Then choose the most interesting ones for your poem.

   - **Create a sensory chart.** Many poems appeal to the senses. List sights, smells, sounds, tastes, and touch sensations about your topic to generate details for your poem.

3. **Choosing a Form . . .** There are two basic ways to decide on a form for your poem:

   - **Use a traditional form.** There are many books that define traditional forms and give examples. Browse the pages to find a form that suits your purpose.

     —or—

   - **Just start writing.** As you write your first lines, a form may suggest itself. Otherwise, you can simply draft your poem as a paragraph and later add line breaks and indents.

■ WRITING

4. Drafting Your Poem . . . The most important secret to writing a first draft is this: Turn off the critical part of your brain and turn on the playful part. Everyone has something worth saying in a poem, so just start writing and have fun. When you lose steam, check your details list or sensory chart for inspiration.

■ REVISING

5. Improving Your Poem . . . After your first draft is finished, read through it and circle the strongest, most interesting words, phrases, and lines. Cross out the weaker parts, or replace them with something better. If needed, move parts to improve the arrangement of ideas.

- ■ **Improving a free-verse poem:** Experiment by breaking your lines in different places. Sometimes just moving one word from the end of one line to the beginning of the next makes all the difference. Experiment with indentation, too. (Notice the line breaks and indentations in the rap poem on page 169, for example.)

- ■ **Improving a traditional poem:** Use a dictionary, thesaurus, and rhyming dictionary to find just the right words to suit your poem's rhythm, or syllable count and rhyme. Don't be afraid to change a line to fit in a new word that seems especially suited to your poem.

■ EDITING AND PROOFREADING

6. Polishing Your Poem . . . Cutting is the most important part of editing a poem. With the removal of unnecessary words, the remaining words take on new power. In a traditional form, where line length is critical, you will need to replace rather than cut weak words.

Also, check your spelling and punctuation. If you choose to use nonstandard spelling and punctuation for effect, make sure those differences seem intentional, not accidental.

■ PUBLISHING

7. Sharing Your Poem . . . Be sure to share your poetry. Check www. Poets.org and similar Web sites to learn about poetry organizations in your state. Many poetry organizations host public readings and publish magazines, calendars, and the like. Ask your teacher or librarian about poetry contests in your area, too.

Sample Free-Verse Poem

A free-verse poem does not rhyme like traditional poetry. Nor does it follow a traditional rhythm pattern. Instead, each free-verse poem finds its own rhythm and makes its own form.

In free verse, poetic techniques such as assonance, consonance, and alliteration often take the place of rhyme to give the poem an interesting sound. Line breaks add emphasis to words at the end of one line and the beginning of the next. Some lines may be indented or staggered across the page for visual interest or to change the flow of the poem.

Free-verse poetry is about inventiveness and experimentation, as in this example by student writer Elena Coplon.

Picky Eater

My little sister doesn't
Like ripe

Tomatoes or any other
Red food.

She prefers her apples
Glossy green.

Yellow grapefruit suits her
Tastes best.

She says she's wary of
Red berries,

And won't even eat
Crimson candies,

Though once I saw her sneak a
Maraschino cherry.

I think mainly she likes
Not liking things.

> Short stanzas ending in paired words give the poem a playful feeling.

> The author has chosen to punctuate normally but to capitalize the first word of each line.

> Breaking the pattern of paired ending words signals the poem's finish.

Take NOTE The author of "Picky Eater" has used several poetic sound techniques. Notice the examples of alliteration, assonance, and consonance. (See page 170.)

Sample **Prose Poem**

A prose poem looks like prose (regular writing), but it reads like poetry. It doesn't have line breaks, indentation, or rhyme; but it does use poetic imagery, and it may use other poetic techniques such as personification, metaphor, rhythm, consonance, and so on. In the example below, student writer Haydon Tobeck takes an unusual look at housing.

The poem begins with an interesting idea.

It builds an image in the reader's mind.

Here, the poem takes a fanciful turn.

Because the meaning is not spelled out, the reader is invited to make his or her own meaning.

Your House

What if everybody, when born, was given a house to live in? Picture your mother and father getting together and, as best they know how, setting a foundation, nailing together some walls, and putting on a roof. So there you are from the start, in this strange house, trying to find all the doors and learn the layout of the rooms.

Now imagine that, like a turtle, you have to keep this house your whole life. You can maybe remodel here and there, tear out a wall if you're really brave, and make an addition or two. But you can't just tear it to the ground and start over, because you have to live somewhere in the meantime.

The safest thing to do would be to just slap on a new coat of paint once in awhile, when the neighbors start complaining.

Sample **Tanka**

A tanka is an unrhymed mood poem that originated in Japan. It generally deals with feelings about life, seasons, or love. Tanka in English are five lines long. Lines one and three are short (often five syllables); the other lines are longer (often seven syllables). There is a turn in thought near the middle of the poem, after line two or line three. Most tanka are untitled, as in this example by student writer Erin Shimada.

The first part of the poem creates an image.

The second part reflects on that image.

A dandelion

sprouting from a cracked sidewalk

on this sunny day.

Tomorrow both will be gone,

but for now they have the sun.

Sample Tercet

A tercet, a favorite form of poet William Carlos Williams, is made up of three-line stanzas. A tercet can be as long as you like. Often, the rhyme scheme is *aba, bcb, cdc,* and so on; although not all tercets rhyme. In the example below, student writer Albertina Hald describes a favorite pastime.

Running

Each line in this tercet has two stressed syllables.

When you start on a run
Your body is awkward
Cold muscles feel drawn

Finding a rhythm is hard
Your stride feels too short
And your brain is bored

Near rhymes (breathing, feeling, and so on) keep the poem more relaxed than strict rhymes.

Your side may hurt
Just focus on breathing
Make your brain do its part

You'll soon lose that feeling
Your joints will loosen
Then you'll really be running

The poem reaches a turning point, from the effort of running to the joy of running.

And you'll know the reason
Why people have legs
Running, a person

The author ends with a figure of speech (a simile).

Feels free as a dog
Released from its leash
To dash for the finish

Sample **Rap Poem**

In this poem, student writer Rico Deloy uses rap techniques to explain what rap is all about. Notice the energy created by the poem's distinctive rhythm and rhyme.

Rap Lesson

Rap!

> **It's about attitude:**

Stylin', smilin', and feelin' good,

Don't have to be rude. Don't have to be crude.

Don't have to be cruel. But gotta be cool.

And gotta be hot, or else it's just not

Rap!

> **It's rhythm: four beats to each measure,**

A rhyming treasure, a work of pleasure,

Effort that sounds like effortless leisure,

Words building up a rhythmic pressure,

It's

Rap!

> **Move your feet to the beat of the street.**

It's complete. Nothing else can compete with the heat

of

Rap!

Internal rhyme —"cruel" and "cool" for example— adds to the poem's rhythm.

Rap line lengths vary, but each line has four beats (stressed syllables).

The poem ends by repeating its opening word, "Rap!"

HELP FILE

To make sure your poetry is the best it can be, check it carefully for these important elements:

- **Imagery appeals to the reader's senses. While some poems use more imagery than others, nearly all poems include at least some sense details.**
- **Mood conveys a feeling. The best poems lead readers to feel a certain way, without specifically telling them how to feel.**
- **Word play makes a poem fun to read and hear. Good poems use unexpected words and phrases to keep the reader interested.**

Poetry Terms

Alliteration is the repetition of initial consonant sounds in words:

> "It is the <u>h</u>appy <u>h</u>eart that breaks." —Sarah Teasdale, "Moonlight"

Assonance is the repetition of vowel sounds without repeating consonants:

> "Let the <u>u</u>nknowable t<u>ou</u>ch the b<u>u</u>ckle <u>o</u>f my spine."
> —Mary Oliver, "Little Summer Poem Touching the Subject of Faith"

Ballad is a poem in verse form that tells a story.

Blank verse is an unrhymed form of poetry. Each line normally consists of 10 syllables in which every other syllable is stressed.

Caesura is a pause or sudden break in a line of poetry.

Canto is a main division of a long poem.

Consonance is the repetition of consonant sounds. Although it is similar to alliteration, consonance is not limited to the first letters of words:

> "above his blon<u>d</u> <u>d</u>etermine<u>d</u> hea<u>d</u> the sacred flag of truth unfurle<u>d</u>"
> —e. e. cummings, "Two VIII"

Couplet is a pair of lines of verse of the same length that usually rhyme.

Enjambment is letting a sentence or thought run from one line to another.

Foot is the smallest repeated pattern of stressed and unstressed syllables in a poetic line. (See *Meter, Rhythm,* and *Verse.*)

- *Iambic*: an unstressed followed by a stressed syllable
- *Anapestic*: two unstressed followed by a stressed syllable
- *Trochaic*: a stressed followed by an unstressed syllable
- *Dactylic*: a stressed followed by two unstressed syllables
- *Spondaic*: two stressed syllables
- *Pyrrhic*: two unstressed syllables

Free verse is poetry that does not have a regular meter or rhyme scheme.

Haiku is a form of Japanese poetry that has three lines: the first and third short (usually five syllables) and the second longer (usually seven syllables). The subject of the haiku has traditionally been nature:

> Behind me the moon
> Brushes shadows of pine trees
> Lightly on the floor.

Heroic couplet (closed couplet) consists of two successive rhyming lines that contain a complete thought.

Line break is an important element of free-verse poetry, affecting the way a poem looks on a page, and causing the reader's eye to pause at particular words.

Lyric is a short verse that is intended to express the emotions of the author.

Meter is the patterned repetition of stressed and unstressed syllables in a line of poetry. (See *Foot, Rhythm,* and *Verse.*)

Onomatopoeia is the use of a word whose sound suggests its meaning, as in *clang, buzz,* and *twang.*

Refrain is the repetition of a line or phrase of a poem at regular intervals, especially at the end of each stanza.

Repetition is the repeating of a word or an idea for emphasis or for rhythmic effect: "someone gently rapping, rapping at my chamber door."

Rhyme is the similarity or likeness of sound in two words. *Sat* and *cat* are perfect rhymes because the vowel and final consonant sounds are exactly the same. *Stone* and *frown* are imperfect rhymes because their endings sound similar but not identical.

- *End rhyme* is the rhyming of words at the ends of two or more lines.
- *Internal rhyme* occurs when rhyming words appear within a line of poetry: "You break my eyes with a look that buys sweet cake."

Rhythm is the regular or random occurrence of sound in poetry. Regular rhythm is called *meter.* Random occurrence of sound is called *free verse.*

Sonnet is a poem in 14 lines of iambic pentameter. (See *Foot* and *Verse.*)

- *The Italian (Petrarchan) sonnet* has two parts: an octave (eight lines) and a sestet (six lines), usually rhyming *abbaabba, cdecde.* Often, a theme is given in the octave and a response in the sestet.
- *The Shakespearean (English or Elizabethan) sonnet* consists of three quatrains and a final rhyming couplet. The rhyme scheme is *abab, cdcd, efef, gg.* Usually, the theme is set forth in the quatrains and a response appears in the final couplet.

Stanza is a division of poetry named for the number of lines it contains:

- *Couplet:* two-line stanza
- *Triplet:* three-line stanza
- *Quatrain:* four-line stanza
- *Quintet:* five-line stanza
- *Sestet:* six-line stanza
- *Septet:* seven-line stanza
- *Octave:* eight-line stanza

Verse is a metric line of poetry. It is named according to the kind and number of feet composing it: iambic pentameter, for example. (See *Foot, Meter,* and *Rhythm.*)

- *Monometer:* one foot
- *Dimeter:* two feet
- *Trimeter:* three feet
- *Tetrameter:* four feet
- *Pentameter:* five feet
- *Hexameter:* six feet
- *Heptameter:* seven feet
- *Octometer:* eight feet

Academic
WRITING

Writing Expository Essays   173

Other Forms of Expository Writing   183

Writing Persuasive Essays   197

Other Forms of Persuasive Writing   207

Writing a Position Paper   221

"Expository writing is as much about thinking as it is about writing."

—Jim Burke

Writing
EXPOSITORY Essays

The expository essay is the basic form of writing assigned in many of your classes. You write expository essays about important concepts covered in your reading and in class discussions. You explore topics related to your course work. You compose procedure (how-to) papers, or take essay tests. Anytime you inform, explain, examine, discuss, or interpret in writing, you are developing an expository essay.

Expository essays follow the thesis-statement-plus-support structure. That is, a successful expository essay includes a clear thesis statement *(identifying an important or interesting aspect of a topic)* with effective supporting ideas *(examples, quotations, paraphrases,* and so on). The best essays begin and end with quality information, so the key is to work with a solid base of facts and details right from the start.

Preview

- **Writing Guidelines**

- **Sample Expository Essay**

- **Assessment Rubric**

WRITING GUIDELINES

Expository Essay

The primary purpose of an expository essay is to share information with your reader. You are not trying to change anyone's mind or influence opinions. Instead, you are attempting to pass on as much valuable information as you can about a topic.

Before you begin, be sure you understand the requirements for the assignment. Here are three things that you should do:

- **Analyze** the assignment word for word. Locate any key terms (*define, compare, classify,* etc.) and know what they mean.

- **Restate** the assignment in your own words.

- **Find out** what standards will be used to evaluate your essay.

■ PREWRITING

1. **Choosing a Subject . . .** Usually, an expository writing assignment will start with a general subject or a writing prompt related to your course work. You need to find a *specific* topic that meets the requirements of the assignment. If your topic is too broad, you will have too much information to deal with. If the topic is too narrow, you will not find enough information to write an essay.

   ✱ Once you find an interesting topic, you need to discover the specific focus or angle for your paper. This focus will further limit your topic and help you plan your writing.

General Subject ➡	*Specific Topic* ➡	*Limited Focus*
International sports	**Formula One auto racing**	**Improvements in driver safety**
Democracy in action	**Women's suffrage in the United States**	**Elizabeth Cady Stanton's role in the movement**

2. **Gathering Details . . .** Investigate a number of resources about your topic. Refer to print and online sources, consult knowledgeable people, and make your own observations. (See pages 46–49 for gathering strategies and graphic organizers that can help you.) Gather different types of information including facts, statistics, examples, anecdotes, and quotations. (See the next page.)

Types of Information

Without quality information, you cannot effectively develop an expository essay. Here are different types of information that you can gather.

Facts ■ are specific statements that can be proven to be true. Cite the source of facts unless they are common knowledge. In the sample essay on pages 180–181, the writer gives these facts about improved helmets:

> **Helmets are light but very strong, made from the same materials that are used to manufacture bulletproof vests.**

> **In addition, drivers wear clear tear-off strips on the visors of their helmets so that if the faceplate becomes dirty, it can be quickly pulled off to expose a clean surface.**

Statistics ■ are factual statements that include a numerical value. Cite the sources of statistics unless they are common knowledge. In the sample essay on pages 180–181, the writer uses a statistic to prove a point about the dangers of Formula One racing in the past.

> **The Grand Prix has claimed the lives of dozens of drivers over the years, including 19 racers during the sixties and seventies (Tytler 1).**

Quotations ■ are the exact words of experts or authorities. The source of a quotation must be cited. In the sample essay, the writer quotes from the official Formula One Web site:

> **According to the official Formula One Web site, the purpose of the HANS system is "to massively reduce the loading [stress] caused to a driver's head and neck during the rapid deceleration caused by an accident."**

Paraphrases ■ restate in your own words what someone else has said. The source of a paraphrase must be cited. (See pages 278-279). In the sample essay, the writer paraphrases from a book about car safety:

> **Built-in fire extinguishers in the cockpit and engine areas can be activated by the driver or by rescuers arriving at the scene of a wreck. These extinguishers must work even if the car's electrical system is disabled (Burgess-Wise 127).**

Anecdotes ■ are brief stories that make a point. Cite the source of an anecdote, unless it comes from personal experience. In the sample essay, the writer begins with an anecdote to get the reader's attention.

> **During the first lap of a Grand Prix race in Melbourne, Australia, Martin Brundle's car hit another racer at 185 miles per hour. Spinning into the air, Brundle's B & H Jordan broke into pieces, spraying debris across the track. The race was stopped as the fragments of the car were cleared (Burgess-Wise 139).**

■ **PREWRITING (CONTINUED)**

3. **Forming a Thesis Statement . . .** The thesis statement should identify the limited focus that you plan to address in your essay. A thesis statement usually appears at the end of the first paragraph. You may need to write two or three versions of this statement before you get it just right. The following formula can help you form a thesis statement.

A specific topic	+	a limited focus	=	an effective thesis statement.
Formula One racing		improvements in driver safety		In recent years, Formula One racing has made dramatic improvements in driver safety.

4. **Selecting Main Points . . .** After you have written your thesis statement, you need to decide what main points you want to use to support it. A line diagram can help you do this. Write your thesis statement in the top part and the main supporting points beneath it. Here is a line diagram for the essay on pages 180–181.

Line Diagram

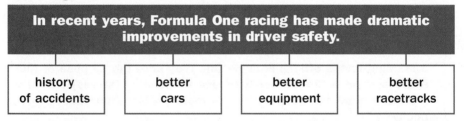

In recent years, Formula One racing has made dramatic improvements in driver safety.

| history of accidents | better cars | better equipment | better racetracks |

HELP FILE

Remember that you may need to use three different levels of detail to complete an idea or to make a point.

Level 1: **A main point is often stated in the topic sentence of a paragraph.**
The driver's helmet and clothing have also become much safer.

Level 2: **Clarifying sentences support the main point.**
In 2003, the Grand Prix made another mandatory improvement to helmet design—the Head-and-Neck Support (HANS) system.

Level 3: **Completing sentences add information (details, examples, quotations, etc.) to complete the explanation.**
The HANS system uses a carbon-fiber collar and three support straps to greatly reduce the risk of whiplash-type injuries to the head, neck, and spinal column.

5. **Creating an Outline . . .** Once you have selected your main points, you are ready to create an outline for your essay. In a *topic outline*, main points and details appear as phrases. In a *sentence outline*, main points and details appear as complete sentences.

✽ Information for the beginning and ending paragraphs is not included in the outline.

Sample Topic Outline

  I. History of driver safety problems in Formula One
     A. Bad accidents at start
     B. Hazards due to the course
     C. Hazards due to the cars
 II. Modifications to cars
     A. Single-shell construction and cockpit survival cell
     B. Fire extinguishers
     C. Escape system
III. Modifications to driver equipment
     A. Helmet improvements
     B. Head-and-Neck Support system
     C. Fireproof clothes
 IV. Modifications to racetracks
     A. Track improvement
     B. Medical service upgraded

Sample Sentence Outline

  I. Driver safety wasn't always a primary concern in Formula One racing.
     A. There is a history of bad accidents.
     B. The courses have included hills and hairpin turns.
     C. The cars are the fastest in the world and jockey for position.
 II. Many safety modifications have been made to cars.
     A. The body shell and cockpit survival cell are very strong.
     B. Each car has several fire extinguishers.
     C. Drivers can quickly escape after an accident.
III. Modifications have improved driver equipment.
     A. Helmets are stronger and lighter.
     B. The new Head-and-Neck Support system prevents spinal injuries.
     C. All clothing is fireproof.
 IV. Modifications have made the racetracks safer.
     A. Improvements in track layout help prevent crashes.
     B. Rescue and medical services are only seconds away.

■ **WRITING**

6. **Connecting Your Ideas . . .** As you write your first draft, focus
   on getting all of your ideas on paper. Each part of the draft—the
   beginning, middle, and ending—plays an important role. To develop
   your first draft, refer to the suggestions below and to the sample essay
   on pages 180–181.

Beginning Your opening paragraph should capture the reader's attention and state your thesis. Here are some ways to capture your reader's
attention:

1. Tell a dramatic or exciting story (anecdote) about the topic.
2. Ask an intriguing question or two.
3. Provide a few surprising facts or statistics.
4. Provide an interesting quotation.
5. Explain your personal experience or involvement with the topic.

Middle The middle paragraphs should support your thesis statement.
They provide information that fully explains the thesis statement. For
example, in the essay about safety measures in Grand Prix racing,
each middle paragraph focuses on one main aspect of improved safety.
Follow your own outline while writing this section.

Ending Your closing paragraph should summarize your thesis and leave
the reader with something to think about. Here are some strategies for
creating a strong closing.

1. Review your main points.
2. Emphasize the special importance of one main point.
3. Answer any questions the reader may still have.
4. Draw a conclusion and put the information in perspective.
5. Provide a final significant thought for the reader.

■ REVISING

7. **Improving Your Writing . . .** Carefully read your essay, looking for ways to improve it. Be prepared to do some adding, cutting, and rearranging. The following questions can guide your revision.

- ■ **Ideas:** *Does my thesis statement focus on an important part of the topic? Have I effectively supported the thesis? Should I add or delete any ideas or details?*

- ■ **Organization:** *Does my essay contain clearly developed beginning, middle, and ending parts? Do my main points and details appear in the best possible order? Have I used transitions to connect my ideas?*

- ■ **Voice:** *Do I sound knowledgeable about, and interested in, my topic?*

- ■ **Word Choice:** *Have I used specific nouns and verbs? Have I defined unfamiliar terms?*

- ■ **Sentence Fluency:** *Do my sentences read smoothly? Have I varied the sentence beginnings and lengths?*

■ EDITING AND PROOFREADING

8. **Checking for Conventions . . .** After you have revised your essay, it's time to make sure your work is correct. The following questions can guide your editing.

- ■ **Conventions:**

    Have I correctly cited information in my essay?

    Have I checked my use of end punctuation, commas, and quotation marks?

    Have I used correct capitalization for proper nouns, titles, and quoted material?

    Have I checked for spelling errors and watched for easily confused words (to, too, two)?

[HOT LINK] See "Assessment Rubric," page 182, for a helpful revising and editing guide.

Sample **Expository Essay**

In this essay, student writer Riley Carruthers shares details about an important international sport, Formula One racing. He focuses on a critical aspect of this sport—improved driver safety.

Buckling Up Is Not Enough

During the first lap of a Grand Prix race in Melbourne, Australia, Martin Brundle's car hit another racer at 185 miles per hour. Spinning into the air, Brundle's B&H Jordan broke into pieces, spraying debris across the track. The race was stopped as the fragments of the car were cleared. According to *The Ultimate Race Car*, the unhurt Brundle ran to the pits, climbed into his reserve car, and drove out in time for the restart (Burgess-Wise 139). This story says a great deal about the Grand Prix's current approach to driver safety. **In recent years, Formula One racing has made dramatic improvements in driver safety.**

Safety wasn't always a primary concern on the Formula One racing circuit. When the Grand Prix began in 1906, the race ran on city streets and country roads, and accidents involving drivers and spectators were common. Modern Grand Prix courses are used only for racing, but they are unlike the ovals used in NASCAR racing. Grand Prix races are held on "road courses" that include a variety of curves, hills, hairpin turns, and other challenges. The speed of Formula One cars adds another complication. They are the fastest race cars in the world, hurtling through race courses at incredible speeds. As a result, the Grand Prix has claimed the lives of dozens of drivers over the years, including 19 racers during the sixties and seventies (Tytler 1). Recently, though, these numbers have been dramatically reduced.

Many safety improvements have been made to the cars themselves. Cars are required to be constructed as a crash-absorbing single shell, with a cockpit survival cell made of indestructible carbon fiber. A four-point harness of belts holds the driver within the cell. Built-in fire extinguishers in the cockpit and engine areas can be activated by the driver or by rescuers arriving at the scene of a wreck. These extinguishers must work even if the car's electrical system is disabled (Burgess-Wise 127). The steering wheel of a Formula One car can be removed in a matter of seconds, and by simply releasing two bolts, the seat can be pulled out with the driver still strapped in place. In addition, sturdy hoops that protect the driver during rollovers are mandatory, as are the internal and external circuit breakers that guard against electrical fires.

The driver's helmet and clothing have also become much safer. Helmets are light but very strong, made from the same materials that are used to manufacture bulletproof vests. In addition, drivers wear clear tear-off strips on the visors of their helmets so that if the faceplate becomes dirty, it can be quickly pulled off to expose a clean surface. In 2003, the Grand Prix made another mandatory improvement to helmet design—the Head-and-Neck Support (HANS) system. According to the official Formula One Web site, the purpose of the HANS system is "to massively reduce the loading [stress] caused to a driver's head and neck during the rapid deceleration caused by an accident." The HANS system uses a carbon-fiber collar and three support straps to greatly reduce the risk of whiplash-type injuries to the head, neck, and spinal column. The driver's clothes also provide protection. Every item the driver wears, from long underwear and overalls to boots and gloves, is fireproof and capable of protecting against intense heat. Even the colorful sponsor patches and the thread used to sew them on are fireproof.

Grand Prix racetracks also have undergone major improvements in the name of driver safety. Banked turns and wide gravel run-out pads have reduced crashes on curves. Many sharp turns have been located specifically to force drivers to reduce speeds. Every race has ambulances and a medical evacuation helicopter on hand, with a fully equipped medical center on the grounds. Doctors are posted around the track and can reach the scene of any accident within seconds.

Formula One racing is still all about speed, but now it's about safety, too. Whether the race is in Australia, Japan, Argentina, the United States, or Europe, the Grand Prix features the same strict safety requirements. As a result, there has not been a fatal accident during a Formula One race or time trial since 1994 (Tytler 2). While the element of risk contributes to the thrill of Formula One racing, technology and skilled personnel help make this high-stakes sport as safe as it can possibly be. ■

The writer demonstrates a clear understanding of the subject.

An official Web site is cited.

The closing provides a significant final detail.

Assessment Rubric

Use this rubric as a guide when you evaluate your expository writing. The rubric is organized according to the traits of writing described in your handbook. (See pages 21–26.)

Ideas

The writing . . .

_____ develops a clearly expressed thesis statement.

_____ contains specific facts, examples, anecdotes, paraphrases, or quotations to support the thesis.

_____ thoroughly informs the reader.

Organization

_____ includes clear beginning, middle, and ending parts.

_____ presents ideas in logically ordered paragraphs.

_____ uses transitions as needed to link sentences and paragraphs.

Voice

_____ speaks clearly and knowledgeably.

_____ shows that the writer is truly interested in the topic.

Word Choice

_____ explains or defines unfamiliar terms.

_____ contains specific nouns and active verbs.

Sentence Fluency

_____ flows smoothly from one idea to the next.

_____ shows a variety of sentence lengths and structures.

Conventions

_____ adheres to the basic rules of writing.

_____ follows the appropriate guidelines for presentation. (See pages 30–32.)

"Essays are experiments
in making sense of things."
—Scot Russell Sanders

Other Forms of
EXPOSITORY WRITING

Expository writing is a particularly effective way to learn because it requires you to form a thesis that you can explain and support. As you put your ideas on paper, you increase your understanding of new concepts and subjects.

The best expository writing interprets and cites current research on a topic. It flows logically from one main point to the next. And it is the end product of careful writing and reviewing.

The specialized essays in this chapter show five different types of expository writing; the guidelines for each essay suggest ways to make challenging information clear to your reader. Learning how to write these essays will improve your ability to analyze complex ideas and express them to others.

Preview

- **Process Essay**
- **Essay of Definition**
- **Cause-Effect Essay**
- **Comparison-Contrast Essay**
- **Essay of Opposing Ideas**

Writing Guidelines **Process Essay**

In a process essay, you explain how something works or how to do or make something. Your challenge is to write clearly and completely so that the reader can easily follow the explanation. To do that, you must have a thorough understanding of your topic.

■ PREWRITING

1. **Choosing a Topic** . . . If your assignment is to explain how something works, review your class notes or text for ideas. For example, in a science class you might explain how a cut heals or a seed germinates. In a more general assignment, you might explain a certain job or chore, a hobby, or a special talent—like changing a flat tire or designing a Web site.

2. **Gathering Details** . . . List facts and details about your topic as they come to mind, or freewrite an instant version of your essay. Either activity will tell you how much you already know about your topic . . . and how much you need to find out. Collect additional information as necessary.

3. **Planning and Organizing** . . . Arrange the information you have collected according to the steps in the process. Also write down the main point you want your audience to understand or appreciate.

■ WRITING AND REVISING

4. **Connecting Your Ideas** . . . Write your first draft freely, working in details according to your prewriting and planning. As you develop your writing, be sure you cover all the steps in the process you are explaining. (You may want to use a bulleted list to present the steps.)

5. **Improving Your Writing** . . . Review your first draft for *ideas, organization,* and *voice.* Make sure all necessary information is included and the steps are in chronological order.

6. **Improving Your Style** . . . Check your *word choice* and *sentence fluency* to make sure that everything is stated clearly and effectively.

■ EDITING AND PROOFREADING

7. **Checking for Conventions** . . . Look for errors in punctuation, mechanics, and grammar. Use the rubric on page 182 as a final check of your revising and editing.

8. **Preparing a Final Copy** . . . Make a neat final copy of your essay.

Sample Process Essay

In the following process essay, the writer describes how one of nature's most devastating forces—a tsunami—develops.

An Unbelievable Force

The introductory paragraph ends with the focus statement (boldfaced).

On December 26, 2004, a tsunami struck Indonesia and the coastal areas around the Indian Ocean. A tsunami (the Japanese word for "harbor wave") is one of the most destructive forces in nature, and the Indonesian surge caused devastation as far away as Africa ("tsunami," etymology). Many people believe that a tsunami is simply a big wave that moves forward until it hits the shore or some other object, but the process is more complex than that. **A tsunami is really a huge transfer of energy from the crust of the earth to a body of water.**

The process is introduced.

Unlike typical ocean waves caused by storms, a tsunami begins with a fault line in the seabed. Faults are where two or more of the earth's tectonic plates meet and rub against each other. When one plate suddenly slips, an earthquake occurs. An earthquake beneath the ocean can cause one plate to thrust up over another, and a tsunami begins to form.

The process is described step-by-step.

When the underwater earthquake lifts the continental plate and all the water above it, tremendous energy is released. The force moves upward through the water until it gets near the surface. There, the energy spreads out horizontally like ripples in a pool. This enormous energy is not apparent on the surface, however, and the outwardly spreading waves may be only a few feet high. The power of the tsunami is still under the surface, moving as fast as 500 miles per hour.

As the surge heads toward the shore, the immense energy does not have enough water to carry it. The water nearer the land gets sucked back out to sea to feed the growing wave. People who witness tsunamis first notice that the ocean is suddenly receding, as it does at low tide. Then the wave rushes onshore in the form of a wall of water that can be as high as 90 feet and as wide as several hundred miles. The power of this wall of water can be unbelievable (12:19).

The closing shares key statistics about the topic.

The tsunami of 2004 was the result of an earthquake that measured 9.3 on the Richter scale, one of the highest readings in 40 years. The surge traveled at about 500 miles per hour but slowed down as it reached shallow water. Its energy shifted from speed to power as it built a wave 65 feet high—a wall of water that carried away trees, buildings, and the lives of *an estimated 300,000* people (Lambourne 1–3). ■

Writing Guidelines Essay of Definition

An essay of definition provides a detailed explanation of a term or concept. The term may be complicated (*inflation, cancer,* or *democracy*) or may mean different things to different people (*love, courage,* or *fairness*). The essay may include dictionary definitions, personal definitions, negative definitions (*telling what the word does not mean*), examples, comparisons, quotations, and anecdotes (*stories*).

■ PREWRITING

1. **Selecting a Topic . . .** Select a term or concept that is complex enough to require some real thought on your part. If no topic comes to mind, write freely about your course work, about current events, or about your personal life. Also consider terms people misuse or use too often.

2. **Gathering Details . . .** Collect information about your topic by referring to dictionaries, interviews, song lyrics, personal anecdotes, newspapers, the Internet, and so on.

3. **Focusing Your Thoughts . . .** Plan how you want to arrange the details. You may want to begin with a dictionary definition, include a quotation or two, follow with an important comparison, and so on. Experiment with a number of combinations.

■ WRITING AND REVISING

4. **Connecting Your Ideas . . .** Write an opening that introduces your topic and states your thesis. Develop the middle paragraphs that define the topic in different ways. Create a closing that thoughtfully sums up the topic.

5. **Improving Your Writing . . .** Review your first draft, paying special attention to the *ideas, organization,* and *voice.* Add, cut, rearrange, and rewrite parts as necessary.

6. **Improving Your Style . . .** Focus next on your *word choice* and *sentence fluency.* Make sure that you use the best words and sentences to express your ideas.

■ EDITING AND PROOFREADING

7. **Checking for Conventions . . .** Review your revised copy for punctuation, mechanics, and grammar. Use the rubric on page 182 to check your revising and editing.

8. **Preparing a Final Copy . . .** Write or type a neat final copy.

Sample Essay of Definition

In the following essay, student writer Christia Wood explains multiple definitions for the word *romance*. Notice how she ties these definitions together in her concluding paragraph.

"Isn't it Romantic?"

When someone uses the word *romance*, the images that come to mind are long-stemmed roses, soft music, and chocolates in a heart-shaped box. **Romance has more meanings than *love*, however. It may also refer to a family of languages, a heroic tale, or a particular period in the arts.**

In the first case, *Romance* (with a capital R) refers to languages that have descended from Latin. These include French, Italian, Portuguese, Spanish, and even Romanian, among others. Because Latin was the language of the Roman Empire, the term "Romance" reflects those origins.

After the fall of the Roman Empire, fantastic tales of heroism, adventure, and the supernatural became popular in Europe during the Middle Ages. Troubadours and traveling actors spread stories of noble knights battling evil ogres, dragons, and other monsters. Because many of these tales originated in southern Europe, where the Romance languages were spoken, the stories themselves came to be known as romances.

Often, these romances featured a damsel in distress, who was rescued by a knight according to a code of chivalry. In France, especially, chivalric tales became extremely popular. In these stories, knights would dedicate themselves to the honor of a lady, as in the story of Sir Lancelot and Queen Guinevere. It isn't difficult to see, then, where the link between courtship, love, and the modern use of the word *romance* began.

Later, during the early nineteenth century, poets such as Wordsworth, Coleridge, Byron, Keats, and Shelley used the term *Romantic* to refer to a new type of poetry. They were reacting against the previous period, the Age of Reason. Poetry of the Romantic period sought to regain a sense of wonder and intense feeling. It focused on nature rather than on science, on human emotions and human rights rather than the progress of nations. Of course, one of the emotions it sometimes dealt with was feelings of love, especially between pure and simple people.

Romance means much more than just hearts and flowers. It can refer to the languages that descended from Latin, to heroic tales that were first told in those languages, and to a particular period of history for poetry. Of course, running through all of these is the common thread of love, so the modern use of the word *romance* has its place, too. ∎

The first paragraph identifies the topic and states the focus of the essay (boldfaced).

Each middle paragraph helps define the topic.

The closing reviews the word's key meanings and tells how they relate to modern usage.

Writing Guidelines Cause-Effect Essay

In a cause-effect essay, you present a thoughtful analysis of a timely topic. Your essay might focus on one cause and show its many effects, or it might focus on one effect and show all the causes that led up to it. The most important step in writing a good cause-effect essay is deciding which organization fits the topic best.

■ PREWRITING

1. **Selecting a Topic ...** Consider recent experiences, conversations, and headlines for possible ideas. A cause-effect essay could focus on an improved situation in your school, a recent development in medicine, an exciting discovery, or a milestone in history. Also consider events that have changed your life.

2. **Gathering Details ...** Once you have a topic in mind, use a graphic organizer to list what you already know about it. (See pages 48-49.) If you need more information, refer to a variety of sources.

3. **Focusing Your Thoughts ...** Plan your essay by establishing a thesis as well as an effective order for presenting your ideas. *Remember:* Focus on one cause and show its effects, or focus on one effect and show the causes that led up to it.

■ WRITING AND REVISING

4. **Connecting Your Ideas ...** Write an opening that introduces your topic and states your thesis (connecting the causes and effects). Develop the middle paragraphs that explain the thesis statement and a closing that restates the thesis in an interesting way.

5. **Improving Your Writing ...** Carefully examine your first draft for *ideas, organization,* and *voice.* Ask at least one other person to react to your work as well. Add, cut, rearrange, or rewrite parts as necessary.

6. **Improving Your Style ...** Check your *word choice* and *sentence fluency* to make sure your essay reads smoothly and clearly.

■ EDITING AND PROOFREADING

7. **Checking for Conventions ...** Look for errors in punctuation, mechanics, and spelling in your revised writing. Use the rubric on page 182 as a final revising and editing guide.

8. **Preparing a Final Copy ...** Make a neat final copy of your essay. Proofread this copy before sharing. it.

Sample Cause-Effect Essay

In this essay, a student examines the effects of a new graduated driver's license law in his state.

The Many Effects of GDL Laws

The opening gains the reader's attention and identifies the thesis (boldfaced).

When my older sister turned 16, she got a learner's permit, took a driving class, and had her regular license six months later. Now I've turned 16, but my experience is going to be different. Many states, including our own, have passed new graduated driver's licensing (GDL) laws. These laws lengthen the time it takes to get an unrestricted driver's license. **Wherever GDL laws are passed, they have had many effects on young drivers.**

The most obvious effect of GDL laws is a longer period of restricted driving. Graduated licensing adds a stage of restricted driving between the learner's permit and the regular license. This stage can last for up to two years, and it restricts the learner's driving. For example, people with restricted licenses can have only one passenger riding with them. In addition, intermediate-stage drivers are held to a "zero tolerance" policy for alcohol and drug abuse. Of course, these activities are already illegal, but now if teenagers are caught, they lose their driver's licenses, even if they aren't anywhere near a car. Teen drivers under GDL laws are much more restricted than they were under the older licensing laws (*Rules of the Road*).

Each middle paragraph develops one effect.

The new GDL laws also have a strong effect on reducing the number of accidents caused by teenage drivers. Prior to GDL laws, the National Highway Traffic Safety Administration found that 16-year-old drivers were twice as likely as adult drivers to be in fatal crashes. As to nonfatal crashes, 16-year-olds had three times more accidents than 17-year-olds, five times more than 18-year-olds, and two times more than 85-year-olds. In states that have adopted GDL laws, these statistics are turning around ("Research Update"). For example, Florida experienced a 20 percent drop in teen traffic fatalities during its first year under GDL laws. Lawmakers hope that the GDL laws will have the same effect in our state.

Sources of information are cited.

The new laws also have a big impact on alcohol and drug use among young drivers. According to the National Survey on Drug Use and Health, GDL laws have reduced the level of teen alcohol and drug abuse ("Graduated"). The laws hit substance abuse with a one-two punch. Of course, the "zero tolerance" policy discourages students from getting involved with drugs or alcohol, but the restrictions on night driving also make students think twice about driving to parties where people will be drinking and using drugs. Many of today's teens may avoid getting involved in substance abuse because of GDL laws.

The new GDL laws will probably have one more positive effect: reducing the high cost of insurance for young drivers. Insurance companies make young drivers pay very high rates because, statistically, teenagers are much more likely to get involved in accidents than other drivers are. As the statistics change, the rates for teenage drivers should change as well. After all, the Insurance Institute for Highway Safety has been a major advocate of GDL laws. As more states establish strong GDL laws, young drivers and their parents will have cash to spend on things other than insurance.

In the United States, car crashes are still the leading cause of death among people from 15 to 20 years of age ("Crashes"). Maybe when more states adopt GDL laws, that statistic will change. Other countries that have GDL laws have drastically reduced the number of teenage traffic fatalities. It's never easy to wait for something important, but sometimes the wait is worth it. ■

Understanding Two-Part Essays

Expository essays often follow a two-part organizational plan. Here are typical expository two-part essay forms:

- ■ **Cause-Effect Essay**
- ■ **Comparison-Contrast Essay**
- ■ **Essay of Opposing Ideas**
- ■ **Problem-Solution Essay.** If the essay focuses on a problem and solution in the past, the essay is expository. If the essay focuses on a current problem and promotes a specific solution, the essay is persuasive.

NOTE The key to all two-part essays is organization. The reader must clearly understand both parts and how they relate to one another. The following pages will explain how to write more two-part expository forms.

Writing Guidelines
Comparison-Contrast Essay

A comparison-contrast essay examines the similarities and differences between two topics. The two topics can come from a wide range of categories, including books, people, events, experiments, products, places, and experiences. Just make sure that the topics come from the same category and are worthy of comparison.

■ PREWRITING

1. **Selecting a Topic . . .** Unless you already have two topics in mind, review your class notes or text for ideas. You may also want to brainstorm ideas with classmates or write freely about your course work, noting potential topics as they come to mind.

2. **Gathering Details . . .** Make a list of the similarities and differences between your topics using a graphic organizer. (See page 49.)

3. **Reviewing Your Work . . .** Study your list of details to determine if you need more information. Then decide whether your essay will emphasize similarities or differences or present a balanced view.

4. **Focusing Your Thoughts . . .** Write a thesis statement. Then plan your writing accordingly. (You can do a point-by-point comparison, or you can address each topic separately.)

■ WRITING AND REVISING

5. **Connecting Your Ideas . . .** In the opening part, introduce your topics and state your thesis. Make your comparisons in the middle paragraphs. In the closing, sum up what you have learned.

6. **Improving Your Writing . . .** Carefully review your first draft, checking your *ideas*, *organization*, and *voice*. Ask yourself the following question: *Have I helped the reader better understand the similarities and differences between the two topics?*

7. **Improving Your Style . . .** Also check your first draft for *word choice* and *sentence fluency*.

■ EDITING AND PROOFREADING

8. **Checking for Conventions . . .** Watch for errors in punctuation, mechanics, and grammar. Use the rubric on page 182 for a final check.

9. **Preparing a Final Copy . . .** Make a neat final copy and proofread it.

Sample Comparison-Contrast Essay

In the following essay, the student writer compares her relationship with friends at two different schools in light of a personal struggle she has dealt with.

If Only They Knew

The writer's personal story leads the reader into the essay.

Anorexia nervosa is an eating disorder that I struggled with for the majority of my middle school years and a portion of my high school years. My classmates at Riverview High School were aware of my disorder, and it greatly affected the way they treated me. At the start of my junior year, I transferred to Madison High School. I decided not to tell anyone at that school about my eating disorder since I was mostly recovered by that time. **Even though my friends at Riverview and Madison all showed concern for my well-being, I felt much more comfortable with the students at Madison.**

The thesis is identified (boldfaced).

At Riverview, lunchtime was usually a nightmare for me. I would enter the cafeteria, and in my mind, all eyes would fix themselves upon my gangly figure. I would take my place at a table full of friends and try to enjoy a "normal" lunch. The problem was that I would not always eat lunch, and that greatly concerned my friends. They would watch to make sure that I was eating properly, almost forcing food into my mouth. Sometimes I would pretend to eat and then drop pieces of food into a napkin and throw it out with the trash. When some of my friends found out, they were furious, which seemed to cause even more trouble. Lunch was obviously not my favorite time of the day, and it involved a lot of stress.

A point-by-point comparison is made throughout the essay. (The first point is lunchtime.)

Strangely, I stopped dreading lunch when I started at Madison. No one knew that I had an eating disorder, so they did not care what I ate. This lifted an enormous amount of stress from my life. I finally had the freedom to eat what I wanted without being harassed. It was still hard for me to eat in front of other people, which is common for anorexics, but I was able to put some of my fears aside. I began to enjoy lunch instead of disposing of it.

With my Riverview friends, instead of chatting about boys and other "girl things," we would discuss my disorder. Girls would follow me into the bathroom, and instead of styling their hair, they would check to see if I was throwing up. We never got to gossip together like normal girls because we had to focus on anorexia instead. All I really wanted to talk about was how cute Mike Reynolds looked that day.

I was totally shocked to find that all the life-and-death conversations disappeared when I went to Madison. It was so much fun to talk about the little things that occurred in everyday life. The subject of eating disorders rarely came up, and when it did, I was not the focus. I loved having the freedom to go into the bathroom without being followed. High school is meant to be filled with frivolous chatter, and at Madison I participated in more than my fair share.

I found that the students at Riverview had made many generalizations about my character, and their behavior was guided by those generalizations. Their natural instincts told them to help me. I appreciated their concern, but they never took the time to find out who I was as a person. They knew me only as an anorexic. My friends cared about my health, but they failed to care about me. Truthfully, all I wanted was for them to love me for me and not to obsess over my shortcomings.

The people at Madison took the time to know who I really was. They had no idea that I had been an anorexic, so that particular stereotype did not color their opinions of me. I was finally recognized for my talents and achievements, not my failures. I was honored as a good student. I was also honored as a cheerleader, and no one cared how I looked in my skirt. I could finally be viewed as a real person. I liked the way that people saw me at Madison, and I was no longer afraid to show my true character and personality.

> "The people at Madison took the time to know who I really was."

My days as an anorexic taught me many lessons that I would not trade for the world. They taught me about life and how to be a better friend. I learned about the joys of routine tasks such as eating lunch. I learned to appreciate the simple things in life, like the gossip shared by a group of teenage girls. I gained an understanding of what true character is. I hold no grudges against those who so desperately tried to help me. In fact, I owe them a great debt. And I appreciate the people who helped me to see that there is more to life than having an eating disorder. ∎

The writer interprets the actions of each set of friends.

The closing paragraph sums up what the writer has learned.

Writing Guidelines
Essay of Opposing Ideas

An essay of opposing ideas explains two different points of view about an important issue. The essay should show both sides fairly, not arguing for one or the other. This type of writing works well to explain any controversy that concerns the reader.

■ **PREWRITING**

1. **Selecting a Topic . . .** In a small group, or on your own, produce a list of some of the hottest topics in your world (*grades, driving, college, underage drinking, relationships, the generation gap, culture clash,* and so forth). Review your list for potential topics.

2. **Gathering Details . . .** After you choose a topic, collect information as needed using the following strategy: Fold a piece of paper in two, lengthwise. On one side of the fold, list the facts and details related to one main viewpoint. On the other side of the fold, list facts related to the other side of the issue.

3. **Focusing Your Thoughts . . .** Review your collecting and think about the focus and shape of your essay. Ask yourself the following questions: *How can I show both sides of the issue? How can I balance the arguments for each side? What message do I want to get across?*

■ **WRITING AND REVISING**

4. **Connecting Your Ideas . . .** Create an opening paragraph that introduces the issue and states your thesis. Develop middle paragraphs that explain each main viewpoint. Write an ending that summarizes the topic and leaves the reader with a final thought.

5. **Improving Your Writing . . .** Carefully review your first draft, paying special attention to *ideas, organization,* and *voice.* Ask yourself the following question: *Have I addressed both viewpoints fairly and completely?* Revise as necessary.

6. **Improving Your Style . . .** Check your *word choice* and *sentence fluency* to make sure you have created a clear, easy-to-read essay.

■ **EDITING AND PROOFREADING**

7. **Checking for Conventions . . .** Review your writing for errors in punctuation, mechanics, and grammar.

8. **Preparing a Final Copy . . .** Make a neat final copy and proofread it.

Sample **Essay of Opposing Ideas**

In this essay, the writer examines a critical national debate—securing American borders against terrorism. Notice that the writer presents both sides of the debate in an evenhanded way.

On the Border

The opening introduces the topic and states the thesis (boldfaced).

Terrorism is a relatively new threat in the United States. Before the first attack on the World Trade Center in 1993, foreign terrorists had not successfully attacked a target on United States soil. Other countries—including Russia, Spain, and the United Kingdom—have had decades of experience dealing with terrorists. But since the horrific second attack on the World Trade Center, defending our borders against terrorists has emerged as a key issue in America. However, some people are concerned that tighter security may jeopardize American freedoms. **So a critical debate has developed between those individuals who want tighter immigration policies and those who are concerned about the negative effects such policies could have on the American way of life.**

Points of agreement are identified.

Some basic reforms of the immigration system are clearly needed. For example, the United States should keep better track of people, such as students who come into the country on a temporary basis. The immigration department also needs to document visiting aliens more closely, and to identify those foreign visitors known to have questionable intentions against the United States. Few people would dispute reforms like these.

One side of the debate is examined.

Such measures, however, don't go far enough for some people. An editorial in the *Chatterton Daily News* recently said that the threat of terror "demands that the United States completely revamp its immigration policy and restrict the rights of aliens to travel within this country" (Davis A23). Those who demand tighter security want immigrants to be required to show the proper paperwork to receive public services. They also back "English-only" laws that proclaim English as the only official language in this country. In what seems to be the ultimate restriction, some individuals are asking for a moratorium on all legal immigration.

Some of these proposed changes will affect the ways that United States citizens go about their lives. A few states already require people to prove that they are citizens in order to register to vote. In addition, they require all voters to present an official picture ID every time they vote. If, as some people suggest, citizens are required to carry national photo IDs, the country would begin to resemble a police state rather than "the land of the free and the home of the brave."

The other side of the debate is examined.

Those concerned with maintaining the American way of life believe that such restrictions take away the freedoms of citizens and immigrants alike. The United States has always been a nation of immigrants. Severely restricting immigration simply seems un-American to them. In their minds, if terrorism forces the United States to surrender its free society, the terrorists will have won. Then there are those who suggest that tighter restrictions could harm the American economy. Tighter restrictions, they reason, would turn away legal foreign business partners, tourists, students, and honest immigrants. That is why Daniel Griswold from the Cato Institute suggests that we refrain from any drastic measures: "We should post a yield sign on the Statue of Liberty, not a stop sign" (Greenya). The economy in this country depends on open borders.

The United States Department of Homeland Security acknowledges that balancing immigration with the threat of terrorism is a challenge. The department's goal is "to secure our borders while respecting the privacy of our visitors . . . helping us demonstrate that we remain a welcoming nation and that we can keep America's doors open and our nation secure" ("US-VISIT"). In other words, terrorism must be prevented as much as freedom must be protected.

The closing puts the debate into perspective.

No one knows for sure how this debate will play itself out. But in time, measures will likely be enacted to protect our country as effectively as possible while still welcoming legitimate, productive immigrants—whether their names be Nguyen, O'Connor, Gonzales, or Al-Hewar. That would be the American way as established by our founding fathers. ◼

"The best advice on writing I've ever received is 'write with authority.'"

— Cynthia Ozick

Writing
PERSUASIVE Essays

Persuasive writing requires all the understanding and logic you can muster. First, you must learn all you can about your topic to establish a solid knowledge base. Then you must do these three things: (1) form a thoughtful opinion about it, (2) gather evidence to support the opinion, and (3) consider opposing points of view. Finally, you must connect all your thoughts in an essay that sounds truly convincing. Persuasive writing succeeds when it presents a solid argument from start to finish.

Your goal is to convince the reader to accept your point of view, and, perhaps, to rethink his or her own feelings about the topic. Careful study and research are to persuasive writing what imagination and intuition are to creative writing.

Preview

- **Writing Guidelines**
- **Avoiding Logical Fallacies**
- **Sample Persuasive Essay**
- **Assessment Rubric**

Writing Guidelines
Persuasive Essays

The goal of persuasive writing is to convince the reader to accept your line of thinking about a debatable topic.

■ PREWRITING

1. **Selecting a Topic . . .** Usually, a persuasive writing assignment involves a subject related to your course work. You will, however, need to make sure that the topic you choose is controversial (inspiring differing opinions) and specific enough for an essay. The following chart shows the difference between expository and persuasive topics.

Topics for an Expository Essay	Topics for a Persuasive Essay
How creatine works as a diet supplement	High school athletes should avoid creatine.
Bilingual education is used to teach English to immigrants.	Bilingual education benefits both English language learners and mainstream students.

2. **Gathering Details . . .** Try one of the following two activities to gather your own thoughts about your topic first.

   Dialogue: Create a dialogue between two people (one of whom may be you) who disagree about the topic. Keep the dialogue going long enough to uncover a good number of ideas about the topic.

   List: Simply list your thoughts about the topic in one column and opposing points of view in another column.

   Collect: After recording your own thoughts, collect information.
   - **Books** Your textbooks will provide a solid foundation, giving you the key facts about many topics.
   - **Magazines and Newspapers** Primary news magazines (*Time, Newsweek,* etc.) and newspapers will give you up-to-date information about current issues. (See pages 360-361 for help.)
   - **Web Sites** Refer to the Internet for information about your topic, but always make sure that you check the reliability of the sites. (See page 341 for help.)
   - **Personal Resources** Conduct surveys, carry out interviews, observe, attend conferences, and so on.

3. **Forming an Opinion Statement . . .** After reviewing the information you have gathered, express in a sentence your opinion about the topic. You may need to write several versions of this statement before it says what you want it to say. The following formula can help you form an opinion statement, which will serve as the thesis of your essay.

Types of Opinion Statements

A specific topic +	your feeling about it	= an effective opinion statement.
Bilingual education	benefits both English learners and mainstream students	Bilingual education benefits both English learners and mainstream students.

Opinion statements fall into three main categories: claims of truth, claims of value, and claims of policy.

- **Claims of truth** state that an idea is or is not true.

  In the long run, bilingual students perform better in the classroom.

- **Claims of value** state that something does or does not have worth.

  Bilingual education benefits English learners and mainstream students.

- **Claims of policy** state that something should or should not be done.

  Bilingual education should be promoted as the most appropriate form of education for English learners.

HELP FILE

Qualifiers are terms that make an opinion easier to support. Notice the difference between the two opinions below:

Without bilingual education, English learners soon become overwhelmed and drop out of school.

Without bilingual education, many English learners soon become overwhelmed, and some drop out of school.

"Many" and "some" qualify the opinion, changing it from an all-or-nothing claim to one that is easier to defend. Here are some other useful qualifiers:

almost	usually	maybe	probably
often	few	most	in most cases
if . . . then . . .	likely	may	frequently

4. **Planning and Organizing Your Thoughts . . .** Once you have your opinion statement, list in the best order the main points that support your opinion. You may also organize your thoughts using an outline or some other graphic organizer. The writer of the sample essay on pages 204–205 planned the main part of his essay using the modified, user-friendly outline shown below. (The information in the outline is arranged in three main parts: background information, key supporting points, and concessions.)

Sample Modified Outline

Opinion Statement: Bilingual education benefits English learners and mainstream students.

Background Information

    I. Bilingual education has three main goals.
        A. Students should learn new academic skills.
        B. They should improve their native language skills.
        C. They should become proficient in English.
    II. The process of bilingual learning varies.
        A. Students may start with learning in the native language.
        B. They may move next to a sheltered classroom.
        C. When ready, they are mainstreamed.

Key Supporting Points

    I. English learners deserve a fair chance.
        A. English-only classes don't work.
        B. Holding students back sends the wrong message.
    II. Mainstream students benefit from bilingual education.
        A. Learning two languages is highly valued.
        B. The United States is far behind in bilingual learning.

Concessions

    I. Some see bilingual education as a threat.
        A. But the goal of bilingual education is to get English learners into mainstream classrooms.
        B. Bilingualism is part of our heritage.
    II. Some people feel bilingual education sends the wrong message.
        A. However, immigrant parents feel it is essential that their children learn English.
        B. Bilingual education validates native languages.

■ **WRITING**

5. **Connecting Your Ideas . . .** A traditional persuasive-essay structure is described below. This structure is followed in the modified outline (page 200) and essay (pages 204–205) in this chapter. Consider using this pattern to guide your own writing.

Setting Up a Persuasive Essay

- ■ **Introduce the topic:** In your beginning paragraph, capture your reader's interest and state your opinion.

- ■ **Give background information:** In the second paragraph, provide the reader with the information that is needed to understand your topic.

- ■ **Support your opinion:** In each of the next paragraphs, support your opinion. Try to cover one or two key points per paragraph. Develop these points with details from credible sources. (Each main point should support and validate your opinion.)

- ■ **Make concessions:** Answer one or two opposing opinions to show that you have considered differing points of view. Then bring your reader back to your opinion. (See below.)

- ■ **Wrap up your argument:** In your closing paragraph, reaffirm your opinion to make sure the reader remembers it. You may also offer one last thought about your topic.

Making Concessions

When you make a concession, you address other opinions about your topic. Making a concession often strengthens your overall argument. Consider the following concession from the sample essay:

> Some people are concerned that bilingual education is a threat to English and this country's traditions. This is obviously not the case . . .

The phrase "some people are concerned that" introduces this concession. The information that follows *answers* the concern. Here are some other useful expressions for making concessions:

even though	I agree that	I cannot argue with
while it is true that	admittedly	granted
I will admit	you're right	I accept the fact

Avoiding Logical Fallacies

As you write your persuasive essay, avoid using faulty logic. This page shows common logical fallacies. (Also see pages 477–478.)

10 Fallacies to Avoid

1. **Appeals to ignorance** use a lack of evidence to prove something.
   Who has ever heard of an English learner wanting a sink-or-swim environment?

2. **Appeals to pity/sentimentality** go overboard with the emotions.
   Think of all those poor kids who don't speak a word of English!

3. **Bandwagoning** promotes an idea by saying "everyone else believes this."
   Get on board with the bilingual revolution, or get left behind.

4. **Generalizations** claim that something is true with all people in all cases.
   Opponents to bilingual education haven't looked at the facts.

5. **Circular reasoning** uses a fact to prove itself.
   Bilingual education is supported by bilingual educators.

6. **Either-or thinking** provides only two extreme options.
   Either the nation funds bilingual education, or no new students will learn English.

7. **Half-truths** present only one side of a situation.
   Immigrant parents support bilingual education. (Many do not.)

8. **Oversimplification** reduces a complex situation to a cliche.
   Bilingual education is the past and the future.

9. **Slanted language** presents ideas in an unfair way.
   Intelligent people support bilingual education.

10. **Testimonials** use the endorsement of famous people who have no real authority.
    Many television personalities appeared at a rally to support bilingual education.

■ REVISING

6. **Improving Your Writing . . .** Carefully review your first draft. Have a classmate look over your essay as well. Then use the following questions to make changes that will strengthen your writing.

Ideas ——————
Have I selected a timely, controversial topic?
Have I expressed a clear opinion about it?
Have I provided strong support for my opinion?
Have I addressed other points of view?

Organization ——————
Do I have a clear beginning, middle, and ending?
Have I followed an effective organizational plan?
Have I used transitions to connect my ideas?

Voice ——————
Do I sound knowledgeable?
Do I speak confidently, even when I consider other viewpoints?

Word Choice ——————
Have I used specific nouns and active verbs?
Have I used qualifiers to limit my statements?

Sentence Fluency ——
Do my sentences read smoothly?
Have I varied my sentence beginnings and lengths?

■ EDITING AND PROOFREADING

7. **Checking for Conventions . . .** Check quotations and source citations for correctness. Then ask yourself the following questions:

Conventions ——————
Have I used capital letters for first words and proper nouns?
Have I used commas correctly and checked end punctuation?
Have I checked spelling?
Have I checked for usage errors and other grammatical problems?

■ PUBLISHING

8. **Preparing a Final Copy . . .** Prepare a neat final copy of your essay. Proofread it and share it with others. Find out if your essay changes anyone's opinion about your subject.

Sample Persuasive Essay

In this persuasive essay, student writer Noelle Green argues in favor of bilingual education. Notice that this essay follows the traditional organization. (See page 201.)

Speaking in Two Worlds

Getting a good education means being taught the skills that are needed to find success after graduation. A good education would never mean losing valuable skills. Unfortunately, that's what can happen to many immigrant students. They often lose their native language while they learn English. In an age in which knowing two languages is so valued, bilingual education is more important than ever. **Bilingual education benefits English learners and mainstream students.**

Bilingual education has three main goals: to teach English learners new academic skills, to help them keep and improve their native language skills, and to ensure that they become proficient in English. This process can take anywhere from one to six years and can be carried out in many different ways. For example, English learners can be taught in their native language while they take English-as-a-second-language classes. Then they move into "sheltered" classes where translation is used as needed. Once English learners become proficient in English, they are taught in mainstream English classes. It is important not to do this too quickly or else they could lose their native language. According to a study by the United States Department of Education, students perform better in the long run when they are fluent in both their native language and English.

All students should be given a fair opportunity to learn no matter what their background. The National Association for Bilingual Education (NABE) explains that alternatives like "English-only" classes or "sink-or-swim" methods are unfair. Immigrant students are often held back a grade or more—not because they aren't smart enough, but because they can't learn new academic skills and English at the same time. Students can become overwhelmed and drop out of school. This can easily have a negative impact on their whole lives and on society (Krashen).

Mainstream students in this country also can benefit from bilingual education. They have the opportunity to participate in sheltered classes with English learners to learn a second language. In today's global market, bilingual ability is highly valued. The United States falls far behind other nations in terms of training students to be bilingual. This is partly because many immigrants feel pressure to learn English at the price of losing their native language. Why not use the great foreign language resource that immigrants bring to this nation at no charge (Snow and Hakuta 386)?

Some people are concerned that bilingual education is a threat to English and this country's traditions. This is obviously not the case, since the ultimate goal is to teach English learners in mainstream English classes. James Crawford, author of *Hold Your Tongue*, writes that "bilingualism is as American as apple pie—and has been ever since this nation's beginnings." After all, members of the Continental Congress rejected John Adam's proposal to make English the national language because they felt it threatened democracy and freedom. They realized that what brought the people of this nation together was not race, culture, religion, or language, but a shared desire to live in a land of liberty and equality.

Another argument against bilingual education is that it sends the wrong message to immigrants. The claim is that immigrants will think they don't need to learn English. However, the American Civil Liberties Union cites a study in which "98% of Latinos surveyed said they felt it is 'essential' that their children learn to read and write English 'perfectly' " (qtd. in Fishman 82). Bilingual education provides the English education that immigrants want. At the same time, it validates their native language and gives them a sense of pride in their heritage.

The United States welcomes immigrants with the promise of opportunity, equality, freedom, and a better life. Bilingual education is the best way to fulfill that promise for immigrant students. It validates and celebrates the newcomers' cultures while teaching them the skills they'll need to be successful in this country. At the same time, mainstream students in this country have the chance to attain highly valued bilingual skills, right from the source. Bilingual education teaches newcomers not only English but also the language of freedom and equality for all. That's a language everyone can understand. ■

Counter-arguments are addressed.

A direct quotation is cited.

In the closing paragraph, the writer solidifies her opinion.

Assessment Rubric

Use this rubric as a checklist to assess the effectiveness of your persuasive essays. The rubric is arranged according to the traits of writing described in the handbook. (See pages 21–26.)

Ideas

The writing . . .

_____ addresses a timely, debatable topic.

_____ presents a clear opinion and logical argument.

_____ counters opposing points of view.

Organization

_____ follows a logical plan from paragraph to paragraph.

_____ uses transitions to connect ideas.

Voice

_____ sounds confident and convincing.

_____ demonstrates the writer's knowledge about the topic.

Word Choice

_____ defines and explains unfamiliar terms.

_____ uses specific nouns and verbs with the appropriate connotation.

Sentence Fluency

_____ creates a smooth flow of thought from sentence to sentence.

_____ includes different types and lengths of sentences.

Conventions

_____ follows the basic rules of writing.

_____ accurately cites sources in the essay.

_____ adheres to the appropriate guidelines for presentation.

"It is not best that we should all think alike;
it is the difference of opinion which makes
horse races."

—Mark Twain

Other Forms of
PERSUASIVE WRITING

The history of the United States is filled with great moments of persuasion. From Thomas Paine's *Common Sense* to Martin Luther King's "I Have a Dream," Americans have responded to compelling arguments. Because democracy depends on free choice and open debate, persuasion is one of its basic elements.

This chapter will give you practice in the many ways that you can express your opinion. From the highly personal pet peeve to the classic essay of argumentation, you will learn how to be persuasive about issues small and large.

Preview

- **Pet Peeve Essay**
- **Editorial**
- **Personal Commentary**
- **Problem-Solution Essay**
- **Essay of Argumentation**

Writing Guidelines Pet Peeve Essay

In a pet peeve essay, you react to a common everyday annoyance. Although it may seem minor, an annoyance like this often has the power to affect you for days on end. Be sure to share enough specific details so that your reader can understand what you are going through and how you feel.

■ PREWRITING

1. **Selecting a Topic ...** You may choose something that really annoys you or something that is just irritating enough to be memorable. For ideas, review your personal journal or think about a typical day in your life.

2. **Gathering Details ...** Once you have a topic in mind, ask yourself the following questions: *Why is this issue annoying to me? Why do I react the way I do? What is ironic about the situation or my reaction to it?*

3. **Focusing Your Thoughts ...** Determine how you want to write about your pet peeve: *Am I going to focus on one specific experience or discuss the topic in more general terms?* Also consider the voice or tone of your writing: *Am I going to be serious, playful, or sarcastic?*

■ WRITING AND REVISING

4. **Connecting Your Ideas ...** Freely develop your first draft, working in the thoughts and details you've collected as well as anything new that occurs to you. Let your unique voice come through in your writing.

5. **Improving Your Writing ...** Read over your first draft (silently and aloud), making sure it forms a meaningful and engaging whole. Also have a classmate react to your work. Then revise your essay, focusing on the *ideas, organization,* and *voice* of your pet peeve.

6. **Improving Your Style ...** Check your *word choice* and *sentence fluency,* making sure even the smallest parts help you get your point across. Use the rubric on page 206 as a final revising check.

■ EDITING AND PROOFREADING

7. **Checking for Conventions ...** Review your revised writing, checking for punctuation, mechanics, and grammar errors. Use the rubric on page 206 as a final editing check.

8. **Preparing a Final Copy ...** Write or type a neat final copy of your pet peeve essay and proofread this copy before sharing it with others.

Sample Pet Peeve Essay

In the following essay, a student outlines how he and other teens are treated in local businesses. His unique writing voice truly engages the reader.

A Crime I Didn't Commit

The opening introduces the topic and states the focus (boldfaced).

Imagine that someone in your neighborhood broke the law, and a judge put the whole neighborhood on probation. How fair would that be? Well, it happens every day to high schoolers. Just because some students have shoplifted, all of us are treated like shoplifters. **Even though I'd never steal, store employees look at me like I'm some kind of criminal mastermind.**

For example, during one lunch period, my friend Danny and I went to the Grab 'n' Go on chili dog Tuesday. We arrived to find a line of students waiting outside. A new sign in the window told the story: "NO MORE THAN TWO STUDENTS AT A TIME." After 15 minutes, we finally got in, but the store manager laid the evil eye on us. I asked him about the new sign, and he said, "You kids are lifting too much stuff." *You kids? Too much stuff!* Not only were we assumed to be shoplifters, but brilliant, greedy shoplifters!

Anecdotes explain the problem in an engaging way.

The Grab 'n' Go isn't an isolated case. Earlier this year, a department store worker told me to leave my backpack at the front of the store. When I asked who was going to keep an eye on my stuff, she said, "Don't worry. It isn't going anywhere." In other words, I had to risk losing my stuff so that the store wouldn't have to risk losing theirs. "Don't worry," I replied, "I don't need to shop here anymore."

The most annoying thing, though, is the way employees watch my friends and me. It's almost spooky. Once, at a drugstore, I went down an aisle and found a guy standing on a crate, stocking the shelves. He was watching my hands more than he was watching his own. I showed him that my hands were empty. He got down off his crate and rushed off, as if he was going to get the store manager. How crazy is that?

The closing gives an amusing suggestion that helps make the point.

You know, this kind of prejudice can go both ways. I work at the CD Crib, and every day I see adults commit a terrible crime. They put on a set of headphones and sort of dance to the music. Talk about bad! Tomorrow, I'm going to put a sign in the window: "NO MORE THAN TWO ADULTS LISTENING TO MUSIC AT A TIME." ■

Writing Guidelines Editorial

In an editorial, you present a brief essay of opinion about a timely and important topic. An effective editorial suggests a new course of action or a possible solution to a problem. When writing an editorial, make sure to state your position clearly and directly and provide solid evidence to support it.

■ PREWRITING

1. **Selecting a Topic . . .** If you don't already have a topic in mind, read stories in your local newspaper. You might also try writing general categories such as "school," "sports," "entertainment," and "environment." Then, under each of the headings, list current topics. Select one you have strong feelings about.

2. **Gathering Details . . .** Jot down everything you know and feel about your topic. Then refer to other sources of information if necessary.

3. **Focusing Your Thoughts . . .** Review the details you have gathered and write an opinion statement telling how you feel about the topic. Then use a table diagram (see page 224) to list reasons that support your opinion. Make sure to consider opposing arguments to counter.

■ WRITING AND REVISING

4. **Connecting Your Ideas . . .** Build your argument in the most logical way. (You may want to save your best point for last.) Remember that editorials are published in the newspaper, so use a strong, to-the-point style and write brief paragraphs.

5. **Improving Your Writing . . .** Review your first draft, paying special attention to *ideas, organization,* and *voice.* Ask yourself the following questions: *Do I clearly state my opinion? Do I support it well? Do I sound sincere and confident?* Add, cut, and rearrange ideas as needed.

6. **Improving Your Style . . .** Consider your *word choice* and *sentence fluency.* Make sure your words and sentences are varied and clearly communicate your opinion.

■ EDITING AND PROOFREADING

7. **Checking for Conventions . . .** Check for errors in punctuation, mechanics, and grammar. Use the rubric on page 206 as a final check for your revising and editing.

8. **Preparing a Final Copy . . .** Write or type a neat final copy of your editorial; proofread this copy before sharing it with others.

Sample Editorial

The writer of the following editorial argues that art classes actually improve student performance on tests. She cites many sources.

Let There Be Art

The opening introduces the topic and states the writer's opinion (boldfaced).

The Clintondale School Board is proposing to eliminate art classes next year. Last week's *Clintondale Gazette* quotes the board president, Bill Howland, as saying, "The board needs to decide which programs are necessary and which ones are not" (A5). Superintendent Melvin Ambrose adds that the district should focus on preparing students for exit exams. **These concerns are important, but the board should consider just how necessary art really is for students' success.**

First of all, art improves visual literacy. The International Visual Literacy Association defines visual literacy as a group of competencies "fundamental to normal human learning" (Avgerinou). Art helps students better understand visual information presented in math, science, English, and social studies. Art also equips students to understand the images they see on TV and the Internet. In addition, art teaches students how to present their ideas in a visual way. Whether they are creating graphs for science or diagrams for social studies, students need art.

Each middle paragraph deals with a benefit of art. Information from other sources is cited.

Art also prepares students for business. The Business Circle for Arts Education in Oklahoma states the following: "Businesses understand that art education strengthens student problem-solving and critical thinking skills . . ." ("Facts"). Art courses require students to solve problems in order to create a finished project. This project-based training is important in the real world, where employers ask workers to come up with creative solutions to problems.

What about those all-important tests? Who needs art to pass them? James Catterall, education professor at UCLA, says that students who are highly involved in the arts have higher standardized test scores than those who are not as involved. Results on college entrance exams like the SAT show a similar pattern. Dr. Catterall adds that this trend applies to students of all economic levels, including those from low-income backgrounds (Leroux and Grossman).

The ending recognizes the opposing viewpoint and ends on a strong note.

My own experience in art supports what these experts are saying. I learn best by doing. Of course, the school board has to figure out how to stretch school funds, but it should be careful not to make cuts that will do more harm than good. Preserving art in the schools is a necessity. ■

Writing Guidelines
Personal Commentary

In a personal commentary, you react thoughtfully to some aspect of your life. In this way, a commentary is one step removed from an editorial. An editorial expresses a specific opinion about a newsworthy event, often calling for a particular course of action. A commentary makes a more even-handed and reflective statement about life. Andy Rooney is famous for the personal commentaries he shares on television.

■ PREWRITING

1. **Selecting a Topic . . .** Think about recent experiences or conversations and review your journal entries. A commentary could focus on school life *(athletes)*, popular culture *(tattoos)*, or life in general *(growing up)*.

2. **Gathering Details . . .** Write freely about your topic to determine what you already know about it and what you need to find out. Gather information from other sources as needed.

3. **Focusing Your Thoughts . . .** Review your freewriting and other notes and ask at least one of your classmates to react to your ideas. Then state a possible focus for your work—a sentence (or two) expressing the main point you want to convey in your commentary.

■ WRITING AND REVISING

4. **Connecting Your Ideas . . .** Think of an engaging way to start your commentary. Then write your first draft, working in the observations and details that support your focus.

5. **Improving Your Writing . . .** Carefully review your first draft, paying special attention to *ideas, organization,* and *voice*. Ask yourself the following questions: *Is my focus clear and well supported? Do I sound sincere and interested?* Get another reader's opinion. Then add, cut, and rearrange ideas as needed.

6. **Improving Your Style . . .** Make sure your words clearly communicate your ideas and your sentences are varied and read smoothly.

■ EDITING AND PROOFREADING

7. **Checking for Conventions . . .** Check for errors in punctuation, mechanics, and grammar. Use the rubric on page 206 as a final check for your revising and editing.

8. **Preparing a Final Copy . . .** Write or type a neat final copy.

Sample Personal Commentary

In this personal commentary, student writer Matt Ostwalt focuses on the pressures of high school athletics. It is his contention that the emphasis on winning takes most of the fun out of participating in sports. See if you agree.

The Demands of Winning

The opening connects with the reader and states the focus (boldfaced).

As a wrestler, I know how much fun it is to win. In fact, there are few things that I enjoy more. However, I think it is important that we teach athletes how to love a sport and enjoy it for all it has to offer. **Competitiveness is great, but sometimes the pressures of being the best can overload teenagers.**

Personal reflections enhance the commentary.

I see and hear wrestlers day in and day out talk about how hard it is to love the sport because of the demands it takes to be the best. Pressure to win is laid upon wrestlers in many different ways. For example, our coach is a great coach, and I know that he cares about every one of his wrestlers, but every time that I walk out on that mat, I hear his words echoing in my mind: "You are a West Lincoln wrestler; and you will win." How can I not feel pressure to win, and anguish after losing, with that in mind? So if I do lose, I go home and mope around because I feel that I have let my coach and myself down. However, this doesn't last long because homework has to be done, and I have to sleep sometime, too. Then there is the never-ending concern with making weight for the next match.

I often wonder what I am doing to myself. I wonder if it would be any different if I still loved what I did, or if I were not as good as I am. If I had a penny for every time I have these thoughts, I could balance the budget.

In closing, the writer remembers an earlier time.

I remember how much fun wrestling was in eighth grade, even though I did not win a single match. I always loved practices, and I always thought they ended too quickly. I know I would miss wrestling if I decided to quit. I just wish I could return to the time when making weight was not a problem and when losing did not matter as long as I gave 100 percent. Now when I walk off that mat, I know I have given 100 percent, but it never seems to be enough. ■

Writing Guidelines
Problem-Solution Essay

In a problem-solution essay, you provide the reader with a detailed analysis of a topic—from a clear statement of the problem to a full discussion of possible solutions. It is important to examine your topic from a number of different angles before proposing any solutions.

■ PREWRITING

1. **Selecting a Topic . . .** If your assignment is related to a specific course, review your text and class notes for possible topics. Otherwise, think about the things students complain about most: homework, school spirit, jobs, grades, and so on. Or consider problems that have come up recently in your neighborhood or in your personal life.

2. **Gathering Details . . .** Write out your problem in a clear statement. Then research it thoroughly, collecting information about its history and causes. List possible solutions. Consider why different solutions may or may not work well.

3. **Focusing Your Thoughts . . .** Review your collecting to decide if you are dealing with a manageable problem and if you have enough background information to write intelligently about it. (You may need to gather more facts and statistics.)

■ WRITING AND REVISING

4. **Connecting Your Ideas . . .** Develop your first draft, discussing the problem and possible solutions as clearly and completely as you can. In the opening part of your essay, give enough background information to help the reader fully understand the subject.

5. **Improving Your Writing . . .** Review your first draft asking yourself the following questions: *Will the reader believe the problem is serious? Will the reader believe my solution will work? Do I sound knowledgeable?* Add, cut, and rework ideas as needed in your essay.

6. **Improving Your Style . . .** Check the sentences and words in your essay to make sure they communicate your ideas.

■ EDITING AND PROOFREADING

7. **Checking for Conventions . . .** Check for errors in punctuation, mechanics, and grammar. Use the rubric on page 206 for a final check.

8. **Preparing a Final Copy . . .** Make a neat final copy and proofread it.

Sample Problem-Solution Essay

In this essay, student writer Terrance Masters discusses the very real problem of conflict and violence in schools. He convinces the reader of the seriousness of the problem and the value of the solution.

A quotation helps the reader focus on the problem.

Grace Under Fire

"The passions are the same in every conflict, large or small."
—Mason Cooley

The opening identifies the problem and introduces the solution.

Two friends have an argument that breaks up their friendship forever, even though neither one can remember how the whole thing got started. This tragedy happens over and over in high schools across the country. Conflict may be unavoidable, but when people lose sight of the real issues, their arguments can become personal and spiral out of control. In fact, according to "Youth Violence," a report by the surgeon general, "In our country today, the greatest threat to the lives of children and adolescents is not disease or starvation or abandonment, but the terrible reality of violence" (2). Given that this is the case, why aren't students taught to manage conflict the way they are taught to solve math problems, drive cars, or stay physically fit? **The best solution to the problem of youth violence is to teach students strategies for conflict resolution.**

A key point from a report is paraphrased.

First of all, students need to realize that conflict is inevitable. In the report "Violence Among Middle School and High School Students," the United States Department of Justice indicates that most violent incidents between students begin with "a relatively minor affront but escalate from there" (2). In other words, a fight could start over the fact that one student eats a peanut butter sandwich each lunchtime. Laughter over the sandwich can lead to insults, which in turn can lead to violence. The problem isn't in the sandwich, but in the way students deal with the conflict. They need to learn that conflicts may be unavoidable, but they also can provide an opportunity to improve friendships. According to safeyouth.org, "If resolved positively, conflicts can actually help strengthen relationships and build greater understanding."

Another key point is quoted.

Once students recognize that conflict is inevitable, they can practice the golden rule of conflict resolution: stay calm. Escalation begins with strong emotions. Pausing a moment to take a deep breath inflates the lungs and deflates the conflict. A person can also maintain control by intentionally relaxing his or her face and body. After all, in any conflict, it is better to look "cool" than "hot." Once the student feels calmer, he or she should choose words that will calm the other person down as well. Profanity, name-calling, accusations, and exaggerations only add fuel to the emotional fire. On the other hand, neutral words spoken at a normal volume can quench the fire before it explodes out of control.

After both sides have calmed down, they can enact another key strategy for conflict resolution: listening. Listening allows the two sides to understand each other. One person should describe his or her side, and the other person should listen without interrupting. Afterward, the listener can ask nonthreatening questions to clarify the speaker's position. Then the two people should reverse roles.

Finally, students need to consider what they are hearing. This doesn't mean trying to figure out what's wrong with the other person. It means understanding what the real issue is and what both sides are trying to accomplish. For example, a shouting match over a peanut butter sandwich might happen because one person thinks the other person is unwilling to try new things. Students need to ask themselves questions such as these: *How did this start? What do I really want? What am I afraid of? How can this conflict be resolved?* As the issue becomes clearer, the conflict often simply fades away. Even if it doesn't, careful thought helps both sides figure out a mutual solution.

There will always be conflict in schools, but that doesn't mean there needs to be violence. When students in Atlanta instituted a conflict resolution program, "64 percent of the teachers reported less physical violence in the classroom; 75 percent of the teachers reported an increase in student cooperation; and 92 percent of the students felt better about themselves" (www.esrnational.org). Learning to resolve conflicts can help students deal with friends, teachers, parents, bosses, and coworkers. In that way, conflict resolution is a fundamental life skill that should be taught in schools across the country. ■

The solution is carefully analyzed.

The closing revisits the problem and expands on the solution.

Writing Guidelines
Essay of Argumentation

The purpose of an essay of argumentation is to convince the reader to accept your point of view on an important topic that you have strong, genuine feelings about. The quality of your argument depends on your ability to support your point of view with solid facts and details and to counter significant opposing viewpoints. (See pages 201–202 and 477–478 for help.)

■ PREWRITING

1. **Selecting a Topic . . .** Review your texts or class notes for possible topics. Also think about issues or problems you hear debated locally or nationally. Test a topic by identifying a reasonable claim and listing at least two supporting points for it.

2. **Gathering Details . . .** Collect your own thoughts about the topic; then refer to books, magazines, newspapers, and the Internet for additional information.

3. **Focusing Your Thoughts . . .** Review the information you have gathered. Then write an opinion statement in which you state your claim. Afterward, create a table diagram (see below) to list supporting, arguments and counterarguments.

4. **Planning and Organizing . . .** Decide on the best arrangement of your argument. Consider this pattern: Introduce your opinion and give any background information the reader needs. Then include your main support in order of importance and answer opposing arguments.

We need to consider better ways to measure student abilities than the current exit exam.				
The exit exam uses "objective" questions, which do not accurately show how much students have learned.	Authentic assessment, which measures knowledge by having students do something real, gives a better measure.	Portfolios allow authentic assessment throughout the year and take the burden of grading off the state.	Project-based learning programs use projects tailored to individual students to assess learning.	Opponents of authentic assessment want a more objective system, but "objective" tests can actually hamper learning.

■ WRITING

5. **Connecting Your Ideas . . .** Write the first draft of your argument, using your prewriting and planning as a guide. Here is a basic essay model to follow:

> **Beginning:** Get your reader's attention, introduce the topic, and provide your opinion statement.

> **Middle:** Provide background information the reader needs to understand, give each of your supporting points, and answer major objections to your viewpoint.

> **Ending:** Revisit your opinion and leave the reader with a final thought.

■ REVISING

6. **Improving Your Writing . . .** Review your essay, asking yourself the following questions:

   - **Ideas:** *Have I created a strong opinion statement? Have I provided support for my opinion? Have I answered objections?*

   - **Organization:** *Does my beginning introduce the topic and provide my opinion statement? Does the middle create a strong argument? Does the ending revisit my point of view and leave the reader with a final thought?*

   - **Voice:** *Have I used a tone appropriate to my topic?*

   - **Word Choice:** *Have I used a suitable level of language?*

   - **Sentence Fluency:** *Do my sentences read smoothly? Have I used a variety of types and beginnings?*

■ EDITING AND PROOFREADING

7. **Checking for Correctness . . .** Edit your work, asking yourself these questions:

   - **Conventions:** *Have I used correct punctuation? Have I checked my essay for mechanics and grammar?*

8. **Preparing a Final Copy . . .** Write or type a neat final copy of your essay; proofread this copy before sharing it with others.

Sample **Essay of Argumentation**

In the following essay, Sarah King argues that standardized exit exams do not fully measure what a student has learned. She uses quotations, paraphrases, and analyses to build her argument.

An Incomplete Picture

The writer
outlines other
opinions
before
stating her
own.

The exit exam is coming, and like many other high-school students, I wonder if it is the best way to prove that I deserve to graduate. Teachers have warned us about this test, saying our futures depend on it. Politicians have praised the test for making sure that no child gets "left behind." However, many professional educators feel that exit exams show which students have crammed rather than which students have learned. I have to agree. **We need to consider better ways to measure student abilities than the current exit exam.**

The writer
quotes and
paraphrases
what others
have written
in order to
support her
argument.

The main problem with the exit exam is that it is an objective test, with true-false, multiple-choice, matching, and fill-in-the-blank questions. As a result, teachers prep their classes by teaching strategies for answering these kinds of questions. Students who score well often know more about test strategy than about the material covered. In his paper "The Case for Authentic Assessment," educator Grant Wiggins writes, "What most defenders of traditional tests fail to see is that it is the form, not the content of the test that is harmful to learning . . . students come to believe that learning is cramming" (3). Wiggins feels that "authentic assessment" is a more realistic way to evaluate learning.

The writer
anticipates
the reader's
questions and
uses them
to build her
argument.

What is authentic assessment, and how can our exit exam be changed to include it? Authentic assessment requires students to demonstrate knowledge by doing something "real" rather than by simply answering questions. For example, according to the Center on Education Policy, many state tests ask students to write an essay in response to a prompt. The essay is a form of authentic assessment, and it gives a more complete picture of the student's ability to think and write. However, writing an essay on demand is still a somewhat artificial exercise, and it adds a great deal of cost and time to the grading process.

Is there a form of authentic assessment that would show true student ability without costing the state a lot of time and money? Many educators suggest using portfolios. A portfolio is a collection of work that shows how well a student has learned certain concepts and skills. For example, a writing portfolio can include a student's expository, persuasive, and narrative essays. A science portfolio can include experiments, demonstrations, and presentations.

The writer
provides
thoughtful
analysis.

As an assessment tool, portfolios have many benefits over exit exams. Portfolios allow students to create real products over an extended period of time. They also provide many assessment opportunities throughout the process. Since the grading is done by the teacher throughout the year instead of by the state at one particular time, the portfolio does not require a lot more time and money. The skill of putting together a portfolio can help students apply for colleges and for jobs. Portfolios also encourage students to demonstrate their ability in many different media.

Some schools would suggest an even more radical form of authentic assessment. Walden III, an alternative school operating in Wisconsin since the early 1970s, outlines its basic ideas on its Web site:

- Assessments are based on "benchmark" standards that students must achieve;
- assessments are individualized for each student;
- rigorous research is expected; and
- each student must complete a major project, called a "rite of passage," in order to graduate. (Mission)

At a school like this, assessment isn't something done on one Thursday morning during the student's senior year, but all through high school.

The writer
counters
objections to
her opinion.

Of course, authentic assessment has its critics. Some people say that it doesn't provide precise statistics about which students and districts are doing better than others. While objective tests provide these statistics, it's debatable whether these tests really show knowledge and ability. Other people claim that authentic assessments are more expensive and harder to manage than traditional tests. This is true only if the state tries to shoulder the whole load. Instead, by trusting the assessments done by the teachers who are already assigning and grading the students' works, the state doesn't need to do any of the paper shuffling.

The closing
reviews the
writer's main
points.

Our state needs to rethink its assessment policy. While objective tests can be useful, they aren't a fair basis for deciding whether students can graduate from high school. Even worse, if succeeding on traditional tests becomes the only focus of schools, students will be less prepared to function in the real world. The state should consider adding an essay to provide some authentic assessment. Better yet, the state should ditch the exam format altogether and use student portfolios. Then teachers and students can stop cramming and start learning. ■

"Truth springs from argument amongst friends." —David Hume

Writing a
POSITION PAPER

Expository writing informs the reader, and persuasive writing argues for one point of view or another. These two modes can be combined in an *informed argument*—otherwise known as a position paper.

In a position paper, you present more than meaningful facts. You also study the facts and offer a specific interpretation of them. Drawing on all your writing and researching skill, a position paper provides the reader with a new perspective about a complex or controversial issue.

Writing a position paper requires higher-level thinking, including analysis, synthesis, and evaluation. Mastering this ultimate form of academic writing can someday put you at the top of your chosen career field. After all, in 1905, Albert Einstein wrote a position paper on the special theory of relativity and, in doing so, changed our understanding of the universe.

Preview

- **Writing Guidelines**
- **Sample Position Paper**
- **Assessment Rubric**

Writing Guidelines **Position Paper**

Your goal in a position paper is to trace your particular line of thinking on an issue. Rather than argue for or against something, you will inform, explain, analyze, and speculate.

■ PREWRITING

1. **Selecting a Topic** ... The best position papers deal with debatable issues. Current events, especially controversial ones, can provide excellent topics for position papers. Think about new trends in subjects that interest you, such as science, technology, medicine, health, archaeology, politics, fashion, music, or entertainment. Test possible topics by creating a T-chart like the one below. You need to be sure that there are at least two sides to the debate.

Topic Idea: Peer-to-Peer (P2P) Music File Sharing

P2P USERS	RECORD COMPANIES
• File sharing is fun.	• File sharing is piracy.
• Music lovers should be free to share music, especially if it is out of print.	• Copyrighted music must always be protected, and music pirates should be prosecuted.
• The technology has many legal uses.	• The technology should be outlawed.

2. **Gathering Details** ... Once you have selected a topic, begin gathering details. Check books, newspapers, magazines, Web sites, news reports, and documentaries for current articles about your topic. Also consider primary sources of information. Here are some suggestions:

   ■ Attend a meeting where the issue is discussed.
   ■ Interview authorities on the topic.
   ■ Analyze original documents, such as transcripts of trials.
   ■ Attend a special exhibit at a museum or school.

⌐HELP FILE

Before you can establish a position, you must immerse yourself in the topic. As you read and learn, your own position will naturally develop. Think of yourself as an investigative journalist, discovering new information and putting that information into perspective.

3. **Developing Your Position Statement . . .** The basis for your position paper is a *position statement*, which is similar to the thesis or opinion statement of a persuasive essay. In the case of a position statement, though, the emphasis is on the *idea* rather than on your opinion.

   Your position statement, which should put your informed argument into focus, has two main jobs: (1) to show knowledge of the topic and (2) to provide a specific perspective.

Sample Position Statements

■ Despite the reluctance of politicians and oil companies to recognize the facts (*knowledge about the topic*), the evidence for global warming is everywhere (*a specific perspective*).

■ In wartime, news agencies are sometimes accused of compromising national security (*knowledge about the topic*), but the United States is more secure due to its free press (*a specific perspective*).

■ Recording companies need to understand that they cannot regulate file-sharing technology (*a specific perspective*) the way they regulate the sale of physical objects such as tapes and CD's (*knowledge about the topic*).

HELP FILE

Since your position statement is crucial to your paper, take extra time to get it right. This checklist can help you refine your position statement. Keep working on the statement until you can check off each item.

Position Statement Checklist

The position statement . . .

_____ identifies a limited, specific topic,

_____ shows knowledge of the topic,

_____ provides a specific perspective,

_____ is stated clearly and directly,

_____ can be supported by facts and interpretations, and

_____ meets the requirements of the assignment.

4. **Supporting Your Position . . .** Once you have written a position statement, you need to develop support for it. Remember that you must do more than simply report facts. You must interpret those facts and put them into perspective. Here is a series of steps for developing support for your position:

- **Background.** Since a position paper presents an *informed* argument, you need to spend some time informing the reader about your issue. This part of your paper will convince the reader that you *understand* your topic.

- **Interpretation.** Next, your paper needs to provide an interpretation of the facts given. Do so by sharing different points of view on the issue and making connections and comparisons between them. In this part of the paper, you *analyze* the issue in depth.

- **Evaluation.** The careful analysis you do of the facts should lead naturally into an evaluation of the different points of view. As you sort through the facts, your own perspective naturally emerges. In this part of the paper, you *develop* your position.

- **Expansion.** Once you have established your position, you should show how it applies to life and to the future of the issue. In this part of the paper, you *apply* your position to the world at large and *create* or *synthesize* a vision of the future for this issue.

Table Diagram

Here is a table diagram that shows the support used in the peer-to-peer file-sharing position paper. (See pages 228–230.)

Recording companies need to understand that they cannot regulate file-sharing technology the way they regulate the sale of physical objects such as tapes and CD's.			
Background	**Interpretation**	**Evaluation**	**Expansion**
Despite admitting many benefits of peer-to-peer file sharing, recording companies consider it piracy.	Peer-to-peer file sharing does little to diminish the sales of tapes and CD's, and actually helps some musicians find an audience.	Historically, right-to-privacy issues have prevailed over copyright enforcement, and technological changes require recording companies to rethink their approach.	Recording companies should base contracts on performances, license P2P rights, and otherwise use file-sharing technology.

5. **Outlining Your Paper** . . . An outline can help you organize the support for your paper. It lists the main points and supporting details of your paper. Use Roman numerals (I, II, III) for the main points and capital letters (A, B, C) for supporting details. The sentence outline below corresponds with the sample essay on pages 228–230.

Position: Recording companies need to understand that they cannot regulate file-sharing technology the way they regulate the sale of physical objects such as tapes and CD's.

I. **Background:** Members of the Recording Industry Association of America (RIAA) are recording companies trying to protect their financial interests.
   A. The RIAA calls peer-to-peer (P2P) networking "online piracy."
   B. They admit the benefits of digital technology.
      —quotation from RIAA
   C. RIAA members think more people sharing music means fewer people buying it.

II. **Interpretation:** There's no question that copyright is an important part of music; those who write and perform music deserve to profit from their work.
   A. A Harvard study shows that P2P does not hurt the industry.
      —quotation from oreillynet.com
   B. Online sharing helps some musicians promote themselves.
      —sites like Independent Music Online
      —quotation from August Christopher

III. **Evaluation:** Money is always an important factor, but the consumer's right to privacy may be the most emotional part of the issue.
   A. Bill of Rights privacy protection extends to Internet users.
   B. Record companies want Internet service providers (ISP's) to identify music sharers.
   C. ISP's, sometimes colleges, get drawn into privacy litigation.
      —lawsuit of Leadbetter vs. Comcast

IV. **Evaluation:** Innovation in technology makes change for the music industry inevitable.
   A. Historically, right to privacy trumps copyright.
      —legal, purposes of hardware and software
      —VCR's legal despite illegal copies of films
   B. MP3 players make legal and illegal copies, and the only way to regulate their use is to invade privacy.
   C. Technological innovation shouldn't be suppressed.

Expansion: In a world with nearly 6.4 billion people, enforcing copyright laws on individuals seems outdated, not to mention nearly impossible.

■ WRITING

6. **Creating Your Beginning . . .** Your beginning has two main duties: to get the reader's attention and to state your position. Here are some strategies for capturing your reader's attention:

   ■ **Start with a powerful quotation:** Quoting someone embroiled in the issue can put the reader in the center of the controversy.

   "Downloading illegal copies is no different than shoplifting CD's out of a record store, and uploading those recordings for others to illegally copy is no different than handing out stolen CD's on the street corner," said Cary H. Sherman of the Recording Industry Association of America.

   ■ **Ask a question:** A provocative question can draw the reader quickly into the issue. Make sure the question cannot be answered simply "yes" or "no."

   How many pirates do you know? According to the recording industry, you may know hundreds . . .

   ■ **Create a personal connection:** A quick anecdote can help you create commonality with the reader. *Remember:* If you choose this option, you should quickly shift to a more formal, objective voice after you share the anecdote.

   My friends and I like music, and we dig through the history of popular tunes from the 1950s to the present—looking for connections.

7. **Creating Your Middle . . .** Develop your middle paragraphs using your outline as a guide. Make sure to use transitions to connect your sentences and paragraphs.

8. **Creating Your Ending . . .** The ending of your position paper should expand upon your position statement. Here are some strategies to try:

   ■ **State your position in a new way:** Review your position in the light of the support you have provided.

   In a world with nearly 6.4 billion people, enforcing copyright laws on individuals seems outdated, not to mention nearly impossible.

   ■ **Apply your position to life:** Strengthen your position by showing how it would work in the real world.

   For example, the industry could base musicians' contracts on live performance revenue, so artists' earnings would then be a more accurate reflection of their talent.

   ■ **Think about the future:** Project what will happen next.

   Recording companies will have to move ahead, away from the traditional delivery system that has served them well for so long.

■ REVISING

9. Improving Your Writing . . . When you revise your position paper, you add new information, cut unnecessary details, rearrange the order of sentences and paragraphs, and rework passages that sound flat. The six traits of writing can help you know what parts to revise.

■ **Ideas:** *Do I have a clear position statement? Have I effectively supported my position? Do I include quotations, paraphrases, analyses, interpretations, and evaluations? Have I avoided plagiarism?*

■ **Organization:** *Does my beginning capture the reader's attention and introduce my position? Does my middle inform the reader and provide strong support for my position? Is each paragraph unified, with all sentences supporting the topic sentence? Does the ending expand on my position?*

■ **Voice:** *Does my writing sound knowledgeable and convincing? Have I used a formal voice?*

■ **Word Choice:** *Do I define any unfamiliar terms or acronyms? Do I use specific, concrete nouns and active verbs?*

■ **Sentence Fluency:** *Do my sentences read smoothly? Do I vary the beginnings, types, and lengths of my sentences? Do I avoid sentence errors?*

■ EDITING AND PROOFREADING

10. Checking for Conventions . . . When you edit and proofread, make sure your work adheres to the rules of English.

■ **Conventions:** *Have I checked for punctuation, mechanics, and grammar errors? Have I cited my sources correctly? Have I used the rubric on page 231 as a final check of my revising and editing?*

11. Preparing a Final Copy . . . When you have finished editing your work, write or print out a clean final copy. Make sure to proofread it before sharing it.

⌐HELP FILE

By their very nature, position papers make excellent speeches, class presentations, or topics for forensics discussions. Consider presenting your paper in one of these forms. Each is a type of *publication*, a word that means simply "making ideas public."

Sample Position Paper

In this sample position paper, student writer Claire Baughn creates an informed argument about the controversial topic of peer-to-peer music sharing systems. The side notes show how Claire developed her position.

Face the Music

The writer makes a personal connection, and then shifts to a formal voice for her position statement.

My friends and I like music, and we dig through the history of popular tunes from the 1950s to the present—looking for connections. Books and magazines are helpful, but the Internet is our main source of information. When we find interesting things, including cuts from old recordings, we share them. What seems like fun to us, however, is seen as unlawful activity by others. Anyone who uses computer technology like peer-to-peer (P2P) networking to share copyrighted music is risking being sued by the music industry. What the industry is finding out, however, is that prosecuting people who use widely available technology isn't stopping the activity. **Recording companies need to understand that they cannot regulate file-sharing technology the way they regulate the sale of physical objects such as tapes and CD's.**

One middle paragraph focuses on providing background.

Members of the Recording Industry Association of America (RIAA) are recording companies trying to protect their financial interests. The RIAA terms P2P networking as "online piracy" even while admitting that "digital technology brings music to a wider public, affords niche artists access to their audiences, makes our vast musical heritage widely available, and distributes old, new and unusual music . . ." ("Online Piracy"). Unfortunately, RIAA members think that more people sharing music means fewer people buying it, so they are targeting P2P services and their users with copyright infringement lawsuits.

The writer interprets the background information she provides.

There's no question that copyright is an important part of music; those who write and perform music deserve to profit from their work. But are musicians really being hurt by P2P's and other file-sharing devices? A recent study shows that the music industry is affected very little. Researchers from Harvard University have published a study showing that sharing music on P2P networks has no effect on CD sales: "While downloads occur on a vast scale, most users are likely individuals who would not have bought the album even in the absence of file sharing" ("Harvard Researchers"). In fact, not only does P2P sharing not hurt musicians—it actually helps some artists promote their music. These musicians avoid the traditional industry middleman, delivering the end product directly to the consumer. They make music because they love it—not to become millionaires. A popular Nashville band, August Christopher, sells its music on its own Web site and on independent sites such as Independent Music Online. August Christopher also has quite a following for its live shows. Criss Cheatham, a member of the band, says, "I played over 300 shows in 2004, the bills are paid, I love my family, and as a result, I consider myself extremely successful" ("Interview").

The writer evaluates differing views and further establishes her position.

Money is always an important factor, but the consumer's right to privacy may be the most emotional part of the issue. Privacy is guaranteed by implication in the Bill of Rights (protected by a number of amendments), and it should apply to Internet users as much as to anyone else. However, the RIAA's approach to discouraging the downloading of copyrighted material requires Internet service providers (ISP's) to identify individuals whose Internet addresses indicate music sharing. (In a number of cases, the ISP is a college or university, drawing them into the fray, as well.) In one instance, Dawnell Leadbetter's ISP gave up her identity to RIAA, and the association threatened her with a lawsuit if she did not pay a $4,500 fine. In a twist that may indicate the shape of things to come, the Seattle-area mother of two teenagers is fighting her ISP with a lawsuit of her own ("Comcast Sued"). She claims that her ISP had no right to disclose her identity.

Additional evaluation strengthens the writer's position.

Innovation in technology makes change for the music industry inevitable. For years, technology has been a nearly constant source of frustration for copyright holders of all kinds. Sharing and recording technologies are difficult to outlaw because they have other purposes. For example, the Supreme Court ruled in 1984 that VCR's were legal and could not be restricted even though some of them were used to make illegal copies (Borland). One can see how this principle might apply today. There are now ways to use MP3 players to make direct transfers of music without using the Internet, but certainly not all owners will utilize the player to this end. Technology will continue to innovate to overcome problems such as viruses spread by commercial file-sharing sites (Best), and the RIAA is not helping anyone by attempting to halt these information-age advances.

In a world with nearly 6.4 billion people, enforcing copyright laws on individuals seems outdated, not to mention nearly impossible. The industry's attempt to control every copy of a song is not the answer. P2P networking isn't going away, so the music industry will have to change to deal with it. For example, the industry could base musicians' contracts on live performance revenue, so artists' earnings would then be a more accurate reflection of their talent. The recording companies' income could be enhanced by fees for the right to host music sharing, similar to the licensing fees that radio stations pay for the right to play copyrighted music. In addition, special taxes could be attached to devices like CD burners that are routinely used to copy music ("Germany"). Recording companies will have to move ahead, away from the traditional delivery system that has served them well for so long. It's simply time for the music industry to face the music, and adapt to new innovations in technology. ■

> The ending paragraph expands upon the writer's position.

HELP FILE

Avoiding Plagiarism

Whenever your writing draws from another source, you must be careful to avoid plagiarism. Plagiarism occurs anytime you present another person's words or ideas as your own. Here's how to avoid plagiarism:

- **Paraphrase** important information from other sources, putting the ideas into your own words.
- **Quote** material from other sources when the original wording is especially powerful. But don't overdo it! Quotations are most effective when they are used sparingly.
- **Document** your sources, crediting them in parentheses and on a works-cited page.

✱ For more information about documenting sources, see pages 281-308 (MLA style) or pages 309-319 (APA style).

Assessment Rubric

Use this rubric as a checklist to assess the effectiveness of your position paper. The rubric is arranged according to the traits of writing described in the handbook. (See pages 21–26.)

Ideas

The writing . . .

_____ presents a clear position concerning a debatable issue.

_____ includes many different types of support.

_____ provides facts and interprets them.

Organization

_____ begins by capturing the reader's attention and stating the position.

_____ develops the position throughout the middle paragraphs.

_____ ends by expanding on the writer's position.

Voice

_____ presents information with a knowledgeable, formal voice.

Word Choice

_____ defines unfamiliar terms and acronyms.

_____ uses specific, concrete nouns and active verbs.

Sentence Fluency

_____ moves smoothly from sentence to sentence.

_____ includes a variety of sentence lengths and types.

Conventions

_____ contains no misspellings or errors in punctuation.

_____ cites all sources correctly.

_____ follows the appropriate format guidelines.

Responding to
LITERATURE

Personal Responses to Literature   233

Writing a Book Review   239

Writing a Literary Analysis   245

"Reading is actually plunging into one's own identity and, one hopes, emerging stronger than before."

—Amalia Kahana-Carmon

Personal
RESPONSES TO LITERATURE

How do you react after attending an incredible concert or seeing a great movie? If you're like most people, you can't wait to talk about it. Movies and music can do that to you. Are you just as quick to talk about a good book? Books are usually complex, containing many levels of meaning, and your feelings about your reading may develop slowly from chapter to chapter. Instead of going crazy over a good book, you may need time to think and reflect before reacting.

Writing about your reading helps you explore your opinion about a book (or other piece of literature). It allows you to respond to the text on a personal level—to agree with it, question it, and analyze it. Your personal response to literature can be anything from a journal entry to an imaginary dialogue with a character. This chapter includes writing guidelines as well as samples of different types of personal responses to literature.

Preview

- **Letter to the Author**
- **Dialogue**
- **Journal Entries**
- **Starting Points for Journal Writing**

Writing Guidelines Personal Responses

In a personal response to literature, you express your thoughts and feelings about a book, a short story, a play, a poem, or an essay. For example, you may choose to write a letter to an author or develop a dialogue based on your reading. The guidelines below will help you explore your feelings about what you read.

■ PREWRITING

1. **Selecting a Topic . . .** Write about a piece of literature that you are currently reading or that you have just finished reading. Explore your overall feelings, focus on a specific part of the text, or think about important questions you have.

2. **Identifying a Form . . .** After choosing a piece of literature, take into account the form of your response. Perhaps you will write a letter to the author, develop a dialogue with a character, or create a new scene.

3. **Gathering Details . . .** Use listing or freewriting to collect your thoughts and feelings about your topic.

4. **Focusing Your Thoughts . . .** Keeping the purpose and form of your writing in mind, choose ideas that you want to include in your response.

■ WRITING AND REVISING

5. **Connecting Your Ideas . . .** Write your ideas in a natural, straightforward way. Use your planning and prewriting as a general guide to creating a first draft.

6. **Improving Your Writing . . .** Review your first draft, paying specific attention to your *ideas, organization,* and *voice.* Ask yourself the following questions: *Have I presented my ideas clearly? Have I included enough specific details? Are my beginning, middle, and ending effective?*

7. **Improving Your Style . . .** Check your *word choice* and *sentence fluency* to be sure they communicate your ideas clearly.

■ EDITING AND PROOFREADING

8. **Checking for Conventions . . .** Correct any errors in punctuation, mechanics, and grammar. Use the rubric on page 244 as a final revising and editing check.

9. **Preparing a Final Copy . . .** Type or neatly write a final copy of your response; proofread your copy one last time before sharing it.

Sample Response: Letter to the Author

In this letter to the author, student writer Benjamin Draves shares his thoughts and feelings about Chinua Achebe's novel *Things Fall Apart.* Notice that Benjamin tells what he enjoyed most about the book and what he has questions about.

201 Pine Drive
Pershing, Texas
March 31, 2005

Dear Mr. Achebe,

Recently I finished reading *Arrow of God* in class, and I decided to also read *Things Fall Apart.* What I find unique about both of these novels is your strong insight into colonialism in Africa.

Benjamin explains what he enjoyed in the novel.

In *Things Fall Apart,* I especially enjoyed the character of Okonkwo. He is hardworking, strong, and respected, but at the same time he is fearful and angry and prone to making mistakes. This makes him a believable character, a kind of everyman that I can relate to. Okonkwo's extreme living conditions make me really care about him and make his life that much more tragic.

He then focuses on a question he has.

Mr. Achebe, there was one thing that I was confused about. Okonkwo, like most of the men in the Ibo society, viewed the majority of women as weak and foolish. However, the priestess of Agbala is one of the most significant figures in the Ibo village. Her decisions have a great effect on Okonkwo's life throughout the book. Why is it that Okonkwo and the other men hold one woman in such high regard and have hardly any respect for their wives and daughters?

The ending tells what Benjamin learned from this novel.

This book shows me that our greatest strengths can sometimes also be our greatest weaknesses. For example, Okonkwo does not show feelings other than anger because he does not want to appear fearful or weak. However, his fear of losing control in a changing society drives him to a tragic end. What you write shows that if we do not face our weaknesses and fears, everything we work for and believe in can fall apart.

Sincerely,

Benjamin Draves

Sample Response: Dialogue

In this response, student writer Ali Washington creates a dialogue between himself and Daniel Dreiberg from *Watchmen*, a graphic novel by Alan Moore and Dave Gibbons. Through this conversation, the writer attempts to understand the actions of Dreiberg and the other characters in the story.

Dialogue with Daniel Dreiberg

> **The conversation is written in script form, much like a scene from a play.**

Me: When people think about superheroes, they probably think of amazing powers. As Nite Owl, you had only your training, your wits, and your inventions. That's one of the reasons I really identified with you as a hero.

Daniel: No one I know has superpowers except Jon Osterman, Dr. Manhattan.

Me: Many of the other heroes are much less human than you. It's hard to get inside the heads of Dr. Manhattan, Rorschach, and Ozymandius.

Daniel: But even though Dr. Manhattan has amazing powers, he still has human failings. He's godlike, but not all-seeing. He makes mistakes. Everyone does.

Me: Rorschach's mistakes hurt people.

Daniel: Rorschach is interesting because he feels that what he does—no matter how horrible—is not a mistake. Like the inkblot test he's named for, he shows people only what's really inside themselves. It's that blank identity that allows Rorschach to impose his own brand of justice on others.

Me: He once said that he was " . . . free to scrawl (his) own design on this morally blank world."

> **Daniel's explanation of his actions provides an interesting "self-analysis."**

Daniel: That's it exactly. He's not the only one who feels that way; he's just the one who's most up-front about it. Everyone feels that to one degree or another.

Me: Is that why you became a hero, Daniel, to remake the world?

Daniel: Yes . . . and no. It's complicated. We're all trying to do the right thing, but we're only fallible humans.

Me: So the main dilemma facing you is . . . ?

Daniel: Does anyone, no matter how noble, have the right to impose his or her will on anyone else? That's a question we all have to answer for ourselves.

Me: What's *your* answer?

Daniel: I just . . . don't know. ■

Sample Journal Entries

Another effective way to respond to your reading is to write in a personal journal or a reader-response journal. Here are sample journal responses.

Response to a Novel

Christine Quale explains her thoughts about a choice an author made.

I liked that Daniel Quinn chose to make Ishmael a gorilla. The major theme of *Ishmael* is that humans cannot survive unless they listen to others living on earth. Ishmael says, "Man is not alone on this planet. He is part of a community." If Ishmael had been human, his lessons would have had less impact. . . .

Response to a Play

Patrick Rivard explores one character in the play *The Road to Mecca*.

After her husband dies, Helen has visions of a "Mecca" and begins to express what is in her imagination. By doing this, she is freeing herself from what would have been a meaningless life, but Helen also becomes an outcast from the community. A few people admire her, though they may not know why, and they remain good friends with her. Throughout the play, Helen shows the other characters how to express their thoughts, feelings, and imaginations. . . .

Response to a Short Story

Renee Tolby thinks about an event in "Recitatif" by Toni Morrison.

The most important event in this story is when Maggie falls down in the apple orchard, even though the narrator, Twyla, does not recognize it as important. Every time Twyla meets with her childhood friend, Roberta, the subject comes up. As the truth is revealed about what happened to Maggie, Twyla learns about herself and Roberta. . . .

Response to an Essay

Denice Jackson connects with Gary Soto's essay "Looking for Work."

This essay reminds me of the time that I decided to earn money to buy a new bike. My grandmother and aunt needed help mowing their lawns and trimming the tall bushes. By August, I had enough money to buy my own bike. At the end of his essay, Soto says, "I took advantage and decided to look for work. I felt suddenly alive. . . ." That's the same way I felt after my summer of yard work. . . .

Starting Points for Journal Writing

The following questions can help you react to the books you read. Use this list if you cannot think of a starting point for your writing. Choose a question, and push yourself to write about it from different angles.

■ PERSONAL CONNECTIONS

1. What were your feelings after reading the opening chapters of the book? After reading half of the book? After finishing the book?

2. What parts of the book made you laugh, cry, cringe, or smile?

3. What connections do you see between the book and your own life?

4. What is the most important word, passage, or event in the book?

5. Who else should read this book? Why?

6. How does this book relate to other literature you have read?

■ POINTS OF INTEREST

1. What is the most significant sentence in the book? Why?

2. What is the most surprising part of the book?

3. Do some parts of the book seem especially believable or unbelievable?

4. Do you like or dislike how the book ends? Why?

5. What confuses you or makes you wonder in this book?

■ STRICTLY IN CHARACTER

1. In what ways do you relate to any of the characters?

2. Do any of the characters remind you of someone you know?

3. Which character would you most like to be in this book? Why?

4. What would you and your favorite character talk about?

■ CAREFUL REFLECTIONS

1. Why do you think the author chose the title of the book?

2. What was the author saying about life and living?

3. Has reading the book helped you or changed you in some way?

4. What have you learned from reading this book?

5. What questions about the book would you like answered?

"I am a part of all that I have read."

—John Kieran

Writing a
BOOK REVIEW

Everyone has his or her own personal tastes. While you may love Mexican food, your best friend may go for Italian dishes. While you may dig the blues, your brother may like rap or reggae. The same is true of the books you read. While you may enjoy science fiction or fantasy, the next person may enjoy modern dramas.

One way to share your personal taste in literature is to review the books you read. A book review is a brief essay expressing your personal opinion about a book's value. An effective book review is informative and enjoyable to read. It highlights key parts of a book without giving away the whole story. It provides thoughtful explanations and reflections to support your main points. Most importantly, it helps readers decide if they should read the book themselves.

Preview

- ■ Book Review: Fiction
- ■ Book Review: Nonfiction
- ■ Sample Mini-Reviews
- ■ Assessment Rubric

Writing Guidelines **Book Review**

In a review, you express your opinion about the value of a book you have read. It's important to support your feelings with thoughtful explanations and specific references to the book itself. Use the following guidelines when you review books (short stories, poems, movies, and so on).

■ PREWRITING

1. **Selecting a Topic** . . . Think about books that have really captured your attention. Focus on titles that you've recently read so that the details are still fresh in your mind.

2. **Gathering Details** . . . Collect your initial thoughts and feelings about your subject through freewriting. Or, if you want to work more systematically, list in one column the book's strong points and in another column its weak points. Continue exploring and collecting ideas as needed.

3. **Focusing Your Thoughts** . . . Review the details you have gathered, and choose the most interesting ideas to include in your review. *Remember:* Use direct quotations to support your main points when appropriate.

■ WRITING AND REVISING

4. **Connecting Your Ideas** . . . Introduce the book in the first part of the review. Highlight the key actions or elements in the middle part and make your recommendations about the book in the closing part.

5. **Improving Your Writing** . . . Review your first draft, focusing on *ideas, organization,* and *voice.* Consider the following questions: *Can readers follow my ideas? Will they understand how I feel about the book and why?* Revise as needed.

6. **Improving Your Style** . . . Check your review for *word choice* and *sentence fluency* to make sure that it reads clearly.

■ EDITING AND PROOFREADING

7. **Checking for Conventions** . . . Look for errors in punctuation, mechanics, and grammar. Use the rubric on page 244 as a final check of your revising and editing.

8. **Preparing a Final Copy** . . . Write or type a clean final copy of your review. Proofread the final copy before sharing it with others.

Sample Book Review: Fiction

The subject of Kya Hubble's book review is the novel *Girl With a Pearl Earring* by Tracy Chevalier.

Painted With Words

The beginning introduces the book and provides background information.

Inspired by the work of Dutch painter Johannes Vermeer, Tracy Chevalier creates the fascinating novel *Girl With a Pearl Earring*. Set in seventeenth-century Holland, the story comes to life through Chevalier's artistic use of historical details.

The book begins with the introduction of Griet, a 16-year-old girl living with her family. When two strangers come to the house, Griet listens to their conversation and thinks, "I could hear rich carpets in their voices, books and pearls and fur" (3). As a result of this meeting, Griet is hired to be a maid in the house of Johannes Vermeer, an artist.

Griet's daily tasks provide insight into what life was like for a servant, and she clearly understands her role. All the household clothing and linen have to be washed, dried, and ironed by hand. Groceries have to be bought every day from the local butchers, vegetable sellers, and bakers. Silver requires regular polishing to maintain its shine. Griet's life becomes consumed by her domestic duties: "I was new and young—it was to be expected I would have the hardest tasks" (21). Then Vermeer asks her to work in his studio, too.

The middle part highlights key features in the story.

As Vermeer's studio assistant, Griet learns about paints and painting. Paints are painstakingly mixed from ground natural materials: bones, white lead, madder (herb), and lapis lazuli (gemstone). Griet discovers "that the finer the materials were ground, the deeper the colour" (115). Explanations of the painting process reveal how much work goes into the creation of one piece.

Chevalier's use of imagery gives the book a strong sense of place and time. Griet and the Vermeer children "watched the boats go up and down the canal, full on their way to market with cabbages, pigs, flowers, wood, flour, strawberries, horseshoes" (46). As Griet does the daily shopping, she passes horses and carts rumbling past Town Hall, girls making lace, and shoppers making purchases in Market Square. These details help the reader envision Delft as it was in the mid-1600s.

The closing emphasizes the book's appeal.

This book weaves an imaginative tale about the story behind a Vermeer painting. Chevalier's imagery breathes beauty and believability into *Girl With a Pearl Earring*. If you have ever looked at a painting and wondered about the story behind it, then you should read this book. ■

Sample Book Review: Nonfiction

Student writer Jeremy Hawkins reviews *Tuesdays with Morrie*, a true story by Mitch Albom about the lessons taught by a former professor.

The Lessons of Death

"Once you learn how to die, you learn how to live."
—*Morrie Schwartz (82)*

The beginning introduces the book and provides background information.

In *Tuesdays with Morrie,* writer Mitch Albom shares a touching story about his former professor, Morrie Schwartz, who is dying from Lou Gehrig's disease. As Albom describes Schwartz's heart-wrenching decline, uplifting lessons about life are revealed.

Albom is a young college student in the 1970s when he has his first class with Morrie Schwartz. He is caught off guard by the friendliness and thoughtful concern of his professor. They regularly meet one-on-one during Albom's sophomore year. By the end of college, Albom finishes an honors thesis with Schwartz's help and encouragement. After graduation, though, Albom loses touch with his mentor.

The writer highlights the main character's strength.

It isn't until Albom sees a 1995 *Nightline* interview featuring Schwartz that former student and professor are reunited. Although it has been a long time, Morrie welcomes Albom with open arms. Always a teacher at heart, Morrie wants to share what he is learning through the process of dying. Morrie points out the reality of life: "Everyone knows they're going to die, but nobody believes it" (81). Albom feels like a student again as Morrie shares his insights. The "final paper" is intended to be this book.

Morrie has a lot to say on important matters of family, emotions, money, death, forgiveness, and fear of aging. As Albom puts it, "Morrie would walk that final bridge between life and death, and narrate the trip" (19). It is striking to note the upbeat tone in Morrie's thoughts. For example, Morrie says that one should put a daily limit on self-pity. "A little each morning, a few tears, and that's all" (57). Cry and then move on. That is amazing advice from a man unable to stand on his own.

The final paragraph stresses the book's importance.

The key feature of this book is Morrie's powerful message. His heartfelt wisdom is not just the result of his age. It is through his experience with dying that Morrie finds incredible clarity in evaluating the major issues of life. Death may be a difficult topic, but somehow this story leaves the reader inspired rather than depressed. Anyone who reads this book should be prepared to laugh, to cry, and, most importantly, to learn. ■

Sample Mini-Reviews

Mini-reviews of books, movies, videos, and CD's are popular in student newspapers, literary magazines, and online magazines.

A Review of *How to Dismantle an Atomic Bomb*

The writer analyzes the title and songs of the album.

The CD *How to Dismantle An Atomic Bomb* by U2 has the distinctive U2 sound of rhythmic guitar, layered sounds, and Bono's powerful vocals. The music ranges from upbeat to haunting. Every time I listen to the CD, I like it more and more.

The album title implies that the band is reacting to the dangerous political climate of the world. Indeed, the songs declare the importance of love and faith in difficult times. "Original of the Species," for example, focuses on faith in yourself. I think every teenager wants to know what makes him or her special. One line says, "Come on now—show your soul." This song celebrates and encourages each and every listener.

U2 has been together for more than 20 years, and the band continues to produce quality work. This CD is a great collection of songs. I recommend it to anyone who likes creative and thoughtful music.

A Review of *The Aviator*

Most people remember billionaire Howard Hughes for his eccentric behavior toward the end of his life. *The Aviator,* directed by Martin Scorsese, focuses on what Hughes achieves in aviation and film from the late 1920s through the 1940s.

The writer uses the director's quote to emphasize the main character's struggle.

Leonardo DiCaprio portrays Hughes as driven, determined, and undeniably disturbed. Hughes's passion for making movies is secondary to his love of airplanes. During a test flight, Hughes is almost killed in a horrific crash. After that, he increasingly succumbs to mental illness. He shuts himself away from his staff and his lavish Hollywood lifestyle, emerging only briefly to defend himself against false allegations of government funding misuse. However, it's painfully obvious that Hughes can't escape his declining mental condition.

The Aviator presents a colorful portrait of Howard Hughes. It shows how close genius and madness really lie. The same obsessive personality traits that drive Hughes to the pinnacle of success in his early life drive him to paranoia and confusion later on. Scorsese sums up Hughes' plight, saying ". . . there's a lot that goes on in the story that has to do with accumulating, greed, and how much is enough."

Assessment Rubric

This rubric is a helpful checklist for evaluating reviews. It follows the traits of writing described in your handbook on pages 21–26.

Ideas

The writing . . .

_____ discusses one piece of literature (music, movie, performance).

_____ emphasizes one or more key factors (character, plot, setting, theme).

_____ includes specific details and direct references from the work.

_____ maintains a clear and consistent view from beginning to end.

Organization

_____ includes an effective beginning, an informative and thoughtful middle part, and a strong conclusion.

_____ presents ideas in an organized manner (perhaps offering the strongest point first or last).

Voice

_____ sounds believable and informed.

_____ reflects the writer's clear understanding of the text.

Word Choice

_____ defines or clarifies any new terms or unfamiliar words.

_____ shows careful choice of words.

Sentence Style

_____ flows smoothly from one idea to the next.

Conventions

_____ follows the standards of punctuation, grammar, and spelling.

_____ observes the correct guidelines for presentation.

"Life-transforming ideas have always
come to me through books."

—bell hooks

Writing a
LITERARY ANALYSIS

In a personal response, you explore your thoughts and feelings about a piece of literature. In a review, you discuss the merits of a particular book or series of stories. And in a literary analysis, you present your understanding or interpretation of a literary work. Writing an effective literary analysis requires a high level of critical thinking on your part.

The starting point for meaningful analysis is your honest response to a piece of literature. You may like how the story line develops in a novel. You may find the actions of a short-story character intriguing. Then again, you may wonder why a writer spends so much time developing a certain image in a poem. Any one of these ideas could lead to an effective analysis.

Base your analysis on a close and careful reading of the piece of literature. Then present your ideas in a carefully planned essay, connecting all of your main points with specific references to the text.

Preview

■ **Writing Guidelines**
■ **Literary Analysis: Novel**
■ **Literary Analysis: Essay**
■ **Ideas for Literary Analysis**
■ **Literary Terms**

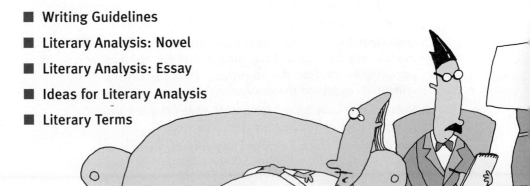

Writing Guidelines Literary Analysis

A literary analysis calls for a close examination of a novel, short story, poem, play, or essay. For example, you might analyze an intriguing character in a novel, interpret a powerful image in a poem, or evaluate the strength of the thesis in an essay. Here are the steps to creating a literary analysis.

■ PREWRITING

1. **Choosing a Topic . . .** Sometimes a teacher will assign literature for you to analyze. If not, choose a piece of writing that speaks to you.

2. **Finding a Focus . . .** Zero in on what interests you most in the literature, such as its intriguing ideas, compelling characters, or distinctive imagery. If no idea comes to mind, freewrite about the text.

3. **Organizing Your Essay . . .** Write a sentence that clearly states the thesis (focus) of your analysis. Outline the main points that support your thesis. Finally, gather details to support your main points.

■ WRITING

4. **Connecting Your Ideas . . .** In the opening part, draw readers into your analysis and identify your thesis. In the middle, support your thesis using quotations, paraphrases, analyses, and so on. (See page 247.) In the closing, restate the thesis, emphasize the importance of one main point, or make a connection with life in general.

■ REVISING

5. **Improving Your Writing . . .** Review your first draft and add, delete, move, or rework sections as needed. Use the following questions:

- **Ideas:** *Have I selected an interesting piece of literature? Have I focused my analysis with a clear thesis statement? Have I included convincing support from the text?*

- **Organization:** *Does my beginning name the title and the author and include a thesis statement? Do my middle paragraphs analyze the literature? Does my ending effectively conclude the analysis?*

- **Voice:** *Do I sound knowledgeable about the literature? Is my voice appropriate for my audience?*

- **Word Choice:** *Have I defined any unfamiliar terms? Is my word choice appropriate for my topic and audience?*

- **Sentence Fluency:** *Do my sentences flow smoothly? Do my sentences vary in length and structure?*

■ **EDITING AND PROOFREADING**

6. Checking for Conventions . . . Check for punctuation, capitalization, spelling, and grammar errors. Also ask a classmate to help you look for errors. Use the rubric on page 244 as a final check for your revising and editing.

7. Preparing a Final Copy . . . Create a clean final copy of your analysis. Proofread the copy one last time before sharing it.

Creating a Literary Analysis

In a literary analysis, it's important to support your thesis by referring to textual evidence in the piece of literature. (See the samples below.)

■ **Quotations** are word-for-word statements from a piece of literature. They are enclosed in quotation marks. Quote the author's exact words when they create a very clear image.

■ **Paraphrases** provide the author's meaning without using the author's exact words. Paraphrase the author's words to get quickly to a big idea.

When the dog's owner discovers him there, Christopher says he did not kill the dog, but he gets in a scuffle with the police and lands in jail.

■ **Inferences** state assumptions based on facts or deductions. Use inferences to tell what is implied but not outwardly shown in a piece of literature.

Like most autistic people, Christopher has trouble reading even simple facial expressions. He describes people's clothing and hands, not their faces, as if it is too painful to look them in the eye.

■ **Analyses** break down information into smaller parts. Analyze details by relating them to each other or to the work of literature as a whole.

All these facts make Christopher alone in his social world, which demonstrates the very meaning of the word autism.

■ **Interpretations** give a specific angle or view of the ideas in a piece of literature. Interpret the ideas in literature by applying them to life in general.

Handon uses the theme of mystery to show how deeply mysterious human expressions, language, and relationships are to a person with autism.

Sample Literary Analysis: Novel

In the following literary analysis, a student explores the theme of mystery in the novel *The Curious Incident of the Dog in the Night-Time*.

The Limits of Being Normal

Sherlock Holmes once asked Dr. Watson about "the curious incident of the dog in the night-time." When Watson pointed out that the dog did nothing in the night-time, Holmes responded, "That was the curious incident." Anyone familiar with Sherlock Holmes would recognize his ruthlessly logical approach to solving a mystery. In *The Curious Incident of the Dog in the Night-Time*, Mark Haddon introduces a detective who has the same obsession with discovering the truth. Christopher John Francis Boone is a 15-year-old autistic savant who has trouble understanding other people's thoughts and feelings but knows every prime number up to 7,057. **As Christopher investigates the mysterious death of a neighborhood dog, Haddon uses the theme of mystery to explore the complexities of human interaction.**

The story begins when Christopher discovers a crime scene across the street. A large black poodle named Wellington lies dead, and Christopher kneels to cradle the dog. When the dog's owner discovers him there, Christopher says he did not kill the dog, but he gets in a scuffle with the police and lands in jail. After his father comes to get him out, Christopher pledges to solve the mystery of Wellington's death. Christopher finds one clue after another while investigating the crime scene and interviewing neighbors about the incident. He also uses deductive logic, listing possible motives for killing a dog and narrowing his list of suspects.

As Christopher investigates the killing, Haddon brings him into direct confrontation with a deeper mystery: other human beings. Like most autistic people, Christopher has trouble reading even simple facial expressions. He describes people's clothing and hands, not their faces, as if it is too painful to look them in the eye. At one point, he says that people look at him when they speak, trying to see what he is thinking, but he can't see what they are thinking. People are confusing to Christopher. By contrast, he likes dogs because he can always tell what they are thinking; they have only four moods —"happy, sad, cross and concentrating"—and they don't lie since they can't talk (4). All these facts make Christopher alone in his social world and demonstrate the very meaning of the word *autism*. In fact, Christopher has a recurrent favorite dream: "And in the dream nearly everyone on the earth is dead . . . and eventually there is no one left in the world" except people with autism (198). This dream shows how alone he truly is.

Haddon deepens the theme of mystery by exploring the complexities of human language. For example, Christopher never lies. A lie means saying something happened that didn't happen, and Christopher cannot see the point of it. For him, the only things worth speaking about are facts and mathematics. Christopher also doesn't understand jokes because they require him to think about one word in two or three ways at once. "If I try to say the joke to myself, making the word mean the three different things at the same time, it is like hearing three different pieces of music at the same time, which is uncomfortable and confusing . . . " (8). In the same way, Christopher dislikes metaphors such as "apple of my eye." He writes, "When I try and make a picture of the phrase in my head, it just confuses me because imagining an apple in someone's eye doesn't have anything to do with liking someone a lot . . . "(15).

Christopher's quest for truth leads him inevitably to discover even deeper mysteries. Two years before the beginning of the story, Christopher's mother died of a sudden heart attack. At that time, Mrs. Shears, the neighbor woman who owned Wellington, became a family friend who helped them deal with their grief. Her friendship with the Boones ended on the night that Wellington was killed—but the question is whether the friendship ended because of the dog's death, or the dog died because the friendship ended. As Christopher attempts to answer this question, he strips away years' worth of lies and discovers the truth.

At the beginning of the book, Christopher writes, "This is a murder mystery novel" (4), but it is much more than that. Haddon uses the theme of mystery to show how deeply mysterious human expressions, language, and relationships are to a person with autism. At first, the book seems to show the limitations of being autistic, but in the end, it shows the limits of being normal. Christopher himself describes it best in the final sentence of the book: "And I know I can do this because I went to London on my own, and because I solved the mystery of Who Killed Wellington? . . . . and I was brave and I wrote a book and that means I can do anything" (221). ∎

Sample Short Literary Analysis: Novel

In this short analysis, student writer Kyran Dasra explores the theme of materialism in F. Scott Fitzgerald's novel *The Great Gatsby*.

Glittering Outside but Empty Inside

In F. Scott Fitzgerald's novel *The Great Gatsby*, Jay Gatsby gathers "enchanted objects" in a desperate attempt to fill the emptiness of his heart. **Although Gatsby seems fond of his sprawling mansion, splendid car, and exquisite wardrobe, his luxurious lifestyle does not bring him peace or satisfaction.**

The beginning paragraph identifies the thesis (boldfaced).

As Fitzgerald introduces Gatsby, the reader is overwhelmed by descriptions of a lavish lifestyle. Elaborate weekend parties glitter late into the night. Most of the guests don't even know Gatsby, but they are happy to enjoy the festivities. Gatsby spends his time standing "alone on the marble steps and looking from one group to another with approving eyes" (51). It's as if Gatsby is a theater director, gathering props and actors to stage a magnificent although artificial performance.

The middle paragraphs use textual evidence to support the thesis.

Gatsby longs to be with his lost love, Daisy. In fact, he chose his mansion for its location across the bay from Daisy's home. After five years apart, Daisy and Gatsby are finally reunited. As he shows Daisy the mansion, he stares "around at his possessions in a dazed way, as though in her actual and astounding presence none of it was any longer real" (88). However, even Daisy is just another object to own, rather than a person to be embraced. Gatsby confides to his friend Nick, "Her voice is full of money" (115). The focus of Gatsby's hollow life has become possessions.

In closing, the writer links the thesis with today's society.

On the outside, Gatsby is a distinguished figure with every luxury to gild his days, but on the inside, Gatsby finds himself to be truly empty, without any type of meaningful relationship. This point is made clear when Gatsby is seen strolling along his velvet lawn. He reaches into the darkness, straining to see the green light that marks the end of Daisy's dock—forever beyond his reach, forever just a dream. Even though this novel is set in the 1920s, it's easy to see the same story told today. When will people learn that all that glitters is not gold? ▪

HELP FILE

Can you find examples of quotations, paraphrases, and analyses in the essay above? By learning to recognize and understand these types of details, you'll be better equipped to use them in your own literary analysis.

Sample Short Literary Analysis: Essay

In this analysis, student writer David Foxx examines the main point in an essay by Richard Rodriguez.

To Turn Around Three Times

The beginning identifies the main point of the analysis.

"The teenage years are the best years of your life," my uncle once told me. My dad said he was crazy, that being a teenager can be a very difficult time. I think they both were right. **In the essay "Growing Up in Los Angeles," Richard Rodriguez creates a compelling definition of adolescence and then extends the definition to refer to our whole culture.**

Rodriguez defines adolescence using a series of contrasts. He contrasts being a child and having children, obeying adult rules and reinventing adult rules, battling for eternal youth and being overcome by "inevitabilities and consequences." According to Rodriguez, "The balancing trick of American adolescence is to stand in-between—neither to be a child nor an adult" (348).

The middle analyzes the author's definition of adolescence.

He then extends this definition to apply to our whole culture. The first immigrants to this country "imagined themselves adolescent, orphans" fleeing their fatherland to find a "land without history or meaning" (346). Those immigrants then wrote literature about their adolescent ideals, including books such as *The Adventures of Huckleberry Finn*. When the age of Hollywood dawned, the country began selling the ideal of eternal youth to the world, and the Baby Boom Generation "transformed youth into a lifestyle, a political manifesto, an aesthetic, a religion" (347). Our nation was born in adolescence, and remains in it still.

The middle also interprets key ideas in the essay.

Our national obsession with youth has some less-than-positive results, though. Today's teenagers often have to take care of their siblings because their parents refuse to grow up. Adolescents in L.A. carry weapons because the streets are so dangerous. Gangs form to give kids the only real families they have ever known. Rodriguez describes today's youth as "tough and cynical as ancients." And he asks, "Have adults become the innocents?" (344). To a large extent, the answer has to be yes.

The ending provides the reader a final intriguing thought.

Teenagers certainly aren't innocents, and youthful dangers aren't new. Think of Huck Finn, who had to escape an abusive, alcoholic father and flee with a runaway slave. Rodriguez believes these dangers have a purpose: "American teenagers are supposed to innovate, to improvise, to rebel, to turn around three times before they harden into adults" (344). In that way, the teenage years are simultaneously the best and worst years of a person's life—the dangerous, wonderful chance to grow up. ■

Ideas for Literary Analysis

Theme

1. What concepts—such as *courage*, *betrayal*, or *trust*—does the writer explore?
2. What social issues—such as *racism*, *loneliness*, or *tradition*—shape the story?
3. What lesson does the main character or the reader learn?

Characters

1. How does a character change from the beginning of the writing to the end?
2. What factors influence the actions of a character (*setting, conflicts, relationships,* and so on)?
3. How does the author use thoughts, words, and actions to reflect the personality of a character?
4. How does the author use action and dialogue to make characters seem believable?
5. How do supporting characters shape the story?

Plot

1. How does the author use external or internal conflict throughout the story?
2. How does the author create a sense of growing suspense?
3. How do plot twists shape the story?
4. What impact does the climax have on the rest of the story?
5. What pattern of fiction does the story follow? (See page 153.)

Setting

1. What effect does the setting have on the characters?
2. What does the story reveal about life in a specific time and place?
3. How would you describe the setting: realistic, fantastic, or some combination?

Style

1. How does the author use imagery to create the overall mood of the piece?
2. How do dialogue and description shape the writing?
3. What key figures of speech does the author use? How do these add to the writing?

Literary Terms

The terms on the following pages describe the different types and elements of literature. This information will help you to discuss and write about the novels, poems, and other literary works you read. (Poetry terms begin on page 170.)

Allegory is a story in which people, things, and actions represent an idea or a generalization about life; allegories often have a strong moral or lesson.

Allusion is a literary reference to a familiar person, place, thing, or event. (See pages 124 and 463.)

Analogy is a comparison of two or more similar objects, suggesting that if they are alike in certain respects, they will probably be alike in other ways as well. (See pages 124 and 463.)

Anecdote is a short account of an interesting event used to make a point. (See page 124.) Abe Lincoln was famous for his anecdotes, especially this one:

> Two fellows, after a hot dispute over how long a man's legs should be in proportion to his body, stormed into Lincoln's office one day and confronted him with their problem. Lincoln listened intently to the arguments given by each of the men and after some reflection rendered his verdict: "This question has been a source of controversy for untold ages," he said, slowly and deliberately, "and it is about time it should be definitely decided. It has led to bloodshed in the past, and there is no reason to suppose it will not lead to the same in the future.
>
> "After much thought and consideration, not to mention mental worry and anxiety, it is my opinion, all side issues being swept aside, that a man's lower limbs, in order to preserve harmony of proportion, should be at least long enough to reach from his body to the ground."

Antagonist is the person or force working against the protagonist, or hero, of the work.

Autobiography is an author's account of her or his own life.

Biography is the story of a person's life written by another person.

Caricature is a picture or an imitation of a person's features or mannerisms exaggerated in a comic or absurd way. (See the caricature of Abe Lincoln above.)

Character sketch is a short piece of writing that reveals or shows something important about a person or fictional character.

Characterization is the method an author uses to create believable people.

Climax is usually the most intense point in a story. A series of struggles or conflicts build a story or play toward the climax. (See "Plot line.")

Comedy is literature in which human errors or problems appear funny. Comedies end on a happy note.

Conflict is the problem or struggle in a story that triggers the action. There are five basic types of conflict:

- **Person vs. Person:** One character in a story has a problem with one or more of the other characters.

- **Person vs. Society:** A character has a problem with some element of society: the school, the law, the accepted way of doing things.

- **Person vs. Self:** A character has a problem deciding what to do in a certain situation.

- **Person vs. Nature:** A character has a problem with nature: heat, cold, a tornado, an avalanche, or any other element of nature.

- **Person vs. Fate (God):** A character must battle what seems to be an uncontrollable problem. Whenever the conflict is an unbelievable or strange coincidence, it can be attributed to fate or an act of God.

Context is the set of facts or circumstances surrounding an event or a situation in a piece of literature.

Denouement is the final resolution or outcome of a play or story.

Dialogue is the conversation carried on by the characters in a literary work.

Diction is word choice based on correctness, clearness, or effectiveness.

- **Archaic** words are those that are old-fashioned and no longer sound natural when used, as "I believe thee not" for "I don't believe you."

- **Colloquialism** is an expression that is usually accepted in informal situations and certain locations, as in "He really gets my goat."

- **Jargon** (technical diction) is the specialized language used by a specific group, such as computer users: *override, interface, download.*

- **Profanity** is language that shows disrespect for something regarded as sacred. **Vulgarity** is language that is generally considered crude and offensive. They are sometimes used in fiction to add realism.

- **Slang** is the informal language used by a particular group of people; it is used in fiction to lend color and feeling: *awesome, chill, no way.*

Didactic literature instructs or presents a moral or religious statement.

Drama is the form of literature known as plays; but drama also refers to the type of serious play that is often concerned with the leading character's relationship to society.

Dramatic monologue is a literary work (or part of a literary work) in which a character is speaking about him- or herself as if another person were present. The words of the speaker reveal something important about his or her character. (See "Soliloquy.")

Empathy is putting yourself in someone else's place and imagining how that person must feel. The phrase "What would you do if you were in my shoes?" is a request for one person to empathize with another.

Epic is a long narrative poem that tells of the deeds and adventures of a hero.

Epigram is a brief, witty saying or poem often dealing with its subject in a satirical manner:

> **"There never was a good war or a bad peace."**   —Ben Franklin

Epiphany is a sudden perception (moment of understanding) that causes a character to change or act in a certain way.

Epitaph is a short poem or verse written in memory of someone.

Epithet is a word or phrase used in place of a person's name; it is characteristic of that person: Alexander the Great, Material Girl, Ms. Know-It-All.

Essay is a piece of prose that expresses an individual's point of view; usually, it is a series of closely related paragraphs that combine to make a complete piece of writing.

Exaggeration is overstating or stretching the truth for special effect.

> **"My shoes are killing me!"**

Exposition is writing that is intended to explain something that might otherwise be difficult to understand. In a play or novel, it would be the portion that gives the background or situation surrounding the story.

Fable is a short fictional narrative that teaches a lesson. It usually includes animals that talk and act like people.

Falling action is the part of a play or story that leads from the climax or turning point to the resolution.

Farce is literature based on a humorous and improbable plot.

Figurative language is language used to create a special effect or feeling. (See "Figure of speech.")

Figure of speech is a literary device used to create a special effect or feeling by making some type of interesting or creative comparison.

■ **Antithesis** is an opposition, or contrast, of ideas:

"It was the best of times, it was the worst of times . . ."

—Charles Dickens, *A Tale of Two Cities*

■ **Hyperbole** (hī-pər-bə-lē) is an exaggeration or overstatement:

"I have seen this river so wide it had only one bank."

—Mark Twain, *Life on the Mississippi*

■ **Metaphor** is a comparison of two things in which no word of comparison (*as* or *like*) is used:

"A green plant is a machine that runs on solar energy."

—*Scientific American*

■ **Metonymy** (mə-tŏn-ə-mē) is the substituting of one word for another related word:

The White House has decided to create more public service jobs.

(*White House* is substituted for *president*.)

■ **Personification** is a literary device in which the author speaks of or describes an animal, object, or idea as if it were a person:

"The rock stubbornly refused to move."

■ **Simile** is a comparison of two things using the words *like* or *as*:

"She stood in front of the altar, shaking like a freshly caught trout."

—Maya Angelou, *I Know Why the Caged Bird Sings*

■ **Understatement** is a way of emphasizing an idea by talking about it in a restrained manner:

"Aunt Polly is prejudiced against snakes." (She was terrified of them.)

—Mark Twain, *Adventures of Tom Sawyer*

Flashback is returning to an earlier time for the purpose of making something in the present more clear. (See page 124.)

Foil is someone who serves as a contrast or challenge to another character.

Foreshadowing is giving hints or clues of what is to come later in a story. (See page 125.)

Genre refers to a category or type of literature based on its style, form, and content. The mystery novel is a literary genre.

Gothic novel is a type of fiction that is characterized by gloomy castles, ghosts, and supernatural happenings—creating a mysterious and sometimes frightening story. Bram Stoker's *Dracula* is probably the best known gothic novel still popular today.

Hubris, derived from the Greek word *hybris*, means "excessive pride." In Greek tragedy, hubris is often viewed as the flaw that leads to the downfall of the tragic hero.

Imagery is the use of words to create a certain picture in the reader's mind. Imagery is usually based on sensory details:

> **"The sky was dark and gloomy, the air was damp and raw, the streets were wet and sloppy."** —Charles Dickens, *The Pickwick Papers*

Impressionism is the recording of events or situations as they have been impressed upon the mind. A writer shares her impressions of flying in an airplane for the first time:

> **"As the plane broke through the clouds, I felt like I had entered a new world. The clouds stretched into eternity like a puffy mountain range. Subtle colors of pink and lavender touched the landscape. I longed to dive into the perfect softness of the beckoning blanket."**

Irony is using a word or phrase to mean the exact opposite of its literal or normal meaning. There are three kinds of irony:

- **Dramatic** irony, in which the reader or the audience sees a character's mistakes or misunderstandings, but the character does not;
- **Verbal** irony, in which the writer says one thing and means another: "The best substitute for experience is being thirteen"; and
- Irony of **situation**, in which there is a great difference between the purpose of a particular action and the result.

Local color is the use of language and details that are common in a certain region of the country:

> **"Memphis ain't a bad town, for them that like city life."**
>
> —William Faulkner, *Light in August*

Malapropism is the type of pun, or play on words, that results when two words become jumbled in the speaker's mind. The term comes from a character in Sheridan's comedy *The Rivals*. The character, Mrs. Malaprop, is constantly mixing up her words, as when she says "as headstrong as an allegory [she means *alligator*] on the banks of the Nile."

Melodrama is an exaggerated form of drama (as in television soap operas) characterized by heavy use of romance, suspense, and emotion.

Memoir is writing based on the writer's memory of a particular time, place, or incident. *Reminiscence* is another term for *memoir*.

Mood is the feeling a text arouses in the reader: happiness, peacefulness, sadness, and so on.

Moral is the particular value or lesson the author is trying to get across to the reader. The "moral of the story" is a common phrase in Aesop's fables.

Motif is the term for an often-repeated idea or theme in literature. In *The Adventures of Huckleberry Finn*, Huck is constantly in conflict with the "civilized" world. This conflict becomes a motif throughout the novel.

Myth is a traditional story that attempts to justify a certain practice or belief or to explain a natural phenomenon.

Narration is writing that relates an event or a series of events: a story.

Narrator is the person who is telling the story.

Naturalism is an extreme form of realism in which the author tries to show the relation of a person to the environment or surroundings. Often, the author finds it necessary to show the ugly or raw side of that relationship.

Novel is a lengthy fictional story with a plot that is revealed by the speech, action, and thoughts of the characters.

Novella is a prose work longer than the standard short story, but shorter and less complex than a full-length novel.

Oxymoron is a combination of contradictory terms as in *jumbo shrimp*, *tough love*, or *cruel kindness*.

Parable is a short descriptive story that illustrates a particular belief or moral.

Paradox is a statement that seems contrary to common sense, yet may, in fact, be true: "The coach considered this a good loss."

Parody is a form of literature that intentionally uses comic effect to mock a literary work or style.

Pathetic fallacy is a form of personification giving human traits to nature: *cruel sea, howling wind, dancing water.*

Pathos is a Greek root meaning "suffering" or "passion." It usually describes the part in a play or story that is intended to elicit pity or sorrow from the audience or reader.

Picaresque novel is a work of fiction consisting of a lengthy string of loosely connected events. It usually features the adventures of a rogue living by his or her wits. Mark Twain's *Huckleberry Finn* is a picaresque novel.

Plot is the action or sequence of events in a story. It is usually a series of related incidents that build upon one another as the story develops. There are five basic elements in a plot line. (See below.)

Plot line is the graphic display of the action or events in a story: *exposition, rising action, climax, falling action,* and *resolution*.

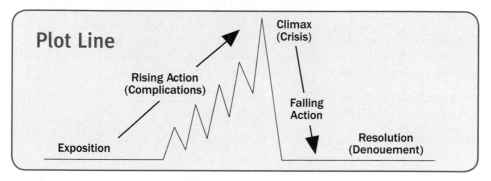

Poetic justice is a term that describes a character "getting what he deserves" in the end, especially if what he deserves is punishment. The purest form of poetic justice is when one character plots against another but ends up being caught in his or her own trap.

Point of view is the vantage point from which the story is told. In the first-person point of view, the story is told by one of the characters: "I remember the summer I turned sixteen." In the third-person point of view, the story is told by someone outside the story: "The old man shuffled across the street. He looked down at the ground as he walked." There are three types of third-person points of view:

- **Omniscient** point of view allows the narrator to share the thoughts and feelings of all the characters.
- **Limited** point of view allows the narrator to share the thoughts and feelings of one central character.
- **Camera view** (objective view) allows the storyteller to record the action from his or her own point of view, being unaware of any of the characters' thoughts or feelings.

Protagonist is the main character or hero of the story.

Pseudonym (also known as a "pen name") means "false name" and applies to the name a writer uses in place of his or her given name. "Mark Twain" is a pseudonym for Samuel Langhorne Clemens.

Quest features a main character who is seeking to find something or achieve a goal. In the process, this character encounters and overcomes a series of obstacles, returning wiser and more experienced.

Realism is literature that attempts to represent life as it really is.

Renaissance, which means "rebirth," is the period of history following the Middle Ages. This period began late in the fourteenth century and continued through the fifteenth and sixteenth centuries. The term now applies to any period of time in which intellectual and artistic interest is revived or reborn.

Resolution, or denouement, is the portion of the play or story in which the problem is solved. It comes after the climax and falling action and is intended to bring the story to a satisfactory end. (See "Plot line.")

Rising action is the series of struggles that builds a story or play toward a climax. (See "Plot line.")

Romanticism is a literary movement with an emphasis on the imagination and emotions.

Sarcasm is the use of praise to mock someone or something, as in "She's a real winner" or "No one cuts pizza like Clyde."

"No one cuts pizza like Clyde."

Satire is a literary tone used to make fun of human vice or weakness, often with the intent of correcting or changing the subject of the attack.

Setting is the time and place in which the action of a literary work occurs.

Short story is a brief fictional work. It usually contains one major conflict and at least one main character.

Slapstick is a form of low comedy that often includes exaggerated, sometimes violent action. The "pie in the face" routine is a classic piece of slapstick.

Slice of life is a term that describes the type of realistic or naturalistic writing that accurately reflects what life is really like. This is done by giving the reader a sample, or slice, of experience.

Soliloquy is a speech delivered by a character when he or she is alone on stage. It is as though the character is thinking out loud.

Stereotype is a form that does not change. A "stereotyped" character has no individuality and fits the mold of that particular kind of person.

Stream of consciousness is a style of writing in which the thoughts and feelings of the writer are recorded as they occur.

Style is how the author uses words, phrases, and sentences to form his or her ideas. Style is also thought of as the qualities and characteristics that distinguish one writer's work from the work of others.

Symbol is a person, a place, a thing, or an event used to represent something else: the dove is a symbol of peace. Characters in literature may be symbols of good or evil.

Theme is the statement about life that a writer is trying to get across in a piece of writing. In most cases, the theme will be implied rather than directly spelled out.

Tone is the overall feeling, or effect, created by a writer's use of words. This feeling may be serious, humorous, or satiric.

Total effect is the general impression a literary work leaves on the reader.

Tragedy is a literary work in which the hero is destroyed by some character flaw or by forces beyond his or her control.

Tragic hero is a character who experiences an inner struggle because of a character flaw. That struggle ends in the defeat of the hero.

Transcendentalism is a philosophy that requires human beings to go beyond (transcend) reason in their search for truth. It assumes that an individual can arrive at the basic truths of life through spiritual insight if he or she takes the time to think seriously about them.

Research
WRITING

Writing the Research Paper   263

Writing Responsibly   273

MLA Documentation Style   281

Sample MLA Research Paper   299

APA Documentation Style   309

"My idea of research is to look at the thing from all sides; the person who has seen the animal, how the animal behaves, and so on."

—Marianne Moore

Writing the
RESEARCH PAPER

What does it mean to be a researcher? To Jerry Ellis it meant walking 900 miles along the infamous Cherokee Trail of Tears and sharing what he learned in his book *Walking the Trail.* To Mari Sandoz it meant fulfilling a promise to her father that she would write about his struggles on the Nebraska frontier. The end result was her book *Old Jules,* an amazing portrait of pioneering.

In each of these cases, the writers investigated subjects that truly interested them. If you do the same, making each of your research projects an active quest for information, you will soon learn what it means to be a researcher.

Remember: A research paper is a carefully planned essay that shares information or proves a point. It may include ideas from books, Web sites, documents, interviews, observations, and so on. Most school research papers are at least five pages long and may also require a title page, an outline, and a list of works cited.

Preview

- **Research Update**
- **Writing Guidelines**
- **Tips for Writing a Thesis Statement**
- **Searching Tips**
- **Writing Tips**

Research Update

In most cases, students head straight to the library or Internet to find published information (books, articles, encyclopedia entries, postings) for their research papers. However, many teachers also expect their students to collect firsthand information by conducting interviews, distributing questionnaires, making visits, participating in activities, and writing letters. These firsthand experiences make researching much more active and meaningful for students.

The I-Search Paper

One method of research that focuses on firsthand information is the I-Search paper. An I-Search begins with an individual's curiosity about something. One person may wonder what it takes to become an emergency-room nurse. Another may wonder about the world of scuba diving.

After identifying a personal interest, the I-Searcher sets out to find information and answers through visits, observations, and interviews. I-Searchers use books and magazines only when recommended by someone they've contacted for information. (They use people first, print material second.) An I-Search paper becomes the story of a person's own searching adventure, telling what the I-Searcher wanted to know and what he or she found out or learned.

A Personalized Approach

Here are some recommendations for your next research project:

- **Get involved.** Start by selecting a topic that interests you, and then carry out as much firsthand research as possible.

- **Keep a journal.** Consider writing in a journal during the project. Thinking and writing about your work will help you make sense of new information, refocus your thinking, and evaluate your progress.

- **Personalize it.** The more information you gain from your own thinking and exploring, the more you will enjoy the research process—and the more readers will appreciate the result.

FAQ **How has the Internet changed the research process?**

On the upside, the Internet is a quick and convenient source of information. You can access an unlimited number of resources almost immediately. On the downside, the Internet provides so much information that settling on a few quality sources may be difficult. Anyone can publish anything on the Net, so you must learn how to judge between what is accurate and responsible and what may be inaccurate and irresponsible. (See pages 341 and 349.)

Writing Guidelines **Research Paper**

■ **PREWRITING**

Selecting a Topic

1. **Understanding the Project . . .** When you are assigned a research paper, your teacher will probably suggest a few general subject areas. It will be up to you to explore these for a specific writing idea that meets the assignment requirements and genuinely interests you.

   Suppose that in a science class you're given the general subject "water resources." Your teacher asks you to decide on a specific water resource (a city well, a river, a lake, and so on) and then examine its use and misuse.

2. **Searching for Topics . . .** To begin, review your class text and notebook for writing ideas. Also talk with your classmates about the assignment, or write about "water resources" in a journal to see what you can discover. Your teacher may also suggest some helpful sources of information.

Sample Cluster

Consider using a cluster (or web) to organize your ideas. Write the general subject in the center; then cluster ideas (possible topics) around it.

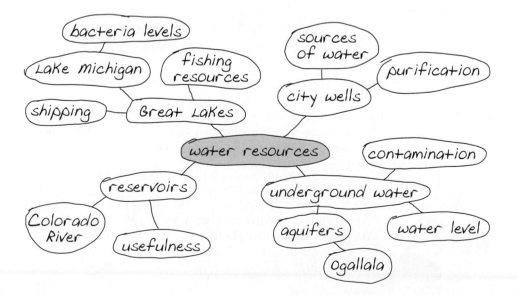

3. **Evaluating a Possible Topic ...** If you can answer *yes* to each of the following questions, your topic is probably worth exploring:

- Am I truly interested in the topic?
- Does it meet the requirements of the assignment?
- Do I have access to enough information?
- Is the topic limited enough?

The last question is very important. You couldn't, for example, write a research paper about "underground water." Where would you begin or end? Nor could you write about "aquifers" (a source of underground water). The topic is still too general. However, the "Ogallala Aquifer" would be a topic limited enough to cover adequately in a research paper.

4. **Focusing Your Efforts ...** If necessary, do some general research to learn more about your specific topic. (This may include talking to others.) Then decide on a focus for your research—something that truly interests you about the topic. The chart below shows how this selecting process works.

THE SELECTING PROCESS

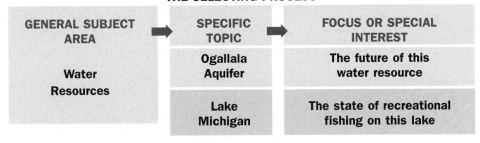

GENERAL SUBJECT AREA	SPECIFIC TOPIC	FOCUS OR SPECIAL INTEREST
Water Resources	Ogallala Aquifer	The future of this water resource
	Lake Michigan	The state of recreational fishing on this lake

5. **Writing a Thesis Statement ...** Once you have discovered what truly interests you about your topic, you are ready to write a thesis statement. This sentence serves as the controlling idea for your research, and it expresses what you believe your research will prove. (See the next page for guidelines and samples. Then see page 268 for "Prewriting, Searching for Information.")

Take NOTE

At this point, you are writing a working thesis statement. As you learn more about your topic, you may change your mind about it. Then you can revise your thesis accordingly.

TIPS for Writing a Thesis Statement

An effective thesis statement tells readers specifically what you plan to write about in your paper. It also serves as a personal guide to keep you on track as you research your topic.

The Process at Work

A thesis statement usually takes a stand or expresses a specific feeling or feature of your topic. Write as many versions as it takes to hit upon the one that sets the right tone for your writing. The following formula can be used to form your thesis statement:

> **A specific topic** *(The Ogallala Aquifer)*
> **+ a particular stand, feeling, or feature** *(is in jeopardy unless the use of irrigation changes)*
> _____
> **= an effective thesis statement.**

Sample Thesis Statements

Writing Assignment:	Research paper about a social issue
Specific Subject:	Homeless people
Thesis Statement:	Who are the homeless **(topic)**, and what are the reasons for their predicament **(particular feature)**?
Writing Assignment:	Research paper about human growth and development
Specific Subject:	Personality traits
Thesis Statement:	An individual's peer group **(particular stand)** shapes certain personality traits **(topic)**.
Writing Assignment:	Analysis of a novel
Specific Subject:	*Frankenstein* by Mary Shelley
Thesis Statement:	Mary Shelley's novel *Frankenstein* **(topic)** focuses on the theme of friendship **(particular feature)**.

Thesis Checklist

Make sure that your thesis statement . . .

____ **identifies a limited, specific topic,**

____ **focuses on a particular feature or feeling about the topic,**

____ **is stated in a clear sentence (or sentences),**

____ **can be supported with convincing facts and details, and**

____ **meets the requirements of the assignment.**

■ **PREWRITING**

Searching for Information

6. **Preparing a Preliminary Bibliography . . .** Look for a wide variety of resources related to your thesis statement by talking to others, searching the library, and checking the Internet.

   ■ Keep track of your sources on your computer or on index cards.

   ■ Arrange your sources alphabetically by the author's last name.

   ■ Number each entry in your computer list, or number each card in the upper right-hand corner.

Sample Bibliography Card

Sample Note Card

Lewis, Jack. "The Ogallala Aquifer: ②
An underground Sea."
~~~~ Journal Nov/Dec 1990; 42
ⅰburg Public Library
p://www.ebscohost.com>
11/5/2000

Depletion of the aquifer—the problem ②
 -11 percent of water pumped
  out since 1930
 -more than 170,000 weeks
  "sucking it dry"
 -some wells in CO, KS, and TX
  already dry

7. **Taking Notes . . .** As you conduct your research, take notes and write out quotations related to your thesis. (See page 280 for more information.)

   ■ Keep notes on cards of the same size and style (four-by-six-inch cards are recommended).

   ■ Record important details, along with the page numbers where this information can be found. Also place the number of the related bibliography card in the upper right-hand corner.

   ■ Place quotation marks around word-for-word quotations.

   ■ Use an ellipsis (. . .) when you leave words out of a quotation. (See page 505.) Use brackets around words you add to quotations.

   ■ Look up unfamiliar words. If you find that a particular word is important, copy its definition onto the same note card.

   ■ Give each card a descriptive heading: *Depletion of the aquifer— the problem).*

Searching TIPS

To help organize your research and note taking, try writing some basic questions you would like to answer in your report. Any time you find information that answers a question, take notes on it.

Sample Questions

1. What is an aquifer?
2. What is the Ogallala Aquifer?
3. How did the Ogallala Aquifer come to exist?
4. Who uses the aquifer water?
5. How does center-pivot irrigation work?
6. Why is irrigation necessary?

8. **Using Primary Sources . . .** Collect as much firsthand information as possible. Consider writing letters to experts, distributing surveys, conducting interviews, and so on. (See pages 340–341 and 344–346 for help.)

■ **PREWRITING**

Designing a Writing Plan

9. **Organizing Your Research . . .** Arrange your note cards into their most logical order; then use them to construct a writing plan (which lists in order or outlines the main points you want to cover in your paper). Use the headings on your note cards or your list of searching questions to form your writing-plan list. Here is a plan for the sample research paper in this handbook. (See pages 300–307.)

Sample Writing Plan

1. Introduction--presents topic and thesis
2. Background and history of the Ogallala Aquifer
3. Problems with current water use
4. The impact of center-pivot irrigation
5. Changing farm practices
6. Applying new technologies
7. Conclusion--summing up main points

10. **Continuing Your Research . . .** Search for any additional information that may be needed to develop your thesis. Revise your thesis if learning more about the topic has changed your mind about it. Also revise your writing plan, if necessary, as you continue your research.

"When you're writing nonfiction, there's no use getting into a writing schedule until you've done the [research] and you have the material."

—Tom Wolfe

■ WRITING THE FIRST DRAFT

1. **Developing Your Introduction . . .** Your introduction should do two things. The first part should say something interesting, surprising, or important about the topic to gain the reader's attention. (See the list below for ideas.) The second part should identify the thesis of your research. (See page 55 for a sample introductory paragraph.)

   - Start with a revealing story or quotation.
   - Give important background information.
   - Offer a series of interesting or surprising facts.
   - Provide important definitions.
   - State your reason for choosing this topic.

2. **Writing the Body . . .** The next step is to write the main part of your research paper, the part that supports or proves your thesis. There are two ways to proceed. You can write freely as ideas come to mind, or you can work systematically, carefully following your notes and writing plan.

Writing Freely To proceed in this way, put your writing plan and note cards aside, and write as much as you can on your own. Refer to your note cards only when you need a quotation, specific facts, or figures.

After you have completed this first writing, review your plan and your note cards to see if you have missed or misplaced any important points. Then continue writing, filling in or reorganizing ideas as you go along.

Writing Systematically To work in a systematic fashion, carefully follow your writing plan and note cards right from the start. Begin by laying out the first section of note cards (those covering the first main point in your plan). Then write a general statement that covers the first main point. Using the note cards you have in front of you, add supporting facts and details. Repeat this process until you have dealt with all the main points in your plan.

Writing TIPS

- Use your own words as much as possible. Include the ideas of others (paraphrases) or direct quotations only when they add significant support to your thesis. (See pages 275–280.)

- Present your ideas honestly and clearly. If you feel strongly about your research and have something meaningful to say, you are more likely to write an interesting paper.

- Keep your readers in mind. What do they already know about your subject? What do they need to know? How can you keep their interest?

- Work to achieve a formal to semiformal style. Avoid fragments, abbreviations, informal expressions, and slang.

- Present only ideas that you can support with facts and details.

3. **Writing the Conclusion . . .** The final section of your paper should leave readers with a clear understanding of the importance of your research. Summarize the main points you have made and draw a final conclusion. In a more personal approach, you may discuss how your research has strengthened or changed your thinking about your topic. (See page 58 for a sample concluding paragraph.)

■ REVISING

1. **Improving Your Writing . . .** Expect to make many changes in your first draft before it says what you want it to say. Make sure that your introduction gains your reader's attention and identifies your thesis, that each paragraph in the body develops a main point about your topic, and that your conclusion ties everything together.

[HOT LINK] See "Assessment Rubric," page 308, for a helpful revising and editing guide.

2. **Seeking Advice . . .** Have at least one person (writing peer, teacher, family member) review your first draft. Share any concerns you have about your writing. Ask this person if he or she found any parts confusing or if they have any questions. (See pages 73-78.)

3. **Documenting Your Sources . . .** Give credit in your paper for ideas and direct quotations that you have used from different sources. In addition, put the works-cited section together, listing all of the sources you have cited in your paper. (See pages 281-298 for MLA guidelines and pages 309–319 for APA guidelines.)

"Punctuation marks are the road signs
that guide the reader." —Patricia T. O'Connor

■ EDITING AND PROOFREADING

1. **Checking for Accuracy . . .** Carefully edit your revised writing for accuracy. First, make sure that your documentation is accurate. Then check your work for spelling, grammar, and punctuation errors.

MLA or APA Documentation Style

Pages 281-298 provide formatting guidelines following MLA (Modern Language Association) documentation style. The guidelines for APA (American Psychological Association) begin on page 309.

2. **Completing Your Final Copy . . .** If you use a computer, print your final copy on good-quality paper. Do not justify your right margins. Leave a one-inch margin on all sides. Double-space your entire paper, including long quotations and the works-cited section.

   Number your pages beginning with the first page of your paper and continue through the works-cited section. Type your last name before each page number. Place the page numbers in the upper right-hand corner, one-half inch from the top and even with the right-hand margin. (See pages 300-307 for a sample final copy.)

3. **Adding Identifying Information . . .** Type your name, the name of the instructor, the course title, and the date in the upper left-hand corner of the first page of the paper. (Begin one inch from the top and double-space throughout.) Center the title (double-space before and after); then type the first line of the paper. (See page 301.)

4. **Proofreading Your Final Copy . . .** Check the final draft from beginning to end for errors. When you submit your research paper, it should be as error-free as you can possibly make it.

┌HELP FILE

If your teacher requires a title page, center the title one-third of the way down from the top of the page; then center your name, the name of your teacher, and any additional information two-thirds of the way down. If you need to submit a final outline, make sure it follows the final version of your paper. (See page 300.)

> "Everyone has a right to an opinion,
> but no one has a right to be wrong
> about the facts."
>
> —Anonymous

Writing RESPONSIBLY

Philosopher Kenneth Burke describes life as an unending conversation. Each of us arrives on the scene long after the conversation has begun. We listen awhile to gain a sense of the discussion. Eventually, we speak our own thoughts. Some people agree with us; others disagree, and we refine our statements accordingly. Others may take up what we have said and make their own statements about it. In this way, the conversation goes on.

The research paper is a smaller model of that process. After choosing a topic, you research to find what others have said about it. As you learn, you pose new questions that lead to further research. Eventually you present your understanding in a paper, crediting those people whose ideas influenced your own.

Giving credit is more than just a matter of being fair. It also lends authority to your writing, and it gives readers the opportunity to consult those sources for themselves so that they can further their own understanding. In other words, by citing your sources, you place your thoughts firmly within the ongoing conversation of life.

Preview

- **Using Sources**
- **Avoiding Plagiarism**
- **Examples of Plagiarism**
- **Writing Paraphrases**
- **Sample Paraphrases**
- **Using Quoted Material**

Using Sources

What does *research* mean? Simply put, research means "searching out answers to your questions."

Beginning Your Research

- **Start early.** Give yourself plenty of time to do your research project. The sooner you start, the more you can relax and enjoy the process, and the easier it will be to find sources.
- **Consider your topic.** What do you already know about your topic? If you had to write your paper right now, what would you write?
- **Ask questions.** What do you wonder about your topic? Make a list of questions; then think about sources for finding answers.
- **Begin with the basics.** For most topics, an encyclopedia or Web search will turn up basic information. Use these sources to get an overview.

Reflecting on Your Research

- **Think about what you have read.** How has your initial research affected your thinking about the topic?
- **Ask more questions.** What new, more informed questions do you have as a result of your reading?
- **Refine your topic, if necessary.** What new ideas occur to you regarding the topic? Do you need to adjust your topic?

Doing Further Research

- **Focus your efforts.** Look for more answers to your informed questions.
- **Use the best sources.** Look for trustworthy books, periodicals, and Web pages that specifically answer your questions. Also, remember to consider using personal surveys, interviews, and letters to experts.

Presenting Your Results

- **Make the topic your own.** Your research paper should not just repeat other people's ideas. First and foremost, it should present your own thoughts and understanding of the topic.
- **Paraphrase or quote appropriately.** To support your ideas, paraphrase or quote credible sources as needed. But remember: References to other sources should be used to enhance or support your own thinking. (See page 420.)
- **Credit your sources.** Let your reader know the source of each idea you summarize or quote.

Avoiding Plagiarism

You owe it to your sources and your readers to give credit for anyone else's ideas or words that you use in your research paper. If you don't, you may be guilty of *plagiarism*—the act of presenting someone else's ideas as your own. (See pages 276-277 for examples.)

Forms of Plagiarism

- **Submitting another writer's paper:** The most blatant form of plagiarism is to put your name on someone else's work (another student's paper, an essay bought from a "paper mill," the text of an article from the Internet, and so on) and turn it in as your own.

- **Using copy-and-paste:** It is unethical to copy phrases, sentences, or larger sections from a source and paste them into your paper without giving credit for the material. Even if you change a few words, this is still plagiarism.

- **Neglecting necessary quotation marks:** Whether it's just a phrase or a larger section of text, if you use the exact words of a source, they must be put in quotation marks and identified with a citation.

- **Paraphrasing without citing a source:** Paraphrasing (rephrasing ideas in your own words) is an important research skill. However, paraphrased ideas must be credited to the source, even if you reword the material entirely.

- **Confusing borrowed material with your own ideas:** While taking research notes, it is important to identify the source of each idea you record. That way, you won't forget whom to credit as you write your paper.

Other Source Abuses

- **Using sources inaccurately:** Make certain that your quotation or paraphrase accurately reflects the meaning of the original. Do not misrepresent the original author's intent.

- **Overusing source material:** Your paper should be primarily your words and thoughts, supported by outside sources. If you simply string together quotations and paraphrases, your voice will be lost.

- **"Plunking" source material:** When you write, smoothly incorporate any information from an outside source. Dropping in or "plunking" a quotation or paraphrased idea without comment makes your writing seem choppy and disconnected.

- **Relying too heavily on one source:** If your writing is dominated by one source, readers may doubt the depth and integrity of your research.

Original Article

The excerpt below about the Ogallala Aquifer is an original source article. Take note of the examples of plagiarism that follow the article.

Ancient Water for the Future by James Stator

The Ogallala Aquifer has helped transform the Great Plains states into a great agricultural region. The aquifer is a huge, natural underground reservoir that extends through most of the Plains states. These states experience very little rainfall compared to other parts of the country, and without irrigation, they could not support agriculture. **Thanks to the Ogallala, farmers can make a living in this semiarid region, producing beef and grain in record amounts.** How important is the aquifer to the country? The United States Department of Agriculture estimates that 65 percent of all irrigated land in the country is supplied by that aquifer.

For some time, scientists have worried about the Ogallala Aquifer. This great water system has been tapped beyond its capacity to replenish itself, and as a result, the aquifer has shrunk drastically. According to _Choices_, a farm magazine, the Ogallala showed significant losses as early as the 1970s, which forced policy makers to figure out how this limited resource can be properly used and conserved.

The aquifer directly provides water for every aspect of life on the Great Plains. The Docking Institute of Public Affairs in 2001 found that current practices take too much water from the Ogallala. For example, the institute noted that in one year Kansas pumped 2 million more acre-feet from the aquifer than was replaced by rain. The rain and snow that renew the aquifer cannot keep up with the demands of modern irrigation and growing cities.

Farmers are worried. They appreciate how important the aquifer is to life on the Great Plains. Farmers know their livelihood is at risk, so they have found ways to cut back their use of water from the Ogallala. Rotation of crops and new irrigation methods have reduced water loss due to evaporation. The Department of Agriculture has determined that water levels have not dropped as rapidly as was predicted. Unfortunately, conservation is not a simple matter. More and more people are living in the aquifer states, and they need water as well. In addition, demands by other western cities ultimately impact the amount of water available to replenish the Ogallala. A collapse of the aquifer would be a serious blow to the vast agricultural enterprise as well as a devastating shock to water-starved cities. . . .

Examples of Plagiarism

Below are the three common types of plagiarism, sometimes committed on purpose and sometimes by accident. The plagiarized text is shown in bold type.

Using copy-and-paste

■ In this sample, the writer pastes in two sentences from the original article without using quotation marks or a citation.

The Plains states in the country are typically flat and dry, but **the Ogallala Aquifer has helped transform the Great Plains states into a great agricultural region. Thanks to the Ogallala, farmers can make a living in this semiarid region, producing beef and grain in record amounts.** The aquifer allows farmers in the United States to export food to the world. That's one reason why the Great Plains became known as the

Paraphrasing without citing a source

■ Below the writer accurately paraphrases (restates) a passage from the original article, but she includes no citation.

Since the 1970s, researchers have been concerned about the alarming depletion of the Ogallala. State agricultural experts have scrambled to see how to save the great aquifer. Too many demands on the Ogallala have overwhelmed the capacity to replenish this magnificent reservoir.

Neglecting necessary quotation marks

■ In the sample below, the writer cites the source of the exact words that she uses from the original article, but she doesn't enclose these words in quotation marks.

In the early days of irrigation, crops were bountiful, and everyone was pleased. Today, things are different. In "Ancient Water for the Future," James Stator states that **farmers are worried. They appreciate how important the aquifer is to life on the Great Plains. Farmers know their livelihood is at risk, so they have found ways to cut back their use of water from the Ogallala.** These farmers realize that they cannot afford to lose this life-giving source of water.

Writing Paraphrases

There are two ways to share information from another source: (1) quote the source directly, or (2) paraphrase the source. When you quote directly, you include the exact words of the author and put quotation marks around them. When you paraphrase, you use your own words to restate someone else's ideas. In either case, you must cite your source. To paraphrase, follow the steps below.

1. **Skim the selection first** to get the overall meaning.

2. **Read the selection carefully;** pay attention to key words and phrases.

3. **List the main ideas** on a piece of paper, without looking at the selection.

4. **Review the selection** again.

5. **Write your paraphrase;** restate the author's ideas in your own words.
   - Stick to the essential information (drop anecdotes and details).
   - State each important idea clearly and concisely.
   - Put quotation marks around ideas taken directly from the source.
   - Arrange the ideas into a smooth, logical order.

6. **Check your paraphrase** for accuracy by asking these questions:
   - Have I kept the author's ideas and viewpoints clear in my paraphrase? Have I quoted where necessary?
   - Have I cut out enough of the original? Too much?
   - Could another person understand the author's main idea by reading my paraphrase?

HELP FILE

A *quotation*, a *paraphrase*, and a *summary* are all ways of referencing a source.

Quoting: A quotation states the words of a source exactly. Quoting should be used sparingly in a research paper so that your writing doesn't sound like a patchwork of other people's statements. Use a quotation only when the exact words of the source are essential.

Paraphrasing: In a paraphrase, you recast an idea from a source into your own words. Paraphrasing demonstrates that you understand the idea, and it maintains your voice within your paper. In a research paper, paraphrasing is more commonly used than quoting or summarizing.

Summarizing: A summary is a condensed version of an entire source. In a research paper, there is seldom any need to summarize an entire work unless that work is the subject of the paper. For example, you might summarize the plot of *King Lear* in a research paper about that play.

Sample Paraphrases

Following the original passage below from a book by Travis Taylor, you'll find two sample paraphrases, both properly cited.

ORIGINAL PASSAGE

Kyudo, which means "the way of the bow" in Japanese, is the Zen martial art of archery. It was adapted into traditional Buddhist practice from medieval Japanese archers who used seven-foot asymmetrical bows called yumi. Although kyudo lacks the widespread popularity of karate or judo, it is often regarded as one of the most intensive martial arts in existence, taking an estimated 30 years to master.

The standard execution of kyudo involves a series of specific actions, including assuming the proper posture, approaching the intended target, nocking the arrow, drawing it, releasing it, and then repeating the process. After the second arrow has been released, the archer approaches the target, withdraws the arrows, and thus completes the exercise.

There is far more to kyudo, however, than simply shooting arrows. For every movement, the archer must maintain a specific posture, inhaling and exhaling at predetermined points throughout the exercise. The repetitive action and deep breathing greatly relaxes the archer—heightening his alertness and lowering his stress.

BASIC PARAPHRASE WITH QUOTATION

Kyudo is the Zen martial art of archery. It was adapted from medieval traditional Japanese archery into a spiritual and physical exercise. "The standard execution of kyudo involves a series of specific actions, including assuming the proper posture, approaching the intended target, nocking the arrow, drawing it, [and] releasing it . . . " (Taylor 26). An archer's sense of balance comes from focused breathing and balanced posture, which lessen stress and increase the archer's ability to concentrate (Taylor 26).

BASIC PARAPHRASE

Kyudo is the Zen martial art of archery. It was adapted from medieval Japanese archery into a spiritual and physical exercise. Through a series of specific actions, the archer prepares and shoots an arrow into a target and then repeats the action one more time. The archer's sense of balance comes from focused breathing and balanced posture, which lessen stress and increase the archer's ability to concentrate (Taylor 26).

Using Quoted Material

A quotation can be a single word or an entire paragraph. Choose quotations carefully, keep them as brief as possible, and use them only when they are necessary. When you do quote material directly, be sure that the capitalization, punctuation, and spelling are the same as that in the original work. Clearly mark changes for your readers: (1) changes within the quotation are enclosed in brackets [like this]; (2) explanations are enclosed in parentheses at the end of the quotation before closing punctuation (like this).

Short Quotations

If a quotation is four typed lines or fewer, work it into the body of your paper and put quotation marks around it.

Long Quotations

Quotations of more than four typed lines (MLA) or more than 40 words (APA) should be set off from the rest of the writing by indenting each line one inch (MLA) and double-spacing the material. When quoting two or more paragraphs, indent the first line of each paragraph one-fourth inch (MLA). (See "In-Text Citations" on page 310 for APA rules about long quotations.) Do not use quotation marks for set-off quotations. (See page 501.)

NOTE: Place the parenthetical reference after the final punctuation mark of the quotation. Generally, a colon is used to introduce quotations set off from the text. (See page 495.1.)

Quoting Poetry

When quoting up to three lines of poetry (or lyrics), use quotation marks and work the lines into your writing. Use a diagonal (/) to show where each line of the poem ends. For quotations of four lines or more, indent each line 10 spaces (and double-space the same as the rest of the text). Do not use quotation marks.

NOTE: To show that you have left out a line or more of verse in a longer quotation, make a line of spaced periods the approximate length of a complete line of the poem.

Partial Quotations

If you want to leave out part of the quotation, use an ellipsis to signify the omission. An ellipsis (. . .) is three periods with a space before and after each one. (See page 505.)

NOTE: Anything you take out of a quotation should not change the author's original meaning.

"Adam was the only man who, when he said
a good thing, knew that nobody had said it
before him."
                                        —Mark Twain

MLA Documentation Style

Most academic disciplines have their own manuals of style for
research paper documentation. The Modern Language Association style
manual (*MLA Handbook for Writers of Research Papers*), for example,
is widely used in the humanities (literature, philosophy, history, etc.),
making it the most popular manual in high school and college writing
courses.

This chapter will provide you with guidelines for citing sources
according to the MLA style manual. Included is a special section on citing
sources from the Internet, including a Web-site address for obtaining
updated information. (For complete information about the MLA style,
refer to the latest version of the *MLA Handbook*.)

Preview

- Citing Sources: In-Text Citations
- MLA Works-Cited List: Overview
- Works-Cited Entries: Books
- Works-Cited Entries: Periodicals
- Works-Cited Entries: Online Sources
- Works-Cited Entries: Other Sources

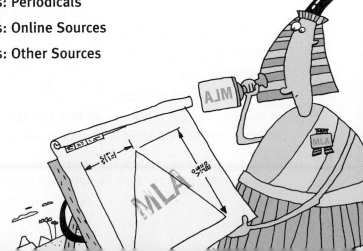

Citing Sources

Guidelines for In-Text Citations

The simplest way to credit a source is to insert the information (usually the author and page number) in parentheses after the words or ideas taken from that source. These in-text citations (often called "parenthetical references") refer to the "Works Cited" page at the end of your paper. (See page 307.)

Points to Remember

- Make sure each in-text citation clearly points to an entry in your list of works cited. Use the word or words by which the entry is alphabetized.
- Keep citations brief and integrate them into your writing.
- When paraphrasing rather than quoting, make it clear where your borrowing begins and ends. Use stylistic cues to distinguish the source's thoughts ("Kalmbach points out . . .") from your own ("I believe . . .").
- For inclusive page numbers larger than ninety-nine, give only the two digits of the second number (113–14, not 113–114).
- At the end of a sentence, place your parenthetical citation before the end punctuation.
- For titles, use italics.

Model In-Text Citations

One Author: A Complete Work

You must give the author's last name in a parenthetical citation unless it is already mentioned in the text. An in-text citation could name an editor, a translator, a speaker, or an artist instead if that is how the entry is listed in the works cited.

WITH AUTHOR IN TEXT (This is the preferred method.)

In *No Need for Hunger*, Robert Spitzer recommends that the U.S. government develop a new foreign policy to help Third World countries overcome poverty.

WITHOUT AUTHOR IN TEXT

No Need for Hunger recommends that the U.S. government develop a new foreign policy to help Third World countries overcome poverty (Spitzer).

NOTE Do not offer page numbers when citing complete works, articles in alphabetized encyclopedias, one-page articles, and unpaginated sources.

One Author: Part of a Work

List the necessary page numbers in parentheses if you borrow words or ideas from a particular source. Leave a space between the author's last name and the page reference. No abbreviation or punctuation is needed.

WITH AUTHOR IN TEXT

Bullough writes that genetic engineering was dubbed "eugenics" by a cousin of Darwin's, Sir Francis Galton, in 1885 (5).

WITHOUT AUTHOR IN TEXT

Genetic engineering was dubbed "eugenics" by a cousin of Darwin's, Sir Francis Galton, in 1885 (Bullough 5).

Two or More Works by the Same Author(s)

In addition to the author's last name(s) and page number(s), include a shortened version of the title of the work when you are citing two or more works by the same author(s).

WITH AUTHOR IN TEXT

Wallerstein and Blakeslee claim that divorce creates an enduring identity for children of the marriage (*Unexpected Legacy* 62).

WITHOUT AUTHOR IN TEXT

They are intensely lonely despite active social lives (Wallerstein and Blakeslee, *Second Chances* 51).

NOTE When including both author(s) and title in a parenthetical reference, separate them with a comma, as shown above.

A Work by Two or Three Authors

Give the last names of every author in the same order that they appear in the works-cited section. (The correct order of the authors' names can be found on the title page of the book.)

Students learned more than a full year's Spanish in ten days using the complete supermemory method (Ostrander and Schroeder 51).

A Work by Four or More Authors

Give the first author's last name as it appears in the works-cited section followed by *et al.* (meaning *and others*).

Communication on the job is more than talking; it is "inseparable from your total behavior" (Culligan et al. 111).

A Work Authored by an Agency, a Committee, or Another Organization

If a book or other work was written by an organization, it is said to have a *corporate author*. If the corporate name is long, include it in the text to avoid disrupting the flow of your writing. After the full name has been used at least once, use a shortened form in subsequent references. For example, *Task Force* may be used for *Task Force on Education for Economic Growth*.

> **The thesis of the Task Force's report is that economic success depends on our ability to improve large-scale education and training (113–14).**

An Anonymous Work

When there is no author listed, give the title or a shortened version of the title as it appears in the works-cited section.

> **Statistics indicate that drinking water can make up 20 percent of a person's total exposure to lead (*Information* 572).**

Two or More Works Included in One Citation

To cite multiple works within a single parenthetical reference, separate the references with a semicolon.

> **In Medieval Europe, Latin translations of the works of Rhazes, a Persian scholar, were a source of medical knowledge (Albala 22; Lewis 266).**

A Work Referred to in Another Work

If you must cite an indirect source—that is, information from a source that is quoted from another source—use the abbreviation *qtd. in* (quoted in) before the indirect source in your reference.

> **Paton improved the conditions in Diepkloof (a prison) by "removing all the more obvious aids to detention. The dormitories are open at night: the great barred gate is gone" (qtd. in Callan xviii).**

Quoting Verse

Do not use page numbers when referencing classic verse plays and poems. Instead, cite them by division (act, scene, canto, book, part) and line, using Arabic numerals for the various divisions unless your instructor prefers Roman numerals. Use periods to separate the various numbers.

> **In the first act of the play named after him, Hamlet comments, "How weary, stale, flat and unprofitable, / Seem to me all the uses of this world" (1.2.133–134).**

NOTE A slash, with a space on each side, shows where a new line of verse begins.

Quoting Verse *(continued)*

If you are citing lines only, use the word *line* or *lines* in your first reference and numbers only in additional references.

> In book five of Homer's *Iliad,* the Trojans' fear is evident: "The Trojans were scared when they saw the two sons of Dares, one of them in fright and the other lying dead by his chariot" (lines 22–24).

Verse quotations of more than three lines should be indented one inch (ten spaces). Do not add quotation marks. Each line of the poem or play begins a new line of the quotation.

> In "Song of Myself" poet Walt Whitman claims to belong to everyone:
>> I am of old and young, of the foolish as much as the wise,
>> Regardless of others, ever regardful of others,
>> Maternal as well as paternal, a child as well as a man,
>> Stuffed with the stuff that is coarse, and stuffed with the stuff
>>> that is fine, . . . (16:326–329)

Quoting Prose

To cite prose from fiction, list more than the page number if the work is available in several editions. Give the page reference first, and then add a chapter, section, or book number, if appropriate.

> In *The House of the Spirits*, Isabel Allende describes Marcos, "dressed in mechanic's overalls, with huge racer's goggles and an explorer's helmet" (13; ch. 1).

When you are quoting any sort of prose that takes more than four typed lines, indent each line of the quotation one inch (ten spaces) and double-space it; do not add quotation marks. In this case, you put the parenthetical citation (the pages and chapter numbers) outside the end punctuation mark of the quotation itself. (See "Long Quotations" on page 280.)

> Allende describes the flying machine that Marcos has assembled:
>> The contraption lay with its stomach on terra firma, heavy and sluggish and looking more like a wounded duck than like one of those newfangled airplanes they were starting to produce in the United States. There was nothing in its appearance to suggest that it could move, much less take flight across the snowy peaks. (12; ch. 1)

MLA Works-Cited List: Overview

The works-cited section lists all of the sources you have referred to in your text. It does not include sources you may have read but did not refer to in your paper. Begin your list on a new page and number each page. The guidelines that follow describe the form of the works-cited section.

1. Type the page number in the upper-right corner, one-half inch from the top of the page, with your last name before it.
2. Center the title *Works Cited* (not in italics) one inch from the top; then double-space before the first entry.
3. Begin each entry flush with the left margin. If the entry runs more than one line, indent additional lines one-half inch (five spaces) or use the hanging indent function on your computer.
4. Double-space lines within each entry and between entries.
5. List each entry alphabetically by author's last name. If there is no author, use the first word of the title (disregard *A, An, The*).
6. Identify the medium of publication for each work (Print, Web, Television, DVD, etc.).

   ■ A basic entry for a book would be as follows:

   Author's last name, First name. *Book Title.* **City: Publisher, date. Medium.**

   Opie, John. *Ogallala: Water for a Dry Land.* **Lincoln: U of Nebraska P, 1993. Print.**

   NOTE: Use a single space after all punctuation in a works-cited entry.

   ■ A basic entry for a periodical would be as follows:

   Author's last name, First name. "Article Title." *Periodical Title* **date: page nos. Medium.**

   Stearns, Denise Heffernan. "Testing by Design." *Middle Ground* **Oct. 2000: 21–25. Print.**

   ■ A basic entry for an online entry would be as follows:

   Author's last name, First name. "Title." *Site Title.* **Site Sponsor. Date of posting or last update. Medium. Date accessed.**

   Tenenbaum, David. "Dust Never Sleeps." *The Why Files.* **U of Wisconsin, Board of Regents. 28 July 1999. Web. 26 April 2010.**

   NOTE: In online entries, include the URL (after the date accessed) only if your reader cannot find the source without it.

Works-Cited Entries: Books

The entries that follow illustrate the information needed to cite books, sections of a book, pamphlets, and government publications. The possible components of these entries are listed in order below:

1. **Author's name**
2. **Title of a part of the book** (an article in the book or a foreword)
3. **Title of the book**
4. **Name of editor or translator**
5. **Edition**
6. **Number of volume**
7. **Name of series**
8. **Place of publication, publisher, year of publication**
9. **Page numbers** (if citation is to only a part of the work)
10. **Medium** ("Print.")

NOTE In general, if any of these components do not apply, they are not included in the works-cited entry. However, in the rare instance that a book does not state publication information, use the following abbreviations in place of information you cannot supply:

n.p.	No place of publication given
n.p.	No publisher given
n.d.	No date of publication given
n. pag.	No pagination given

Additional Guidelines

■ List only the city for the place of publication. If several cities are listed, give only the first.

■ Additionally, note that publishers' names should be shortened by omitting articles (*a, an, the*), business abbreviations (Co., Inc.), and descriptive words (Books, Press). Cite the surname alone if the publisher's name includes the name of one person. If it includes the names of more than one person, cite only the first of the surnames. Abbreviate University Press as UP. Also use standard abbreviations whenever possible. (See pages 513 and 514.)

A Work by One Author

> Baghwati, Jagdish. *In Defense of Globalization*. New York: Oxford UP,
>   2004. Print.

Two or More Books by the Same Author

List the books alphabetically according to title. After the first entry,
substitute three hyphens for the author's name.

> Dershowitz, Alan M. *Rights from Wrongs*. New York: Basic Books, 2005.
>   Print.
>
> ---. *Supreme Injustice: How the High Court Hijacked Election 2000*.
>   Oxford: Oxford UP, 2001. Print.

A Work by Two or Three Authors

> Haynes, John Earl, and Harvey Klehr. *In Denial: Historians, Communism, &*
>   *Espionage*. San Francisco: Encounter Books, 2003. Print.

NOTE List the authors in the same order as they appear on the title page.
Reverse only the name of the first author.

A Work by Four or More Authors

> Schulte-Peevers, Andrea, et al. *Germany*. Victoria: Lonely Planet, 2000.
>   Print.

A Work Authored by an Agency, a Committee, or Another Organization

> Exxon Mobil Corporation. *Great Plains 2000*. Lincolnwood: Publications
>   Intl., 2001. Print.

An Anonymous Book

> *Chase's Calendar of Events 2002*. Chicago: Contemporary, 2002. Print.

A Single Work from an Anthology

> Mitchell, Joseph. "The Bottom of the Harbor." *American Sea Writing*.
>   Ed. Peter Neill. New York: Library of America, 2000. 584–608. Print.

Two or More Works from the Same Anthology or Collection

Cite the collection once with complete publication information (see *Forbes*
below). Then cite individual entries (see *Joseph* below) by listing the author,
title of the piece, editor of the collection, and page numbers.

> Forbes, Peter, ed. *Scanning the Century*. London: Penguin, 2000. Print.
> Joseph, Jenny. "Warning." Forbes 335–36.

One Volume of a Multivolume Work

Cooke, Jacob Ernest, and Milton M. Klein, eds. *North America in Colonial Times*. Vol. 2. New York: Scribner's, 1998. Print.

NOTE If you cite two or more volumes in a multivolume work, give the total number of volumes after each title. Offer specific references to volume and page numbers in the parenthetical reference in your text, like this: (8:112–14).

Salzman, Jack, David Lionel Smith, and Cornel West. *Encyclopedia of African-American Culture and History*. 5 vols. New York: Simon, 1996. Print.

An Introduction, a Preface, a Foreword, or an Afterword

To cite the introduction, preface, foreword, or afterword of a book, list the author of the part first. Then identify the part by type, with no quotation marks or underlining, followed by the title of the book. Next, identify the author of the work, using the word *By*. (If the book author and the part's author are the same person, give just the last name after *By*.) For a book that gives cover credit to an editor instead of an author, identify the editor as usual. Finally, list any page numbers for the part being cited.

Barry, Anne. Afterword. *Making Room for Students*. By Celia Oyler. New York: Teachers College, 1996. Print.

Lefebvre, Mark. Foreword. *The Journey Home*. Vol. 1. Ed. Jim Stephens. Madison: North Country, 1989. ix. Print.

Second and Subsequent Edition

An edition refers to the particular publication you are citing, as in the third (3rd) edition.

Joss, Molly W. *Looking Good in Presentations*. 3rd ed. Scottsdale: Coriolis, 1999. Print.

An Edition with Author and Editor

The term *edition* also refers to the work of one person that is prepared by another person, an editor.

Shakespeare, William. *A Midsummer Night's Dream*. Ed. Jane Bachman. Lincolnwood: NTC, 1994. Print.

A Translation

Lebert, Stephan, and Norbert Lebert. *My Father's Keeper*. Trans. Julian Evans. Boston: Little, 2001. Print.

An Article in a Familiar Reference Book

It is not necessary to give full publication information for familiar reference works (encyclopedias, dictionaries). List the edition and publication year. If an article is initialed, check the index of authors for the author's full name.

> **Lum, P. Andrea. "Computed Tomography."** *World Book.* **2000 ed. Print.**

A Government Publication

State the name of the government (country, state, and so on) followed by the name of the agency. Most federal publications are published by the Government Printing Office (GPO).

> **United States. Dept. of Labor. Bureau of Labor Statistics.** *Occupational*
> *Outlook Handbook 2000–2001.* **Washington: GPO, 2000. Print.**

A Book in a Series

Give series name and number (if any) before the publication information.

> **Paradis, Adrian A.** *Opportunities in Military Careers.* **VGM Opportunities**
> **Series. Lincolnwood: VGM Career Horizons, 1999. Print.**

A Book with a Title Within Its Title

If the title contains a title normally in quotation marks, keep the quotation marks and italicize the entire title.

> **Stuckey-French, Elizabeth.** *"The First Paper Girl in Red Oak, Iowa" and*
> *Other Stories.* **New York: Doubleday, 2000. Print.**

If the title contains a title that is normally italicized, do not italicize that title in your entry:

> **Harmetz, Aljean.** *The Making of* **The Wizard of Oz:** *Movie, Magic, and*
> *Studio Power in the Prime of MGM.* **New York: Hyperion, 1998. Print.**

A Pamphlet, Brochure, Manual, or Other Workplace Document

Treat any such publication as you would a book.

> **Grayson, George W.** *The North American Free Trade Agreement.* **New York:**
> **Foreign Policy Assn., 1993. Print.**

If publication information is missing, list the country of publication [in brackets] if known. Use *n.p.* (no place) if the country or the publisher is unknown and *n.d.* if the date is unknown, just as you would for a book.

> *Pedestrian Safety.* **[United States]: n.p., n.d. Print.**

Works-Cited Entries: Periodicals

The possible components of periodical entries are listed in order below:

1. **Author's name**
2. **Title of article** (in quotation marks)
3. **Name of periodical** (italicized)
4. **Series number or name** (if relevant)
5. **Volume number** (for a scholarly journal)
6. **Issue number**
7. **Date of publication** (abbreviate all months but May, June, July)
8. **Page numbers**
9. **Medium** ("Print")

NOTE If any of these components do not apply, they are not listed.

An Article in a Weekly or Biweekly Magazine

List the author (if identified), article title (in quotation marks), publication title (italicized), full date of publication, and page numbers for the article. Do not include volume and issue numbers. End with the medium.

> **Goodell, Jeff. "The Uneasy Assimilation."** *Rolling Stone* **6–13 Dec. 2001: 63–66. Print.**

An Article in a Monthly or Bimonthly Magazine

As for a weekly or biweekly magazine, list the author (if identified), article title (in quotation marks), and publication title (italicized). Then identify the month(s) and year of the issue, followed by page numbers for the article. Do not give volume and issue numbers. End with the medium.

> **"Patent Pamphleteer."** *Scientific American* **Dec. 2001: 33. Print.**

An Article in a Scholarly Journal

Rather than month or full date of publication, scholarly journals are identified by volume number. List the volume number immediately after the journal title, followed by a period and the issue number, and then the year of publication (in parentheses). End with the page numbers of the article, as usual, followed by the medium.

> **Chu, Wujin. "Costs and Benefits of Hard-Sell."** *Journal of Marketing Research* **32.2 (1995): 97–102. Print.**

A Printed Interview

Begin with the name of the person interviewed.

> **Cantwell, Maria. "The New Technocrat." By Erika Rasmusson. *Working Woman* Apr. 2001: 20–21. Print.**

> **NOTE** If the interview is untitled, *Interview* (no italics) follows the interviewee's name.

A Newspaper Article

> **Bleakley, Fred R. "Companies' Profits Grew 48% Despite Economy." *Wall Street Journal* 1 May 1995, Midwest ed.: 1. Print.**

> **NOTE** Cite the edition of a major daily newspaper (if given) after the date (1 May 1995, Midwest ed.: 1). If a local paper's name does not include the city of publication, add it in brackets (not underlined) after the name.

To cite an article in a lettered section of the newspaper, list the section and the page number (A4). If the sections are numbered, however, use a comma after the year (or the edition); then indicate sec. 1, 2, 3, and so on, followed by a colon and the page number (sec. 1:20). An unsigned newspaper article follows the same format:

> **"Bombs—Real and Threatened—Keep Northern Ireland Edgy." *Chicago Tribune* 6 Dec. 2001, sec. 1: 20. Print.**

A Newspaper Editorial

If an article is an editorial, put *Editorial* (no italics) after the title.

> **"Hospital Power." Editorial. *Bangor Daily News* 14 Sept. 2004: A6. Print.**

A Letter to the Editor

To identify a letter to the editor, put *Letter* (no italics) after the author's name.

> **Sory, Forrest. Letter. *Discover* July 2001: 10. Print.**

A Review

Begin with the author (if identified) and title of the review. Use the notation *Rev. of* (no italics) between the title of the review and that of the original work. Identify the author of the original work with the word *by* (no italics). Then follow with publication data for the review.

> Olsen, Jack. "Brains and Industry." Rev. of *Land of Opportunity*, by Sarah
>> Marr. *New York Times* 23 Apr. 1995, sec. 3: 28. Print.

NOTE If you cite the review of a work by an editor or a translator, use *ed.* or *trans.* instead of *by.*

An Unsigned Article in a Periodical

If no author is identified for an article, list the entry alphabetically by title among your works cited (ignoring any initial *A, An,* or *The*).

> "Feeding the Hungry." *Economist*. 371.8374 (2004): 74. Print.

An Article with a Title or Quotation Within Its Title

> Morgenstern, Joe. "Sleeper of the Year: *In the Bedroom* Is Rich Tale of
>> Tragic Love." *Wall Street Journal* 23 Nov. 2001: W1. Print.

NOTE Use single quotation marks around the shorter title if it is a title normally punctuated with quotation marks.

An Article Reprinted in a Loose-Leaf Collection

The entry begins with original publication information and ends with the name of the loose-leaf volume (*Youth*), editor, volume number, publication information including name of the information service (SIRS), and the article number.

> O'Connell, Loraine. "Busy Teens Feel the Beep." *Orlando Sentinel* 7 Jan.
>> 1993: E1+. Print. *Youth*. Ed. Eleanor Goldstein. Vol. 4. Boca Raton:
>> SIRS, 1993. Art. 41.

An Article with Pagination That Is Not Continuous

For articles that are continued on a nonconsecutive page, whatever the publication type, add a plus sign (+) after the first page number.

> Garrett, Robyne. "Negotiating a Physical Identity: Girls, Bodies and
>> Physical Education." *Sport, Education & Society* 9 (2004): 223+.
>> Print.

Works-Cited Entries: Online Sources

Online sources fall into three general categories: Nonperiodical sources (such as common Web sites), scholarly articles published or republished online, and periodicals collected in a database. The following guidelines explain the contents of each type of reference.

Nonperiodical Sources

1. Author's name
2. Title of work, in quotation marks (article or section) or italics (larger work)
3. Title of site (if separate from the work), italicized
4. Version or edition
5. Site sponsor or publisher (or "N.p.")
6. Date of publication (or "n.d.")
7. Medium of publication ("Web")
8. Date of access

NOTE Do not include the URL (Web address) unless your reader cannot find the source without it, or your instructor requires it. In that case, list the URL within angle brackets (< >) after the date of access. If you must break a long URL across lines of text, do so only after a double or single slash, and do not add a double or single hyphen.

Scholarly Articles Published or Republished Online

1. Information for print version (without the medium "Print")
2. Medium of publication ("Web")
3. Date of access

Periodicals in a Database

1. Information for print version (without the medium "Print")
2. Title of database (italicized)
3. Medium of publication ("Web")
4. Date of access

NOTE If no page numbers are available for an article in a database, use the abbreviation "n. pag."

A Personal Site

After the author's name, list the site title (italicized) or a description such as *Home page* or *Online posting* (no italics), whichever is appropriate. Follow with the date of publication or most recent update, if available, the medium, and your date of visit.

> **Mehuron, Kate. Home page. N.p., 30 Sept. 2004. Web. 31 Jan. 2010.**

A Professional Site

Generally, no author is identified for a professional site, so the entry begins with the article site title. Use the copyright date if no date of update is given. Conclude with the medium and your date of access.

> **"Challenges."** *BP Global.* **BP p.l.c., 2005. Web. 17 June 2009.**

An Article in an Online Periodical

Begin with the author's name, the article title in quotation marks, the italicized name of the site, and the date of publication. Include page numbers (or other sections) if numbered. Close with the medium and date of access.

> **Dickerson, John. "Nailing Jello."** *Time.com.* **Time, 5 Nov. 2001. Web. 9 Dec. 2009.**

An Article in an Online Reference Work

Unless the author of the entry is identified, begin with the entry name in quotation marks. Follow with the usual online publication information.

> **"Eakins, Thomas."** *Britannica Online Encyclopedia.* **Encyclopedia Britannica, 2008. Web. 26 Sept. 2009.**

An Article in an Online Service

Begin with the information for the print source, followed by the database name (in italics), the medium, and the date of access.

> **Davis, Jerome. "Massacre in Kiev."** *Washington Post* **29 Nov. 1999, final ed.: C12.** *ProQuest.* **Web. 28 Dec. 2008.**

An Online Governmental Publication

As with a governmental publication in print, begin with the name of the government (country, state, and so on) followed by the name of the agency. After the publication title, add the electronic publication information.

> **United States. Dept. of Labor. Office of Disability Employment Policy.**
> ***Emergency Preparedness for People with Disabilities.* Apr. 2004. Web.**
> **12 Sept. 2009.**

When citing the *Congressional Record,* the date, page numbers, and medium are all that is required.

> ***Cong. Rec.* 5 Feb. 2002: S311–15. Web.**

An Online Multimedia Resource: Painting, Photograph, Musical Composition, Film or Film Clip, Etc.

After the usual information for the type of work being cited, add electronic publication information.

> **Goya, Francisco de. *Saturn Devouring His Children.* 1819-1823. Museo**
> **del Prado, Madrid. Web. 13 Dec. 2009.**

An E-Mail Communication

Identify the author of the e-mail, and then list the subject line of the e-mail as a title, in quotation marks. Next, include a description of the entry, including the recipient—usually *Message to the author* (no italics), meaning you, the author of the paper. Finally, give the date of the message and the medium of delivery.

> **Barzinji, Atman. "Re: Frog Populations in Wisconsin Wetlands." Message**
> **to the author. 1 Jan. 2010. E-Mail.**

Other Sources: Primary, Personal, and Multimedia

The following examples of works-cited entries illustrate how to cite sources such as television or radio programs, films, live performances, works of art, and other miscellaneous nonprint sources.

A Periodically Published Database on CD-ROM, Diskette, or Magnetic Tape

Citations for materials published on CD-ROM, diskette, or magnetic tape are similar to those for print sources, with these added considerations:

1. The publisher and vendor of the publication may be different, in which case both must be identified.

2. Because of periodic updates, multiple versions of the same database may exist, which calls for citation if possible of both the date of the document cited and the date of the database itself.

> "Bunker Hill Monument to Get $3.7M Makeover." *Boston Business Journal* 13 June 2005. CD-ROM. *Business Dateline.* ProQuest. July 2005.

> Malleron, Jean-Luc, and Alain Juin. *Database of Palladium Chemistry.* Version 1.1. Burlington, MA: Academic Press, 2002. CD-ROM.

Computer Software

If you use an encyclopedia or other reference book recorded on disk, use the form below. If available, include publication information for the printed source.

> *Microsoft Encarta Deluxe 2005.* Redmond: Microsoft, 2005. DVD.

A Television or Radio Program

> "Another Atlantis?" *Deep Sea Detectives.* The History Channel. 13 June 2005. Television.

A Film

The director, distributor, and year of release follow the title. Other information may be included if pertinent.

> *The Aviator.* Dir. Martin Scorsese. Perf. Leonardo DiCaprio. Miramax Films, 2004. DVD.

A Video Recording

Cite a filmstrip, slide program, videocassette, or DVD just as you would a film.

> *Beyond the Da Vinci Code.* **A&E Home Video, 2005. DVD.**

An Audio Recording

If you are not citing a CD, indicate LP, Audiocassette, or Audiotape. If you are citing a specific song on a musical recording, place its title in quotation marks before the title of the recording.

> **Welch, Jack.** *Winning.* **Harper Audio, 2005. Audiotape.**

An Interview by the Author (Yourself)

> **Brooks, Sarah. Personal interview. 15 Oct. 2009.**

A Cartoon or Comic Strip (in Print)

> **Luckovich, Mike. "The Drawing Board." Cartoon.** *Time*
> **17 Sept. 2001: 18. Print.**

A Lecture, a Speech, an Address, or a Reading

If there is a title, include it in quotation marks after the speaker's name.

> **Annan, Kofi. Oslo City Hall, Oslo, Norway. 10 Dec. 2001. Lecture.**

A Map or Chart

Follow the format for an anonymous book, adding *Map* or *Chart* (no italics).

> *Wisconsin Territory.* **Map. Madison: Wisconsin Trails, 1988. Print.**

NOTE The availability of information on computer networks can change from day to day, so we strongly recommend that you print out a copy of the material you are accessing. For additional information on citing sources in MLA style, visit our Web site at www.thewritesource.com/mla.htm.

"The guiding question in research
is 'so what?' Answer that question
in every sentence you write."

—Donald W. McClosky

Sample MLA RESEARCH Paper

Meaningful research requires a lot of time to develop because there is so much searching, planning, writing, and revising involved. That is why your teachers assign research projects over an extended period of time. Always follow whatever timetable they give you, and keep time on your side as much as possible. Your teachers know what it takes to develop a worthwhile finished product.

Also take time to preview the sample paper in this chapter. First skim the paper to get an overview of its structure. Then do a careful reading, looking closely at the different parts: title page, outline, introduction, supporting paragraphs, and so on. The side notes, which highlight important features in the paper, will also be helpful as you prepare to write your own research paper.

Preview

- **Title Page and Outline**
- **Sample Research Paper**
- **Assessment Rubric**

Title Page and Outline

MLA style does not require a title page or an outline; however, if you are instructed to include a title page or an outline with your research paper, use the samples below as your guide.

The Ogallala: Preserving the
Great American Desert

Allison De Jong
Mr. Schelhaas
Environmental Science
20 November 2010

TITLE PAGE

Center the title one-third of the way down the page; center author information two-thirds of the way down.

The Ogallala: Preserving the

Great American Desert

Introduction—The Ogallala Aquifer transformed the Great American Desert, but its future is in jeopardy.

  I. Background of the problem

    A. Formation of the Ogallala Aquifer

    B. Explanation of aquifers

    C. Size and location of the Ogallala Aquifer

  II. The nature and extent of the problem

    A. Irrigation depleting the aquifer

    B. Advances in center-pivot irrigation a huge factor

    C. Not everyone wants to conserve

  III. The solution: limited pumping and sustainable farming practices

    A. Positive changes in the last decade

    B. New technologies: gypsum blocks, LEPA

    C. Cooperation and long-term view

Conclusion—For the Ogallala Aquifer to survive, users must change their attitudes and learn to conserve.

RESEARCH PAPER OUTLINE

Center the title one inch from the top of the page. Double-space throughout.

Sample Research Paper

├── 1" ──┤   1"   1/2"   ├── 1" ──┤

De Jong 1

A complete
heading is
provided.

Allison De Jong

Mr. Schelhaas

Environmental Science

20 November 2010

The title is
centered.

The Ogallala: Preserving the
Great American Desert

Long ago, the middle of the North American continent was a
treeless prairie covered by tall grasses and roaming buffalo. When
European settlers came, they called this area the Great American
Desert. Today, this "desert" is covered with fields of wheat,
corn, and alfalfa made possible by center-pivot irrigation. My
grandfather used to sell center-pivot systems, and when my family
drove to my grandparents' home in Nebraska, we would count how
many "sprinklers" were watering each section of land. At the time,
I didn't know that this water was being pumped from something
called the Ogallala Aquifer, a huge underground water supply.
Throughout the years, this aquifer has made the Great American
Desert one of the best farming areas in the world. Unfortunately,
the Ogallala Aquifer's future as a valuable resource is in jeopardy
unless citizens of the Plains states reduce their water consumption.

Double
spacing
is used
throughout
the paper.

The writer
introduces
her subject
and states
her thesis
(in red).

Subheadings
help readers
follow the
organization.

Background of the Problem

To understand why the problem is important, it is necessary
to know some basic facts about the Ogallala Aquifer. This
underground reservoir covers 174,000 square miles. According to
John Opie, author of *Ogallala: Water for a Dry Land*, the Ogallala
was formed over the course of millions of years as the land flooded,
dried out, and flooded again. As centuries passed, glaciers melted,
carrying water, silt, and rocks from the Rockies down to the Great
Plains to form the Ogallala. Dirt, clay, and rocks accumulated

1"

De Jong 2

above it so that the waters of the Ogallala can now be reached at depths of 300 feet beneath the surface (29–35). Some people think that the Ogallala is a huge underground lake, but this idea is wrong. As Erla Zwingle puts it, an aquifer such as the Ogallala is like a "gigantic underground sponge" (83). The water fills in the spaces between the sand, silt, clay, and gravel that make up the Ogallala formation. This gigantic sponge ranges in thickness from one foot to more than 1,000 feet; the average thickness, however, is about 200 feet (Zwingle 85). The aquifer reaches its deepest points under the state of Nebraska, which is not surprising because most of the Ogallala's water lies beneath this state. The rest lies under Colorado, Kansas, New Mexico, Oklahoma, South Dakota, Texas, and Wyoming.

The Ogallala Aquifer is the largest "underground sponge" in the United States. It contains more than 977 trillion gallons, or three billion acre-feet, of water. (An acre-foot is 325,851 gallons, or the amount of water it would take to cover an acre to the depth of one foot.) According to Jack Lewis in the *EPA Journal*, the water contained in the aquifer is enough to fill Lake Huron plus one-fifth of Lake Ontario. "If pumped out over the United States," Lewis writes, "the High Plains aquifer would cover all 50 states with one and one-half feet of water."

The Nature and the Extent of the Problem

Each year, at least 7.8 trillion gallons of water are drawn up from the Ogallala Aquifer to irrigate the crops planted on the High Plains. These crops are the main food source for our entire country. Tragically, irrigation is depleting the aquifer faster than it can replenish itself, and that is the problem. In fact, only the tiniest fraction of the water is ever replaced in the Ogallala Aquifer. If the water were ever fully depleted, the aquifer would

De Jong 3

need 6,000 years to refill naturally (Zwingle 83). The only way the Ogallala can be replenished is by water seeping down through the layers of soil until it reaches the aquifer. This water comes from the small amount of precipitation in the region, as well as from streams, reservoirs, canals, and irrigation (Opie 37–39).

A question serves as a transition to a new paragraph.

How serious is the problem? Since 1930, in much of the Texas Panhandle, over half the aquifer has gone dry (McGuire). The volume of water has decreased because the use of irrigation has increased so much since World War II. In 1949, 2.1 million acres were under irrigation. In 1980, the amount of irrigated land rose to 13.7 million acres; and in 1997, it rose to 13.9 million acres (McGuire). The land presently under irrigation in the Texas Panhandle alone is equal to the size of New Jersey (Thorpe). Water for all of this land is supplied by irrigation wells, and the number of wells has exploded over the decades—from just 170 in 1930 to more than 150,000 today (Nebel and Wright 279).

Multiple sources of important facts are cited in this paragraph.

A long quotation is introduced.

The biggest technological advance that has made this irrigation explosion possible is the center-pivot irrigation system. John Opie explains the system:

A quotation longer than four lines is indented one inch (ten spaces).

> The center pivot is a 1300-foot-long pipe that is held eight feet off the ground by a row of seven or more towers on large wheels. Sprinklers are attached at regular intervals along the pipe, pointing up or down. One end of the pipe is set in the middle of a 160-acre quarter section around which the pipe and wheeled towers circle. (146)

The water pumped through the pipe triggers a mechanism that causes the system to roll in a large circle. All of the crops within the circle receive a generous amount of water.

If you were flying over the Great Plains between Minneapolis and Denver in the summertime, you would see thousands of green

De Jong 4

circles, showing how farmers have irrigated their land. With center-pivot irrigation, crop production on one acre increases 600 to 800 percent compared to dry-land farming (Lewis). Today, 15 percent of all of the United States' wheat, corn, and sorghum grows on Ogallala-watered land, and 40 percent of American beef cattle feed on the grain and water of the Ogallala (Nebel and Wright 279).

These paragraphs are linked by using a key phrase (center-pivot irrigation) and a transitional word (however).

Center-pivot irrigation, however, has dramatically lowered the aquifer's water level. Even though farmers have known for decades that this was happening, they have continued to pump and spray as much water as they felt was necessary. When a drought hit in the mid-1970s, the water level of the Ogallala began to lower drastically in some areas because of overuse and lack of replenishment. In some parts of Texas, water levels dropped as much as 200 feet. Farmers who lived above shallow parts of the aquifer could not pump enough water for their crops at that time. More recently, state and local governments have worked to educate farmers about optimal water use, and they have imposed limits on how much can be drawn each year. Still, these limits are designed only to slow the rate at which the aquifer is depleted, not to stop that depletion altogether.

As Joe Patoski explains, in Texas a "rule of capture" law from the 1800s makes imposing even those limits difficult. Upheld by the Texas Supreme Court in 1904 and again in 1999, this law says the owner of the land also owns all the water he or she can pump out of it, even if that means running a neighbor's wells dry (121, 185). While wastage is prohibited, nothing stops a business from "water mining" and selling that water somewhere else.

A quotation reinforces one of the writer's main points.

The "court upheld the Ozarka Water Company's right to capture water under its property and bottle it, throwing out a lawsuit filed by neighboring East Texas landowners who claimed their

De Jong 5

wells, creeks, and streams were running dry thanks to Ozarka"
(185). Other organizations, including corporate giant Alcoa and a
business group known as Mesa Water, plan to mine the water from
their land and sell it to cities like El Paso and San Antonio (120).

The Solution: Sustainable Farming Practices

Because people's lives and the land itself are at stake, citizens
and businesses in the Plains states need to change their attitudes
about the use of this resource. The key is to accept annual
limitations on pumping and to follow what are called "sustainable
farming practices." These practices promote the careful use of the
aquifer so that it will serve the area indefinitely. If people accept
changes in irrigation methods, water regulations, and personal
consumption controls, water from the Ogallala Aquifer could serve
the area for thousands of years.

In the past decade, some positive changes have already taken
place. In areas of the Great Plains, some farmers are giving
their water to local towns. The towns use the water first, filter
it, and pump it to farmers to use on their crops. In this way, the
water is used twice before it drains back into the aquifer. Other
farmers are working on zero depletion, which is "gradually and
voluntarily pump[ing] less water according to a plan based on [a
farmer's] estimated supply" (Zwingle 103). The goal of this plan
is to maintain the water table at its current level so that water is
preserved for future generations.

Using less water means that farmers must rethink their
farming practices. For some farmers, cutting back means returning
to dry-land farming. This is being done in some areas of Texas
and Kansas because the water level has dropped so low that it
has become too expensive to pump water to the surface. However,
choosing dry-land farming does not mean farmers use no irrigation

No citation is needed for common knowledge available in many sources.

Brackets [ ] indicate that the writer has added something to a quotation.

De Jong 6

at all. It does mean more careful use of available water. Instead of drenching their fields "just to be sure," farmers must use better irrigation methods to give their crops only the water they need.

New technologies have been developed to help farmers figure out exactly how much water to use and how to irrigate without waste. For example, some farmers bury special gypsum blocks in the soil. Two electrodes in the blocks help farmers figure out how much water the soil actually needs. A second device that prevents water waste is low-energy precision application (LEPA). In a LEPA system, the nozzles of the center-pivot sprinklers are close to the ground, rather than several feet above it. LEPA reduces evaporation by as much as 95 percent (Gerston and Mosely). Most farmers in the market for new irrigation equipment are buying LEPA systems because they are so efficient.

These technological advances have done much to make sure the Ogallala Aquifer has a future. But cooperation and having a long-term view are just as important. Although farmers in the Great Plains have resisted in the past, they are now accepting the idea of sustainability. They are more willing to conserve water for future farmers. Because many Plains cities also use this water, state and local officials must work together to conserve municipal water supplies. In addition, businesses in the region must accept and practice water conservation.

In the end, citizens of the Plains states need to change their attitudes about their water consumption and think about the future. They must maintain the Ogallala Aquifer as a sustainable resource. The survival of this amazing underground sponge, as well as the survival of the farms and the cities of the Great American Desert, depends on it.

A summary of new technologies adds to the reader's understanding of possible solutions.

The writer analyzes the solutions to the problem.

The conclusion echoes the introduction and presents the challenge to act responsibly.

De Jong 7

Works Cited

Gerston, Jan, and Lynn Mosely. "Shorter Irrigation Cycles Boost
Crop Yields." *Texas Water Savers* Spring 1997. Texas Water
Resources Institute. Web. 29 Oct. 2010.

Lewis, Jack. "The Ogallala Aquifer: An Underground Sea." *EPA
Journal* 16.6 (Nov./Dec. 1990): 42. *MasterFILE Premier*.
EBSCOhost. Web. 6 Nov. 2010.

McGuire, V. L. "Water-Level Changes in the High Plains Aquifer,
Predevelopment to 2001, 1999 to 2000, and 2000 to 2001." *U.S.
Geological Survey*. Fact Sheet FS-078-03 (2003). Web. 2 Nov.
2010.

Nebel, Bernard J., and Richard T. Wright. *Environmental Science*.
8th ed. Upper Saddle River: Prentice Hall, 2002. Print.

Opie, John. *Ogallala: Water for a Dry Land*. Lincoln: U of
Nebraska P, 2000. Print.

Patoski, Joe Nick. "Boone Pickens Wants to Sell You His Water."
Texas Monthly 29.8 (Aug. 2001): 118+. *MasterFILE Premier*.
EBSCOhost. Web. 3 Nov. 2010.

Thorpe, Helen. "Waterworld." *Texas Monthly* 23.9 (Sept. 1995): 44.
MasterFILE Premier. EBSCOhost. Web. 6 Nov. 2010.

Zwingle, Erla. "Wellspring of the High Plains." *National
Geographic* Mar. 1993: 80–109. Print.

"Works Cited" is centered one inch from the top.

Sources are listed in alphabetical order.

Double spacing is used throughout.

Second and third lines are indented five spaces.

Assessment Rubric

Use this rubric as a checklist to evaluate your research writing. The rubric is arranged according to the traits of writing described in your handbook. (See pages 21–26.)

Stimulating Ideas

The writing . . .

_____ focuses on an important part of a subject, expressed in a thesis statement.

_____ effectively supports or develops the thesis with facts and details from a variety of sources.

_____ gives credit, when necessary, for ideas from other sources.

Logical Organization

_____ includes a clearly developed beginning, middle, and ending.

_____ presents supporting information in an organized manner (one main point per paragraph).

Engaging Voice

_____ speaks in a sincere and knowledgeable voice.

_____ shows that the writer is truly interested in the subject.

Original Word Choice

_____ explains or defines any unfamiliar terms.

_____ employs a formal level of language.

Effective Sentence Style

_____ flows smoothly from one idea to the next.

_____ shows variation in sentence structure.

Correct, Accurate Copy

_____ adheres to the rules of grammar, spelling, and punctuation.

_____ follows MLA or APA guidelines for documentation.

"Man's mind, stretched to new ideas, never goes back to its original dimensions."

—Oliver Wendell Holmes

APA Documentation Style

The research documentation style developed by the Modern Language Association (MLA) works well for literary papers. However, for papers in social science and social studies, the documentation style of the American Psychological Association (APA) is often used.

This chapter explains basic APA style and gives examples of the typical kinds of sources you may need to document. Because the style continues to evolve, the Write Source maintains a Web site with the most up-to-date information about documenting electronic sources and a sample APA research paper at www.thewritesource.com/apa.htm.

Remember: Always follow your teacher's directions for documentation style. Your teacher may have special requirements or ask for certain exceptions to the usual APA style.

Preview

- APA Paper Format
- Citing Sources: In-Text Citations
- Reference List: An Overview
- Reference Entries: Books
- Reference Entries: Periodicals
- Reference Entries: Online Sources
- Reference Entries: Other Sources

APA Paper **Format**

This overview gives formatting guidelines for a student research paper, not for an article to be submitted to a journal. Ask your teacher for special requirements he or she may have.

Title Page ■ On the first page, include your paper's title, your name, and your teacher's name on three separate lines. Double-space and center the lines beginning approximately one-third of the way down from the top of the page. Place the running head (an abbreviated title) in the upper left corner and the page number 1 in the upper right.

Abstract ■ On the second page, include an abstract—a 150- to 250-word paragraph summarizing your paper. Place the title *Abstract* approximately one inch from the top of the page and center it. Include the running head upper left and page number 2 upper right.

Body ■ Format the body of your paper as follows:

Margins: Leave a one-inch margin on all four sides of each page (1-1/2 inches on the left for papers to be bound).

Running Head and Page Numbers: Continue the running head throughout in the upper left corner and the page number in the upper right.

Line Spacing: Double-space your entire paper, unless your teacher allows single spacing for tables, titles, and so on.

Headings: If you need only one or two levels of headings, the first is centered, boldface, using upper- and lowercase text. The second is flush left, boldface, in upper- and lowercase text.

In-Text Citations ■ Within your paper, give credit by including the author and year in a citation. For quotations and other specific references, add the page number to the citation. (See page 311.) If a quotation runs 40 words or more, type it in block style, five spaces in from the left margin, with all lines flush left along that new margin. If it is more than one paragraph, indent the first line of the second and later paragraphs another five spaces.

References ■ Place full citations for all sources in an alphabetized list at the end of your paper. Start this list on a separate page, with the running head and page number in place, and the title *References* one inch from the top. (See pages 313–319.)

Citing **Sources**

In-Text Citations

In-text citations must include the author and date of the sources, either within the sentence or in parentheses. Each citation must be matched to an entry in the alphabetized list of references at the end of your paper.

> **According to a 2002 essay by Patrick Marshall . . .**
>
> **According to a recent essay by Patrick Marshall (2002) . . .**
>
> **According to a recent essay (Marshall, 2002) . . .**

One Author

Place the author's last name and the date of the work in parentheses. If you cite a specific part, give the page number, chapter, or section, using the appropriate abbreviations (p. or pp., chap., or sec.).

> **. . . Bush's 2002 budget was based on revenue estimates that "now appear to have been far too optimistic" (Lemann, 2003, p. 48).**

> **NOTE** When citing two works by the same author published in the same year, arrange them alphabetically by title in the reference list. Add a small *a* after the date of the first work, a small *b* after the second, and so on. Then use these letters in your in-text citations.

> **Gene therapy holds great promise for the future (Gormann, 2000a).**

Two Authors

If a work has two authors, identify both in every citation of that work. Separate their names with an ampersand in any parenthetical reference.

> **A rise in global temperature and a decrease in atmospheric oxygen led to the mass extinction during the Late Permian Period (Huey & Ward, 2005).**

Three to Five Authors

Mention all authors—up to five—in the first citation of a work.

> **Love changes not just who we are, but who we can become, as well (Lewis, Amini, & Lannon, 2000).**

After the first citation, list only the first author followed by *et al.* (the Latin abbreviation for *et alii*, meaning "and others").

> **These discoveries lead to the hypothesis that love actually alters the brain's structure (Lewis et al., 2000).**

Six or More Authors

If your source has six or more authors, refer to the work by the first author's name followed by "et al." in all parenthetical references. However, be sure to list all the authors (up to seven) in your references list.

Among children 13 to 14 years old, a direct correlation can be shown between cigarette advertising and smoking (Lopez et al., 2004).

A Work Authored by an Agency, a Committee, or Another Organization

The organization name acts as the author name. For the first citation, place abbreviations in square brackets; then use only the abbreviation.

First text citation: (National Institute of Mental Health [NIMH], 2010)

Subsequent citations: (NIMH, 2010)

A Work with No Author

If your source lists no author, use the first two or three words of the title (capitalized normally) instead.

. . . including a guide to low-impact exercise ("Staying Healthy," 2004).

A Work Referred to in Another Work

When using a source that is referred to in another source, try to find and cite the original. If that isn't possible, credit the source by adding "as cited in" within the parentheses.

. . . theorem given by Ullman (as cited in Hoffman, 2009).

NOTE Your reference list will have an entry for Hoffman (not Ullman).

Two or More Works in One Reference

When citing two or more works within one parenthetical reference, list the sources in alphabetical order, separating them with semicolons.

These near-death experiences are reported with conviction (Rommer, 2000; Sabom, 1998).

NOTE Arrange two or more works by the same author(s) by year of publication, separated by commas. (McIntyre & Ames, 1992, 1995)

Personal Communications

Cite letters, e-mail messages, phone conversations, and so on, as "personal communications," with their full date. Do not list them in your references.

The management team expects to finish hiring this spring (R. Fouser, personal communication, December 14, 2010).

Reference List: An Overview

The reference list includes all of the retrievable sources cited in a paper. It begins on a separate page and follows the format below.

Page Numbers Continue the numbering scheme from the paper: place the running head in the upper left corner.

Title Place the title "References" approximately one inch from the top of the page and center it.

Entries List the entries alphabetically by author's last name. If no author is given, then list by title (disregarding *A, An,* or *The*).

- Double-space between all lines (including between the title "References" and the first entry).
- Capitalize only the first word (and any proper nouns) of book and article titles; capitalize the names of periodicals in the standard upper- and lowercase manner.
- Begin each entry at the left margin and indent additional lines of the entry five to seven spaces. (See the examples below.)

Format for a Book Entry

Author's last name, Initials for first name and middle name. (year). *Book title.* Location: Publisher.

NOTE: For the location, give the city and the postal abbreviation for the state. Outside of the United States, include the state or province and the country.

Format for a Periodical Entry

Author's last name, Initials. (date). Article title. *Periodical Title, volume number* (issue number if paginated by issue), page numbers.

Format for an Online Periodical Entry

Author's last name, Initials. (date). Article title. *Periodical Title, volume number* (issue number), pages. doi:code.

NOTE: If no DOI (digital object identifier) is available, use a "Retrieved from URL" statement instead. If the content is likely to change, use a "Retrieved date from URL" format.

Reference Entries:
Books and Other Documents

A Book by One Author

Guttman, J. (1999). *The gift wrapped in sorrow: A mother's quest for healing.* Palm Springs, CA: JMJ Publishing.

A Book by Two or More Authors

Lynn, J., & Harrold, J. (1999). *Handbook for mortals: Guidance for people facing serious illness.* New York, NY: Oxford University Press.

NOTE Follow the first author's name with a comma; then join the two authors' names with an ampersand (&) rather than "and." List up to seven authors; abbreviate subsequent authors as "et al."

An Anonymous Book

If an author is listed as "Anonymous," treat it as the author's name. Otherwise, follow this format:

American Medical Association essential guide to asthma. (2003). New York, NY: American Medical Association.

A Chapter from a Book

Tattersall, I. (2002). How did we achieve humanity? In *The monkey in the mirror* (pp. 138–168). New York, NY: Harcourt.

A Single Work from an Anthology

Nichols, J. (2005). Diversity and stability in language. In B. D. Joseph & R. D. Janda (Eds.), *The handbook of historical linguistics* (pp. 283–310). Malden, MA: Blackwell.

NOTE When editors' names appear in the middle of an entry, follow the usual order: initial first, surname last.

One Volume of a Multivolume Edited Work

Salzman, J., Smith, D. L., & West, C. (Eds.). (1996). *Encyclopedia of African-American culture and history* (Vol. 4). New York, NY: Simon & Schuster Macmillan.

A Group Author as Publisher

> Amnesty International. (2000). *Hidden scandal, secret shame: Torture and ill-treatment of children.* New York, NY: Author.

NOTE If the publication is a brochure, identify it as such in brackets after the title.

An Edited Work, One in a Series

When a work is part of a larger series or collection, make a two-part title of the series and the particular volume you are citing.

> Hunter, S., & Sundel, M. (Eds.). (1998). *Sage sourcebooks for the human services: Vol. 7. Midlife myths: Issues, findings and practice implications.* Newbury Park, CA: Sage Publications.

An Edition Other Than the First

> Trimmer, J. (2001). *Writing with a purpose* (13th ed.). Boston, MA: Houghton Mifflin.

An Article in a Reference Book

> Lewer, N. (1999). Non-lethal weapons. In *World encyclopedia of peace* (pp. 279–280). Oxford, UK: Pergamon Press.

NOTE If no author is listed, begin the entry with the title of the article.

A Technical or Research Report

> Ball, J., & Evans Jr., C. (2001). *Safe passage: Astronaut care for exploration missions.* Washington, DC: Institute of the National Academics.

A Government Publication

> National Renewable Energy Laboratory. (2003). *Statistical wind power forecasting for U.S. wind farms* (NREL Publication No. CP-500-35087). Springfield, VA: U.S. Department of Commerce.

NOTE If the document is not available from the Government Printing Office (GPO), the publisher would be either "Author" or the separate government department that published it.

Reference Entries: **Periodicals**

A Magazine Article, Author Given

Silberman, S. (2001, December). The geek syndrome. *Wired, 9(12),*
174–183.

A Magazine Article, No Author Given

Arctic ozone wiped out by solar storms. (2005, March). *New Scientist,*
185(2490), 17.

An Article in a Scholarly Journal, Consecutively Paginated

Epstein, R., & Hundert, E. (2002). Defining and assessing professional
competence. *JAMA, 287,* 226–235.

NOTE Here are the features of a basic reference to a scholarly journal:

- last name and initial(s) as for a book reference,
- year of publication,
- title of article in lowercase, except for the first word; title not italicized
  or in quotations,
- title and volume number of journal italicized, and
- inclusive page numbers.

A Journal Article, Paginated by Issue

Lewer, N. (1999, summer). Nonlethal weapons. *Forum, 14(2),* 39–45.

NOTE When the page numbering of the issue starts with page 1, the issue number (not italicized) is placed in parentheses after the volume number.

A Journal Article, Two Authors

Newman, P. A., & Nash, E. R. (2005). The unusual southern hemisphere
stratosphere winter of 2002. *Journal of the Atmospheric Sciences,*
62(3), 614–628.

A Journal Article, More Than Six Authors

Watanabe, T., Bihoreau, M-T., McCarthy, L., Kiguwa, S., Hishigaki, H.,
Tsaji, A., et al. (1999, May 1). A radiation hybrid map of the rat
genome containing 5,255 markers. *Nature Genetics, 22,* 27–36.

An Abstract of a Scholarly Article (from a Secondary Source)

Yamamoto, S., & Nakamura, A. (2000). A new model of continuous dust production from the lunar surface. *Astronomy & Astrophysics, 356,* 1112–1118. Abstract taken from CDS Bibliographic Service, 2005.

NOTE When the dates of the article and the secondary-source abstract differ, the reference in your text would cite both dates, the original first, separated by a slash (2001/2002). When the abstract is obtained from the original source, the description Abstract is placed in brackets following the title (but before the period).

A Newspaper Article, Author Given

Stolberg, S. C. (2002, January 4). Breakthrough in pig cloning could aid organ transplants. *The New York Times*, pp. 1A, 17A.

NOTE For newspapers, use "p." or "pp." before the page numbers; if the article is not on continuous pages, give all the page numbers, separated by commas.

A Newspaper Article, No Author Given

AOL to take up to $60 billion charge. (2002, January 8). *Chicago Tribune*, sec. 3, p. 3.

A Letter to the Editor

Cohen, E. (2005, May 9). Don't overlook benefits of medical spending [Letter to the editor]. *The Milwaukee Journal Sentinel*, p. 9A.

NOTE The "A" means that the letter is in the newspaper's A section.

A Review

Updike, J. (2001, December 24). Survivor/believer [Review of the book *New and Collected Poems 1931–2001*]. *The New Yorker*, 118–122.

A Newsletter Article

Newsletter article entries are very similar to newspaper article entries; only a volume number is added.

Teaching mainstreamed special education students. (2002 February). *The Council Chronicle, 11,* 6–8.

Reference Entries: **Online Sources**

APA style prefers a reference to the print or fixed-media form of a source, even if the source is available online. Even if an online article has been changed from the print version or has additional information, follow the same general format for the author, date, and title elements of print sources, but follow it with a DOI (if possible) or a "Retrieved from" statement. (See page 313.)

Online Document:

Author, A.A. (year). Title of work. doi or "Retrieved from" statement.

Bittlestone, R. (2005). *Odysseus unbound.* doi:10.2277/0521853575

American Psychological Association. (2000, January). Successful aging: The second 50. *APA Monitor.* Retrieved May 6, 2010, from http:// www.apa.org/monitor/jan00/cs.html

Periodical, Different from Print Version or Online Only

Author, A., & Author, B. (year, month day). Title of article, chapter, or Web page. *Title of Periodical, volume number,* inclusive page numbers if available. doi or "Retrieved from" statement.

Nicholas, D., Huntington, P., & Williams, P. (2001, May 23). Comparing web and touch screen transaction log files. *Journal of Medical Internet Research, 3.* Retrieved Nov. 15, 2009, from http:// www.jmir.org/2001/2/e18/index.htm

NOTE If additional information (podcast, map, etc.) has been included in the online version, use the description "Supplemental material" in brackets after the article title.

A Document from an Online Database

If the database identifies the print source, list that information only. Add a "Retrieved from" statement only if the source cannot be found otherwise or is likely to change (such as a wiki page).

Author, A., & Author, B. (year). Title of article. Title of Periodical, volume number, inclusive page numbers.

Belsie, Laurent. (1999). Progress or peril? *Christian Science Monitor, 91*(85), 15.

NOTE If the document cited is an abstract, include [*Abstract*] after the title.

Reference Entries: **Other Sources**

The following citation entries are examples of audiovisual media sources and sources available electronically.

A Television or Radio Broadcast

Crystal, L. (Executive Producer). (2005, February 11). *The newshour with Jim Lehrer* [Television broadcast]. New York, NY, and Washington, DC: Public Broadcasting Service.

An Audio Recording

Give the name and function (author, speaker, performer, compiler, and so on) of the originators or primary contributors. Indicate the recording medium (CD, record, cassette, and so on) in brackets, following the title.

Kim, E. (Author, Speaker). (2000). *Ten thousand sorrows* [CD]. New York, NY: Random House.

A Motion Picture

Give the name and function of the director, producer, or both. If the motion picture's circulation was limited, provide the distributor's name and complete address in parentheses.

Jackson, P. (Director). (2003). *The lord of the rings: Return of the king* [Motion picture]. United States: New Line Productions, Inc.

A Lecture, Speech, Reading, or Dissertation

For an unpublished paper presented at a meeting, indicate when the paper was presented, at what meeting, in what location.

Lycan, W. (2002, June). *The plurality of consciousness.* Paper presented at the meeting of the Society for Philosophy and Psychology, New York, NY.

For an unpublished doctoral dissertation, place the dissertation's title in italics, even though the work is unpublished. Indicate the school at which the writer completed the dissertation.

Roberts, W. (2001). *Crime amidst suburban wealth* (Unpublished doctoral dissertation). Bowling Green State University, Bowling Green, OH.

Workplace
WRITING

Writing Business Letters   **321**

Special Forms of Workplace Writing   **329**

"In the workplace, you don't write for a grade, you write for a living." —Jim Franke, electrical contractor

Writing
BUSINESS LETTERS

People in the workplace write business letters to do many things—such as share ideas, promote products, and ask for help. Putting a message in writing gives the writer time to think about, organize, and edit what he or she wants to say. In addition, a written message becomes a record of important details for both the sender and the recipient.

Students also write business letters to get things done. Letters connect the writer with experts and organizations that offer information, provide internships, help solve problems, and much more.

Preview

- **Parts of a Business Letter**
- **Writing Guidelines**
- **Informative Letter**
- **Application Letter**
- **Sending Your Letter**
- **Assessment Rubric**

Parts of a Business Letter

A business letter presents complete information in the order below.

Heading
The heading gives the writer's complete address, either printed in the letterhead or typed out, plus the date. (If the address is part of the letterhead, place only the date in the upper left-hand corner.)

Inside Address
The inside address gives the reader's name and complete mailing address (including the company name). If you're not sure which person to address or how to spell his or her name, call the company and ask. If the person's title is a single word or very short, place it after the name, separated by a comma. Longer titles go on a separate line.

Salutation
The salutation personalizes the letter. Use *Dear* with people only, not department or company names. Place a colon after the name. (Also see "Avoiding Sexism" at 562.1.)

Body
The body contains your message in single-spaced paragraphs (no indents) with double spacing between them. The body of your letter is organized in three parts: (1) the beginning states why you are writing, (2) the middle provides all the needed details, and (3) the ending focuses on what should happen next.

Complimentary Closing
The closing politely ends the message with a parting word or phrase— *Sincerely, Yours sincerely, Yours truly,*—followed by a comma. Capitalize only the first word of complimentary closings.

Signature
The signature makes the letter official. It includes the writer's handwritten name and corresponding typed name.

Initials, Enclosures, Copies
When someone types the letter for the writer, that person's *lowercased initials* appear after the writer's capitalized initials, separated by a colon.

If a document (brochure, form, copy) is *enclosed* with the letter, the word *Enclosure* or the abbreviation *Encl.* appears below the initials.

If a *copy* of the letter is sent elsewhere, type "cc:" and follow with the name of the person or department receiving the copy.

Sample **Business Letter**

Heading

Monroe Chamber of Commerce
105 East Bay Road
Monroe, LA 31404-1832
October 19, 2006

Four to Seven Spaces

Inside Address

Ms. Charlotte Williams, Manager
Belles Lettres Books
1617 Delta Mall Road
Monroe, LA 31404-0012

Double Space

Salutation

Dear Ms. Williams:

Double Space

Welcome to the Monroe business community. As
the Chamber's executive director, I'd like to thank
you for opening your store in the Delta Mall. Belles
Lettres Books is a welcome addition to the town's
economy, especially with the store's emphasis
on Southern authors. I wish you success.

Body

I would like to invite you to join our Chamber of
Commerce. Membership gives you a voice in your
community and access to promotional materials.

If you decide to join, I could set up a ribbon-cutting
ceremony, which would provide some useful news
coverage. Call me at 944-0645 or e-mail me at
<alein@chamber.org> if you have any questions.

Double Space

Complimentary Closing

Sincerely,

Signature

Ardith Lein   *Four Spaces*

Ardith Lein

Double Space

Initials
Enclosures
Copies

AL:nk
Encl. membership brochure
cc: Peter Sanchez, Membership Chairperson

Writing Guidelines **Business Letters**

■ PREWRITING

1. **Considering Your Audience . . .** Who is your reader, and how will he or she feel about your message?

2. **Determining Your Purpose . . .** Jot down your reason for writing or what you want your reader to know or do.

3. **Gathering Details . . .** Collect the information you will need for your letter. Think about the best way to organize and present it.

■ WRITING AND REVISING

4. **Organizing the Details . . .** Organize your letter in three parts.

   Beginning: Introduce the message by stating the topic and purpose of your letter.

   Middle: Present whatever information is appropriate for the kind of letter you are writing. Use a voice that fits your purpose—persuasive, informative, and so on.

   Ending: Focus on the outcome. What do you want the reader to do, and when, and how? Is there an action you will take?

5. **Improving Your Writing . . .** Revise your first draft, asking these questions:
   - **Ideas:** *Is my main point clear? Are my details accurate and complete?*
   - **Organization:** *Does each paragraph develop one main idea?*
   - **Voice:** *Do I use a polite, respectful tone?* (See pages 561-563.)

6. **Improving Your Style . . .** Revise for style, asking these questions:
   - **Word Choice:** *Do I use clear, natural words?*
   - **Sentence Fluency:** *Have I written smooth-flowing sentences?*

■ EDITING AND PROOFREADING

7. **Checking for Conventions . . .** Check for errors in punctuation, mechanics, and grammar. Use the rubric on page 328 as a final check of your work.

8. **Preparing a Final Copy . . .** Neatly type or keyboard your letter. Center it on the page and keep the margins even on both sides. Address the envelope, add correct postage, and mail your letter. (See page 327.)

Sample Informative Letter

4213 Minnow Lane
Medford, MA 02052
March 6, 2006

Geoffrey Gosbin
164 12th Street, NW
Somerville, MA 02044

Dear Geoffrey:

Beginning
Explain why you are writing.

Thanks for your letter praising our school's Web page! As for your request, I'd be happy to help you build a Web page for your school's Environmental Awareness Club.

First, you need a Web page-maker program. You may download one from the Internet or buy one separately.

Middle
Supply necessary details.

Second, you'll need a plan for your page. A good page has a clear, concise, and interesting design. Here are a few points to think about:
- Explain who you are and what you're about.
- Don't overdo the graphics; they can really slow things down.
- Include some links to sites that would be interesting to a visitor.
- Include a FAQ (frequently asked questions) section.

Ending
Establish a plan of action and end politely.

Let's get together next Wednesday in your computer lab at 3:30 p.m. I'll take you through a sample page. If you're ready with your design plan, we can dig right in.

Sincerely,

Brian Krygsman

Brian Krygsman
Computer Coordinator

Sample Application Letter

326 Ash Boulevard
Florence, OR 97439-3216
March 23, 2006

Dr. Ray Peters
Communications Department Chair
St. Xavier College
32 Fountain Street
Omaha, NE 68102-6070

Dear Dr. Peters:

Beginning
Explain how you learned about the position.

In response to the brochure I received from St. Xavier College, I am applying for a position on the staff of the *Xavier News*. I have enclosed a recommendation from my high school English teacher as well as several articles that I wrote for my high school newspaper, *The Florence Flier*.

Middle
Describe your qualifications.

I have been on the staff of *The Florence Flier* for four years, and this year I am the editor. I have always enjoyed English, and I plan on majoring in journalism at St. Xavier College. I am an organized, creative person, and I have never missed a deadline. In addition to writing and editing, I do layout work.

Ending
Politely offer additional information and thank the reader.

If you would like more information, please let me know by calling 555-997-3205 anytime during the day or by e-mailing me at <greensleeves@aol.com>. Thank you for considering my application. I look forward to hearing from you.

Sincerely,

Allison Emerson

Allison Emerson

Encl. recommendation and newspaper articles

Sending Your Letter

Addressing the Envelope

Address the envelope correctly so your letter can be delivered promptly. Place the return address in the upper left corner, the destination address in the center, and the correct postage in the upper right corner. Make sure that the destination and return addresses on the envelope match the inside address and heading on the letter.

```
ANDREA MCGRADY
2518 FOURTH AVE SW
COLUMBUS OH 43230                              postage



              MR TIM LINDON
              1286 ELM ST NW
              COLUMBUS OH 43230
```

There are two acceptable forms for addressing the envelope: the older, traditional form and the new form preferred by the postal service.

Traditional Form	Postal Service Form
Ms. Theresa Chang	MS THERESA CHANG
Goodwill Industries	GOODWILL INDUSTRIES
9200 Wisconsin Avenue	9200 WISCONSIN AVE
Bethesda, MD 20814-3896	BETHESDA MD 20814-3896

Official United States Postal Service

ENVELOPE GUIDELINES

- Capitalize everything in the address and leave out all punctuation.
- Use the list of common abbreviations found in the *National ZIP Code Directory*. (See page 513.2.) Use numerals rather than words for numbered streets and avenues (9TH AVE SE, 3RD ST NE).
- If you know the ZIP + 4 code, use it. You can get this information by phoning one of the postal service's ZIP-code information units.

Assessment Rubric

Use this rubric as a checklist to evaluate your business writing. The rubric addresses the traits of writing. (See pages 21–26.)

Ideas

The writing . . .

_____ focuses on an appropriate topic.

_____ develops a clearly expressed goal or purpose.

_____ includes details the reader needs to know.

Organization

_____ includes a clear beginning, middle, and ending.

_____ arranges details logically, using appropriate transitions.

Voice

_____ speaks knowledgeably and sincerely about the topic.

_____ uses a voice that fits the purpose (persuasive, informative, and so on).

_____ uses a level of language appropriate to the reader.

Word Choice

_____ uses plain language, specific nouns, and vivid verbs.

_____ defines terms the reader might be unfamiliar with.

Sentence Fluency

_____ flows easily from one thought to another.

_____ includes sentences with varied beginnings and lengths.

Conventions

_____ adheres to the basic rules of writing.

_____ follows the appropriate business-letter format.

"When writing instructions, don't assume anything.
If the person knew what to do,
he or she wouldn't need instructions."

—Dennis Walstra, plumbing contractor

Special Forms of
WORKPLACE Writing

All organizations need people who not only speak well but also write effectively. Whether you become an engineer or an electrician, a lab technician or a social worker, good writing will help you get a job and do your job. Writing will also help you do your job right now as you plan projects, request help, and gather needed materials to complete your schoolwork.

A written message holds several advantages over a phone call or a personal conversation: (1) You have time to think about and edit what you want to say. (2) Both parties have an official record of the message. (3) The written word is often taken more seriously. (4) Written forms of communication can be sent to many people at once.

Preview

- **Writing Guidelines and Samples**
- **Memos**
- **E-Mail Messages**
- **Brochures**
- **Résumés**

Writing Guidelines Memos

Memos are short messages in which you ask and answer questions, describe procedures, give short reports, and remind others about deadlines and meetings. Memos create a flow of information within an organization, whether it's a classroom, an entire school, or a workplace.

■ PREWRITING

1. **Considering Your Audience . . .** Think about who is going to receive your memo and why.

2. **Determining Your Purpose . . .** Jot down your reason for the memo.

3. **Gathering Details . . .** Ask yourself what your reader needs to know and gather the necessary details.

■ WRITING AND REVISING

4. **Preparing the Heading . . .** Begin your memo by typing "Memo" and centering it. Include a heading that contains the following information:

Date:	the month, day, and year
To:	the reader's name
From:	your first and last name (You may initial before sending.)
Subject:	the memo's topic in a clear, simple statement

5. **Organizing the Body . . .** Organize the message into three parts:

Beginning:	State why you are writing the memo.
Middle:	Provide all the necessary details. Consider listing the most important points rather than writing them out.
Ending:	Focus on what should happen next—the action or response you would like from the reader or readers.

6. **Improving Your Writing . . .** Ask yourself these questions:
   - **Ideas:** *Is my topic clear? Is my purpose obvious?*
   - **Organization:** *Do I have an effective beginning, middle, and ending?*
   - **Voice:** *Have I used a positive, friendly tone?*
   - **Word Choice:** *Have I explained any unfamiliar terms?*
   - **Sentence Fluency:** *Does my memo read smoothly?*

■ EDITING AND PROOFREADING

7. **Checking for Conventions . . .** Use the rubric on page 328.

Sample **Memo**

Memo

Date: October 12, 2006

To: Mr. Marcus

From: Danielle White

Subject: Mid-project report on history paper

Beginning
State why you are writing.

Here's an update on my history paper about China. At first I had trouble finding information on my topic, but I've made this progress.

1. I went to the library, and Ms. Pate showed me how to use the computer for my search.

2. After I showed you my project proposal, I took your advice to look at either Chinese dating practices or wedding traditions, but not both.

Middle
Give the necessary details.

3. After researching both topics, I found several sources on Chinese wedding traditions, but only a few on dating practices. So I will write about present-day Chinese wedding customs.

4. I found a Web site with information about Chinese wedding traditions at <www.travelchinaguide.com>.

5. For my primary research, I interviewed Donna Sung, our foreign exchange student from Shanghai, about her experiences with weddings in China.

Ending
Focus on what should happen next.

I will finish my first draft by next Wednesday and will be on schedule for the deadlines I gave you in my project proposal.

Writing Guidelines **E-Mail Messages**

Electronic mail helps you send, receive, and store messages quickly through computer networks. In spite of e-mail's delivery speed, it still takes time to write a good message in the first place. The guidelines below will help you.

■ PREWRITING

1. **Considering Your Audience . . .** Think about who your reader will be and your purpose for e-mailing this person.

2. **Gathering Details . . .** Gather all the details that your reader needs to know.

■ WRITING AND REVISING

3. **Organizing the Body . . .** Organize your e-mail message in three parts:

   Beginning: Complete your e-mail header, making sure your subject line is precise. Expand on the subject in the first sentences of your e-mail, getting right to the point.

   Middle: Fill in the details of your message, but keep all of your paragraphs short. Double-space between paragraphs. Try to limit your message to one or two screens and use numbers, lists, and headings to organize your thoughts.

   Ending: Let your reader know what follow-up action is needed and when. Then end politely.

4. **Improving Your Writing . . .** Revise by asking these questions:
   - **Ideas:** *Is my message accurate, complete, and clear?*
   - **Organization:** *Do I have an effective beginning, middle, and ending?*
   - **Voice:** *Is my tone appropriate for the topic and the reader?*

5. **Improving Your Style . . .** Ask yourself the following:
   - **Word Choice:** *Have I used clear, everyday language?*
   - **Sentence Fluency:** *Does my message read smoothly?*

■ EDITING AND PROOFREADING

6. **Checking for Conventions . . .** Check your message for errors in punctuation, mechanics, and grammar. Use the rubric on page 328 as a final check.

Sample E-Mail

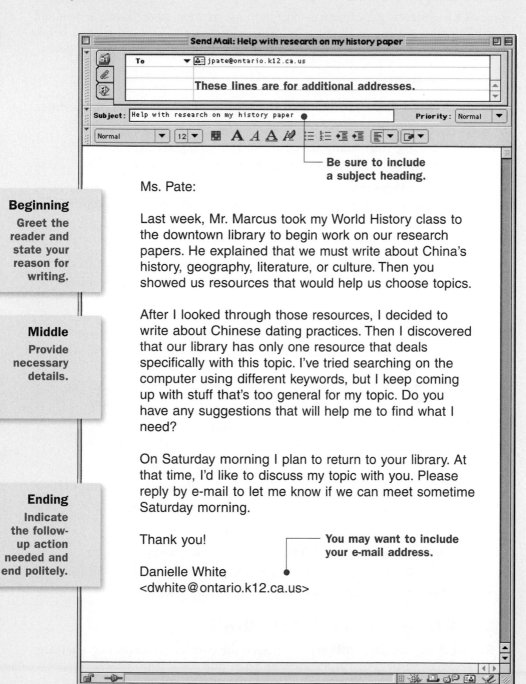

Send Mail: Help with research on my history paper

To ▼ jpate@ontario.k12.ca.us

These lines are for additional addresses.

Subject: Help with research on my history paper ●   Priority: Normal ▼

Normal ▼ 12 ▼

Be sure to include a subject heading.

Ms. Pate:

Beginning
Greet the reader and state your reason for writing.

Last week, Mr. Marcus took my World History class to the downtown library to begin work on our research papers. He explained that we must write about China's history, geography, literature, or culture. Then you showed us resources that would help us choose topics.

Middle
Provide necessary details.

After I looked through those resources, I decided to write about Chinese dating practices. Then I discovered that our library has only one resource that deals specifically with this topic. I've tried searching on the computer using different keywords, but I keep coming up with stuff that's too general for my topic. Do you have any suggestions that will help me to find what I need?

Ending
Indicate the follow-up action needed and end politely.

On Saturday morning I plan to return to your library. At that time, I'd like to discuss my topic with you. Please reply by e-mail to let me know if we can meet sometime Saturday morning.

Thank you!   You may want to include your e-mail address.

Danielle White
<dwhite@ontario.k12.ca.us>

Writing Guidelines **Brochures**

A brochure is an effective tool you can use for advertising a product, promoting a cause, or sharing helpful information. The guidelines below will help you produce a brochure that does just what you want it to do.

■ PREWRITING

1. **Selecting a Topic . . .** Think of the service or product that you want to promote or sell.

2. **Considering Your Audience . . .** Consider who your audience will be and what kind of brochure will work best.

3. **Gathering Details . . .** Think about what your reader needs to know about this product or service in order to be convinced of its value.

■ WRITING AND REVISING

4. **Organizing the Body . . .** Organize your brochure into three parts:

    Beginning: State the main point in bold type, either as a question and an answer or as a large headline, at the top.

    Middle: State your message fully but concisely, using as few words as possible. Fill in the details using bulleted lists. Add facts, figures, and testimonials to verify the quality of your product or service.

    Ending: Include reader-response instructions, offering all the necessary names, addresses, and phone numbers.

5. **Designing Your Brochure . . .** Design your brochure with large headlines, attention-grabbing visuals, and interesting graphics.

6. **Improving Your Writing . . .** Revise by using the following questions:
   - **Ideas:** *Is my message clear? Do I answer the reader's questions?*
   - **Organization:** *Do I use headings, lists, and graphics?*
   - **Voice:** *Does my writing voice sound persuasive?*

7. **Improving Your Style . . .** Ask yourself these questions:
   - **Word Choice:** *Have I chosen precise words to convey my message?*
   - **Sentence Fluency:** *Does my brochure read smoothly?*

■ EDITING AND PROOFREADING

8. **Checking for Conventions . . .** Check for correct punctuation, spelling, and mechanics. Use the rubric on page 328 for a final check.

9. **Preparing a Final Copy . . .** Proofread the final draft of your brochure.

Sample Brochure

The size of brochures can vary. This sample brochure was designed on a standard sheet of paper folded in half.

Front
The main point is stated boldly.

Save a Life— Give Blood!

Your student council invites you to help others by participating in our school's blood drive.

Thursday, October 20, 2005
8–11 a.m. and 1–3 p.m.
School Cafeteria

Inside
Bulleted lists highlight details.

Why should you give?

- Accident victims, people who need surgery, and people with blood disorders need your help.
- Community blood banks must be resupplied because . . .
  - all types of blood are constantly in demand.
  - blood has a limited shelf life and must be replaced often.

When and where can you give?

- Thursday, October 20, in the school cafeteria from 8 to 11 a.m. or 1 to 3 p.m.
- Information about community blood bank hours is available in the school office.

Who should donate?

- Any healthy person 17 or older
- Someone who hasn't donated within 60 days

Remember . . .

- Bring a signed parental-release form with you. They are available in the school office.
- Bring identification—driver's license or school I.D.
- Be prepared to fill out a medical questionnaire.
- Eat before and after your donation and drink plenty of fluids.
- Giving blood is . . .
  A CHANCE TO HELP OTHERS.

Ending
The writer gives a final message.

Writing Guidelines Résumés

Your résumé presents you—your skills, knowledge, and experiences—to a prospective employer. There are two forms of résumés:

A **chronological** résumé lists work experiences and education by date. Chronological résumés work best when you've held a number of jobs.

A **functional** résumé lists skills you may have acquired at home or at school; it lists your educational history (mention any special awards), plus your job history. Functional résumés are a good choice when you have little work experience.

■ PREWRITING

1. **Gathering Details . . .** Think about your immediate and long-term goals. Then list the following: (1) a job objective showing what kind of job you want; (2) your schooling, work experience, extracurricular and volunteer activities, and hobbies, including the dates; (3) responsibilities and related skills; (4) teachers, employers, and other people in the community who could act as references for you.

■ WRITING AND REVISING

2. **Organizing the Body . . .** Shape your résumé into three parts:

   Beginning: Provide personal data and a job objective.

   Middle: Choose the type of résumé that will best fit your needs: chronological or functional. Depending on your choice, list your skills, achievements, education, and work experience in the appropriate way.

   Ending: Either list the names of your references or indicate that references are available upon request.

3. **Improving Your Writing . . .** Ask yourself the following questions:
   - **Ideas:** *Have I included specific, accurate, and complete details?*
   - **Organization:** *Does the format highlight my strengths?*
   - **Voice:** *Have I used a serious, factual tone?*
   - **Word Choice:** *Have I considered each word carefully?*
   - **Sentence Fluency:** *Are all my ideas parallel in structure?*

■ EDITING AND PROOFREADING

4. **Checking for Conventions . . .** Check for errors in punctuation, mechanics, and grammar. Use the rubric on page 328.

5. **Preparing a Final Copy . . .** Proofread your résumé before using it.

Sample **Functional Résumé**

Adam Thoral
567 West Highland Road
Tiewing, FL 34207-2367
Phone: (111) 943-7125
E-mail: a_thoral@tiewing.net

Job Objective: Take part in a summer environmental studies program.

Environmental Science Skills:
- Wrote three research papers based on environmental issues: "Effects of Gulf War on Nature"; "The Rain Forest: Why Do We Need It?"; and "North American Environmental Disasters"
- Subscribe to the following environmental magazines: *Earth Awareness* and *Endangered Environment*
- Completed wilderness survival training through Boy Scouts

Communication Skills:
- Team worker: led group projects at school, participated in scouting events, served as crew leader at fast-food restaurant
- Well acquainted with writing memos, letters, and e-mail
- Worked to promote environmental bills (Bills 104, 235)

Organizational Skills:
- Organized an Earth Day community cleanup at school
- Helped set up a school recycling program
- Assisted Mr. Carper, my biology teacher, in lab preparations

Education:
- 11th grader, Tiewing High School
- Course work: Environmental Science, Biology, Chemistry

Awards/Activities:
- Boy Scouts (2001–present)
- Peer Tutor at Tiewing High School (2005–2006)
- First Aid and CPR certification—Tiewing Hospital (2005)

Work History:
2005 (Summer) Internship in environmental studies and public relations at Landzone Industries in Tiewing
2005–2006 Restaurant crew leader—supervised three workers

References available upon request

Searching for
INFORMATION

Types of Information   339

Using the Internet   347

Using the Library   353

"I use not only all the brains I have,
but all I can borrow."

—Woodrow Wilson

Types of
INFORMATION

You've just been assigned a six-page research report on a health-related issue. Quality information, your teacher tells you, must be the foundation of your report. But what is quality information? Where do you find it, what does it look like, and how do you really determine its quality?

These questions are important. In an information age, computers, TV, and print media remind you every day that you're swimming in a sea of information. To find what you need, you must first know where to look, and then how to determine the quality of the information available to you. Finally, you need to know how to use the information you choose.

Preview

- **Primary vs. Secondary Sources**
- **Evaluating Information**
- **Information Packages and Places**
- **Conducting Surveys and Interviews**

Primary vs. Secondary Sources

Information sources can be divided into two categories—*primary* and *secondary*.

Primary Sources

A **primary source** is an original source. This source (a diary, a person, an event, a survey, and so on) informs you directly, not through another person's explanation or interpretation. You're working with primary sources when you . . .

- observe an event to get firsthand information.
- survey or interview people to gather and tabulate their responses.
- do experiments to understand cause-and-effect relationships.
- analyze original documents, such as the Constitution.

Secondary Sources

A **secondary source** is *not* an original source. A secondary source is one that contains information other people have gathered and interpreted. It is at least once removed from the original. Secondary sources extend, analyze, interpret, or evaluate the primary information. You're working with secondary sources when you . . .

- read a magazine article.
- refer to an encyclopedia.
- consult a nonfiction book.
- watch a documentary on television.
- visit a Web site.

Primary Source	Secondary Source
Interview with a teacher about bilingual education	Journal article reviewing the status of bilingual education
Survey of students about learning a second language	Newspaper article about careers for bilingual individuals
Observations of mainstream students participating in sheltered bilingual classes	Documentary about language learning in schools

Evaluating Information

Once you've found what you think is the right information for your needs, put it to the test. On the surface, all information looks the same. It all seems to be valid and trustworthy. But not all information is created or recorded equally. It's your responsibility to sort it out before presenting it to your reader. The questions below should help.

> ✱ Be especially cautious in evaluating information on the Internet. While there is an incredible amount of information available on the Net, there's also a lot of misinformation.

Quality Control

Is the source an expert? ■ An expert is someone who has mastered a subject area, someone who is regarded as an authority. But be careful—when experts go outside their fields of expertise, they may not have much authority.

Is the information current? ■ A book on computers written five years ago may be ancient history by now. But a book on Abraham Lincoln could be 40 years old and still be the best source on the market.

> ✱ If your information comes from a Web site, when was it created and when was it last updated? Are the hyperlinks in the site functional?

Is the information complete? ■ Try to see the whole picture. If your source provides data from an experimental group, you should be given results from another group for comparison. If your source shows you highlights, ask to see the "lowlights," too.

Is the information accurate? ■ Check for obvious factual errors, analysis that doesn't make sense, and results that don't add up. Unfortunately, errors don't come with little red flags that say "Oops." You've got to detect them the old-fashioned way—carefully checking your information and thinking about it.

Is your source biased? ■ A *bias* means, literally, a tilt toward one side. Biased sources—such as political "spin doctors," corporate spokespersons, or TV infomercials—have everything to gain by slanting facts their way. Ask, "Why was this source created?"

Take NOTE

Slanted language or distorted statistics reveal many sorts of biases to watch out for—bias toward (or against) a region of the country, a political party, males or females, a certain race or ethnic group, and so on.

Information **Packages**

Information comes in all shapes and sizes. Look at the chart below to get an overview of the kinds of information available, and how that information may be packaged.

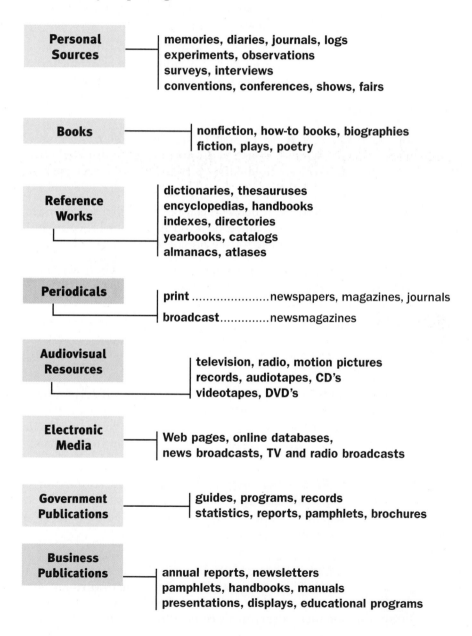

Personal Sources
- memories, diaries, journals, logs
- experiments, observations
- surveys, interviews
- conventions, conferences, shows, fairs

Books
- nonfiction, how-to books, biographies
- fiction, plays, poetry

Reference Works
- dictionaries, thesauruses
- encyclopedias, handbooks
- indexes, directories
- yearbooks, catalogs
- almanacs, atlases

Periodicals
- print .... newspapers, magazines, journals
- broadcast.............. newsmagazines

Audiovisual Resources
- television, radio, motion pictures
- records, audiotapes, CD's
- videotapes, DVD's

Electronic Media
- Web pages, online databases, news broadcasts, TV and radio broadcasts

Government Publications
- guides, programs, records
- statistics, reports, pamphlets, brochures

Business Publications
- annual reports, newsletters
- pamphlets, handbooks, manuals
- presentations, displays, educational programs

Information **Places**

Information places are sites where information packages can be located. For your research, consider the places listed below. What information packages can be found at these sites?

libraries	public	
	school	
	special	legal, medical
		government
		business
		research
computer resources	personal computers	files
		programs
	networks	e-mail
		Internet
		online services
mass media	radio, television	
	print	
learning sites	museums, zoos	
	science centers	
	special places	parks, nature centers
		historical sites
		plants and facilities
government	municipal	
	state	
	national	
research sites	laboratories	
	testing centers	
conference sites	shows, fairs, exhibits	
	conventions	
workplace	corporate databases	
	Web sites	

Conducting **Surveys**

One source of information available to all people is the survey. You can use surveys to collect facts and opinions from a logical audience. To get quality information using a survey, follow these guidelines:

1. Find a focus. Limit your purpose and target an audience.

2. Ask clear questions.

- Ask questions that are clear, precise, and complete.
- Use words that are objective (not biased or slanted).
- Make answering relatively easy.
- Offer answer options that are complete and do not overlap.

3. Match your questions to your purpose.

- Open-ended questions bring in a wide variety of answers and more complex information, but they take time to complete and the answers are hard to summarize and compile.
- Closed questions give respondents easy answer options, and the answers are easy to tabulate. Closed questions can provide two choices (*yes* or *no*, *true* or *false*), multiple choices, a rating or scale (*poor 1 2 3 excellent*), or a blank to fill.

4. Organize your survey so that it's easy to complete.

- In the introduction, state who you are and why you need the information. Explain how to complete the survey and when and where to return it.
- Guide readers with numbers, instructions, and headings.
- Begin with basic questions and end with any necessary complex, open-ended questions. Move in a logical order from one point to the next.
- Give respondents enough room to answer questions.

5. Test your survey.

- Ask a friend or a classmate to read your survey and help you revise it before printing it.
- Check how your survey works with a small test group.

6. Conduct your survey.

- Distribute the survey to a clearly defined group in a way that won't prejudice the sampling (random or cross-section).
- Get responses from a good sample (at least 10 percent) of your target group and tabulate them carefully and objectively.

Sample **Survey**

The introduction provides essential information.

Confidential Survey About Learning a Second Language

My name is Noelle Green, and I am conducting research about bilingual education in our school. I'd like to hear from you, McKinley High School students. Please answer the questions below by circling or filling in your responses. Then drop your survey in the box outside room 103 by Friday, February 10. Your responses will remain confidential.

The survey begins with clear, basic questions.

1. What is your gender?   **male   female**

2. What grade are you in?   **9   10   11   12**

3. What is your first language? _____

4. Are you learning a second language?   **yes   no**

Note: If you circled "no," you may turn in your survey at this point.

5. How long have you been learning the second language?

   1 year   2   3   4   5   6 years or more

The survey covers the topic thoroughly.

6. How are you learning this language?

   foreign language class   bilingual class   tutor   other

7. How would you rate your mastery of the second language?

   very little   1 2 3 4 5   proficient knowledge

8. Describe the best way to learn a second language.

   _____
   _____
   _____

The survey asks open-ended questions.

9. How will you use a second language? _____
   _____
   _____

10. How important is it to be bilingual?

    not important   1 2 3 4 5   very important

✱ The results of this survey would add valuable firsthand information to an essay about the merits of bilingual education. (See pages 204–205.)

Conducting **Interviews**

The purpose of an interview is simple. In order to get information, you talk with someone who is an expert on your topic. Use the guidelines below whenever you conduct an interview.

1. **Prepare for the interview** by doing your homework about the topic and your interviewee.

   ■ Arrange the interview in a thoughtful way. Explain your purpose, the process, and the topics to be covered.

   ■ Write questions for each of the specific ideas you want to cover in the interview. The 5 W's and H *(Who? What? Where? When? Why? and How?)* are important for good coverage.

   ■ Organize your questions in a logical order so that the interview moves smoothly from one subject to the next.

   ■ Write the questions on the left side of a page. Leave room for quotations, information, and impressions on the right side.

2. **During the interview,** try to relax so that your conversation seems natural and sincere.

   ■ Provide some background information about yourself, your project, and your plans for using the interview information.

   ■ Use recording equipment only if you have the interviewee's permission.

   ■ Jot down key facts, quotations, and impressions.

   ■ Listen actively. Show that you're listening through your body language—eye contact, nods, smiles. Pay attention not only to what the person says but also to how he or she says it.

   ■ Be flexible. If the person looks puzzled by a question, rephrase it. If the discussion gets off track, redirect it. Based on the interviewee's responses, ask follow-up questions. (If time allows, don't limit yourself to your planned questions only.)

3. **After the interview,** do the following:

   ■ As soon as possible, review your notes. Fill in responses you remember but couldn't record at the time.

   ■ Document your interview by interviewee's name, type of interview (personal interview, telephone interview), and date.

   ■ Thank the interviewee with a note, e-mail, or a phone call.

   ■ If necessary, ask the interviewee to check that your information and quotations are accurate.

   ■ Offer to send the interviewee a copy of your writing.

> "Cyberspace can give you more homework help than 10 libraries combined, and it's open 24 hours a day."
>
> —Preston Gralla

Using the
INTERNET

The Internet can be a writer's greatest resource or a writer's biggest waste of time. It can answer the most pressing questions you have about a topic, or it can lead to a great deal of frustration. The outcome all depends upon how you use the Internet. There are so many links to explore, so many flashy elements involved, that you can easily get lost. And, as with any technology, it's frustrating to need something in a hurry and not really know how or where to find it. However, if you plan ahead before logging on, and stay focused on your original purpose for browsing, the Net will take you to resources you never would have imagined.

In this chapter, we'll discuss how to use the Net for research and communication. (*Note:* Publishing on the Net is discussed in "Publishing Your Writing" on pages 38–39.)

Preview

- **Researching on the Net**
- **Communicating on the Net**
- **Netiquette**

Researching on the Net

One of the best things about the Internet is the wealth of information it makes available. Of course, you have to know how to find that information, how to evaluate it for accuracy, and how to save it for later use.

Locating Information

Your first research task as an Internet user is to find relevant and trustworthy sources of information.

USING AN INTERNET ADDRESS

Sometimes you will have the address of an Internet location, perhaps from a book, a periodical, or a teacher. Type the address into the bar at the top of your browser window; then press the "Enter" or "Return" key. Your browser will send a request for the site across your Internet connection and load it, if it's available.

USING A SEARCH ENGINE

If you don't have any Internet addresses for your topic, a search engine can help you look for sites. (For word-search tips, see page 349.)

Browser Searching ■ Some browsers have an Internet-search function built into them. Just type words about your topic into the address bar or search bar, then press "Return" or "Enter," and your browser will supply a list of suggested sites. Select one of those links to load that site.

Web Search Engines ■ The Web offers many different search engines. (See the Write Source site, www.thewritesource.com, for a recommended list.) Some use robot programs to search the Net; others accept recommendations submitted by individuals; most combine these two approaches. When you type a term into a search engine's input box, the search engine scans its database for matching sites. Then the engine returns recommendations for you to explore. (Most search engine sites also provide topic headings you can explore yourself rather than trusting the engine to do your searching.)

CONDUCTING A PAGE SEARCH

To find information quickly within a file, use the available document search functions. Just as your word processor can seek a particular word within a document, most Web browsers can "scan" the text of an Internet document. See your browser's help files to learn how.

Word-Search **TIPS**

Mastery of search engines lies in how you phrase your searches.

- **Enter a single word** to seek sites that contain that word or a derivative of it. The term *apple* yields sites containing the word *apple*, *apples*, *applet*, and so on.

- **Enter more than one word** to seek sites containing any of those words. The words *apple* and *pie* yield sites containing *apple* only and *pie* only, as well as those containing both words (together or not).

- **Use quotation marks** to find an exact phrase. The term *"apple pie"* (together in quotation marks) yields only sites with that phrase.

- **Use Boolean symbols (+ or -)** to shape your search. The phrase *+apple +pie* (without quotation marks) yields sites containing *both* words, though not necessarily as a phrase. The phrase *+apple -pie* yields sites with apple but not pie.

Note: Check the instructions on your favorite search engine to learn how to best use it.

Evaluating Information

It isn't always easy to judge the usefulness of information on the Net. Here are some guidelines to help you.

Consider the Source ■ Government and education sites are usually reliable, as are most nonprofit-organization and professional-business sites. Some private sites, however, are less accurate.

Compare Sources ■ If you find the same information at more than one reliable site, it is probably accurate.

Seek the Original Source ■ For news, try to find the original source, if possible. Otherwise, consider the information carefully.

Check with a Trusted Adult ■ Ask your parents, a teacher, a librarian, or a media specialist to help you judge the accuracy of what you find.

─HELP FILE─

Keep the following five points in mind when you evaluate the usefulness of a Net source: Is the information (1) reasonable, (2) reliable, (3) accurate, (4) current, and (5) complete?

Saving Information

There are several ways—including the four listed below—to preserve information once you find it.

Bookmark ■ Your Web browser can save a site's address for later use. Look for a "bookmark" or "favorites" option on your menu bar. But keep in mind that sites change, so a bookmark may become outdated.

Printout ■ You can print a hard copy of a Net document to keep. Be sure to note the details you'll need for citing the source in your work.

Electronic Copy ■ You can save a Net document to your computer or to a disc as text. Web browsers allow you to save a page as "source," which preserves the formatting. Unless your browser can create a "Web archive," however, you must save the page's graphics separately.

E-Mail ■ One quick way of saving is to send the current page address as e-mail to your personal account. That's especially helpful when you're not at your own computer.

Sample **Web Page**

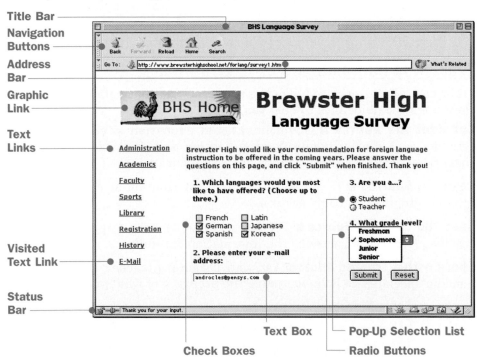

Communicating on the Net

Writers usually thrive in a community of other writers, and the Net allows such a community to converse in many new ways.

Chat Rooms ■ Chat rooms are sites where people can hold real-time conversations. You can find them through any search engine. Most are identified by topic. Pay attention to your Netiquette (see page 352) if you wish to be taken seriously and benefit from a chat room.

Mailing Lists ■ Mailing lists are group discussions of a topic by e-mail, often managed by an automated program. The messages come directly to your e-mail account. Check a search engine to find an automated mailing list about your topic.

Message Boards ■ Many organizations on the Internet provide online message boards devoted to one topic or another. Some message boards are open to the public; others are "members only." On a message board, people can post items for others to read and respond to. Some college courses are conducted online in a message-board format.

Online Writing Labs ■ Some schools maintain an online writing lab (OWL) on their Web site or Internet server. An OWL can be a great place to post your work in progress and have it critiqued by other writers and teachers. Ask your teacher if your school has such a site.

Navigation TIPS

Here are a few basic browser skills to help you "navigate" the Net.

- **Surfing Links:** You know to click on an underlined word or a highlighted image to use a Web link. You will find that not all pages underline or highlight their links. To check for a suspected link, move your mouse cursor over the spot. If the cursor changes in shape or color, you've found a link.

- **Back and Forward:** Your browser keeps a history of sites you visit each time you're online. Click the back arrow on your browser's toolbar to go back one site or the forward arrow to move ahead again. Clicking the right mouse button on these arrows (or holding the only mouse button down) shows a list of recently visited sites.

- **Returning Home:** If you get lost or confused while on the Net, click on the "home" symbol of your browser's toolbar to return your browser to its starting place.

Netiquette

Chatting and posting messages on the Net pose special challenges. It's almost as immediate as speaking face-to-face, but Net users don't have the visual cues that speakers do, and they can't hear the tone of voice. This means that the intent of a message can be misunderstood. To help solve this problem, Net users have developed "Netiquette." Proper Netiquette will help you communicate effectively online.

Message Clarity ■ The most important part of Netiquette is being careful as you write. Make your message as clear as possible before you send it. Also, don't assume that the recipient will remember a previous e-mail or post; add a reminder about the topic in your message. When responding to a message, it may help to quote part of it in your own.

Note: In your replies, don't quote a previous message entirely. Many people pay for their Internet connection by the minute and don't appreciate downloading long quotations of earlier messages.

Emoticons ■ Often, to add a certain tone to part of an online message, people use smiley faces or other emoticons. These sideways faces :-) are made up of keyboard characters.

Long Messages ■ If your message is long, it's polite to add "Long Message" to the subject line. That way people are prepared before they open the text itself.

Don't SHOUT ■ On the Net, words in capital letters mean SHOUTING. Don't send your messages in all capital letters. Such messages are harder to read, and people consider them rude.

Note: You can, however, use all capitals to emphasize words, such as to represent the title of a book (MOBY DICK, for example). For lighter emphasis, bracket the word in asterisks. (Netiquette *is* a virtue.)

Net Abbreviations ■ To speed the flow of communication, people on the Net use many abbreviations: LOL for "laughing out loud," TTFN for "ta-ta for now," and so on. If you see an abbreviation you don't know, don't be afraid to politely ask the user what it means.

Accuracy ■ Though writing e-mail and other electronic feedback is easy and fast, don't let that be an excuse for sloppiness. Proofread your message; check spacing between words and between sentences. Follow correct punctuation rules and use paragraphs just as you would in a nonelectronic message.

"Knowledge is of two kinds.
We know the subject ourselves,
or we know where we can find
information upon it."

—Samuel Johnson

Using the LIBRARY

Collecting information in the library is like detective work—it requires time, thought, and an inspired use of clues. Experienced information detectives know that one of their best informants is the librarian. An expert in information storage and retrieval, the librarian can help you conduct your research in any one of your classes.

Good detectives, though, don't depend on others to do all their searching. They get to know their way around, just as you need to do if you're going to use the library most effectively. This chapter will help.

Preview

- **Using the Computer Catalog**
- **Using the Card Catalog**
- **Selecting Reference Works**
- **Finding Articles in Periodicals**
- **Using a Dictionary**
- **Using a Thesaurus**
- **Using a Book**

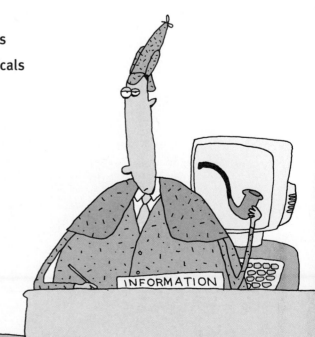

Using the **Computer Catalog**

A computer catalog contains all the information you need to use your library efficiently. Computer catalogs differ from card catalogs in their organization and operation but provide the same information. Most are easy to use; just follow the instructions on the screen. Below is a typical start-up screen.

```
Welcome to the Rapid City Public
Access On-Line Catalog
Databases:
    1. author, title, subject searching
    2. general periodical index
    3. information about system libraries
To make a selection, type a number and
then press [RETURN]>>>
```

You will be prompted to make a series of choices that will take you to a screen that gives the same information you would find on a catalog card. Print out the screen (if the computer allows you to) or write down the information you need.

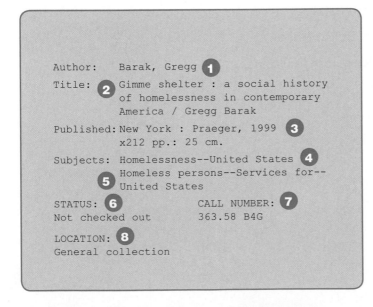

```
Author:    Barak, Gregg  ❶
Title:  ❷ Gimme shelter : a social history
           of homelessness in contemporary
           America / Gregg Barak
Published: New York : Praeger, 1999  ❸
           x212 pp.: 25 cm.
Subjects:  Homelessness--United States  ❹
        ❺ Homeless persons--Services for--
           United States
STATUS:  ❻          CALL NUMBER:  ❼
Not checked out       363.58 B4G

LOCATION:  ❽
General collection
```

❶ Author's name

❷ Title heading

❸ Publisher; copyright date

❹ Descriptive information

❺ Subject heading(s)

❻ Library status

❼ Call number

❽ Location information

Keyword Searching

Probably the greatest advantage of using an online catalog is being able to do *keyword searching*. This means that if you know only part of the title or author's name, you can still find the work.

Keyword Searches for Titles ■ If you know only one word in a book's title, use it as your *keyword*. The computer will show you all titles that contain the word, and you can scan the list to find the title you're looking for.

> **Important Note:** If you know several words in a title, use all of them; the computer will give you a shorter list to scan. (Use the most unusual word if you are limited to one keyword.)

Keyword Searches for Authors ■ If you know only an author's last name, the computer will show you all authors with that last name. You can scan the list to find the author you're looking for. (Some computers can find your author even if you know only the first few letters of the name, or if you spell the name incorrectly.)

Keyword Searches for Subjects ■ If you want to search by subject, using a keyword is similar to a regular subject search. However, a keyword search often turns up a longer list of books than a regular subject search.

Refining a Keyword Search

Computer catalogs vary. Some computer catalogs allow you to refine (broaden or narrow) your keyword search using ordinary words and phrases. Other search systems allow you to use "Boolean operators"—the words *and*, *or*, and *not*. Examples of how Boolean operators work are shown below.

Keywords you enter:	The computer will show you . . .
civil war	listings that contain the words *civil war.*
civil war **and** United States	listings that contain both *civil war* and *United States;* this might be the U.S. Civil War or other civil wars in which the U.S. played a role.
civil war **or** rebellion	listings that contain either *civil war* or *rebellion;* this would be civil wars anywhere, as well as events that were called *rebellions* instead of *wars.*
civil war **not** United States	listings that contain *civil war* but not *United States* (in other words, civil wars outside the U.S.).

Using the **Card Catalog**

A card catalog consists of drawers filled with index cards filed in alphabetical order. For each book or other resource, the catalog contains at least three cards:

- a subject card (filed under the general subject of the book),
- an author card (filed under the author's last name), and
- a title card (filed under the book's title).

Note: Books that cover more than one subject often have more than one subject card.

The different kinds of cards allow you to use whatever clues you have (the subject you're researching, an author's name, or a book title) to find the materials you need. When you've found a card for the book you want, the most important piece of information to record is the call number.

Sample Catalog Cards

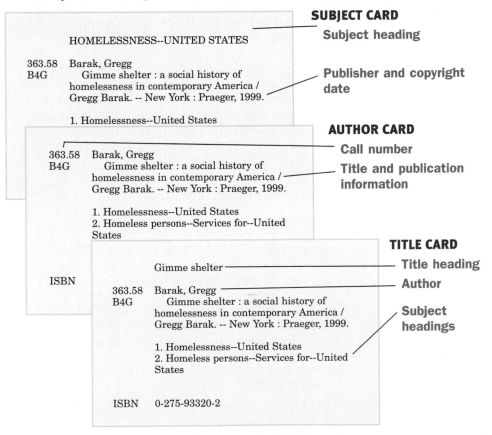

SUBJECT CARD
Subject heading

HOMELESSNESS--UNITED STATES

363.58   Barak, Gregg
B4G   Gimme shelter : a social history of
homelessness in contemporary America /
Gregg Barak. -- New York : Praeger, 1999.

Publisher and copyright date

1. Homelessness--United States

AUTHOR CARD
Call number

363.58   Barak, Gregg
B4G   Gimme shelter : a social history of
homelessness in contemporary America /
Gregg Barak. -- New York : Praeger, 1999.

Title and publication information

1. Homelessness--United States
2. Homeless persons--Services for--United States

ISBN

TITLE CARD
Title heading

Gimme shelter

Author

363.58   Barak, Gregg
B4G   Gimme shelter : a social history of
homelessness in contemporary America /
Gregg Barak. -- New York : Praeger, 1999.

Subject headings

1. Homelessness--United States
2. Homeless persons--Services for--United States

ISBN   0-275-93320-2

The **Call Number**

If you know how to read a call number, it can tell you a great deal about the book—including where to find it in the library.

The Dewey Decimal System

Call numbers are based on the classification system used by libraries to organize their materials. The most common system is the Dewey decimal system. The Dewey decimal system divides books into 10 main subject classes, with 100 numbers assigned to each class.

000-099 **General Works** • Encyclopedias, handbooks, and other books that cover many subjects

100-199 **Philosophy**

200-299 **Religion** • Books on religions or religious topics

300-399 **Social Sciences** • Books on education, government, law, economics, and other social sciences

400-499 **Languages** • Dictionaries and books about grammar

500-599 **Sciences** • Books about biology, chemistry, all other sciences, and math

600-699 **Technology** • Books about engineering, inventions, medicine, and cookbooks

700-799 **Arts and Recreation** • Books on painting, music, and other arts; sports and games

800-899 **Literature** • Poetry, plays, essays, and famous speeches

900-999 **History, Travel, and Geography**

Other Divisions

The 10 major subject classes are broken down into divisions, sections, and subsections—each with its own topic and number. The table below shows an example of each level of the Dewey decimal system.

Divisions of the Dewey Decimal Class Number

Number	Topic	Level
900	History	Class
970	History of North America	Division
973	History of the United States	Section
973.7	History of the U.S. Civil War	Subsection
973.74	History of Civil War Songs	Sub-subsection

Locating Books by Call Number

The Dewey decimal system determines a book's *class number*, which is the most important part of its call number. But the call number includes other information, too. Depending on which library you use, the call number may include the following items:

■ the first letter or letters of the author's last name,

■ a cutter number assigned by the librarian, and

■ the first letter of the first significant word in the title.

Sample Call Number

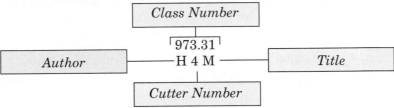

	Class Number	
	973.31	
Author	—H 4 M—	Title
	Cutter Number	

┌─**HELP FILE**─────────────────────────────

Fiction books and biographies are not classified according to the Dewey decimal system. Most fiction is shelved in a separate section of the library, alphabetized by the author's last name. (However, classic fiction is classified as literature and shelved in that Dewey decimal subject class.) Biographies, too, are in a separate section and are shelved alphabetically by the last name of the person written about.

Using the Call Number to Find the Book

To find a book in the library, you must read the call number carefully. Note that 973.2 is a higher number than 973.198 and will come after it on the shelf. (See illustration.)

Also, there may be many books with the same Dewey decimal number. In that case, you must use the rest of the call number to find the right book.

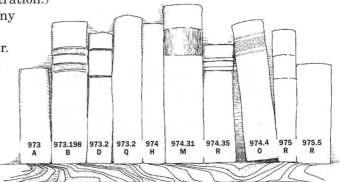

973	973.198	973.2	973.2	974	974.31	974.35	974.4	975	975.5
A	B	D	Q	H	M	R	O	R	R

Selecting **Reference Works**

The reference section is where you'll find dictionaries, thesauruses, encyclopedias, and other reference works, including the following:

Almanacs are regular (usually annual) publications filled with facts and statistics. Originally, almanacs were used as community calendars and basic information books. Today they're broader in scope and cover everything from politics to sports.

The World Almanac and *Information Please® Almanac* both present information on many topics such as business, politics, history, religion, social programs, sports, education, and the year's major events.

Atlases are books of detailed maps and related information. They include information on countries, transportation, languages, climate, and more.

The Rand McNally Commercial Atlas and Marketing Guide includes maps of the United States and its major cities as well as information on transportation and communication, economics, and population.

Street Atlas USA on CD-ROM allows you to call up street maps for any place in the United States.

Biographical Dictionaries contain minibiographies of many famous people, usually listed in alphabetical order.

Current Biography is published monthly and annually. Each article includes a photo of the individual, a biographical sketch, and information concerning the person's birth date, address, occupation, and so on.

Directories are lists of people and groups. (Directories are now widely used on the Internet.)

The National Directory of Addresses and Telephone Numbers provides nationwide coverage of companies, associations, schools, and so on.

Guides and Handbooks offer guidelines and models for exploring a topic, a program, an area of knowledge, or a profession.

Occupational Outlook Handbook, published by the Department of Labor, explores the job market—where jobs are or will be and how to prepare for the workplace.

Yearbooks cover major developments in specific areas of interest during the previous year.

Statistical Abstract of the United States: The National Data Book provides statistical information about the United States, from population figures to data on geography, social trends, politics, employment, and business.

Finding Articles in **Periodicals**

When you want to find articles in periodicals (magazines, journals, and newspapers), start with the periodical indexes. You will find them in the reference or periodical section of the library. Some will be in printed volumes; some may be on CD-ROM or computer.

Readers' Guide to Periodical Literature

The *Readers' Guide to Periodical Literature* is available in nearly all libraries. It indexes articles that appear in widely read magazines, so it is a good place to look for articles on a specific topic. Begin by finding the volume that covers the time period you are researching (perhaps you want only recent articles, or you are looking for details of an event that happened two years ago, and so on). Use the following guidelines to help you look up your topic:

- Articles are listed alphabetically by topic and by author.

- Some topics are divided into subtopics, with each article listed under the appropriate subtopic.

- Cross-references refer you to related topic entries where you may find more articles.

HELP FILE

Check to see which periodicals your library subscribes to before you search the *Readers' Guide.* That way, you won't spend time writing down information about articles that aren't available at your library.

Locating Articles

Once you've found a listing on your topic, write down the essential information: the name and issue date of the magazine, and the title and page numbers of the article. You may need to write this information on a call slip and give the slip to the librarian, who will get the periodical for you. Or, you may need to find the periodical yourself. Your library may have periodicals in printed form, on CD-ROM, or on microfilm.

Take NOTE

While the *Readers' Guide* is a common periodical index, most libraries have other indexes, too. The *General Periodicals Index,* for example, is similar to the *Readers' Guide* and is on computer. Some indexes list articles from a single publication, such as the *New York Times.*

Sample **Entries in a Periodical Guide**

The sample page below shows the type of information provided on a page in a periodical guide to literature. (Two articles are listed on this page.)

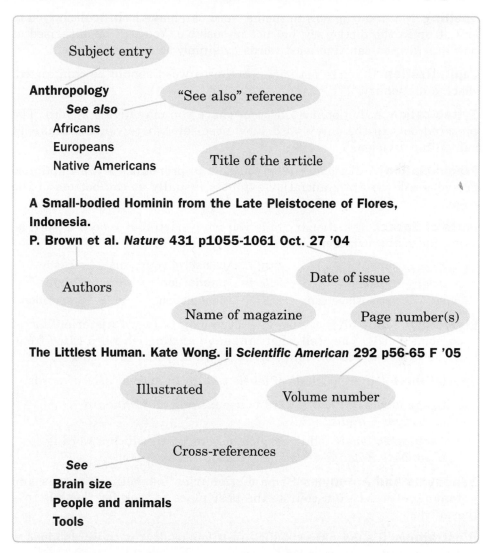

Subject entry

Anthropology
 See *also* "See also" reference
 Africans
 Europeans
 Native Americans Title of the article

A Small-bodied Hominin from the Late Pleistocene of Flores, Indonesia.
P. Brown et al. *Nature* **431 p1055-1061 Oct. 27 '04**

Authors

Date of issue

Name of magazine

Page number(s)

The Littlest Human. Kate Wong. il *Scientific American* **292 p56-65 F '05**

Illustrated

Volume number

Cross-references

 See
Brain size
People and animals
Tools

Finding Articles in Periodicals on the Web

There are Web sites that allow you to search for articles in periodicals. You can read some articles right on the Web. For other articles, only an abstract (summary) is provided. To read the complete article you would have to locate the periodical in a library.

Using a **Dictionary**

A dictionary gives many types of information, including the 10 types listed below.

Spelling Not knowing how to spell a word can make it difficult for you to look it up in the dictionary, but not impossible. You will be surprised at how quickly you can find most words by simply sounding them out.

Capitalization If you're not sure whether a word should be capitalized, check a dictionary.

Syllabication A dictionary tells you where you may divide a word. The centered dots in the entry word show precisely where you can make an end-of-line division.

Pronunciation A dictionary tells you how to pronounce a word and also provides a key to pronunciation symbols, usually at the bottom of the page.

Parts of Speech A dictionary tells you what part(s) of speech a word is, using these abbreviations:

n	noun	*tr.v*	transitive verb	*adj*	adjective
pron	pronoun	*interj*	interjection	*adv*	adverb
vi	intransitive verb	*conj*	conjunction	*prep*	preposition

Etymology Many dictionaries give etymologies (word histories) for at least some words. They tell what language an English word came from, how the word entered our language, and when it was first used.

Special Uses Different kinds of labels tell about special uses of words.

> **Usage labels** tell how a word is used: *slang, nonstandard (nonstand.), dialect (dial.),* etc.

> **Geographic labels** tell the region or country in which a word is used: *New England (NewEng.), Canada (Can.),* etc.

Synonyms and Antonyms Some dictionaries list both synonyms and antonyms of words. (Of course, the best place to look for these is in a thesaurus.)

Illustrations If a definition is difficult to make clear with words alone, a picture or drawing is provided.

Meanings Many dictionaries list all the meanings of a word. Some list meanings chronologically, with the oldest meaning first, followed by newer meanings. Other dictionaries list a word's most common meaning first, followed by less common meanings. Always read all the meanings listed to make sure you are using the word appropriately.

Sample **Dictionary Page**

GUIDE WORDS	**bossism-•-Botswana** 168

Botany Bay An inlet of the Tasman Sea in SE Australia.
botch (bŏch) *tr.v.* **botched, botch•ing, botch•es 1.** To ruin through clumsiness. **2.** To make or perform clumsily; bungle. **3.** To repair or mend clumsily. ❖ *n.* **1.** A ruined or defective piece of work: "*I have made a miserable botch of this description*" (Nathaniel Hawthorne). **2.** A hodgepodge. [ME *bocchen*, to mend.] —**botch′er** *n.* —**botch′y** *adj.*

SYNONYMS *botch, blow, bungle, fumble, muff* These verbs mean to harm or spoil through inept or clumsy handling: *botch a repair; blow an opportunity; bungle an interview; fumbled my chance; muffed the painting job.*

bot•fly also **bot fly** (bŏt′flī′) *n.* Any of various stout two-winged flies, chiefly of the genera *Gasterophilus* and *Oestrus*, having larvae that are parasitic on various animals.
both (bōth) *adj.* One and the other; relating to or being two in conjunction: *Both guests came.* ❖ *pron.* The one and the other: *Both are mad.* ❖ *conj.* Used with *and* to link two things in a coordinated phrase or clause: *both he and I.* [ME *bothe* < ON *bādhar.* See **to-** in App.]

USAGE NOTE *Both* is used to indicate that the action or state denoted by the verb applies individually to each of two entities.

Bo•tha (bō′tə, -tä′), **Louis** 1862–1919. South African general and first prime minister of South Africa (1910–19).
Botha, Pieter Willem b. 1916. South African prime minister (1978–89) who upheld apartheid.
both•er (bŏth′ər) *v.* **-ered, -er•ing, -ers** —*tr.* **1.** To disturb or anger, esp. by minor irritations; annoy. **2a.** To make agitated or nervous; fluster. **b.** To make confused or perplexed; puzzle. **3.** To intrude on without warrant; disturb. **4.** To give trouble to. —*intr.* **1.** To take the trouble; concern oneself. **2.** To cause trouble. ❖ *n.* A cause or state of disturbance. ❖ *interj.* Used to express annoyance or mild irritation. [Prob. < dialectal *bodder*, poss. of Celt. orig.]
both•er•a•tion (bŏth′ə-rā′shən) *n.* The act of bothering or the state of being bothered. ❖ *interj.* Used to express annoyance or irritation.
both•er•some (bŏth′ər-səm) *adj.* Causing bother.
Both•ni•a (bŏth′nē-ə), **Gulf of** An arm of the Baltic Sea between Sweden and Finland.
Both•well (bŏth′wĕl′, -wəl, bŏth′-), **4th Earl of.** Title of James Hepburn. 1536?–78. Scottish noble and third husband of Mary Queen of Scots, whose second husband, Lord Darnley, he murdered (1567).
bo tree (bō) *n.* See **pipal.** [Partial transl. of Sinhalese *bo-gaha*, tree of wisdom (because it was the tree under which the Buddha was enlightened) : *bo*, wisdom (< Pali *bodhi* < Skt. *bodhiḥ*, enlightenment; see **bheudh-** in App.) + *gaha*, tree.]
bot•ry•oi•dal (bŏt′rē-oid′l) also **bot•ry•oid** (bŏt′rē-oid′) *adj.* Shaped like a bunch of grapes. Used esp. of mineral formations: *botryoidal hematite.* [< Gk. *botruoeidēs* : *botrus*, bunch of grapes + *-oeidēs*, -oid.] —**bot′ry•oi′dal•ly** *adv.*
bo•try•tis (bō-trī′tĭs) *n.* **1.** Any of various fungi of the genus *Botrytis* responsible for numerous fruit and vegetable diseases. **2.** Noble rot. [NLat., genus name < Gk. *botrus*, bunch of grapes.]
Bot•swa•na (bŏt-swä′nə) Formerly **Bech•u•a•na•land** (bĕch-wä′nə-lănd′, bĕch′ōō-ä′-) A country of S-central Africa; gained independence from Great Britain in 1966. Cap. Gaborone. Pop. 1,443,000. —**Bot•swa′nan** *adj. & n.*

Botswana

SYNONYMS

MEANING

USAGE

SPELLING OF RELATED FORMS

ETYMOLOGY (History)

PRONUNCIATION

SPELLING AND CAPITAL LETTERS

SYLLABICATION AND PART OF SPEECH

ILLUSTRATION

Using a **Thesaurus**

A thesaurus is, in a sense, the opposite of a dictionary. You go to a dictionary when you know the word but need the definition. You go to a thesaurus when you know the general definition but need a specific word. For example, you might want a noun that means *fear*—the kind of fear that causes worry. You need the word to complete the following sentence:

Dana experienced a certain amount of _____ over the upcoming exam.

If you have a thesaurus in dictionary form, simply look up the word *fear* as you would in a dictionary. If, however, you have a traditional thesaurus, first look up your word in the index. You might find this entry:

FEAR 860
Fearful painful 830
timid 862

The numbers in the index entry (for example, 860) are guide numbers, not page numbers. When you look up number 860 in the thesaurus, you will find a long list of synonyms for *fear*. You may need to look up some in a dictionary to help you decide which is exactly right for your sentence. *Anxiety* means "a state of uneasiness, worry, and fear"; it's a good choice.

Dana experienced a certain amount of <u>anxiety</u> over the upcoming exam.

259   PERSONAL AFFECTIONS   859-861

860. FEAR—*N.* **fear,** timidity, diffidence, apprehensiveness, fearfulness, solicitude, anxiety, care, apprehension, misgiving, mistrust, suspicion, qualm, hesitation.

 trepidation, flutter, fear and trembling, perturbation, tremor, restlessness, disquietude, funk *[colloq.].*

 fright, alarm, dread, awe, terror, horror, dismay, consternation, panic, scare; stampede *[of horses].*

 V. **fear,** be afraid, apprehend, dread, distrust; hesitate, falter, wince, flinch, shy, shrink, fly.

 tremble, shake, shiver, shudder, flutter, quake, quaver, quiver, quail.

 frighten, fright, terrify, inspire (*or* excite) fear, bulldoze *[colloq.],* alarm, startle, scare, dismay, astound; awe; strike terror, appall, unman, petrify, horrify.

 Adj. **afraid,** frightened, alarmed, fearful, timid, timorous, nervous, diffident, fainthearted, tremulous, shaky, apprehensive.

 ✱ Review the entire list of synonyms in the thesaurus entry before choosing a word. Also, consider both the word's meaning and connotation.

Using a **Book**

Knowing the parts of a book can help you find information easily and quickly. Note that an appendix, a glossary, a bibliography, and an index are typically found only in nonfiction books.

- The **title page** is usually the first printed page in a book. It gives (1) the full title of the book, (2) the author's name, (3) the publisher's name, and (4) the place of publication.

- The **copyright page** follows the title page. Here you will find the year the copyright was issued. (When you are looking for up-to-date facts, be sure to check the book's copyright.)

- The **preface, foreword,** or **introduction** come before the table of contents and give an overview of what the book is about and why it was written.

- The **table of contents** lists the names and numbers of the major divisions of the book and the page on which each begins. The table of contents can give you a good overview of what the book is about.

- The **body** is the main text of the book.

- An **epigraph** is a quotation at the beginning of a chapter or a division; an epigraph sets forth the main idea.

- A **footnote** is placed at the bottom of a page and either gives the source of information used in the text or adds useful information. (Endnotes have the same function but appear at the end of a chapter or after the body of the book.)

- An **appendix** may follow the body. It provides additional information, often in the form of maps, charts, tables, diagrams, or documents.

- A **glossary** may follow the appendix. It is an alphabetical list of key words and definitions related to the topic of the book.

- The **bibliography** may list sources used by the author, suggestions for further reading, or both.

- The **index** is an alphabetical list of all the topics covered in the book, with the page number(s) on which each topic is covered.

Take NOTE
The index is probably the most useful part of any reference book. It tells you, first, whether the book contains the information you need and, second, where you can find it.

READING
Skills

Reading Graphics   367

Critical Reading Skills   373

Improving Vocabulary Skills   385

"Understanding the purpose and function of information graphics will help you develop your rhetorical reading skills."

—John C. Bean, Virginia A. Chappell,

and Alice M. Gillam

Reading
GRAPHICS

Graphics combine a strong visual element with a few key words to communicate an important piece of information. Common graphics include graphs, tables, diagrams, and maps.

A good graphic can make complex information easy to understand. It can show in one picture what it might take hundreds of words to tell. That's why a graphic usually makes a big impression. It registers almost immediately in the reader's mind.

The main purpose of all graphics is to show how facts relate to one another. Different graphics show different types of relationships. For example, a line graph shows how something changes over time, and a picture diagram shows how all the parts of something fit together. This chapter will help you read and understand the most common types of graphics.

Preview

- **Graphs**
- **Tables**
- **Diagrams**
- **Maps**

Graphs

Graphs show how different pieces of information are related. The most common kinds of graphs are line graphs, pie graphs, and bar graphs.

Line Graph ■ A line graph shows how things change over time. It starts with an L-shaped grid. The horizontal line of the grid stands for passing time (minutes, years, centuries). The vertical line of the grid shows the subject of the graph. The line graph below shows the estimated amounts of carbon dioxide emitted into the atmosphere from 1995 to 2004.

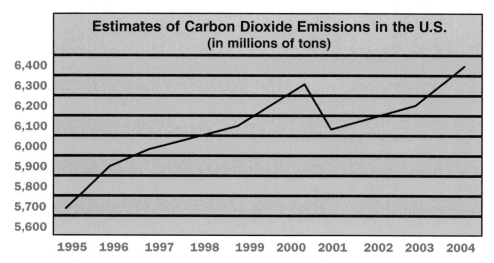

Pie Graph ■ A pie graph shows proportions and how each proportion, or part, relates to the other parts as well as to the whole pie. The pie graph below shows what percentage of immigrant groups in the United States in 2003 came from different global regions.

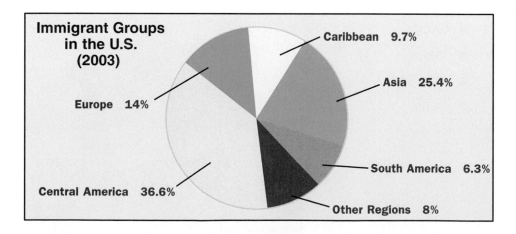

Bar Graph ■ A bar graph uses bars (sometimes called columns) to stand for the subjects of the graph. Unlike line graphs, bar graphs do not show how things change over time. Instead, like a snapshot, they show how things compare at one time.

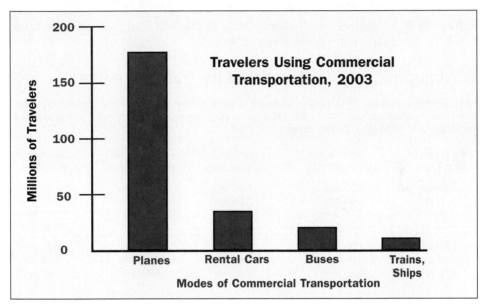

Stacked Bar Graph ■ A stacked bar graph gives more detailed information than a regular bar graph. Besides comparing the bars, it compares parts within the bars themselves.

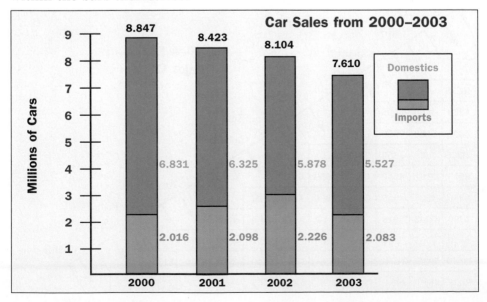

Tables

A table organizes detailed information in a clear and convenient way. Most tables have rows (going across) and columns (going down). Rows contain one set of details, while columns contain another.

Schedule ■ A common and useful table is the schedule. Read schedules carefully because each one is a bit different.

Washington, D.C., to New York City Train Schedule

Reading this schedule: Find the time you want to arrive in New York City in the right-hand column. Read straight across, to your left, on the same line to your pickup point; that is the time you will leave from that point. (Disregard all other times.)

Lv **Washington, D.C.** Union Station	Lv **Baltimore, MD** BWI Airport Station	Lv **Philadelphia, PA** 30th Street Station	Lv **Newark, NJ** North Broad Street	Ar **New York City** Penn Station
5:00 am	5:35 am	6:57 am	7:58 am	8:14 am
6:00 am	5:36 am	7:58 am	8:59 am	9:12 am
7:30 am	8:10 am	10:00 am	11:15 am	11:35 am
8:00 am	8:35 am	9:50 am	10:00 am	10:14 am
1:00 pm	1:35 pm	2:57 pm	4:00 pm	4:20 pm
3:00 pm	3:30 pm	4:45 pm	5:40 pm	5:55 pm
6:00 pm	6:35 pm	7:45 pm	8:45 pm	9:00 pm

Distance Table ■ Another common kind of table is a distance, or mileage, table. To read a distance table, find the place you're starting from and the place you're going to. Then find the place where the row and the column meet. That will show the distance in miles from one place to another.

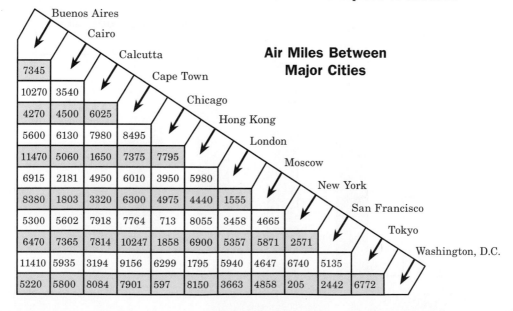

Air Miles Between Major Cities

Buenos Aires	Cairo	Calcutta	Cape Town	Chicago	Hong Kong	London	Moscow	New York	San Francisco	Tokyo	Washington, D.C.
7345											
10270	3540										
4270	4500	6025									
5600	6130	7980	8495								
11470	5060	1650	7375	7795							
6915	2181	4950	6010	3950	5980						
8380	1803	3320	6300	4975	4440	1555					
5300	5602	7918	7764	713	8055	3458	4665				
6470	7365	7814	10247	1858	6900	5357	5871	2571			
11410	5935	3194	9156	6299	1795	5940	4647	6740	5135		
5220	5800	8084	7901	597	8150	3663	4858	205	2442	6772	

Diagrams

A diagram is a drawing designed to show how something is constructed, how its parts relate to one another, or how it works.

Picture Diagram ■ A picture diagram is just that—a picture or drawing of the subject. The diagram below shows a cross section of a human heart and identifies the important parts, including the veins and arteries attached to the heart.

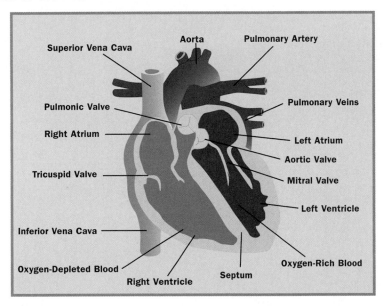

Line Diagram ■ A line diagram uses lines, symbols, and words to show the relationships among people, places, things, or ideas. A family tree is a type of line diagram. The diagram below shows relationships among languages with Latin as their origin.

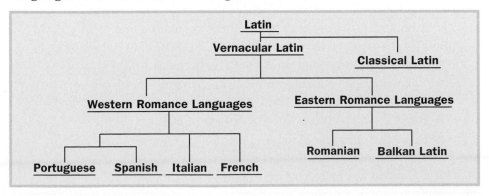

Maps

A map may show a continent, a country, a state, a city, or another geographic area. There are many kinds of maps (political maps, road maps, topographical maps, weather maps, etc.), each serving a different purpose.

Weather Map ■ A weather map has a language all its own, made up of words, symbols, and colors. Study the map's key to unlock its language.

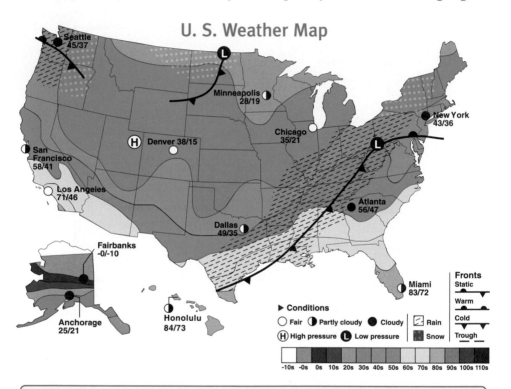

U. S. Weather Map

TIPS for Reading Graphics

Although no two graphs, tables, diagrams, or maps are exactly alike, there are some general guidelines you can use:

■ Read the title or caption (to get the big picture).

■ Read the labels or column headings (to get a better idea of what the chart is covering).

■ Read the data (to get specific information).

■ Read the paragraph above or below the chart (to provide background information).

■ Read the key or footnotes (to clarify the details).

"To read without reflecting
is like eating without digesting."
—Edmund Burke

CRITICAL READING Skills

Most of the reading you do in school is critical reading: careful
reading for the purpose of understanding and interpreting information.
As you probably know, critical reading takes effort. You sometimes need
to read a text more than once, especially if the material is difficult. You
often need to refer to other parts of the book as you read (the *glossary,
appendix*, and *index*, for example). You may even need to use other
resources (*atlases, dictionaries*, or *handbooks*) to help you. Above all,
you need to concentrate and think about what you're reading.

This chapter gives you strategies that will help you with your critical
reading. You'll learn specific skills that will help you now and in the
future, even with the most challenging texts.

Preview

- ■ **Strategies for Critical Reading**
- ■ **Patterns of Nonfiction**
- ■ **Reading and Reacting to Nonfiction**
- ■ **Reading and Reacting to Fiction**
- ■ **Reading Poetry**

Strategies for **Critical Reading**

Critical reading puts you mentally on the edge of your seat. It trains you to meet any reading challenge. It shows you how to learn as much as possible from a text. You read critically in these ways:

- Reading with total focus
- Reading actively, with a purpose and a plan
- Reading to digest, not simply to swallow
- Reading to apply information to other tasks

Read Critically

To become a critical reader, apply the following guidelines to each reading assignment.

1. **Be purposeful.** When you read, know your goal. Ask yourself how this text fits into the course or what this reading adds to your understanding.

2. **Be prepared.** Instead of coming at the text cold, get ready for it. Set aside enough time for the task and gather the necessary materials (pens, notebooks, dictionary).

3. **Be active.** Preview the chapter, Web site, or journal article to get the big picture. Preview titles, headings, and graphics to gain a sense of the whole. Look for the main ideas, and take clear notes on important information and ideas. (See page 375–380.)

4. **Be curious and engaged.** Ask yourself questions about what you are reading. Make the writer's interests your own. Turn the reading process into a conversation with the text.

5. **Be open and fair.** Read the entire piece, respecting what the writer says even as you evaluate it.

6. **Be a little distant.** Keep a critical distance from the reading. Hold an argument at arm's length so that you can examine it fairly. Developing a healthy critical distance allows you to measure the value of what you are reading.

7. **Be thorough.** If the reading has been difficult, reread challenging parts and try to connect them to what you do understand. Summarize what you've read.

Take NOTE
Reading assignments sometimes take unexpected turns. A reading with a serious purpose may include passages marked by humor, while a comical reading may have a serious intent. Stay open to the unexpected.

Patterns of Nonfiction

Knowing some of the common patterns of nonfiction makes it easier to understand your assigned reading. Five of these patterns are reviewed in this chapter: *description, chronological order, comparison/contrast, main idea/supporting details,* and *cause and effect.* Knowing these patterns can help you take notes as you read.

Description

Description focuses on sensory details (how something looks, sounds, and feels) to give you a clear picture of the topic. When a selection follows the description pattern, you can use mapping to help you take notes.

Mount Everest, the world's highest mountain at 29,028 feet, towers over the border between Nepal and Tibet. Its Nepali name is *Sagarmatha,* which means "Forehead in the Sky."

Everest is clothed with gigantic glaciers that make their way down its slopes—usually slowly, but sometimes in huge, thundering avalanches of snow and ice that bury entire valleys. Temperatures vary greatly. In January, the average temperature at the summit is -33° Fahrenheit; low temperatures drop to -76°F. The "warmest" month is July, when the average temperature is -2°F.

From June through September, monsoon season brings screaming winds and blinding snowstorms. Winter winds whip around the summit at more than 175 miles per hour—stronger than a Category 5 hurricane.

Mapping

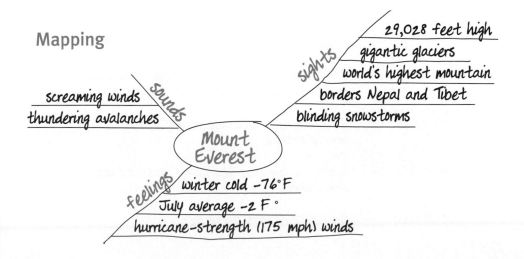

Chronological Order

When a selection relates information in chronological order, you can use a time line to help you take notes. A time line lists events in the order in which they happen.

Today when we think of technology, we think of things like computers and satellites. But the story of technology begins at least 12,000 years ago (in about 10,000 B.C.E.). That's when people first began to use metal to make tools and utensils. The first metal to be used was copper. It was a big improvement over stone because coppersmiths could heat it and mold it into any needed shape.

The earliest evidence of people combining copper with tin to make bronze dates from about 4500 B.C.E. in Thailand. Bronze was much harder than copper and could be shaped into a sharp edge. With the invention of bronze, people were able to make knives, swords, and other weapons.

Around 3000 B.C.E., iron became the metal of choice. It was even harder than bronze and easier to come by because there was plenty of it near the earth's surface. The process of making steel—a strong, hard, flexible alloy (mixture) of iron and carbon—was first developed around 1400 but wasn't perfected until the 1800s.

Time Line

History of Modern Metals

10,000 B.C.E.	Copper was the first metal to be used for tools.
4500 B.C.E.	In Thailand, copper and tin were combined to make bronze, a harder metal than copper.
3000 B.C.E.	Iron was used because it was harder and more plentiful.
1400 C.E.	Early steelmaking technology combined iron and carbon.
1800 C.E.	Steelmaking was perfected.

Comparison/Contrast

The comparison/contrast pattern introduces two (or more) topics and then tells how they are the same and how they are different. A Venn diagram is a helpful way to organize comparison/contrast notes.

There are many similarities between the two world wars, but also some important differences. In both wars, Great Britain, France, and Russia (the Soviet Union in World War II) were the main Allies until the United States joined them late in the conflict. In both wars, Germany was the primary adversary. In World War I, Germany was joined by Austria-Hungary, Turkey, and Bulgaria; in World War II, Germany's partners were Japan and Italy. (Italy had been an Allied nation in World War I.) Germany and its partners lost both wars.

WW II caused about four times as many deaths as WW I (about 55 million compared to about 14 million) and had a far greater impact on world politics, leaving the United States and Soviet Union as powerful leaders.

Venn Diagram

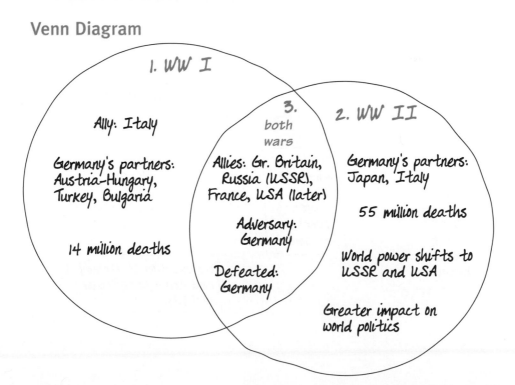

1. WW I

Ally: Italy

Germany's partners: Austria-Hungary, Turkey, Bulgaria

14 million deaths

3. both wars

Allies: Gr. Britain, Russia (USSR), France, USA (later)

Adversary: Germany

Defeated: Germany

2. WW II

Germany's partners: Japan, Italy

55 million deaths

World power shifts to USSR and USA

Greater impact on world politics

Main Idea/Supporting Details

This pattern begins with one main idea and goes on to give details (facts, figures, examples) that explain the main idea. A table organizer can help you organize your notes.

William Shakespeare is widely believed to be the greatest playwright of all time. There are several hallmarks of Shakespeare's work that have earned him this honor. Perhaps most important, Shakespeare's plays portray universal human emotions and behaviors in a way that is both sharply accurate and deeply moving. Audiences can identify with characters who experience the same kinds of problems, weaknesses, and feelings that all human beings experience. Second, Shakespeare expressed his characters' most powerful emotions in the equally powerful language of poetry. This successful blend of poetry and drama is an unparalleled achievement. Third, Shakespeare also mixes comedy with tragedy to dramatize the unpredictable nature of pleasure and pain in life. These qualities combine to give Shakespeare's works unmatched depth and texture.

Table Organizer

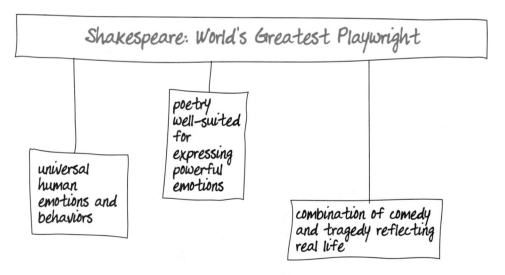

Cause and Effect

The cause-and-effect pattern shows the relationships between two or more events or situations. Cause-and-effect relationships can take on a variety of forms: one cause with many effects, many causes that create one final effect (as in the excerpt below), and other variations. When a selection features cause-and-effect relationships, you can use an organizer like the one below to help you take notes.

> **Economic, political, and philosophical causes combined to bring about the French Revolution. France was in financial crisis because of war expenditures (including loans to American revolutionaries) and luxury-loving kings and queens. The middle class and peasants were taxed heavily, while the clergy and wealthy nobility paid nothing. Although the common people made up four-fifths of the population, they had only one-third of the vote in the French legislature. Therefore, they had no political power to change the tax laws. Dissatisfaction with this state of affairs was fueled by philosophers throughout Europe who were promoting philosophical ideas such as "government by majority rule" and "the inalienable rights of all human beings, regardless of their social or economic status." When efforts to reform the French government failed, a full-scale revolt began.**

Cause-and-Effect Organizer

Subject: The French Revolution

Causes:	Effects:

Economic Crisis
  common people—heavily taxed
  for war debts
	resentment of luxury-loving royalty
	and untaxed clergy and nobility

Political Power
  common people—no power
  to make changes (4/5 of
  population with 1/3 of vote)
	dissatisfaction over inability to
	change tax laws

Philosophical Ideas
  inalienable rights,
  majority rule
	attempts to reform fail
	
	Final Effect: Revolution

Reading Nonfiction: SQ3R

An effective reading technique for all patterns of nonfiction is the SQ3R method. SQ3R stands for the five steps in this reading process: *survey, question, read, recite,* and *review.*

Before You Read . . .

Survey ■ The first step in the SQ3R study method is "survey." When you survey a reading assignment, you try to get a general idea of what the assignment is about. You look briefly at each page, paying special attention to the headings, chapter titles, illustrations, and boldfaced type. It is also a good idea to read the first and last paragraphs.

Question ■ As you do your survey, you should begin to ask questions about the material—questions that you hope to find the answers to as you read. One quick way of doing this is to turn the headings and subheadings into questions. Asking questions will make you an "active" rather than a "passive" reader, keeping you involved and thinking about what is coming up next.

As You Read . . .

Read ■ Read the material carefully from start to finish. Look for main ideas in each paragraph or section. Take notes as you read. (See the next page. Also see pages 375-379.) Read the difficult parts slowly. (Reread them if necessary.) Use context to help you figure out the most difficult passages. (See page 388.) Look up unfamiliar words or ideas, and imagine the events, people, places, or things you are reading about.

Recite ■ One of the most valuable parts of the SQ3R method is the reciting step. It is very important that you recite out loud what you have learned from your reading. Stop at the end of each page, section, or chapter to answer the *Who? What? When? Where? Why?* and *How?* questions. This step is a way of testing yourself on how well you understand what you have read. You may then reread if necessary.

After You Read . . .

Review ■ The final step is to review. If you have some questions about the assignment, answer them immediately. If you have no questions, summarize the assignment in a short writing. You may also make an outline, note cards, flash cards, and illustrations to help you review and remember what you have read.

Reacting to **Nonfiction**

The excerpt below comes from Henry David Thoreau's essay "Civil Disobedience." The side notes show how one student reacted to this reading. She makes observations, asks question, summarizes certain parts, and connects ideas to other subjects. Whenever you are reading a challenging nonfiction text, you should react to it in the same way.

I think of Martin Luther King and Ghandi when I read this part about a "just man in prison."

Thoreau writes long, rambling sentences.

What does Thoreau mean that "truth is stronger than error"?

Thoreau believes that being in the minority is not a reason to give up.

Is Thoreau more concerned about rebelling against the government or the evil of slavery?

Excerpt from "Civil Disobedience"

Under a government which imprisons any unjustly, the true place for a just man is also in prison. The proper place to-day, the only place which Massachusetts has provided for her freer and less desponding spirits, is in her prisons, to be put out and locked out of the State by her own act, as they have already put themselves out by their principles. It is there that the fugitive slave, and the Mexican prisoner on parole, and the Indian come to plead the wrongs of his race, should find them; on that separate, but more free and honorable ground, where the State places those who are not with her, but against her—the only house in a slave State in which a free man can abide with honor. If any think that their influence would be lost there, and their voices no longer afflict the ear of the State, that they would not be as an enemy within its walls, they do not know by how much truth is stronger than error, nor how much more eloquently and effectively he can combat injustice who has experienced a little in his own person. Cast your whole vote, not a strip of paper merely, but your whole influence. A minority is powerless while it conforms to the majority; it is not even a minority then; but it is irresistible when it clogs by its whole weight. If the alternative is to keep all just men in prison, or give up war and slavery, the State will not hesitate which to choose. If a thousand men were not to pay their tax bills this year, that would not be a violent and bloody measure, as it would be to pay them, and enable the State to commit violence and shed innocent blood. This is, in fact, the definition of a peaceable revolution, if any such is possible. If the tax-gatherer, or any other public officer, asks me, as one has done, "But what shall I do?" my answers is, "If you really wish to do anything, resign your office." When the subject has refused allegiance, and the officer has resigned his office, then the revolution is accomplished. But even suppose blood should flow. Is there not a sort of blood shed when the conscience is wounded? Through this wound a man's real manhood and immortality flow out, and he bleeds to an everlasting death, I see the blood flowing now. . . .

Reading **Fiction**

Fiction isn't fact, but good fiction is true. Fiction uses made-up characters and events to show something that is true about life. That's why reading fiction is a great way to learn. Here are some things to think about and explore as you read fiction. (See pages 241–242 for more.)

Before You Read . . .

■ Learn something about the author and his or her other works.

■ React thoughtfully to the title and opening pages.

As You Read . . .

■ Identify the following story elements: *setting, tone, main characters, theme*, and *central conflict*.

■ Always keep the plot in mind and try to predict what will happen next.

■ Record your personal thoughts (or draw, list, cluster them) in a reading journal as you progress through the story. (See the next page.)

■ Think about the characters and the things they do.

● What motivates the characters?

● Have I known similar characters in life or in literature?

● Have I faced situations similar to the ones faced by the main characters?

● Would I have reacted in the same way?

■ Think about how the time and place in which the author lives (or lived) may have influenced the story.

■ Notice the author's style and word choice. (See pages 124–126.)

● How effectively has the author used literary devices?

● Why did the author use a particular word or phrase?

■ Discuss the story with others who are reading it.

After You Read . . .

■ Think about the changes the main character undergoes. Often, this is the key to understanding fiction.

■ Determine the story's main message or theme; then decide how effectively this message is communicated.

Reacting to **Fiction**

The excerpt below comes from Nathaniel Hawthorne's novel *The Scarlet Letter*. The side notes show how one student reacted to this reading. He makes observations, defines unfamiliar words, asks questions, and so on. Whenever you are reading a challenging piece of fiction, you should react to it in the same way.

From *The Scarlet Letter*, Chapter 2, "The Market-Place"

Hester seems ashamed but still proud.

She makes her mark of shame look gorgeous.

Hawthorne's language sounds "lady-like."

"Evanescent" means "quickly disappearing."

What is a "halo of the misfortune and ignominy?"

When the young woman—the mother of this child—stood fully revealed before the crowd, it seemed to be her first impulse to clasp the infant closely to her bosom; not so much by an impulse of motherly affection, as that she might thereby conceal a certain token, which was wrought or fastened into her dress. In a moment, however, wisely judging that one token of her shame would but poorly serve to hide another, she took the baby on her arm, and, with a burning blush, and yet a haughty smile, and a glance that would not be abashed, looked around at her townspeople and neighbours. On the breast of her gown, in fine red cloth, surrounded with an elaborate embroidery and fantastic flourishes of gold thread, appeared the letter A. It was so artistically done, and with so much fertility and gorgeous luxuriance of fancy, that it had all the effect of a last and fitting decoration to the apparel which she wore; and which was of a splendor in accordance with the taste of the age, but greatly beyond what was allowed by the sumptuary regulations of the colony.

The young woman was tall, with a figure of perfect elegance, on a large scale. She had dark and abundant hair, so glossy that it threw off the sunshine with a gleam, and a face which, besides being beautiful from regularity of feature and richness of complexion, had the impressiveness belonging to a marked brow and deep black eyes. She was lady-like, too, after the manner of the feminine gentility of those days; characterized by a certain state and dignity, rather than by the delicate, evanescent, and indescribable grace, which is now recognized as its indication. And never had Hester Prynne appeared more lady-like, in the antique interpretation of the term, than as she issued from the prison. Those who had before known her, and had expected to behold her dimmed and obscured by a disastrous cloud, were astonished, and even startled, to perceive how her beauty shone out, and made a halo of the misfortune and ignominy in which she was enveloped. It may be true, that, to a sensitive observer, there was something exquisitely painful in it. . . .

Reading Poetry

The poet Archibald MacLeish once said that "a poem should not *mean*, but *be*." That may sound a bit odd at first, but this explanation just might point you in the right direction when it comes to reading a poem.

You shouldn't expect to grasp everything a poem has to offer in one reading, especially if the poem is lengthy or complex. In fact, it usually takes at least three readings to begin to appreciate everything about a poem. Here are some strategies to help you get the most out of the poetry you read.

First Reading

- Read the poem all the way through at your normal reading speed to gain on overall first impression.
- Jot down your immediate reaction to the poem.

Second Reading

- Read the poem again—out loud, if possible. Pay attention to the sound of the poem.
- Read slowly and carefully observing the punctuation, spacing, and special treatment of words and lines.
- Note examples of sound devices in the poem—alliteration, assonance, rhyme. (See pages 170–171.) This will help you understand the proper phrasing and rhythm of the poem.
- Think about what the poem is saying or where the poem is going.

Third Reading

- Try to identify the type of poem you're reading. Does this poem follow the usual pattern of that particular type? If not, why not?
- Determine the literal sense of the poem. What is the poem about? What does the poem seem to say about its topic?
- Look carefully for figurative language in the poem. How does this language—metaphors, similes, personification, symbols—support or add to the poem? (See pages 124–126.)

Take NOTE Do a 10-minute freewriting when you finish reading. Write down everything you can about the poem. Relate what you've read to what you know or have experienced.

> "Words are one of our chief means
> of adjusting to life."
>
> —Bergen Evans

Improving
VOCABULARY Skills

According to writer Bill Bryson, "What sets English apart from other languages is the richness of its vocabulary." For example, there are about 200,000 English words in common use today. (This figure does not include technical or scientific terms.) Now, to be sure, no one person understands and regularly uses all of these words. However, those individuals who continually add more of them to their vocabulary have a distinct learning advantage.

As your vocabulary grows, your reading rate and comprehension level naturally grow, too. A large vocabulary also helps you communicate more efficiently, allowing you to say exactly what you mean. The best way to improve your vocabulary is to increase the amount of reading and writing that you do. This chapter suggests additional strategies for learning new words.

Preview

- Quick Guide
- Using Context
- Using Word Parts

Quick Guide

Building Your Vocabulary

Many experts agree that the most important thing you can do to improve your grades is to increase your vocabulary. Here are some ways to do that:

Use context. Study the various kinds of context clues. (See pages 387–388.) Then use them when you encounter new words in your reading. You'll be amazed at how many definitions you can figure out on your own.

Learn common word roots, prefixes, and suffixes. With a knowledge of these word parts, you can often infer the meaning of a word. (See pages 389–399.)

Keep a vocabulary notebook. Include the definition, pronunciation, and part of speech for each word. If you've found the new word in your reading, copy the sentence it came from into your notebook. Words learned in context are more likely to be remembered than words learned in isolation.

Make flash cards. Print the new word on the front of an index card with the definition on the back. Carry the cards with you and flip through them when you're waiting in line with nothing to do.

Refer to your dictionary. Every time you look up a word, put a dot next to it in your dictionary. When a word has two or more dots, include it in your flash cards.

Study the origins of words. Pay attention to the etymologies (history of words) in the dictionary. Many of these are interesting enough to help you remember a word.

Make a CD. Record yourself reading new words along with their definitions. Instead of listening to music when you're walking or driving somewhere, pop in your vocabulary CD. (Nobody will ever know.)

Use a thesaurus. Check a thesaurus to find all the synonyms for a common word or phrase, such as *move slowly*. For starters, there are *glide*, *stroll*, and *wander;* but these words are not interchangeable. To make full use of these choices, you need to learn the subtle differences between the connotations of these words.

"It's a fact that your working vocabulary doesn't grow after you're about 11, unless you read."

—Lynne Reid Banks

Using **Context**

Whenever you come across an unfamiliar word, you can use the words and ideas surrounding it to figure out the word's meaning. You can use synonyms, definitions, descriptions, and other kinds of specific information to help you understand the meaning of a new word. Below are six context clues that you can use to unlock the meaning of words. (The unfamiliar words are in bold; the familiar words or phrases—the context clues—are in blue.)

1. **Synonyms and Antonyms**
   The old man asked if I could **traverse** the creek; I said I could cross it easily. He seemed uncertain that I could do it, but I was **resolute**.

2. **Comparisons and Contrasts**
   Outside, the **tempest** raged like a hurricane. Confined to the house by their concerned mother, Jeremy was **restive**, but Adam contentedly read a book.

3. **Definitions and Descriptions**
   The woman wore a red **mantilla** that covered her head and shoulders.

4. **Words in a Series**
   The **dulcimer**, fiddle, and banjo are popular in the Appalachian region.

5. **Cause and Effect**
   Because no one volunteered to clean up the gym, the principal declared the work session would be **mandatory** for all sophomores.

6. **Tone and Setting**
   The **sinister** sound came from a long, dark passageway that had been hidden behind a bookcase. As we crept into the blackness, the stale, damp air made us feel as if we were being drawn into a dungeon.

HELP FILE

A context clue does not always appear in the same sentence as the word you don't know. You may need to look in surrounding sentences and paragraphs.

*"All my life I've looked at words as though
I were seeing them for the first time."*

—Ernest Hemingway

Using Indirect Clues

Some forms of context, such as examples, results, or general statements, are not as direct as the six types listed on the previous page. Still, indirect clues can be helpful. The more clues you find, the closer you are to discovering the specific meaning of a word and the overall intent of the passage it is part of.

NOW YOU TRY IT

See how well you can use context. Look carefully at the words in purple in the following passage taken from Jack London's *Call of the Wild*. Then look for direct and indirect context clues to help you understand the meaning of those words.

In addition to the clues available in this single paragraph, the reader of this novel would have the advantage of having read the first 46 pages. Considering that, there is a good chance he or she could figure out the meaning of at least some of the words in purple. See how well you do—now that you understand more about using context.

They made Sixty Miles, which is a fifty-mile run, on the first day; and the second day saw them booming up the Yukon well on their way to Pelly. But such splendid running was achieved not without great trouble and **vexation** on the part of Francois. The **insidious** revolt led by Buck had destroyed the **solidarity** of the team. It no longer was as one dog leaping in the traces. The encouragement Buck gave the rebels led them into all kinds of petty **misdemeanors**. No more was Spitz a leader greatly to be feared. The old awe departed, and they grew equal to challenging his authority. Pike robbed him of half a fish one night and gulped it down under the protection of Buck. Another night Dub and Joe fought Spitz and made him forego the punishment they deserved. And even Billee, the good-natured, was less good-natured, and whined not half so **placatingly** as in former days. Buck never came near Spitz without snarling and bristling **menacingly**. In fact, his conduct approached that of a bully, and he was given to **swaggering** up and down before Spitz's very nose.

Using **Word Parts**

Many English words are a combination of word parts (prefixes, suffixes, and roots). If you know the meanings of the parts, you can figure out the meanings of words that contain these parts.

Rejuvenate combines

- the prefix *re* (meaning *again*),
- the root *juven* (meaning *young*), and
- the suffix *ate* (meaning to *make*).

   To *rejuvenate* is "to make young again."

Orthodontist combines

- the root *ortho* (meaning *straight*),
- the root *dont* (meaning *tooth*, *teeth*), and
- the suffix *ist* (meaning a *person who*).

   An *orthodontist* is "a person who straightens teeth."

HELP FILE

English words that are not a combination of word parts are called *base words*. A base word cannot be divided into parts. However, base words can be combined with other base words and with prefixes and suffixes.

base word	base word + base word	base word + prefix	base word + suffix
ground	Background	underground	groundless
hand	handshake	forehand	handful

FAQ

How can I improve my vocabulary?

You already know and use many common prefixes, suffixes, and roots every day. To improve your speaking and writing vocabulary, study the meanings of prefixes, suffixes, and roots that are not familiar to you. The following pages contain nearly 500 word parts. Scan the pages until you come to a word part that is new to you.

Learn its meaning(s) and at least one of the sample words listed. Then apply your knowledge as you encounter new words in your textbooks, your favorite magazines, and even as you surf the Net. You'll see a payoff almost immediately.

Prefixes

Prefixes are those "word parts" that come *before* the root words (*pre* = before). Depending upon its meaning, a prefix changes the intent, or sense, of the base word. As a skilled reader, you will want to know the meanings of the most common prefixes and then watch for them when you read.

a, an [not, without] amoral (without a sense of moral responsibility), atypical, atom (not cuttable), apathy (without feeling), anesthesia (without sensation)

ab, abs, a [from, away] abnormal, abduct, absent, avert (turn away)

acro [high] acropolis (high city), acrobat, acronym, acrophobia (fear of height)

ambi, amb [both, around] ambidextrous (skilled with both hands), ambiguous, amble

amphi [both] amphibious (living on both land and water), amphitheater

ante [before] antedate, anteroom, antebellum, antecedent (happening before)

anti, ant [against] anticommunist, antidote, anticlimax, antacid

be [on, away] bedeck, belabor, bequest, bestow, beloved

bene, bon [well] benefit, benefactor, benevolent, benediction, bonanza, bonus

bi, bis, bin [both, double, twice] bicycle, biweekly, bilateral, biscuit, binoculars

by [side, close, near] bypass, bystander, by-product, bylaw, byline

cata [down, against] catalog, catapult, catastrophe, cataclysm

cerebro [brain] cerebral, cerebrum, cerebellum

circum, circ [around] circumference, circumnavigate, circumspect, circular

co, con, col, com [together, with] copilot, conspire, collect, compose

coni [dust] coniosis (disease that comes from inhaling dust)

contra, counter [against] controversy, contradict, counterpart

de [from, down] demote, depress, degrade, deject, deprive

deca [ten] decade, decathlon, decapod (10 feet)

di [two, twice] divide, dilemma, dilute, dioxide, dipole, ditto

dia [through, between] diameter, diagonal, diagram, dialogue (speech between people)

dis, dif [apart, away, reverse] dismiss, distort, distinguish, diffuse

dys [badly, ill] dyspepsia (digesting badly), dystrophy, dysentery

em, en [in, into] embrace, enslave

epi [upon] epidermis (upon the skin, outer layer of skin), epitaph, epithet

eu [well] eulogize (speak well of, praise), euphony, euphemism, euphoria

ex, e, ec, ef [out] expel (drive out), ex-mayor, exorcism, eject, eccentric (out of the center position), efflux, effluent

extra, extro [beyond, outside] extraordinary (beyond the ordinary), extrovert, extracurricular

for [away or off] forswear (to renounce an oath)

fore [before in time] forecast, foretell (to tell beforehand), foreshadow

hemi, demi, semi [half] hemisphere, demitasse, semicircle (half of a circle)

hex [six] hexameter, hexagon

homo [man] Homo sapiens, homicide (killing man)

hyper [over, above] hypersensitive (overly sensitive), hyperactive

hypo [under] hypodermic (under the skin), hypothesis

il, ir, in, im [not] illegal, irregular, incorrect, immoral

in, il, im [into] inject, inside, illuminate, illustrate, impose, implant, imprison

infra [beneath] infrared, infrasonic

inter [between] intercollegiate, interfere, intervene, interrupt (break between)

intra [within] intramural, intravenous (within the veins)

intro [into, inward] introduce, introvert (turn inward)

macro [large, excessive] macrodent (having large teeth), macrocosm

mal [badly, poorly] maladjusted, malady, malnutrition, malfunction

meta [beyond, after, with] metaphor, metamorphosis, metaphysical

mis [incorrect, bad] misuse, misprint

miso [hate] misanthrope, misogynist

mono [one] monoplane, monotone, monochrome, monocle

multi [many] multiply, multiform

neo [new] neopaganism, neoclassic, neophyte, neonatal

non [not] nontaxable (not taxed), nontoxic, nonexistent, nonsense

ob, of, op, oc [toward, against] obstruct, offend, oppose, occur

oct [eight] octagon, octameter, octave, octopus

paleo [ancient] paleoanthropology (pertaining to ancient humans), paleontology (study of ancient life-forms)

para [beside, almost] parasite (one who eats beside or at the table of another), paraphrase, paramedic, parallel, paradox

penta [five] pentagon (figure or building having five angles or sides), pentameter, pentathlon

per [throughout, completely] pervert (completely turn wrong, corrupt), perfect, perceive, permanent, persuade

peri [around] perimeter (measurement around an area), periphery, periscope, pericardium, period

poly [many] polygon (figure having many angles or sides), polygamy, polyglot, polychrome

post [after] postpone, postwar, postscript, posterity

pre [before] prewar, preview, precede, prevent, premonition

pro [forward, in favor of] project (throw forward), progress, promote, prohibition

pseudo [false] pseudonym (false or assumed name), pseudopodia

quad [four] quadruple (four times as much), quadriplegic, quadratic, quadrant

quint [five] quintuplet, quintuple, quintet, quintile

re [back, again] reclaim, revive, revoke, rejuvenate, retard, reject, return

retro [backward] retrospective (looking backward), retroactive, retrorocket

se [aside] seduce (lead aside), secede, secrete, segregate

self [by oneself] self-determination, self-employed, self-service, selfish

sesqui [one and a half] sesquicentennial (one and one-half centuries)

sex, sest [six] sexagenarian (sixty years old), sexennial, sextant, sextuplet, sestet

sub [under] submerge (put under), submarine, substitute, subsoil

suf, sug, sup, sus [from under] sufficient, suffer, suggest, support, suspend

super, supr [above, over, more] supervise, superman, supernatural, supreme

syn, sym, sys, syl [with, together] system, synthesis, synchronize (time together), synonym, sympathy, symphony, syllable

trans, tra [across, beyond] transoceanic, transmit (send across), transfusion, tradition

tri [three] tricycle, triangle, tripod, tristate

ultra [beyond, exceedingly] ultramodern, ultraviolet, ultraconservative

un [not, release] unfair, unnatural, unknown

under [beneath] underground, underlying

uni [one] unicycle, uniform, unify, universe, unique (one of a kind)

vice [in place of] vice president, viceroy, vice admiral

Numerical Prefixes

Prefix	Symbol	Multiples and Submultiples	Equivalent	Prefix	Symbol	Multiples and Submultiples	Equivalent
tera	T	10^{12}	trillionfold	centi	c	10^{-2}	hundredth part
giga	G	10^{9}	billionfold	milli	m	10^{-3}	thousandth part
mega	M	10^{6}	millionfold	micro	u	10^{-6}	millionth part
kilo	k	10^{3}	thousandfold	nano	n	10^{-9}	billionth part
hecto	h	10^{2}	hundredfold	pico	p	10^{-12}	trillionth part
deka	da	10	tenfold	femto	f	10^{-15}	quadrillionth part
deci	d	10^{-1}	tenth part	atto	a	10^{-18}	quintillionth part

Suffixes

Suffixes come at the end of a word. Very often a suffix will tell you what kind of word it is part of (noun, adverb, adjective, and so on). For example, words ending in *-ly* are usually adverbs.

able, ible [able, can do] capable, agreeable, edible, visible (can be seen)

ade [result of action] blockade (the result of a blocking action), lemonade

age [act of, state of, collection of] salvage (act of saving), storage, forage

al [relating to] sensual, gradual, manual, natural (relating to nature)

algia [pain] neuralgia (nerve pain)

an, ian [native of, relating to] African, Canadian, Floridian

ance, ancy [action, process, state] assistance, allowance, defiance, truancy

ant [performing, agent] assistant, servant

ary, ery, ory [relating to, quality, place where] dictionary, bravery, dormitory

ate [cause, make] liquidate, segregate (cause a group to be set aside)

cian [having a certain skill or art] musician, beautician, magician, physician

cule, ling [very small] molecule, ridicule, duckling (very small duck), sapling

cy [action, function] hesitancy, prophecy, normalcy (function in a normal way)

dom [quality, realm, office] freedom, kingdom, wisdom (quality of being wise)

ee [one who receives the action] employee, nominee (one who is nominated), refugee

en [made of, make] silken, frozen, oaken (made of oak), wooden, lighten

ence, ency [action, state of, quality] difference, conference, urgency

er, or [one who, that which] baker, miller, teacher, racer, amplifier, doctor

escent [in the process of] adolescent (in the process of becoming an adult), obsolescent, convalescent

ese [a native of, the language of] Japanese, Vietnamese, Portuguese

esis, osis [action, process, condition] genesis, hypnosis, neurosis, osmosis

ess [female] actress, goddess, lioness

et, ette [a small one, group] midget, octet, baronet, majorette

fic [making, causing] scientific, specific

ful [full of] frightful, careful, helpful

fy [make] fortify (make strong), simplify, amplify

hood [order, condition, quality] manhood, womanhood, brotherhood

ic [nature of, like] metallic (of the nature of metal), heroic, poetic, acidic

ice [condition, state, quality] justice, malice

id, ide [a thing connected with or belonging to] fluid, fluoride

ile [relating to, suited for, capable of] missile, juvenile, senile (related to being old)

ine [nature of] feminine, genuine, medicine

ion, sion, tion [act of, state of, result of] contagion, aversion, infection (state of being infected)

ish [origin, nature, resembling] foolish, Irish, clownish (resembling a clown)

ism [system, manner, condition, characteristic] heroism, alcoholism, Communism

ist [one who, that which] artist, dentist

ite [nature of, quality of, mineral product] Israelite, dynamite, graphite, sulfite

ity, ty [state of, quality] captivity, clarity

ive [causing, making] abusive (causing abuse), exhaustive

ize [make] emphasize, publicize, idolize

less [without] baseless, careless (without care), artless, fearless, helpless

ly [like, manner of] carelessly, quickly, forcefully, lovingly

ment [act of, state of, result] contentment, amendment (state of amending)

ness [state of] carelessness, kindness

oid [resembling] asteroid, spheroid, tabloid, anthropoid

ology [study, science, theory] biology, anthropology, geology, neurology

ous [full of, having] gracious, nervous, spacious, vivacious (full of life)

ship [office, state, quality, skill] friendship, authorship, dictatorship

some [like, apt, tending to] lonesome, threesome, gruesome

tude [state of, condition of] gratitude, multitude (condition of being many), aptitude

ure [state of, act, process, rank] culture, literature, rupture (state of being broken)

ward [in the direction of] eastward, forward, backward

y [inclined to, tend to] cheery, crafty, faulty

Roots

A *root* is a base upon which other words are built. Knowing the root of a difficult word can go a long way toward helping you figure out its meaning—even without a dictionary. For that reason, learning the following roots will be very valuable in all your classes.

acer, acid, acri [bitter, sour, sharp] acrid, acerbic, acidity (sourness), acrimony

acu [sharp] acute, acupuncture

ag, agi, ig, act [do, move, go] agent (doer), agenda (things to do), agitate, navigate (move by sea), ambiguous (going both ways), action

ali, allo, alter [other] alias (a person's other name), alibi, alien (from another place), alloy, alter (change to another form)

alt [high, deep] altimeter (a device for measuring heights), altitude

am, amor [love, liking] amiable, amorous, enamored

anni, annu, enni [year] anniversary, annually (yearly), centennial (occurring once in 100 years)

anthrop [man] anthropology (study of mankind), philanthropy (love of mankind), misanthrope (hater of mankind)

anti [old] antique, antiquated, antiquity

arch [chief, first, rule] archangel (chief angel), architect (chief worker), archaic (first, very early), monarchy (rule by one person), matriarchy (rule by the mother)

aster, astr [star] aster (star flower), asterisk, asteroid, astronomy (star law), astronaut (star traveler, space traveler)

aud, aus [hear, listen] audible (can be heard), auditorium, audio, audition, auditory, audience, ausculate

aug, auc [increase] augur, augment (add to; increase), auction

auto, aut [self] autograph (self-writing), automobile (self-moving vehicle), author, automatic (self-acting), autobiography

belli [war] rebellion, belligerent (warlike or hostile)

bibl [book] Bible, bibliography (list of books), bibliomania (craze for books), bibliophile (book lover)

bio [life] biology (study of life), biography, biopsy (cut living tissue for examination)

brev [short] abbreviate, brevity, brief

cad, cas [to fall] cadaver, cadence, caducous (falling off), cascade

calor [heat] calorie (a unit of heat), calorify (to make hot), caloric

cap, cip, cept [take] capable, capacity, capture, reciprocate, accept, except, concept

capit, capt [head] decapitate (to remove the head from), capital, captain, caption

carn [flesh] carnivorous (flesh eating), incarnate, reincarnation

caus, caut [burn, heat] caustic, cauterize (to make hot, to burn)

cause, cuse, cus [cause, motive] because, excuse (to attempt to remove the blame or cause), accusation

ced, ceed, cede, cess [move, yield, go, surrender] procedure, secede (move aside from), proceed (move forward), cede (yield), concede, intercede, precede, recede, success

centri [center] concentric, centrifugal, centripetal, eccentric (out of center)

chrom [color] chrome, chromosome (color body in genetics), chromosphere, monochrome (one color), polychrome

chron [time] chronological (in order of time), chronometer (time measured), chronicle (record of events in time), synchronize (make time with, set time together)

cide, cise [cut down, kill] suicide (killing of self), homicide (human killer), pesticide (pest killer), germicide (germ killer), insecticide, precise (cut exactly right), incision, scissors

cit [to call, start] incite, citation, cite

civ [citizen] civic (relating to a citizen), civil, civilian, civilization

clam, claim [cry out] exclamation, clamor, proclamation, reclamation, acclaim

clud, clus, claus [shut] include (to take in), conclude, claustrophobia (abnormal fear of being shut up, confined), recluse (one who shuts himself away from others)

cognosc, gnosi [know] recognize (to know again), incognito (not known), prognosis (forward knowing), diagnosis

cord, cor, cardi [heart] cordial (hearty, heartfelt), concord, discord, courage, encourage (put heart into), discourage (take heart out of), core, coronary, cardiac

corp [body] corporation (a legal body), corpse, corpulent

cosm [universe, world] cosmic, cosmos (the universe), cosmopolitan (world citizen), cosmonaut, microcosm, macrocosm

crat, cracy [rule, strength] democratic, autocracy

crea [create] creature (anything created), recreation, creation, creator

cred [believe] creed (statement of beliefs), credo (a creed), credence (belief), credit (belief, trust), credulous (believing too readily, easily deceived), incredible

cresc, cret, crease, cru [rise, grow] crescendo (growing in loudness or intensity), concrete (grown together, solidified), increase, decrease, accrue (to grow)

crit [separate, choose] critical, criterion (that which is used in choosing), hypocrite

cur, curs [run] concurrent, current (running or flowing), concur (run together, agree), incur (run into), recur, occur, precursor (forerunner), cursive

cura [care] curator, curative, manicure (caring for the hands)

cycl, cyclo [wheel, circular] Cyclops (a mythical giant with one eye in the middle of his forehead), unicycle, bicycle, cyclone (a wind blowing circularly, a tornado)

deca [ten] decade, decalogue, decathlon

dem [people] democracy (people-rule), demography (vital statistics of the people: deaths, births, and so on), epidemic (on or among the people)

dent, dont [tooth] dental (relating to teeth), denture, dentifrice, orthodontist

derm [skin] hypodermic (injected under the skin), dermatology (skin study), epidermis (outer layer of skin), taxidermy (arranging skin; mounting animals)

dict [say, speak] diction (how one speaks, what one says), dictionary, dictate, dictator, dictaphone, dictatorial, edict, predict, verdict, contradict, benediction

doc [teach] indoctrinate, document, doctrine

domin [master] dominate, dominion, predominant, domain

don [give] donate, condone

dorm [sleep] dormant, dormitory

dox [opinion, praise] doxy (belief, creed, or opinion), orthodox (having the correct, commonly accepted opinion), heterodox (differing opinion), paradox (contradictory)

drome [run, step] syndrome (run-together symptoms), hippodrome (a place where horses run)

duc, duct [lead] produce, induce (lead into, persuade), seduce (lead aside), reduce, aqueduct (water leader or channel), viaduct, conduct

dura [hard, lasting] durable, duration, endurance

dynam [power] dynamo (power producer), dynamic, dynamite, hydrodynamics

endo [within] endoral (within the mouth), endocardial (within the heart), endoskeletal

equi [equal] equinox, equilibrium

erg [work] energy, erg (unit of work), allergy, ergophobia (morbid fear of work), ergometer, ergonomic

fac, fact, fic, fect [do, make] factory (place where workers make goods of various kinds), fact (a thing done), manufacture, amplification, confection

fall, fals [deceive] fallacy, falsify

fer [bear, carry] ferry (carry by water), coniferous (bearing cones, as a pine tree), fertile (bearing richly), defer, infer, refer

fid, fide, feder [faith, trust] confidante, Fido, fidelity, confident, infidelity, infidel, federal, confederacy

fila, fili [thread] filament (a single thread or threadlike object), filibuster, filigree

fin [end, ended, finished] final, finite, finish, confine, fine, refine, define, finale

fix [attach] fix, fixation (the state of being attached), fixture, affix, prefix, suffix

flex, flect [bend] flex (bend), reflex (bending back), flexible, flexor (muscle for bending), inflexibility, reflect, deflect

flu, fluc, fluv [flowing] influence (to flow in), fluid, flue, flush, fluently, fluctuate (to wave in an unsteady motion)

form [form, shape] form, uniform, conform, deform, reform, perform, formative, formation, formal, formula

fort, forc [strong] fort, fortress (a strong place), fortify (make strong), forte (one's strong point), fortitude, enforce

fract, frag [break] fracture (a break), infraction, fragile (easy to break), fraction (result of breaking a whole into equal parts), refract (to break or bend)

gam [marriage] bigamy (two marriages), monogamy, polygamy (many spouses or marriages)

gastr(o) [stomach] gastric, gastronomic, gastritis (inflammation of the stomach)

gen [birth, race, produce] genesis (birth, beginning), genetics (study of heredity), eugenics (well born), genealogy (lineage by race, stock), generate, genetic

geo [earth] geometry (earth measurement), geography (earth writing), geocentric (earth centered), geology

germ [vital part] germination (to grow), germ (seed; living substance, as the germ of an idea), germane

gest [carry, bear] congest (bear together, clog), congestive (causing clogging), gestation

gloss, glot [tongue] glossary, polyglot (many tongues), epiglottis

glu, glo [lump, bond, glue] glue, agglutinate (make to hold in a bond), conglomerate (bond together)

grad, gress [step, go] grade (step, degree), gradual (step-by-step), graduate (make all the steps, finish a course), graduated (in steps or degrees), progress

graph, gram [write, written] graph, graphic (written, vivid), autograph (self-writing, signature), graphite (carbon used for writing), photography (light writing), phonograph (sound writing), diagram, bibliography, telegram

grat [pleasing] gratuity (mark of favor, a tip), congratulate (express pleasure over success), grateful, ingrate (not thankful)

grav [heavy, weighty] grave, gravity, aggravate, gravitate

greg [herd, group, crowd] gregarian (belonging to a herd), congregation (a group functioning together), segregate (tending to group aside or apart)

helio [sun] heliograph (an instrument for using the sun's rays to send signals), heliotrope (a plant that turns to the sun)

hema, hemo [blood] hemorrhage (an outpouring or flowing of blood), hemoglobin, hemophilia

here, hes [stick] adhere, cohere, cohesion

hetero [different] heterogeneous (different in birth), heterosexual (with interest in the opposite sex)

homo [same] homogeneous (of same birth or kind), homonym (word with same pronunciation as another), homogenize

hum, human [earth, ground, man] humus, exhume (to take out of the ground), humane (compassion for other humans)

hydr, hydra, hydro [water] dehydrate, hydrant, hydraulic, hydraulics, hydrogen, hydrophobia (fear of water)

hypn [sleep] hypnosis, Hypnos (god of sleep), hypnotherapy (treatment of disease by hypnosis)

ignis [fire] ignite, igneous, ignition

ject [throw] deject, inject, project (throw forward), eject, object

join, junct [join] adjoining, enjoin (to lay an order upon, to command), juncture, conjunction, injunction

juven [young] juvenile, rejuvenate (to make young again)

lau, lav, lot, lut [wash] launder, lavatory, lotion, ablution (a washing away), dilute (to make a liquid thinner and weaker)

leg [law] legal (lawful; according to law), legislate (to enact a law), legislature, legitimize (make legal)

levi [light] alleviate (lighten a load), levitate, levity (light conversation; humor)

liber, liver [free] liberty (freedom), liberal, liberalize (to make more free), deliverance

liter [letters] literary (concerned with books and writing), literature, literal, alliteration, obliterate

loc, loco [place] locality, locale, location, allocate (to assign, to place), relocate (to put back into place), locomotion (act of moving from place to place)

log, logo, ogue, ology [word, study, speech] catalog, prologue, dialogue, logogram (a symbol representing a word), zoology (animal study), psychology (mind study)

loqu, locut [talk, speak] eloquent (speaking well and forcefully), soliloquy, locution, loquacious (talkative), colloquial (talking together; conversational or informal)

luc, lum, lus, lun [light] translucent (letting light come through), lumen (a unit of light), luminary (a heavenly body; someone who shines in his or her profession), luster (sparkle, shine), Luna (the moon goddess)

magn [great] magnify (make great, enlarge), magnificent, magnanimous (great of mind or spirit), magnate, magnitude, magnum

man [hand] manual, manage, manufacture, manacle, manicure, manifest, maneuver, emancipate

mand [command] mandatory (commanded), remand (order back), mandate

mania [madness] mania (insanity, craze), monomania (mania on one idea), kleptomania, pyromania (insane tendency to set fires), maniac

mar, mari, mer [sea, pool] marine (a soldier serving on shipboard), marsh (wetland, swamp), maritime (relating to the sea and navigation), mermaid (fabled sea creature, half fish, half woman)

matri [mother] maternal (relating to the mother), matrimony, matriarchate (rulership of women), matron

medi [half, middle, between, halfway] mediate (come between, intervene), medieval (pertaining to the Middle Ages), Mediterranean (lying between lands), mediocre, medium

mega [great, million] megaphone (great sound), megalopolis (great city; an extensive urban area including a number of cities), megacycle (a million cycles), megaton

mem [remember] memo (a reminder), commemoration (the act of remembering by a memorial or ceremony), memento, memoir, memorable

meter [measure] meter (a metric measure), voltameter (instrument to measure volts), barometer, thermometer

micro [small] microscope, microfilm, microcard, microwave, micrometer (device for measuring small distances), omicron, micron (a millionth of a meter), microbe (small living thing)

migra [wander] migrate (to wander), emigrate (one who leaves a country), immigrate (to come into the land)

mit, miss [send] emit (send out, give off), remit (send back, as money due), submit, admit, commit, permit, transmit (send across), omit, intermittent (sending between, at intervals), mission, missile

mob, mot, mov [move] mobile (capable of moving), motionless (without motion), motor, emotional (moved strongly by feelings), motivate, promotion, demote, movement

mon [warn, remind] monument (a reminder or memorial of a person or an event), admonish (warn), monitor, premonition (forewarning)

mor, mort [mortal, death] mortal (causing death or destined for death), immortal (not subject to death), mortality (rate of death), mortician (one who prepares the dead for burial), mortuary (place for the dead, a morgue)

morph [form] amorphous (with no form, shapeless), metamorphosis (a change of form, as a caterpillar into a butterfly), morphology

multi [many, much] multifold (folded many times), multilinguist (one who speaks many languages), multiped (an organism with many feet), multiply

nat, nasc [to be born, to spring forth] innate (inborn), natal, native, nativity, renascence (a rebirth, a revival)

neur [nerve] neuritis (inflammation of a nerve), neurology (study of nervous systems), neurologist (one who practices neurology), neural, neurosis, neurotic

nom [law, order] autonomy (self-law, self-government), astronomy, gastronomy (art or science of good eating), economy

nomen, nomin [name] nomenclature, nominate (name someone for an office)

nov [new] novel (new, strange, not formerly known), renovate (to make like new again), novice, nova, innovate

nox, noc [night] nocturnal, equinox (equal nights), noctilucent (shining by night)

numer [number] numeral (a figure expressing a number), numeration (act of counting), enumerate (count out, one by one), innumerable

omni [all, every] omnipotent (all-powerful), omniscient (all-knowing), omnipresent (present everywhere), omnivorous

onym [name] anonymous (without name), synonym, pseudonym (false name), antonym (name of opposite meaning)

oper [work] operate (to labor, function), cooperate (work together)

ortho [straight, correct] orthodox (of the correct or accepted opinion), orthodontist (tooth straightener), orthopedic (originally pertaining to straightening a child), unorthodox

pac [peace] pacifist (one for peace only; opposed to war), pacify (make peace, quiet), Pacific Ocean (peaceful ocean)

pan [all] panacea (cure-all), pandemonium (place of all the demons, wild disorder), pantheon (place of all the gods in mythology)

pater, patr [father] paternity (fatherhood, responsibility), patriarch (head of the tribe, family), patriot, patron (a wealthy person who supports as would a father)

path, pathy [feeling, suffering] pathos (feeling of pity, sorrow), sympathy, antipathy (feeling against), apathy (without feeling), empathy (feeling or identifying with another), telepathy (far feeling; thought transference)

ped, pod [foot] pedal (lever for a foot), impede (get the feet in a trap, hinder), pedestal (foot or base of a statue), pedestrian (foot traveler), centipede, tripod (three-footed support), podiatry (care of the feet), antipodes (opposite feet)

pedo [child] orthopedic, pedagogue (child leader; teacher), pediatrics (medical care of children)

pel, puls [drive, urge] compel, dispel, expel, repel, propel, pulse, impulse, pulsate, compulsory, expulsion, repulsive

pend, pens, pond [hang, weigh] pendant pendulum, suspend, appendage, pensive (weighing thought), ponderous

phil [love] philosophy (love of wisdom), philanthropy, philharmonic, bibliophile, Philadelphia (city of brotherly love)

phobia [fear] claustrophobia (fear of closed spaces), acrophobia (fear of high places), hydrophobia (fear of water)

phon [sound] phonograph, phonetic (pertaining to sound), symphony (sounds with or together)

photo [light] photograph (light-writing), photoelectric, photogenic (artistically suitable for being photographed), photosynthesis (action of light on chlorophyll to make carbohydrates)

plac [please] placid (calm, peaceful), placebo, placate, complacent

plu, plur, plus [more] plural (more than one), pluralist (a person who holds more than one office), plus (indicating that something more is to be added)

pneuma, pneumon [breath] pneumatic (pertaining to air, wind, or other gases), pneumonia (disease of the lungs)

pod (see ped)

poli [city] metropolis (mother city), police, politics, Indianapolis, Acropolis (high city, upper part of Athens), megalopolis

pon, pos, pound [place, put] postpone (put afterward), component, opponent (one put against), proponent, expose, impose, deposit, posture (how one places oneself), position, expound, impound

pop [people] population, populous (full of people), popular

port [carry] porter (one who carries), portable, transport (carry across), report, export, import, support, transportation

portion [part, share] portion (a part; a share, as a portion of pie), proportion (the relation of one share to others)

prehend [seize] comprehend (seize with the mind), apprehend (seize a criminal), comprehensive (seizing much, extensive)

prim, prime [first] primacy (state of being first in rank), prima donna (the first lady of opera), primitive (from the earliest or first time), primary, primal, primeval

proto [first] prototype (the first model made), protocol, protagonist, protozoan

psych [mind, soul] psyche (soul, mind), psychiatry (healing of the mind), psychology, psychosis (serious mental disorder), psychotherapy (mind treatment), psychic

punct [point, dot] punctual (being exactly on time), punctuation, puncture, acupuncture

reg, recti [straighten] regiment, regular, regulate, rectify (make straight), correct, direction

ri, ridi, risi [laughter] deride (mock, jeer at), ridicule (laughter at the expense of another, mockery), ridiculous, derision

rog, roga [ask] prerogative (privilege; asking before), interrogation (questioning; the act of questioning), derogatory

rupt [break] rupture (break), interrupt (break into), abrupt (broken off), disrupt (break apart), erupt (break out), incorruptible (unable to be broken down)

sacr, sanc, secr [sacred] sacred, sanction, sacrosanct, consecrate, desecrate

salv, salu [safe, healthy] salvation (act of being saved), salvage, salutation

sat, satis [enough] satient (giving pleasure, satisfying), saturate, satisfy (to give pleasure to; to give as much as is needed)

sci [know] science (knowledge), conscious (knowing, aware), omniscient (knowing everything)

scope [see, watch] telescope, microscope, kaleidoscope (instrument for seeing beautiful forms), periscope, stethoscope

scrib, script [write] scribe (a writer), scribble, manuscript (written by hand), inscribe, describe, subscribe, prescribe

sed, sess, sid [sit] sediment (that which sits or settles out of a liquid), session (a sitting), obsession (an idea that sits stubbornly in the mind), possess, preside (sit before), president, reside, subside

sen [old] senior, senator, senile (old; showing the weakness of old age)

sent, sens [feel] sentiment (feeling), consent, resent, dissent, sentimental (having strong feeling or emotion), sense, sensation, sensitive, sensory, dissension

sequ, secu, sue [follow] sequence (following of one thing after another), sequel, consequence, subsequent, prosecute, consecutive (following in order), second (following "first"), ensue, pursue

serv [save, serve] servant, service, preserve, subservient, servitude, conserve, reservation, deserve, conservation

sign, signi [sign, mark, seal] signal (a gesture or sign to call attention), signature (the mark of a person written in his or her own handwriting), design, insignia (distinguishing marks)

simil, simul [like, resembling] similar (resembling in many respects), assimilate (to make similar to), simile, simulate (pretend; put on an act to make a certain impression)

sist, sta, stit [stand] persist (stand firmly; unyielding; continue), assist (to stand by with help), circumstance, stamina (power to withstand, to endure), status (standing), state, static, stable, stationary, substitute (to stand in for another)

solus [alone] soliloquy, solitaire, solitude, solo

solv, solu [loosen] solvent (a loosener, a dissolver), solve, absolve (loosen from, free from), resolve, soluble, solution, resolution, resolute, dissolute (loosened morally)

somnus [sleep] insomnia (not being able to sleep), somnambulist (a sleepwalker)

soph [wise] sophomore (wise fool), philosophy (love of wisdom), sophisticated

spec, spect, spic [look] specimen (an example to look at, study), specific, aspect, spectator (one who looks), spectacle, speculate, inspect, respect, prospect, retrospective (looking backward), introspective, expect, conspicuous

sphere [ball, sphere] stratosphere (the upper portion of the atmosphere), hemisphere (half of the earth), spheroid

spir [breath] spirit (breath), conspire (breathe together; plot), inspire (breathe into), aspire (breathe toward), expire (breathe out; die), perspire, respiration

string, strict [draw tight] stringent (drawn tight; rigid), strict, restrict, constrict (draw tightly together), boa constrictor (snake that constricts its prey)

stru, struct [build] construe (build in the mind, interpret), structure, construct, instruct, obstruct, destruction, destroy

sume, sump [take, use, waste] consume (to use up), assume (to take; to use), sump pump (a pump that takes up water), presumption (to take or use before knowing all the facts)

tact, tang, tag, tig, ting [touch] contact, tactile, intangible (not able to be touched), intact (untouched, uninjured), tangible, contingency, contagious (able to transmit disease by touching), contiguous

tele [far] telephone (far sound), telegraph (far writing), television (far seeing), telephoto (far photography), telecast

tempo [time] tempo (rate of speed), temporary, extemporaneously, contemporary (those who live at the same time), pro tem (for the time being)

ten, tin, tain [hold] tenacious (holding fast), tenant, tenure, untenable, detention, content, pertinent, continent, obstinate, abstain, pertain, detain

tend, tent, tens [stretch, strain] tendency (a stretching; leaning), extend, intend, contend, pretend, superintend, tender, extent, tension (a stretching, strain), pretense

terra [earth] terrain, terrarium, territory, terrestrial

test [to bear witness] testament (a will; bearing witness to someone's wishes), detest, attest (bear witness to), testimony

the, theo [God, a god] monotheism (belief in one god), polytheism (belief in many gods), atheism, theology

therm [heat] thermometer, therm (heat unit), thermal, thermostat, thermos, hypothermia (subnormal temperature)

thesis, thet [place, put] antithesis (place against), hypothesis (place under), synthesis (put together), epithet

tom [cut] atom (not cuttable; smallest particle of matter), appendectomy (cutting out an appendix), tonsillectomy, dichotomy (cutting in two; a division), anatomy (cutting, dissecting to study structure)

tort, tors [twist] torture (twisting to inflict pain), retort (twist back, reply sharply), extort (twist out), distort (twist out of shape), contort, torsion (act of twisting, as a torsion bar)

tox [poison] toxic (poisonous), intoxicate, antitoxin

tract, tra [draw, pull] tractor, attract, subtract, tractable (can be handled), abstract (to draw away), subtrahend (the number to be drawn away from another)

trib [pay, bestow] tribute (to pay honor to), contribute (to give money to a cause), attribute, retribution, tributary

turbo [disturb] turbulent, disturb, turbid, turmoil

typ [print] type, prototype (first print; model), typical, typography, typewriter, typology (study of types, symbols), typify

ultima [last] ultimate, ultimatum (the final or last offer that can be made)

uni [one] unicorn (a legendary creature with one horn), unify (make into one), university, unanimous, universal

vac [empty] vacate (to make empty), vacuum (a space entirely devoid of matter), evacuate (to remove troops or people), vacation, vacant

vale, vali, valu [strength, worth] valiant, equivalent (of equal worth), validity (truth; legal strength), evaluate (find out the value), value, valor (value; worth)

ven, vent [come] convene (come together, assemble), intervene (come between), venue, convenient, avenue, circumvent (come or go around), invent, prevent

ver, veri [true] very, aver (say to be true, affirm), verdict, verity (truth), verify (show to be true), verisimilitude

vert, vers [turn] avert (turn away), divert (turn aside, amuse), invert (turn over), introvert (turn inward), convertible, reverse (turn back), controversy (a turning against; a dispute), versatile (turning easily from one skill to another)

vic, vicis [change, substitute] vicarious, vicar, vicissitude

vict, vinc [conquer] victor (conqueror, winner), evict (conquer out, expel), convict (prove guilty), convince (conquer mentally, persuade), invincible (not conquerable)

vid, vis [see] video, television, evident, provide, providence, visible, revise, supervise (oversee), vista, visit, vision

viv, vita, vivi [alive, life] revive (make live again), survive (live beyond, outlive), vivid, vivacious (full of life), vitality

voc [call] vocation (a calling), avocation (occupation not one's calling), convocation (a calling together), invocation, vocal

vol [will] malevolent, benevolent (one of goodwill), volunteer, volition

volcan, vulcan [fire] volcano (a mountain erupting fiery lava), volcanize (to undergo volcanic heat), Vulcan (Roman god of fire)

volvo [turn about, roll] revolve, voluminous (winding), voluble (easily turned about or around), convolution (a twisting)

vor [eat greedily] voracious, carnivorous (flesh eating), herbivorous (plant eating), omnivorous (eating everything), devour

zo [animal] zoo (short for zoological garden), zoology (study of animal life), zodiac (circle of animal constellations), zoomorphism (being in the form of an animal), protozoa (one-celled animals)

The Human Body

capit	head	gastro	stomach	osteo	bone
card	heart	glos	tongue	ped	foot
corp	body	hema	blood	pneuma	breathe
dent	tooth	man	hand	psych	mind
derm	skin	neur	nerve	spir	breath

STUDY
Skills

Improving Classroom Skills   **401**

Listening and Note-Taking Skills   **407**

Writing to Learn   **415**

Test-Taking Skills   **423**

Taking Exit and Entrance Exams   **437**

"Everyone teaches, everyone learns."

—Arnold Bennett

Improving
CLASSROOM Skills

To do well in school you must do well individually and as a member of a group. Individually, you must manage your time and complete your assignments. As a group member, you need to listen to others, observe, respond, and ask questions.

Inside the classroom, you're part of a learning team. Your teacher heads up the team, introduces new concepts, and assigns the reading and other activities that give you the information you need to understand the concepts. Your job is to supply the enthusiasm and effort. Without that personal commitment, learning will not happen. This section of your handbook covers the skills you need to succeed in school, both as an individual and as a member of a group.

Preview

- **Group Skills**
- **Planning Skills**
- **Completing Assignments**

The ability to use group skills (also called "people skills") is very important for success in school, at home, and in the workplace.

Group Skills

You've probably worked on your share of group projects, so you already know that group work doesn't always go smoothly. Developing the following skills will help you work well with others: *listening, observing, cooperating, clarifying,* and *responding.*

Listening

Group members must listen carefully to one another, focusing on *what* is being said, not on *who* is saying it. As you listen to an idea, think about how it relates to the group and to the group's goals. Take notes and ask questions after the speaker finishes sharing the idea.

Listen actively. Good listeners are active listeners. This means you should let the speaker know you are listening by making eye contact, nodding your head, and remaining attentive. You can also let the speaker know you have been listening by asking a good question, summarizing what has been said, or offering a compliment or comment.

Listen accurately. Hearing is not the same as listening. Hearing involves your ears; listening involves your ears and your mind. Always think about what you hear. Listen with pen in hand. Jot down a word, phrase, or question to help you remember what is being said and what you want to add. Then, when the speaker stops, offer your ideas.

Know when—and how—to interrupt. If you are a good listener, you will sooner or later have a comment, a question, or an important fact to add. Even so, interrupting someone who is speaking is not usually a good idea. If you feel you must interrupt the speaker, say, "Excuse me, Janet, when you finish I have something to add." Sometimes it is also necessary to interrupt a group member who has wandered off the topic. When that happens, you can say, "Excuse me, but I think we should get back to the main point."

Learn how to respond when you are interrupted. When you are interrupted without good reason by a group member, you can say, "I wasn't finished making my point yet," or "Could you please wait until I'm finished?" Whatever you say, say it courteously. (You can discourage interruptions by keeping what you say to the point.)

Observing

Observing means paying attention to the body language and tone of voice of each group member.

Watch body language. At times you can "see" what a person is saying or feeling. Pay attention to body language, which can tell you how people are feeling about the discussion.

Listen to tone of voice. Remember, it's not always what people say; it's how they say it. A person's tone of voice can tell you a lot about how that person is feeling.

Cooperating

Cooperating means using common sense and common courtesy.

Contribute your ideas. Share your ideas, and, if your idea builds on someone else's, give that person credit. ("I like what Eduardo said, and he gave me the idea that we could . . . ")

Challenge ideas, not people. Challenge the idea, not the person who contributed it. Say something like "David, I'm not sure that idea will work, because . . . " instead of "You're not thinking straight."

Never use put-downs. Put-downs must be avoided in group work. They disrupt the group and destroy members' self-confidence.

Cooperating means "working together."
It means using common sense and common
courtesy—and sharing a common goal.

Clarifying

Clarifying means listening closely, asking questions, and giving clear examples.

Ask questions. When a group gets bogged down or loses direction, a good question can help members refocus. You might, for example, say, "Tom, what do you think about our plan?"

Offer to explain or clarify. If what you say is long or complex, you can end by asking, "Are there any questions?"

Request help or clarification when needed. If you're not sure you understand something, summarize it and ask, "Is that right, or did I miss something?"

Responding

When you work in a group, nearly everything you say and do is a response to what someone else has said or done. First you hear others' statements and observe their behavior. You take a moment to think about the ways you could respond. Then you choose your response.

Think before responding. Imagine someone making the statement "Blind Alley is a dumb group." Before you knew about group skills, you might have responded with "Yeah, well, I think you're dumb." If you ever do respond in this way, you're headed into a dead-end argument instead of a discussion.

But you can choose a better response. You can avoid an argument by saying, "Everyone is entitled to his or her own opinion." You can open up the discussion by asking, "Why do you feel they're dumb?" Or "What do you mean by 'dumb'?"

Learn how to disagree. Never say, "I disagree *with you*." Say instead, "I disagree. I think Blind Alley is a great group." This is disagreeing with the idea, not the speaker. You may also list your reasons for disagreeing. Then again, instead of saying "I disagree," you can ask the speaker a few questions, questions showing that important points have been left out.

Making Decisions

It's important to understand how groups make decisions and that decisions made by a group can be as democratic as its members like. Here are some of the ways decisions are made.

Leader's Choice The group leader makes a decision based on choices offered by group members.

Expert's Choice An expert is invited to give advice or make the decision for the group.

Poll A vote or survey taken of individuals outside the group is conducted to guide the group's decision.

Voting Group members vote on a list of choices.

Consensus Group members continue to discuss choices until everyone in the group agrees.

Planning Skills

Nothing much happens without a plan. Think of any accomplishment—from writing a terrific research paper to being elected president, from winning a game to sending people to the moon. No matter what you think of, it happened because someone made a plan and put that plan into action.

Now consider your life. What do you think will happen if you don't make a plan? Hmm. . . . On the other hand, if you do make a plan, you can achieve just about anything you set out to do.

Time-Management Basics

Managing time is a must-have planning skill. You have a limited amount of time, and an unlimited number of things you could do with it. You must use your time to do the things that will help you reach your goals and achieve your dreams.

Break big tasks into smaller tasks. Big achievements and big assignments can't be completed in a day. But they'll never be completed if you don't pick a day and begin. When you have a big job to do, figure out how much of it you can tackle each day and each week until it's done. Then pick a day to begin.

Keep a schedule. Buy or make a planning calendar and put all your important "things to do" on it. That way you won't forget, get sidetracked, or end up with too much to do the night before a deadline. Try to plan out a week in advance, so there's time for everything.

Plan your study time. Good advice, but most of us seldom take it. Good planning means having everything you need where you need it. Schedule your study time as early in the day as you can, take short breaks, keep snacks to a minimum, interact with the page by asking questions (out loud, if no one objects), and summarize what you've learned before you finish.

Be disciplined, but flexible. Stick to your schedule as much as possible. When you have to make a change (you may get sick, or someone may cancel or change an appointment), look for the best way to adjust your schedule. If play rehearsal is cancelled, use that time to get ahead on your assignments, so you'll have time to go to a makeup rehearsal next week.

Completing Assignments

Right now, schoolwork is a big part of your life. If you plan your assignments so that you can do a good job and finish on time, you're well on your way to developing planning skills that will serve you for a lifetime.

Plan Ahead

Before you sit down . . .

- **Know what you're doing.** Before you sit down to work on your assignments, know exactly what your assignments are and when they are due.

- **Know your time frame.** Figure out how much time each assignment will take. (The more you do this, the better you'll get at it.)

- **Break things down.** Remember, break big assignments into smaller ones, and do a little each day.

- **Keep a schedule.** Write your assignments on your weekly and daily planning calendars.

- **Have a regular study spot.** Find a spot that's quiet, well lighted, and stocked with supplies (pens and pencils, highlighters, paper, dictionary, handbook, and so on).

- **Have a regular study time.** Having a set time to study will help you get into the right frame of mind and use your time well. Choose a time when you're alert.

Do the Work

When you sit down . . .

- **Review directions carefully.** Before you begin, make sure you know what you're supposed to do.

- **Use study strategies.** See the "Critical Reading Skills" chapter on pages 373–384 for helpful strategies and guidelines.

- **Stay focused.** Avoid distractions such as phone calls and television.

- **Plan breaks and rewards.** Plan to get a certain amount of work done before you take a break. Keep your breaks short and do something that refreshes you. Reward yourself when you finish for the day or complete a big project.

- **Keep a list of questions.** Make notes about anything you don't understand, so you can look for further information or ask your teacher or a classmate questions.

"A good listener is not only popular everywhere,
but after awhile he gets to know something."

—Wilson Mizner

LISTENING and NOTE-TAKING Skills

Experts have long told us that people remember only about half of what they hear—even if they're tested immediately after hearing it. A couple of months later, that percentage drops to 25 percent. That may be no big deal if you're listening to your favorite morning disc jockey, but if you only remember 25 percent of what you heard in your history class, you may be in big trouble.

Listening is a skill, and like all other skills, it can be improved with time and practice. The same is true for note taking. In fact, the two skills work hand in hand: You will be a better listener if you take good notes, and you will take better notes if you listen carefully. This section of your handbook introduces guidelines and strategies designed to improve both your listening and note-taking skills. And, if you read carefully, you may just pick up a bonus or two along the way.

Preview

- **Improving Listening Skills**
- **Improving Note-Taking Skills**
- **Using a Note-Taking Guide**
- **Quick Guide: Creating a Shorthand System**

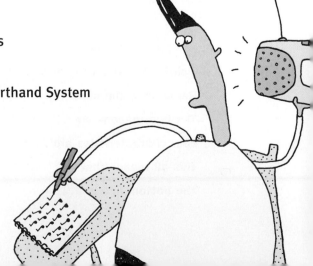

Improving **Listening** Skills

Someone (probably an English teacher) once observed that there must be a reason why people have two ears and only one mouth. Not everyone takes the hint, though; plenty of people still do more talking than listening. Maybe that's because listening takes effort. To really listen, you have to concentrate on what is being said, and concentration is work. Plus, there are all kinds of things that can make listening extra challenging: being distracted by noise, being tired, being too hot or too cold, and so on.

It takes determination to listen well.

1. **Prepare to listen and keep a goal in mind.**
   Take time to figure out why you are listening (to gather information about a subject, to learn how to . . .). Then keep an open mind about the speaker and the topic.

2. **Listen carefully.**
   Listen not only to what the speaker is actually saying but also to what the speaker is implying (saying between the lines). The speaker's voice, tone, volume, facial expressions, and gestures can all help tell you what's really important.

3. **Listen for the facts.**
   Listen to find out the *who, when, where, what, why,* and *how* of something. This will help you learn how to pull important facts out of what you hear and arrange them in a way that makes them easier to remember.

4. **Separate fact from opinion.**
   Listen for bias or opinion disguised as fact. (See page 481.)

5. **Listen for signals.**
   Your instructor will often tell you exactly what is important. He or she may not use a megaphone to say, "Now hear this!" but it may be almost as obvious.

   Examples: And don't forget to . . .

   Remember, the best way to . . . is . . .

   The two reasons are . . .

   Four characteristics are . . .

   This all means that . . .

   The bottom line is . . .

6. Listen for patterns of organization.

Textbooks and lectures often follow "patterns of organization." If you can discover how a speaker has organized information and where she or he is going with the material, you have important signposts to follow. Discovering a speaker's pattern of organization is a listening skill that will increase your capacity to learn. (See page 457.)

7. Listen for details.

Don't be satisfied with understanding the general drift of a story or a lecture. Pay full attention to what a speaker is saying. If you allow the details to slip through the cracks, you are less likely to remember what is being said. Details, examples, and anecdotes help a lecture come to life, and they also provide helpful hooks for your memory.

8. Listen to directions.

How often have you sat down, ready to begin an assignment, only to be confused because you could not remember exactly what the teacher asked you to do? Your ability to listen to directions is vital. You may be able to e-mail your teacher to ask for the directions again, but he or she may not be too impressed.

9. Think about what is being said.

Ask yourself how this material relates to you. What can you relate it to in your personal life to help you remember? How might you use the information in the future?

10. Put the lecture into your own words.

Put the speaker's statements into your own words as you take notes. Identify each main point and draw conclusions about its importance. This is one way you can begin to own the material.

The highest level of listening involves empathy—listening to the world through the ears of the speaker.

Improving **Note-Taking** Skills

Note taking is an active approach to learning, one that gets you personally involved in the learning process and helps you focus on and organize the information you need to study and learn.

The most important thing to understand about note taking is that you need to do more than simply listen and write. You need to *listen, think, react, question, summarize, organize, label,* and *write.*

Be Prepared

■ **Do your assigned reading before you come to class.** That way you can follow what is being discussed and don't have to look at the floor every time your teacher asks a question.

■ **Have a separate notebook for each class** and an extra pen or two.

■ **Label and date your notes** at the beginning of each class period.

Be Attentive

■ **Listen for any special instructions,** rules, or guidelines your teacher may have regarding notebooks and note taking.

■ **Write your notes as neatly as time will allow;** leave space in the margin for working with your notes later.

■ **Begin taking notes immediately.** Don't wait for something new or earthshaking before you begin taking notes.

■ **Relate the material to something in your life** by writing a brief personal observation or reminder.

■ **Use your own words** rather than copying exactly what you hear.

Be Concise

■ **Summarize the main ideas,** listing only the necessary details. Remember, taking good notes does not mean writing down everything.

■ **Condense information.** Write your notes in phrases and lists rather than complete sentences.

■ **Use abbreviations, acronyms, and symbols** (U.S., av., in., ea., lb., vs., @, #, $, %, &, +, =, w/o).

■ **Develop your own shorthand method.** (See page 414.)

■ **Draw simple illustrations, charts, or diagrams** in your notes whenever they will make a point clearer.

Be Organized

- **Use a note-taking guide.** Choose the guide that best fits your needs, or create a variation of your own. (See pages 412-413.)
- **Write a title or heading** for each new topic covered in your notes.
- **Leave wide margins or skip a line or two between main ideas.** When you're reviewing later, you'll have room to add study notes.
- **Listen for transitions** or signal words to help you organize your notes. Number all ideas and information presented in sequence or time order.
- **Use a special system of marking** your notes to emphasize important information (underline, highlight, star, check, indent).
- **Label or mark** information that is related by cause and effect, by comparison or contrast, or by any other special way.

Be Smart

- **Always copy down** (or summarize) what the teacher puts on the board or projects on an overhead.
- **Ask questions** when you don't understand something.
- **Circle those words or ideas** that you will need to look up later.
- **Don't let your notes sit** until it is time to review for a test. Read over the notes you have taken within 24 hours and recopy, add details, highlight, or summarize as necessary.
- **Jot down key words in the left-hand column.** Cover your notes and try to restate what was said about each key word.
- **Share your note-taking techniques,** abbreviations, or special markings with others; then learn from what they share with you.

Tips for Remembering Your Notes

- Relate the material to your life.
- Recite ideas and facts out loud.
- Draw diagrams, illustrations, and clusters.
- Write about it, using your own words.
- Study it with someone or teach it to someone.
- Visualize it.
- Study your most difficult material first.
- Use acronyms, rhymes, raps, and flash cards.

Using a **Note-Taking Guide**

Note taking helps you listen better in class, organize your ideas more effectively, and remember more of what you read or hear. And the better the notes you take, the more help they can be. That's why note-taking guides have become so popular. By using the correct guide for each situation, you can make the most of your efforts. A note-taking guide can help you develop an efficient note-taking system to coordinate your textbook, lecture, and review notes.

Keeping Text and Class Notes Together

If your teacher follows the textbook closely, you can use your reading notes as a classroom note-taking guide. As you follow your notes, you'll be prepared to answer any questions your teacher may ask and you'll be ready to take additional notes as well. Simply follow along and jot down anything that helps to clarify or adds to your understanding of the material.

Use the left two-thirds of your paper for reading notes; use the right one-third for class notes.

Use this format when a teacher follows the text closely.

Chapter 10: The Disinherited	
Outlined Reading Assignment	Class Notes
I. The Clash of Cultures	Early settlers had
A. Pioneer attitude toward	few problems; as
Native Americans	more trappers and
1. Uncultured	hunters moved in,
a. Lacked civilization	conflicts started.
b. Lacked religion	Native Americans
2. Easily exploited	labeled pagans.
a. Swindled in trades	
b. Set against other tribes	
3. No property rights	
a. A squatter on govt. land	Some argued that
b. False promises	because Native
c. Forced off land	Americans did not
B. Native American reaction	have the right to
to treatment	vote, they could not
1. Attitudes	own property.
a. Disappointment	
b. Bitterness	
2. Resulting Action	
a. Move	Serious clashing of
1) To designated areas	the cultures
2) farther west	followed.
b. Defend	
c. Attack	

Adding a Review Column

If you want to keep all your notes together, you can add a third column at the left of your page. Leave this review column blank during class; but after class, read through your notes and add key words and phrases that summarize what is in each section of your notes. This will help you review and remember your notes.

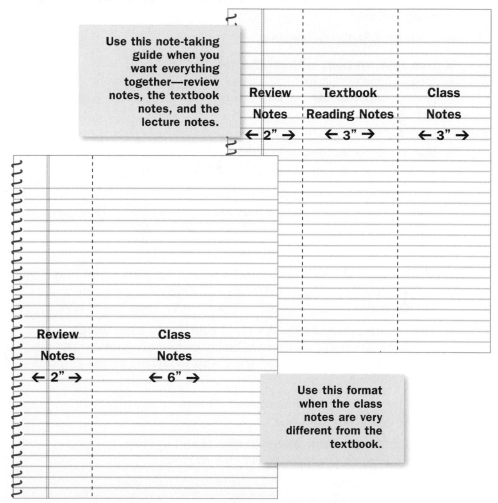

Use this note-taking guide when you want everything together—review notes, the textbook notes, and the lecture notes.

Review Notes	Textbook Reading Notes	Class Notes
← 2" →	← 3" →	← 3" →

Review Notes	Class Notes
← 2" →	← 6" →

Use this format when the class notes are very different from the textbook.

Keeping Text and Class Notes Separate

If your teacher does not base his or her lecture on the class text, you may want to keep your class and textbook notes separate. In that case, your class notes will have only two columns—a wide right column for lecture notes and a narrow left column where you can add review notes.

Quick Guide

Creating a Shorthand System

You will be taking a lot of notes during your high school career. Start now to develop your own personal shorthand system. Here are some guidelines:

■ **Omit all articles (*a, an, the*).**

■ **Use abbreviations without the periods.**

meas	max	min	p	pp
prev	approx	etc	esp	incl
reg	lg	sm	lbs	st
pres	Jan			

■ **Use common mathematical and technical symbols.**

+ − = × % # < > ÷ ↑ ↓ $ ||

■ **Eliminate vowels from words.**

mdl for *middle*   *psbl* for *possible*

■ **Use word beginnings.**

intro for *introduction*   *psych* for *psychology*

✻ Use your abbreviations consistently. Otherwise, you may end up wondering if *psych* means *psychology, psychiatry,* or *psychic*.

■ **Create abbreviations for the most commonly used words.**
Review your notes to find the most commonly used words for each class. Write them and their abbreviations at the front of your notebook.

PNS for *parasympathetic nervous system*
QE for *quadratic equation*

■ **Keep adding to your personal shorthand system.**
Here are some examples to get you started:

w/	*with*	*w/o*.......	*without*
ex	*for example*	*b/c*	*because*
b4........	*before*	*SB*........	*should be*
SNB	*should not be*	*2*	*two, to, too*

"The man who has ceased to learn ought not to be allowed to wander around loose."

—M. M. Coady

Writing to
LEARN

Writing about a particular topic to understand it better—that's what writing to learn is all about. It's really that simple. When you write to learn, you are *not* trying to show how well you can write or how much you already know about a topic; you are writing to learn more.

When you write to learn, you should write freely and naturally. Most writing-to-learn activities are short, spontaneous, and exploratory. They are almost never graded or corrected for mechanical errors. Some educators now believe that writing to learn is the best way to truly learn anything, from math to music. This chapter includes a variety of writing-to-learn strategies that you can try.

Preview

- **Learning Logs**
- **Writing-to-Learn Activities**
- **Writing a Paraphrase**
- **Writing a Summary**

Learning Logs

A learning log is a notebook in which you take notes of a different kind. It is a place where you can dig deeper into what you have learned from lectures, class discussions, group projects, experiments, and reading assignments. Approach writing in your learning log the same way you approach writing in your journal. (See pages 132-134.)

Keeping a Learning Log

A learning log gets you actively involved in your course work and gives you the opportunity to freely explore important ideas. This free flow of ideas and questions promotes true learning. Here are some specific ideas for writing in a learning log.

- **Write a summary** of a learning experience (lecture, discussion, and so on). Add your own conclusions, telling what information you found most valuable or interesting, what opinions you agreed with or disagreed with, and why.

- **Personalize new ideas and concepts.** Consider how this new information relates to what you already know.

- **Write about what you still want to know** about a topic. Brainstorm ways to find this information.

- **Discuss your course work with a particular audience:** a young child, a foreign exchange student, an alien from another planet, an object.

- **Question what you are learning.** How important are the concepts you are learning? One way to discover this is to write a dialogue.

- **Express ideas and information in pictures,** charts, and maps.

- **Start a glossary** of important and interesting vocabulary words. Use these words in your log entries.

- **Argue *for* or *against* a topic.** The topic can be anything that comes up in a discussion, in a lecture, or in your reading.

- **Write about how you are doing in a certain class.** Are you learning as much as you can, or doing as well as you had hoped? Is some of the material hard for you? What can you do to improve?

Sample Learning Logs

The sample learning-log entries below were written in response to an article in a science magazine and a lecture in a chemistry class. Notice how both entries are personalized.

Response to a Science Article

I just read an article in a science magazine about mosquitoes and the diseases they can carry. I thought flies and mosquitoes were a pain just because they bite. But it turns out that you can get more than an itchy bump from a mosquito. They can carry viruses that cause serious diseases such as malaria and encephalitis. Doctors think that, in all of history, more people have died of malaria than any other disease. Malaria was even one of the reasons why the Roman Empire fell. In 1999, seven people in New York City died from encephalitis caused by mosquito bites. Health officials are very concerned about this recent outbreak.

Response to a Chemistry Lecture

Our teacher used the *Hindenburg* as an example of how noble gases are different from other elements. The *Hindenburg* was a zeppelin—a huge, cylinder-shaped, flying balloon that could carry passengers. It was filled with hydrogen—which is not a noble gas—and reacted with oxygen in the air, causing the zeppelin to burn. Thirty-six people died. If helium had been used instead, it also would have kept the zeppelin airborne, but it wouldn't have burned. This is because it is a noble gas, meaning it doesn't interact with other elements. That's why balloons and dirigibles use helium now, not hydrogen. This got me thinking about how what you don't know can hurt you. Chemistry can actually be useful in real life!

Writing-to-Learn Activities

Writing to learn is essentially exploratory writing. What form it takes is strictly up to you, as long as it encourages thinking and learning. You might be perfectly satisfied with free, nonstop writing; others might find clustering or listing meaningful. Still others might enjoy a variety of writing activities similar to those that follow.

Admit Slips ■ Admit slips are brief pieces of writing called for by the teacher at the beginning of class, like an admission ticket. An admit slip can be a summary of last night's reading, a question about class material, a request for the teacher to review a particular point, or anything else that makes sense to you.

Debates ■ Try splitting your mind into two persons. Have one side disagree with your thinking on a subject, and have the other side defend it. Keep the debate going as long as you can.

Dialogues ■ In a dialogue, you create an imaginary conversation between yourself and a character (a historical figure, for example) or between two characters (from a story, for example). Dialogue can bring information to life, helping you to better understand a particular subject or historical period.

Dramatic Scenarios ■ In a dramatic scenario, you project yourself into a unit of study and develop a scenario (plot) that can be played out in writing. If the unit is World War II, for example, you may put yourself in President Truman's shoes the day before he decided to drop the first atomic bomb.

Exit Slips ■ Write a note at the end of class, evaluating, questioning, or summarizing something about the day's lesson. Turn in your exit slip to your teacher before you leave the classroom.

First Thoughts ■ Write down your immediate impressions about a topic you are preparing to study. These writings will help you focus on the new subject matter.

How-To Writing ■ Write instructions or directions on how to perform a certain task in order to clarify and remember the information.

Instant Versions ■ In an instant version of a paper or report, you write a final draft immediately—no prewriting, no planning. Writing instant versions can help you find a focus and discover what you know (or don't know) about the subject.

Nutshelling ■ Try writing down, in one sentence, the importance of something you've heard, seen, or read.

Personal Summary ■ Summarize a section of reading or a lecture—putting the material into your own words and relating it to your own life whenever possible.

> **I remember hearing only bad things about cholesterol. I know a man who has been on a low-cholesterol diet for many years. He still has high levels of "bad" cholesterol in his blood. Why does the body produce something that can cause such serious problems as heart attacks? Then I heard there's good cholesterol and that eating certain things can produce "good" cholesterol instead of the "bad." So why doesn't a diet low in LDL- and VLDL-cholesterol automatically mean only HDL, or good cholesterol, will be produced?**

Picture Outlines ■ Instead of using a traditional format, you can organize your thoughts into a picture outline. For example, a picture outline can easily capture the main points from a lecture on the makeup and function of a particular organ.

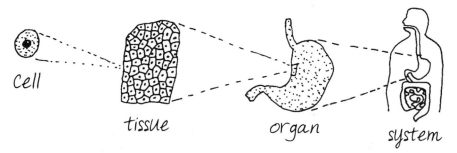

Cell   tissue   organ   system

Predicting ■ Stop at a key point in a book or lesson and write what you think will happen next. Predicting works especially well with materials that have a strong cause-and-effect relationship.

Pointed Questions ■ Keep asking yourself *why* in your writing until you run out of answers.

Role-Playing ■ Imagine yourself in a different role (a reporter, a historical or fictional character, an animal) and write about a topic from this new point of view.

Stop 'n' Write ■ At any point in a reading assignment, stop and write about what you've just read. This allows you to evaluate your understanding of the topic.

Unsent Letters ■ Write a letter to anyone (or anything) on a topic related to the subject you are studying. Unsent letters allow you to personalize the subject matter and then share it with another person—real or imagined.

Writing a **Paraphrase**

A paraphrase is a type of summary that is written in your own words. It is particularly good for clarifying the meaning of a difficult or symbolic piece of writing (some poems, proverbs, documents). Because it often includes your interpretation, it is sometimes longer than the original.

Writing Guidelines

1. **Skim the passage** or selection quickly.

2. **Then read the passage carefully,** noting key words and ideas.

3. **Look up any unfamiliar words.**

4. **Summarize each idea** of the passage in a clear statement.

5. **Expand or reword the text to make it clearer,** maintaining the meaning and tone of the original.

SAMPLE PARAPHRASE

Notice that the paraphrase below translates some of the out-of-date language (*faculties*, *thither*) into words that make sense to modern readers. Notice, too, how the paraphrase replaces the male pronouns in the original with gender-free words without changing Emerson's meaning.

ORIGINAL PASSAGE

Each man has his own vocation. The talent is the call. There is one direction in which all space is open to him. He has faculties silently inviting him thither to endless exertion. He is like a ship in a river; he runs against obstructions on every side but one; on that side all obstruction is taken away, and he sweeps serenely over a deepening channel into an infinite sea.

—Ralph Waldo Emerson, "Spiritual Laws"

Paraphrase

Ralph Waldo Emerson said that everyone has a calling in life. All people have abilities, talents, and energies silently inviting them to their life's work. Those who respond to their calling are like ships in a river flowing toward the sea. There are banks on both sides, and there is only one direction in which to move with ease. Those who try to avoid that one direction will run into obstacles wherever they turn. And, like ships moving surely to the sea, those who follow their true calling will move with great peace of mind toward the open sea of unlimited possibilities.

Writing a **Summary**

Writing an effective summary is an excellent way to understand and remember what you have read. Follow the guidelines below and read through the model on the next page.

Writing Guidelines

1. **Skim the selection** first to get the overall meaning.

2. **Read the selection carefully,** paying particular attention to key words and phrases. (Check the meaning of any words you're unsure of.)

3. **List the main ideas** on your own paper—without looking at the selection.

4. **Review the selection** a final time so that you have the overall meaning clearly in mind as you begin to write.

5. **Write a summary** of the major ideas, using your own words except for those few words in the original that cannot be changed. Keep the following points in mind as you write:

   ■ Your opening (topic) sentence should be a clear statement of the main idea of the original selection.

   ■ Stick to the essential information. Names, dates, times, places, and similar facts are usually essential; examples, descriptive details, and adjectives are usually not needed.

   ■ Try to state each important idea in one clear sentence.

   ■ Use a concluding sentence that ties all of your thoughts together and brings the summary to an effective end.

6. **Check your summary** for accuracy and conciseness. Ask yourself the following questions:

   ■ Have I included all of the main ideas?

   ■ Have I cut or combined most of the descriptive details? (Your summary should be about one-half the length of the original.)

   ■ Will another person understand the main points simply by reading my summary?

HELP FILE

To write a *précis* (a special form of summary), do the following:
■ Keep the same voice and perspective as the original.
■ Use paraphrases instead of direct quotations.
■ Be brief.

Sample **Summary**

Notice that the opening sentence of the summary below contains both a definition of the topic and the main point of the summary. The writer then lists the key details and concludes with a thought-provoking statement.

ORIGINAL TEXT

"Acid rain" is precipitation with a high concentration of acids. The acids are produced by sulfur dioxide, nitrogen oxide, and other chemicals that are created by the burning of fossil fuels. Acid rain is known to have a gradual, destructive effect on plant and aquatic life.

The greatest harm from acid rain is caused by sulfur dioxide, a gas produced from coal. As coal is burned in large industrial and power plant boilers, the sulfur it contains is turned into sulfur dioxide. This invisible gas is funneled up tall smokestacks and released into the atmosphere some 350–600 feet above the ground. As a result, the effects of the gas are seldom felt immediately. Instead, the gas is carried by the wind for hundreds and sometimes thousands of miles before it floats back down to earth. For example, sulfur dioxide produced in Pennsylvania at noon on Monday may not show up again until early Tuesday when it settles into the lakes and soil of rural Wisconsin.

Adding to the problem is the good possibility that the sulfur dioxide has undergone a chemical change while in flight. By simply taking on another molecule of oxygen, the sulfur dioxide could be changed to sulfur trioxide. Sulfur trioxide, when mixed with water, creates sulfuric acid—a highly toxic acid. If the sulfur trioxide enters a lake or stream, the resulting acid can kill fish, algae, and plankton. This, in turn, can interrupt the reproductive cycle of other life-forms, causing a serious imbalance in nature. If the sulfuric acid enters the soil, it can work on metals such as aluminum and mercury and set them free to poison both the soil and water.

SUMMARY

"Acid rain," the term for precipitation that contains a high concentration of harmful chemicals, is gradually damaging our environment. The greatest harm from acid rain is caused by sulfur dioxide, a gas produced from the burning of coal. This gas, which is released into the atmosphere by industries using coal-fired boilers, is carried by the wind for hundreds of miles. By the time this gas has floated back to earth, it has often changed from sulfur dioxide to sulfur trioxide. Sulfur trioxide, when mixed with water, forms sulfuric acid. This acid can kill both plant and aquatic life and upset the cycle of life.

"A question asked in the right way
often points to its own answer."

—Edward Hodnett

TEST-TAKING Skills

What's the secret to doing well on tests? The key is preparation. This is true of any test—essay, objective, or standardized. To be well prepared, start with an effective test-taking plan.

Your plan should include a process for organizing the test material, reviewing it, remembering it, and, finally, using it on the test itself. Having a good plan will reduce "test anxiety" and give you the best chance to succeed. Studying the guidelines and samples in this chapter will help you improve your test-taking skills.

Preview

- Taking Essay Tests
- Tips for Taking Essay Tests
- Taking Objective Tests
- Tips for Taking Classroom Tests
- Taking Standardized Tests
- Tips for Taking Standardized Tests
- Taking District or State Writing Tests

Taking Essay Tests

Essay tests are challenging. They require you to respond in writing to a thought-provoking prompt or question. The following strategies will help you respond to essay-test prompts.

Understanding the Prompt

Read an essay-test prompt several times until you are sure that you understand it. Pay special attention to the *key word* in the prompt. For example, if you are asked to *contrast* two things, show their differences. If, instead, you simply *discuss* the topics, your test score will suffer.

Key Words

The following key terms are often used in essay prompts. Each term is explained and used in an essay-test prompt.

Classify ■ To classify is to group things because they are alike or similar. Classification questions are often used in science classes. Organize your essay so that the groups are clearly identified.

> **Classify the following forms of water according to the three physical states: clouds, steam, snow, drizzle, dew, water vapor, and frost.**

Compare ■ To compare is to show how things are similar and different, with the greater emphasis on similarities.

> **Compare the English and American Bills of Rights.**

Contrast ■ To contrast is to show how things are different in one or more important ways.

> **Contrast how a writer might use dramatic monologue and soliloquy.**

Define ■ To define is to give a clear definition or meaning for a term. A definition often identifies how an item is different from other items in the same category or class.

> **Define deductive reasoning. (Your definition might point out how deductive reasoning differs from inductive reasoning.)**

Describe ■ To describe is to tell how something looks or to give a general impression of it.

> **Describe Scout's appearance on the night of the Halloween party.**

Diagram ■ To diagram is to explain something using a flowchart, a map, or some other graphic device. The important parts of graphics are labeled.

> **Draw a diagram showing the layers of the skin.**

Discuss ■ To discuss is to talk about an issue from all sides.

> **Discuss the spread of democracy in the former USSR.**

Evaluate ■ To evaluate is to make a judgment, to give the pluses and minuses backed up with evidence (facts, figures, and so on).

> **Evaluate the impact of home computers on everyday life.**

Explain ■ To explain is to make clear, to analyze, to show a process. Although it is similar to the term *discuss*, *explain* places more emphasis on cause-and-effect relationships and step-by-step sequences.

> **Explain the greenhouse effect on Earth's atmosphere.**

Illustrate ■ To illustrate means to show a law, rule, or principle through specific examples and instances. A drawing or graphic may be part of the answer.

> **Illustrate how a bill becomes law in this state.**

Justify ■ To justify is to defend a position or point of view. A justification stresses the advantages over the disadvantages.

> **Justify the opinion that presidents should be limited to one six-year term.**

Outline ■ To outline is to organize a set of facts or ideas by listing main points and subpoints. An effective outline shows how topics or ideas fit together.

> **Outline the events in the Tom Robinson affair.**

Prove ■ To prove means to bring out the truth by giving evidence, facts, and examples to back up your point.

> **Attempt to prove that capital punishment is not an effective deterrent to crime.**

Review ■ To review is to reexamine or to summarize the major points of a topic, usually in chronological (time) order or in order of importance.

> **Review the events leading to the beginning of World War I.**

State ■ To state means to present a concise statement of a position, fact, or point of view.

> **State your reasons for having taken the position you hold on states' rights.**

Summarize ■ To summarize is to present the main points of an issue in a shortened form. Details, illustrations, and examples are usually omitted.

> **Summarize the main reasons for the French Revolution.**

Planning and Writing the Essay-Test Answer

To develop an effective response to an essay-test prompt, follow the four steps listed below.

1. **Read the prompt** several times. Pay special attention to the key word as it applies to the topic.

2. **Rephrase the prompt** into a thesis statement that clearly states the main point. It often works well to drop the key word from your thesis statement.

   Prompt: Explain the greenhouse effect.

   Thesis statement: The greenhouse effect causes Earth's atmosphere to retain heat and to become warmer.

3. **Outline or list the main points** you plan to cover in your answer. Time will probably not allow you to include all supporting details.

4. **Write your essay** (or paragraph). Begin with your thesis statement (or topic sentence). Add the necessary background information and then include your main supporting details, following your outline of main points.

HELP FILE

Beginning with the thesis statement is not the only strategy to use. You may, in fact, want to lead up to it. At other times, you may decide to use an *implied thesis* in which the main point of your response is developed indirectly rather that stated and supported directly.

Sample **One-Paragraph Response**

If you feel that one paragraph can adequately answer the prompt, simply use the main points of your outline to support your topic sentence.

Question: Explain the greenhouse effect.

> **The greenhouse effect causes Earth's atmosphere to retain heat and to become warmer.** The process begins when the sun's rays warm the planet. Earth's surface reflects some of this heat back toward space in the form of infrared radiation. However, certain gases in the atmosphere absorb this reflected radiation, emitting it back to the planet as heat. This causes the temperature of the atmosphere to rise. The more greenhouse gases, the greater the greenhouse effect. This is why some people are worried that Earth will get too warm if gases like carbon dioxide and methane continue to increase in the atmosphere.

Sample **Multiparagraph Answer**

If the prompt is too complex to handle in one paragraph, include only your thesis statement and any necessary background information in your opening paragraph. Begin each middle paragraph by forming one of the main points from your outline into a topic sentence. Support this topic sentence with examples, reasons, or other details. Your ending paragraph should summarize your thoughts.

Prompt: Contrast how a writer might use dramatic monologue and soliloquy.

I. Explanation + Examples
   A. Soliloquy: <u>Romeo and Juliet</u>
   B. Dramatic monologue: "My Last Duchess"
II. Uses
   A. Soliloquy: Reveals a character's thoughts
   B. Dramatic monologue: Shows how characters relate to one another

---

Although both techniques involve a single speaker, soliloquy and dramatic monologue have different purposes and effects in literature. In a soliloquy, the speaker thinks out loud and is usually alone. This happens often in Shakespeare's plays. One of the most famous soliloquies occurs in *Romeo and Juliet* when Juliet speaks from her heart near the start of the balcony scene. During a dramatic monologue, a character speaks to someone who remains silent, a situation like hearing a person talking on the phone. In Robert Browning's poem "My Last Duchess," the Duke talks about his former wife to another man, whose reactions we do not hear.

Writers often use soliloquies to reveal a character's thoughts. In the balcony scene, Juliet is unaware that Romeo can hear her, so she says things to herself that she would not tell anyone else. It's clear that she has strong feelings for Romeo, and she is embarrassed when he speaks and reveals his presence. Juliet wishes she could take back her words, but the soliloquy has done its job: We (and Romeo) know her true thoughts, and the romance picks up speed.

A dramatic monologue shows how a character relates to others. The Duke in "My Last Duchess" is talking to a man who has been sent to find out whether the Duke would be a good husband. The Duke should show how considerate he is. Instead, he brags about how he dominated his first wife and thus is a totally unlikable character.

Literary characters can be interesting for what they do, but they are sometimes even more interesting for what they say. Soliloquy and dramatic monologue are two methods that writers use to tell readers what their characters are really like. Even though only one character is speaking in both cases, the effects can be very different.

TIPS for Taking **Essay Tests**

Make sure you are ready both mentally and physically for the test. Keep up with your schoolwork, prepare for the test, and get enough rest.

- **Listen carefully to your teacher's final instructions.**

    How much time do you have to complete the test?

    Do all the questions count equally?

    Can you use any aids (dictionary, handbook, notes)?

    Are there any corrections, changes, or additions to the test?

- **Begin the test immediately and watch the time carefully.**

    Don't spend so much time on one question that you run out of time for the others.

- **Read each question carefully, paying special attention to the key words.** (See pages 424-425.)

    Ask the teacher to clarify anything you may not understand about the questions.

- **Rephrase each question into a thesis statement (or topic sentence) for your essay answer.**

- **Think before you write.**

    List your main points in a brief outline. Do this on scrap paper or on the back of the test paper.

- **Write a strong topic sentence for each paragraph, using a main point from your outline.**

    Include the appropriate supporting details in an organized way.

- **Write concisely.**

    Don't use abbreviations or nonstandard language.

- **In each question, first write about the points you know well.**

    Work on the remaining points as time permits.

- **Keep your test paper neat with reasonable margins.**

    Neatness is always important, and readability is a must on an exam.

- **Revise and proofread as carefully as time permits.**

Taking **Objective Tests**

The following guidelines will help you answer the common types of questions on objective tests.

True/False Test

- **Read the entire question before answering.** Often the first part of the statement will be true or false, while the second half will be just the opposite. For an answer to be true, the entire statement must be true.
- **Read each word and number.** Pay special attention to names, dates, and numbers that are similar and could easily be confused.
- **Beware of true/false statements that contain words like *all, every, always,* and *never*.** These statements are often false.
- **Watch for statements that contain more than one negative word.** Example: It is *un*likely ice will *not* melt when the temperature rises above 32° F. Read these statements very carefully.

Matching Test

- **Read through both lists quickly before you begin answering.** Notice items that are similar, and pay special attention to their differences, so you won't mix them up.
- **When matching word to word, determine the part of speech of each word.** If a word is a verb, match it with another verb.
- **When matching a word to a phrase, read the phrase first and look for the word it describes.**
- **Cross out each answer as you find it**—unless you are told that the answer can be used more than once.
- **Use capital letters rather than lowercase letters** since they are less likely to be misread by the person correcting the test.

Multiple-Choice Test

- **Read the directions to determine whether you are looking for the correct answer or the best answer.** Also check to see if a question can have more than one correct answer.
- **Read the first part of the question, looking for negative words like *not, never, except,* and *unless.***
- **Try to answer the question in your mind before looking at the choices.**
- **Read all the choices before selecting your answer.** This is especially important on tests in which you must select the *best* answer.

TIPS for Taking **Classroom Tests**

Organizing and Preparing Test Material

- Ask the teacher about what will be on the test.
- Ask how the material will be tested (true/false, multiple choice, essay).
- Review your class notes and recopy important sections.
- Get any notes or materials you may have missed from the teacher or another student.
- Set up specific times to study for tests; don't let other activities interfere.
- Look over quizzes and exams you took earlier in that class.
- Attempt to predict test questions and write practice answers for them.
- Make a list of questions to ask the teacher or another student.

Reviewing and Remembering Test Material

- Begin reviewing early. Don't wait until the night before the test.
- Look for patterns of organization in the material you study (cause/effect, comparison, chronological, and so on).
- Use maps, lists, diagrams, acronyms, rhymes, or any other special memory aids.
- Use flash cards or note cards to review material.
- Recite material out loud (whenever possible) as you review.
- Study with others only after you have studied well by yourself.
- Test your knowledge of a subject by teaching or explaining it to someone else.
- Review difficult material just before going to bed the night before the exam or just before the test.

Tip Whenever possible, relate the test material to your personal life or to other subjects you know about.

Taking **Standardized Tests**

You will take a number of standardized tests throughout high school. These tests measure your skills, progress, and achievement in nearly every subject—English, science, social studies, math, and reading.

Standardized test questions follow certain formats, and knowing about these formats can prepare you for your next testing experience. The guidelines below and the information on the following pages will help you prepare.

Guidelines for Standardized Tests

1. **Listen carefully to the instructions.** Most standardized tests follow very strict guidelines; there is a clear procedure for you to follow and a definite time limit.

2. **Read the directions carefully.** Most standardized tests have specific directions for each section, and no two sections are exactly alike.

   Note: If you just skim the directions, or any other part of the tests, you may miss some important information.

3. **Plan your time.** Standardized tests allow you a certain amount of time for each section. Plan your use of that time based on the number of questions, the difficulty level, and your own strengths and weaknesses.

4. **Answer the easy questions first.** If you're really unsure about certain questions, go back to them later.

5. **Read all the choices.** Don't answer a question until you've read all the choices; many choices are worded similarly to test your true understanding.

6. **Make educated guesses.** Unless you're told not to, select an answer for every question. First, eliminate choices that are obviously incorrect; then use logic to choose from the remaining answers.

7. **Double-check your answers.** As time permits, check each of your answers to make sure you haven't made any foolish mistakes or missed any questions.

Take NOTE Mark your answer sheet correctly and clearly. If you need to change an answer, erase it completely. Also make sure that you keep your place and that your answers end up next to the correct numbers.

TIPS for Taking **Standardized Tests**

Vocabulary

The vocabulary section of standardized tests usually contains two types of questions: *synonym* and *antonym*. Synonym questions ask you to find a word that has the same meaning; antonym questions ask for the opposite meaning of a word.

Synonym   BIBLIOPHILE   (A) soldier   (B) artist   (C) lover of books   (D) music lover   (E) child

Antonym   PRELUDE   (A) forerunner   (B) ending   (C) interruption   (D) test   (E) conference

Sentence Completion

Sentence completions test your understanding of how words work within sentences. Each blank indicates that something has been omitted. Choose the set of words that best fits the meaning of the sentence. Be sure to consider all choices before marking your answer.

In an effort to _____ their controversial decision, the committee _____ an open meeting where the public could ask questions.

   (A) explain . . . canceled   **(B)** disavow . . . suggested

   (C) clarify . . . scheduled   **(D)** ignore . . . proposed

Multiple Choice

The key to multiple-choice questions is to read the directions carefully. (The example below requires finding the sentence error.) Always read all the choices before selecting your answer.

Multiple Choice   1. I <u>enjoy</u> eating in a <u>good</u> restaurant and
                               A   B

                   <u>to go</u> to a movie <u>afterward</u>.   <u>No error.</u>
                    C   D   E

Reading Comprehension

You may be asked to read a passage and answer questions about it. The tips below can help you handle these types of comprehension questions:

- Read the passage carefully but as quickly as possible.
- Read all the choices before choosing the best answer.
- Eliminate choices that are clearly incorrect.

Taking District or State **Writing Tests**

When you take a writing test, your goal is to compose a clear, unified piece of writing within a limited amount of time. These tests can vary greatly from one situation to the next.

Writing Situations

■ In one situation, you might be given an open-ended writing prompt:

Describe an experience that really changed one of your beliefs.

■ In another situation, you might be given a clearly defined scenario to write about:

Write a letter to your school board either defending or opposing a proposal that would allow students to graduate from high school a semester early.

■ In still another situation, you might be given a prompt related to a piece of literature you should be familiar with:

The Reverend Mr. Collins and Wickham (in *Pride and Prejudice*) possess undesirable character traits. Explore these traits in a brief essay.

■ Then again, you might be given a prompt related to a piece of literature that you must read *during* the test:

In "An Unfortunate Event," the story you have just read, Essie has to make a difficult decision involving her friends. Write an essay in which you explain how Essie's character and her standards help her make her decision.

Preparing Yourself

How can you prepare for writing situations like the ones listed above? Here are some suggestions:

■ Keep up with your content-area reading and note taking.

■ Work to improve your reading skills. Pay special attention to the ways in which meaning is expressed in stories and poems.

■ Put forth a real effort in all writing assignments. That alone will increase your confidence.

■ Write often—in and out of the classroom.

■ Learn to use an abbreviated form of the writing process.

■ Practice writing impromptu pieces. (See pages 435–436 for prompts.)

The Timed Writing Process

The challenge in writing tests is to select the best of what you know and write about it clearly and effectively—in a limited time frame. Perhaps the most important quality you can bring to this experience is confidence, and confidence develops as you practice and work at your writing.

Use the following graphic to help you plan how much time you will spend on each part of the writing process. For example, if you are limited to 30 minutes, you should spend about 5 minutes on prewriting, 20 minutes on writing, and 5 minutes on revising and editing.

Prewriting	Writing	Revising / Editing
5 minutes	20 minutes	5 minutes

Steps to Follow

When you must write in a timed situation, follow these basic steps. (Also see page 451.)

1. Read the prompt carefully, looking for the key words.

2. Restate the focus of the prompt in a thesis statement.

3. Collect your thoughts by listing or clustering the main supporting points you want to include.

4. Arrange these thoughts and details in the best possible order.

5. Reword your thesis statement, if necessary, to reflect your plan.

6. Introduce your topic in a clear and engaging way.

7. Write your essay, always keeping your overall point (and the time limit) clearly in mind.

8. Add a conclusion that summarizes your main points and effectively brings your writing to a close.

9. Leave enough time to review the entire essay from start to finish.

Take NOTE To practice your timed-writing skills, review your class notes at regular intervals, and imagine a test prompt about the material your notes cover. Then develop a freely written essay that responds to the test prompt. Use the steps above as a general guide.

Assessing Timed Writing

What do evaluators look for when they assess a timed writing? They focus most of their attention on content and form.

1. **Evaluators look at the content,** the ideas you put forth in the writing. *Does the writing display a good working knowledge of the subject? Does it contain a reasonable thesis or focus statement and plenty of supporting detail?*

2. **They also look at the form of the writing,** the way you put the ideas together. *Does the writing contain a beginning, a middle, and an ending? Are the supporting details arranged in a logical order?*

HELP FILE

Evaluators understand the difference between a timed writing and one produced over an extended period. They know that impromptu essays do not display the polish that a piece developed under more relaxed circumstances can possess. Keep this in mind as you write.

Sample Writing Prompts

Listed below are sample writing prompts used in a state writing test. (Students were directed to write a two- to five-paragraph essay on one of the prompts. They had 90 minutes to complete their work.) The samples will give you an idea of what to expect on your own writing tests.

WRITING PROMPT 1

Suppose your school district is considering a twelve-month school year. The superintendent is your audience. Write a persuasive letter defending or opposing the idea of a twelve-month school year. Include your reasons for taking a particular position and support these reasons with examples.

WRITING PROMPT 2

Write an informative essay in which you identify the biggest or most significant problem you have ever solved. Provide the necessary background information to introduce the problem and a clear explanation of your solution. Consider whether you reached your solution by design or by accident.

WRITING PROMPT 3

"The only way to help yourself is to help others." Discuss the truth of these words, presenting examples from some or all of the following: literature, history, current events, biography, or personal experience. Be specific.

Prompts for Practice

Use the prompts listed below as starting points for timed writing practice.

Think and Write About . . .

current news stories
world problems
local problems
notable people
occupations and professions
nature
education and learning
places and events
art or music
food and drink
cars and travel
language and communication
manners and morals
laws and justice
social concerns
customs and habits
money and costs
government and politics
the media

Read and Respond to . . .

short articles from magazines
    or newspapers
song lyrics and poems
quips, quotes, or short stories
classroom literature

Listen and Respond to . . .

news broadcasts
interviews
music videos
short films
recited poetry

Analyze and Write About . . .

unusual statistics
quotations
proverbs
cliches
euphemisms

Describe . . .

a favorite photograph
a flock of birds in flight
a person who is totally organized
a person who is great to work with
someone who has an unusual hobby or
    collection
someone who has influenced you
someone who is one of a kind
someone you met once or knew briefly
a high school dance (or other event)

Compare . . .

original / imitation
middle school / high school
winter / summer
like / love
mother / father
one class to another
'60s / '90s
musicians or musical groups
movies or TV programs
old friends / new friends
bad days / good days
alligator / crocodile
wisdom / knowledge
opinion / belief

Cause and Effect . . .

What causes tornadoes?
What causes rainbows?
What causes misunderstandings?
What causes cancer?
What causes sunburn?
What causes violence?
What causes prejudice?
What causes pain?
What causes war?
Why are there schools?
Why are there towns?
Why do we worship sports stars?
Why do we get angry?

"Knowledge is power."
—Sir Francis Bacon

Taking Exit and Entrance
EXAMS

Some school districts and states use high school exit exams to determine whether students will graduate. Referred to as high-stakes tests, these assessments are designed to measure what you have learned in high school, including how well you write. In addition, the SAT and ACT tests help colleges and universities decide whether or not you will be admitted. Recently these tests have added a writing component as well.

There are two sections related to writing on exit and entrance exams. One section asks multiple-choice questions, and the other section provides writing prompts. This chapter will help you prepare for both parts.

Preview

- Multiple-Choice Questions
- Writing Tests Based on Prompts
- Persuasive Responses
- Responses to Literature

Multiple-Choice Questions

For writing-related multiple-choice questions, you must decide if a sentence or passage contains some type of error. You may be asked to identify the error (if, in fact, one exists) or to correct it.

Testing Use of Conventions

Multiple-choice questions may deal with the rules of language: punctuation, capitalization, spelling, grammar, and usage. Here are the types of questions you may be asked.

1. *Brazil is a vast <u>country, it</u> is almost as big as the United States.*

   The best choice for the underlined section is
   - **A.** NO CHANGE
   - **B.** country: it
   - **C.** country; it
   - **D.** country it

   ■ This item focuses on punctuation. The answer is **C**.

2. *A hush <u>past</u> over the crowd as Kurt, our best gymnast, fell from the high bar. Coach Bryant and I ran over and tried to determine <u>whether</u> he was injured, but we wouldn't <u>know</u> if his ankle was <u>all right</u> until the next day when X-rays were taken.*

   Which one of the underlined words is not the right word?
   - **A.** past
   - **B.** whether
   - **C.** know
   - **D.** all right

   ■ This item focuses on words that sound the same and are often mixed up in writing—*passed/past, weather/whether, know/no,* and *alright/all right.* The answer is **A**.

3. *"It's over <u>they're</u>," the salesperson said, pointing out the store's sale item.*

   The best choice for the underlined section is
   - **A.** "It's over their,"
   - **B.** "Its over there,"
   - **C.** "Its over they're,"
   - **D.** "It's over there,"

   ■ This item also focuses on words that sound the same and are often mixed up in writing—*it's/its* and *their/there/they're.* The answer is **D**.

4. *According to our* <u>science</u> *teacher, the* <u>Mesozoic Era</u> *came after the* <u>Permia Period</u>.

Which one of the underlined words has a capitalization error?
    A. science
    B. Mesozoic Era
    C. Permian Period
    D. NONE

    ■ This item focuses on capitalization. The answer is **D**.

5. *According to the most reliable calculations, the Leaning Tower of Pisa* <u>have existed</u> *for at least 650 years.*

Which of the following is the correct change for the underlined words?
    A. NO CHANGE
    B. will have existed
    C. exists
    D. has existed

    ■ This item focuses on verb tenses and subject-verb agreement. The answer is **D**.

6. *He and the other players sat in* <u>silence;</u> *they* <u>were</u> *stunned by* <u>thier</u> *sudden defeat.*

Which of the underlined items should be corrected?
    A. He
    B. silence;
    C. thier
    D. Both B and D

    ■ This item focuses on spelling. The answer is **C**.

Take **NOTE**

When you answer multiple-choice questions, keep these points in mind:

■ **Read the question carefully.** *Remember*: You will be asked to analyze a brief passage, to determine if it contains an error, and, possibly, to correct the error.

■ **Watch for negatives.** When directions contain words such as *not, none, never,* and *except,* make sure you understand what is being asked.

■ **Read each answer carefully.** Watch for answers such as "Both A and B," "All of the above," or "None of the above."

■ **Eliminate some answers.** Cross out choices you know are not correct before you make a choice.

Testing Sentence Revision Skills

Other multiple-choice questions may test your ability to revise sentences. These questions cover such skills as combining sentences, fixing ambiguous wording, creating parallel structure, correcting dangling modifiers, and eliminating sentence errors. (See the "Proofreader's Guide.")

Read the following sentences and choose the best revision. If the original is the best choice, the answer is D.

1. *The weather which consisted of seven straight days of rain. It ruined our vacation.*
   - **A.** The weather, which consisted of seven straight days of rain, ruined our vacation.
   - **B.** The weather consisted of seven straight days of rain. And it ruined our vacation.
   - **C.** The weather that consisted of seven straight days of rain. It ruined our vacation.
   - **D.** NO CHANGE

   ■ This item focuses on sentence fragments and sentence combining. The answer is **A**.

2. *Whipping the willow's branches back and forth, we huddled at the screen door to watch the wind.*
   - **A.** To watch the wind, we huddled at the screen door, whipping the willow's branches back and forth.
   - **B.** We huddled at the screen door to watch the wind whipping the willow's branches back and forth.
   - **C.** Watching the wind whipping the willow's branches back and forth at the screen door, we huddled.
   - **D.** NO CHANGE

   ■ This item focuses on misplaced modifiers. The answer is **B**.

3. *Natasha went to the restaurant and ate a sub sandwich and drank a diet cola and then she went back to work.*
   - **A.** Natasha went to the restaurant and ate a sub sandwich and drank a diet cola. Then she went back to work.
   - **B.** Natasha went to the restaurant, and ate a sub sandwich, and drank a diet cola. Then she went back to work.
   - **C.** Natasha went to the restaurant, where she had a sub sandwich and a diet cola before going back to work.
   - **D.** NO CHANGE

   ■ This item focuses on rambling or awkward sentences. The answer is **C**.

4. *I like sushi better than my brother.*

    A. I like sushi more better than my brother.

    B. I like sushi better than my brother does.

    C. I like sushi even better than my brother.

    D. NO CHANGE

    ■ This item focuses on incomplete comparisons.
The answer is **B**.

5. *No one saw Saul's boat sink after the lightning hit it, which Saul thought was just one more example of his bad luck.*

    A. Saul thought it was just one more example of his bad luck that no one saw his boat sink after the lightning hit it.

    B. No one saw Saul's boat sink after the lightning hit it. Saul thought it was just one more example of his bad luck.

    C. After the lightning hit Saul's boat, no one saw it sink. Saul thought it was just one more example of his bad luck.

    D. NO CHANGE

    ■ This item focuses on ambiguous wording. The answer is **A**.

6. *The car raced down the highway. The highway had ice on it. The car leaned into a sharp curve. It spun out of control and slid over the embankment.*

    A. The car raced down the highway, and the highway had ice on it. The car leaned into a sharp curve and spun out of control and slid over the embankment.

    B. The car raced down the icy highway. The car leaned into a sharp curve and spun out of control. It slid over the embankment.

    C. The car raced down the icy highway, leaned into a sharp curve, spun out of control, and slid over the embankment.

    D. NO CHANGE

    ■ This item focuses on sentence combining. The answer is **C**.

7. *The basketball player, with one black sock and one yellow one, scored the most points.*

    A. The basketball player, with one black sock and one yellow one scored the most points.

    B. The basketball player with one black sock and one yellow one, scored the most points.

    C. The basketball player with one black sock and one yellow one scored the most points.

    D. NO CHANGE

    ■ This item focuses on restrictive/nonrestrictive phrases and clauses. The answer is **C**.

Testing Paragraph Revision Skills

Some questions are based on an extended reading sample. These questions test your paragraph-revising skills. It is important to read the sample carefully and refer to it as you try to answer the questions.

Sample **Essay**

(1) A dog has a wet nose. (2) Whether you think of that nose as annoying or cute, it is much more complex than it seems. (3) A dog's nose is part of a highly developed system that is good for the dog but even better for mankind.

(4) The dog's acute sense of smell serves humans in many ways. (5) Tracker dogs have a long history of tracing escaped criminals and missing children. (6) Some dogs focus on finding people trapped alive in avalanches and collapsed buildings, while others are trained to hunt for the corpses of those who have not survived. (7) Patrol dogs sniff around border checkpoints for things like explosives and illegal drugs. (8) But the most amazing benefits are those emerging in medicine. (9) Medical companion dogs can detect oncoming epileptic seizures, high blood pressure, heart attacks, migraines, and low blood sugar. (10) The most recent medical "miracle" is that dogs seem to be able to smell certain kinds of cancer before they are measurable by lab tests.

(11) The anatomy or structure of a dog's nose helps explain its sophisticated sense of smell. (12) The wetness itself is important. (13) It allows the dog to smell better by making odors stronger. (14) Then behind the nose itself, there are two other important olfactory organs—the receptors and the brain. (15) Inside the dog's nose is a very large number of smell receptors—25 times more than in humans. (16) These receptors are not active in the dog's normal breathing but come into play during sniffing. (17) The sensations from the receptors go to a part of the dog's brain that is four times larger than the corresponding part in a human brain. (18) These organs together give the dog the ability to sense odor in concentrations 100 million times lower than humans can. (19) But although dogs smell much more than humans do, they are not overwhelmed; they can sort out many layers of odor at the same time.

(20) Dogs have been thought of as man's best friend for a long time. (21) They wag their tails and seem to enjoy human company. (22) Their personalities are only part of the story, though. (23) Sometimes dogs need obedience lessons. (24) Scientists are probably only beginning to understand how important the family dog can be.

1. *Which of the following would be better than sentence 1?*

   A. On a sleepy Saturday morning, you suddenly wake up because you feel your dog's cold, wet nose on your hand— a signal that it's time to let him outside.

   B. I'd like to talk about a dog's nose.

   C. A dog's nose is an extraordinarily perceptive device.

   D. NO CHANGE

   ■ This item focuses on openings or introductions. The answer is **A**.

2. *Which of the following sentences should be deleted?*

   A. Sentence 8

   B. Sentence 13

   C. Sentence 23

   D. NONE

   ■ This item focuses on paragraph unity. The answer is **C**.

3. *Which of the following would be the best addition to the beginning of sentence 12?*

   A. On the other hand,

   B. First of all,

   C. Likewise,

   D. In other words,

   ■ This item focuses on transitions. The answer is **B**.

4. *Which sentence best paraphrases the focus of the essay?*

   A. Medical science is learning more and more about how dogs can help humans.

   B. Humans cannot get along without a dog's help.

   C. Dogs should be given greater respect.

   D. A dog's keen sense of smell has wide-ranging benefits to humans.

   ■ This item focuses on the main idea or thesis. The answer is **D**.

5. *If you were to add a sentence to the end of the essay, which of the following would best reflect the way the writer feels about the topic?*

   A. Dogs can be pretty goofy, but sometimes they're a big help.

   B. The preponderance of evidence says that dogs are beneficial.

   C. All I can say about dogs is, "Cool!"

   D. The animals that have long been considered faithful companions may also be able to help people live better lives.

   ■ This item focuses on tone. The answer is **D**.

Testing Editing Skills

Some writing tests include questions that assess your editing skills. These questions require you to find a usage or grammatical error in a sentence.

In the following sentences, choose the underlined section that contains an error. If there is no error, choose D.

1. Inez <u>heard the phone ringing</u>, <u>answered it</u>, and <u>has taken the message</u>.
                A   **B**   **C**

    D. NO ERROR

    ■ This item focuses on parallel structure. The answer is **C**.

2. We <u>recommend</u> that new rules <u>be considered</u> <u>at this point in time</u>.
            A   **B**   **C**

    D. NO ERROR

    ■ This item focuses on ineffective expressions, or "deadwood." The answer is **C**.

3. She <u>had</u> a habit of speaking <u>too</u> softly <u>when she was saying something</u>.
        A   **B**   **C**

    D. NO ERROR

    ■ This item focuses on wordiness, or redundancy. The answer is **C**.

4. Sam, an apprentice, <u>he</u> was afraid he would lose <u>his</u> job, but the boss
                         A   **B**

    <u>thought</u> Sam was doing good work.
     C

    D. NO ERROR

    ■ This item focuses on double subjects. The answer is **A**.

5. As she <u>swung</u> her bat at the ball, <u>it</u> whistled <u>through</u> the air.
           A   **B**   **C**

    D. NO ERROR

    ■ This item focuses on indefinite reference. The answer is **B**.

6. One of my <u>friend's</u> favorite books <u>are</u> ***To Kill*** <u>***a***</u> ***Mockingbird***.
                   A   **B**   **C**

    D. NO ERROR

    ■ This item focuses on subject-verb agreement. The answer is **B**.

Writing Tests **Based on Prompts**

Some state and district exit exams require you to respond to a writing prompt in the form of an essay, a narrative, or a letter. You may be prompted to write from your own experience, or you may be asked to read one or two short passages and respond to them. These writings are usually timed, but some states and districts give students as much time as they need.

College entrance tests like the ACT and SAT also include a timed-writing section. The prompts on these tests ask you to support your point of view on a topic. The essays are evaluated on clarity, consistency, level of detail, and appropriateness. While correctness is important, evaluators understand that you are working within a limited time frame.

Whether you are preparing for an exit exam or a college entrance test, keep the following tips in mind:

1. **Understand the basic forms of writing.** Be sure that you know how to write the following:
   - **Expository Essay**
   - **Persuasive Essay**
   - **Personal (Biographical) Narrative**
   - **Business Letter**
   - **Response to Literature**

2. **Follow the writing process.**
   - **Prewrite.** Take some time to plan your writing. Write a thesis or focus statement and jot down supporting ideas in a simple outline.
   - **Write.** Begin in an interesting way and state your thesis or focus; include details and examples to support your thesis in the middle part; and restate your main idea in the closing.
   - **Revise.** Make as many revisions and corrections as time allows.

3. **Remember the traits of writing.**
   - **Ideas.** It's not enough to state an opinion or offer a position; you need to provide good reasons to support what you believe.
   - **Organization.** Write with purpose. Start with an organized plan (outline) and stick to it.
   - **Voice.** Sound confident, interested, and sincere.
   - **Word Choice.** Use specific nouns and verbs. Be as original and fresh as possible in the language that you use.
   - **Sentence Fluency.** Express your ideas in sentences that read smoothly from one to the next.
   - **Conventions.** Keep your writing as error free as possible.

Persuasive **Responses**

Most writing prompts require a persuasive response. Whenever you are asked to take a position on an issue and defend that position, you are involved in persuasive writing.

A persuasive prompt may be very general in nature, or it may relate specifically to an issue familiar to high school students. For example, a general prompt might ask writers to take a position on the need for rules; a more specific prompt might ask if year-round school should be required. (The following sample is a general prompt.)

Sample Prompt

Some parents and educators feel that students need specific limitations and rules to guide them in their growth. Others maintain that students can grow only when they are allowed to make most of their own decisions about what is good for them.

How do you feel about this debate? Do students thrive when they are given rules to live by, or are they better off learning by trial and error? Defend your position.

The student responding to the prompt took a few minutes to write an opinion (thesis) statement and list main reasons in support of the opinion.

> My feeling is that the most effective rules are the ones that will help students now and in the future.
>
> A. Avoid rules that have no long-term value.
> B. Promote rules that help students focus on the future.
> C. One of my dad's rules helped me.

Sample Response

Next, the student developed his response. He pays as much attention to each part—the beginning, the middle, and the ending—as time permits.

An opening question leads up to the opinion statement (underlined).

A Ruling on Rules

Do kids need rules, or is it more important for them to find out on their own what works and what doesn't work? It all depends on what the rules are supposed to accomplish. <u>My feeling is that the most effective rules are the ones that will help students now and in the future.</u>

Each middle paragraph develops one main point.

Some of the most frustrating rules are the ones that don't seem necessary in the long term. For example, unreasonable dress and grooming codes are particularly annoying. What lasting benefit do they have? Boys have been sent home for wearing their hair too long. What is gained by regulating hairstyles? It seems to me that learning about appropriate grooming is something that students can safely learn on their own. It won't really ruin a person's life to look back at a yearbook picture in 10 years and laugh at the hairstyles.

On the other hand, most students respect rules and requirements that help them stay focused on the future. It seems that every day the world gets more confused about what's important, so it's definitely useful to have a few guidelines for staying on track. Students may complain about having to take required courses (especially the ones they don't like), doing community service, and reading books during summer vacation, but at least they can see that there are clear reasons for these requirements. The future depends much more on what a person has learned and how he or she relates to others than on the clothes the person wears in high school.

The writer uses a personal anecdote to support a main idea.

My own lesson in rules happened when I was in eighth grade. Because I got all C's on my first-quarter report card, Dad said that I was limited to one hour of TV on school nights. Of course, I was upset and said my freedom was being taken away. Dad stood firm, and my grades improved dramatically. More importantly, I got out of the habit of wasting time when I should be doing something more useful. I probably wouldn't have come up with the TV rule on my own, and as a result, my life may have been much different.

The closing paragraph concedes an opposing viewpoint.

I realize that people who come up with rules mean well. They, too, are trying to remove distractions and smooth the way to success for students. However, some of their rules are more about individual preference than about learning lessons for the future. Good intentions don't always make good rules.

Responses to Literature

Prompts may be based on literature that you have read prior to the exam or on selections that you read during the test. Here are some tips on writing responses to literature:

- **Write a thesis (focus) statement.** Reword the prompt so that it applies to the literature you're writing about.
- **Briefly outline your main points.** Support your thesis statement with convincing details.
- **Avoid summarizing the literature.** Follow the plan in your outline; don't simply retell a story or paraphrase a poem.
- **Include comments on the author's techniques.** Point out literary devices (symbols, repetition, ambiguity, word choice) that reveal the author's purpose.
- **Make direct references to the text.** Quote or paraphrase important excerpts to support your analysis.

Sample Prompt and Reading Sections

Many poets have written about the role leaders play in history. The two poems that follow are examples. In "Ozymandias," Percy Bysshe Shelley reflects on the legacy of Egyptian king Rameses II (Ozymandias in Greek texts), who lived from 1304–1237 B.C.E. In "O Captain! My Captain!" Walt Whitman writes about the legacy of U.S. President Abraham Lincoln, assassinated in 1865. What do these two poems have to say about the role of a leader?

Ozymandias

I met a traveller from an antique land
Who said: Two vast and trunkless legs of stone
Stand in the desert. Near them, on the sand,
Half sunk, a shattered visage lies, whose frown,
And wrinkled lip, and sneer of cold command,
Tell that its sculptor well those passions read
Which yet survive, stamped on these lifeless things,
The hand that mocked them and the heart that fed;
And on the pedestal these words appear:
"My name is Ozymandias, king of kings:
Look on my works ye mighty, and despair!"
Nothing beside remains. Round the decay
Of that colossal wreck, boundless and bare
The lone and level sands stretch far away.

—Percy Bysshe Shelley (1792–1822)

O Captain! My Captain!

O Captain! my Captain! our fearful trip is done,
The ship has weather'd every rack, the prize we sought is won,
The port is near, the bells I hear, the people all exulting,
While follow eyes the steady keel, the vessel grim and daring;
        But O heart! heart! heart!
            O the bleeding drops of red,
                Where on the deck my Captain lies,
                  Fallen cold and dead.

O Captain! my Captain! rise up and hear the bells;
Rise up—for you the flag is flung—for you the bugle trills,
For you bouquets and ribbon'd wreaths—for you the shores a-crowding,
For you they call, the swaying mass, their eager faces turning;
        Here Captain! dear father!
            This arm beneath your head!
                It is some dream that on the deck,
                  You've fallen cold and dead.

My Captain does not answer, his lips are pale and still,
My father does not feel my arm, he has no pulse nor will,
The ship is anchor'd safe and sound, its voyage closed and done,
From fearful trip the victor ship comes in with object won;
        Exult O shores, and ring O bells!
            But I with mournful tread,
                Walk the deck my Captain lies,
                  Fallen cold and dead.

—Walt Whitman (1819–1892)

Sample Response Plan

Taken together, these two poems suggest that effective leadership is not about power and authority, but instead about the ability to inspire people.

A. Ozymandias' achievements have turned to dust.

    1. Only wreckage and "lifeless things" remain.

    2. Emptiness and desert lie all around.

    3. His inscription is now ironic.

B. Captain's achievements live on in his people.

    1. The "ship" has survived its dangers.

    2. People crowd the shore with bells and victory wreaths.

    3. His legacy is that of a hero.

Sample **Response**

In the response below, the student wrote an opening that introduces the topic and ends with a thesis statement. The middle paragraphs develop the ideas from the outline. The ending revisits and emphasizes the thesis.

The opening asks a question that the essay will answer.

It ends with a thesis statement (underlined).

History is filled with tales of leaders—some great, and some terrible. What does it take to be a great leader? In the poems "Ozymandias" and "O Captain! My Captain!" Percy Bysshe Shelley and Walt Whitman describe two very different types of leaders and their effects on the world. <u>Taken together, the poems suggest that effective leadership is not about power and authority, but instead about the ability to inspire people.</u>

The first middle paragraph discusses one poem.

"Ozymandias" describes an authority figure with the power to have an enormous stone statue raised in his honor. This ruler declared himself the "king of kings" and flaunted his strength in the face of other rulers, telling them to "look on my works ye mighty, and despair!" Shelley uses images of fear and domination to describe Ozymandias. His "sneer of cold command" keeps people in line during his life, but in death, his greatness fades. Ironically, all that now remains of his monument are a few ruined pieces in the emptiness of a vast desert. The word "despair" now reflects the fleetingness of the king's power.

The next middle paragraph discusses the other poem.

By contrast, the "Captain" has devoted himself to guiding the ship of state through troubled times to safety. "The prize we sought is won," the poet says, and the people cheer the return of their "dear father!" They crowd the shore with "bugle trills," with "bouquets and ribbon'd wreaths." The Captain has inspired his people, and they love him because of it. Unfortunately, the Captain has given his very life in service. Despite the victory of the state, the poet weeps for the loss of the leader—a very different reaction than we see for Ozymandias. The Captain's legacy will live on. In fact, the poem itself becomes a memorial to this great leader.

The concluding paragraph revisits the thesis statement.

As long as the United States survives, Lincoln's sacrifice will be remembered by its people. He held the country together through a great crisis and became one of our great heroes. On the other hand, Rameses II is remembered only for the ruins he left behind. He is mocked by his own inscription. <u>The lesson would seem to be that the best leader is one who sacrifices for others, not one who commands others for his own glory.</u>

Tips for Responding to Test Prompts

Responding to a prompt in an "on-demand" writing environment requires a special set of skills. The following tips can help you create your best response.

Before you write . . .

- **Know how much time you have.** Structure your response according to the clock. Use an accelerated approach for a 25-minute response but take more time with prewriting and revising if you have 60 or 75 minutes.

- **Study the prompt.** Watch for key words that will help you answer the following questions:
  Subject: What general subject am I supposed to write about?
  Focus: What is my specific focus for this topic?
  Form: What form should my response take (essay, letter, story)?
  Audience: Who is my audience (peers, parents, teachers)?
  Purpose: What should my writing do (explain, persuade, tell a story)?

- **Plan your response.** Write your thesis or opinion statement and use a brief outline or graphic organizer to plan your writing.

During your writing . . .

- **Write an effective opening paragraph.** Capture your reader's attention, introduce the topic, and state your thesis.

- **Develop the middle part.** Begin each paragraph with a topic sentence (main point) that supports your thesis. Each topic sentence should answer "why" your thesis is valid. Use different types of details, including quotations, paraphrases, and analyses. For persuasive writing, answer any major objections to your opinion.

- **Write a strong closing paragraph.** Complete your writing by providing a final thought or by restating your thesis. For persuasive writing, consider a call to action.

After you've written a first draft . . .

- **Read your work.** Watch for places where adding, cutting, or moving details will make your work stronger.

- **Check for conventions.** Correct any errors you find.

Speaking, Thinking, and Viewing
SKILLS

Speech Skills **453**

Multimedia Reports **465**

Thinking Skills **469**

Viewing Skills **479**

*"It takes more than three weeks
to prepare a good impromptu speech."*

—William Zinsser

SPEECH Skills

The bell rings, and over the noise of shuffling backpacks, Mrs. Goff says, "Remember that your speech topics are due next Wednesday." As you leave class, your stomach churns.

If public speaking makes you nervous, you aren't the only one. Reports show that public speaking is one of the most common fears. Still, since you'll give many speeches in school and in the workplace, now is the time to conquer that fear.

The best way to calm your nerves is to be well prepared. Planning and practicing a speech prepares you for the moment of truth. This chapter will guide you through the speech-making process. It will help you get ready for those "talks" you'll be giving—both in school and in life.

Preview

- ■ **Planning Your Speech**
- ■ **Writing Your Speech**
- ■ **Preparing Your Speech Script**
- ■ **Sample Outline, Note Cards, and Manuscript**
- ■ **Rehearsing and Presenting Your Speech**
- ■ **A Closer Look at Style**

Planning Your Speech

Planning a speech is a lot like planning any other type of writing. You need to pay close attention to your purpose, topic, audience, and details. The following guidelines will help you plan a successful speech.

Determine Your Purpose

The purpose is what you intend your speech to do: to inform, to persuade, or to demonstrate.

- **Informative speeches** educate by providing information. This type of speech needs plenty of interesting details. (See page 175.)
- **Persuasive speeches** argue for or against something. A persuasive speech needs to develop a convincing and logical argument. (See pages 201-202.)
- **Demonstration speeches** show how to do something or how something works. A clear, step-by-step explanation is the key to this kind of speech.

Select a Topic

Choose a specific topic that interests you and will appeal to your audience. Here are the three steps to finding the right topic for your speech.

- **Choose a topic** that meets the requirements and purpose of the assignment.
- **Learn about your topic** by conducting research and thinking carefully about it.
- **Focus on a specific topic** that you can comfortably cover in the allotted time. See the chart below.

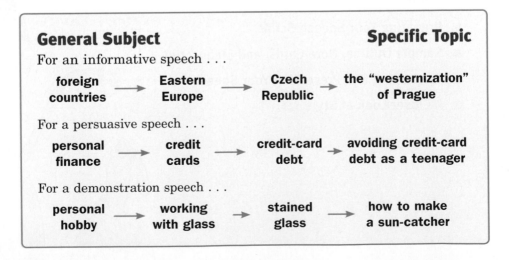

General Subject   **Specific Topic**

For an informative speech . . .

foreign countries → Eastern Europe → Czech Republic → the "westernization" of Prague

For a persuasive speech . . .

personal finance → credit cards → credit-card debt → avoiding credit-card debt as a teenager

For a demonstration speech . . .

personal hobby → working with glass → stained glass → how to make a sun-catcher

Consider Your Audience

As you think about your audience, keep the following suggestions in mind.

- **Choose your topic carefully:** Your audience will be more attentive if you pick a topic that interests them.
- **Be clear:** Listeners should understand the point of your speech immediately.
- **Anticipate questions:** Imagine questions the audience might have, and answer them in your speech. This helps keep the audience connected.
- **Make it enjoyable:** Use thought-provoking questions, intriguing details, and a little humor (if appropriate).
- **Be brief:** Make your point within the allotted time.

* Once you've thought about your purpose, subject, and audience, try writing a thesis or purpose statement. (See page 267.)

Collect Interesting Details

After you have determined your purpose, selected a specific topic, and considered your audience, it's time to collect information. To get started, consider the following sources.

- **Search your memory:** If you base your speech on a personal experience, write down everything you remember about it. Focus on facts, details, and feelings.
- **Interview people:** Find people with experience or knowledge related to your topic.
- **Get firsthand experience:** Learn about your topic in a hands-on way, especially if you are planning a demonstration speech.
- **Explore the Internet:** Surf the Internet to find relevant Web sites and newsgroups (but make sure to use other sources, too).
- **Search the library:** Make sure to check different library resources, including books, magazines, pamphlets, and videos.

Take NOTE

Look for photographs, models, graphs, maps, artifacts, and other materials. Showing such items can make a speech clearer and more interesting, especially a demonstration speech. And, of course, you can create your own graphics or charts as well.

Writing Your Speech

After you've finished your basic planning, you need to select your best details and organize them into an effective speech. The way you organize your details depends primarily on (1) the kind of speech you are giving and (2) the kind of script or notes you plan to use. (See pages 458–461 for sample scripts.)

If you are giving a short demonstration speech, you may want to use only a few note cards. If you are going to inform your audience, you may decide a well-organized outline would work best. And, if you are giving a persuasive speech, you may want to use a word-for-word script (manuscript). Whatever approach you choose, you need to be well prepared with an effective introduction, body, and conclusion.

Introduction

A good introduction sets the tone and direction of the speech. Your opening should get the audience's attention, introduce the topic, and state your purpose or thesis.

Start-Up Ideas: Use one or more of these ideas to get the audience's attention and help them focus on your topic.

- Ask a thoughtful question.

- Tell a dramatic story or funny anecdote.

- Use interesting visual aids or give a short demonstration.

- Share a quotation that relates to your topic.

- Make a strong statement about the importance of the topic.

Stating Your Thesis

After you've thought about your purpose, topic, and audience (and gathered some information), you need to write a thesis statement to focus your speech. Start with the phrase "My purpose is . . ." and finish with your specific topic or idea. You may decide to include your thesis in your introduction but make sure to rewrite it so that it sounds natural and genuine.

"My purpose is to persuade my classmates that credit cards must be used wisely to avoid the trap of long-term debt."

Body

While writing the body of your speech, focus on making each fact or detail into an interesting, complete thought. Clear descriptions and concise explanations will make it easier for your listeners to follow along. Support your opinions with enough logical reasons and solid facts to convince your audience. Here are six effective ways to organize your speech.

Order of Importance: Arrange information according to its significance: most important to least or least important to most.

> **Example:** A persuasive speech on the benefits of buying a hybrid car

Chronological Order: Arrange information according to time—the order in which events take place.

> **Example:** A demonstration speech on building a model airplane

Comparison-Contrast: Give information about topics by comparing them (showing similarities) and contrasting them (showing differences).

> **Example:** An informative speech about football and rugby

Cause and Effect: Present information to reveal the causes and effects concerning a specific circumstance, problem, or process.

> **Example:** An informative speech about the effects of smoking

Problem-Solution: Describe a problem and offer a solution.

> **Example:** A persuasive speech about lonely shut-ins and a new student visitation program

Order of Location: Arrange information according to the location of different parts of a topic.

> **Example:** An informative speech about parts of a car engine

Conclusion

Conclude your speech by focusing on your key points. A good conclusion helps your audience understand what they have learned, why it's important, and what (if anything) they should do about it. Consider these ideas for your conclusion:

- **Share a final relevant story or eye-opening fact.**

  (Try ending an informative speech this way.)

- **Emphasize the importance of your topic.**

  (Try ending a persuasive speech this way.)

- **Summarize your most important ideas.**

  (Try ending a demonstration speech this way.)

Preparing Your Speech Script

Once you have written the general draft of your speech, it's time to prepare the speech script. You can use an *outline*, *note cards*, or a word-for-word *manuscript*. (See the following four pages.)

Sample Outline

To create a speech outline, follow the guidelines and model below.

1. Write your opening statement word for word.
2. Write each main point as a sentence.
3. Use phrases to list important details (facts, dates, numbers).
4. Include notes [in brackets] to cue yourself to use visual aids.
5. Write out quotations word for word.
6. Write your closing statement word for word.

Avoid the Crunch

Let's say that you decide to buy a CD that's $10, and the cashier says, "That will be $30, please. If you don't have $30, just pay a little each month for the next 17 years." Sound ridiculous? Teenagers do it every day, creating credit card debts that will follow them into adulthood.

I. Many students sign up for credit cards without reading the fine print. [hold up application form]
  A. Introductory rate of 0%
  B. Standard rate of 15%
  C. Default rate of 30%
II. What does this mean to you?
  A. Can't pay $2,000 balance
  B. Pay monthly minimum of 2%
  C. Pay back in 12 years @ $4,000
III. Teenage bankruptcy is increasing.
  A. Bankruptcy for ages 18–25 at all-time high in 2000
  B. More bankrupt young people than college graduates
IV. So how do you maintain a good credit report?
  A. Know credit limit
  B. Pay off balance
  C. Pay on time

What is the lesson here? As a teenager, making bad decisions with a credit card can have a negative impact on student loans, future jobs, and even buying your own house. But, if you read the fine print, spend wisely, and pay promptly, you'll be on your way to building a solid financial foundation.

Sample **Note Cards**

If you decide to use note cards, write out your entire introduction and conclusion on separate note cards. For the body of your speech, write one point per card, along with specific details. Clearly number your cards.

①

Introduction
Let's say that you decide to buy a CD that's $10, and the cashier says, "That will be $30, please. If you don't have $30, just pay a little each month for the next 17 years." Sound ri~~diculous~~? Teenagers do it every day, creating credit—
low them into

②

Many students sign up, without considering the fine print.
    —Introductory rate 0%.
      —After six months, the standard rate 15%
        —Late or missed payment, 30%

③

What does this mean to you?
    —You don't have enough money to pay a $2,000 balance
    —You pay the monthly minimum of
2% or at least
    —Takes almos
    —Clark Howa

④

Some overwhelmed students file for bankruptcy.
    —Bankruptcy filings for people 18-25 high in 2000

⑤

Conclusion
What is the lesson here? As a teenager, making bad decisions with a credit card can have a negative impact on student loans, future jobs, and even buying your own house. But if you read the fine print, spend wisely, and pay promptly, you'll be on your way to building a solid financial foundation.

Sample **Manuscript Speech**

If you use a word-for-word manuscript, write it to be heard, not read. Mark your copy to guide your presentation. Student Terence Hatcher used wavy lines to add feeling and brackets to show a visual aid. (See "Marking Your Speech" on page 462.) In the manuscript below, Terence develops his thesis by showing the audience how the problem could affect their lives.

Avoid the Crunch

The speaker begins with an anecdote.

Let's say that you decide to buy a CD that's $10, and the cashier says, "That will be $30, please. If you don't have $30, just pay a little each month for the next 17 years." Sound ridiculous? Teenagers do it every day, creating credit card debts that will follow them into adulthood.

He holds up a credit application.

Credit card companies are hoping to cash in by targeting students. Plush toys, T-shirts, and snacks are "freebies" intended to lure potential customers. Sociologist Robert Manning states, "The credit card marketers sign high school kids at college fairs. They get paid by the number of applications they turn in." Many students sign up without considering the fine print. [hold up credit card application form] Can you see what's written here? No? Let me read from a typical credit card application form. "Introductory rate of **0%**." That means you pay nothing on the balance of your credit card. Sounds great, right? Let me keep reading. "After the promotional period of six months, the standard rate of **15%** will be applied. However, if you default or fail to pay, the rate will be raised to **30%**."

The speaker quotes an expert to support his argument.

What does this mean to you? Let's say you spend $2,000 during the first six months. Then the interest rate zooms up to 15%. You decide to start paying off the balance, but you don't have enough money to pay the whole thing, because you only work weekends at Big Burger. So you pay the monthly minimum of 2% or at least $25 a month. How long do you think it would take to pay off the original $2000 balance? [ask for guesses] Not only would it take **almost 12 years**, but you would also end up spending about **$4,000**! As radio talk show host Clark Howard says, " . . . what you really need to know is that you are ripping yourself off because you are not paying off that balance."

The speaker points out the importance of the topic.

Some students are so overwhelmed by debt that they file for bankruptcy, which is a legal cancellation of debt. Writer Cindy Landrum gathered the following statistics: "Bankruptcy filings for people ages 18–25 were at an all-time high in 2000, numbering almost 150,000, a **tenfold increase** in just five years. More young adults filed for bankruptcy than graduated from college in 2001."

For up to 10 years, bankruptcy will be a nasty stain on your credit report.

"Your credit report is often called your <u>second resume</u>," according to Dr. Flora Williams in her book *Climbing the Steps to Financial Success*. A credit report covers your history of borrowing, bill payment, and debt owed. If you use your credit card irresponsibly, your credit card company will make negative comments on your credit report. Banks, college loan officers, employers, and landlords can request your credit report.

So how do you maintain a positive credit report? Here are four key points:

1. **Use your credit card wisely.** Keep track of what you are buying. Know how long it will take you to pay for each item. Don't be tempted by the latest laptop or video game system that you can't afford.
2. **Know your credit limit.** Going over the limit may result in fines or even cancellation of your account.
3. **Pay off the balance,** or at least more than the minimum.
4. **Pay on time.** This is the simplest way to avoid late fees and credit damage.

The closing paragraph encourages the audience to reflect on the subject.

What is the lesson here? As a teenager, making bad decisions with a credit card can have a negative impact on student loans, future jobs, and even buying your own house. It takes common sense and hard work to avoid the pitfalls of credit card debt, but if you read the fine print, spend wisely, and pay promptly, you'll be on your way to building a **solid** financial foundation. ■

Rehearsing and Presenting Your Speech

Practice your speech until you feel comfortable giving it. Ask a friend or family member to listen and give feedback. Another option is to use a tape recorder or video recorder so that you can hear and see yourself. As you rehearse, keep the following points in mind.

Before You Speak

- Organize your visual aids and any equipment. Make sure everything is ready.
- Check your outline, note cards, or manuscript to make sure they are in order.
- Stand, slowly walk to the front, and face the audience.

As You Speak

- Speak loudly and clearly.
- Don't rush through your speech. Read carefully if you're using a manuscript. Glance at your note cards or outline if that's what you're using.
- Concentrate on what you're saying and add feeling to important words or phrases.
- Use appropriate gestures to emphasize your points.
- Look at your audience and communicate with your facial expressions.

After You Speak

- If appropriate, ask the audience if they have any questions.
- Thank your audience, gather your speech and visual aids, and walk quietly back to your seat.

Marking Your Speech

As you rehearse your speech, decide which words or phrases to emphasize, where to pause, and where to add visual aids. Use the following symbols to mark the copy of your speech.

Curved line or italic .... for additional <u>feeling</u> or *emotion*
Underlining or boldface ....for greater <u>volume</u> or **emphasis**
Dash, diagonal, ellipsis..............for a pause—or a break in the flow
Brackets .... [for actions or visual aids]

A Closer Look at **Style**

More than any other modern president, John F. Kennedy is remembered for the appealing style and tone of his speeches. The following portions of his speeches show how style and tone can help strengthen the spoken word. The tone, or appeal, is listed above each excerpt.

Allusion ■ An allusion is a reference to a familiar person, place, or thing.

Appeal to the Democratic Principle

One hundred years of delay have passed since President Lincoln freed the slaves, yet their heirs, their grandsons, are not fully free. (Radio and Television address, 1963)

Analogy ■ An analogy is a comparison of an unfamiliar idea to a simple, familiar one. The comparison is usually quite lengthy, suggesting several points of similarity. An analogy is especially useful when attempting to explain a difficult or complex idea.

Appeal to Common Sense

In our opinion the German people wish to have one united country. If the Soviet Union had lost the war, the Soviet people themselves would object to a line being drawn through Moscow and the entire country defeated in war. We wouldn't like to have a line drawn down the Mississippi River. . . . (Interview, November 25, 1961)

Anecdote ■ An anecdote is a short story told to illustrate a point.

Appeal to Pride, Commitment

Frank O'Connor, the Irish writer, tells in one of his books how as a boy, he and his friends would make their way across the countryside, and when they came to an orchard wall that seemed too high and too doubtful to try and too difficult to permit their voyage to continue, they took off their hats and tossed them over the wall—and then they had no choice but to follow them. This nation has tossed its cap over the wall of space, and we have no choice but to follow it. Whatever the difficulties, they will be overcome. (San Antonio Address, November 21, 1963)

Antithesis ■ Antithesis balances or contrasts one word or idea against another, usually in the same sentence.

Appeal to Common Sense, Commitment

Let us never negotiate out of fear. But let us never fear to negotiate. (Inaugural Address, 1961)

Mankind must put an end to war, or war will put an end to mankind. (Address to the United Nations, 1961)

Irony ■ Irony is creating a result that is opposite of what is expected or appropriate; an odd coincidence.

Appeal to Common Sense

They see no harm in paying those to whom they entrust the minds of their children a smaller wage than is paid to those to whom they entrust the care of their plumbing. (Vanderbilt University, 1961)

Negative Definition ■ A negative definition describes something by telling what it is *not* rather than, or in addition to, what it is.

Appeal for Commitment

. . . members of this organization are committed by the Charter to promote and respect human rights. Those rights are not respected when a Buddhist priest is driven from his pagoda, when a synagogue is shut down, when a Protestant church cannot open a mission, when a cardinal is forced into hiding, or when a crowded church service is bombed. (United Nations, September 20, 1963)

Parallel Structure ■ Parallel structuring means repeating phrases or sentences that are similar in meaning and structure; repetition means repeating words or phrases to create rhythm and emphasis.

Appeal for Commitment

Let every nation know, whether it wishes us well or ill, that we shall pay any price, bear any burden, meet any hardship, support any friend, oppose any foe, in order to assure the survival and the success of liberty. (Inaugural Address, 1961)

Quotations ■ Quotations, especially of well-known individuals, can be effective in nearly any speech.

Appeal for Emulation or Affiliation

At the inauguration, Robert Frost read a poem which began "the land was ours before we were the land's"—meaning, in part, that this new land of ours sustained us before we were a nation. And although we are now the land's—a nation of people matched to a continent—we still draw our strength and sustenance . . . from the earth. (Dedication Speech, 1961)

Rhetorical Question ■ A rhetorical question is a question that is asked to emphasize a point, not to get an answer.

Appeal to Common Sense, Democratic Principle

"When a man's ways please the Lord," the Scriptures tell us, "he maketh even his enemies to be at peace with him." And is not peace, in the last analysis, basically a matter of human rights—the right to live out our lives without fear of devastation—the right to breathe air as nature provided it—the right of future generations to a healthy existence? (Commencement Address, 1963)

"Computers are incredibly fast, accurate, and stupid; humans are incredibly slow, inaccurate, and brilliant; together they are powerful beyond imagination."

—Albert Einstein

MULTIMEDIA Reports

Studies show that you absorb information much more quickly when you encounter it through more than one sense. That's one reason you take notes during a lecture: Listening engages your sense of hearing, while writing notes reinforces what you hear. Speakers often use visual aids, too, so that you can hear and see the ideas at the same time.

Personal computers now allow you to make your presentations and reports multisensory. As a speaker, you can carry an entire library of visual aids on a portable computer, connect it to a video monitor or projector, and show slides, film clips, and animated graphics to support an oral presentation. As an author, you can enhance a written report with colorful on-screen graphics and then distribute it on disc or via the Internet to create an interactive report.

In this chapter, you'll find writing guidelines for creating a multimedia presentation and an interactive report. You can find a sample presentation and report on the Write Source Web site: www.thewritesource.com.

Preview

- **Multimedia Presentation**
- **Interactive Report**
- **Creating a Storyboard**

Writing Guidelines
Multimedia Presentation

Using a visual aid during an oral report helps to create a multimedia presentation. It's the same when your teacher uses a chalkboard or an overhead projector to illustrate a point; or when a businessperson makes a presentation supported by posters, charts, and other graphics.

More and more, the computer is being employed for multimedia presentations. As the presenter speaks, the audience looks at a screen where the information is reinforced and clarified.

■ PREWRITING

1. **Selecting a Topic . . .** Select a topic that is right for your audience and appropriate for a multimedia presentation.

2. **Gathering Details . . .** Collect information about your topic in the same way you would if you were making a speech. (See pages 453–464.)

■ WRITING AND REVISING

3. **Creating a Design . . .** Create a graphic design for your pages. Be certain it is appropriate in tone for your topic and your audience—businesslike for a serious topic, lighthearted for a humorous speech, and so on. Remember, visuals should never detract from your message. They should add to or highlight important points.

4. **Creating Pages . . .** Create a new page for each main idea in your outline. (See the storyboard on page 468.) If an idea has several parts, present them one at a time on that page (if your computer program allows). Each click of the mouse button should reveal a new detail.

5. **Fine-Tuning Your Presentation . . .** Practice delivering your speech while clicking through the multimedia pages. Try it with a sample audience (a group of friends or family), if possible. Insert separate pages for statements or quotations that need emphasis. Also add sound and animation if they help your message.

6. **Revising for Style and Accuracy . . .** Check that the words on screen are clear and concise. They must help listeners grasp your message, not confuse them.

■ EDITING AND PROOFREADING

7. **Preparing a Final Version . . .** Check spelling, punctuation, usage, and other mechanics. *Remember:* On screen, errors are glaringly obvious.

Writing Guidelines
Interactive Report

From news journals on the Web to encyclopedias on CD, the shape of written information has changed in recent years. Many publishers now use hypertext to present information in an interactive format. In hypertext, certain words and images on screen serve as links to other information. By selecting that link, the viewer interacts with the computer to load the linked information to the screen.

■ PREWRITING

1. **Selecting a Topic . . .** One way to select a topic is to start with a finished report and then make it interactive. Nearly any report will work—a research paper, an informational essay, a speech manuscript, and so on. (See pages 454–455.)

■ WRITING AND REVISING

2. **Creating a Design . . .** Devise a graphic design that is appropriate for your topic and your audience.

3. **Creating Pages . . .** Create a new page for each main idea in your report. Include a separate page for your title and perhaps another for *The End*. If an idea has several parts, and your software allows, have the parts appear on screen one at a time.

4. **Creating Links . . .** Put *Back* and *Next* links on the pages to lead readers through the report. Add any other links you need—for notes, definitions of terms, sound recordings, film clips, and so on. (See the *Target* box on the storyboard on page 468.)

   ✳ You can dress up your report with any appropriate animation and sound (such as a *click* or *beep* when a link is selected), but don't let the sounds and animation distract your audience.

5. **Fine-Tuning Your Presentation . . .** Have someone try out your interactive report and ask that person for comments. Correct any problems you discover.

6. **Revising for Style and Accuracy . . .** Check that the words on screen are clear and concise. They must help readers grasp your message, not confuse them.

■ EDITING AND PROOFREADING

7. **Preparing a Final Version . . .** Make sure that your text is free of mechanical errors so that your report is taken seriously.

Creating a **Storyboard**

The storyboard below demonstrates one way to turn the model speech on pages 460–461 into a multimedia presentation or an interactive report. The tan boxes below show notes for pages of a multimedia presentation in simple step-by-step order. The white boxes show added links and pages for an interactive report. To view the final versions of the presentation and report, visit www.thewritesource.com/mm.htm.

Sample **Storyboard**

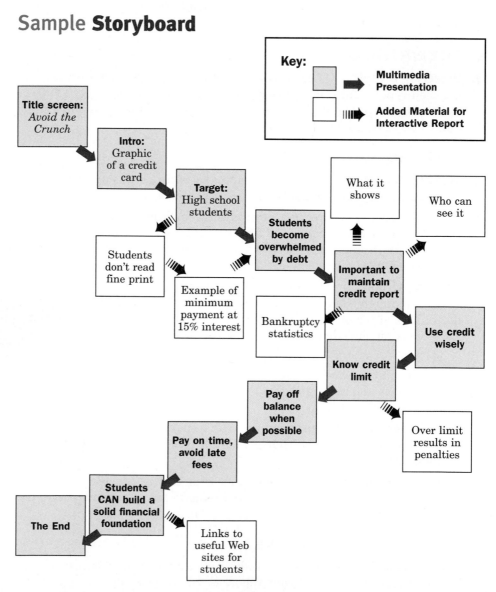

Key:

➡ **Multimedia Presentation**

➡ **Added Material for Interactive Report**

Title screen: *Avoid the Crunch*

Intro: Graphic of a credit card

Target: High school students

Students don't read fine print

Example of minimum payment at 15% interest

Students become overwhelmed by debt

What it shows

Who can see it

Important to maintain credit report

Bankruptcy statistics

Use credit wisely

Know credit limit

Pay off balance when possible

Over limit results in penalties

Pay on time, avoid late fees

Students CAN build a solid financial foundation

Links to useful Web sites for students

The End

"The whole of science is nothing more than
a refinement of everyday thinking."

—Albert Einstein

THINKING Skills

Have you ever been asked to compare two things in an English paper or on a history test? Easier said than done, right? Or how about defining or classifying a simple term in science class? Not so simple? The truth is, thinking can be hard work, especially in some of your tougher classes.

Don't worry. There are many strategies for accomplishing your most challenging thinking tasks. This chapter will help you learn how to use six types of thinking in your day-to-day schoolwork: *recalling, understanding, applying, analyzing, synthesizing,* and *evaluating.* Effective use of these will help you make decisions, solve problems, ask questions, and think more logically.

Preview

- **Guidelines for Thinking and Writing**
- **Types of Thinking**
- **Using Evidence and Logic**

Guidelines for Thinking and Writing

Whenever you are asked to . . .

Be ready to . . .

RECALL ⟶ Remember what you have learned

underline	circle
list	match
name	label
cluster	define

- collect information
- list details
- identify or define key terms
- remember main points

UNDERSTAND ⟶ Explain what you have learned

explain	review
summarize	restate
describe	cite

- give examples
- restate important details
- tell how something works

APPLY ⟶ Use what you have learned

change	illustrate
do	model
demonstrate	show
locate	organize

- select the most important details
- organize information
- explain a process
- show how something works

ANALYZE ⟶ Break down information

break down	rank
examine	compare
contrast	classify
tell why	

- carefully examine a subject
- group it into important parts
- make connections and comparisons

SYNTHESIZE ⟶ Shape information into a new form

combine	connect
speculate	design
compose	create
predict	develop
invent	imagine

- invent a better way of doing something
- blend the old with the new
- predict or hypothesize (make an educated guess)

EVALUATE ⟶ Judge the worth of information

recommend	judge
criticize	argue
persuade	rate
convince	assess
weigh	

- point out a subject's strengths and weaknesses
- evaluate its clarity, accuracy, value, and so on
- convince others of its value/worth

Types of Thinking

Recalling Information

The most basic type of thinking you use in school is **recalling.** This type of thinking is needed when you are asked to remember and repeat what you have learned in class. To help you recall information, do the following:

- Listen carefully in class and take notes.
- Read your assignments carefully.
- Review and study the information so that you know it well.

Recalling

Your teachers will give very few writing assignments that only require you to recall information. However, you may encounter test questions that ask you to use only this level of thinking. When answering multiple-choice, matching, fill-in-the-blank, and short-answer questions on a test, you need to recall information. On a history test about the Peloponnesian War, a student might be asked to answer the following questions by recalling information.

Directions: Fill in the blanks to correctly complete the sentences below.

1. The Peloponnesian War was the conflict in Greece that started in the year _431 B.C.E._ and ended in _404 B.C.E._ .

2. The alliance of Greek city-states that the Athenians led was called the _____ Delian League _____ .

3. The Spartan infantry that fought the Athenians were called _____ hoplites _____ .

Directions: Write three sentences, each telling an important fact about the Peloponnesian War.

1. _In the early years of the war, Pericles was the leader of the Athenians._

2. _The Athenians tried to help a group of barbarians called the Segestans attack Spartan colonies in Sicily._

3. _The Persians gave the Spartans money to build a fleet to fight the Athenian navy._

Understanding Information

Your teachers will often ask you to recall factual information and show that you truly **understand** it. One way teachers can measure how well you understand something is to have you write about it in your own words.

When you explain, describe, or tell how something works, you are displaying an understanding of the subject. To help you understand information, do the following:

■ Use critical reading and note-taking strategies.
(See pages 373-384 and 410-414.)

■ Rewrite the information in your own words.

■ Explain the information to someone else.

Understanding

Often, you will be asked to show understanding by writing an essay or a paragraph. In the following assignment, a student needs to (1) recall important facts and details and (2) use this information to show a clear understanding of the situation. (Graphic organizers, charts, or maps can also be used to show understanding.)

Assignment: Explain how the Athenians went, in just a few decades, from being the most powerful city-state in Greece to being conquered by the Spartans.

Athens was the dominant force in ancient Greece because of its great navy and its role as the head of the Greek city-states. The Peloponnesian War started because Athens demanded heavy taxes from its neighbors and constantly competed with Sparta for dominance in the region. After several bloody battles, sieges, and a horrible plague within its own walls, Athens found its supply lines disrupted, its navy weakened, and its armies defeated. In the year 404 B.C.E., the Athenians had no choice but to surrender unconditionally to Sparta and its allies.

Applying Information

When you are **applying** information, you must be able to use what you have learned to demonstrate, show, or relate something. For example, using your computer manual to help you set up your computer requires you to apply the information from the manual to the job. To help you apply information, do the following:

- Select the most important facts and details.

- Think about how you could use this information.

- Organize the information in the way that best meets your specific needs. (See page 52.)

Applying

Sometimes you will be asked to apply information to a situation in your own world. To do this, you need to know the important facts and understand the main themes in a body of information. Then you must apply this understanding to your own experience. In the assignment below, a student must do this kind of thinking.

Assignment: What is one of the main lessons you have learned from the Peloponnesian War? Relate this lesson to an action or experience in your own world.

I learned that taking advantage of others can have harmful effects on everyone involved. I know someone who was always asking people for favors and borrowing things, but he never gave anything back or did anything for others. He borrowed my favorite sweatshirt once when he had no jacket. I never saw it again. His friends stopped wanting to be around him, and no one would help him out when he needed it. They all felt they were being taken advantage of. If he had stopped taking so much from people or had started giving some of it back, he would have gotten along just fine. Now no one trusts him, and all his friends have turned against him. It reminds me of how poorly Athens treated its one-time friends and neighbors. Eventually, they turned against Athens and sided with its enemy, Sparta.

Analyzing Information

When you compare and contrast, rank things in order of importance, or give reasons, you are **analyzing** information. Analyzing means breaking down information into smaller parts. To help you analyze information, do the following:

- ■ Identify the important parts that make up the whole.
- ■ Determine how the parts are related to one another.

Analyzing

When you must analyze information, first figure out what kind of analysis to do (compare and contrast, rank things, give reasons, and so on). Then decide which facts and details to use and how to organize them. The following assignment asks a student to analyze by comparing and contrasting.

> **Assignment:** Athenian democracy from the time of the Peloponnesian War has been an example for Western civilization. However, our ideas of government have changed greatly since Athenian culture flourished. Highlight some of the main differences between the Athenian and United States forms of government.
>
> *Although the United States government is rooted in the traditions of Athenian democracy, there are still many differences between the two. First, the fact that Athens was a city-state and was smaller than the United States meant that it didn't need a system of federal, state, and city governments. Second, in ancient Greece, only male citizens could vote, whereas in today's U.S. system, any citizen over the age of 18 can vote. Third, the democracy of the Athenians involved its citizens directly, whereas the U.S. government relies on representatives rather than on direct citizen action. American democracy evolved into its present form to meet the demands of our complex society, a society that has little in common with ancient Athens.*

✱ A Venn diagram can help you organize your thoughts whenever you are asked to compare and contrast. (See page 377.)

Synthesizing Information

When you combine information with new ideas, or use information to create something, you are **synthesizing.** Common ways of synthesizing information are predicting, inventing, and redesigning. In each case, you have to reshape the information you already have. To help you synthesize information, do the following:

■ Think of ways to combine the information with other ideas.
   (For example, information about the Peloponnesian War, plus a student's knowledge of space travel, could turn into a science-fiction story about a war on another planet.)

■ Put the information in a different form.
   (Knowledge about the Peloponnesian War could serve as the starting point for a play, a ballad, a feature article, or another choice.)

Synthesizing

The same thing that makes synthesizing a challenge also makes it fun: You get to use your imagination. Suppose a student is asked to use information about a period of time or an event like the Peloponnesian War to write a week-long journal as if he or she were actually there. This would require synthesizing—putting existing information into a new, creative form. The paragraph that follows is a single journal entry.

Assignment: Write a series of journal entries as if you were alive at the time of the Peloponnesian War.

I spent several hours today at the shrine to Athena praying for an end to this war. How long has it been that we have been living in the midst of constant fighting? My father tells me that he can remember a time when we Athenians were the strongest of all the Greeks. Now, no doubt, it is just a matter of time before the Spartans enter our city. Has Athena forsaken the city that was named after her? Maybe we have done something to anger the gods. I remember my uncle telling horrible stories of what the soldiers did to our neighbors to the north when they were out collecting the taxes Athens demanded. That money helped build our fleet of ships. We were truly the lords of the sea! Maybe the gods resented that.

Evaluating Information

When you are asked to express your opinion about an important issue, or to discuss the good and bad points about something, you are **evaluating.** Evaluating is an advanced level of thinking that requires a thorough understanding and analysis of a subject. To help you evaluate information, do the following:

- Learn as much as you can about a subject before you try to evaluate it.
- Recall, review, organize, and analyze the information as needed.
- Weigh all sides of the subject or issue carefully.

Evaluating

An effective evaluation is based on information. Start with a sentence that identifies your overall opinion, or evaluation. Then add facts and details that support your evaluation. Note how the paragraph below contains a great deal of supporting information.

Assignment: In one paragraph, evaluate the overall effects of the Peloponnesian War on Greece.

The Peloponnesian War changed Greece forever. Although Athens abused its power by demanding heavy tributes from other Greeks, its removal from power meant that the militaristic Spartans became the dominant force in Greece. In many ways, the Spartans were even more demanding than the democratic Athenians. The oppressive government that the Spartans set up in Athens led to a series of revolts, a number of tyrannical leaders, and general conflict. All this caused further suffering. In the end, the war weakened the entire region for many years. It weakened it so much that all of Greece became vulnerable to foreign enemies, including the Macedonians to the north. Greece also became vulnerable to new uprisings from within. This once proud and stable region never fully recovered from those years of war and unrest.

Using **Evidence and Logic**

An argument is a chain of reasons that a person uses to support a claim or an opinion. To use argument well, you need to know (1) how to draw logical conclusions from sound evidence and (2) how to recognize and avoid false arguments, or logical fallacies.

The **logical fallacies** described in this section are the bits of fuzzy or misguided thinking that often crop up in our own speaking and writing, as well as in advertisements, political appeals, editorials, and persuasive essays. You should first look them over so that you can recognize them in what you read or hear. Then avoid them in your own writing and thinking.

Fallacies of Thinking

Appeal to Ignorance ■ A person commits this logical fallacy by maintaining that because no one has ever proved a claim, it must therefore be false. Appeals to ignorance unfairly shift the burden of proof to someone else.

> **Example:** Show me one study that proves seat belts save lives.

Appeal to Pity ■ This fallacy may be heard in courts of law when a lawyer begs for leniency because his client's mother is ill, his brother is out of work, and on and on. The tug on the heartstrings can also be heard in the classroom when a student says to the teacher, "May I have another day on this paper? I worked till my eyeballs fell out, but it's still not done."

> **Example:** Imagine what it must have been like for him. If anyone deserves a break, he does.

Bandwagon ■ Another form of ineffective logic in an argument is the appeal to everyone's sense of wanting to belong or be accepted. By suggesting that everyone else is doing this or wearing that or going here or there, you can avoid the real question—"Is this idea or claim a valid one or not?"

> **Example:** Everyone on the team wears brand X shoes. It's the only way to go.

Broad Generalization ■ A broad generalization takes in everything and everyone at once, allowing no exceptions. For example, a generalization about voters might be, "All voters spend too little time reading about a candidate and too much time being swayed by 30-second sound bites." It may be true that quite a few voters are guilty of this error, but it is unfair to suggest that this is true of all voters. Here's another example:

> **Example:** All teenagers spend too much time watching television.

Circular Thinking ■ This fallacy occurs when you assume, in a definition or an argument, the very point you are trying to prove. Note how circular this sort of reasoning is.

> **Example:** **I love Mr. Baldwin's class because I'm always happy in there.** (But what's special about the class?)

Either-Or Thinking ■ Either-or thinking consists of reducing a solution to two possible extremes: "America: Love it or leave it." "Put up or shut up." This fallacy of thinking eliminates all the possibilities in the middle.

> **Example:** **Either this community votes to build a new school or the quality of education will drop dramatically.**

Half-Truths ■ Avoid building your argument with evidence or statements that contain part of the truth but not the whole truth. These kinds of statements are called half-truths. They are especially misleading because they leave out "the rest of the story." They are partly true and partly untrue at the same time.

> **Example:** **The new recycling law is bad because it will cost more money than it saves.**
> (Maybe so; but it will also save the environment.)

Oversimplification ■ Beware of phrases like "It all boils down to . . . " or "It's a simple question of . . . . " Almost no dispute among reasonably intelligent people is "a simple question." Anyone who feels, for example, that capital punishment "all boils down to" protecting society ought to question a doctor, an inmate on death row, the inmate's family, a sociologist, or a religious leader for other points of view.

> **Example:** **Capital punishment protects society.**

Slanted Language ■ By choosing words that carry strong positive or negative feelings, a person can distract the audience and lead them away from the valid arguments being made. The philosopher Bertrand Russell once illustrated the bias involved in slanted language when he compared three synonyms for the word *stubborn*: "I am *firm*. You are *obstinate*. He is *pigheaded*."

> **Example:** **No one in his right mind would ever do anything that dumb.**

Testimonial ■ You can take Jack Horkheimer's word on the composition of Saturn's rings, but the moment he starts promoting a product, watch out! If the testimonial or statement comes from a recognized authority in the field, great. If it comes from a person famous in another field, it can be misleading.

> **Example:** **Sports hero: "I've tried every cold medicine on the market, and—believe me—nothing works like No Cold."**

"News is the first rough draft of history."

—Ben Bradlee

VIEWING Skills

If you're an American teenager, you probably spend about 20 hours a week watching TV. You watch music videos, sitcoms, sporting events, and countless commercials.

Have you ever stopped to consider how this viewing shapes your ideas, opinions, and actions? Does TV influence what you like or don't like? Does it shape what you think is true or important? Does it affect the way you spend your time or your money? In all probability, television has a huge impact on your life.

The same may be true of the World Wide Web. From banner ads to mass e-mailings, from personal sites to corporate press releases, people behind the Web seek to influence the way you think. That's why it's important for you to think about, and question, what you see on TV and on the Web. This chapter will help you with viewing tips and guidelines.

Preview

- **Watching Television News**
- **Reviewing Videos**
- **Watching Commercials**
- **Viewing Web Sites**

Watching Television News

You've probably heard of *active reading;* it means "thinking as you read." It follows, then, that active viewing requires you to think as you view. This is especially true when you are watching the news. You need to think about each news story and test it for the following three qualities: *completeness, correctness,* and *balance.*

Completeness

A good news story is complete. It answers *Who? What? When? Where? Why?* and sometimes *How?* On Thursday, January 13, 2005, the following information was reported by several news agencies. Notice how the 5 W's and H are answered in the first sentence.

On Friday, scientists will view Saturn's largest
├──WHEN──┤├──WHO──┤├─────────────WHAT───────

moon, Titan, when the Hugens probe lands
───────────────┤├───────HOW──────────────

on the surface and broadcasts pictures of a place
├──────WHERE──────┤ ├──────HOW───────┤

that might harbor life.
├─────────WHY─────────┤

When viewing the news, always listen carefully for the context of each story. The above story went on to explain that the viewing of Titan is the first collaboration between NASA, the European Space Agency, and Italy's space program. All three groups believe that the study will provide answers about the solar system and life itself. This kind of background information will give you a better understanding of the importance of the story.

Viewing TIP

Remember to watch the entire news story before you come to any conclusions about its importance or relevance for you. The last few facts in a story can be crucial to its overall impact.

Correctness

Correctness means the story states only known facts, and states them accurately. For example, imagine that an apartment building is on fire, and firefighters are at the scene. A resident who has been rescued says a family is still trapped in the burning building, but firefighters have searched all the apartments and found no one. There are three ways this story could be reported—two could easily mislead the audience.

Possibly Incorrect:
Both of the following statements are possibly incorrect:

"An apartment building is burning, and a family is trapped inside."

"An apartment building is burning, but all residents have been rescued."

Correct:
To be correct, the news story should say the following:

"An apartment building is burning. One resident who was rescued says other people are still trapped inside. However, firefighters say they have searched the building and found no one. We will update the story as more information comes in."

Balance

Balance is the opposite of *bias*. A balanced story presents all sides of an event or issue fairly. Balance is affected by the following factors:

Story Order ■ Viewers expect the most important story to come first in a newscast, the next most important to come second, and so on. Is the story in an appropriate position for its importance?

People Interviewed ■ Are people of equal reliability interviewed to speak for differing views? Are they given equal time?

Pictures Shown ■ Do the pictures make one person or one side of the story look good and another person or viewpoint look bad? Or do most of the pictures focus on only one person or viewpoint?

Word Choice ■ The following sentences could be about the same event: "More than 50 people were injured." "Minor injuries were reported." The first sentence makes the event seem more serious.

Take NOTE

One important but often overlooked issue is whether a given news story is included in a newscast. Are there important events and issues in your community (or in the world) that aren't being covered by TV news?

Writing Guidelines
Reviewing Videos

Video presentations (films, TV sitcoms, documentaries) use pictures, action, dialogue, and music to present information. Writing a review will help you think through what a video says and how well it says it.

■ PREWRITING

1. **Considering the Purpose** . . . Before viewing, consider the purpose of the video program. Do you think that the video will inform, entertain, tell a story, or persuade? What questions do you have about the topic?

2. **Taking Notes** . . . While viewing, write down key words and ideas, but avoid taking too many notes. After viewing, do a freewriting in which you summarize what you saw and heard.

3. **Finding a Focus** . . . Think about what you want to focus on in your review—the plot, characters, subject, theme, or visual images.

4. **Developing a Thesis** . . . With your focus in mind, view the video again (if possible). Then develop a thesis that clearly states the point you plan to make in your writing.

■ WRITING AND REVISING

5. **Writing a First Draft** . . . Divide your review into three parts:

   Beginning: Introduce the video and present your focus as either a thesis statement or a question. If necessary, give a brief summary of the video as background for your review.

   Middle: Apply your thesis to different parts of the video. For each point, provide and discuss supporting details.

   Ending: Summarize what you've covered in your review and leave your readers with something to think about.

6. **Improving Your Writing** . . . Ask yourself the following questions: *Do I have a clear thesis and strong support? Have I reported details in the best order? Do I sound knowledgeable?*

7. **Improving Your Style** . . . Ask yourself the following questions: *Do I define unfamiliar terms? Do my sentences read smoothly?*

■ EDITING AND PROOFREADING

8. **Checking for Conventions** . . . Check for errors in punctuation, mechanics, and grammar. Make a final copy and proofread it.

Sample **Video Review**

In the essay below, student Sharise Morgan reviews a documentary about global warming. She considers the evidence presented in the program and draws her own conclusions about it.

A Global Problem

The writer gets the reader's attention, names the documentary, and gives the focus.

"So, you think global warming won't affect you?" This is the question posed by Alan Alda in a *Scientific American Frontiers* documentary entitled "Hot Planet, Cold Comfort." Some people don't care about global warming. They simply shrug and smile, hoping their chilly homes in the north will become balmy resorts. Other people doubt whether global warming is real at all. This documentary, however, provides compelling evidence about the change to the world climate and some shocking predictions of what is to come.

The writer cites specific examples from the documentary.

Perhaps the most troubling change is occurring in the Atlantic Ocean. According to Ruth Curry, a researcher at the Woods Hole Oceanographic Institution, global warming is endangering the Gulf Stream current. This huge circulation carries hot water away from the equator toward Europe and carries cold water from the arctic to the equator. The Gulf Stream has been called the heat pump of the Atlantic. However, because so much of the polar ice cap is melting, a thick layer of freshwater now sits atop the deep saltwater that used to pump southward. This change has weakened the flow of the Gulf Stream and may stop it entirely. If this happens, Europe could become much colder very quickly.

Another alarming trend is taking place in Alaska. Glaciers are melting at a rate of six feet per year, and tundra shrubs are being displaced by species that used to grow hundreds of miles farther south. These changes are causing extinctions of certain plants and animals. Also, the arctic tundra used to be a "carbon sink," meaning that it took more carbon dioxide out of the air than it released. Now the permafrost is melting, though, and the carbon stored in the peat is pouring into the air. The tundra has turned from a carbon sink into a carbon pump. Since carbon dioxide is the chief greenhouse gas, the warming of the Arctic is only accelerating the greenhouse effect.

The conclusion interprets the meaning of the information.

"Hot Planet, Cold Comfort" shows that evidence of climate change appears in many surprising ways across the globe. In places, the greenhouse effect will lead to drastic changes in temperatures, increased storm action, and mass extinctions of certain plants and animals. Unless the countries of our hot planet soon reach an agreement about emission of greenhouse gases, many people, indeed, will be left out in the cold. ■

Watching **Commercials**

The purpose of a commercial is to persuade viewers to buy something. And while some commercials come right out and ask you to buy a product, many rely on more subtle, unspoken messages. Here are some common unspoken messages, and why you should be aware of them.

FAMOUS FACES

Super athletes, movie stars, TV actors, and other celebrities appear in commercials for everything from shoes to soft drinks. The unspoken message:

If you want to be like the rich and famous, buy what they buy!

Of course, there is no real connection between the stars and the products. In fact, many of these celebrities don't even use the products they sell on TV. They just make millions trying to convince *you* to use them.

PERFECT PEOPLE

Even the "regular people" in commercials aren't really so "regular." Most are actors who are made to seem real, but more attractive, better dressed, smarter, nicer, and funnier than most real people. The unspoken message:

If you buy this product, you are smart, hip, cool, and funny.

WARM, FUZZY FEELINGS

How good can a hamburger or a phone call make you feel? Really good, if you believe the commercials that use smiling faces, gentle voices, kind words, and soft music to create warm, fuzzy feelings. The unspoken message:

Buy this, and you'll feel good, too.

SPECIAL EFFECTS

Have you ever noticed that products in commercials can do the most amazing things? Bicycles fly. A celebrity action figure actually becomes a celebrity. A family walks into a chain restaurant and is suddenly transported to a tropical paradise. The unspoken message:

If you buy this product, wonderful things will happen to you, too.

HELP FILE

Advertisers use a special tactic in commercials for children and teen-agers. The actors in these commercials are always a few years older than the target audience. For example, a commercial advertising a product for high school students might use college students as actors. Why? Advertisers know most young people admire people who are a little older.

Viewing **Web Sites**

Like television, the Internet is a popular source of information and entertainment; and like television, the Internet requires critical viewing. When you surf the Net, you need to know what you're getting into. To determine the reliability of a particular Web site, ask appropriate questions and be on the lookout for red flags. (See page 349.)

Questions to Ask

- Who created the Web site and supplied the content? Look for a person's name and some information about her or him: education, professional training, experience, current organization, job title, and so on.
- What organization (if any) sponsors the Web site? What can you find out about the organization?
- Is there an e-mail address you can use to contact the author or organization with questions or comments?
- When was the site last updated? This is especially important if you need up-to-date information.
- Is the information accurate? You can answer this question by comparing it to information found in other sources.

Red Flags to Watch For

- The site is anonymous—no author or organization name is listed.
- The content is poorly written, with many errors and misspellings.
- The information proves inaccurate when compared to other sources.
- The information is one-sided, not recognizing other viewpoints.
- The site presents facts and figures without naming a source for the information.
- The opinions stated are not backed by facts.
- The language is unreasonable, unfair, or even hateful.

Take NOTE To find out how reliable a Web site is, check out the site's links, learn more about the site's author or the sponsoring organization, or look for recommendations and reviews of the site.

PROOFREADER'S
Guide

Marking Punctuation 487

Checking Mechanics 507

Using the Right Word 523

Parts of Speech 533

Using the Language 550

"Cut out all those exclamation marks. An exclamation mark is like laughing at your own joke."

—F. Scott Fitzgerald

Marking
PUNCTUATION

Period

487.1 At the End of a Sentence

Use a **period** at the end of a sentence that makes a statement, requests something, or gives a mild command.

> (Statement) **The man who does not read good books has no advantage over the man who can't read them.**
> —Mark Twain

> (Request) **Please bring your folders and notebooks to class.**

> (Mild command) **Listen carefully so that you don't make the same mistake again.**

NOTE: It is not necessary to place a period after a statement that has parentheses around it and is part of another sentence.

> **One time, when my friend was driving, our teacher, Mr. Spock (we called him that because he had funny ears and showed no emotion), told her to make a left turn, and she quickly responded by turning on the windshield wipers.**
> —Chris Kanarick, "They're Driving Me Crazy"

487.2 After an Initial or an Abbreviation

Place a period after an initial or an abbreviation.

> **Ms.   Sen.   D.D.S.   M.F.A.   M.D.   Jr.   U.S.   p.m.   a.m.**
> **Edna St. Vincent Millay   Booker T. Washington   D. H. Lawrence**

NOTE: When an abbreviation is the last word in a sentence, use only one period at the end of the sentence.

> **Jaleesa eyed each door until she found the name Fletcher B. Gale, M.D.**

487.3 As a Decimal Point

A period is used as a decimal point.

> **New York City has around 7.3 million people; its last budget was $33.4 billion.**

Question Mark

488.1 Direct Question

Place a **question mark** at the end of a direct question.

> **Now what? I wondered. Do I go out and buy a jar of honey and stand around waving it? How in the world am I supposed to catch a bear?**
> > —Ken Taylor, "The Case of the Grizzly on the Greens"
>
> **Where did my body end and the crystal and white world begin?**
> > —Ralph Ellison, *Invisible Man*

When a question ends with a quotation that is also a question, use only one question mark, and place it within the quotation marks.

> **On road trips, do you remember driving your parents crazy by asking, "Are we there yet?"**

NOTE: Do *not* use a question mark after an indirect question.

> **Out on the street, I picked out a friendly looking old man and asked him where the depot was.** —Wilson Rawls, *Where the Red Fern Grows*

488.2 To Show Uncertainty

Use a question mark within parentheses to show uncertainty.

> **This summer marks the 20th season (?) of the American Players Theatre.**

488.3 Short Question Within a Sentence

Use a question mark for a short question within parentheses.

> **We crept so quietly (had they heard us?) past the kitchen door and back to our room.**

Use a question mark for a short question within dashes.

> **Maybe somewhere in the pasts of these humbled people, there were cases of bad mothering or absent fathering or emotional neglect—what family surviving the '50s was exempt?—but I couldn't believe these human errors brought the physical changes in Frank.**
> > —Mary Kay Blakely, *Wake Me When It's Over*

Exclamation Point

488.4 To Express Strong Feeling

Use the **exclamation point** (sparingly) to express strong feeling. You may place it after a word, a phrase, or a sentence.

> **"That's not the point," said Wangero. "These are all pieces of dresses Grandma used to wear. She did all this stitching by hand. Imagine!"**
> > —Alice Walker, "Everyday Use"

Comma

489.1 Between Two Independent Clauses

Use a **comma** between two independent clauses that are joined by a coordinating conjunction (*and, but, or, nor, for, yet, so*).

I wanted to knock on the glass to attract attention, but I couldn't move.

—Ralph Ellison, *Invisible Man*

NOTE: Do not confuse a sentence containing a compound verb for a compound sentence.

I had to burn her trash and then sweep up her porches and halls.

—Anne Moody, *Coming of Age in Mississippi*

489.2 To Separate Adjectives

Use commas to separate adjectives that *equally* modify the same noun. (Note: Do not use a comma between the last adjective and the noun.)

Bao's eyes met the hard, bright lights hanging directly above her.

—Julie Ament, student writer

A Closer Look To determine whether adjectives modify equally—and should, therefore, be separated by commas—use these two tests:

1. Shift the order of the adjectives; if the sentence is clear, the adjectives modify equally. (In the example below, *hot* and *smelly* can be shifted and the sentence is still clear; *usual* and *morning* cannot.)

2. Insert *and* between the adjectives; if the sentence reads well, use a comma when *and* is omitted. (The word *and* can be inserted between *hot* and *smelly,* but *and* does not make sense between *usual* and *morning.*)

> **Matty was tired of working in the hot, smelly kitchen and decided to take her usual morning walk.**

489.3 To Separate Contrasted Elements

Use commas to separate contrasted elements within a sentence.

Since the stereotypes were about Asians, and not African Americans, no such reaction occurred.

—Emmeline Chen, "Eliminating the Lighter Shades of Stereotyping"

Comma (continued)

490.1 To Enclose Parenthetical Elements

Use commas to separate parenthetical elements, such as an explanatory word or phrase, within a sentence.

> **They stood together, away from the pile of stones in the corner, and their jokes were quiet, and they smiled rather than laughed.**
>
> —Shirley Jackson, "The Lottery"
>
> **Allison meandered into class, late as usual, and sat down.**

490.2 To Set Off Appositives

A specific kind of explanatory word or phrase called an **appositive** identifies or renames a preceding noun or pronoun.

> **Benson, our uninhibited and enthusiastic Yorkshire terrier, joined our family on my sister's fifteenth birthday.**   —Chad Hockerman, student writer

NOTE: Do not use commas with *restrictive appositives*. A restrictive appositive is essential to the basic meaning of the sentence.

> **Twenty-one-year-old student Edna E. Rivera almost had a nose job but changed her mind.**   —Andrea Lo and Vera Perez

490.3 Between Items in a Series

Use commas to separate individual words, phrases, or clauses in a series. (A series contains at least three items.)

> **I'd never known anything about having meat, vegetables, and a salad all at the same meal.** (Three nouns in a series)
>
> **I took her for walks, read her stories, and made up games for her to play.** (Three phrases in a series)   —Anne Moody, *Coming of Age in Mississippi*

NOTE: Do not use commas when all the words in a series are connected with *or, nor,* or *and.*

> **Her fingernails are pointed and manicured and painted a shiny red.**
>
> —Carson McCullers, "Sucker"

490.4 After Introductory Phrases

Use a comma after an introductory participial phrase.

> **Determined to finish the sweater by Thanksgiving, my grandmother knits night and day.**

Use a comma after an introductory prepositional phrase.

> **In the oddest places and at the strangest times, my grandmother can be found knitting madly away.**

NOTE: You may omit the comma if the introductory phrase is short.

> **Before breakfast my grandmother knits.**

491.1 After Introductory Clauses

Use a comma after an introductory adverb (subordinate) clause.

After the practice was over, Tina walked home.

NOTE: A comma is also used if an adverb clause follows the main clause and begins with *although, even though, while,* or another conjunction expressing a contrast.

Tina walked home, even though it was raining very hard.

However, a comma is not used if the adverb clause following the main clause is needed to complete the meaning of the sentence.

Tina practiced hard because she feared losing.

491.2 To Set Off Nonrestrictive Phrases and Clauses

Use commas to set off **nonrestrictive** (unnecessary) clauses and participial phrases. A nonrestrictive clause or participial phrase adds information that is not necessary to the basic meaning of the sentence. For example, if the clause or phrase (in **red**) were left out in the two examples below, the meaning of the sentences would remain clear. Therefore, commas are used to set them off.

The Altena Fitness Center and Visker Gymnasium, which were built last year, are busy every day. (nonrestrictive clause)

Students and faculty, improving their health through exercise, use both facilities throughout the week. (nonrestrictive phrase)

Do not use commas to set off **restrictive** (necessary) clauses and participial phrases. A restrictive clause or participial phrase adds information that the reader needs to know in order to understand the sentence. For example, if the clause and phrase (in **red**) were dropped from the examples below, the meaning wouldn't be the same. Therefore, commas are *not* used.

The handball court that has a sign-up sheet by the door must be reserved.
The clause identifies which handball court must be reserved.
(restrictive clause)

Individuals wanting to use this court must sign up a day in advance.
(restrictive phrase)

A Closer Look: **That and Which** Use *that* to introduce restrictive (necessary) clauses; use *which* to introduce nonrestrictive (unnecessary) clauses. When the two words are used in this way, the reader can quickly distinguish necessary information from unnecessary information.

The treadmill that monitors heart rate is the one you must use. The reader needs the information to find the right treadmill.

This treadmill, which we got last year, is required for your program. The main clause tells the reader which treadmill to use; the other clause gives additional, unnecessary information.

Comma (continued)

492.1 To Set Off Dates

Use commas to set off items in a date.

He began working out on December 1, 2004, but quit by May 1, 2005.

However, when only the month and year are given, no commas are needed.

He began working out in December 2004 but quit by May 2005.

492.2 To Set Off Items in Addresses

Use commas to set off items in an address. (No comma is placed between the state and ZIP code.)

Mail the box to Friends of Wildlife, Box 402, Spokane, Washington 20077.

When a city and state (or country) appear in the middle of a sentence, a comma follows the last item in the address.

Several charitable organizations in Juneau, Alaska, pool their funds.

492.3 To Set Off Dialogue

Use commas to set off the speaker's exact words from the rest of the sentence.

"It's like we have our own government," adds Tanya, a 17-year-old squatter.
—Kyung Sun Yu and Nell Bernstein, "Street Teens Forge a Home"

492.4 To Set Off Interjections

Use a comma to separate an interjection or a weak exclamation from the rest of the sentence.

Hey, how am I to know that a minute's passed?
—Nathan Slaughter and Jim Schweitzer, *When Time Dies*

492.5 To Set Off Interruptions

Use commas to set off a word, a phrase, or a clause that interrupts the movement of a sentence. Such expressions usually can be identified through the following tests: (1) They may be omitted without changing the meaning of a sentence. (2) They may be placed nearly anywhere in the sentence without changing its meaning.

For me, well, it's just a good job gone!

—Langston Hughes

As a general rule, the safest way to cross this street is with the light.

493.1 In Numbers

Use commas to separate numerals in large numbers in order to distinguish hundreds, thousands, millions, and so forth.

1,101   **25,000**   **7,642,020**

493.2 In Direct Address

Use commas to separate a noun of direct address from the rest of the sentence. A *noun of direct address* is the noun that names the person(s) spoken to.

"But, Mother Gibbs, one can go back; one can go back there again. . . . "

—Thornton Wilder, *Our Town*

493.3 To Enclose Titles or Initials

Use commas to enclose a title or initials and names that follow a surname.

Until Martin, Sr., was 15, he never had more than three months of schooling in any one year.   —Ed Clayton, *Martin Luther King: The Peaceful Warrior*

Hickok, J. B., and Cody, William F., are two popular Western heroes.

493.4 For Clarity or Emphasis

You may use a comma for clarity or for emphasis. There will be times when none of the traditional rules call for a comma, but one will be needed to prevent confusion or to emphasize an important idea.

It may be that those who do most, dream most. (emphasis)

—Stephen Leacock

What the crew does, does affect our voyage. (clarity)

Semicolon

493.5 To Join Two Independent Clauses

Use a **semicolon** to join two or more closely related independent clauses that are not connected with a coordinating conjunction. (Independent clauses can stand alone as separate sentences.)

I did not call myself a poet; I told people I wrote poems.

—Terry McMillan, "Breaking Ice"

Silence coated the room like a layer of tar; not even the breathing of the 11 Gehad made any sound.   —Gann Bierner, "The Leap"

NOTE: When independent clauses are especially long or contain commas, a semicolon may punctuate the sentence, even though a coordinating conjunction connects the clauses.

We waited all day in that wide line, tired travelers pressing in from all sides; and when we needed drinks or sandwiches, I would squeeze my way to the cafeteria and back.

Semicolon (continued)

494.1 With Conjunctive Adverbs

A semicolon is used *before* a conjunctive adverb (with a comma after it) when the word connects two independent clauses in a compound sentence. (Common conjunctive adverbs are *also, besides, finally, however, indeed, instead, meanwhile, moreover, nevertheless, next, still, then, therefore,* and *thus.*)

"I am faced with my imminent demise; therefore, life becomes a very precious thing."
— Amy Taylor, "AIDS Can Happen Here!"

494.2 To Separate Groups That Contain Commas

A semicolon is used to separate groups of words that already contain commas.

Every Saturday night my brother gathers up his things—goggles, shower cap, and snorkel; bubble bath, soap, and shampoo; tapes, stereo, and rubber duck—and heads for the tub.

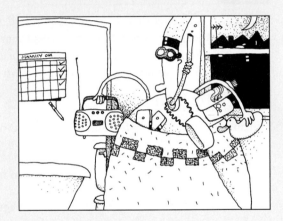

Colon

494.3 After a Salutation

Use a **colon** after the salutation of a business letter.

Dear Judge Parker: **Dear Governor Whitman:**

494.4 Between Numerals Indicating Time

Use a colon between the hours, minutes, and seconds of a number indicating time.

8:30 p.m.   **9:45 a.m.**   **10:24:55**

494.5 For Emphasis

Use a colon to emphasize a word, a phrase, a clause, or a sentence that explains or adds impact to the main clause.

His guest lecturers are local chefs who learn a lesson themselves: Homeless people are worth employing.
—Beth Brophy, "Feeding Those Who Are Hungry"

495.1 To Introduce a Quotation

Use a colon to formally introduce a quotation, a sentence, or a question.

> **Directly a voice in the corner rang out wild and clear: "I've got him! I've got him!"**
> —Mark Twain, *Roughing It*

495.2 To Introduce a List

A colon is used to introduce a list.

> **I got all the proper equipment: scissors, a bucket of water to keep things clean, some cotton for the stuffing, and needle and thread to sew it up.**
> —Joan Baez, *Daybreak*

A Closer Look Do not use a colon between a verb and its object or complement, or between a preposition and its object.

> **Incorrect:** Min has: a snowmobile, an ATV, and a canoe.
> **Correct:** **Min has plenty of toys: a snowmobile, an ATV, and a canoe.**

> **Incorrect:** Dad watches a TV show about: cooking wild game.
> **Correct:** **Dad watches a TV show about a new subject: cooking wild game.**

495.3 Between a Title and a Subtitle

Use a colon to distinguish between a title and a subtitle, volume and page, and chapter and verse in literature.

> **Writers INC: A Student Handbook for WRITING and LEARNING**
> **Encyclopedia Americana IV: 211**　　　　**Psalm 23:1-6**

Hyphen

495.4 In Compound Words

Use the **hyphen** to make compound words.

> **great-great-grandfather**　　　**maid-in-waiting**　　　**three-year-old**
> **It was taller than my-dad-and-me-on-his-shoulders tall.**
> —Kristen Frappier, "The Corn"

NOTE: A dash is indicated by two hyphens--without spacing before or after--in all handwritten material. Don't use a single hyphen when a dash is required.

495.5 To Join Letters and Words

Use a hyphen to join a capital letter or lowercase letter to a noun or participle. (Check your dictionary.)

> **T-shirt**　　　**Y-turn**　　　**G-rated**　　　*x*-axis

Hyphen (continued)

496.1 Between Numbers and Fractions

Use a hyphen to join the words in compound numbers from *twenty-one* to *ninety-nine* when it is necessary to write them out.

twenty-five	forty-three	seventy-nine	sixty-two

Use a hyphen between the numerator and denominator of a fraction, but not when one or both of those elements are already hyphenated.

four-tenths	five-sixteenths	(7/32) seven thirty-seconds

496.2 In a Special Series

Use hyphens when two or more words have a common element that is omitted in all but the last term.

The ship has lovely two-, four-, or six-person cabins.

496.3 To Join Numbers

Use a hyphen to join numbers indicating the life span of a person or the score in a contest or a vote.

We can thank Louis Pasteur (1822–1895) for pasteurized milk.

In the 2000 Rose Bowl, Wisconsin defeated Stanford 17–9.

496.4 To Divide a Word

Use a hyphen to divide a word, only between its syllables, at the end of a line of print. Always place the hyphen after the syllable at the end of the line—never before a syllable at the beginning of the following line.

Guidelines for Dividing with Hyphens

1. Always leave enough of the word at the end of the line so that the word can be identified.
2. Always divide a compound word between its basic units: *sister-in-law,* not *sis-ter-in-law.*
3. Avoid dividing a word of five or fewer letters: *paper, study, July.*
4. Avoid dividing the last word in a paragraph.
5. Never divide a one-syllable word: *rained, skills, through.*
6. Never divide a one-letter syllable from the rest of the word: *omit-ted,* not *o-mitted.*
7. When a vowel is a syllable by itself, divide the word after the vowel: *epi-sode,* not *ep-isode.*
8. Never divide abbreviations or contractions: *shouldn't,* not *should-n't.*
9. Never divide the last word in more than two lines in a row.

497.1 To Prevent Confusion

Use a hyphen with prefixes or suffixes to avoid confusion or awkward spelling.

re-create (not *recreate*) the image   **re-cover (not *recover*) the sofa**

497.2 To Create New Words

Use a hyphen to form new words beginning with the prefixes *self-, ex-, all-,* and *half-*. Also use a hyphen to join any prefix to a proper noun, a proper adjective, or the official name of an office. Use a hyphen before the suffix *-elect*.

self-contained	**ex-governor**	**all-inclusive**	**half-painted**
pre-Cambrian	**mid-December**	**president-elect**	

Use a hyphen to join the prefix *great* to names of relatives, but do not use a hyphen to join *great* to other words.

great-aunt, great-grandfather (correct)   **great-hall** (incorrect)

497.3 To Form an Adjective

Use the hyphen to join two or more words that serve as a single adjective (a single-thought adjective) before a noun.

In real life I am a large, big-boned woman with rough, man-working hands.
—Alice Walker, "Everyday Use"

Use common sense to determine whether a compound adjective might be misread if it is not hyphenated. Generally, hyphenate a compound adjective that is composed of a noun + adjective, . . .

oven-safe handles   **book-smart student**

a noun + participle (*ing* or *ed* form of a verb), . . .

line-dried clothes   **bone-chilling story**

or a phrase.

heat-and-serve meal   **off-and-on relationship**

A Closer Look When words forming the adjective come after the noun, do not hyphenate them.

In real life I am large and big boned.

When the first of these words is an adverb ending in *-ly,* do not use a hyphen; also, do not use a hyphen when a number or a letter is the final element in a single-thought adjective.

delicately prepared pastry (adverb ending in *-ly*)

class B movie (letter is the final element)

Apostrophe

498.1 In Contractions

Use an **apostrophe** to show that one or more letters have been left out of a word group to form a contraction.

hadn't – _o_ is left out   **they'd – _woul_ is left out**   **it's – _i_ is left out**

NOTE: Use an apostrophe to show that one or more numerals or letters have been left out of numbers or words in order to show special pronunciation.

class of '99 – _19_ is left out   **g'day – _ood_ is left out**

498.2 To Form Plurals

Use an apostrophe and _s_ to form the plural of a letter, a number, a sign, or a word discussed as a word.

B – B's   **C – C's**   **8 – 8's**   **+ – +'s**   **_and_ – _and_'s**

Ms. D'Aquisto says our conversations contain too many _like_'s and _no way_'s.

NOTE: If two apostrophes are called for in the same word, omit the second one.

Follow closely the _do's_ and _don'ts_ (not _don't's_) on the checklist.

498.3 To Form Singular Possessives

Add an apostrophe and _s_ to form the possessive of most singular nouns.

Spock's ears   **Captain Kirk's singing**   **the ship's escape plan**

NOTE: When a singular noun ends with an _s_ or a _z_ sound, you may form the possessive by adding just an apostrophe. When the singular noun is a one-syllable word, however, you usually add both an apostrophe and an _s_ to form the possessive.

San Carlos' government (or) San Carlos's government (two-syllable word)

Ross's essay (one-syllable word) **The class's field trip** (one-syllable word)

498.4 To Form Plural Possessives

The possessive form of plural nouns ending in _s_ is usually made by adding just an apostrophe.

students' homework   **bosses' orders**

A Closer Look It will help you punctuate correctly if you remember that the word immediately before the apostrophe is the owner.

girl's guitar (_girl_ is the owner)   **boss's order** (_boss_ is the owner)

girls' guitar (_girls_ are the owners)   **bosses' order** (_bosses_ are the owners)

499.1 In Compound Nouns

Form the possessive of a compound noun by placing the possessive ending after the last word.

the secretary of the interior's (singular) **agenda**
her lady-in-waiting's (singular) **day off**

If forming a possessive of a plural compound noun creates an awkward construction, you may replace the possessive with an *of* phrase. (All four forms below are correct.)

their fathers-in-law's (plural) **birthdays**
or **the birthdays of their *fathers-in-law*** (plural)

the ambassadors-at-large's (plural) **plans**
or **the plans of the *ambassadors-at-large*** (plural)

499.2 With Indefinite Pronouns

Form the possessive of an indefinite pronoun by placing an apostrophe and an *s* on the last word. (See 559.2.)

everyone's   **anyone's**   **somebody's**

499.3 To Express Time or Amount

Use an apostrophe and an *s* with an adjective that is part of an expression indicating time or amount.

a penny's worth   **today's business**   **this morning's meeting**
yesterday's news   **a day's wage**   **a month's pay**

499.4 To Show Shared Possession

When possession is shared by more than one noun, use the possessive form for the last noun in the series.

Hoshi, Linda, and Nakiva's water skis (All three own the same skis.)
Hoshi's, Linda's, and Nakiva's water skis (Each owns her own skis.)

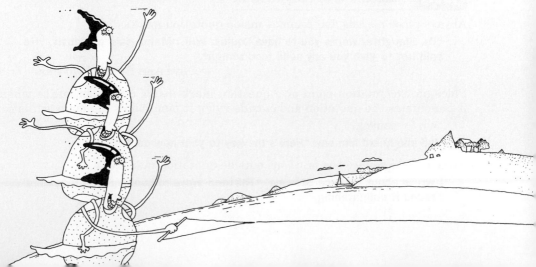

Quotation Marks

500.1 To Punctuate Titles

Use **quotation marks** to punctuate titles of songs, poems, short stories, one-act plays, lectures, episodes of radio or television programs, chapters of books, unpublished works, electronic files, and articles found in magazines, newspapers, encyclopedias, or online sources. (For punctuation of other titles, see 502.2.)

> **"Santa Lucia"** (song)
>
> **"The Chameleon"** (short story)
>
> **"Twentieth-Century Memories"** (lecture)
>
> **"Affordable Adventures"** (magazine article)
>
> **"Dire Prophecy of the Howling Dog"** (chapter in a book)
>
> **"Dancing with Debra"** (television episode)
>
> **"Miss Julie"** (one-act play)

500.2 For Special Words

You may use quotation marks (1) to distinguish a word that is being discussed, (2) to indicate that a word is unfamiliar slang, or (3) to point out that a word is being used in a special way.

> **(1) A commentary on the times is that the word "honesty" is now preceded by "old-fashioned."**
> —Larry Wolters
>
> **(2) I . . . asked the bartender where I could hear "chanky-chank," as Cajuns called their music.**
> —William Least Heat-Moon, *Blue Highways*
>
> **(3) Tom pushed the wheelchair across the street, showed the lady his "honest" smile . . . and stole her purse.**

NOTE: You may use italics (underlining) in place of quotation marks in each of these three situations. (See 502.3.)

500.3 Placement of Punctuation

Always place periods and commas inside quotation marks.

> **"Dr. Slaughter wants you to have liquids, Will," Mama said anxiously. "He said not to give you any solid food tonight."**
> —Olive Ann Burns, *Cold Sassy Tree*

Place an exclamation point or a question mark *inside* quotation marks when it punctuates the quotation and *outside* when it punctuates the main sentence.

> **"Am I dreaming?"**
>
> **Had she heard him say, "Here's the key to your new car"?**

Always place semicolons or colons outside quotation marks.

> **I wrote about Wallace Stevens' "Thirteen Ways of Looking at a Blackbird"; I found it enlightening.**

Quick Guide

Marking Quoted Material

501.1 To Set Off Quoted Passages

Place quotation marks before and after the words in direct quotations.

"Just come to a game," he pleads. "You'll change your mind."

—Sandra Lampe, "Batter UP!"

In a quoted passage, put brackets around any word or punctuation mark that is not part of the original quotation.

(Original) **Conservation pundits point to it as the classic example of the impossibility of providing good government service.**

(Quotation) **"Conservation pundits point to it [the U.S. Postal Service] as the classic example of the impossibility of providing good government service."** —Brad Branan, "Dead Letter Office?"

NOTE: If you quote only part of the original passage, be sure to construct a sentence that is both accurate and grammatically correct.

Much of the restructuring of the Postal Service has involved "turning over large parts of its work to the private sector."

501.2 For Long Quotations

If you quote more than one paragraph, place quotation marks before each paragraph and at the end of the last paragraph (Example A). If a quotation has more than four lines on a page, you may set it off from the text by indenting 10 spaces from the left margin (block form). Do not use quotation marks either before or after the quoted material, unless they appear in the original. Double-space the quotation. (Example B).

Example A "_____   **Example B**

501.3 For Quoting a Quotation

Use single quotation marks to punctuate a quotation **within** a quotation. Use double quotation marks in order to distinguish a quotation **within** a quotation within a quotation.

"For tomorrow," said Mr. Botts, "read 'Unlighted Lamps.'"

Sue asked, "Did you hear Mr. Botts say, 'Read "Unlighted Lamps"'?"

Italics (Underlining)

502.1 Handwritten and Printed Material

Italics is a printer's term for a style of type that is slightly slanted. In this sentence, the word *happiness* is printed in italics. In material that is handwritten or typed on a machine that cannot print in italics, underline each word or letter that should be in italics.

> **My Ántonia is the story of a strong and determined pioneer woman.**
> (printed)
> **Willa Cather's <u>My Ántonia</u> describes pioneer life in America.**
> (typed or handwritten)

502.2 In Titles

Use italics to indicate the titles of magazines, newspapers, pamphlets, books, full-length plays, films, videos, radio and television programs, book-length poems, ballets, operas, paintings, lengthy musical compositions, cassettes, CD's, legal cases, and the names of ships and aircraft. (For punctuation of other titles, see 500.1.)

Newsweek (magazine)	**Cold Sassy Tree** (book)
Shakespeare in Love (film)	**Law & Order** (television program)
Caring for Your Kitten (pamphlet)	**Hedda Gabler** (full-length play)
Chicago Tribune (newspaper)	

NOTE: Punctuate one title within another title as follows:

> **"Is <u>ER's</u> Reality Trustworthy?"** (title of TV program in an article)

502.3 For Special Uses

Use italics for a number, letter, or word that is being discussed or used in a special way. (Sometimes quotation marks are used for this reason. See 500.2.)

> **I hope that this letter <u>I</u> stands for <u>incredible</u> and not <u>incomplete</u>.**

502.4 For Foreign Words

Use italics for foreign words that have not been adopted into the English language; also use italics for scientific names.

> **The voyageurs—tough men with natural <u>bonhomie</u>—discovered the shy <u>Castor canadensis</u>, or North American beaver.**

Parentheses

503.1 To Set Off Explanatory Material

You may use **parentheses** to set off explanatory or added material that interrupts the normal sentence structure.

Benson (our dog) sits in on our piano lessons (on the piano bench), much to the teacher's surprise and amusement.

—Chad Hockerman, student writer

NOTE: Place question marks and exclamation points within the parentheses when they mark the added material.

Ivan at once concluded (the rascal!) that I had a passion for dances, and . . . wanted to drag me off to a dancing class.

—Fyodor Dostoyevsky, "A Novel in Nine Letters"

503.2 With Full Sentences

When using a full "sentence" within another sentence, do not capitalize it or use a period inside the parentheses.

And, since your friend won't have the assignment (he was just thinking about calling you), you'll have to make a couple more calls to actually get it.

—Ken Taylor, "The Art and Practice of Avoiding Homework"

When the parenthetical sentence comes after the main sentence, capitalize and punctuate it the same way you would any other complete sentence.

They kiss and hug when they say "hello," and I love this. (In Korea, people are much more formal; they just shake hands and bow to each other.)

—Sue Chong, "He Said I Was Too American"

NOTE: For unavoidable parentheses within parentheses (. . . [. . .] . . .), use brackets. Avoid overuse of parentheses by using commas instead.

Diagonal

503.3 To Show a Choice

Use a **diagonal** (also called a *slash*) between two words, as in *and/or,* to indicate that either is acceptable.

Press the load/eject button.

Don't worry; this is indoor/outdoor carpet.

503.4 When Quoting Poetry

When quoting more than one line of poetry, use a diagonal to show where each line of poetry ends. (Insert a space on each side of the diagonal.)

I have learned not to worry about love; / but to honor its coming / with all my heart.

—Alice Walker, "New Face"

Dash

504.1 To Indicate a Sudden Break

Use a **dash** to indicate a sudden break or change in the sentence.

> **Near the semester's end—and this is not always due to poor planning—some students may find themselves in a real crunch.**

NOTE: Dashes are often used in place of commas. Use dashes when you want to give special emphasis; use commas when there is no need for emphasis.

504.2 To Set Off an Introductory Series

Use a dash to set off an introductory series from the clause that explains the series.

> **A good book, a cup of tea, a comfortable chair—these things always saved my mother's sanity.**

504.3 To Set Off Parenthetical Material

You may use a dash to set off parenthetical material—material that explains or clarifies a word or a phrase.

> **A single incident—a tornado that came without warning—changed the face of the small town forever.**

504.4 To Indicate Interrupted Speech

Use a dash to show interrupted or faltering speech in dialogue.

> **SOJOURNER: Mama, why are you—**
> **MAMA: Isabelle, do as I say!**
>
> —Sandy Asher, *A Woman Called Truth*

504.5 For Emphasis

Use a dash to emphasize a word, a series, a phrase, or a clause.

> **After years of trial and error, Belther made history with his invention—the unicycle.**

Quick Guide

Ellipsis

505.1 To Show Omitted Words

Use an **ellipsis** (three periods with one space before and after each period) to show that one or more words have been omitted in a quotation.

(Original)
We the people of the United States, in order to form a more perfect Union, establish justice, insure domestic tranquility, provide for the common defense, promote the general welfare, and secure the blessings of liberty to ourselves and our posterity, do ordain and establish this Constitution for the United States of America.

—Preamble, U.S. Constitution

(Quotation)
"We the people . . . in order to form a more perfect Union . . . establish this Constitution for the United States of America."

505.2 At the End of a Sentence

If words from a quotation are omitted at the end of a sentence, place the ellipsis after the period that marks the conclusion of the sentence.

"Five score years ago, a great American, in whose symbolic shadow we stand, signed the Emancipation Proclamation. . . . But one hundred years later, we must face the tragic fact that the Negro is still not free."

—Martin Luther King, Jr., "I Have a Dream"

NOTE: If the quoted material is a complete sentence (even if it was not complete in the original), use a period, then an ellipsis.

(Original)
I am tired; my heart is sick and sad. From where the sun now stands I will fight no more forever.

—Chief Joseph of the Nez Percé

(Quotation)
"I am tired. . . . From where the sun now stands I will fight no more forever."
or
"I am tired. . . . I will fight no more. . . . "

505.3 To Show a Pause

Use an ellipsis to indicate a pause.

I brought my trembling hand to my focusing eyes. It was oozing, it was red, it was . . . it was . . . a tomato!

—Laura Baginski, student writer

Brackets

506.1 To Set Off Clarifying Information

Use **brackets** before and after words that are added to clarify what another person has said or written.

> **"They'd [the sweat bees] get into your mouth, ears, eyes, nose. You'd feel them all over you."**
> —Marilyn Johnson and Sasha Nyary, "Roosevelts in the Amazon"

NOTE: The brackets indicate that the words *the sweat bees* are not part of the quotation but were added for clarification.

506.2 To Set Off Added Words

Place brackets around comments that have been added to a quotation.

> **"Congratulations to the astronomy club's softball team, which put in, shall we say, a 'stellar' performance."** [groans]

506.3 Around an Editorial Correction

Place brackets around an editorial correction inserted within quoted material.

> **"Brooklyn alone has 8 percent of lead poisoning [victims] nationwide," said Marjorie Moore.**
> —Donna Actie, student writer

NOTE: Place brackets around the letters *sic* (Latin for "as such"); the letters indicate that an error appearing in the material being quoted was made by the original speaker or writer.

> **"'When I'm queen,' mused Lucy, 'I'll show these blockheads whose [*sic*] got beauty and brains.'"**

Punctuation Marks

´	Accent, acute	,	Comma	(–)	Parentheses
`	Accent, grave	†	Dagger	.	Period
'	Apostrophe	—	Dash	?	Question mark
*	Asterisk	/	Diagonal/Slash	"–"	Quotation marks
{ }	Brace	¨ (ü)	Dieresis	§	Section
[ ]	Brackets	. . .	Ellipsis	;	Semicolon
^	Caret	!	Exclamation point	~	Tilde
(ç)	Cedilla	-	Hyphen	_____	Underscore
^	Circumflex	...	Leaders		
:	Colon	¶	Paragraph		

"English spelling is weird . . .
or is it wierd?"

—Irwin Hill

Checking
MECHANICS

Capitalization

507.1 Proper Nouns and Adjectives

Capitalize proper nouns and proper adjectives (those derived from proper nouns). The chart below provides a quick overview of capitalization rules. The pages following explain some specific rules of capitalization.

Capitalization at a Glance

Names of people	Alice Walker, Matilda, Jim, Mr. Roker
Days of the week, months	Sunday, Tuesday, June, August
Holidays, holy days	Thanksgiving, Easter, Hanukkah
Periods, events in history	Middle Ages, the Battle of Bunker Hill
Official documents	Declaration of Independence
Special events	Elgin Community Spring Gala
Languages, nationalities, religions	French, Canadian, Islam
Political parties	Republican Party, Socialist Party
Trade names	Oscar Mayer hot dogs, Pontiac Sunbird
Official titles used with names	Mayor John Spitzer, Senator Feinstein
Formal epithets	Alexander the Great
Geographical names	
Planets, heavenly bodies	Earth, Jupiter, the Milky Way
Continents	Australia, South America
Countries	Ireland, Grenada, Sri Lanka
States, provinces	Ohio, Utah, Nova Scotia
Cities, towns, villages	El Paso, Burlington, Wonewoc
Streets, roads, highways	Park Avenue, Route 66, Interstate 90
Landforms	the Rocky Mountains, the Sahara Desert
Bodies of water	Yellowstone Lake, Pumpkin Creek
Buildings, monuments	Elkhorn High School, Gateway Arch
Public areas	Times Square, Sequoia National Park

Capitalization (continued)

508.1 First Words

Capitalize the first word of every sentence, including the first word of a full-sentence direct quotation.

> **The crowd was quiet. A girl whispered, "I hope it's not Nancy," and the sound of her whisper reached the edges of the crowd.**
> > —Shirley Jackson, "The Lottery"

508.2 Sentences in Parentheses

Capitalize the first word in a sentence enclosed in parentheses, but do not capitalize the first word if the parenthetical appears within another sentence.

> **Shamelessly she winked at me and grinned again. (That grin! She could have taken it off her face and put it on the table.)**
> > —Jean Stafford, "Bad Characters"
> **Damien's aunt (she's a wild woman) plays bingo every Saturday night.**

508.3 Sentences Following Colons

Capitalize the first word in a complete sentence that follows a colon when (1) you want to emphasize the sentence or (2) the sentence is a quotation.

> **When we quarreled and made horrible faces at one another, Mother knew what to say: "Your faces will stay that way, and no one will marry you."**

508.4 Sections of the Country

Capitalize words that indicate particular sections of the country; do not capitalize words that simply indicate direction.

> **Mr. Johnson is from the Southwest.** (section of the country)
> **After moving north to Montana, he had to buy winter clothes.** (direction)

508.5 Certain Religious Words

Capitalize nouns that refer to the Supreme Being, the word *Bible,* the books of the Bible, and the names for other holy books.

> **God   Jehovah   the Lord   the Savior   Allah   Bible   Genesis**

508.6 Titles

Capitalize the first word of a title, the last word, and every word in between except articles (*a, an, the*), short prepositions, and coordinating conjunctions. Follow this rule for titles of books, newspapers, magazines, poems, plays, songs, articles, films, works of art, photographs, and stories.

> ***Cold Sassy Tree   Washington Post   "Nothing Gold Can Stay"***
> ***A Midsummer Night's Dream   "The Diary of a Madman"***

509.1 Letters

Capitalize the letters used to indicate form or shape.

U-turn   I-beam   S-curve   T-shirt   V-shaped

509.2 Organizations

Capitalize the name of an organization, an association, or a team.

Lake Ontario Sailors   American Indian Movement   Democratic Party

509.3 Abbreviations

Capitalize abbreviations of titles and organizations. (Some other abbreviations are also capitalized. See pages 513–514.)

AAA   CEO   NAACP   M.D.   Ph.D.

509.4 Words Used as Names

Capitalize words like *father, mother, uncle,* and *senator* when they are used as titles with a personal name or when they are substituted for proper nouns (especially in direct address).

We've missed you, Aunt Lucinda! (*Aunt* is part of the name.)

I hope Mayor Bates arrives soon. (*Mayor* is part of the name.)

A Closer Look To test whether a word is being substituted for a proper noun, simply read the sentence with a proper noun in place of the word. If the proper noun fits in the sentence, the word being tested should be capitalized; if the proper noun does not work in the sentence, the word should not be capitalized.

Did Mom (Sue) say we could go? (*Sue* works in this sentence.)

Did your mom (Sue) say you could go? (*Sue* does not work here.)

NOTE: Usually the word is not capitalized if it follows a possessive—*my, his, your*—as it does in the second sentence above.

509.5 Titles of Courses

Capitalize words like *sociology* and *history* when they are used as titles of specific courses; do not capitalize these words when they name a field of study.

Who teaches History 202? (title of a specific course)

It's the same professor who teaches my sociology course. (a field of study)

NOTE: The words *freshman, sophomore, junior,* and *senior* are not capitalized unless they are part of an official title.

Rosa is a senior this year and is in charge of the Senior Class Banquet.

Plurals

510.1 Most Nouns

Form the **plurals** of most nouns by adding *s* to the singular.

cheerleader – cheerleaders   wheel – wheels   crate – crates

510.2 Nouns Ending in *sh, ch, x, s,* and *z*

Form the plurals of nouns ending in *sh, ch, x, s,* and *z* by adding *es* to the singular.

lunch – lunches   dish – dishes   mess – messes   fox – foxes

510.3 Nouns Ending in *y*

The plurals of common nouns that end in *y*—preceded by a consonant—are formed by changing the *y* to *i* and adding *es.*

fly – flies   jalopy – jalopies

The plurals of nouns that end in *y* and are preceded by a vowel are formed by adding only an *s.*

donkey – donkeys   monkey – monkeys

NOTE: Form the plurals of all proper nouns ending in *y* by adding *s.*

We have three Kathys in our English class.

510.4 Nouns Ending in *o*

The plurals of nouns ending in *o*—preceded by a vowel—are formed by adding an *s.*

radio – radios   rodeo – rodeos   studio – studios   duo – duos

The plurals of most nouns ending in *o* and preceded by a consonant are formed by adding *es.*

echo – echoes   hero – heroes   tomato – tomatoes

Exception: Musical terms always form plurals by adding *s.*

alto – altos   banjo – banjos   solo – solos   piano – pianos

510.5 Nouns Ending in *f* or *fe*

Form the plurals of nouns that end in *f* or *fe* in one of two ways: if the final *f* sound is still heard in the plural form of the word, simply add *s;* but if the final *f* sound becomes a *v* sound, change the *f* to *ve* and add *s.*

Plural ends with *f* sound: roof – roofs; chief – chiefs
Plural ends with *v* sound: wife – wives; loaf – loaves

NOTE: Several words are correct with either ending.

Plural ends with either sound: hoof – hooves/hoofs

511.1 Irregular Spelling

A number of words form a plural by taking on an irregular spelling.

crisis – crises	child – children	radius – radii
criterion – criteria	goose – geese	die – dice

NOTE: Some of these words are now acceptable with the commonly used *s* or *es* ending.

index – **indices/indexes**   **cactus** – **cacti/cactuses**

Some nouns remain unchanged when used as plurals.

deer   sheep   salmon   aircraft   series

511.2 Words Discussed as Words

The plurals of symbols, letters, numbers, and words being discussed as words are formed by adding an apostrophe and an *s*.

Dad yelled a lot of *wow*'s and *yippee*'s when he saw my A's and B's.

NOTE: You may omit the apostrophe if it does not cause any confusion.

the three R's or Rs   YMCA's or YMCAs

511.3 Nouns Ending in *ful*

Form the plurals of nouns that end in *ful* by adding an *s* at the end of the word.

two tankfuls   three pailfuls   four mouthfuls

NOTE: Do not confuse these examples with *three pails full* (when you are referring to three separate pails full of something) or *two tanks full*.

511.4 Compound Nouns

Form the plurals of most compound nouns by adding *s* or *es* to the important word in the compound.

brothers-in-law   maids of honor   secretaries of state

511.5 Collective Nouns

A collective noun may be singular or plural depending upon how it's used. A collective noun is singular when it refers to a group considered as one unit; it is plural when it refers to the individuals in the group.

The class was on its best behavior. (group as a unit)

The class are preparing for their final exams. (individuals in the group)

If it seems awkward to use a plural verb with a collective noun, add a clearly plural noun such as *members* to the sentence.

The class members are preparing for their final exams.

You may also change the collective noun into a possessive followed by a plural noun that describes the individuals in the group.

The class's students are preparing for their final exams.

Numbers

512.1 Numerals or Words

Numbers from one to nine are usually written as words; numbers 10 and over are usually written as numerals.

two   seven   nine   10   25   106   1,079

Exception: Numbers being compared or contrasted should be kept in the same style.

8 to 11 years old   eight to eleven years old

You may use a combination of numerals and words for very large numbers.

1.5 million   3 billion to 3.2 billion   6 trillion

If numbers are used infrequently in a piece of writing, you may spell out those that can be written in no more than two words.

ten   twenty-five   two hundred   fifty thousand

512.2 Numerals Only

Use numerals for the following forms: decimals, percentages, chapters, pages, addresses, phone numbers, identification numbers, and statistics.

26.2	**8 percent**	**Highway 36**	**chapter 7**
pages 287-89	**July 6, 1945**	**44 B.C.E.**	**a vote of 23 to 4**

Always use numerals with abbreviations and symbols.

8%   10 mm   3 cc   8 oz   90° C   24 mph   76.9%

512.3 Words Only

Use words to express numbers that begin a sentence.

Fourteen students "forgot" their assignments.

NOTE: Change the sentence structure if this rule creates a clumsy construction.

Clumsy: ***Six hundred thirty-nine* teachers were laid off this year.**

Better: **This year, 639 teachers were laid off.**

Use words for numbers that come before a compound modifier if that modifier includes another number.

They made twelve 10-foot sub sandwiches for the picnic.

512.4 Time and Money

If time is expressed with an abbreviation, use numerals; if it is expressed in words, spell out the number.

4:00 A.M. (or) four o'clock

If an amount of money is spelled out, so is the currency; if a symbol is used, use a numeral.

twenty dollars (or) $20

Abbreviations

513.1 Formal and Informal Abbreviations

An **abbreviation** is the shortened form of a word or phrase. Some abbreviations are always acceptable in both formal and informal writing:

Mr. Mrs. Jr. Ms. Dr. a.m. (A.M.) p.m. (P.M.)

NOTE: In most of your writing, you **do not** abbreviate the names of states, countries, months, days, or units of measure. Do not abbreviate the words *Street, Road, Avenue, Company,* and similar words, especially when they are part of a proper name. Also, do not use signs or symbols (%, &, #, @) in place of words. The dollar sign, however, is appropriate with numerals ($325).

513.2 Correspondence Abbreviations

United States

	Standard	Postal
Alabama	Ala.	AL
Alaska	Alaska	AK
Arizona	Ariz.	AZ
Arkansas	Ark.	AR
California	Calif.	CA
Colorado	Colo.	CO
Connecticut	Conn.	CT
Delaware	Del.	DE
District of Columbia	D.C.	DC
Florida	Fla.	FL
Georgia	Ga.	GA
Guam	Guam	GU
Hawaii	Hawaii	HI
Idaho	Idaho	ID
Illinois	Ill.	IL
Indiana	Ind.	IN
Iowa	Iowa	IA
Kansas	Kan.	KS
Kentucky	Ky.	KY
Louisiana	La.	LA
Maine	Maine	ME
Maryland	Md.	MD
Massachusetts	Mass.	MA
Michigan	Mich.	MI
Minnesota	Minn.	MN
Mississippi	Miss.	MS
Missouri	Mo.	MO
Montana	Mont.	MT
Nebraska	Neb.	NE
Nevada	Nev.	NV
New Hampshire	N.H.	NH
New Jersey	N.J.	NJ
New Mexico	N.M.	NM
New York	N.Y.	NY
North Carolina	N.C.	NC
North Dakota	N.D.	ND
Ohio	Ohio	OH
Oklahoma	Okla.	OK
Oregon	Ore.	OR
Pennsylvania	Pa.	PA
Puerto Rico	P.R.	PR
Rhode Island	R.I.	RI
South Carolina	S.C.	SC
South Dakota	S.D.	SD
Tennessee	Tenn.	TN
Texas	Texas	TX
Utah	Utah	UT
Vermont	Vt.	VT
Virginia	Va.	VA
Virgin Islands	V.I.	VI
Washington	Wash.	WA
West Virginia	W.Va.	WV
Wisconsin	Wis.	WI
Wyoming	Wyo.	WY

Canadian Provinces

	Standard	Postal
Alberta	Alta.	AB
British Columbia	B.C.	BC
Labrador	Lab.	NL
Manitoba	Man.	MB
New Brunswick	N.B.	NB
Newfoundland	N.F.	NL
Northwest Territories	N.W.T.	NT
Nova Scotia	N.S.	NS
Nunavut		NU
Ontario	Ont.	ON
Prince Edward Island	P.E.I.	PE
Quebec	Que.	QC
Saskatchewan	Sask.	SK
Yukon Territory	Y.T.	YT

Addresses

	Standard	Postal
Apartment	Apt.	APT
Avenue	Ave.	AVE
Boulevard	Blvd.	BLVD
Circle	Cir.	CIR
Court	Ct.	CT
Drive	Dr.	DR
East	E.	E
Expressway	Expy.	EXPY
Freeway	Fwy.	FWY
Heights	Hts.	HTS
Highway	Hwy.	HWY
Hospital	Hosp.	HOSP
Junction	Junc.	JCT
Lake	L.	LK
Lakes	Ls.	LKS
Lane	Ln.	LN
Meadows	Mdws.	MDWS
North	N.	N
Palms	Palms	PLMS
Park	Pk.	PK
Parkway	Pky.	PKY
Place	Pl.	PL
Plaza	Plaza	PLZ
Post Office Box	P.O. Box	PO BOX
Ridge	Rdg.	RDG
River	R.	RV
Road	Rd.	RD
Room	Rm.	RM
Rural	R.	R
Rural Route	R.R.	RR
Shore	Sh.	SH
South	S.	S
Square	Sq.	SQ
Station	Sta.	STA
Street	St.	ST
Suite	Ste.	STE
Terrace	Ter.	TER
Turnpike	Tpke.	TPKE
Union	Un.	UN
View	View	VW
Village	Vil.	VLG
West	W.	W

514.1 Other Common Abbreviations

abr. abridged; abridgment
AC, ac alternating current
ack. acknowledge; acknowledgment
acv actual cash value
A.D. in the year of the Lord (Latin *anno Domini*)
AM amplitude modulation
A.M., a.m. before noon (Latin *ante meridiem*)
ASAP as soon as possible
avg., av. average
BBB Better Business Bureau
B.C. before Christ
B.C.E. before the Common Era
bibliog. bibliographer; bibliography
biog. biographer; biographical; biography
C 1. Celsius 2. centigrade 3. coulomb
c. 1. circa (about) 2. cup
cc 1. cubic centimeter 2. carbon copy
CDT, C.D.T. central daylight time
C.E. of the Common Era
chap. chapter
cm centimeter
c.o., c/o care of
COD, C.O.D 1. cash on delivery 2. collect on delivery
co-op. cooperative
CST, C.S.T. central standard time
cu., c cubic
D.A. district attorney
d.b.a. doing business as
DC, dc direct current
dec. deceased
dept. department
DST, D.S.T. daylight saving time
dup. duplicate
DVD digital video disc
ea. each
ed. edition; editor
EDT, E.D.T. eastern daylight time
e.g. for example (Latin *exempli gratia*)
EST, E.S.T. eastern standard time
etc. and so forth (Latin *et cetera*)
ex. example
F Fahrenheit
FM frequency modulation
F.O.B., f.o.b. free on board
ft foot
g 1. gram 2. gravity
gal. gallon
gloss. glossary
GNP gross national product
hdqrs, HQ headquarters

HIV human immunodeficiency virus
Hon. Honorable (title)
hp horsepower
HTML hypertext markup language
Hz hertz
ibid. in the same place (Latin *ibidem*)
id. the same (Latin *idem*)
i.e. that is (Latin *id est*)
illus. illustration
inc. incorporated
IQ, I.Q. intelligence quotient
IRS Internal Revenue Service
ISBN International Standard Book Number
Jr., jr. junior
K 1. kelvin (temperature unit) 2. Kelvin (temperature scale)
kc kilocycle
kg kilogram
km kilometer
kn knot
kw kilowatt
l liter
lat. latitude
lb, lb. pound (Latin *libra*)
l.c. lowercase
lit. literary; literature
log logarithm
long. longitude
Ltd., ltd. limited
m meter
M.A. master of arts (Latin *Magister Artium*)
Mc, mc megacycle
M.C., m.c. master of ceremonies
M.D. doctor of medicine (Latin *medicinae doctor*)
mdse. merchandise
mfg. manufacturing
mg milligram
mi. 1. mile 2. mill (monetary unit)
misc. miscellaneous
ml milliliter
mm millimeter
mpg, m.p.g. miles per gallon
mph, m.p.h. miles per hour
MS 1. manuscript 2. Mississippi 3. multiple sclerosis
Ms., Ms title of courtesy for a woman
MST, M.S.T. mountain standard time
neg. negative
N.S.F., n.s.f. not sufficient funds
oz, oz. ounce
PA 1. public-address system 2. Pennsylvania
pct. percent
pd. paid
PDT, P.D.T. Pacific daylight time

PFC, Pfc. private first class
pg., p. page
P.M., p.m. after noon (Latin *post meridiem*)
P.O. 1. personnel officer 2. purchase order 3. postal order; post office 4. (also **p.o.**) petty officer
pop. population
POW, P.O.W. prisoner of war
pp. pages
ppd. 1. postpaid 2. prepaid
PR, P.R. 1. public relations 2. Puerto Rico
P.S. post script
psi, p.s.i. pounds per square inch
PST, P.S.T. Pacific standard time
PTA, P.T.A. Parent-Teachers Association
qt. quart
RF radio frequency
RN registered nurse
R.P.M., rpm revolutions per minute
R.S.V.P., r.s.v.p. please reply (French *répondez s'il vous plaît*)
SASE self-addressed stamped envelope
SCSI small computer system interface
SOS 1. international distress signal 2. any call for help
Sr. 1. senior (after surname) 2. sister (religious)
ST standard time
St. 1. saint 2. strait 3. street
std. standard
syn. synonymous; synonym
TBA to be announced
tbs, tbsp tablespoon
TM trademark
tsp teaspoon
UHF, uhf ultra high frequency
UPC universal product code
UV ultraviolet
V 1. *Physics:* velocity 2. *Electricity:* volt 3. volume
V.A., VA Veterans Administration
VHF, vhf very high frequency
VIP *Informal:* very important person
vol. 1. volume 2. volunteer
vs. versus
W 1. *Electricity:* watt 2. *Physics:* (also **w**) work 3. west
whse., whs. warehouse
wkly. weekly
w/o without
wt. weight
yd yard (measurement)

Acronyms and Initialisms

515.1 Acronyms

An **acronym** is a word formed from the first (or first few) letters of words in a phrase. Even though acronyms are abbreviations, they require no periods.

radar **radio detecting and ranging**
CARE **Cooperative for American Relief Everywhere**
NASA **National Aeronautics and Space Administration**
VISTA **Volunteers in Service to America**
LAN **local area network**

515.2 Initialisms

An **initialism** is similar to an acronym except that the initials used to form this abbreviation are pronounced individually.

CIA **Central Intelligence Agency**
FBI **Federal Bureau of Investigation**
FHA **Federal Housing Administration**

515.3 Common Acronyms and Initialisms

ADD	attention deficit disorder	**LLC**	limited liability company
AIDS	acquired immunodeficiency syndrome	**MADD**	Mothers Against Drunk Driving
AKA	also known as	**MRI**	Magnetic Resonance Imaging
ATM	automatic teller machine	**NASA**	National Aeronautics and Space Administration
BMI	body mass index	**NATO**	North Atlantic Treaty Organization
CD	compact disc		
DMV	Department of Motor Vehicles	**OPEC**	Organization of Petroleum-Exporting Countries
ETA	expected time of arrival	**OSHA**	Occupational Safety and Health Administration
FAA	Federal Aviation Administration		
FTC	Federal Trade Commission	**PAC**	political action committee
FCC	Federal Communications Commission	**PDF**	portable document format
FDA	Food and Drug Administration	**PETA**	People for the Ethical Treatment of Animals
FDIC	Federal Deposit Insurance Corporation	**PIN**	personal identification number
FEMA	Federal Emergency Management Agency	**PSA**	public service announcement
		ROTC	Reserve Officers' Training Corps
FYI	for your information	**SADD**	Students Against Destructive Decisions
GPS	global positioning system		
HDTV	high-definition television	**SUV**	sport utility vehicle
IRS	Internal Revenue Service	**SWAT**	Special Weapons and Tactics
IT	information technology	**TDD**	telecommunications device for the deaf
JPEG	Joint Photographic Experts Group		
LCD	liquid crystal display	**VA**	Veterans Administration

Quick Guide

Spelling Rules

516.1 Write *i* before *e*

Write *i* before *e* except after *c,* or when sounded like *a* as in *neighbor* and *weigh.*

> **relief   receive   perceive   reign   freight   beige**
>
> **Exceptions:** There are a number of exceptions to this rule, including these: **neither, leisure, seize, weird, species, science.**

516.2 Words with Consonant Endings

When a one-syllable word (*bat*) ends in a consonant (*t*) preceded by one vowel (*a*), double the final consonant before adding a suffix that begins with a vowel (*batting*).

> **sum—summary   god—goddess**

NOTE: When a multisyllable word (*control*) ends in a consonant (*l*) preceded by one vowel (*o*), the accent is on the last syllable (*con trol´*), and the suffix begins with a vowel (*ing*)—the same rule holds true: double the final consonant (*controlling*).

> **prefer—preferred   begin—beginning**
> **forget—forgettable   admit—admittance**

516.3 Words with a Silent *e*

If a word ends with a silent *e,* drop the *e* before adding a suffix that begins with a vowel. Do not drop the *e* when the suffix begins with a consonant.

> **state—stating—statement   like—liking—likeness**
> **use—using—useful   nine—ninety—nineteen**

Exceptions: judgment, truly, argument, ninth

516.4 Words Ending in *y*

When *y* is the last letter in a word and the *y* is preceded by a consonant, change the *y* to *i* before adding any suffix except those beginning with *i.*

> **fry—fries—frying   hurry—hurried—hurrying   lady—ladies**
> **ply—pliable   happy—happiness   beauty—beautiful**

When *y* is the last letter in a word and the *y* is preceded by a vowel, do not change the *y* to *i* before adding a suffix.

> **play—plays—playful   stay—stays—staying   employ—employed**

Important reminder: Never trust your spelling to even the best spell-checker. Use a dictionary for words your spell-checker may not cover.

Commonly Misspelled Words

A

abbreviate
abrupt
abscess
absence
absolute (ly)
absorbent
absurd
abundance
accede
accelerate
accept (ance)
accessible
accessory
accidentally
accommodate
accompany
accomplice
accomplish
accordance
according
account
accrued
accumulate
accurate
accustom (ed)
ache
achieve (ment)
acknowledge
acquaintance
acquiesce
acquired
actual
adapt
addition (al)
address
adequate
adjourned
adjustment
admirable
admissible
admittance
advantageous
advertisement
advertising
advice (n.)
advisable

advise (v.)
aerial
affect
affidavit
again
against
aggravate
aggression
agreeable
agreement
aisle
alcohol
alignment
alley
allotted
allowance
all right
almost
already
although
altogether
aluminum
always
amateur
amendment
among
amount
analysis
analyze
ancient
anecdote
anesthetic
angle
annihilate
anniversary
announce
annoyance
annual
anoint
anonymous
answer
antarctic
anticipate
anxiety
anxious
anything
apartment
apologize
apparatus

apparent (ly)
appeal
appearance
appetite
appliance
applicable
application
appointment
appraisal
appreciate
approach
appropriate
approval
approximately
architect
arctic
argument
arithmetic
arouse
arrangement
arrival
article
artificial
ascend
ascertain
asinine
assassin
assess (ment)
assignment
assistance
associate
association
assume
assurance
asterisk
athlete
athletic
attach
attack (ed)
attempt
attendance
attention
attitude
attorney
attractive
audible
audience
authority
automobile

autumn
auxiliary
available
average
awful
awfully
awkward

B

bachelor
baggage
balance
balloon
ballot
banana
bandage
bankrupt
bargain
barrel
basement
basis
battery
beautiful
beauty
become
becoming
before
beggar
beginning
behavior
being
belief
believe
beneficial
benefit (ed)
between
bicycle
biscuit
blizzard
bookkeeper
bough
bought
bouillon
boundary
breakfast
breath (n.)
breathe (v.)
brief

brilliant
Britain
brochure
brought
bruise
budget
bulletin
buoyant
bureau
burglar
bury
business
busy

C

cafeteria
caffeine
calendar
campaign
canceled
candidate
canister
canoe
can't
capacity
capital
capitol
captain
carburetor
career
caricature
carriage
cashier
casserole
casualty
catalog
catastrophe
caught
cavalry
celebration
cemetery
census
century
certain
certificate
cessation
challenge
changeable

character (istic)
chauffeur
chief
chimney
chocolate
choice
choose
Christian
circuit
circular
circumstance
civilization
clientele
climate
climb
clothes
coach
cocoa
coercion
collar
collateral
college
colloquial
colonel
color
colossal
column
comedy
coming
commence
commercial
commission
commit
commitment
committed
committee
communicate
community
comparative
comparison
compel
competent
competition
competitively
complain
complement
completely
complexion
compliment
compromise
concede

conceive
concerning
concert
concession
conclude
concrete
concurred
concurrence
condemn
condescend
condition
conference
conferred
confidence
confidential
congratulate
conscience
conscientious
conscious
consensus
consequence
conservative
considerably
consignment
consistent
constitution
contemptible
continually
continue
continuous
control
controversy
convenience
convince
coolly
cooperate
cordial
corporation
correlate
correspond
correspondence
corroborate
cough
couldn't
council
counsel
counterfeit
country
courage
courageous
courteous

courtesy
cousin
coverage
creditor
crisis
criticism
criticize
cruel
curiosity
curious
current
curriculum
custom
customary
customer
cylinder

D

daily
dairy
dealt
debtor
deceased
deceitful
deceive
decided
decision
declaration
decorate
deductible
defendant
defense
deferred
deficit
definite (ly)
definition
delegate
delicious
dependent
depositor
depot
descend
describe
description
desert
deserve
design
desirable
desirous
despair

desperate
despise
dessert
deteriorate
determine
develop
development
device
devise
diamond
diaphragm
diarrhea
diary
dictionary
difference
different
difficulty
dilapidated
dilemma
dining
diploma
director
disagreeable
disappear
disappoint
disapprove
disastrous
discipline
discover
discrepancy
discuss
discussion
disease
dissatisfied
dissipate
distinguish
distribute
divide
divine
divisible
division
doctor
doesn't
dominant
dormitory
doubt
drudgery
dual
duplicate
dyeing
dying

E

eagerly
earnest
economical
economy
ecstasy
edition
effervescent
efficacy
efficiency
eighth
either
elaborate
electricity
elephant
eligible
eliminate
ellipse
embarrass
emergency
eminent
emphasize
employee
employment
emulsion
enclose
encourage
endeavor
endorsement
engineer
English
enormous
enough
enterprise
entertain
enthusiastic
entirely
entrance
envelop (v.)
envelope (n.)
environment
equipment
equipped
equivalent
especially
essential
establish
esteemed
etiquette

evidence
exaggerate
exceed
excellent
except
exceptionally
excessive
excite
executive
exercise
exhaust (ed)
exhibition
exhilaration
existence
exorbitant
expect
expedition
expenditure
expensive
experience
explain
explanation
expression
exquisite
extension
extinct
extraordinary
extremely

F

facilities
fallacy
familiar
famous
fascinate
fashion
fatigue (d)
faucet
favorite
feasible
feature
February
federal
feminine
fertile
fictitious
field
fierce
fiery
finally

financially
foliage
forcible
foreign
forfeit
forgo
formally
formerly
fortunate
forty
forward
fountain
fourth
fragile
frantically
freight
friend
fulfill
fundamental
furthermore
futile

G

gadget
gangrene
garage
gasoline
gauge
genealogy
generally
generous
genius
genuine
geography
ghetto
ghost
glorious
gnaw
government
governor
gracious
graduation
grammar
grateful
gratitude
grease
grief
grievous
grocery
grudge

gruesome
guarantee
guard
guardian
guerrilla
guess
guidance
guide
guilty
gymnasium
gypsy
gyroscope

H

habitat
hammer
handkerchief
handle (d)
handsome
haphazard
happen
happiness
harass
harbor
hastily
having
hazardous
height
hemorrhage
hesitate
hindrance
history
hoarse
holiday
honor
hoping
hopping
horde
horrible
hospital
humorous
hurriedly
hydraulic
hygiene
hymn
hypocrisy

I

iambic
icicle
identical
idiosyncrasy
illegible
illiterate
illustrate
imaginary
imaginative
imagine
imitation
immediately
immense
immigrant
immortal
impatient
imperative
importance
impossible
impromptu
improvement
inalienable
incidentally
inconvenience
incredible
incurred
indefinitely
indelible
independence
independent
indictment
indispensable
individual
inducement
industrial
industrious
inevitable
inferior
inferred
infinite
inflammable
influential
ingenious
ingenuous
inimitable
initial
initiation
innocence
innocent

inoculation
inquiry
installation
instance
instead
institute
insurance
intellectual
intelligence
intention
intercede
interesting
interfere
intermittent
interpret (ed)
interrupt
interview
intimate
invalid
investigate
investor
invitation
iridescent
irrelevant
irresistible
irreverent
irrigate
island
issue
itemized
itinerary
it's (it is)

J

janitor
jealous (y)
jeopardize
jewelry
journal
journey
judgment
justice
justifiable

K

kitchen
knowledge
knuckle

L

label
laboratory
lacquer
language
laugh
laundry
lawyer
league
lecture
legal
legible
legislature
legitimate
leisure
length
letterhead
liability
liable
liaison
library
license
lieutenant
lightning
likable
likely
lineage
liquefy
liquid
listen
literary
literature
livelihood
living
logarithm
loneliness
loose
lose
losing
lovable
lovely
luncheon
luxury

M

machine
magazine
magnificent
maintain

maintenance
majority
making
management
maneuver
manual
manufacture
manuscript
marriage
marshal
material
mathematics
maximum
mayor
meanness
meant
measure
medicine
medieval
mediocre
medium
memorandum
menus
merchandise
merit
message
mileage
millionaire
miniature
minimum
minute
mirror
miscellaneous
mischief
mischievous
miserable
misery
missile
missionary
misspell
moisture
molecule
momentous
monotonous
monument
mortgage
municipal
muscle
musician
mustache
mysterious

N

naive
naturally
necessary
necessity
negligible
negotiate
neighborhood
nevertheless
nickel
niece
nineteenth
ninety
noticeable
notoriety
nuclear
nuisance

O

obedience
obey
oblige
obstacle
occasion
occasionally
occupant
occur
occurred
occurrence
offense
official
often
omission
omitted
operate
opinion
opponent
opportunity
opposite
optimism
ordinance
ordinarily
original
outrageous

P

pageant
paid
pamphlet

paradise
paragraph
parallel
paralyze
parentheses (pl.)
parenthesis (s.)
parliament
partial
participant
participate
particularly
pastime
patience
patronage
peculiar
perceive
perhaps
peril
permanent
permissible
perpendicular
perseverance
persistent
personal (ly)
personnel
perspiration
persuade
phase
phenomenon
philosophy
physician
piece
planned
plateau
plausible
playwright
pleasant
pleasure
pneumonia
politician
possess
possession
possible
practically
prairie
precede
precedence
preceding
precious
precisely
precision

predecessor
preferable
preference
preferred
prejudice
preliminary
premium
preparation
presence
prevalent
previous
primitive
principal
principle
priority
prisoner
privilege
probably
procedure
proceed
professor
prominent
pronounce
pronunciation
propaganda
prosecute
protein
psychology
publicly
pumpkin
purchase
pursue
pursuing
pursuit

Q

qualified
quantity
quarter
questionnaire
quiet
quite
quotient

R

raise
rapport
realize
really

recede
receipt
receive
received
recipe
recipient
recognition
recognize
recommend
recurrence
reference
referred
rehearse
reign
reimburse
relevant
relieve
religious
remember
remembrance
reminisce
rendezvous
renewal
repetition
representative
requisition
reservoir
resistance
respectably
respectfully
respectively
responsibility
restaurant
rheumatism
rhyme
rhythm
ridiculous
route

S

sacrilegious
safety
salary
sandwich
satisfactory
Saturday
scarcely
scene
scenery
schedule

science
scissors
secretary
seize
sensible
sentence
sentinel
separate
sergeant
several
severely
shepherd
sheriff
shining
siege
significance
similar
simultaneous
since
sincerely
skiing
soldier
solemn
sophisticated
sophomore
sorority
source
souvenir
spaghetti
specific
specimen
speech
sphere
sponsor
spontaneous
stationary
stationery
statistic
statue
stature
statute
stomach
stopped
straight
strategy
strength
stretched
studying
subsidize
substantial
substitute

subtle
succeed
success
sufficient
summarize
superficial
superintendent
superiority
supersede
supplement
suppose
surely
surprise
surveillance
survey
susceptible
suspicious
sustenance
syllable
symmetrical
sympathy
symphony
symptom
synchronous

T

tariff
technique
telegram
temperament
temperature
temporary
tendency
tentative
terrestrial
terrible
territory
theater
their
therefore
thief
thorough (ly)
though
throughout
tired
tobacco
together
tomorrow
tongue
tonight

touch
tournament
tourniquet
toward
tragedy
traitor
tranquilizer
transferred
treasurer
tried
truly
Tuesday
tuition
typical
typing

U

unanimous
unconscious
undoubtedly
unfortunately
unique
unison
university
unnecessary
unprecedented
until
upper
urgent
usable
useful
using
usually
utensil
utilize

V

vacancies
vacation
vacuum
vague
valuable
variety
various
vegetable
vehicle
veil
velocity
vengeance

vicinity
view
vigilance
villain
violence
visibility
visible
visitor
voice
volume
voluntary
volunteer

W

wander
warrant
weather
Wednesday
weird
welcome
welfare
where
whether
which
whole
wholly
whose
width
women
worthwhile
worthy
wreckage
wrestler
writing
written
wrought

Y

yellow
yesterday
yield

Steps to Becoming a Better Speller

1. **Be patient.**
   Becoming a good speller takes time.

2. **Check the correct pronunciation of each word you are attempting to spell.**
   Knowing the correct pronunciation of a word can help you remember its spelling.

3. **Note the meaning and history of each word as you are checking the dictionary for pronunciation.**
   Knowing the meaning and history of a word provides you with a better notion of how the word is properly used, and this can help you remember its spelling.

4. **Before you close the dictionary, practice spelling the word.**
   Look away from the page and try to "see" the word in your mind. Then write it on a piece of paper. Check your spelling in the dictionary; repeat the process until you are able to spell the word correctly.

5. **Learn some spelling rules.**
   This handbook contains four of the most useful rules. (See page 516.)

6. **Make a list of the words that you often misspell.**
   Select the first 10 and practice spelling them.

   STEP A: Read each word carefully; then write it on a piece of paper. Check to see that you've spelled it correctly. Repeat this step for the words that you misspelled.

   STEP B: When you have finished your first 10 words, ask someone to read them to you as you write them again. Then check for misspellings. If you find none, congratulations! (Repeat both steps with your next 10 words, and so on.)

7. **Write often.**

"There is little point in learning to spell if you have little intention of writing."

—Frank Smith

"The difference between the right word and the nearly right word is the same as that between lightning and the lightning bug."

—Mark Twain

Using the
RIGHT WORD

a lot ■ *A lot* (always two words) is a vague descriptive phrase that should be used sparingly.

> **"You can observe a lot just by watching."** — Yogi Berra

accept, except ■ The verb *accept* means "to receive" or "to believe"; the preposition *except* means "other than."

> **The principal accepted the boy's story about the broken window, but she asked why no one except him saw the ball accidentally slip from his hand.**

adapt, adopt ■ *Adapt* means "to adjust or change to fit"; *adopt* means "to choose and treat as your own" (a child, an idea).

> **After a lengthy period of study, Malcolm X adopted the Islamic faith and adapted to its lifestyle.**

affect, effect ■ The verb *affect* means "to influence"; the verb *effect* means "to produce, accomplish, complete."

> **Ming's hard work effected an A on the test, which positively affected her semester grade.**

The noun *effect* means the "result."

> **Good grades have a calming effect on parents.**

aisle, isle ■ An *aisle* is a passage between seats; an *isle* is a small island.

> **Many airline passengers on their way to the Isle of Capri prefer an aisle seat.**

all right ■ *All right* is always two words (not *alright*).

allusion, illusion ■ *Allusion* is an indirect reference to someone or something; *illusion* is a false picture or idea.

> **My little sister, under the illusion that she's movie-star material, makes frequent allusions to her future fans.**

already, all ready ■ *Already* is an adverb meaning "before this time" or "by this time." *All ready* is an adjective meaning "fully prepared."

NOTE: Use *all ready* if you can substitute *ready* alone in the sentence.

> Although I've already had some dessert, I am all ready for some ice cream from the street vendor.

altogether, all together ■ *Altogether* means "entirely." The phrase *all together* means "in a group" or "all at once."

> "There is altogether too much gridlock," complained the Democrats. All together, the Republicans yelled, "No way!"

among, between ■ *Among* is used when speaking of more than two persons or things. *Between* is used when speaking of only two.

> The three of us talked among ourselves to decide between going out or eating in.

amount, number ■ *Amount* is used for bulk measurement. *Number* is used to count separate units. (See also *fewer, less.*)

> A number of chocolate bars contain a substantial amount of caffeine.

annual, biannual, semiannual, biennial, perennial ■ An *annual* event happens once every year. A *biannual* or *semiannual* event happens twice a year. A *biennial* event happens every two years. A *perennial* event is one that is persistent or constant.

> Dad's annual family reunion gets bigger every year.
> We're going shopping at the department store's semiannual white sale.
> Due to dwindling attendance, the county fair is now a biennial celebration.
> A perennial plant persists for several years.

anyway ■ Do not add an *s* to *anyway*.

ascent, assent ■ *Ascent* is the act of rising or climbing; *assent* is "to agree to something after some consideration" (or such an agreement).

> The group's ascent of the butte was completed with the assent of the landowner.

bad, badly ■ *Bad* is an adjective. *Badly* is an adverb.

> This apple is bad, but one bad apple doesn't always ruin the whole bushel.
> In today's game, Ross passed badly.

base, bass ■ *Base* is the foundation or the lower part of something. *Bass* is a deep sound or tone. *Bass* (when pronounced like *class*) is a fish.

beside, besides ■ *Beside* means "by the side of." *Besides* means "in addition to."

> **Mother always grew roses beside the trash bin. Besides looking nice, they also gave off a sweet smell that masked odors.**

board, bored ■ *Board* is a piece of wood. *Board* is also an administrative group or council.

> **The school board approved the purchase of fifty 1- by 6-inch pine boards.**

Bored is the past tense of the verb "bore," which may mean "to make a hole by drilling" or "to become weary out of dullness."

> **Watching television bored Joe, so he took his drill and bored a hole in the wall where he could hang his new clock.**

brake, break ■ *Brake* is a device used to stop a vehicle. *Break* means "to separate or to destroy."

> **I hope the brakes on my car never break.**

bring, take ■ *Bring* suggests the action is directed toward the speaker; *take* suggests the action is directed away from the speaker.

> **I'll bring home some garbage bags so you can take the trash outside.**

can, may ■ *Can* suggests ability while *may* suggests permission.

> **"Can I go to the mall?" means "Am I physically able to go to the mall?"**
>
> **"May I go to the mall?" asks permission to go.**

capital, capitol ■ The noun *capital* refers to a city or to money. The adjective *capital* means "major or important." *Capitol* refers to a building.

> **The state capital is home to the capitol building for a capital reason. The state government contributed capital for its construction.**

cent, sent, scent ■ *Cent* is a coin; *sent* is the past tense of the verb "send"; *scent* is an odor or a smell.

> **For thirty-seven cents, I sent my girlfriend a mushy love poem in a perfumed envelope. She adored the scent but hated the poem.**

cereal, serial ■ *Cereal* is a grain, often made into breakfast food. *Serial* relates to something in a series.

> **Mohammed enjoys reading serial novels while he eats a bowl of cereal.**

chord, cord ■ *Chord* may mean "an emotion" or "a combination of musical tones sounded at the same time." A *cord* is a string or a rope.

> **The guitar player strummed the opening chord to the group's hit song, which struck a responsive chord with the audience.**

chose, choose ■ *Chose* (chōz) is the past tense of the verb *choose* (chōōz).

Last quarter I chose to read Martin Luther King's *Strength to Love*—a book that says it takes strength to choose a nonviolent response to injustice.

coarse, course ■ *Coarse* means "rough or crude"; *course* means "a path or direction taken." *Course* also means "a class or a series of studies."

Fletcher, known for using coarse language, was barred from the golf course until he took an etiquette course.

complement, compliment ■ *Complement* refers to that which completes or fulfills. *Compliment* is an expression of admiration or praise.

Kimberly smiled, thinking she had received a compliment, when Carlos said that her new chihuahua complemented her personality.

continual, continuous ■ *Continual* refers to something that happens again and again with some breaks or pauses; *continuous* refers to something that keeps happening, uninterrupted.

Sunlight hits Iowa on a continual basis; sunlight hits Earth continuously.

counsel, council ■ When used as a noun, *counsel* means "advice"; when used as a verb, it means "to advise." *Council* refers to a group that advises.

The student council counseled all freshmen to join at least one school club. That's good counsel.

desert, dessert ■ The noun *desert* (dez´ert) refers to barren wilderness. *Dessert* (di zûrt´) is food served at the end of a meal.

The scorpion tiptoed through the moonlit desert, searching for dessert.

The verb *desert* (di zûrt´) means "to abandon"; the noun *desert* (di zûrt´) means "deserved reward or punishment."

The burglar's hiding place deserted him when the spotlight swung his way; his subsequent arrest was his just desert.

die, dye ■ *Die* (dying) means "to stop living." *Dye* (dyeing) is used to change the color of something.

different from, different than ■ Use *different from* in a comparison of two things. *Different than* should be used only when followed by a clause.

Yassine is quite different from his brother.

Life is different than it used to be.

farther, further ■ *Farther* refers to a physical distance; *further* refers to additional time, quantity, or degree.

Alaska extends farther north than Iceland does. Further information can be obtained in an atlas.

fewer, less ■ *Fewer* refers to the number of separate units; *less* refers to bulk quantity.

Because we have fewer orders for cakes, we'll buy less sugar and flour.

flair, flare ■ *Flair* refers to style or natural talent; *flare* means "to light up quickly" or "burst out" (or an object that does so).

Ronni was thrilled with Jorge's flair for decorating—until one of his strategically placed candles flared, marring the wall.

good, well ■ *Good* is an adjective; *well* is nearly always an adverb. (When *well* is used to describe a state of health, it is an adjective: He was happy to be well again.)

The strange flying machines worked well and made our team look good.

heal, heel ■ *Heal* means "to mend or restore to health." A *heel* is the back part of a foot.

Achilles died because a poison arrow pierced his heel and caused a wound that would not heal.

healthful, healthy ■ *Healthful* means "causing or improving health"; *healthy* means "possessing health."

Healthful foods build healthy bodies.

hear, here ■ You *hear* with your ears. *Here* means "the area close by."

heard, herd ■ *Heard* is the past tense of the verb "hear"; *herd* is a large group of animals.

hole, whole ■ A *hole* is a cavity or hollow place. *Whole* means "complete."

idle, idol ■ *Idle* means "not working." An *idol* is someone or something that is worshipped.

The once-popular actress, who had been idle lately, wistfully recalled her days as an idol.

immigrate, emigrate ■ *Immigrate* means "to come into a new country or environment." *Emigrate* means "to go out of one country to live in another."

Martin Ulferts immigrated to this country in 1882. He was only three years old when he emigrated from Germany.

imply, infer ■ *Imply* means "to suggest or express indirectly"; *infer* means "to draw a conclusion from facts." (A writer or speaker implies; a reader or listener infers.)

Dad implied by his comment that I should drive more carefully, and I inferred that he was concerned for both me and his new car.

insure, ensure ■ *Insure* means "to secure from financial harm or loss." *Ensure* means "to make certain of something."

To ensure that you can legally drive that new car, you'll have to insure it.

it's, its ■ *It's* is the contraction of "it is." *Its* is the possessive form of "it."

It's hard to believe, but the movie *Shrek* still holds its appeal for my little sister—even after repeated viewings.

later, latter ■ *Later* means "after a period of time." *Latter* refers to the second of two things mentioned.

Later that year we had our second baby and adopted a stray kitten. The latter was far more welcomed by our toddler.

lay, lie ■ *Lay* means "to place." *Lay* is a transitive verb. (See 539.3.)

Lay your books on the big table.

Lie means "to recline," and *lay* is the past tense of *lie*. *Lie* is an intransitive verb. (See 539.3.)

In this heat, the children must lie down for a nap. Yesterday they lay down without one complaint. Sometimes they have lain in the hammocks to rest.

lead, led ■ *Lead* (lēd) is the present tense of the verb meaning "to guide." The past tense of the verb is *led* (lĕd). The noun *lead* (lĕd) is a metal.

We were led along the path that leads to an abandoned lead mine.

learn, teach ■ *Learn* means "to acquire information." *Teach* means "to give information."

I learn better when people teach with real-world examples.

leave, let ■ *Leave* means "to allow something to remain behind." *Let* means "to permit."

Would you let me leave my bike at your house?

lend, borrow ■ *Lend* means "to give for temporary use." *Borrow* means "to receive for temporary use."

I told Mom I needed to borrow $18 for a CD, but she said she could only lend money for school supplies.

like, as ■ When *like* is used as a preposition meaning "similar to," it can be followed only by a noun, pronoun, or noun phrase; when *as* is used as a subordinating conjunction, it introduces a subordinate clause.

If you want to be a gymnast like her, you'd better practice three hours a day as she does.

medal, meddle ■ *Medal* is an award. *Meddle* means "to interfere."

Many parents meddle in the awards process to make sure that their kids receive medals.

metal, mettle ■ *Metal* is a chemical element like iron or gold. *Mettle* is "strength of spirit."

Grandad's mettle during battle left him with some metal in his shoulder.

miner, minor ■ A *miner* digs for valuable ore. A *minor* is a person who is not legally an adult. A *minor* problem is one of no great importance.

The use of minors as miners is no minor problem.

moral, morale ■ A *moral* is a lesson drawn from a story; as an adjective, it relates to the principles of right and wrong. *Morale* refers to someone's attitude.

Ms. Ladue considers it her moral obligation to go to church every day.

The students' morale sank after their defeat in the forensics competition.

past, passed ■ *Passed* is a verb. *Past* can be used as a noun, an adjective, or a preposition.

That old pickup truck passed my sports car! (verb)

Many senior citizens hold dearly to the past. (noun)

Tilly's past life as a circus worker must have been . . . interesting. (adjective)

Who can walk past a bakery without looking in the window? (preposition)

peace, piece ■ *Peace* means "tranquility or freedom from war." *Piece* is a part or fragment.

Grandma often sits and rocks in the peace and quiet of the parlor, enjoying a piece of pie or cake.

peak, peek, pique ■ A *peak* is a high point. *Peek* means "brief look" (or "look briefly"). *Pique*, as a verb, means "to excite by challenging"; as a noun, it is a feeling of resentment.

The peak of Dr. Fedder's professional life was his ability to pique children's interest in his work.

"Take a peek at this slide," the doctor urged her colleague.

pedal, peddle, petal ■ A *pedal* is a foot lever; as a verb, it means "to ride a bike." *Peddle* means "to go from place to place selling something." A *petal* is part of a flower.

Don Miller paints beautiful petals on his homemade birdhouses. Then he pedals through the flea market every weekend to peddle them.

personal, personnel ■ *Personal* means "private." *Personnel* are people working at a particular job.

plain, plane ■ *Plain* means "an area of land that is flat or level"; it also means "clearly seen or clearly understood."

It's plain to see why settlers of the Great Plains had trouble moving west.

Plane means "flat, level"; it is also a tool used to smooth the surface of wood.

I used a plane to make the board plane and smooth.

pore, pour, poor ■ A *pore* is an opening in the skin. *Pour* means "to cause to flow in a stream." *Poor* means "needy or pitiable."

Tough exams on late spring days make my poor pores pour sweat.

principal, principle ■ As an adjective, *principal* means "primary." As a noun, it can mean "a school administrator" or "a sum of money." *Principle* means "idea or doctrine."

His principal gripe is lack of freedom. (adjective)
The principal expressed his concern about the open-campus policy. (noun)
During the first year of a loan, you pay more interest than principal. (noun)

The principle of c*aveat emptor* is "Let the buyer beware."

quiet, quit, quite ■ *Quiet* is the opposite of "noisy." *Quit* means "to stop." *Quite* means "completely or entirely."

quote, quotation ■ *Quote* is a verb; *quotation* is a noun.

The quotation I used was from Woody Allen. You may quote me on that.

real, really, very ■ Do not use *real* in place of the adverbs *very* or *really*.

Mother's cake is usually very (not *real*) tasty, but this one is really stale!

right, write, wright, rite ■ *Right* means "correct or proper"; it also refers to that which a person has a legal claim to, as in *copyright*. *Write* means "to inscribe or record." A *wright* is a person who makes or builds something. *Rite* refers to a ritual or ceremonial act.

Write this down: It is the right of the shipwright to perform the rite of christening—breaking a bottle of champagne on the stern of the ship.

ring, wring ■ *Ring* means "encircle" or "to sound by striking." *Wring* means "to squeeze or twist."

At the beach, Grandma would ring her head with a large scarf. Once, it blew into the sea, so she had me wring it out.

scene, seen ■ *Scene* refers to the setting or location where something happens; it also may mean "sight or spectacle." *Seen* is a form of the verb "see."

Serena had seen her boyfriend making a scene; she cringed.

seam, seem ■ *Seam* (noun) is a line formed by connecting two pieces. *Seem* (verb) means "to appear to exist."

The ragged seams in his old coat seem to match the creases in his face.

set, sit ■ *Set* means "to place." *Sit* means "to put the body in a seated position." *Set* is transitive; *sit* is intransitive. (See 539.3.)

How can you just sit there and watch as I set all these chairs in place?

sight, cite, site ■ *Sight* means "the act of seeing"; a *sight* is what is seen. *Cite* means "to quote," or "to summon" as before a court. *Site* means "location."

> **In her report, the general contractor cited several problems at the downtown job site. For one, the loading area was a chaotic sight.**

sole, soul ■ *Sole* means "single, only one"; *sole* also refers to the bottom surface of the foot. *Soul* refers to the spiritual part of a person.

> **As the sole inhabitant of the island, he put his heart and soul into his farming.**

stationary, stationery ■ *Stationary* means "not movable"; *stationery* refers to the paper and envelopes used to write letters.

steal, steel ■ *Steal* means "to take something without permission"; *steel* is a metal.

than, then ■ *Than* is used in a comparison; *then* tells when.

> **Abigail shouted that her big brother was bigger than my big brother. Then she ran away.**

their, there, they're ■ *Their* is a possessive personal pronoun. *There* is an adverb used to point out location. *They're* is the contraction for "they are."

> **They're a well-dressed couple. Do you see them over there, with their matching jackets?**

threw, through ■ *Threw* is the past tense of "throw." *Through* means "from beginning to end."

> **Through seven innings, Egor threw just seven strikes.**

to, too, two ■ *To* is a preposition that can mean "in the direction of." *To* is also used to form an infinitive. (See 540.3) *Too* means "also" or "very." *Two* is the number.

vain, vane, vein ■ *Vain* means "value-less or fruitless"; it may also mean "holding a high regard for oneself." *Vane* is a flat piece of material set up to show which way the wind blows. *Vein* refers to a blood vessel or a mineral deposit.

> **The vain prospector, boasting about the vein of silver he'd uncovered, paused to look up at the turning weather vane.**

vary, very ■ *Vary* means "to change." *Very* means "to a high degree."

Though the weather may vary from day to day, generally, it is very pleasant.

vial, vile ■ A *vial* is a small container for liquid. *Vile* is an adjective meaning "foul, despicable."

It's a vile job, but someone has to clean these lab vials.

waist, waste ■ *Waist* is the part of the body just above the hips. The verb *waste* means "to spend or use carelessly" or "to wear away or decay"; the noun *waste* refers to material that is unused or useless.

Her waist is small because she wastes no opportunity to exercise.

wait, weight ■ *Wait* means "to stay somewhere expecting something." *Weight* refers to a degree or unit of heaviness.

ware, wear, where ■ *Ware* refers to a product that is sold; *wear* means "to have on or to carry on one's body"; *where* asks the question *in what place?* or *in what situation?*

The designer boasted, "Where can anybody wear my ware? Anywhere."

way, weigh ■ *Way* means "path or route." *Weigh* means "to measure weight" or "to have a certain heaviness."

My dogs weigh too much. The best way to reduce is a daily run in the park.

weather, whether ■ *Weather* refers to the condition of the atmosphere. *Whether* refers to a possibility.

Because of the weather forecast, Coach Pennington didn't know whether or not to schedule another practice.

which, that ■ Use *which* to refer to objects or animals in a nonrestrictive clause (set off with commas). Use *that* to refer to objects or animals in a restrictive clause. (For more information about these types of clauses, see 491.2.)

The birds, which stay in the area all winter, know exactly where the feeders are located. The food that attracts the most birds is sunflower seed.

who, whom ■ Use *who* to refer to people. *Who* is used as the subject of a verb in an independent clause or in a relative clause. *Whom* is used as the object of a preposition or as a direct object.

To whom do we owe our thanks for these pizzas? And who ordered that one with pepperoni and pineapple?

who's, whose ■ *Who's* is the contraction for "who is." *Whose* is a pronoun that can show possession or ownership.

Cody, whose car is new, will drive. Who's going to read the map?

your, you're ■ *Your* is a possessive pronoun. *You're* is the contraction for "you are."

Take your boots if you're going out in that snow.

"Don't be afraid to throw more than one verb in a sentence. I think 'She twisted and fell' is more exciting than 'She twisted. She fell to the ground.' "

—Martyn Godfrey

Parts of
SPEECH

Noun

A **noun** is a word that names something: a person, a place, a thing, or an idea.

> **governor Oregon hospital Buddhism love**

Classes of Nouns

The five classes of nouns are *proper, common, concrete, abstract,* and *collective.*

533.1 Proper Noun

A **proper noun** names a particular person, place, thing, or idea. Proper nouns are always capitalized.

> **Jackie Robinson Brooklyn Ebbets Field World Series Christianity**

533.2 Common Noun

A **common noun** does not name a particular person, place, thing, or idea. Common nouns are not capitalized.

> **person woman president park baseball government**

533.3 Concrete Noun

A **concrete noun** names a thing that is tangible (can be seen, touched, heard, smelled, or tasted). Concrete nouns are either proper or common.

> **child Grand Canyon music aroma pizza Beck**

533.4 Abstract Noun

An **abstract noun** names an idea, a condition, or a feeling—in other words, something that cannot be touched, smelled, tasted, seen, or heard.

> **New Deal greed poverty progress freedom hope**

533.5 Collective Noun

A **collective noun** names a group or a unit.

> **United States Portland Cementers team crowd community**

Forms of Nouns

Nouns are grouped according to their *number, gender,* and *case.*

534.1 Number of a Noun

Number indicates whether the noun is singular or plural.

> A **singular noun** refers to one person, place, thing, or idea.
> **actor   stadium   Canadian   bully   truth   child   person**

> A **plural noun** refers to more than one person, place, thing, or idea.
> **actors   stadiums   Canadians   bullies   truths   children   people**

534.2 Gender of a Noun

Gender indicates whether a noun is masculine, feminine, neuter, or indefinite.

> **Masculine: uncle   brother   men   bull   rooster   stallion**
> **Feminine: aunt   sister   women   cow   hen   filly**
> **Neuter** (without gender):
>   **tree   cobweb   closet**
> **Indefinite** (masculine or feminine):
>   **president   plumber   doctor   parent   flying fish**

534.3 Case of a Noun

Case tells how nouns are related to other words used with them. There are three cases: *nominative, possessive,* and *objective.*

- A **nominative case** noun can be the *subject* of a clause.

  > **Patsy's heart was beating very wildly beneath his jacket. . . . That black horse there owed something to the orphan he had made.**
  > —Paul Dunbar, "The Finish of Patsy Barnes"

  A nominative noun can also be a predicate noun (or predicate nominative), which follows a "be" verb (*am, is, are, was, were, be, being, been*) and renames the subject. In the sentence below, *type* renames *Mr. Cattanzara.*

  > **Mr. Cattanzara was a different type than those in the neighborhood.**
  > —Bernard Malamud, "A Summer's Reading"

- A **possessive case** noun shows possession or ownership.

  > **Like the spider's claw, a part of him touches a world he will never enter.**
  > —Loren Eiseley, "The Hidden Teacher"

- An **objective case** noun can be a direct object, an indirect object, or an object of the preposition.

  > **Marna always gives Mylo science-fiction books for his birthday.**
  > (*Mylo* is the indirect object and *books* is the direct object of the verb "gives." *Birthday* is the object of the preposition "for.")

Pronoun

A **pronoun** is a word used in place of a noun.

> I, you, she, it, which, that, themselves, whoever, me, he, they, mine, ours

535.1 Types of Pronouns

There are three types of pronouns: *simple, compound,* and *phrasal.*

Simple:	I, you, he, she, it, we, they, who, what
Compound:	myself, someone, anybody, everything, itself, whoever
Phrasal:	one another, each other

535.2 Antecedent

All pronouns have antecedents. An **antecedent** is the noun that the pronoun refers to or replaces.

> **Ambrosch was considered the important person in the family. Mrs. Shimerda and Ántonia always deferred to him, though he was often surly with them and contemptuous toward his father.** —Willa Cather, *My Ántonia*
> (*Ambrosch* is the antecedent of *him, he,* and *his.*)

NOTE: Each pronoun must agree with its antecedent. (See page 560.)

535.3 Classes of Pronouns

The six classes of pronouns are *personal, reflexive and intensive, relative, indefinite, interrogative,* and *demonstrative.*

PERSONAL
I, me, my, mine / we, us, our, ours
you, your, yours / they, them, their, theirs
he, him, his, she, her, hers, it, its

REFLEXIVE AND INTENSIVE
myself, yourself, himself, herself, itself, ourselves, yourselves, themselves

RELATIVE
what, who, whose, whom, which, that

INDEFINITE

all	both	everything	nobody	several
another	each	few	none	some
any	each one	many	no one	somebody
anybody	either	most	nothing	someone
anyone	everybody	much	one	something
anything	everyone	neither	other	such

INTERROGATIVE
who, whose, whom, which, what

DEMONSTRATIVE
this, that, these, those

536.1 Personal Pronoun

A **personal pronoun** can take the place of any noun.

Our coach made her point loud and clear when she raised her voice.

■ A **reflexive pronoun** is formed by adding -*self* or -*selves* to a personal pronoun. A reflexive pronoun can be a direct object, an indirect object, an object of the preposition, or a predicate nominative.

Miss Sally Sunshine loves herself. (direct object of *loves*)

Tomisha does not seem herself today. (predicate nominative)

■ An **intensive pronoun** is a reflexive pronoun that intensifies, or emphasizes, the noun or pronoun it refers to.

Leo himself taught his children to invest their lives in others.

The dessert the children had baked themselves tasted . . . interesting.

536.2 Relative Pronoun

A **relative pronoun** relates an adjective clause to the noun or pronoun it modifies.

Students who study regularly get the best grades. Surprise!

The dance, which we had looked forward to for weeks, was canceled.

(The relative pronoun *who* relates the adjective clause to *students*; *which* relates the adjective clause to *dance*.)

536.3 Indefinite Pronoun

An **indefinite pronoun** often refers to unnamed or unknown people or things.

I don't know if you've known anybody from that far back; if you've loved anybody that long, first as an infant, then as a child, then as a man. . . . (The antecedent of *anybody* is unknown.)

—James Baldwin, "My Dungeon Shook: Letter to My Nephew"

536.4 Interrogative Pronoun

An **interrogative pronoun** asks a question.

"Then, who are you? Who could you be? What do you want from my husband?"
—Elie Wiesel, "The Scrolls, Too, Are Mortal"

536.5 Demonstrative Pronoun

A **demonstrative pronoun** points out people, places, or things without naming them.

This shouldn't be too hard. That looks about right.

These are the best ones. Those ought to be thrown out.

NOTE: When one of these words precedes a noun, it functions as an adjective, not a pronoun. (See 545.1.)

That movie bothers me. (*That* is an adjective.)

Forms of Personal Pronouns

The form of a personal pronoun indicates its *number* (singular or plural), its *person* (first, second, third), its *case* (nominative, possessive, or objective), and its *gender* (masculine, feminine, or neuter).

537.1 Number of a Pronoun

Personal pronouns are singular or plural. The singular personal pronouns include *my, him, he, she, it.* The plural personal pronouns include *we, you, them, our.* (*You* can be singular or plural.) Notice in the caption below that the first **you** is singular and the second **you** is plural.

Larry, you need to keep all four tires on the road when turning. Are you still with us back there?

537.2 Person of a Pronoun

The **person** of a pronoun indicates whether the person, place, thing, or idea represented by the pronoun is speaking, is spoken to, or is spoken about.

■ **First person** is used in place of the name of the speaker or speakers.

"We don't do things like that," says Pa; "we're just and honest people. . . . I don't skip debts." —Jesse Stuart, "Split Cherry Tree"

■ **Second person** pronouns name the person or persons spoken to.

"If you hit your duck, you want me to go in after it?" Eugie said.
—Gina Berriault, "The Stone Boy"

■ **Third person** pronouns name the person or thing spoken about.

She had hardly realized the news, further than to understand that she had been brought . . . face to face with something unexpected and final. It did not even occur to her to ask for any explanation.
—Joseph Conrad, "The Idiots"

538.1 Case of a Pronoun

The **case** of each pronoun tells how it is related to the other words used with it. There are three cases: *nominative, possessive,* and *objective.*

■ A **nominative case** pronoun can be the subject of a clause. The following are nominative forms: *I, you, he, she, it, we, they.*

> **I like life when things go well.**
> **You must live life in order to love life.**

A nominative pronoun is a *predicate nominative* if it follows a "be" verb (*am, is, are, was, were, be, being, been*) or another linking verb (*appear, become, feel,* etc.) and renames the subject.

> **"Oh, it's only she who scared me just now," said Mama to Papa, glancing over her shoulder.**
> **"Yes, it is I," said Mai in a superior tone.**

■ **Possessive case** pronouns show possession or ownership. Apostrophes, however, are not used with personal pronouns.

> **But as I placed my hand upon his shoulder, there came a strong shudder over his whole person.**
>
> —Edgar Allan Poe, "The Fall of the House of Usher"

■ An **objective case** pronoun can be a direct object, an indirect object, or an object of the preposition.

> **The kids loved it! We lit a campfire for them and told them old ghost stories.** (*It is the direct object of the verb* loved. *Them is the object of the preposition* for *and the indirect object of the verb* told.)

Number, Person, and Case of Personal Pronouns

	Nominative	Possessive	Objective
First Person Singular	I	my, mine	me
Second Person Singular	you	your, yours	you
Third Person Singular	he	his	him
	she	her, hers	her
	it	its	it

	Nominative	Possessive	Objective
First Person Plural	we	our, ours	us
Second Person Plural	you	your, yours	you
Third Person Plural	they	their, theirs	them

538.2 Gender of a Pronoun

Gender indicates whether a pronoun is masculine, feminine, or neuter.

Masculine: **he   him   his**   Feminine: **she   her   hers**

Neuter (without gender): **it   its**

Verb

A **verb** is a word that expresses action (*run, carried, declared*) or state of being (*is, are, seemed*).

Classes of Verbs

539.1 Linking Verbs

A **linking verb** links the subject to a noun or an adjective in the predicate.

On his skateboard, the boy felt confident. He was the best skater around.

<table>
<tr><td colspan="8" align="center">**Common Linking Verbs**</td></tr>
<tr><td>is</td><td>are</td><td>was</td><td>were</td><td>be</td><td>been</td><td>am</td><td>smell</td></tr>
<tr><td>seem</td><td>grow</td><td>become</td><td>appear</td><td>sound</td><td>taste</td><td>feel</td><td>remain</td></tr>
<tr><td>stay</td><td>look</td><td>turn</td><td>get</td><td></td><td></td><td></td><td></td></tr>
</table>

539.2 Auxiliary Verbs

Auxiliary verbs, or helping verbs, are used to form some of the **tenses** (542.3), the **mood** (544.1), and the **voice** (541.1) of the main verb. (In the example below, the auxiliary verbs are in **red**; the main verbs are in green.)

The long procession was led by white-robed priests, their faces streaked with red and yellow and white ash. By this time the flames had stopped spurting, and the pit consisted of a red-hot mass of burning wood, which attendants were leveling with long branches.

—Leonard Feinberg, "Fire Walking in Ceylon"

<table>
<tr><td colspan="9" align="center">**Common Auxiliary Verbs**</td></tr>
<tr><td>is</td><td>was</td><td>being</td><td>did</td><td>have</td><td>would</td><td>shall</td><td>might</td></tr>
<tr><td>am</td><td>were</td><td>been</td><td>does</td><td>had</td><td>could</td><td>can</td><td>must</td></tr>
<tr><td>are</td><td>be</td><td>do</td><td>has</td><td>should</td><td>will</td><td>may</td><td></td></tr>
</table>

539.3 Action Verbs: Transitive and Intransitive

An **intransitive verb** communicates an action that is complete in itself. It does not need an object to receive the action.

The boy flew on his skateboard. He jumped and flipped and twisted.

A **transitive verb** (red) is an action verb that needs an object (green) to complete its meaning.

The city council passed a strict noise ordinance.

While some action verbs are only transitive *or* intransitive, some can be either, depending on how they are used.

He finally stopped to rest. (intransitive)
He finally stopped the show. (transitive)

540.1 Objects with Transitive Verbs

■ A **direct object** receives the action of a transitive verb directly from the subject. Without it, the transitive verb's meaning is incomplete.

> **The boy kicked his skateboard forward.** (*Skateboard* is the direct object.)

■ An **indirect object** also receives the action of a transitive verb, but indirectly. An indirect object names the person *to whom* or *for whom* something is done. (It can also name the thing *to what* or *for what* something is done.)

> **Then he showed us his best tricks.** (*Us* is the indirect object.)

NOTE: When the word naming the indirect receiver of the action is in a prepositional phrase, it is no longer considered an indirect object.

> **Then he showed his best tricks to us.**
> (*Us* is the object of the preposition *to.*)

Verbals

A **verbal** is a word that is derived from a verb but acts as another part of speech. There are three types of verbals: *gerunds, infinitives,* and *participles.* Each is often part of a verbal phrase.

540.2 Gerunds

A **gerund** is a verb form that ends in *ing* and is used as a noun.

> **Swimming is my favorite pastime.** (subject)
> **I began swimming at the age of six months.** (direct object)
> **Swimming in chlorinated pools makes my eyes red.** (gerund phrase as subject)

540.3 Infinitives

An **infinitive** is a verb form that is usually introduced by *to*; the infinitive may be used as a noun, an adjective, or an adverb.

> **Most people find it easy to swim.** (adverb)
> **To swim the English Channel must be a thrill.** (infinitive phrase as noun)
> **The urge to swim in tropical waters is more common.** (infinitive phrase as adjective)

540.4 Participles

A **participle** is a verb form ending in *ing* or *ed* that acts as an adjective.

> **The farmhands harvesting corn are tired and hungry.** (participial phrase modifies *farmhands*)
> **The cribs full of harvested cobs are evidence of their hard work.** (modifies *cobs*)

Forms of Verbs

A verb has different forms depending on its *voice* (active, passive); *number* (singular, plural); *person* (first, second, third); *tense* (present, past, future, present perfect, past perfect, future perfect); and *mood* (indicative, imperative, subjunctive).

541.1 Voice of a Verb

Voice indicates whether the subject is acting or being acted upon.

- **Active voice** indicates that the subject of the verb is, has been, or will be doing something.

  Baseball great Walter Johnson pitched 50 consecutive scoreless innings.

  For many years Lou Brock held the base-stealing record.

  Use the active voice as much as possible because it makes your writing more direct and lively. (See "Passive Style" on page 120.)

- **Passive voice** indicates that the subject of the verb is being, has been, or will be acted upon.

  Fifty consecutive scoreless innings were pitched by baseball great Walter Johnson.

  For many years the base-stealing record was held by Lou Brock.

  NOTE: With a passive verb, the person or thing creating the action is not always stated.

  The ordinance was overturned.

  (It is not clear who did the overturning in this example.)

TENSE	Active Voice		Passive Voice	
	Singular	Plural	Singular	Plural
PRESENT	I see	we see	I am seen	we are seen
	you see	you see	you are seen	you are seen
	he/she/it sees	they see	he/she/it is seen	they are seen
PAST	I saw	we saw	I was seen	we were seen
	you saw	you saw	you were seen	you were seen
	he saw	they saw	it was seen	they were seen
FUTURE	I will see	we will see	I will be seen	we will be seen
	you will see	you will see	you will be seen	you will be seen
	he will see	they will see	it will be seen	they will be seen
PRESENT PERFECT	I have seen	we have seen	I have been seen	we have been seen
	you have seen	you have seen	you have been seen	you have been seen
	he has seen	they have seen	it has been seen	they have been seen
PAST PERFECT	I had seen	we had seen	I had been seen	we had been seen
	you had seen	you had seen	you had been seen	you had been seen
	he had seen	they had seen	it had been seen	they had been seen
FUTURE PERFECT	I will have seen	we will have seen	I will have been seen	we will have been seen
	you will have seen	you will have seen	you will have been seen	you will have been seen
	he will have seen	they will have seen	it will have been seen	they will have been seen

542.1 Number of a Verb

Number indicates whether a verb is singular or plural. In a clause, the verb (in green below) and its subject (in **red**) must both be singular or both be plural.

- **Singular**

  One large island floats off Italy's "toe."

  Italy's northern countryside includes the spectacular Alps.

  The Po Valley stretches between the Alps and the Apennines Mountains.

- **Plural**

  Five small islands float inside Michigan's "thumb."

  The Porcupine Mountains rise above the shores of Lake Superior.

  High bluffs and sand dunes border Lake Michigan.

542.2 Person of a Verb

Person indicates whether the subject of the verb is first, second, or third person (is speaking, is spoken to, or is spoken about). Usually the form of the verb only changes when the verb is in the present tense and is used with a third-person singular pronoun.

	Singular	Plural
First Person	I sniff	we sniff
Second Person	you sniff	you sniff
Third Person	he/she/it sniffs	they sniff

542.3 Tense of a Verb

Tense indicates time. Each verb has three principal parts: the *present, past,* and *past participle.* All six tenses are formed from these principal parts. The past and past participle of regular verbs are formed by adding *ed* to the present form. The past and past participle of irregular verbs are usually different words; however, a few have the same form in all three principal parts. (See page 543.)

- **Present tense** expresses action that is happening at the present time, or action that happens continually, regularly.

  In September, sophomores smirk and joke about the "little freshies."

- **Past tense** expresses action that is completed at a particular time in the past.

  They forgot that just ninety days separated them from freshman status.

- **Future tense** expresses action that will take place in the future.

  They will remember this in three years when they will be freshmen again.

Common Irregular Verbs and Their Principal Parts

Present Tense	Past Tense	Past Participle	Present Tense	Past Tense	Past Participle	Present Tense	Past Tense	Past Participle
am, be	was, were	been	give	gave	given	show	showed	shown
begin	began	begun	go	went	gone	shrink	shrank	shrunk
bite	bit	bitten	grow	grew	grown	sing	sang, sung	sung
blow	blew	blown	hang	hanged	hanged	sink	sank, sunk	sunk
break	broke	broken	(execute)			sit	sat	sat
bring	brought	brought	hang	hung	hung	slay	slew	slain
catch	caught	caught	(suspend)			speak	spoke	spoken
choose	chose	chosen	hide	hid	hidden, hid	spring	sprang,	sprung
come	came	come	know	knew	known		sprung	
dive	dove	dived	lay	laid	laid	steal	stole	stolen
do	did	done	lead	led	led	strive	strove	striven
drag	dragged	dragged	lie	lay	lain	swear	swore	sworn
draw	drew	drawn	(recline)			swim	swam	swum
drink	drank	drunk	lie	lied	lied	swing	swung	swung
drive	drove	driven	(deceive)			take	took	taken
drown	drowned	drowned	ride	rode	ridden	teach	taught	taught
eat	ate	eaten	ring	rang	rung	tear	tore	torn
fall	fell	fallen	rise	rose	risen	throw	threw	thrown
fight	fought	fought	run	ran	run	wake	waked,	waked,
flee	fled	fled	see	saw	seen		woke	woken
fly	flew	flown	shake	shook	shaken	wear	wore	worn
forsake	forsook	forsaken	shine	shone	shone	weave	weaved,	weaved,
freeze	froze	frozen	(light)				wove	woven
get	got	gotten	shine	shined	shined	wring	wrung	wrung
			(polish)			write	wrote	written

These verbs are the same in all principal parts: *burst, cost, cut, hurt, let, put, set,* and *spread.*

■ **Present perfect tense** expresses action that began in the past but continues in the present or is completed in the present.

> **Our boat has weathered worse storms than this one.**

■ **Past perfect tense** expresses an action in the past that occurs before another past action.

> **They reported, wrongly, that the hurricane had missed the island.**

■ **Future perfect tense** expresses action that will begin in the future and be completed by a specific time in the future.

> **By this time tomorrow, the hurricane will have smashed into the coast.**

544.1 Mood of a Verb

Mood of a verb indicates the tone or attitude with which a statement is made.

■ **Indicative mood** is used to state a fact or to ask a question.

> Sometimes I'd yell questions at the rocks and trees, and across gorges, or yodel, "What is the meaning of the void?" The answer was perfect silence, so I knew. —Jack Kerouac, "Alone on a Mountain Top"

■ **Imperative mood** is used to give a command.

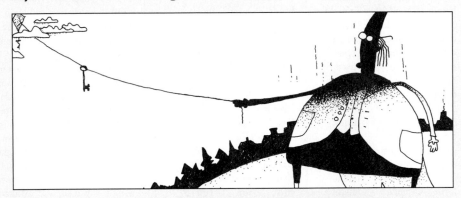

"Whatever you do, don't fly your kite during a storm."
—Mrs. Abiah Franklin

■ **Subjunctive mood** is no longer commonly used; however, careful writers may choose to use it to express the exact manner in which their statements are meant.

> ■ Use the subjunctive *were* to express a condition that is contrary to fact.
> **If I were finished with my report, I could go to the movie.**

> ■ Use the subjunctive *were* after *as though* or *as if* to express an unreal condition.
> **Mrs. Young acted as if she were sixteen again.**

> ■ Use the subjunctive *be* in "that" clauses to express necessity, legal decisions, or parliamentary motions.
> **"It is moved and supported that no more than 6,000,000 quad be used to explore the planet Earth."**
> **"Ridiculous! Knowing earthlings is bound to help us understand ourselves! Therefore, I move that the sum be amended to 12,000,000 quad."**
> **"Stupidity! I move that all missions be postponed until we have living proof of life on Earth."**

Adjective

An **adjective** describes or modifies a noun or a pronoun. The articles *a, an,* and *the* are also adjectives.

> The young **driver** peeked through the big **steering wheel.**

> (*The* and *young* modify *driver; the* and *big* modify *steering wheel.*)

545.1   Types of Adjectives

A **proper adjective** is created from a proper noun and is capitalized.

> In Canada (proper noun), **you will find many cultures and climates.**

> Canadian (proper adjective) **winters can be harsh.**

A **predicate adjective** follows a form of the "be" verb (or other linking verb) and describes the subject.

> Late autumn seems grim **to those who love summer.** (*Grim* modifies *autumn.*)

NOTE: Some words can be either adjectives or pronouns (*that, these, all, each, both, many, some,* etc.). These words are adjectives when they come before the nouns they modify; they are pronouns when they stand alone.

> Jiao made both goals. (*Both* modifies *goals;* it is an adjective.)

> Both were scored in the final period. (*Both* stands alone; it is a pronoun.)

545.2   Forms of Adjectives

Adjectives have three forms: *positive, comparative,* and *superlative.*

- The **positive form** describes a noun or a pronoun without comparing it to anyone or anything else.

  The first game was long and tiresome.

- The **comparative form** (*-er, more,* or *less*) compares two persons, places, things, or ideas.

  The second game was longer and more tiresome than the first.

- The **superlative form** (*-est, most,* or *least*) compares three or more persons, places, things, or ideas.

  The third game was the longest and most tiresome of all.

NOTE: Use *more* and *most* (or *less* and *least*)—instead of adding a suffix—with adjectives of two or more syllables.

Positive	Comparative	Superlative
big	bigger	biggest
helpful	more helpful	most helpful
painful	less painful	least painful

Adverb

An **adverb** describes or modifies a verb, an adjective, or another adverb.

She sneezed loudly. (*Loudly* modifies the verb *sneezed.*)
Her sneezes are really dramatic. (*Really* modifies the adjective *dramatic.*)
The sneeze exploded very noisily. (*Very* modifies the adverb *noisily.*)

An adverb usually tells *when, where, how,* or *how much.*

546.1 Types of Adverbs

Adverbs can be cataloged in four basic ways: *time, place, manner,* and *degree.*

> **TIME** (These adverbs tell *when, how often,* and *how long.*)
> today, yesterday   daily, weekly   briefly, eternally

> **PLACE** (These adverbs tell *where, to where,* and *from where.*)
> here, there   nearby, beyond   backward, forward

> **MANNER** (These adverbs often end in *ly* and tell *how* something is done.)
> precisely   effectively   regally   smoothly   well

> **DEGREE** (These adverbs tell *how much* or *how little.*)
> substantially   greatly   entirely   partly   too

NOTE: Some adverbs can be written with or without the *ly* ending. When in doubt, use the *ly* form.

> slow, slowly   loud, loudly   fair, fairly   tight, tightly   quick, quickly

546.2 Forms of Adverbs

Adverbs of manner have three forms: *positive, comparative,* and *superlative.*

- The **positive form** describes a verb, an adjective, or another adverb without comparing it to anyone or anything else.
  Model X vacuum cleans well and runs quietly.

- The **comparative form** (*-er, more,* or *less*) compares how two things are done.
  Model Y vacuum cleans better and runs more quietly than model X does.

- The **superlative form** (*-est, most,* or *least*) compares how three or more things are done.
  Model Z vacuum cleans best and runs most quietly of all.

Positive	Comparative	Superlative
well	better	best
fast	faster	fastest
remorsefully	more remorsefully	most remorsefully

Preposition

A **preposition** is the first word (or group of words) in a prepositional phrase. It shows the relationship between its object (a noun or a pronoun that follows the preposition) and another word in the sentence. The first noun or pronoun following a preposition is its object.

> **To make a mustache, Natasha placed the hairy caterpillar under her nose.**
> (*Under* shows the relationship between the verb, *placed*, and the object of the preposition, *nose*.)

> **The drowsy insect clung obediently to the girl's upper lip.** (The first noun following the preposition *to* is *lip; lip* is the object of the preposition.)

547.1 Prepositional Phrase

A **prepositional phrase** includes the preposition, the object of the preposition, and the modifiers of the object. A prepositional phrase functions as an adverb or as an adjective.

> **Some people run away from caterpillars.**
> (The phrase functions as an adverb and modifies the verb *run*.)

> **However, little kids with inquisitive minds enjoy their company.**
> (The phrase functions as an adjective and modifies the noun *kids*.)

NOTE: A preposition is always followed by an object; if there is no object, the word is an adverb, not a preposition.

> **Natasha never played with caterpillars before.** (The word *before* is not followed by an object; therefore, it functions as an adverb that modifies *played,* a verb.)

Common Prepositions

aboard	before	from	of	save
about	behind	from among	off	since
above	below	from between	on	subsequent to
according to	beneath	from under	on account of	together with
across	beside	in	on behalf of	through
across from	besides	in addition to	onto	throughout
after	between	in back of	on top of	till
against	beyond	in behalf of	opposite	to
along	by	in front of	out	toward
alongside	by means of	in place of	out of	under
along with	concerning	in regard to	outside of	underneath
amid	considering	inside	over	until
among	despite	inside of	over to	unto
apart from	down	in spite of	owing to	up
around	down from	instead of	past	up to
aside from	during	into	prior to	upon
at	except	like	regarding	with
away from	except for	near	round	within
because of	for	near to	round about	without

Conjunction

A **conjunction** connects individual words or groups of words. There are three kinds of conjunctions: *coordinating, correlative,* and *subordinating.*

548.1 Coordinating Conjunctions

Coordinating conjunctions usually connect a word to a word, a phrase to a phrase, or a clause to a clause. The words, phrases, or clauses joined by a coordinating conjunction are equal in importance or are of the same type.

> **I could tell by my old man's eyes that he *was nervous* and *wanted to smooth things over,* but Syl didn't give him a chance.** —Albert Halper, "Prelude"

(*And* connects the two parts of a compound predicate; *but* connects two independent clauses that could stand on their own.)

548.2 Correlative Conjunctions

Correlative conjunctions are conjunctions used in pairs.

> **They were not only exhausted by the day's journey but also sunburned.**

548.3 Subordinating Conjunctions

Subordinating conjunctions connect two clauses that are *not* equally important, thereby showing the relationship between them. A subordinating conjunction connects a dependent clause to an independent clause in order to complete the meaning of the dependent clause.

> **A brown trout will study the bait before he eats it.** (The clause *before he eats it* is dependent. It depends on the rest of the sentence to complete its meaning.)

Kinds of Conjunctions

COORDINATING: and, but, or, nor, for, yet, so

CORRELATIVE: either, or; neither, nor; not only, but also; both, and; whether, or

SUBORDINATING: after, although, as, as if, as long as, as though, because, before, if, in order that, provided that, since, so that, that, though, till, unless, until, when, where, whereas, while

---

NOTE: Relative pronouns (page 536.2) and conjunctive adverbs (page 494.1) can also connect clauses.

Interjection

An **interjection** communicates strong emotion or surprise. Punctuation (often a comma or an exclamation point) is used to set off an interjection from the rest of the sentence.

> **Oh no! The TV broke. Good grief! I have nothing to do! Yipes, I'll go mad!**

Quick Guide

Parts of Speech

Words in the English language are used in eight different ways. For this reason, there are eight parts of speech.

Noun

A word that names a person, a place, a thing, or an idea

Governor Smith-Jones   Oregon   hospital   religion

Pronoun

A word used in place of a noun

**I   you   she   him   who   everyone   these
neither   theirs   themselves   which**

Verb

A word that expresses action or state of being

float   sniff   discover   seem   were   was

Adjective

A word that describes a noun or a pronoun

young   big   grim   Canadian   longer

Adverb

A word that describes a verb, an adjective, or another adverb

briefly   forward   regally   slowly   better

Preposition

The first word or words in a prepositional phrase (which functions as an adjective or an adverb)

away from   under   before   with   for   out of

Conjunction

A word that connects other words or groups of words.

and   but   although   because   either, or   so

Interjection

A word that shows strong emotion or surprise

Oh no!   Yipes!   Good grief!   Well, . . .

"A sentence should read as if its author, had he
held a plough instead of a pen, could have drawn
a furrow deep and straight to the end."

—Henry David Thoreau

Using the
LANGUAGE
Constructing Sentences

A **sentence** is made up of one or more words that express a complete thought.
A sentence begins with a capital letter; it ends with a period, a question mark,
or an exclamation point.

> **What should we do for our vacation this year? We could go camping.**
> **No, I hate bugs!**

Using Subjects and Predicates

A sentence usually has a **subject** and a predicate. The subject is the part of the
sentence about which something is said. The predicate, which contains the verb,
is the part of the sentence that says something about the subject.

> **Like the pilot, the writer must see faster and more completely than the
> ordinary viewer of life.**
> —Paul Engle, "Salt Crystals, Spider Webs, and Words"

550.1 The Subject

The **subject** is the part of the sentence about which something is said. The
subject is always a noun; a pronoun; or a word, clause, or phrase that functions
as a noun (such as a gerund or a gerund phrase or an infinitive).

> **Wolves howl.** (noun)   **They howl for a variety of reasons.** (pronoun)
> **To establish their turf may be one reason.** (infinitive phrase)
> **Searching for "lost" pack members may be another.** (gerund phrase)
> **That wolves and dogs are similar animals seems obvious.** (noun clause)

■ A **simple subject** is the subject without its modifiers.

> **Most wildlife biologists disapprove of crossbreeding wolves and dogs.**

■ A **complete subject** is the subject with all of its modifiers.

> **Most wildlife biologists disapprove of crossbreeding wolves and dogs.**

■ A **compound subject** is composed of two or more simple subjects.

> **Wise breeders and owners know that wolf-dog puppies can display
> unexpected, destructive behaviors.**

551.1 Delayed Subject

In sentences that begin with *There* or *It* followed by a form of the "be" verb, the subject comes after the verb. The subject is also delayed in questions.

There was nothing in the refrigerator. (The subject is *nothing;* the verb is *was.*)

Where is my sandwich? (The subject is *sandwich;* the verb is *is.*)

551.2 The Predicate

The **predicate** is the part of the sentence that shows action or says something about the subject.

Giant squid do exist.

■ A **simple predicate** is the verb without its modifiers.

One giant squid measured nearly 60 feet long.

■ A **complete predicate** is the simple predicate with all its modifiers.

One giant squid measured nearly 60 feet long.
(*Measured* is the simple predicate; *nearly 60 feet long* modifies *measured.*)

■ A **compound predicate** is composed of two or more simple predicates.

A squid grasps its prey with tentacles and bites it with its beak.

NOTE: A sentence can have a **compound subject** and a **compound predicate**.

Both sperm whales and giant squid live and occasionally clash in the deep waters off New Zealand's South Island.

■ A **direct object** is part of the predicate and receives the action of the verb. (See 540.1.)

Sperm whales sometimes eat giant squid.
(The direct object *giant squid* receives the action of the verb *eat* by answering the question *whales eat what?*)

NOTE: The **direct object** may be compound.

In the past, whalers harvested oil, spermaceti, and ambergris from slain sperm whales.

551.3 Understood Subject and Predicate

Either the subject or the predicate may be "missing" from a sentence, but both must be clearly **understood**.

Who is making supper?
(*Who* is the subject; *is making supper* is the predicate.)

No one.
(*No one* is the subject; the predicate *is making supper* is understood.)

Put on that apron.
(The subject *you* is understood; *put on that apron* is the predicate.)

Using Phrases

A **phrase** is a group of related words that function as a single part of speech. The sentence below contains a number of phrases.

Finishing the race will require running down several steep slopes.

finishing the race (This gerund phrase functions as a subject noun.)

will require (This phrase functions as a verb.)

running down several steep slopes (This gerund phrase functions as an object noun.)

552.1 Types of Phrases

There are several types of phrases: *verb, verbal, prepositional, appositive,* and *absolute.*

- A **verb phrase** consists of a main verb preceded by one or more helping verbs.

  The snow has been falling for three straight days.
  (*Has been falling* is a verb phrase.)

- A **verbal phrase** is a phrase based on one of the three types of verbals: *gerund, infinitive,* or *participle.* (See 540.2, 540.3, and 540.4.)

  - A **gerund phrase** consists of a gerund and its modifiers. The whole phrase functions as a noun.

    Spotting the tiny mouse was easy for the hawk.
    (The gerund phrase is used as the subject of the sentence.)

    Dinner escaped by ducking under a rock.
    (The gerund phrase is the object of the preposition *by.*)

  - An **infinitive phrase** consists of an infinitive and its modifiers. The whole phrase functions either as a noun, an adjective, or an adverb.

    To shake every voter's hand was the candidate's goal.
    (The infinitive phrase functions as a noun used as the subject.)

    Your efforts to clean the chalkboard are appreciated.
    (The infinitive phrase is used as an adjective modifying *efforts.*)

    Please watch carefully to see the difference.
    (The infinitive phrase is used as an adverb modifying *watch.*)

  - A **participial phrase** consists of a past or present participle and its modifiers. The whole phrase functions as an adjective.

    Following his nose, the beagle took off like a jackrabbit.
    (The participial phrase modifies the noun *beagle.*)

    The raccoons, warned by the rustling, took cover.
    (The participial phrase modifies the noun *raccoons.*)

■ A **prepositional phrase** is a group of words beginning with a preposition and ending with a noun or a pronoun. Prepositional phrases function mainly as adjectives and adverbs.

> **Zach won the wheelchair race in record time.** (The prepositional phrase *in record time* is used as an adverb modifying the verb *won*.)
> **Reach for that catnip ball behind the couch.** (The prepositional phrase *behind the couch* is used as an adjective modifying *catnip ball*.)

■ An **appositive phrase,** which follows a noun or a pronoun and renames it, consists of a noun and its modifiers. An appositive adds new information about the noun or pronoun it follows.

> **The Trans-Siberian Railroad, the world's longest railway, stretches from Moscow to Vladivostok.** (The appositive phrase renames *Trans-Siberian Railroad* and provides new information.)

■ An **absolute phrase** consists of a noun and a participle (plus the participle's object, if there is one, and any modifiers). An absolute phrase functions as an adjective that adds information to the entire sentence. Absolute phrases are always set off with commas.

> **Its wheels clattering rhythmically over the rails, the train rolled into town.** (The noun *wheels* is modified by the present participle *clattering*. The entire phrase modifies the rest of the sentence.)

Using Clauses

A **clause** is a group of related words that has both a subject and a predicate.

553.1 Independent and Dependent Clauses

An **independent clause** presents a complete thought and can stand alone as a sentence; a **dependent clause** (also called a *subordinate clause*) does not present a complete thought and cannot stand alone as a sentence.

> **Sparrows make nests in cattle barns** (independent clause) **so that they can stay warm during the winter** (dependent clause).

553.2 Types of Dependent Clauses

There are three basic types of dependent clauses: *adverb, noun,* and *adjective.*

■ An **adverb clause** is used like an adverb to modify a verb, an adjective, or an adverb. Adverb clauses begin with a subordinating conjunction. (See 548.3.)

> **If I study hard, I will pass this test.**
> (The adverb clause modifies the verb *will pass*.)

■ A **noun clause** is used in place of a noun.

> **However, the teacher said that the essay questions are based only on the last two chapters.** (The noun clause functions as a direct object.)

■ An **adjective clause** modifies a noun or a pronoun.

> **Tomorrow's test, which covers the entire book, is half essay and half short answers.** (The adjective clause modifies the noun *test*.)

Using Sentence Variety

A sentence may be classified according to the type of statement it makes, the way it is constructed, and its arrangement of words.

554.1 Kinds of Statements

Sentences can make five basic kinds of statements: *declarative, interrogative, imperative, exclamatory,* or *conditional.*

■ **Declarative sentences** make statements. They tell us something about a person, a place, a thing, or an idea.

The Statue of Liberty stands in New York Harbor.

For over a century, it has greeted immigrants and visitors to America.

■ **Interrogative sentences** ask questions.

Did you know that the Statue of Liberty is made of copper and stands over 150 feet tall?

■ **Imperative sentences** make commands. They often contain an understood subject (*you*) as in the examples below.

Go see the Statue of Liberty.

After a few weeks of physical conditioning, climb its 168 stairs.

■ **Exclamatory sentences** communicate strong emotion or surprise.

Climbing 168 stairs is not a dumb idea!

Just muster some of that old pioneering spirit, that desire to try something new, that never-say-die attitude that made America great!

■ **Conditional sentences** express wishes ("if . . . then" statements) or conditions contrary to fact.

If you were to climb to the top of the statue, then you could share in the breathtaking feeling experienced by many hopeful immigrants.

554.2 Types of Sentence Constructions

A sentence may be *simple, compound, complex,* or *compound-complex.* It all depends on the relationship between independent and dependent clauses.

■ A **simple sentence** can have a single subject or a compound subject. It can have a single predicate or a compound predicate. However, a simple sentence has only one independent clause, and it has no dependent clauses.

My back aches.
(single subject; single predicate)

My teeth and my eyes hurt.
(compound subject; single predicate)

My throat and nose feel sore and look red.
(compound subject; compound predicate)

I must have caught the flu from the sick kids in class.
(independent clause with two phrases: *from the sick kids* and *in class*)

■ A **compound sentence** consists of two independent clauses. The clauses must be joined by a comma and a coordinating conjunction or by a semicolon.

> **I usually don't mind missing school, but this is not fun.**
>
> **I feel too sick to watch TV; I feel too sick to eat.**

NOTE: The comma can be omitted when the clauses are very short.

> **I wept and I wept.**

■ A **complex sentence** contains one independent clause (in black) and one or more dependent clauses (in red).

> **When I get back to school, I'm actually going to appreciate it.**
> (dependent clause; independent clause)
>
> **I won't even complain about math class, although I might be talking out of my head because I'm feverish.**
> (independent clause; two dependent clauses)

■ A **compound-complex sentence** contains two or more independent clauses (in black) and one or more dependent clauses (in red).

> **Yes, I have a bad flu, and because I need to get well soon,**
> **I won't think about school just yet.**
> (two independent clauses; one dependent clause)

555.1 Arrangements of Sentences

Depending on the arrangement of the words and the placement of emphasis, a sentence may also be classified as *loose, balanced, periodic,* or *cumulative.*

■ A **loose sentence** expresses the main thought near the beginning and adds explanatory material as needed.

> **We hauled out the boxes of food and set up the camp stove, all the time battling the hot wind that would not stop, even when we screamed into the sky.**

■ A **balanced sentence** is constructed so that it emphasizes a similarity or a contrast between two or more of its parts (words, phrases, or clauses).

> **The wind in our ears drove us crazy and pushed us on.**
> (The similar wording emphasizes the main idea in this sentence.)

■ A **periodic sentence** is one that postpones the crucial or most surprising idea until the end.

> **Following my mother's repeated threats to ground me for life,**
> **I decided it was time to propose a compromise.**

■ A **cumulative sentence** places the general idea in the middle of the sentence with modifying clauses and phrases coming before and after.

> **With careful thought, and extra attention to detail, I wrote out my plan for being a model teenager, a teen who cared about neatness and reliability.**

Diagramming Sentences

A **graphic diagram** of a sentence is a picture of how the words in that sentence are related and how they fit together to form a complete thought.

556.1 Simple Sentence with One Subject and One Verb

Chris fishes.

| Chris | fishes | | subject | verb |

556.2 Simple Sentence with a Predicate Adjective

Fish are delicious.

| Fish | are \ delicious | | subject | verb \ predicate adjective |

556.3 Simple Sentence with a Predicate Noun and Adjectives

Fishing is my favorite hobby.

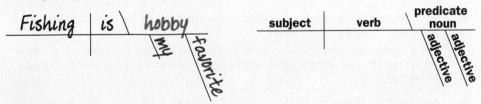

NOTE: When possessive pronouns (*my, his, their,* etc.) are used as adjectives, they are placed on a diagonal line under the word they modify.

556.4 Simple Sentence with an Indirect and Direct Object

My grandpa gave us a trout.

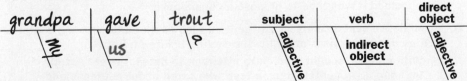

NOTE: Articles (*a, an, the*) are adjectives and are placed on a diagonal line under the word they modify.

557.1 Simple Sentence with a Prepositional Phrase

I like fishing by myself.

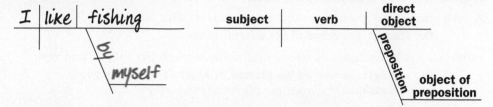

557.2 Simple Sentence with a Compound Subject and Verb

The team and fans clapped and cheered.

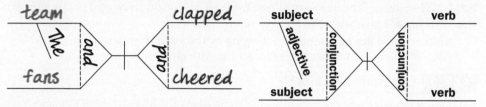

557.3 Compound Sentence

The team scored, and the crowd cheered wildly.

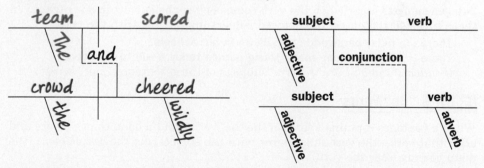

557.4 Complex Sentence with a Subordinate Clause

Before Erin scored, the crowd sat quietly.

Getting **Sentence Parts to Agree**

Agreement of Subject and Verb

A verb must agree in number (singular or plural) with its subject.

> **The student** was **proud of her quarter grades.**

NOTE: Do not be confused by words that come between the subject and verb.

> **The manager, as well as the players,** is **required to display good sportsmanship.** (*Manager,* not *players,* is the subject.)

558.1 Singular Subjects

Singular subjects joined by *or* or *nor* take a singular verb.

> **Neither Bev nor Kendra** is **going to the street dance.**

NOTE: When one of the subjects joined by *or* or *nor* is singular and one is plural, the verb must agree with the subject nearer the verb.

> **Neither Yoshi nor his friends** are **singing in the band anymore.** (The plural subject *friends* is nearer the verb, so the plural verb *are* is correct.)

558.2 Compound Subjects

Compound subjects connected with *and* require a plural verb.

> **Strength and balance** are **necessary for gymnastics.**

558.3 Delayed Subjects

Delayed subjects occur when the verb comes before the subject in a sentence. In these inverted sentences, the delayed subject must agree with the verb.

> **There** are **many hardworking students in our schools.**
> **There** is **present among many young people today a will to succeed.**
> (*Students* and *will* are the true subjects of these sentences, not *there.*)

558.4 "Be" Verbs

When a sentence contains a form of the "be" verb—and a noun comes before and after that verb—the verb must agree with the subject, not the *complement* (the noun coming after the verb).

> **The cause of his problem** was **the bad brakes.**
> **The bad brakes** were **the cause of his problem.**

558.5 Special Cases

Some nouns that are **plural in form but singular in meaning** take a singular verb: *mumps, measles, news, mathematics, economics, gallows, shambles.*

> **Measles** is **still considered a serious disease in many parts of the world.**

Some nouns that are plural in form but singular in meaning take a plural verb: *scissors, trousers, tidings.*

> **The scissors** are **missing again.**

559.1 Collective Nouns

Collective nouns (*faculty, committee, team, congress, species, crowd, army, pair, squad*) take a singular verb when they refer to a group as a unit; collective nouns take a plural verb when they refer to the individuals within the group.

The favored team is losing, and the crowd is getting ugly. (Both *team* and *crowd* are considered units in this sentence, requiring the singular verb *is*.)

The pair were finally reunited after 20 years apart.
(Here, *pair* refers to two individuals, so the plural verb *were* is required.)

559.2 Indefinite Pronouns

Some **indefinite pronouns** are singular: *each, either, neither, one, everybody, another, anybody, everyone, nobody, everything, somebody*, and *someone*. They require a singular verb.

Everybody is invited to the cafeteria for refreshments.

Some **indefinite pronouns** are plural: *both, few, many,* and *several.*

Several like chocolate cake. Many ask for ice cream, too.

NOTE: Do not be confused by words or phrases that come between the indefinite pronoun and the verb.

One of the participants is (not *are*) **going to have to stay late to clean up.**

A Closer Look Some **indefinite pronouns** can be either singular or plural: *all, any, most, none,* and *some*. These pronouns are singular if the number of the noun in the prepositional phrase is singular; they are plural if the noun is plural.

Most of the food complaints are coming from the seniors.
(*Complaints* is plural, so *most* is plural.)

Most of the tabletop is sticky with melted ice cream.
(*Tabletop* is singular, so *most* is singular.)

559.3 Relative Pronouns

When a **relative pronoun** (*who, which, that*) is used as the subject of a clause, the number of the verb is determined by the antecedent of the pronoun. (The antecedent is the word to which the pronoun refers.)

This is one of the books that are required for geography class.
(The relative pronoun *that* requires the plural verb *are* because its antecedent *books* is plural.)

NOTE: To test this type of sentence for agreement, read the "of" phrase first.

Of the books that are required for geography class, this is one.

Agreement of Pronoun and Antecedent

A pronoun must agree in number, person, and gender with its *antecedent*. (The *antecedent* is the word to which the pronoun refers.)

> **Cal brought his gerbil to school.** (The antecedent of *his* is *Cal*. Both the pronoun and its antecedent are singular, third person, and masculine; therefore, the pronoun is said to "agree" with its antecedent.)

560.1 Agreement in Number

Use a **singular pronoun** to refer to such antecedents as *each, either, neither, one, anyone, anybody, everyone, everybody, somebody, another, nobody,* and *a person.*

> **Neither of the brothers likes his (not their) room.**

Two or more singular antecedents joined by *or* or *nor* are also referred to by a **singular pronoun.**

> **Either Connie or Sue left her headset in the library.**

If one of the antecedents joined by *or* or *nor* is singular and one is plural, the pronoun should agree with the nearer antecedent.

> **Neither the manager nor the players were crazy about their new uniforms.**

Use a **plural pronoun** to refer to plural antecedents as well as compound subjects joined by *and.*

> **Jared and Carlos are finishing their assignments.**

560.2 Agreement in Gender

Use a **masculine** or **feminine pronoun** depending upon the gender of the antecedent.

> **Is either Connor or Grace bringing his or her baseball glove?**

When *a person* or *everyone* is used to refer to both sexes or either sex, you will have to choose whether to offer optional pronouns or rewrite the sentence.

> **A person should be allowed to pursue his or her interests.** (optional pronouns)
>
> **People should be allowed to pursue their interests.** (rewritten in plural form)

Using Fair Language

When depicting individuals or groups according to their differences, you must use language that implies equal value and equal respect for all people.

561.1 Addressing Ethnicity

Acceptable General Terms	Acceptable Specific Terms
American Indians, Native Americans	Cherokee, Inuit, Navajo
Asian Americans.	Chinese Americans
Hispanic or Latino.	Mexican Americans

African Americans, blacks
    African American has come into wide acceptance, though the term *black* is preferred by some individuals.

Anglo-Americans (English ancestry), **European Americans**
    Avoid the notion that *American,* used alone, means *white.*

NOTE: Also avoid using *Americans* to mean just *U.S. citizens.*

561.2 Addressing Age

General Age Group	Acceptable Terms
Up to age 12	boys, girls
Between 13 and 19	youth, young people, adolescents
Late teens and 20's	young adults
30's and older.	adults, men, women
70 and older.	older adults, older people (not *elderly*)

561.3 Addressing Disabilities and Impairments

Not Recommended	Preferred
handicapped.	disabled
birth defect	congenital disability
an AIDS victim	person with AIDS
stutter, stammer, lisp	speech impairment (impaired)
deaf.	hearing impairment (impaired)
blind.	visual impairment (impaired)

561.4 Putting People First

People with various conditions should be referred to as simply people who have a certain condition—not as though they *were* their condition *(quadriplegics).*

Not Recommended	Preferred
the retarded.	people with mental retardation
neurotics	patients with neuroses
quadriplegics	people who are quadriplegic

562.1 Avoiding Sexism

■ **Don't** use masculine-only pronouns (*he, his, him*) when you want to refer to a human being in general.

A politician can kiss privacy good-bye when he runs for office.

DO use one of the several ways to avoid sexism:

Reword the sentence:	**Running for office robs a politician of privacy.**
Express in the plural:	**Politicians can kiss privacy good-bye when they run for office.**
Offer optional pronouns:	**A politician can kiss privacy good-bye when he or she runs for office.**

■ **Don't** use a male word in the salutation of a business letter to someone you do not know:

Dear Sir: Dear Gentlemen:

DO address both if you're not sure whether the reader is male or female . . .

Dear Madam or Sir:
Dear Ladies and Gentlemen:

or address a position:

Dear Personnel Officer:
Dear Members of the Big Bird Fan Club:

■ **Don't** give special treatment to one of the sexes:

The men and the ladies came through in the clutch.
Mr. Bubba Gumm, Mrs. Bubba Gumm

DO use equal language for both sexes:

The men and the women came through in the clutch.
Mr. Bubba Gumm, Mrs. Lotta Gumm

562.2 Avoiding Gender Typecasting

■ **Don't** typecast one gender.

DO show both women and men as doctors and nurses, principals and teachers, breadwinners and housekeepers, bosses and secretaries, grocery-store owners and cashiers, pilots and plumbers, etc.

■ **Don't** associate certain qualities like courage, strength, brilliance, creativity, independence, persistence, seriousness, emotionalism, passivity, or fearfulness with only one gender.

DO portray people of both sexes along the whole range of potential human strengths and weaknesses.

563.1 Avoiding Unfair References

■ **Don't** refer to women according to their physical appearance and to men according to their mental abilities or professional status:

The admirable Dr. William Hicks and his wife Sareena, a former model, both showed up at the party.

DO refer to both on the same plane:

Bill and Sareena Hicks showed up at the party.

■ **Don't** take special notice when a woman does a "man's job" or vice versa:

lady doctor   male nurse   coed   steward   policewoman

DO treat men's or women's involvement in a profession in the same way:

doctor   nurse   student   flight attendant   police officer

Not Recommended	Preferred
chairman	chair, presiding officer, moderator
salesman	sales representative, salesperson
mailman	mail carrier, postal worker, letter carrier
fireman	firefighter
businessman	executive, manager, businessperson
congressman	member of Congress, representative, senator
policeman	police officer

563.2 Avoiding Demeaning Portrayals

■ **Don't** portray women as the possessions of men:

Fred took his wife and kids on a vacation.

DO portray women and men, husbands and wives, as equal partners:

Fred and Wilma took their kids on a vacation.

■ **Don't** use demeaning or sexually loaded labels:

the weaker sex   chick, fox   jock
the little woman   stud, hunk   the old man

DO use respectful terms rather than labels; consider what the person might wish to be called:

women, females   attractive woman   athletic man
wife, spouse   handsome man   father, husband, spouse

Student
ALMANAC

Language   565

Science   571

Mathematics   581

Geography   589

Government   603

History   609

"I love the taste of words. They have a taste and a weight and a colour as well as a sound and a shape."

—Philip Pullman

LANGUAGE

This chapter provides various charts and graphs related to the study of language. You'll find the manual alphabet for sign language, a brief history of the English language, traffic signs, and common parliamentary procedures.

Manual Alphabet (Sign Language)

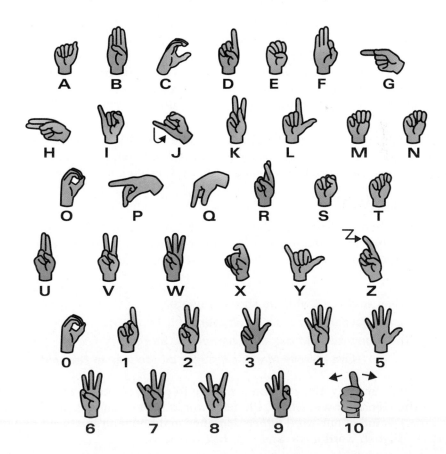

The History of the English Language

Old English

English is part of the **Indo-European** group of languages. (See the bottom of page 567.) When some of the ancient Indo-Europeans migrated west (others migrated in other directions), they developed a number of Germanic dialects. It was these people who invaded the British Isles about 1,000 years ago, bringing with them what we call Old English—the earliest version of English. These **Anglo-Saxons** were warriors, but they enjoyed puns and creating compound words. They called the sea the *whaleroad* (hranrad) and combined the word for nose and hole to give us *nostril*. These features can be seen in *Beowulf*, the most famous Old English poem.

Half of our everyday words come directly from Old English. Here are some of them: *hand, field, tree, house, sun, day, drink, sit, love,* and *live.*

Invasions

Two more invasions affected English. Beginning in 787, the **Vikings** raided their distant cousins in England, bringing with them most of the words in English that begin with *sk-* (*skin, sky, skirt*) and other common words like *die, freckle,* and *window*. Then in 1066, **William of Normandy** (Normandy is in the northwestern part of present-day France) arrived in England, bringing with him knights, clergy, and government officials who spoke French and Latin.

English survived, but it gained a whole new French vocabulary in government (*tax, parliament, royal*), in religion (*sermon, prayer*), in building (*ceiling, porch, curtain*), in law (*judge, attorney, crime*), and so on.

Middle English

English had reasserted itself as a strong language by the time **Geoffrey Chaucer** wrote the *Canterbury Tales* and his other main works (1375–1400). Here are the two opening lines to the *Canterbury Tales* (with a translation in italics):

> **Whan that April with his showres soote,**
> > **(When April's sweet showers)**
> **The droughte of March hath perced to the roote,**
> > **(Have pierced March's drought all the way to the root)**

In Chaucer's day, there began a change in pronunciation. The change is called the **Great Vowel Shift**. Chaucer would have pronounced *hand* with the vowel sound of our word *father*; *soon* he would have pronounced like the modern English word *home* and *ride* like our *seen*.

Early Modern English

The **Renaissance** (1475–1650) brought many new ideas and places into the world of English speakers. They borrowed words from the New World (*tomato, tobacco, alligator, squash*) and from new learning (*thermometer, hydrant, algebra*). The **printing press** made two great works of Early Modern English available to many English speakers: the English Bible (especially the *King James Version*) and the plays of William Shakespeare (1590–1616).

William Shakespeare had a tremendous vocabulary. He used words in new ways (*assassinate*) and created more than 1,700 new words (*obscene, submerged*) and phrases like "vanished into thin air."

Modern English

English continues to grow and to change. (English has the largest vocabulary of any modern language.) In the United States, Modern English has been influenced by every aspect of the **American experience**. This experience includes the contribution of African Americans: Today, Black English Vernacular is an important variety of English. It also includes the contributions of a constant flow of immigrants and their languages (including Spanish, Yiddish, and many other languages) and modern technology (*radar, astronaut, DVD*).

Is English still changing and developing? Of course it is. The latest source for new words is the vast world of **electronics** and the **media**, from video games to worldwide newscasts to the movie industry.

The Indo-European *Family of Languages*

Albanian	Armenian	Balto-Slavic ↓	Celtic ↓	Germanic ↓	Greek	Indo-Iranian ↓	Romance ↓
		Bulgarian	Brenton	Dutch		Bengali	French
		Czech	Irish	English		Farsi	Italian
		Latvian	Scots	German		Hindi	Portuguese
		Lithuanian	Welsh	Scandinavian		Pashto	Romanian
		Polish				Urdu	Spanish
		Russian					
		Serbo-Croatian					
		Slovak					
		Slovenian					
		Ukrainian					

Traffic Signs

Red: Regulatory Signs

These signs are red to get your attention: they tell you to do (or *not do*) something. The red circle and stripe tells you NO.

White and Black: Informational Signs

Informational signs are black and white, and square or rectangular in shape. They provide basic information for pedestrians and drivers.

Yellow: Warning Signs

Yellow signs warn of a possible danger. Many warning signs are diamond shaped.

Green: Directional or Guide Signs

Green signs give traffic directions or provide information on trails and bike routes.

Blue: Service Signs

Blue signs indicate there are services nearby.

Orange: Construction and Slow-Moving Vehicle Signs

Orange signs mean slow down and drive carefully.

Common **Parliamentary Procedures**

Motion	Purpose	Needs Second	Debatable	Amend-able	Required Vote	May Interrupt Speaker	Subsidiary Motion Applied
I. ORIGINAL OR PRINCIPAL MOTION							
1. Main Motion (general) Main Motions (specific)	To introduce business	Yes	Yes	Yes	Majority	No	Yes
a. To take from the table	To consider tabled motion	Yes	No	No	Majority	No	No
b. To reconsider	To reconsider previous motion	Yes	When original motion is	No	Majority	Yes	No
c. To rescind	To nullify or wipe out previous action	Yes	Yes	Yes	Majority or two-thirds	No	No
II. SUBSIDIARY MOTIONS							
2. To lay on the table	To defer action	Yes	No	No	Majority	No	No
3. To call for previous question	To close debate and force vote	Yes	No	No	Two-thirds	No	Yes
4. To limit or extend limits of debate	To control time of debate	Yes	No	Yes	Two-thirds	No	Yes
5. To postpone to a certain time	To defer action	Yes	Yes	Yes	Majority	No	Yes
6. To refer to a committee	To provide for special study	Yes	Yes	Yes	Majority	No	Yes
7. To amend	To modify a motion	Yes	When original motion is	Yes (once only)	Majority	No	Yes
8. To postpone indefinitely	To suppress action	Yes	Yes	No	Majority	No	Yes
III. PRIVILEGED MOTIONS							
9. To raise a point of order	To correct error in procedure	No	No	No	Decision of chair	Yes	No
10. To appeal for a decision of chair	To change decision on procedure	Yes	If motion does not relate to indecorum	No	Majority or tie	Yes	No
11. To withdraw a motion	To remove a motion	No	No	No	Majority	No	No
12. To divide a motion	To modify a motion	No	No	Yes	Majority	No	Yes
13. To object to consideration	To suppress action	No	No	No	Two-thirds	Yes	No
14. To call for division of house	To secure a countable vote	No	No	No	Majority if chair desires	Yes	Yes
15. To suspend rules	To alter existing rules and order of business	Yes	No	No	Two-thirds	No	No
16. To close nominations	To stop nomination of officers	Yes	No	Yes	Two-thirds	No	Yes
17. To reopen nominations	To permit additional nominations	Yes	No	Yes	Majority	No	Yes
IV. INCIDENTAL MOTIONS							
18. To call for orders of the day	To keep assembly to order of business	No	No	No	None unless objection	Yes	No
19. To raise question of privilege	To make a request concerning rights of assembly	No	No	No	Decision of chair	Yes	No
20. To take a recess	To dismiss meeting for specific time	Yes	No, if made when another question is before the assembly	Yes	Majority	No	Yes
21. To adjourn	To dismiss meeting	Yes	No	Yes	Majority	No	No
22. To fix time at which to adjourn	To set time for the continuation of this meeting	Yes	No, if made when another question is before the assembly	Yes	Majority	No	Yes

6-Year **Calendar**

2005

JANUARY
S	M	T	W	T	F	S
						1
2	3	4	5	6	7	8
9	10	11	12	13	14	15
16	17	18	19	20	21	22
23	24	25	26	27	28	29
30	31					

FEBRUARY
S	M	T	W	T	F	S
		1	2	3	4	5
6	7	8	9	10	11	12
13	14	15	16	17	18	19
20	21	22	23	24	25	26
27	28					

MARCH
S	M	T	W	T	F	S
		1	2	3	4	5
6	7	8	9	10	11	12
13	14	15	16	17	18	19
20	21	22	23	24	25	26
27	28	29	30	31		

APRIL
S	M	T	W	T	F	S
					1	2
3	4	5	6	7	8	9
10	11	12	13	14	15	16
17	18	19	20	21	22	23
24	25	26	27	28	29	30

MAY
S	M	T	W	T	F	S
1	2	3	4	5	6	7
8	9	10	11	12	13	14
15	16	17	18	19	20	21
22	23	24	25	26	27	28
29	30	31				

JUNE
S	M	T	W	T	F	S
			1	2	3	4
5	6	7	8	9	10	11
12	13	14	15	16	17	18
19	20	21	22	23	24	25
26	27	28	29	30		

JULY
S	M	T	W	T	F	S
					1	2
3	4	5	6	7	8	9
10	11	12	13	14	15	16
17	18	19	20	21	22	23
24	25	26	27	28	29	30
31						

AUGUST
S	M	T	W	T	F	S
	1	2	3	4	5	6
7	8	9	10	11	12	13
14	15	16	17	18	19	20
21	22	23	24	25	26	27
28	29	30	31			

SEPTEMBER
S	M	T	W	T	F	S
				1	2	3
4	5	6	7	8	9	10
11	12	13	14	15	16	17
18	19	20	21	22	23	24
25	26	27	28	29	30	

OCTOBER
S	M	T	W	T	F	S
						1
2	3	4	5	6	7	8
9	10	11	12	13	14	15
16	17	18	19	20	21	22
23	24	25	26	27	28	29
30	31					

NOVEMBER
S	M	T	W	T	F	S
		1	2	3	4	5
6	7	8	9	10	11	12
13	14	15	16	17	18	19
20	21	22	23	24	25	26
27	28	29	30			

DECEMBER
S	M	T	W	T	F	S
				1	2	3
4	5	6	7	8	9	10
11	12	13	14	15	16	17
18	19	20	21	22	23	24
25	26	27	28	29	30	31

2006

JANUARY
S	M	T	W	T	F	S
1	2	3	4	5	6	7
8	9	10	11	12	13	14
15	16	17	18	19	20	21
22	23	24	25	26	27	28
29	30	31				

FEBRUARY
S	M	T	W	T	F	S
			1	2	3	4
5	6	7	8	9	10	11
12	13	14	15	16	17	18
19	20	21	22	23	24	25
26	27	28				

MARCH
S	M	T	W	T	F	S
			1	2	3	4
5	6	7	8	9	10	11
12	13	14	15	16	17	18
19	20	21	22	23	24	25
26	27	28	29	30	31	

APRIL
S	M	T	W	T	F	S
						1
2	3	4	5	6	7	8
9	10	11	12	13	14	15
16	17	18	19	20	21	22
23	24	25	26	27	28	29
30						

MAY
S	M	T	W	T	F	S
	1	2	3	4	5	6
7	8	9	10	11	12	13
14	15	16	17	18	19	20
21	22	23	24	25	26	27
28	29	30	31			

JUNE
S	M	T	W	T	F	S
				1	2	3
4	5	6	7	8	9	10
11	12	13	14	15	16	17
18	19	20	21	22	23	24
25	26	27	28	29	30	

JULY
S	M	T	W	T	F	S
						1
2	3	4	5	6	7	8
9	10	11	12	13	14	15
16	17	18	19	20	21	22
23	24	25	26	27	28	29
30	31					

AUGUST
S	M	T	W	T	F	S
		1	2	3	4	5
6	7	8	9	10	11	12
13	14	15	16	17	18	19
20	21	22	23	24	25	26
27	28	29	30	31		

SEPTEMBER
S	M	T	W	T	F	S
					1	2
3	4	5	6	7	8	9
10	11	12	13	14	15	16
17	18	19	20	21	22	23
24	25	26	27	28	29	30

OCTOBER
S	M	T	W	T	F	S
1	2	3	4	5	6	7
8	9	10	11	12	13	14
15	16	17	18	19	20	21
22	23	24	25	26	27	28
29	30	31				

NOVEMBER
S	M	T	W	T	F	S
			1	2	3	4
5	6	7	8	9	10	11
12	13	14	15	16	17	18
19	20	21	22	23	24	25
26	27	28	29	30		

DECEMBER
S	M	T	W	T	F	S
					1	2
3	4	5	6	7	8	9
10	11	12	13	14	15	16
17	18	19	20	21	22	23
24	25	26	27	28	29	30
31						

2007

JANUARY
S	M	T	W	T	F	S
	1	2	3	4	5	6
7	8	9	10	11	12	13
14	15	16	17	18	19	20
21	22	23	24	25	26	27
28	29	30	31			

FEBRUARY
S	M	T	W	T	F	S
				1	2	3
4	5	6	7	8	9	10
11	12	13	14	15	16	17
18	19	20	21	22	23	24
25	26	27	28			

MARCH
S	M	T	W	T	F	S
				1	2	3
4	5	6	7	8	9	10
11	12	13	14	15	16	17
18	19	20	21	22	23	24
25	26	27	28	29	30	31

APRIL
S	M	T	W	T	F	S
1	2	3	4	5	6	7
8	9	10	11	12	13	14
15	16	17	18	19	20	21
22	23	24	25	26	27	28
29	30					

MAY
S	M	T	W	T	F	S
		1	2	3	4	5
6	7	8	9	10	11	12
13	14	15	16	17	18	19
20	21	22	23	24	25	26
27	28	29	30	31		

JUNE
S	M	T	W	T	F	S
					1	2
3	4	5	6	7	8	9
10	11	12	13	14	15	16
17	18	19	20	21	22	23
24	25	26	27	28	29	30

JULY
S	M	T	W	T	F	S
1	2	3	4	5	6	7
8	9	10	11	12	13	14
15	16	17	18	19	20	21
22	23	24	25	26	27	28
29	30	31				

AUGUST
S	M	T	W	T	F	S
			1	2	3	4
5	6	7	8	9	10	11
12	13	14	15	16	17	18
19	20	21	22	23	24	25
26	27	28	29	30	31	

SEPTEMBER
S	M	T	W	T	F	S
						1
2	3	4	5	6	7	8
9	10	11	12	13	14	15
16	17	18	19	20	21	22
23	24	25	26	27	28	29
30						

OCTOBER
S	M	T	W	T	F	S
	1	2	3	4	5	6
7	8	9	10	11	12	13
14	15	16	17	18	19	20
21	22	23	24	25	26	27
28	29	30	31			

NOVEMBER
S	M	T	W	T	F	S
				1	2	3
4	5	6	7	8	9	10
11	12	13	14	15	16	17
18	19	20	21	22	23	24
25	26	27	28	29	30	

DECEMBER
S	M	T	W	T	F	S
						1
2	3	4	5	6	7	8
9	10	11	12	13	14	15
16	17	18	19	20	21	22
23	24	25	26	27	28	29
30	31					

2008

JANUARY
S	M	T	W	T	F	S
		1	2	3	4	5
6	7	8	9	10	11	12
13	14	15	16	17	18	19
20	21	22	23	24	25	26
27	28	29	30	31		

FEBRUARY
S	M	T	W	T	F	S
					1	2
3	4	5	6	7	8	9
10	11	12	13	14	15	16
17	18	19	20	21	22	23
24	25	26	27	28	29	

MARCH
S	M	T	W	T	F	S
						1
2	3	4	5	6	7	8
9	10	11	12	13	14	15
16	17	18	19	20	21	22
23	24	25	26	27	28	29
30	31					

APRIL
S	M	T	W	T	F	S
		1	2	3	4	5
6	7	8	9	10	11	12
13	14	15	16	17	18	19
20	21	22	23	24	25	26
27	28	29	30			

MAY
S	M	T	W	T	F	S
				1	2	3
4	5	6	7	8	9	10
11	12	13	14	15	16	17
18	19	20	21	22	23	24
25	26	27	28	29	30	31

JUNE
S	M	T	W	T	F	S
1	2	3	4	5	6	7
8	9	10	11	12	13	14
15	16	17	18	19	20	21
22	23	24	25	26	27	28
29	30					

JULY
S	M	T	W	T	F	S
		1	2	3	4	5
6	7	8	9	10	11	12
13	14	15	16	17	18	19
20	21	22	23	24	25	26
27	28	29	30	31		

AUGUST
S	M	T	W	T	F	S
					1	2
3	4	5	6	7	8	9
10	11	12	13	14	15	16
17	18	19	20	21	22	23
24	25	26	27	28	29	30
31						

SEPTEMBER
S	M	T	W	T	F	S
	1	2	3	4	5	6
7	8	9	10	11	12	13
14	15	16	17	18	19	20
21	22	23	24	25	26	27
28	29	30				

OCTOBER
S	M	T	W	T	F	S
			1	2	3	4
5	6	7	8	9	10	11
12	13	14	15	16	17	18
19	20	21	22	23	24	25
26	27	28	29	30	31	

NOVEMBER
S	M	T	W	T	F	S
						1
2	3	4	5	6	7	8
9	10	11	12	13	14	15
16	17	18	19	20	21	22
23	24	25	26	27	28	29
30						

DECEMBER
S	M	T	W	T	F	S
	1	2	3	4	5	6
7	8	9	10	11	12	13
14	15	16	17	18	19	20
21	22	23	24	25	26	27
28	29	30	31			

2009

JANUARY
S	M	T	W	T	F	S
				1	2	3
4	5	6	7	8	9	10
11	12	13	14	15	16	17
18	19	20	21	22	23	24
25	26	27	28	29	30	31

FEBRUARY
S	M	T	W	T	F	S
1	2	3	4	5	6	7
8	9	10	11	12	13	14
15	16	17	18	19	20	21
22	23	24	25	26	27	28

MARCH
S	M	T	W	T	F	S
1	2	3	4	5	6	7
8	9	10	11	12	13	14
15	16	17	18	19	20	21
22	23	24	25	26	27	28
29	30	31				

APRIL
S	M	T	W	T	F	S
			1	2	3	4
5	6	7	8	9	10	11
12	13	14	15	16	17	18
19	20	21	22	23	24	25
26	27	28	29	30		

MAY
S	M	T	W	T	F	S
					1	2
3	4	5	6	7	8	9
10	11	12	13	14	15	16
17	18	19	20	21	22	23
24	25	26	27	28	29	30
31						

JUNE
S	M	T	W	T	F	S
	1	2	3	4	5	6
7	8	9	10	11	12	13
14	15	16	17	18	19	20
21	22	23	24	25	26	27
28	29	30				

JULY
S	M	T	W	T	F	S
			1	2	3	4
5	6	7	8	9	10	11
12	13	14	15	16	17	18
19	20	21	22	23	24	25
26	27	28	29	30	31	

AUGUST
S	M	T	W	T	F	S
						1
2	3	4	5	6	7	8
9	10	11	12	13	14	15
16	17	18	19	20	21	22
23	24	25	26	27	28	29
30	31					

SEPTEMBER
S	M	T	W	T	F	S
		1	2	3	4	5
6	7	8	9	10	11	12
13	14	15	16	17	18	19
20	21	22	23	24	25	26
27	28	29	30			

OCTOBER
S	M	T	W	T	F	S
				1	2	3
4	5	6	7	8	9	10
11	12	13	14	15	16	17
18	19	20	21	22	23	24
25	26	27	28	29	30	31

NOVEMBER
S	M	T	W	T	F	S
1	2	3	4	5	6	7
8	9	10	11	12	13	14
15	16	17	18	19	20	21
22	23	24	25	26	27	28
29	30					

DECEMBER
S	M	T	W	T	F	S
		1	2	3	4	5
6	7	8	9	10	11	12
13	14	15	16	17	18	19
20	21	22	23	24	25	26
27	28	29	30	31		

2010

JANUARY
S	M	T	W	T	F	S
					1	2
3	4	5	6	7	8	9
10	11	12	13	14	15	16
17	18	19	20	21	22	23
24	25	26	27	28	29	30
31						

FEBRUARY
S	M	T	W	T	F	S
	1	2	3	4	5	6
7	8	9	10	11	12	13
14	15	16	17	18	19	20
21	22	23	24	25	26	27
28						

MARCH
S	M	T	W	T	F	S
	1	2	3	4	5	6
7	8	9	10	11	12	13
14	15	16	17	18	19	20
21	22	23	24	25	26	27
28	29	30	31			

APRIL
S	M	T	W	T	F	S
				1	2	3
4	5	6	7	8	9	10
11	12	13	14	15	16	17
18	19	20	21	22	23	24
25	26	27	28	29	30	

MAY
S	M	T	W	T	F	S
						1
2	3	4	5	6	7	8
9	10	11	12	13	14	15
16	17	18	19	20	21	22
23	24	25	26	27	28	29
30	31					

JUNE
S	M	T	W	T	F	S
		1	2	3	4	5
6	7	8	9	10	11	12
13	14	15	16	17	18	19
20	21	22	23	24	25	26
27	28	29	30			

JULY
S	M	T	W	T	F	S
				1	2	3
4	5	6	7	8	9	10
11	12	13	14	15	16	17
18	19	20	21	22	23	24
25	26	27	28	29	30	31

AUGUST
S	M	T	W	T	F	S
1	2	3	4	5	6	7
8	9	10	11	12	13	14
15	16	17	18	19	20	21
22	23	24	25	26	27	28
29	30	31				

SEPTEMBER
S	M	T	W	T	F	S
			1	2	3	4
5	6	7	8	9	10	11
12	13	14	15	16	17	18
19	20	21	22	23	24	25
26	27	28	29	30		

OCTOBER
S	M	T	W	T	F	S
					1	2
3	4	5	6	7	8	9
10	11	12	13	14	15	16
17	18	19	20	21	22	23
24	25	26	27	28	29	30
31						

NOVEMBER
S	M	T	W	T	F	S
	1	2	3	4	5	6
7	8	9	10	11	12	13
14	15	16	17	18	19	20
21	22	23	24	25	26	27
28	29	30				

DECEMBER
S	M	T	W	T	F	S
			1	2	3	4
5	6	7	8	9	10	11
12	13	14	15	16	17	18
19	20	21	22	23	24	25
26	27	28	29	30	31	

"Science is simply common sense at its best—that is, rigidly accurate in observation, and merciless to fallacy in logic."
—T. H. Huxley

SCIENCE

This chapter contains charts and conversion lists to help you in your science classes. Information about the solar system and a glossary of computer terms are also included.

Weights and Measures

Linear Measure

1 inch	=	2.54 centimeters
1 foot	=	12 inches
		0.3048 meter
1 yard	=	3 feet
		0.9144 meter
1 rod (or pole or perch)	=	5.5 yards or 16.5 feet
		5.029 meters
1 furlong	=	40 rods
		201.17 meters
1 (statute) mile	=	8 furlongs
		1,760 yards
		5,280 feet
		1,609.3 meters
1 (land) league	=	3 miles
		4.83 kilometers

Square Measure

1 square inch	=	6.452 sq. centimeters
1 square foot	=	144 square inches
		929 square centimeters
1 square yard	=	9 square feet
		0.8361 square meter
1 square rod	=	30.25 square rods
		25.29 square meters
1 acre	=	160 square rods
		4,840 square yards
		43,560 square feet
		0.4047 hectare
1 square mile	=	640 acres
		259 hectares
		2.59 square kilometers

(Engineer's chain)

1 link	=	1 foot
		0.3048 meter
1 chain	=	100 feet
		30.48 meters
1 mile	=	52.8 chains
		1,609.3 meters

Surveyor's (Square) Measure

1 square pole	=	625 square links
		25.29 square meters
1 square chain	=	16 square poles
		404.7 square meters
1 acre	=	10 square chains
		0.4047 hectare
1 square mile or		
1 section	=	640 acres
		259 hectares
		2.59 square kilometers
1 township	=	36 square miles
		9,324 hectares
		93.24 square kilometers

Nautical Measure

1 fathom	=	6 feet
		1.829 meters
1 cable's length (ordinary)	=	100 fathoms
		(In the U.S. Navy 120 fathoms or 720 feet = 1 cable's length; in the British Navy 608 feet = 1 cable's length)
1 nautical mile	=	6,076.10333 feet; *by international agreement in 1954*
		10 cables' length
		1.852 kilometers
		1.1508 statute miles; *length of a minute of longitude at the equator*
1 marine league	=	3.45 statute miles
		3 nautical miles
		5.56 kilometers
1 degree of a great circle of the earth	=	60 nautical miles

Weights and Measures

Cubic Measure

1 cubic inch..........	=	16.387 cubic centimeters
1 cubic foot..........	=	1,728 cubic inches
		0.0283 cubic meter
1 cubic yard..........	=	27 cubic feet
		0.7646 cubic meter
1 cord foot...........	=	16 cubic feet
1 cord ....=		8 cord feet
		3.625 cubic meters

Chain Measure
(Gunter's or surveyor's chain)

1 link...............	=	7.92 inches
		20.12 centimeters
1 chain	=	100 links or 66 feet
		20.12 meters
1 furlong	=	10 chains
		201.17 meters
1 mile	=	80 chains
		1,609.3 meters

Dry Measure

1 pint..............	=	33.60 cubic inches
		0.5505 liter
1 quart	=	2 pints
		67.20 cubic inches
		1.1012 liters
1 peck	=	8 quarts
		537.61 cubic inches
		8.8096 liters
1 bushel............	=	4 pecks
		2,150.42 cubic inches
		35.2383 liters

Liquid Measure

4 fluid ounces	=	1 gill
(see next table)		7.219 cubic inches
		0.1183 liter
1 pint...............	=	4 gills
		28.875 cubic inches
		0.4732 liter
1 quart	=	2 pints
		57.75 cubic inches
		0.9463 liter
1 gallon.............	=	4 quarts
		231 cubic inches
		3.7853 liters

Apothecaries' Fluid Measure

1 minim.............	=	0.0038 cubic inch
		0.0616 milliliter
1 fluid dram	=	60 minims
		0.2256 cubic inch
		3.6966 milliliters
1 fluid ounce.........	=	8 fluid drams
		1.8047 cubic inches
		0.0296 liter
1 pint...............	=	16 fluid ounces
		28.875 cubic inches
		0.4732 liter

Circular (or Angular) Measure

1 minute (')	=	60 seconds (")
1 degree (°)	=	60 minutes
1 quadrant or 1 right angle ..	=	90 degrees
1 circle..................	=	4 quadrants
		360 degrees

Avoirdupois Weight

(The grain, equal to 0.0648 gram, is the same in all three tables of weight.)

1 dram or 27.34 grains	=	1.772 grams
1 ounce	=	16 drams
		437.5 grains
		28.3495 grams
1 pound.................	=	16 ounces
		7,000 grains
		453.59 grams
1 hundredweight	=	100 pounds
		45.36 kilograms
1 ton	=	2,000 pounds
		907.18 kilograms

Troy Weight

(The grain, equal to 0.0648 gram, is the same in all three tables of weight.)

1 carat..................	=	3.086 grains
		200 milligrams
1 pennyweight.............	=	24 grains
		1.5552 grams
1 ounce	=	20 pennyweights
		480 grains
		31.1035 grams
1 pound.................	=	12 ounces
		5,760 grains
		373.24 grams

Apothecaries' Weight

(The grain, equal to 0.0648 gram, is the same in all three tables of weight.)

1 scruple	=	20 grains
		1.296 grams
1 dram..................	=	3 scruples
		3.888 grams
1 ounce	=	8 drams
		480 grains
		31.1035 grams
1 pound.................	=	12 ounces
		5,760 grains
		373.24 grams

Miscellaneous

1 palm..................	=	3 inches
1 hand..................	=	4 inches
1 span..................	=	6 inches
1 cubit..................	=	18 inches
1 Biblical cubit	=	21.8 inches
1 military pace	=	2.5 feet

The **Metric** System

In 1975, the United States signed the Metric Conversion Act, declaring a national policy of encouraging voluntary use of the metric system. Today, the metric system exists side by side with the U.S. customary system. The debate on whether the United States should adopt the metric system has been going on for nearly 200 years, leaving the United States the only country in the world not totally committed to adopting the system.

The metric system is considered a simpler form of measurement. It is based on the decimal system (units of 10) and eliminates the need to deal with fractions.

Linear Measure

1 centimeter	=	10 millimeters
		0.3937 inch
1 decimeter	=	10 centimeters
		3.937 inches
1 meter	=	10 decimeters
		39.37 inches
		3.28 feet
1 decameter	=	10 meters
		393.7 inches
1 hectometer	=	10 decameters
		328 feet 1 inch
1 kilometer	=	10 hectometers
		0.621 mile
1 myriameter	=	10 kilometers
		6.21 miles

Volume Measure

1 cubic centimeter	=	1,000 cubic millimeters
		.06102 cubic inch
1 cubic decimeter	=	1,000 cubic centimeters
		61.02 cubic inches
1 cubic meter	=	1,000 cubic decimeters
		35.314 cubic feet

Capacity Measure

1 centiliter	=	10 milliliters
		.338 fluid ounce
1 deciliter	=	10 centiliters
		3.38 fluid ounces
1 liter	=	10 deciliters
		1.0567 liquid quarts
		0.9081 dry quart
1 decaliter	=	10 liters
		2.64 gallons
		0.284 bushel
1 hectoliter	=	10 decaliters
		26.418 gallons
		2.838 bushels
1 kiloliter	=	10 hectoliters
		264.18 gallons
		35.315 cubic feet

Square Measure

1 square centimeter	=	100 square millimeters
		0.15499 square inch
1 square decimeter	=	100 square centimeters
		15.499 square inches
1 square meter	=	100 square decimeters
		1,549.9 square inches
		1.196 square yards
1 square decameter	=	100 square meters
		119.6 square yards
1 square hectometer	=	100 square decameters
		2.471 acres
1 square kilometer	=	100 square hectometers
		0.386 square mile

Land Measure

1 centare	=	1 square meter
		1,549.9 square inches
1 are	=	100 centares
		119.6 square yards
1 hectare	=	100 ares
		2,471 acres
1 square kilometer	=	100 hectares
		0.386 square mile

Weights

1 centigram	=	10 milligrams
		0.1543 grain
1 decigram	=	10 centigrams
		1.5432 grains
1 gram	=	10 decigrams
		15.432 grains
1 decagram	=	10 grams
		0.3527 ounce
1 hectogram	=	10 decagrams
		3.5274 ounces
1 kilogram	=	10 hectograms
		2.2046 pounds
1 myriagram	=	10 kilograms
		22.046 pounds
1 quintal	=	10 myriagrams
		220.46 pounds
1 metric ton	=	10 quintals
		2,204.6 pounds

Handy **Conversion Factors**

TO CHANGE	TO	MULTIPLY BY
acres	hectares	.4047
acres	square feet	43,560
acres	square miles	.001562
Celsius	Fahrenheit	1.8*
		*(then add 32)
centimeters	inches	.3937
centimeters	feet	.03281
cubic meters	cubic feet	35.3145
cubic meters	cubic yards	1.3079
cubic yards	cubic meters	.7646
degrees	radians	.01745
Fahrenheit	Celsius	.556*
		* (after subtracting 32)
feet	meters	.3048
feet	miles (nautical)	.0001645
feet	miles (statute)	.0001894
feet/sec.	miles/hr.	.6818
furlongs	feet	660.0
furlongs	miles	.125
gallons (U.S.)	liters	3.7853
grains	grams	.0648
grams	grains	15.4324
grams	ounces avdp.	.0353
grams	pounds	.002205
hectares	acres	2.4710
horsepower	watts	745.7
hours	days	.04167
inches	millimeters	25.4000
inches	centimeters	2.5400
kilograms	pounds advp. or t.	2.2046
kilometers	miles	.6214
kilowatts	horsepower	1.341
knots	nautical miles/hr.	1.0
knots	statute miles/hr.	1.151
liters	gallons (U.S.)	.2642
liters	pecks	.1135
liters	pints (dry)	1.8162
liters	pints (liquid)	2.1134
liters	quarts (dry)	.9081

TO CHANGE	TO	MULTIPLY BY
liters	quarts (liquid)	1.0567
meters	feet	3.2808
meters	miles	.0006214
meters	yards	1.0936
metric tons	tons (long)	.9842
metric tons	tons (short)	1.1023
miles	kilometers	1.6093
miles	feet	5,280
miles (nautical)	miles (statute)	1.1516
miles (statute)	miles (nautical)	.8684
miles/hr.	feet/min.	88
millimeters	inches	.0394
ounces advp.	grams	28.3495
ounces	pounds	.0625
ounces (troy)	ounces (advp.)	1.09714
pecks	liters	8.8096
pints (dry)	liters	.5506
pints (liquid)	liters	1.4732
pounds ap. or t.	kilograms	.3782
pounds advp.	kilograms	.4536
pounds	ounces	16
quarts (dry)	liters	1.1012
quarts (liquid)	liters	.9463
rods	meters	5.029
rods	feet	16.5
square feet	square meters	.0929
square kilometers	square miles	.3861
square meters	square feet	10.7639
square meters	square yards	1.1960
square miles	square kilometers	2.5900
square yards	square meters	.8361
tons (long)	metric tons	1.1060
tons (short)	metric tons	.9072
tons (long)	pounds	2,240
tons (short)	pounds	2,000
watts	Btu/hr.	3.4129
watts	horsepower	.001341
yards	meters	.9144
yards	miles	.0005682

Ten Ways to **Measure** *When You Don't Have a Ruler*

1. Many floor tiles are 12-inch squares (30.48-cm squares).
2. Paper money is 6-1/8 inches by 2-5/8 inches (15.56 x 6.67 cm).
3. A quarter is approximately 1 inch wide (2.54 cm).
4. A penny is approximately 3/4 of an inch wide (1.9 cm).
5. Typing paper is 8-1/2 inches by 11 inches (21.59 cm x 27.94 cm).

Each of the following items can be used as a measuring device by multiplying its length by the number of times it is used to measure an area in question.

6. A shoelace   7. A tie   8. A belt
9. Your feet—placing one in front of the other to measure floor area
10. Your outstretched arms from fingertip to fingertip

Periodic Table of the Elements

Key

Atomic Number	2
Symbol	He
Atomic Weight (or Mass Number of most stable isotope in parentheses)	Helium 4.00260

Legend
- Alkali metals
- Alkaline earth metals
- Transition metals
- Lanthanide series
- Actinide series
- Other metals
- Nonmetals
- Noble gases

1a	2a	3b	4b	5b	6b	7b	8	8	8	1b	2b	3a	4a	5a	6a	7a	0
1 **H** Hydrogen 1.00797																	2 **He** Helium 4.00260
3 **Li** Lithium 6.941	4 **Be** Beryllium 9.0128											5 **B** Boron 10.811	6 **C** Carbon 12.0115	7 **N** Nitrogen 14.0067	8 **O** Oxygen 15.9994	9 **F** Fluorine 18.9984	10 **Ne** Neon 20.179
11 **Na** Sodium 22.9898	12 **Mg** Magnesium 24.305											13 **Al** Aluminum 26.9815	14 **Si** Silicon 28.0855	15 **P** Phosphorus 30.9738	16 **S** Sulfur 32.064	17 **Cl** Chlorine 35.453	18 **Ar** Argon 39.948
19 **K** Potassium 39.0983	20 **Ca** Calcium 40.08	21 **Sc** Scandium 44.9559	22 **Ti** Titanium 47.88	23 **V** Vanadium 50.94	24 **Cr** Chromium 51.996	25 **Mn** Manganese 54.9380	26 **Fe** Iron 55.847	27 **Co** Cobalt 58.9332	28 **Ni** Nickel 58.69	29 **Cu** Copper 63.546	30 **Zn** Zinc 65.39	31 **Ga** Gallium 69.72	32 **Ge** Germanium 72.59	33 **As** Arsenic 74.9216	34 **Se** Selenium 78.96	35 **Br** Bromine 79.904	36 **Kr** Krypton 83.80
37 **Rb** Rubidium 85.4678	38 **Sr** Strontium 87.62	39 **Y** Yttrium 88.905	40 **Zr** Zirconium 91.224	41 **Nb** Niobium 92.906	42 **Mo** Molybdenum 95.94	43 **Tc** Technetium (98)	44 **Ru** Ruthenium 101.07	45 **Rh** Rhodium 102.906	46 **Pd** Palladium 106.42	47 **Ag** Silver 107.868	48 **Cd** Cadmium 112.41	49 **In** Indium 114.82	50 **Sn** Tin 118.71	51 **Sb** Antimony 121.75	52 **Te** Tellurium 127.60	53 **I** Iodine 126.905	54 **Xe** Xenon 131.29
55 **Cs** Cesium 132.905	56 **Ba** Barium 137.33	57–71* **La** Lanthanum 138.906 / Lanthanides	72 **Hf** Hafnium 178.49	73 **Ta** Tantalum 180.948	74 **W** Tungsten 183.85	75 **Re** Rhenium 186.207	76 **Os** Osmium 190.2	77 **Ir** Iridium 192.22	78 **Pt** Platinum 195.08	79 **Au** Gold 196.967	80 **Hg** Mercury 200.59	81 **Tl** Thallium 204.383	82 **Pb** Lead 207.19	83 **Bi** Bismuth 208.980	84 **Po** Polonium (209)	85 **At** Astatine (210)	86 **Rn** Radon (222)
87 **Fr** Francium (223)	88 **Ra** Radium 226.025	89–103** Actinides	104 **Rf** Rutherfordium (261)	105 **Db** Dubnium (262)	106 **Sg** Seaborgium (263)	107 **Bh** Bohrium (262)	108 **Hs** Hassium (265)	109 **Mt** Meitnerium (266)	110 **Ds** (269)	111 **Rg** (272)	112 **Uub** (285)	113 **Uut** (284)	114 **Uuq** (289)	115 **Uup** (288)	116 **Uuh** (292)	117 **Uus**	118 **Uuo**

*Lanthanides

57 **La** Lanthanum 138.906	58 **Ce** Cerium 140.12	59 **Pr** Praseodymium 140.908	60 **Nd** Neodymium 144.24	61 **Pm** Promethium (145)	62 **Sm** Samarium 150.36	63 **Eu** Europium 151.96	64 **Gd** Gadolinium 157.25	65 **Tb** Terbium 158.925	66 **Dy** Dysprosium 162.50	67 **Ho** Holmium 164.930	68 **Er** Erbium 167.26	69 **Tm** Thulium 168.934	70 **Yb** Ytterbium 173.04	71 **Lu** Lutetium 174.967

**Actinides

89 **Ac** Actinium 227.028	90 **Th** Thorium 232.038	91 **Pa** Protactinium 231.036	92 **U** Uranium 238.029	93 **Np** Neptunium 237.048	94 **Pu** Plutonium (244)	95 **Am** Americium (243)	96 **Cm** Curium (247)	97 **Bk** Berkelium (247)	98 **Cf** Californium (251)	99 **Es** Einsteinium (252)	100 **Fm** Fermium (257)	101 **Md** Mendelevium (258)	102 **No** Nobelium (259)	103 **Lr** Lawrencium (260)

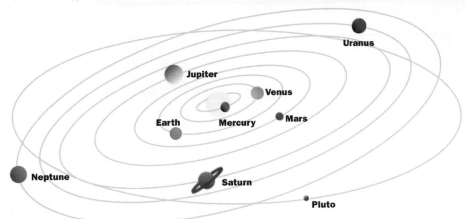

Our Solar System

Our solar system is located in the Milky Way Galaxy. Even though this galaxy contains approximately 100 billion stars, our solar system contains only one star—the sun. The sun, which is the center of our solar system, has nine planets and a myriad of asteroids, meteors, and comets orbiting it. The planets are large, nonluminous bodies that follow fixed elliptical orbits about the sun. (See the illustration above.)

The planets are divided into two categories: the terrestrial planets—Mercury, Venus, Earth, Mars, and Pluto—which resemble Earth in size, chemical composition, and density; and the Jovian planets—Jupiter, Saturn, Uranus, and Neptune—which are much larger in size and have thick, gaseous atmospheres and low densities. (See the table below.)

	Sun	Moon	Mercury	Venus	Earth	Mars	Jupiter	Saturn	Uranus	Neptune	Pluto
Orbital Speed (in mi. per second)		.6	29.8	21.8	18.5	15.0	8.1	6.0	4.2	3.4	3.0
Rotation on Axis	24 days 16 hrs. 48 min.	27 days 7 hrs. 38 min.	59 days	243 days	23 hrs. 56 min.	24 hrs. 37 min.	9 hrs. 55 min.	10 hrs. 39 min.	17 hrs. 8 min.	16 hrs. 7 min.	6 days
Mean Surface Gravity (Earth=1)		0.16	0.38	0.9	1.00	0.38	2.53	1.07	0.91	1.14	0.07
Density (times that of water)	100 (core)	3.3	5.4	5.3	5.5	3.9	1.3	0.7	1.27	1.6	2.03
Mass (times that of Earth)	333,000	0.012	0.056	0.82	6×10^{21} metric tons	0.10	318	95	14.5	17.2	0.0026
Approx. Weight of a 150-Pound Human		24	59	135	150	57	380	161	137	171	11
No. of Satellites	9 planets	0	0	0	1	2	63	33	21	8	1
Mean Distance to Sun (in millions of miles)		93.0	36.0	67.24	92.96	141.7	483.8	887.1	1,783.9	2,796.4	3,666
Revolution Around Sun		365.25 days	88.0 days	224.7 days	365.25 days	687 days	11.86 years	29.46 years	84.0 years	165 years	248 years
Approximate Surface Temp. (degrees Fahrenheit)	10,000° (surface) 27,000,000° (center)	lighted side 260° dark side −280°	−346° to 950°	850°	−126.9° to 136°	−191° to −24°	−236°	−203°	−344°	−360°	−342° to −369°
Diameter (in miles)	865,400	2,155	3,032	7,519	7,926	4,194	88,736	74,978	32,193	30,775	1,423

Computer and Internet **Terms**

Backup: A duplicate copy of a file or program, made in case the original is lost or destroyed.

Binary system: The number system commonly used by computers because the values 0 and 1 can be represented electronically in the computer.

Bit: A unit of computer memory that can store either a 0 or a 1. (See *byte.*)

Blog: (Web log) A private journal available on the Web. Updating a blog is called *blogging*, and a person who does so is a *blogger.*

Bookmark: A command to make a browser save an Internet address, so that the site can be revisited easily.

BPS: (bits per second) A measure of how fast data is transmitted over a network. (Sometimes called *baud rate.*) For example, a modem may have a speed of 56,600 bps.

Browser: A type of program used to view and navigate the World Wide Web.

Bulletin board: A service on the Internet where users can post messages for others to read.

Byte: Eight bits of information acting as a single piece of data. Computer memory is measured in bytes. (See *GB, K,* and *MB.* See also *bit.*)

CD: (compact disk) A type of disk that stores data as tiny dots burned into its surface.

CD burner: A device that allows computer users to burn or store information on a compact disk.

Character: A letter, number, or symbol that appears on a keyboard or on a computer screen.

Chat: A live conversation using the keyboard on the Internet.

Chip: A small piece of silicon containing thousands of electrical elements. Also known as an *integrated circuit.*

Circuit board: A flat board used to hold and connect computer chips and other electrical parts.

Client: The user of an Internet service. The Internet software on a user's machine is "client-side software," for instance. (See *server.*)

Command: An instruction telling a computer to perform a certain task, such as "print."

Compress: To make a file smaller so that it can be easily stored or quickly sent to another computer over a network. Special software is used to compress (and decompress) files.

Computer: A machine that can accept data, process it according to a stored set of instructions, and then output the results.

Control character: A character that is entered by holding down the control key while typing another key.

CPU: (central processing unit) The "brain" of the computer; the part that performs computations and controls all other parts of the system.

Crash: A term used to describe what happens when a computer or program stops working.

CRT: (cathode ray tube) The electronic vacuum tube found in some computer monitors and TV screens.

Cursor: A pointer on the computer screen that shows where the next character typed on the keyboard will appear.

Cyberspace: The imaginary world perceived by humans when using a computer network or a virtual reality program. From William Gibson's novel *Neuromancer.* (See *network, Internet,* and *virtual reality.*)

Data: Information given to or produced by a computer.

Database: A program and a collection of information organized in such a way that a computer can quickly access a certain item or group of items.

Desktop: The monitor screen as it appears when the computer is on but no programs are open.

Directory: The table of contents for all files on a disk.

Disk: A magnetic device used to record computer information. A disk rotates so that information can be stored on its many tracks.

Disk drive: A device that writes and reads information from and to a disk.

Documentation: The printed book or the program that explains how to use a piece of hardware or software.

Domain: In an Internet or e-mail address, the parts that name the server.

Download: To copy a program or file from another computer to your own via a network.

Drag: To move items across the screen by holding down the mouse button while sliding the mouse.

DVD: (digital video disk or digital versatile disk) A high-density compact disk capable of storing high-resolution video. (See *CD*.)

E-mail: (electronic mail) A system that uses telecommunications to send text messages from one computer to another.

Emoticon: Often called a "smiley." A set of characters that, when viewed sideways, resemble a face. Used to add emotion to a message. :-)

Error message: A message, displayed by the computer, that tells what type of error has occurred in a program.

Exit: To leave or quit a program. Also called *close* or *quit*.

FAQ: (frequently asked questions) A list of commonly asked questions and answers.

File: A collection of computer information stored under a single title.

Flame: To post an insulting or inflammatory message on the Internet.

Font: A typeface, or style of type, used by a printer. Most computer systems have several fonts.

Format: To prepare a blank disk for use. Also called *initialize*. Most disks are sold preformatted.

Freeware: Software in the public domain, for which the creator expects no payment.

FTP: (file transfer protocol) A system for transmitting large files on the Internet or a network.

GB: (gigabyte) A measure of computer memory; 1,000 megabytes (MB).

GHz: (gigahertz) A measure of processor speed; a measure of alternating current or electromagnetic frequency equal to a billion hertz.

Graphics: Information displayed as pictures or images.

Hacker: A person who illegally breaks into computers to access files or tamper with systems.

Hard copy: A printed copy; a printout.

Hard drive: A stack of disks permanently mounted inside most computers. The hard drive is for long-term storage of important files and programs (such as the computer's operating system).

Hardware: The electronic and mechanical parts of a computer system. A hard drive is hardware; a program stored on it is software.

Home page: The Web page that gives basic information about a person or an organization. It contains links to other Web pages or sites.

Host: The computer whose programs serve another computer in a computer-to-computer link. (See *server*.)

Hot: (See *hypertext*.)

HTML: (hypertext markup language) The codes that tell a browser how to display text and graphics for a Web page.

Hypertext or Hypermedia: A system of web-like links among pages on the Internet or within a program. A link from a "hot word" or "hot symbol" opens directly to another page.

Icon: A small picture or symbol used to identify computer folders, files, or functions.

Inkjet printer: A printer that uses tiny jets of ink to produce printouts.

Input: Information placed into a computer from a disk drive, keyboard, or other device.

Interactive: A computer program in which the user and the computer exchange information.

Interface: The hardware and software that is used to link one computer or computer device to another. Also the method by which a program communicates to a user.

Internet: A worldwide network of independent computer networks that communicate with one another.

ISP: (Internet service provider) A business that provides its customers access to the Internet. (See *server*.)

K: (kilobyte) A measure of computer memory; 1,024 bytes (about 170 words).

Keyboard: An input device used to enter information on a computer by striking keys.

Laser printer: A printer that uses a laser to produce high-quality printouts.

Link: A connection from one hypertext page to another. A link contains the address for the target page. When the link is selected, the target page loads.

List server: A program that sends e-mail to a set of addresses. Each list server is organized around a particular topic, allowing subscribers to conduct a group discussion by e-mail. Also called a mailing list or a mail server.

Mainframe: A large computer, with many terminals, powerful enough to be used by many people at once.

MB: (megabyte) A measure of computer memory; 1,000 kilobytes (K).

Memory: The chips in the computer that store information and programs while the computer is on.

Menu: A list of choices from which a user can select. Many programs have menus.

Modem: (modulator demodulator) A device that sends data over telephone lines.

Monitor: A video screen that displays information from a computer.

Mouse: A small manual input device that controls the pointer on the screen and sends information to the computer when it is clicked.

Multimedia: A program capable of combining text, graphics, video, voice, music, and animation.

Multiuser: A computer system that can be used by several people at once.

Network: A series of computers (or other devices) connected together in order to share information and programs.

Newsgroup: An ongoing, topic-centered discussion in bulletin-board style.

Online: To be connected to a computer network.

Online service: A business that serves as a network for its users, providing e-mail, chat rooms, and so on. Most online services now also act as Internet providers.

Open: To start a computer program or load a file.

Operating system: A software system that operates a computer. Some common operating systems for personal computers are Windows, Mac OS, and Linux.

Output: Information that a computer sends out to a monitor, printer, modem, or other device.

PC: A personal computer. A small computer, as opposed to a mainframe.

Peripheral: A device such as a monitor, printer, or scanner that is connected to a computer.

Pixel: One dot on the screen. (See *resolution*.)

Post: As a verb, to upload a message to a bulletin board, newsgroup, or list server. As a noun, the message that is posted.

Printer: A device used to print out information from a computer.

Printout: A hard copy; or a computer document printed on paper.

Program: A piece of software or set of instructions that tells a computer what to do.

Programmer: A person who helps write, edit, or produce a computer program.

Prompt: A question or an instruction on the screen that asks the user to make a choice or give information.

Quit: To close a program, removing it from random access memory.

RAM: (random access memory) The part of a computer's memory that stores programs and documents temporarily while you are using them.

Resolution: The number of dots per square inch (dpi) on a computer screen. Images on a screen are made up of tiny dots. The more dots there are, the higher the resolution and the clearer the picture. (See *pixel*.)

ROM: (read-only memory) The part of a computer's memory that holds its permanent instructions. ROM cannot record new data.

Save: To transfer a document to a disk for permanent storage.

Scanner: A device used to read a printed image, picture, or text and save it as an electronic file.

Search engine: A program for locating sites on the Internet. Sometimes called a robot, spider, or web-crawler.

Select: To highlight part of a document to work on or change.

Server: The hosting computer of a network. Software on the server is called "server-side" software, for example. (See *client* and *host*.)

Shareware: Programs intended as demos, to be used freely for a test period, then paid for.

Software: The program that tells a computer how to do a certain task.

Spam: Unrequested e-mails sent to many people at once (often ads); electronic "junk mail."

Spreadsheet: A computer program that displays numbers and text in a worksheet form.

Surfing: Exploring the Net, going from link to link.

Telecommunications: The technology that allows computers to communicate with one another over phone lines, by satellite, etc.

Terminal: A keyboard and a monitor sharing a mainframe with other terminals.

Text file: A computer document made up of ASCII characters only.

Tunneling: The method for exploring an FTP site, beginning at the welcome page and working downward through layers of folders.

Upload: To send a file from your computer to another computer via a network.

URL: (universal resource locator) The text version of the electronic address for a site on the Internet. The URL or Write Source is www.thewritesource.com.

User: A person using a computer.

Virtual reality: A technology that makes users feel present in an environment created by the computer.

Virus: A "bug" that is intentionally put into a computer system to cause problems.

Window: A box on a computer screen in which text and/or graphics are displayed.

Word processor: A program that allows a user to write, revise, edit, save, and print text documents.

WWW: (World Wide Web) A major portion of the Internet, characterized by graphical pages and hypertext links. (See *hypertext*.)

*"I think and think for months and years.
Ninety-nine times, the conclusion is false.
The hundredth time I am right."*

—Albert Einstein

MATHEMATICS

This chapter is your guide to the language of mathematics. It lists and defines many of the common mathematical signs, symbols, shapes, and terms. The chapter also includes helpful math tables.

Basic Math Symbols

+	plus (addition)	<	is less than	°	degree
−	minus (subtraction)	>	is greater than	′	minute (also foot)
×	multiplied by	±	plus or minus	″	second (also inch)
÷	divided by	%	percent	:	is to (ratio)
=	is equal to	$	dollars	π	pi
≠	is not equal to	¢	cents		

Advanced Math Symbols

√	square root		~	is similar to
∛	cube root		≅	is congruent to
≥	is greater than or equal to		∠	angle
≤	is less than or equal to		⊥	is perpendicular to
{ }	set		‖	is parallel to
∴	therefore			

A Chart of Prime Numbers Less Than 500

2	3	5	7	11	13	17	19	23	29	31	37
41	43	47	53	59	61	67	71	73	79	83	89
97	101	103	107	109	113	127	131	137	139	149	151
157	163	167	173	179	181	191	193	197	199	211	223
227	229	233	239	241	251	257	263	269	271	277	281
283	293	307	311	313	317	331	337	347	349	353	359
367	373	379	383	389	397	401	409	419	421	431	433
439	443	449	457	461	463	467	479	487	491	499	

Multiplication and Division Table

A number in the top line (11) multiplied by a number in the extreme left-hand column (12) produces the number where the top line and side line meet (132). A number in the table (208) divided by the number at the top of the same column (16) results in the number (13) in the extreme left column. A number in the table (208) divided by the number at the extreme left (13) results in the number (16) at the top of the column.

1	2	3	4	5	6	7	8	9	10	11	12	13	14	15	16	17	18	19	20	21	22	23	24	25
2	4	6	8	10	12	14	16	18	20	22	24	26	28	30	32	34	36	38	40	42	44	46	48	50
3	6	9	12	15	18	21	24	27	30	33	36	39	42	45	48	51	54	57	60	63	66	69	72	75
4	8	12	16	20	24	28	32	36	40	44	48	52	56	60	64	68	72	76	80	84	88	92	96	100
5	10	15	20	25	30	35	40	45	50	55	60	65	70	75	80	85	90	95	100	105	110	115	120	125
6	12	18	24	30	36	42	48	54	60	66	72	78	84	90	96	102	108	114	120	126	132	138	144	150
7	14	21	28	35	42	49	56	63	70	77	84	91	98	105	112	119	126	133	140	147	154	161	168	175
8	16	24	32	40	48	56	64	72	80	88	96	104	112	120	128	136	144	152	160	168	176	184	192	200
9	18	27	36	45	54	63	72	81	90	99	108	117	126	135	144	153	162	171	180	189	198	207	216	225
10	20	30	40	50	60	70	80	90	100	110	120	130	140	150	160	170	180	190	200	210	220	230	240	250
11	22	33	44	55	66	77	88	99	110	121	132	143	154	165	176	187	198	209	220	231	242	253	264	275
12	24	36	48	60	72	84	96	108	120	132	144	156	168	180	192	204	216	228	240	252	264	276	288	300
13	26	39	52	65	78	91	104	117	130	143	156	169	182	195	208	221	234	247	260	273	286	299	312	325
14	28	42	56	70	84	98	112	126	140	154	168	182	196	210	224	238	252	266	280	294	308	322	336	350
15	30	45	60	75	90	105	120	135	150	165	180	195	210	225	240	255	270	285	300	315	330	345	360	375
16	32	48	64	80	96	112	128	144	160	176	192	208	224	240	256	272	288	304	320	336	352	368	384	400
17	34	51	68	85	102	119	136	153	170	187	204	221	238	255	272	289	306	323	340	357	374	391	408	425
18	36	54	72	90	108	126	144	162	180	198	216	234	252	270	288	306	324	342	360	378	396	414	432	450
19	38	57	76	95	114	133	152	171	190	209	228	247	266	285	304	323	342	361	380	399	418	437	456	475
20	40	60	80	100	120	140	160	180	200	220	240	260	280	300	320	340	360	380	400	420	440	460	480	500
21	42	63	84	105	126	147	168	189	210	231	252	273	294	315	336	357	378	399	420	441	462	483	504	525
22	44	66	88	110	132	154	176	198	220	242	264	286	308	330	352	374	396	418	440	462	484	506	528	550
23	46	69	92	115	138	161	184	207	230	253	276	299	322	345	368	391	414	437	460	483	506	529	552	575
24	48	72	96	120	144	168	192	216	240	264	288	312	336	360	384	408	432	456	480	504	528	552	576	600
25	50	75	100	125	150	175	200	225	250	275	300	325	350	375	400	425	450	475	500	525	550	575	600	625

Decimal Equivalents of Common Fractions

1/2	.5000	1/12	.0833	3/5	.6000	5/6	.8333	7/9	.7778
1/3	.3333	1/16	.0625	3/7	.4286	5/7	.7143	7/10	.7000
1/4	.2500	1/32	.0313	3/8	.3750	5/8	.6250	7/11	.6364
1/5	.2000	1/64	.0156	3/10	.3000	5/9	.5556	7/12	.5833
1/6	.1667	2/3	.6667	3/11	.2727	5/11	.4545	8/9	.8889
1/7	.1429	2/5	.4000	3/16	.1875	5/12	.4167	8/11	.7273
1/8	.1250	2/7	.2857	4/5	.8000	5/16	.3125	9/10	.9000
1/9	.1111	2/9	.2222	4/7	.5714	6/7	.8571	9/11	.8182
1/10	.1000	2/11	.1818	4/9	.4444	6/11	.5455	10/11	.9091
1/11	.0909	3/4	.7500	4/11	.3636	7/8	.8750	11/12	.9167

Math **Terms**

An **absolute value** for any real number is the number of units the number is from zero on the number line. The absolute value of −4, written |−4|, is 4. An absolute value is never negative.

An **angle** is made when two rays (lines) share a common endpoint. An angle is measured in degrees. The three most common angles are *acute*, *obtuse*, and *right* angles.

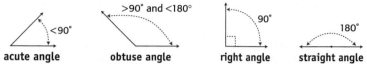

| acute angle | obtuse angle | right angle | straight angle |

Area is the total surface within a closed figure (circle, square, etc). The area of a rectangle is figured by multiplying the length by the width. Area is measured in square units such as square inches or square feet.

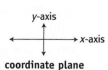

area

The **average** is found by adding a group of numbers together and then dividing that sum by the number of separate numbers (addends). The average of 7, 8, and 9 is 8, because $7 + 8 + 9 = 24$, and $24 \div 3$ (numbers) = 8. This is also called the mathematical *mean*.

Circumference is the measure of distance around the edge of a circle.

A **common denominator** is a multiple shared by the denominators of two or more fractions. For example, 6 is a common denominator of $\frac{1}{2}(\frac{3}{6})$ and $\frac{1}{3}(\frac{2}{6})$; 6 is a multiple of both 2 and 3. To add or subtract fractions, you must find a common denominator; $\frac{1}{2}+\frac{1}{3}=\frac{3}{6}+\frac{2}{6}=\frac{5}{6}$. The lowest common denominator is also called the least common multiple (LCM) of the denominators.

Complementary angles are two angles whose degree measures have a sum of 90.

Congruent (≅) is the term for two figures, angles, or line segments that are the same size and shape.

congruent triangles

A **coordinate plane** is made up of two perpendicular number lines forming a grid. The horizontal number line is called the *x*-axis. The vertical number line is called the *y*-axis. Ordered pairs are used to plot points on the coordinate plane.

y-axis

x-axis

coordinate plane

Coordinates are the numbers in an ordered pair of numbers. The first number is called the *x-coordinate,* and the second number is called the *y-coordinate,* usually expressed as (*x, y*).

Cosine (cos) is a trigonometric function. In a right triangle, the cosine of an angle is found by dividing the adjacent leg by the hypotenuse.

The **denominator** is the bottom number of a fraction. In the fraction $\frac{1}{3}$, the denominator is 3. It indicates the number of parts needed to make a whole unit.

A **diagonal** is a line from one vertex of a quadrilateral to the opposite vertex.

The **diameter** is the length of a straight line through the center of a circle.

diameter

Difference is a word used to indicate the result of subtraction. For example, 2 is the difference of 8 and 6, because $8 - 6 = 2$.

An **equation** is a statement that says two numbers or mathematical expressions are equal to each other ($2 + 10 = 12$ or $x + 4 = 9$). Equations use the equal sign (=).

An **estimate** is a reasonable guess at an answer. If you add 6.24 and 5.19, you can estimate the answer will be around 11, because $6 + 5 = 11$.

To **evaluate** is to find out the value of an expression or to solve for the number an expression stands for.

An **exponent** is the small, raised number to the right of the base number that shows how many times the base is to be multiplied by itself. In the expression 2^3, 3 is the exponent (2 is the base). So, 2^3 means ($2 \times 2 \times 2 = 8$).

An **expression** is a collection of numbers, operation signs, variables, and inclusion symbols (parentheses, brackets, etc.) that stands for a number. ($4 + x$) or $-8 \div t + 6$

A **factor** is a number that is being multiplied. In $4 \times 3 = 12$, the factors are 4 and 3.

Geometry is the study of two-dimensional shapes (circles, triangles), three-dimensional solids (spheres, cubes), and positions in space (points).

The **hypotenuse** is the side opposite the right angle in a right triangle.

Inequality is a mathematical sentence involving one of the symbols <, >, ≤, ≥. (See page 581.)

Integers are the whole numbers (counting numbers) and their opposites ($-2, -1, 0, +1, +2, \ldots$).

An **intersection** is the point where two figures in geometry cross each other.

intersections

An **irrational number** is a real number that cannot be written as a fraction (a non-terminating, non-repeating decimal such as *pi*).

An **isosceles triangle** is a triangle with two sides of equal length and two congruent angles. (See *triangle.*)

A **line** is all points formed by extending a line segment in both directions, without end.

line

Lowest common denominator (See *common denominator.*)

Mean is another word for average. (See *average.*)

The **median** is the middle number when a group of numbers is arranged in order from the least to the greatest, or greatest to least. In 1, 4, 6 the median (middle number) is 4. In 1, 4, 6, 8 the median is 5, halfway between 4 and 6.

The **midpoint** is the point that divides a segment into 2 equal halves. If M is the midpoint between P and Q, then $\overline{PM} \cong \overline{MQ}$.

P   M   Q

midpoint

The **mode** is the number or item occurring most frequently in a list of data. It is possible for a list of data to have more than one mode or to have no mode.

A **monomial** is an expression that is either a single number, a variable, or the product of a number and one or more variables. (A polynomial with one term.)

A **multiple** is a quantity that can be divided by another quantity with zero as the remainder (both 6 and 9 are multiples of 3).

The **numerator** is the top number of a fraction. In the fraction $\frac{5}{6}$, the numerator is 5.

An **obtuse** angle is an angle greater than 90 degrees and less than 180 degrees. (See *angle.*)

Opposite numbers are two numbers whose sum is zero (−2 and +2).

An **ordered pair** is two numbers named in a specific order, used to locate points on a plane (*x, y*).

Order of operations is the order in which expressions must be evaluated. PEMDAS—Parentheses, Exponents, Multiplication and Division (left to right), Addition, and Subtraction (left to right).

The **origin** is the point of intersection of the *x*-axis and *y*-axis on a coordinate plane. All ordered pairs (*x, y*) are referenced from the origin.

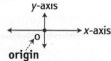
origin

A **parabola** is the graph of a quadratic function.

parabola

Parallel refers to lines that never intersect.

Percent is a way of expressing a number as a fraction of 100. So, $\frac{1}{2}$ expressed as a percentage is $\frac{50}{100}$, which is 50%.

A **perfect square** is the result of multiplying any number or polynomial by itself (4, 9, 16, 25, 36, 49, . . . are perfect squares). For example, $2 \times 2 = 4$, $3 \times 3 = 9$, $4 \times 4 = 16$ . . .

perimeter = 9'

The **perimeter** is the distance around the edge of a multisided figure. If a triangle has three sides, each 3 feet long, its perimeter is 9 feet $(3 + 3 + 3 = 9)$.

Perpendicular refers to two lines that intersect forming right angles (90° angles).

perpendicular lines

Pi (π) is the ratio of the circumference of a circle to its diameter. Pi is approximately 3.14.

Place value is the value of the place of a digit depending on where it is in the number. So, 3,497 is 3 thousands, 4 hundreds, 9 tens, 7 ones. And, .3497 is 3 tenths, 4 hundredths, 9 thousandths, 7 ten-thousandths.

Plane is a term of geometry. Planes can be thought of as flat surfaces that extend indefinitely in all directions and have no thickness.

A **point** is an exact location on a plane.

Point-slope form is an equation of the form $y - y_1 = m (x - x_1)$ for the line passing through a point whose coordinates are (x_1, y_1) and having a slope of m.

A **polynomial** is the sum of two or more monomials. Each monomial is called a term. For example: $4x^2 - 3y + 2 - 8z$

A **positive number** is a number greater than 0.

A **prime number** is a number that cannot be divided evenly by any number except itself and 1. The number 5 is a prime number because it can be divided evenly (without a remainder) only by 1 and 5.

Product is the word used to indicate the result of multiplication. For example, 8 is the product of 2 times 4, because $2 \times 4 = 8$.

Proportion is an equation of the form $\frac{a}{b} = \frac{c}{d}$ that states two ratios are equivalent.

Pythagorean theorem

The **Pythagorean theorem** states that in a right triangle, where c is the hypotenuse, the square of the hypotenuse is equal to the squares of the legs. $a^2 + b^2 = c^2$.

Quadratic formula is a formula for solving a quadratic equation:

$$x = \frac{-b \pm \sqrt{b^2 - 4ac}}{2a}$$

Quotient is the word used to indicate the result of division. For example, if 8 is divided by 4, the quotient is 2, because $8 \div 4 = 2$.

A **radical** is an expression that has a root. (square root, cube root, and so on.)

The **radius** (r) is the distance from the center of a circle to its circumference. (The radius is half the diameter.)

radius

A **ratio** is a way of comparing two numbers by dividing one by the other. The ratio of 3 to 4 is $\frac{3}{4}$. If there are 20 boys and 5 girls in your class, the ratio of boys to girls is $\frac{20}{5}$ ($\frac{4}{1}$ in lowest terms), or $4 : 1$.

A **ray** is a part of a line having one endpoint and extending without end in one direction.

Real numbers are all numbers on the number line, including positive numbers, negative numbers, zero, fractions, and decimals.

Reciprocals are two numbers whose product is 1. The reciprocal of $\frac{2}{3}$ is $\frac{3}{2}$. The multiplication inverse property states that any number times its reciprocal equals 1. $\frac{2}{3} \cdot \frac{3}{2} = 1$

A **rectangle** is a four-sided closed figure with four right angles and with opposite sides parallel and congruent.

A **right angle** is an angle that measures 90 degrees. A right angle is formed when two perpendicular lines meet. (See *angle*.)

A **segment** is part of a line that consists of two points, called endpoints, and all the points between them.

segment

Similar figures are figures that have the same shape but that may differ in size.

Sine ($\sin$) is a trigonometric function. In a right triangle, the sine of an angle is found by dividing the opposite leg by the hypotenuse.

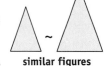

similar figures

Slope is the ratio of the change in y to the change in x of a line, or the ratio of the change in the rise (vertical change) to the run (horizontal change). The variable m is used to denote slope. The slope between 2 points is $\dfrac{y_2 - y_1}{x_2 - x_1}$

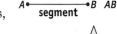

Slope-intercept form is a linear equation of the form $y = mx + b$. (m is the slope and b is the y-intercept).

A **solid** is a three-dimensional figure in geometry, like a cube, a cone, a prism, or a sphere.

solid

A **square** has four sides of equal length and four right angles. *Square* also refers to the product of a number multiplied by itself. The square of 3 is 9 ($3^2 = 9$; $3 \times 3 = 9$). Square also refers to how area is measured.

area = 9
square units

The **square root** of a number is a number that, when multiplied by itself, gives the original number as the product. The symbol for square root is $\sqrt{}$. The square root of 4 is 2, because $2 \times 2 = 4$ or ($\sqrt{4} = 2$).

Standard form is an equation of the form $Ax + By = C$, where A, B, and C are integers and A and B are not both zero.

Sum is a word used to indicate the result of addition. For example, 7 is the sum of 4 and 3, because $4 + 3 = 7$.

Supplementary angles are two angles whose degree measures have a sum of 180.

Tangent (tan) is a trigonometric function. In a right triangle, the tangent of an angle is found by dividing the opposite leg by the adjacent leg.

A **triangle** is a closed figure with three sides. The sum of the angles in every triangle is 180°. Triangles can be classified by *sides:* equilateral, isosceles, or scalene; or by *angles:* right, equiangular, acute, or obtuse.

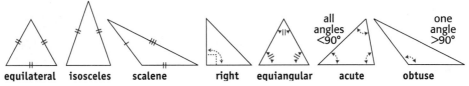

equilateral   isosceles   scalene   right   equiangular   acute   obtuse

A **variable** is a letter that represents a number.

A **vertex** is the point where two sides of a plane (flat) figure meet (corner). The plural of *vertex* is *vertices.*

vertex

x-axis is the horizontal number line in a coordinate plane.

x-intercept is the *x*-coordinate of the point on a line where it intersects the *x*-axis. Here, the value of $y = 0$.

y-axis is the vertical number line on a coordinate plane.

y-intercept is the *y*-coordinate of the point on a line where it intersects the *y*-axis. Here, the value of $x = 0$.

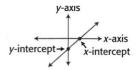

y-axis

y-intercept→   x-axis
x-intercept

> "We are citizens of the world;
> and the tragedy of our times
> is that we do not know this."
> —Woodrow Wilson

GEOGRAPHY

As global citizens, each of us must stay on top of changes in the world. Just as we try to understand key facts about each of the 50 states, we must also try to understand important information about regions and countries in the world. The section that follows will give you the map skills you need to begin your work.

Using the Maps

Finding Direction

Mapmakers use special marks and symbols to show where things are or to give other useful information. Among other things, these marks and symbols show direction (north, south, east, and west). On most maps, north is at the top. But you should always check the **compass rose,** or directional finder, to make sure you know where north is. If there is no symbol, you can assume that north is at the top.

Finding Information

Other important marks and symbols are explained in a box printed on each map. This box is called the legend, or key. It is included to make it easier for you understand and use the map. Below is the United States map legend. (See page 593.) This legend includes state boundaries.

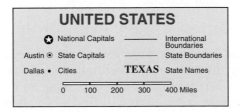

UNITED STATES

✪ National Capitals	——	International Boundaries
Austin ⊙ State Capitals	——	State Boundaries
Dallas • Cities	**TEXAS**	State Names

0   100   200   300   400 Miles

Measuring Distances

0   100   200   300   400 Miles

To measure distances on a map, use the map scale. (See the sample below.) Line up an index card or a piece of paper under the map scale and put a dot on your paper at "0." Put other dots at 100, 200, 300, and so on. You can now measure the approximate distance between points on the map.

Locating Countries

Latitude and longitude lines are another helpful feature of most maps. Latitude and longitude refer to imaginary lines that mapmakers use. Together, these lines can be used to locate any point on the earth.

Latitude

The lines on a map that go from east to west around the earth are called lines of *latitude*. Latitude is measured in degrees, with the equator being 0 degrees (0°). Above the equator, the lines are called *north latitude* and measure from 0° to 90° north (the North Pole). Below the equator, the lines are called *south latitude* and measure from 0° to 90° south (the South Pole). On a map, latitude numbers are printed along the sides.

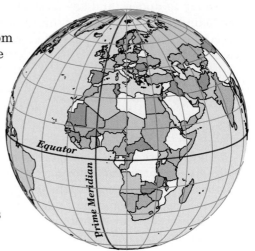

Longitude

The lines on a map that run from the North Pole to the South Pole are lines of *longitude*. Longitude is also measured in degrees. The prime meridian, which runs through Greenwich, England, is 0° longitude. Lines east of the prime meridian are called *east longitude;* lines west of the prime meridian are called *west longitude*. On a map, longitude numbers are printed at the top and bottom.

Coordinates

The latitude and longitude numbers of a country or other place are called its *coordinates*. In each set of coordinates, latitude is given first, then longitude. To locate a certain place on a map using its coordinates, find the point where the two lines cross. (You will find a complete list of coordinates on pages 601-602.)

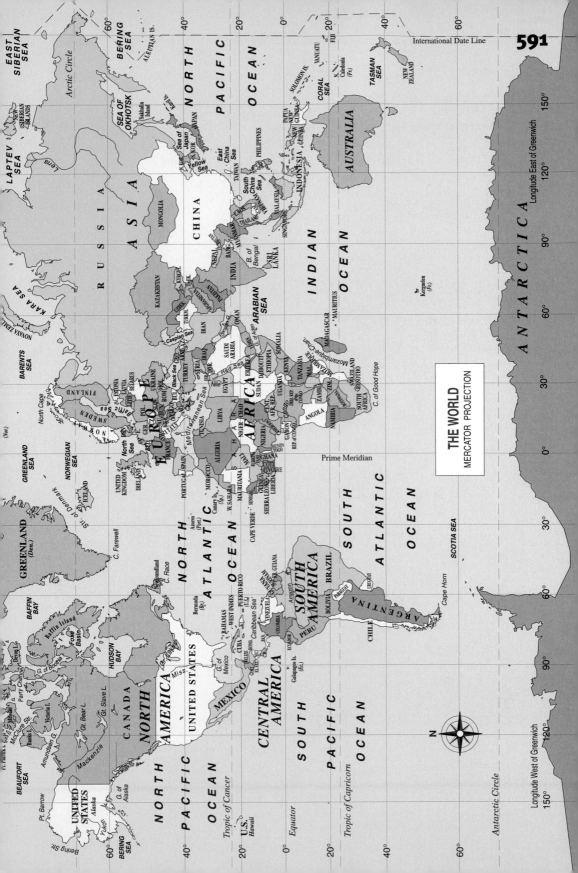

THE WORLD
MERCATOR PROJECTION

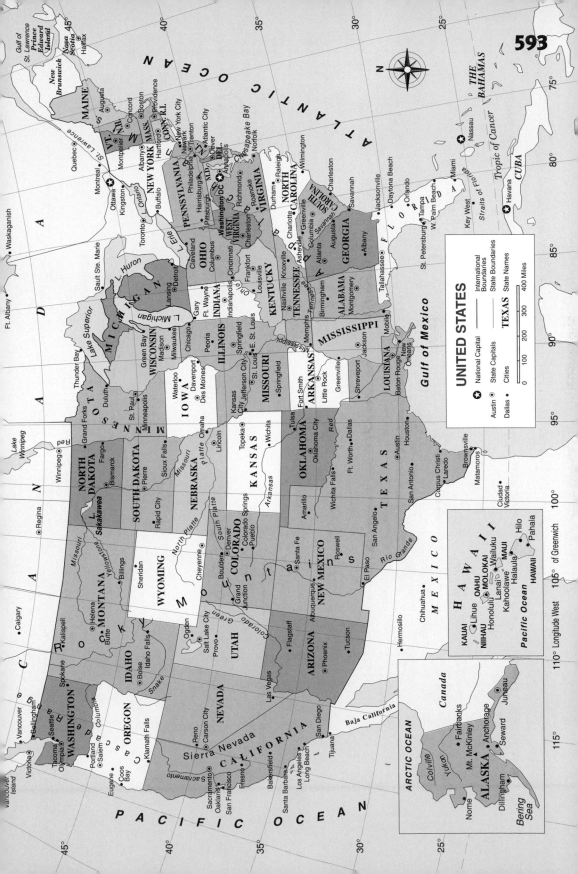

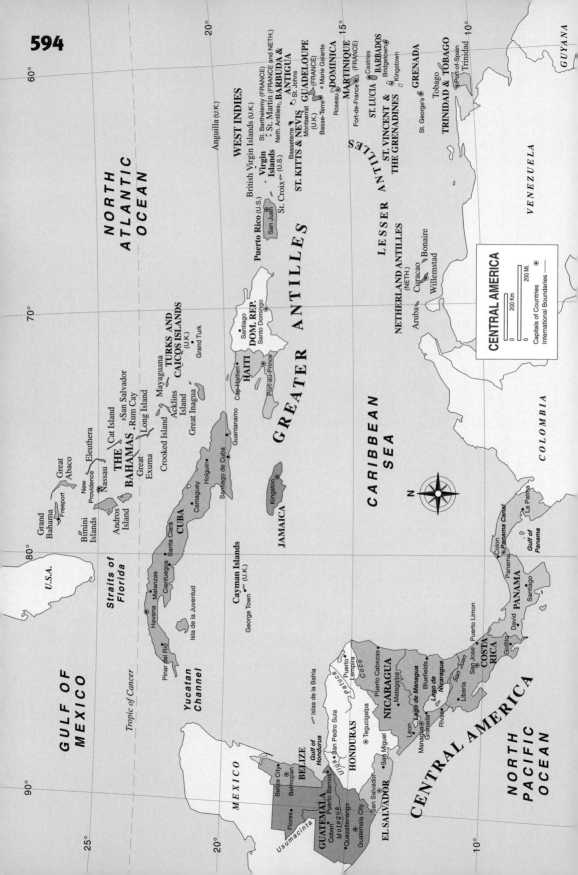

595

Caribbean Sea
West Indies

Pt. Gallinas
G. de Venezuela
Port of Spain
**TRINIDAD &
TOBAGO**

Barranquilla
Maracaibo
Caracas
Cumana
VENEZUELA
Ciudad Guayana

Monteria
Cucuta
San Cristobal
Orinoco
Georgetown
Paramaribo
GUYANA
SURINAME
FR.
GUIANA
(Fr.)
Cayenne

COLOMBIA
Bogota
Boa Vista
Oyapock

Buenaventura
Cali

Pasto
Orinoco

Quito
ECUADOR
Putumayo
Japura
Negro
Branco
Macapa
I. de Marajo
Equator

**NORTH
ATLANTIC
OCEAN**

Guayaquil
Iquitos
Benjamin Constant
Amazon
Manaus
Amazon
Santarem
Belém
Abaetetuba
Sao Luis

G. of
Guayaquil
Marañon
Javari
Jurua
Purus
Madeira
Tapajos
Xingu

Sullana
Chiclayo
Trujillo
Rio Branco
Porto
Velho
Roosevelt
Guapore

Fortaleza
Teresina

PERU
Lima
Ica
B R A Z I L

Natal
Juazeiro do Norte
Recife

Arequipa
**Lake
Titicaca**
Trinidad
BOLIVIA
La Paz
(de facto)
Cochabamba
Santa Cruz
Sucre
(legal)
Cuiaba
Porto Nacional
Sao Francisco
Aracaju
Salvador
Ilhéus

Arica
Mariscal
Estigarribia
Campo
Grande
Brasilia
Goiania

Tocopilla
Paraguay
Belo Horizonte
Vitória

Antofagasta
San Salvador
de Jujuy
PARAGUAY
Asuncion
Parana
Sao Paulo
Santos
Rio de Janeiro

Copiapó
San Miguel
de Tucuman
Resistencia
Encarnación
Curitiba
Paranaguá

La Serena
Ovalle
Cordoba
Salado
Uruguay
Santana do
Livramento
Salto
Porto Alegre
L. dos Patos
Florianópolis

Valparaiso
Santiago
Mendoza
Rosario
Melo
URUGUAY
Montevideo

Concepcion
Santa Rosa
Buenos Aires
La Plata
Rio de la Plata
C. San Antonio

Bahia Blanca
Mar del Plata

Valdivia
Negro
Colorado

Puerto Montt
Ancud
San Carlos
de Bariloche
Pto. Madryn
Chubut
G. San Matias

I. Grande de Chiloé
**ARCHIPIELAGO
de los
CHONOS**
Comodoro
Rivadavia
G. San Jorge

N

Puerto
Aisen
C. Tres Puntas

San Julián

Bahia Grande
Rio Gallegos
Punta Arenas
**FALKLAND
ISLANDS
(U.K.)**
Stanley

I. Santa Inés
I. de los Estados
Cape Horn

**SOUTH GEORGIA
ISLAND
(U.K.)**

SOUTH PACIFIC OCEAN

SOUTH ATLANTIC OCEAN

Tropic of Capricorn

Tropic of Capricorn

Tropic of Capricorn

PANAMA
G. of
Panama

Medellin

A   N   D   E   S   M   O   U   N   T   A   I   N   S

C   H   I   L   E

A   R   G   E   N   T   I   N   A

Araguaia
Tocantins
Parnaiba

Picomayo

Plicomayo

Pilcomayo

80°
70°
60°
50°
40°

10°
0°
10°
20°
30°
40°
50°

90°
80°
70° Longitude West of Greenwich 50°
40°
30°
20°

Legend:

SOUTH AMERICA

0   600 Km.
0   600 Mi.

Capitals of Countries   ⊙
International Boundaries ————

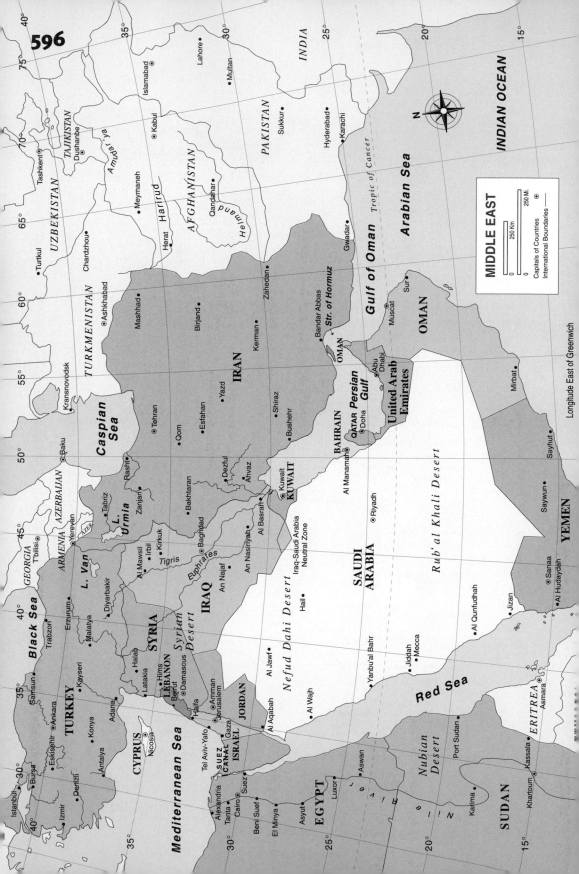

MIDDLE EAST

Capitals of Countries ⊙
International Boundaries

0 ——— 250 Km
0 ——— 250 Mi.

Longitude East of Greenwich

INDIAN OCEAN

Arabian Sea

Gulf of Oman

Tropic of Cancer

Str. of Hormuz

OMAN

Muscat ⊙
Sur •
Mirbat •
Sayhut •

YEMEN

Sanaa ⊙
Saywun •
Al Hudaydah •

UNITED ARAB EMIRATES

Abu Dhabi ⊙

QATAR
Doha ⊙

BAHRAIN
Al Manamah ⊙
Persian Gulf

KUWAIT
Kuwait ⊙

SAUDI ARABIA

Riyadh ⊙
Rub' al Khali Desert
Hail •
Mecca •
Jiddah •
Yanbu'al Bahr •
Al Jawf •
Al Wajh •
Al Aqabah •
Nefud Dahi Desert
Iraq-Saudi Arabia Neutral Zone
Jizan •
Al Qunfudhah •

IRAN

Tehran ⊙
Mashhad •
Birjand •
Zahedan •
Kerman •
Yazd •
Qom •
Estahan •
Shiraz •
Bushehr •
Bandar Abbas •
Gwadar •
Ahvaz •
Deztul •
Bakhtaran •
Zanjan •
Tabriz •
Rasht •

Caspian Sea

AZERBAIJAN
Baku ⊙

ARMENIA
Yerevan ⊙

GEORGIA
Tbilisi ⊙

L. Urmia
L. Van

IRAQ
Baghdad ⊙
Al Mawsil •
Kirkuk •
Irbil •
An Najaf •
An Nasiriyah •
Al Basrah •
Tigris
Euphrates
Syrian Desert

SYRIA
Damascus ⊙
Halab •
Hims •
Latakia •

LEBANON
Beirut ⊙

ISRAEL
Jerusalem ⊙
Tel Aviv-Yato •
Gaza •
Haifa •

JORDAN
Amman ⊙

TURKEY
Ankara ⊙
Istanbul •
Izmir •
Bursa •
Denizli •
Antalya •
Konya •
Adana •
Kayseri •
Eskisehir •
Samsun •
Trabzon •
Erzurum •
Malatya •
Diyarbakir •

CYPRUS
Nicosia ⊙

Black Sea

Mediterranean Sea

TAJIKISTAN
Dushanbe ⊙

UZBEKISTAN
Tashkent ⊙
Turtkul •

TURKMENISTAN
Ashkhabad ⊙
Chardzhou •
Krasnovodsk •

Amu Darya

AFGHANISTAN
Kabul ⊙
Herat •
Meymaneh •
Qandahar •
Harirud
Helmand

PAKISTAN
Islamabad ⊙
Lahore •
Multan •
Sukkur •
Hyderabad •
Karachi •
Gwadar •

INDIA

EGYPT
Cairo ⊙
Alexandria •
Tanta •
Suez •
Beni Suef •
El Minya •
Asyut •
Luxor •
Aswan •

SUEZ CANAL

Nubian Desert

Red Sea

Nile

SUDAN
Khartoum ⊙
Port Sudan •
Kassala •
Karima •

ERITREA
Asmara ⊙

40° 35° 30° 25° 20° 15°

75° 70° 65° 60° 55° 50° 45° 40°

40° 35° 30° 25° 20° 15°

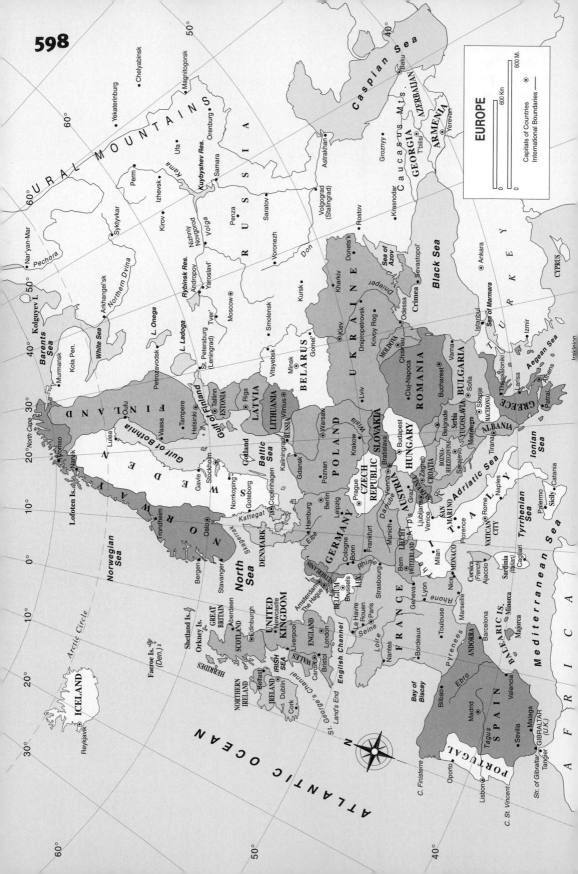

598

EUROPE

Capitals of Countries ⊙
International Boundaries —

600 Km
600 Mi.

599

ARCTIC OCEAN

ATLANTIC OCEAN

GREENLAND

ICELAND

BRITISH ISLES

BARENTS SEA

NORTH SEA

BALTIC SEA

Berlin
Warsaw
Kiev
Moscow
St. Petersburg

London

EUROPE

BLACK SEA

TURKEY
Ankara
Adana
Aleppo
Erzurum
SYRIA
Damascus
LEBANON
Beirut
ISRAEL
Amman
IRAQ
Baghdad
Basra
KUWAIT
BAHRAIN
QATAR
Riyadh
SAUDI ARABIA
Mecca
UN. ARAB EMIR.
Sanaa
YEMEN
Aden

IRAN
Tehran
Mashad
Shiraz
Bandar Abbas
OMAN
Muscat

Tabriz

CASPIAN SEA

KAZAKHSTAN
ARAL SEA
Karaganda
L. Balkhash
Ural'sk
Gur'yev
Krasnovodsk
TURKMENISTAN
Ashgabat
UZBEK.
Tashkent
KYRGYZ.
Bishkek
Alma-Ata
TAJIK.
AFGHANISTAN
Kabul
Herat
Quetta
Islamabad
Srinagar
PAKISTAN
Gwadar
Karachi

RUSSIA

Perm'
Yekaterinburg
Chelyabinsk
Magnitogorsk
Omsk
Tomsk
Novosibirsk
Barnaul
Semipalatinsk
Ob'
Irtysh
Syrdarya
Amudarya
Shache
Hotan
Aksu
Urumqi
SINKIANG

Salekhard
Khanty-Mansiysk
Yenisey
Dudinka
Nordvik

Arctic Circle

Tura
Yakutsk
Krasnoyarsk
Irkutsk
Ulan-Ude
Chita
L. Baykal
Lena

Kirensk
Nordvik

SEVERNAYA ZEMLYA
NOVAYA ZEMLYA
KARA SEA
LAPTEV SEA
NEW SIBERIAN IS.
EAST SIBERIAN SEA

UNITED STATES (Alaska)

BERING SEA

ALEUTIAN IS.

Komandorskiye Is.

Anadyr

Srednekolymsk
Kolyma
Magadan
Kamchatka Pen.
Petropavlovsk-Kamchatskiy

SEA OF OKHOTSK

Nikolayevsk
Komsomol'sk
Skovorodino
Khabarovsk
Amur

Sakhalin I.
KURIL IS.

Hokkaido
Hakodate
Vladivostok

MONGOLIA
Uliastay
Hovd
Ulaanbaatar
Gobi
INNER MONGOLIA

Qiqihar
Changchun
Shenyang
Dandong
N. KOREA
Pyongyang
S. KOREA
Seoul

SEA OF JAPAN

Sendai
Honshu
Tokyo
Nagoya
Hiroshima
Shikoku
Kyushu
Nagasaki
RYUKYU IS. (Jap.)

JAPAN

Beijing
Tianjin
Jihan
Kaifeng
GRAND CANAL
Xi'an
Wuhan
CHINA
TIBET
Lhasa
Thimphu
BHUTAN
NEPAL
Kathmandu
New Delhi
Kanpur
Lanzhou
Jiuquan
Yumen
Chengdu
Chongqing
Changsha
Fuzhou
Guangzhou
HONG KONG
Shanghai
Nanjing
Chang (Yangtze)
Huang

YELLOW SEA
EAST CHINA SEA
Taipei
TAIWAN

Tropic of Cancer

PACIFIC OCEAN

INDIA
Ahmadabad
Daman
Bombay
Hyderabad
Yanam
Bangalore
Mahe
Karikal
Madurai
SRI LANKA
Colombo
Kandy
Madras
New Delhi
Calcutta
Dhaka
BANGLA-DESH
BURMA
Mandalay
Rangoon
Myitkyina
Hanoi
LAOS
Vientiane
THAILAND
Bangkok
CAMBODIA
Phnom Penh
VIETNAM
Ho Chi Minh City
G. of Thailand
G. of Tonkin
SOUTH CHINA SEA
Hainan

MALDIVES
Male

ARABIAN SEA

Socotra

AFRICA

G. of Aden

SEYCHELLES

MADAGASCAR

BAY OF BENGAL

Equator

INDIAN OCEAN

PHILIPPINES
Manila
Luzon
Mindoro
Samar
Leyte
Palawan
Negros
Davao
Mindanao

George Town
Medan
MALAYA
MALAYSIA
Kuala Lumpur
SINGAPORE
Str. of Malacca
Sumatra
Palembang
Jakarta
JAVA
Surabaya
JAVA SEA
Kuching
SARAWAK
BRUNEI
SABAH
Kota Kinabalu
Borneo
Banjarmasin
Makassar Str.
Ujung Pandang
CELEBES SEA
Manado
Celebes
INDONESIA
Flores
Sumbawa
Timor
East Timor
FLORES SEA
BANDA SEA
TIMOR SEA

SUNDA IS.

Broome

AUSTRALIA

Tropic of Capricorn

Perth

ASIA

0   1200 Km
0   1200 Mi.

Capitals of Countries ⊚
International Boundaries ———

60°   Longitude East of Greenwich   80°   100°   120°

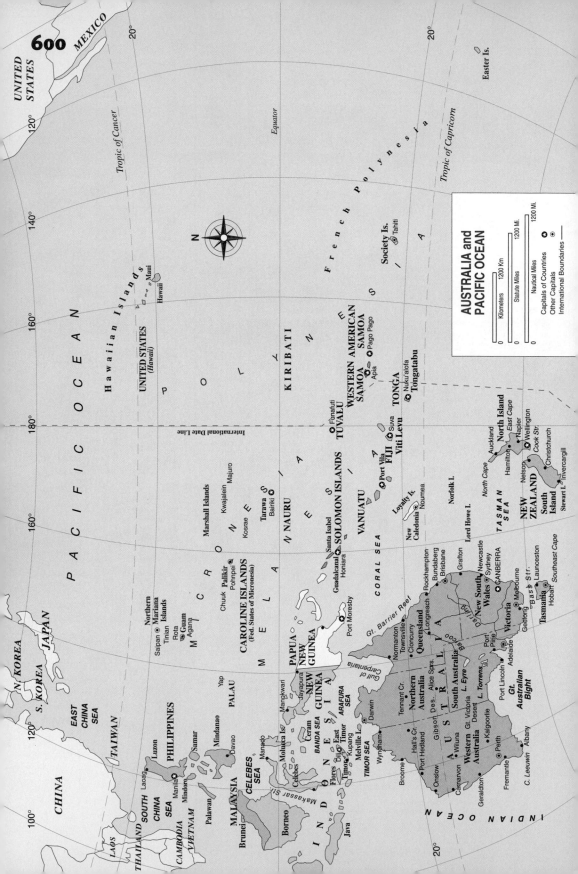

MEXICO

UNITED STATES

Easter Is.

Tropic of Cancer

Equator

Tropic of Capricorn

F r e n c h   P o l y n e s i a

Society Is.
⊛ Tahiti

N

Maui
Hawaii

Hawaiian Islands

UNITED STATES
(Hawaii)

WESTERN AMERICAN
SAMOA   SAMOA
⊛ Pago Pago

KIRIBATI

P O L Y N E S I A

Apia ⊛
Nuku'alofa
⊛ Tongatabu

TONGA

Funafuti ⊛
TUVALU

Auckland
North Cape ● Hamilton ● East Cape
Suva ● Napier
Viti Levu ● Wellington ⊛
Nelson ● Cook Str.
NEW ● Christchurch
ZEALAND South
Island
Stewart I. ● Invercargill

International Date Line

P A C I F I C   O C E A N

Marshall Islands

Kwajalein
Majuro

Kosrae

Tarawa ⊛
Bairiki

N NAURU

M I C R O N E S I A

Chuuk Palikir ⊛
Pohnpei

CAROLINE ISLANDS
(Fed. States of Micronesia)

Santa Isabel
Guadalcanal ⊛ SOLOMON ISLANDS
Honiara

VANUATU

Port Vila ⊛ FIJI

New ● Noumea
Caledonia
Loyalty Is.

Norfolk I.

North Island

TASMAN
SEA

Lord Howe I.

CORAL SEA

Gt. Barrier Reef

Rockhampton
Bundaberg
Brisbane
Grafton
Newcastle
New South
Wales ● Sydney
⊛ CANBERRA
Victoria ● Melbourne
Geelong
Tasmania
Hobart ● Southeast Cape
Launceston
Bass Str.

Normanton
Townsville
Cloncurry
Longreach
Queensland

Gulf of
Carpentaria

Port Moresby

PAPUA
NEW
GUINEA

Mangkwari

NEW GUINEA

Jayapura

I N D O N E S I A

ARAFURA
SEA

BANDA SEA

Ceram

Molucca Is.
Celebes

CELEBES
SEA

Manado

Davao

Mindanao

Samar

Luzon
Manila ●

PHILIPPINES

Mindoro
Palawan

Yap

PALAU

TIMOR SEA

Timor
Flores East
Timor
Kupang

Java

Borneo

Brunei

MALAYSIA

Makassar Str.

I N D I A N   O C E A N

Darwin
Melville I.
Wyndham
Broome
Port Hedland
Onslow
Carnarvon
Geraldton
Fremantle
Perth
C. Leeuwin
Albany

Northern
Australia
Tennant Cr.
Hall's Cr.
Gibson
Des.
Gt. Victoria
Desert
Western
Australia
Kalgoorlie
Wiluna

Alice Sprs.
L. Eyre
L. Torrens
South Australia
Port Lincoln
Port Augusta
Adelaide

A U S T R A L I A

Darling

Murray
Port
Pirie
Port
Lincoln
Gt.
Australian
Bight

CHINA

N. KOREA
S. KOREA
JAPAN

EAST
CHINA
SEA

TAIWAN

CHINA

SOUTH
CHINA
SEA

THAILAND
VIETNAM
CAMBODIA
LAOS

20°
120°
140°
160°
180°
160°
140°
120°
100°
20°

**AUSTRALIA and
PACIFIC OCEAN**

Kilometers   1200 Km
Statute Miles   1200 Mi.
Nautical Miles   1200 Mi.
0
0
0

⊛ Capitals of Countries
⊙ Other Capitals
─── International Boundaries

Index to World Maps

Country	Latitude		Longitude		Country	Latitude		Longitude	
Afghanistan	33°	N	65°	E	France	46°	N	2°	E
Albania	41°	N	20°	E	Gabon	1°	S	11°	E
Algeria	28°	N	3°	E	The Gambia	13°	N	16°	W
Andorra	42°	N	1°	E	Georgia	43°	N	45°	E
Angola	12°	S	18°	E	Germany	51°	N	10°	E
Antigua and Barbuda	17°	N	61°	W	Ghana	8°	N	2°	W
Argentina	34°	S	64°	W	Greece	39°	N	22°	E
Armenia	41°	N	45°	E	Greenland	70°	N	40°	W
Ashgabat	25°	N	95°	E	Grenada	12°	N	61°	W
Australia	25°	S	135°	E	Guatemala	15°	N	90°	W
Austria	47°	N	13°	E	Guinea	11°	N	10°	W
Azerbaijan	41°	N	47°	E	Guinea-Bissau	12°	N	15°	W
Bahamas	24°	N	76°	W	Guyana	5°	N	59°	W
Bahrain	26°	N	50°	E	Haiti	19°	N	72°	W
Bangladesh	24°	N	90°	E	Honduras	15°	N	86°	W
Barbados	13°	N	59°	W	Hungary	47°	N	20°	E
Belarus	54°	N	25°	E	Iceland	65°	N	18°	W
Belgium	50°	N	4°	E	India	20°	N	77°	E
Belize	17°	N	88°	W	Indonesia	5°	S	120°	E
Benin	9°	N	2°	E	Iran	32°	N	53°	E
Bhutan	27°	N	90°	E	Iraq	33°	N	44°	E
Bolivia	17°	S	65°	W	Ireland	53°	N	8°	W
Bosnia-Herzegovina	44°	N	18°	E	Israel	31°	N	35°	E
Botswana	22°	S	24°	E	Italy	42°	N	12°	E
Brazil	10°	S	55°	W	Jamaica	18°	N	77°	W
Brunei Darussalam	4°	N	114°	E	Japan	36°	N	138°	E
Bulgaria	43°	N	25°	E	Jordan	31°	N	36°	E
Burkina Faso	13°	N	2°	W	Kazakhstan	45°	N	70°	E
Burundi	3°	S	30°	E	Kenya	1°	N	38°	E
Cambodia	13°	N	105°	E	Kiribati	0°	N	175°	E
Cameroon	6°	N	12°	E	North Korea	40°	N	127°	E
Canada	60°	N	95°	W	South Korea	36°	N	128°	E
Cape Verde	16°	N	24°	W	Kuwait	29°	N	47°	E
Central African Republic	7°	N	21°	E	Kyrgyzstan	42°	N	75°	E
Chad	15°	N	19°	E	Laos	18°	N	105°	E
Chile	30°	S	71°	W	Latvia	57°	N	25°	E
China	35°	N	105°	E	Lebanon	34°	N	36°	E
Colombia	4°	N	72°	W	Lesotho	29°	S	28°	E
Comoros	12°	S	44°	E	Liberia	6°	N	10°	W
Congo, Dem. Rep. of the	4°	S	25°	E	Libya	27°	N	17°	E
Congo, Republic of the	1°	S	15°	E	Liechtenstein	47°	N	9°	E
Costa Rica	10°	N	84°	W	Lithuania	56°	N	24°	E
Cote d'Ivoire	8°	N	5°	W	Luxembourg	49°	N	6°	E
Croatia	45°	N	16°	E	Macedonia	43°	N	22°	E
Cuba	21°	N	80°	W	Madagascar	19°	S	46°	E
Cyprus	35°	N	33°	E	Malawi	13°	S	34°	E
Czech Republic	50°	N	15°	E	Malaysia	2°	N	112°	E
Denmark	56°	N	10°	E	Maldives	2°	N	70°	E
Djibouti	11°	N	43°	E	Mali	17°	N	4°	W
Dominica	15°	N	61°	W	Malta	36°	N	14°	E
Dominican Rep.	19°	N	70°	W	Marshall Islands	7°	N	172°	E
Ecuador	2°	S	77°	W	Mauritania	20°	N	12°	W
Egypt	27°	N	30°	E	Mauritius	20°	S	57°	E
El Salvador	14°	N	89°	W	Mexico	23°	N	102°	W
Equatorial Guinea	2°	N	9°	E	Micronesia	5°	N	150°	E
Eritrea	17°	N	38°	E	Moldova	47°	N	28°	E
Estonia	59°	N	26°	E	Monaco	43°	N	7°	E
Ethiopia	8°	N	38°	E	Mongolia	46°	N	105°	E
Fiji	19°	S	174°	E	Montenegro	43°	N	19°	E
Finland	64°	N	26°	E	Morocco	32°	N	5°	W

Country	Latitude	Longitude	Country	Latitude	Longitude
Mozambique	18° S	35° E	United Arab Emirates	24° N	54° E
Namibia	22° S	17° E	United Kingdom	54° N	2° W
Nauru	1° S	166° E	United States	38° N	97° W
Nepal	28° N	84° E	Uruguay	33° S	56° W
The Netherlands	52° N	5° E	Uzbekistan	40° N	68° E
New Zealand	41° S	174° E	Vanuatu	17° S	170° E
Nicaragua	13° N	85° W	Venezuela	8° N	66° W
Niger	16° N	8° E	Vietnam	17° N	106° E
Nigeria	10° N	8° E	Wales	53° N	3° W
Northern Ireland	55° N	7° W	Western Samoa	10° S	173° W
Norway	62° N	10° E	Yemen	15° N	44° E
Oman	22° N	58° E	Yugoslavia	44° N	19° E
Pakistan	30° N	70° E	Zambia	15° S	30° E
Palau	8° N	138° E	Zimbabwe	20° S	30° E
Panama	9° N	80° W			
Papua New Guinea	6° S	147° E			
Paraguay	23° S	58° W			
Peru	10° S	76° W			
The Philippines	13° N	122° E			
Poland	52° N	19° E			
Portugal	39° N	8° W			
Qatar	25° N	51° E			
Romania	46° N	25° E			
Russia	60° N	80° E			
Rwanda	2° S	30° E			
St. Kitts and Nevis	17° N	62° W			
Saint Lucia	14° N	61° W			
Saint Vincent and the Grenadines	13° N	61° W			
San Marino	44° N	12° E			
São Tomé and Príncipe	1° N	7° E			
Saudi Arabia	25° N	45° E			
Scotland	57° N	5° W			
Senegal	14° N	14° W			
Serbia	45° N	21° E			
Seychelles	5° S	55° E			
Sierra Leone	8° N	11° W			
Singapore	1° N	103° E			
Slovakia	49° N	19° E			
Slovenia	46° N	15° E			
Solomon Islands	8° S	159° E			
Somalia	10° N	49° E			
South Africa	30° S	26° E			
Spain	40° N	4° W			
Sri Lanka	7° N	81° E			
Sudan	15° N	30° E			
Suriname	4° N	56° W			
Swaziland	26° S	31° E			
Sweden	62° N	15° E			
Switzerland	47° N	8° E			
Syria	35° N	38° E			
Taiwan	23° N	121° E			
Tajikistan	39° N	71° E			
Tanzania	6° S	35° E			
Thailand	15° N	100° E			
Togo	8° N	1° E			
Tonga	20° S	173° W			
Trinidad and Tobago	11° N	61° W			
Tunisia	34° N	9° E			
Turkey	39° N	35° E			
Turkmenistan	40° N	55° E			
Tuvalu	8° S	179° E			
Uganda	1° N	32° E			
Ukraine	50° N	30° E			

TOPOGRAPHIC TALLY TABLE

THE CONTINENTS	Area (Sq Km)	Percent of Earth's Land
Asia	44,026,000	29.7
Africa	30,271,000	20.4
North America	24,258,000	16.3
South America	17,823,000	12.0
Antarctica	13,209,000	8.9
Europe	10,404,000	7.0
Australia	7,682,000	5.2

LONGEST RIVERS	Length (Km)
Nile, *Africa*	6,671
Amazon, *South America*	6,437
Chang Jiang (Yangtze), *Asia*	6,380
Mississippi-Missouri, *North America*	5,971
Ob-Irtysk, *Asia*	5,410
Huang (Yellow), *Asia*	4,672
Congo, *Africa*	4,667
Amur, *Asia*	4,416
Lena, *Asia*	4,400
Mackenzie-Peace, *North America*	4,241

MAJOR ISLANDS	Area (Sq Km)
Greenland	2,175,600
New Guinea	792,500
Borneo	725,500
Madagascar	587,000
Baffin	507,500
Sumatra	427,300
Honshu	227,400
Great Britain	218,100
Victoria	217,300
Ellesmere	196,200
Celebes	178,700
South (New Zealand)	151,000
Java	126,700

THE OCEANS	Area (Sq Km)	Percent Earth's Area Water
Pacific	166,241,000	46.0
Atlantic	86,557,000	23.9
Indian	73,427,000	20.3
Arctic	9,485,000	2.6

"Government is one of the subtlest of the arts . . .
since it is the art of making people live together in
peace and with reasonable happiness."

—Felix Frankfurter

GOVERNMENT

Every country in the world has a government. The purpose of the
government is to make and enforce laws and to protect the rights of its
citizens. Every major country in the world also has a constitution, a basic
set of laws by which the people are governed.

The United States Constitution establishes the form of the federal
government and explains the rights and responsibilities of its citizens.
This section of your handbook takes a closer look at the Constitution and
how it affects the government and the average citizen.

Branches of the U.S. Federal Government

Legislative Branch		Executive Branch	Judicial Branch
Responsibilities			
Makes Laws		Enforces Laws Makes Policy	Interprets Laws
Components			
Congress		President	Supreme Court
Senate	House of Representatives	Vice President	Circuit Courts
President of the Senate	Speaker of the House	Cabinet	District and Special Courts

The **U.S. Constitution**

The U.S. Constitution is made up of three main parts: **a preamble, 7 articles,** and **27 amendments.** The *preamble* states the purpose of the Constitution, the *articles* explain how the government works, and the 10 original *amendments* list the basic rights guaranteed to all American citizens.

Together, the three parts of the Constitution contain the laws and guidelines necessary to set up and run the U.S. national government successfully. Besides giving power to the national government, the U.S. Constitution gives some power to the states and some to the people.

The Preamble

We the people of the United States, in order to form a more perfect Union, establish justice, insure domestic tranquility, provide for the common defense, promote the general welfare, and secure the blessings of liberty to ourselves and our posterity, do ordain and establish this Constitution for the United States of America.

The Articles of the Constitution

The articles of the Constitution explain how the three branches of government work and what each can and cannot do. The articles also explain how the federal and state governments must work together, and how the Constitution can be amended or changed.

ARTICLE 1   explains the legislative branch, how laws are made, and how Congress works.

ARTICLE 2   explains the executive branch, the offices of the President and Vice President, and the powers of the executive branch.

ARTICLE 3   explains the judicial branch, the Supreme Court and other courts, and warns people about trying to overthrow the government.

ARTICLE 4   describes how the United States federal government and the individual state governments work together.

ARTICLE 5   tells how the Constitution can be amended, or changed.

ARTICLE 6   states that the United States federal government and the Constitution are the law of the land.

ARTICLE 7   outlines how the Constitution must be adopted to become official.

The Bill of Rights

To get the necessary votes to approve the Constitution, a number of changes (amendments) had to be made. These 10 original amendments are called the Bill of Rights. They guarantee all Americans some very basic rights, including the right to worship and speak freely and the right to have a jury trial. The first eight amendments grant individual rights and freedoms. The ninth and tenth amendments prevent Congress from passing laws that would deprive citizens of these rights.

AMENDMENT 1   People have the right to worship, to speak freely, to gather together, and to question the government.

AMENDMENT 2   People have the right to bear arms.

AMENDMENT 3   The government cannot have soldiers stay in people's houses without their permission.

AMENDMENT 4   People and their property cannot be searched without the written permission of a judge.

AMENDMENT 5   People cannot be tried for a serious crime without a jury. They cannot be tried twice for the same crime or be forced to testify against themselves. Also, they cannot have property taken away while they are on trial. Any property taken for public use must receive a fair price.

AMENDMENT 6   In criminal cases, people have a right to a speedy and public trial, to be told what they are accused of, to hear witnesses against them, to get witnesses in their favor, and to have a lawyer.

AMENDMENT 7   In cases involving more than $20, people have the right to a jury trial.

AMENDMENT 8   People have a right to fair bail (money given as a promise the person will return for trial) and to fair fines and punishments.

AMENDMENT 9   People have rights that are not listed in the Constitution.

AMENDMENT 10   Powers not given to the federal government are given to the states or to the people.

The **Other Amendments**

The Constitution and the Bill of Rights were ratified in 1791. Since that time, more than 7,000 amendments to the Constitution have been proposed. Because three-fourths of the states must approve an amendment before it becomes law, just 27 amendments have been passed. The first 10 are listed under the Bill of Rights; the other 17 are listed below. (The date each amendment became law is given in parentheses.)

AMENDMENT 11   A person cannot sue a state in federal court. (**1795**)

AMENDMENT 12   The President and Vice President are elected separately. (**1804**)

AMENDMENT 13   Slavery is abolished. (**1865**)

AMENDMENT 14   All persons born in the United States or those who have become citizens enjoy full citizenship rights. (**1868**)

AMENDMENT 15   Voting rights are given to all [adult male] citizens regardless of race, creed, or color. (**1870**)

AMENDMENT 16   Congress has the power to collect income taxes. (**1913**)

AMENDMENT 17   United States Senators are elected directly by the people. (**1913**)

AMENDMENT 18   Making, buying, and selling alcoholic beverages is no longer allowed. (**1919**)

AMENDMENT 19   Women have the right to vote. (**1920**)

AMENDMENT 20   The President's term begins January 20; Senators' and Representatives' terms begin January 3. (**1933**)

AMENDMENT 21   (Repeals Amendment 18) Alcoholic beverages can be made, bought, and sold again. (**1933**)

AMENDMENT 22   The President is limited to two elected terms. (**1951**)

AMENDMENT 23   District of Columbia residents gain the right to vote. (**1961**)

AMENDMENT 24   All voter poll taxes are forbidden. (**1964**)

AMENDMENT 25   If the Presidency is vacant, the Vice President takes over. If the Vice Presidency is vacant, the President names someone and the Congress votes on the choice. (**1967**)

AMENDMENT 26   Citizens 18 years old gain the right to vote. (**1971**)

AMENDMENT 27   No law changing the pay for members of Congress will take effect until after an election of Representatives. (**1992**)

U.S. Presidents

Vice Presidents

	President	Dates	Vice President	
1	George Washington	April 30, 1789 – March 3, 1797	John Adams	**1**
2	John Adams	March 4, 1797 – March 3, 1801	Thomas Jefferson	**2**
3	Thomas Jefferson	March 4, 1801 – March 3, 1805	Aaron Burr	**3**
	Thomas Jefferson	March 4, 1805 – March 3, 1809	George Clinton	**4**
4	James Madison	March 4, 1809 – March 3, 1813	George Clinton	
	James Madison	March 4, 1813 – March 3, 1817	Elbridge Gerry	**5**
5	James Monroe	March 4, 1817 – March 3, 1821	Daniel D. Tompkins	**6**
	James Monroe	March 4, 1821 – March 3, 1825		
6	John Quincy Adams	March 4, 1825 – March 3, 1829	John C. Calhoun	**7**
7	Andrew Jackson	March 4, 1829 – March 3, 1833	John C. Calhoun	
	Andrew Jackson	March 4, 1833 – March 3, 1837	Martin Van Buren	**8**
8	Martin Van Buren	March 4, 1837 – March 3, 1841	Richard M. Johnson	**9**
9	William Henry Harrison*	March 4, 1841 – April 4, 1841	John Tyler	**10**
10	John Tyler	April 6, 1841 – March 3, 1845		
11	James K. Polk	March 4, 1845 – March 3, 1849	George M. Dallas	**11**
12	Zachary Taylor*	March 5, 1849 – July 9, 1850	Millard Fillmore	**12**
13	Millard Fillmore	July 10, 1850 – March 3, 1853		
14	Franklin Pierce	March 4, 1853 – March 3, 1857	William R. King	**13**
15	James Buchanan	March 4, 1857 – March 3, 1861	John C. Breckinridge	**14**
16	Abraham Lincoln	March 4, 1861 – March 3, 1865	Hannibal Hamlin	**15**
	Abraham Lincoln*	March 4, 1865 – April 15, 1865	Andrew Johnson	**16**
17	Andrew Johnson	April 15, 1865 – March 3, 1869		
18	Ulysses S. Grant	March 4, 1869 – March 3, 1873	Schuyler Colfax	**17**
	Ulysses S. Grant	March 4, 1873 – March 3, 1877	Henry Wilson	**18**
19	Rutherford B. Hayes	March 4, 1877 – March 3, 1881	William A. Wheeler	**19**
20	James A. Garfield*	March 4, 1881 – Sept. 19, 1881	Chester A. Arthur	**20**
21	Chester A. Arthur	Sept. 20, 1881 – March 3, 1885		
22	Grover Cleveland	March 4, 1885 – March 3, 1889	Thomas A. Hendricks	**21**
23	Benjamin Harrison	March 4, 1889 – March 3, 1893	Levi P. Morton	**22**
24	Grover Cleveland	March 4, 1893 – March 3, 1897	Adlai E. Stevenson	**23**
25	William McKinley	March 4, 1897 – March 3, 1901	Garret A. Hobart	**24**
	William McKinley*	March 4, 1901 – Sept. 14, 1901	Theodore Roosevelt	**25**
26	Theodore Roosevelt	Sept. 14, 1901 – March 3, 1905		
	Theodore Roosevelt	March 4, 1905 – March 3, 1909	Charles W. Fairbanks	**26**
27	William H. Taft	March 4, 1909 – March 3, 1913	James S. Sherman	**27**
28	Woodrow Wilson	March 4, 1913 – March 3, 1917	Thomas R. Marshall	**28**
	Woodrow Wilson	March 4, 1917 – March 3, 1921		

29 Warren G. Harding* .... March 4, 1921 – Aug. 2, 1923 .... Calvin Coolidge **29**
30 Calvin Coolidge .... Aug. 3, 1923 – March 3, 1925
Calvin Coolidge .... March 4, 1925 – March 3, 1929 .... Charles G. Dawes **30**
31 Herbert C. Hoover .... March 4, 1929 – March 3, 1933 .... Charles Curtis **31**
32 Franklin D. Roosevelt ...... March 4, 1933 – Jan. 20, 1937 .... John N. Garner **32**
Franklin D. Roosevelt .... Jan. 20, 1937 – Jan. 20, 1941 .... John N. Garner
Franklin D. Roosevelt .... Jan. 20, 1941 – Jan. 20, 1945 .... Henry A. Wallace **33**
Franklin D. Roosevelt* .... Jan. 20, 1945 – April 12, 1945 .... Harry S. Truman **34**
33 Harry S. Truman .... April 12, 1945 – Jan. 20, 1949
Harry S. Truman .... Jan. 20, 1949 – Jan. 20, 1953 .... Alben W. Barkley **35**
34 Dwight D. Eisenhower .... Jan. 20, 1953 – Jan. 20, 1957 .... Richard M. Nixon **36**
Dwight D. Eisenhower .... Jan. 20, 1957 – Jan. 20, 1961 .... Richard M. Nixon
35 John F. Kennedy* .... Jan. 20, 1961 – Nov. 22, 1963 .... Lyndon B. Johnson **37**
36 Lyndon B. Johnson .... Nov. 22, 1963 – Jan. 20, 1965
Lyndon B. Johnson .... Jan. 20, 1965 – Jan. 20, 1969 ... Hubert H. Humphrey **38**
37 Richard M. Nixon .... Jan. 20, 1969 – Jan. 20, 1973 .... Spiro T. Agnew **39**
Richard M. Nixon* .... Jan. 20, 1973 – Aug. 9, 1974 .... Gerald R. Ford **40**
38 Gerald R. Ford .... Aug. 9, 1974 – Jan. 20, 1977 .... Nelson A. Rockefeller **41**
39 James E. Carter .... Jan. 20, 1977 – Jan. 20, 1981 .... Walter Mondale **42**
40 Ronald W. Reagan .... Jan. 20, 1981 – Jan. 20, 1985 .... George H. W. Bush **43**
Ronald W. Reagan .... Jan. 20, 1985 – Jan. 20, 1989 .... George H. W. Bush
41 George H. W. Bush .... Jan. 20, 1989 – Jan. 20, 1993 .... J. Danforth Quayle **44**
42 William J. Clinton .... Jan. 20, 1993 – Jan. 20, 1997 .... Albert Gore Jr. **45**
William J. Clinton .... Jan. 20, 1997 – Jan 20, 2001 .... Albert Gore Jr.
43 George W. Bush .... Jan. 20, 2001 – Jan. 20, 2005 .... Richard B. Cheney **46**
George W. Bush .... Jan. 20, 2005 – .... Richard B. Cheney
(*Did not finish term)

Order of Presidential Succession

1. Vice president
2. Speaker of the House
3. President pro tempore of the Senate
4. Secretary of state
5. Secretary of the treasury
6. Secretary of defense
7. Attorney general
8. Secretary of the interior
9. Secretary of agriculture
10. Secretary of commerce
11. Secretary of labor
12. Secretary of health and human services
13. Secretary of housing and urban development
14. Secretary of transportation
15. Secretary of energy
16. Secretary of education
17. Secretary of veterans affairs
18. Secretary of homeland security

"When I want to understand what is happening today or try to decide what will happen tomorrow, I look back."

—Oliver Wendell Holmes

HISTORY

Thousands of years before this time, people migrated across a land bridge from Asia to North America. These people were the ancestors of the Native Americans, who eventually formed different tribal cultures based on the climate, the animals and plants, and the landforms in each particular region. As you'll see on the map below, the tribes lived in one of eight major regions. American history really begins with the Native Americans.

Native American Regions

Historical Time Line

The historical time line that follows will help you better understand history. The time line covers the period from 1500 to the present. You'll notice that the time line is divided into three main parts: **United States and World History, Science and Inventions,** and **Literature and Life.** You'll discover many interesting things on the time line—when watches were invented (1509), when paper money was first used in America (1690), and who developed the first pair of blue jeans (Levi Strauss in 1850).

1500	**1520**	**1540**	**1560**	**1580**

U.S. & WORLD HISTORY

1492 Columbus reaches the West Indies.

1513 Ponce de León explores Florida; Balboa reaches Pacific.

1519 Magellan begins three-year voyage around the world.

1521 Cortez defeats Aztecs and claims Mexico for Spain.

1540 Coronado explores American Southwest for fabled Seven Cities of Gold.

1559 Spanish colony of Pensacola, Florida, lasts two years.

1565 Spain settles St. Augustine, Florida, first permanent European colony.

1570 League of the Iroquois Nations formed.

1588 Englan defeat Spanis Armad rules t seas.

1 Br Parlian se crimina color

SCIENCE & INVENTIONS

1507 Book on surgery is developed.

1509 Watches are invented in Germany.

1530 Bottle corks are invented.

1531 Halley's comet appears.

1543 Copernicus's theory proclaims a sun-centered universe.

1545 French printer Garamond sets first type.

1558 Magnetic compass invented by John Dee.

1565 Pencils invented in England.

1585 Decimals introduced by Dutch mathematic

1590 First paper is use Engla

1 Thermom is inver

LITERATURE & LIFE

1500 Game of bingo developed.

1503 Pocket handkerchiefs are first used.

1512 Michelangelo completes the Sistine Chapel ceiling.

1516 Thomas Moore publishes *Utopia*.

1517 Reformation begins in Europe.

1532 Machiavelli's *The Prince* published.

1538 Mercator draws map with America on it.

1541 Michelangelo completes largest painting, "The Last Judgment."

1564 First horse-drawn coach used in England.

1580 First water closet designed in Bath, England.

1582 Pope Gregory X introduces the calendar still in use today.

Copper coins first m

U.S. POPULATION: (NATIVE AMERICAN)   (SPANISH)

approximately 1,100,000   1,021

1600	1620	1640	1660	1680	1700

1607
England establishes Jamestown, Virginia.

1619
House of Burgesses in Virginia establishes first representative government in colonies.

1654
First Jewish colonists settle in New Amsterdam.

1673
Marquette and Joliet explore Mississippi River for France.

1609
Henry Hudson explores the Hudson River and Great Lakes.

1620
Pilgrims found Plymouth Colony.

1634
Colony of Maryland is founded.

1636
Connecticut and Rhode Island colonies founded.

1664
The Dutch colony of New Netherlands becomes the English colony of New York.

1682
William Penn founds Pennsylvania.

1629
Massachusetts Bay Colony is established.

1608
Telescope is invented.

1641
First cotton factories open in England.

1668
Reflecting telescope invented by Sir Isaac Newton.

1682
Halley's comet is studied by Edmund Halley and named for him.

1609
Galileo makes first observations with telescope.

1643
Torricelli invents the barometer.

1671
First calculation machine invented.

1629
Human temperature measured by physician in Italy.

1650
First pendulum clocks developed by Huygens.

1687
Newton describes gravity and publishes *Principia Mathematica*.

1600
Shakespeare's plays are performed at Globe Theatre in London.

1636
Harvard is the first American college.

1685
First drinking fountain used in England.

1653
First postage stamps used in Paris.

1690
Paper money is used for the first time in America.

1622
January 1 accepted as beginning of the year (instead of March 25).

1640
First book printed in the colonies.

1605
European diseases kill many Native Americans (measles, TB, and smallpox).

1658
First colonial police force created in New Amsterdam.

1697
Tales of Mother Goose written by Charles Perrault.

(ENGLISH)

50	2,302	26,634	75,058	151,507

1700	**1710**	**1720**	**1730**	**1740**

U.S. & WORLD HISTORY

1700
France builds forts at Mackinac and Detroit to control fur trade.

1711
Tuscarora War fought in Carolina.

1718
France founds New Orleans.

1733
James Oglethorpe founds Georgia.

1747
Ohio Company formed to settle Ohio River Valley.

1705
Virginia Act establishes public education.

1733
Molasses Act places taxes on sugar and molasses.

Scotland

England

1707
England (English) and Scotland (Scots) unite and become Great Britain (British).

1735
Freedom of the press upheld during trial of John Peter Zenger.

SCIENCE & INVENTIONS

1701
Seed drill that plants seeds in a row is invented by Jethro Tull.

1712
Thomas Newcomen develops first practical steam engine.

1728
First dental drill is used by Pierre Fauchard.

1742
Benjamin Franklin invent efficient Frankl stove.

1716
First American lighthouse in Boston Harbor.

1732
Sedatives for operations discovered by Thomas Dover.

1735
Rubber found in South America.

1709
The pianoforte (first piano) is invented by Christofori Bartolommeo.

1738
First cuckoo clocks invented in Germany.

LITERATURE & LIFE

1700
The Selling of Joseph by Samuel Sewall is first protest of slavery.

1716
First hot-water home heating system developed.

1731
Ben Franklin begins first subscription library.

1741
Andrew Bedfor publishes first American mag

1701
Yale University is founded.

1719
Robinson Crusoe written by Daniel Defoe.

1733
Poor Richard's Almanac first printed.

1744
John New publishes children's *A Little P Pocket-Bo*

1704
First successful newspaper in colonies, *Boston News-Letter*, is published.

1726
Gulliver's Travels written by Jonathan Swift.

U.S. POPULATION: (ENGLISH COLONIES)

250,888	331,711	466,185	629,445	905,563

1750	1760	1770	1780	1790	1800

1750
The French and Indian War begins.

1750
Flatbed boats and Conestoga wagons begin moving settlers west.

1763
Britain defeats France in French and Indian War.

1765
Stamp Act tax imposed on colonies.

1770
Boston Massacre occurs.

1773
Boston Tea Party occurs.

1775
Revolutionary War begins.

1776
Declaration of Independence signed at Second Continental Congress on July 4.

1781
British surrender at Yorktown October 19.

1781
United colonies adopt Articles of Confederation as first government.

1787
U.S. Constitution is signed.

1789
George Washington elected president.

1789
French Revolution begins.

1794
U.S. Navy created.

1752
Benjamin Franklin discovers lightning is a form of electricity.

1758
Sextant for navigation is invented by John Bird.

1764
"Spinning jenny" for cotton is invented by James Hargreaves.

1770
First steam carriage is invented by French engineer Nicholas Cugnot.

1781
Uranus, first planet not known to ancient world, is discovered.

1783
First balloon is flown by Frenchmen Joseph and Jacques Montgolfier.

1793
Eli Whitney invents cotton gin that takes seeds out of cotton.

1798
Eli Whitney invents mass production.

1752
First general hospital is established in Philadelphia.

1764
Mozart writes first symphony.

1757
Streetlights are installed in Philadelphia.

1769
Venetian blinds are first used.

1776
Paine prints *Common Sense*.

1780
The waltz becomes popular dance.

1782
The American bald eagle is first used as U.S. symbol.

1786
First ice-cream company in America begins production.

1790
Official U.S. census begins.

1790
Supreme Court meets for the first time.

1795
Food canning is introduced.

1799
Rosetta Stone discovered in Egypt.

170,760	1,593,625	2,148,076	2,780,369	3,929,157

1800   1810   1820   1830   1840

U.S. & WORLD HISTORY

1800
Washington, D.C., becomes U.S. capital.

1803
Louisiana Purchase from France doubles U.S. size.

1804
Lewis & Clark explore Louisiana Territory and northwestern United States.

1812–1814
War of 1812 is fought between U.S. and Britain.

1819
U.S. acquires Florida from Spain.

1820
Missouri Compromise signed.

1821
Sierra Leone is established by U.S. for freed slaves.

1830
Indian Removal Act forces Native Americans west of Mississippi River.

1836
Texans defend the Alamo.

1838
Cherokee Nation forced west on "Trail of Tears."

1846
Mexican War begins.

1846
Britain cedes Oregon Country to U.S.

184[ ]
Go[ ] found California

SCIENCE & INVENTIONS

1800
The battery is invented by Count Volta.

1802
Steamboat is built by Robert Fulton.

1808
Chemical symbols are developed by Jöns Berzelius.

1816
Stethoscope invented by Reneé Laënnec.

1817
Erie Canal is begun.

1819
Hans Christian Oestad discovers electromagnetism.

1836
Samuel Morse invents telegraph.

1839
Bicycle is invented by Kirkpatrick Macmillan.

1841
Stapler is patented.

1844
Safety matches produced.

1846
Elias Howe invents sewing machine.

LITERATURE & LIFE

1800
Library of Congress is established.

1804
World population reaches 1 billion.

1806
Gas lighting used in homes.

1812
Army meat inspector, "Uncle Sam" Wilson, becomes U.S. symbol.

1814
Sequoyah creates Cherokee alphabet.

1816
Niépce takes first photograph.

1820
Rip Van Winkle is written by Washington Irving.

1827
Audubon's *Birds of America* is published.

1828
Webster's Dictionary is published.

1830
Mormon Church is founded.

1834
Louis Braille perfects a letter system for the blind.

1845
Thorea[ ] moves [ ] Walden Pond.

18[ ]
Safety p[ ] inven[ ]

18[ ]
Eliza[ ] Black[ ] beco[ ] first fe[ ] do[ ]

U.S. POPULATION:

| 5,308,080 | 7,240,102 | 9,638,453 | 12,860,702 | 17,063,353 |

1850   **1860**   **1870**   **1880**   **1890**   **1900**

1853
National Council of Colored People is founded.

1860
Abraham Lincoln elected 16th president of the U.S.

1861
Civil War begins at Fort Sumter.

1869
Coast-to-coast railroad is finished in Utah.

1863
Battle of Gettysburg.

1872
Yellowstone established as world's first national park.

1862
Merrimac-Monitor Battle.

1876
Custer is defeated at Little Big Horn.

1865
Lincoln is assassinated.

1880
President Garfield assassinated.

1889
Jane Addams founds Hull House in Chicago to help immigrants.

1891
Congress establishes the U.S. Court of Appeals.

1893
New Zealand grants women the right to vote.

1851
Isaac Singer produces sewing machine.

1860
Jean Lenoir builds internal combustion engine.

1874
Barbed wire introduced by Joseph Glidden.

1887
Radio waves produced by Hertz.

1865
Joseph Lister introduces antiseptic practices.

1876
Alexander Graham Bell invents telephone.

1893
First successful U.S. gasoline automobile is built.

1852
Elisha Otis invents elevator.

1877
Thomas Edison invents phonograph.

1866
Alfred Nobel invents dynamite.

1896
Marconi invents wireless radio.

1857
Atlantic cable is completed.

1879
Edison makes incandescent lightbulb.

1898
Curies discover radium.

1850
Levi Strauss produces blue jeans.

1864
Red Cross is established.

1876
National Baseball League established.

1883
Four U.S. time zones are established.

1892
"Pledge of Allegiance" is written by F. Bellamy.

1852
Uncle Tom's Cabin by Harriet Beecher Stowe strengthens anti-slavery movement.

1866
Hires introduces root beer.

1879
Ibsen's *Doll House* and Tolstoy's *War and Peace* published.

1895
Alfred Nobel establishes Nobel Peace Prize.

1888
John Dunlop invents pneumatic bicycle tires.

1873
Zipper invented by Whitcomb Judson.

1855
Alexander Parks produces first synthetic plastic.

1889
Roll film produced by George Eastman.

23,191,876   31,443,321   38,558,371   50,189,209   62,979,766

| **1900** | **1905** | **1910** | **1915** | **1920** |

U.S. & WORLD HISTORY

1900
First Olympics involving women held in Paris.

1903
Wrights' first successful airplane flight.

1909
National Association for the Advancement of Colored People (NAACP) is founded.

1912
Iceberg sinks RMS *Titanic*.

1913
Income Tax established.

1914
Panama Canal opens.

1914
World War I begins.

1917
United States enters World War I.

1917
Bolshevik Revolution starts in Russia.

1918
World War I ends.

1919
League of Nations founded.

1920
Prohibition begins.

1920
Women given vote.

SCIENCE & INVENTIONS

1900
Zeppelin airships developed.

1901
Walter Reed discovers yellow fever is carried by mosquitoes.

1904
New York City opens its subway system.

1905
Albert Einstein announces theory of relativity ($E=mc^2$) of time and space.

$$E=mc^2$$

1911
Greenwich Mean Time established for worldwide time zones.

1913
Henry Ford establishes assembly line for automobiles.

1915
Coast-to-coast telephone system established.

1921
Vaccine for tuberculosis is discovered.

1922
Insulin treatment for diabete discovered

1922
Farnsworth develops electron scanner for television.

LITERATURE & LIFE

1900
American Baseball League established.

1902
First bowl game, the Rose Bowl, is held.

1903
Call of the Wild written by Jack London.

1903
First World Series played.

1905
First nickelodeon movie theater established in Pittsburgh.

1907
Artists Picasso and Braque create cubism.

1913
Arthur Wynne invents the crossword puzzle.

1917
Doughnuts created for the soldier "doughboys" fighting in World War I.

KDKA

1920
First radio station, KDKA, founded in Pittsburgh.

1922
King Tut's tomb discovered

U.S. POPULATION:

| 76,212,168 | 92,228,496 | 106,021,537 |

925   **1930**   **1935**   **1940**   **1945**   **1950**

1927
Charles Lindbergh flies solo across the Atlantic Ocean.

1929
Wall Street stock market crashes.

1931
The 102-story Empire State Building completed as tallest in the world.

1933
President Franklin Roosevelt introduces New Deal to end Great Depression.

1933
Prohibition is repealed.

1939
Germany invades Poland to begin World War II.

1941
U.S. enters World War II after bombing of Pearl Harbor.

1948
Israel becomes a nation.

1945
World War II ends.

1945
United States joins the United Nations.

1949
Communists gain control in China.

926
John Baird demonstrates his television system.

1930
First analog computer invented by Vannevar Bush.

1928
Alexander Fleming develops penicillin.

1929
Clarence Birdseye introduces frozen foods.

1935
Radar is invented.

1938
Modern-type ballpoint pens developed.

1938
First photocopy machine produced.

1939
First jet aircraft flown.

1940
Enrico Fermi develops nuclear reactor.

1947
Edwin Land invents Polaroid camera.

1947
Bell Lab scientists invent transistor.

1947
Raytheon invents the microwave oven.

1927
World population reaches 2 billion.

1927
Wings wins first Academy Award for motion pictures.

1927
First "talking movie," *The Jazz Singer*, made.

1931
"The Star-Spangled Banner" becomes U.S. national anthem.

1937
First full-length animated film, *Snow White*, is made.

1938
Superman "Action Comics" created.

1938
"War of the Worlds" broadcast on radio.

1939
Steinbeck's *Grapes of Wrath* is published.

1947
Jackie Robinson becomes the first black major-league baseball player.

1947
Anne Frank's *Diary of a Young Girl* is published.

1950   **1955**   **1960**   **1965**   **1970**

U.S. & WORLD HISTORY

1950
United States enters Korean War.

1953
Korean War ends.

1955
Rosa Parks refuses to follow segregation rules on Montgomery bus.

1955
Martin Luther King Jr. begins organizing protests against black discrimination.

1959
Alaska becomes 49th state.

1959
Hawaii becomes 50th state.

1961
Alan Shepard becomes first U.S. astronaut in space.

1963
President John F. Kennedy assassinated in Dallas, Texas.

1965
U.S. combat troops sent to Vietnam.

1965
Civil Rights Freedom March from Selma to Montgomery, Alabama.

1968
Martin Luther King Jr. is assassinated.

1969
Neil Armstrong and Buzz Aldrin are first men to walk on moon.

1971
Eighteen-year-olds are given right to vote.

1
President Rich Nixon resig

SCIENCE & INVENTIONS

1951
Fluoridated water discovered to prevent tooth decay.

1953
Watson and Crick map the DNA molecule.

1954
Jonas Salk discovers polio vaccine.

1957
Russia's *Sputnik* satellite is launched.

1958
Stereo long-playing records are produced.

1960
First laser invented by Theodor Maiman.

1963
Cassette music tapes developed.

1967
Cholesterol discovered as a cause of heart disease.

1968
First U.S. heart transplant is performed by surgeon Norman Shumway.

1971
Space probe *Mariner* maps surface of Mar

1972
DDT is banned.

197
Sears Tower (1 stories) built Chicag

LITERATURE & LIFE

1950
Peanuts comic strip produced by Charles Schulz.

1951
Fifteen million American homes have television.

1953
Arthur Miller's *The Crucible* is published.

1957
Theodor "Dr. Seuss" Geisel's *Cat in the Hat* is published.

1957
Elvis Presley is the most popular rock 'n' roll musician in U.S.

1961
Peace Corps is established.

1962
Rachel Carson's *Silent Spring* is published.

1964
The Beatles appear on *The Ed Sullivan Show*.

1969
Sesame Street TV show begins.

1970
First Earth Day is observed.

1970
Dee Brown's *Bury My Heart At Wounded Knee* is published.

1974
World population reaches 4 billion.

U.S. POPULATION:

151,325,798   179,323,175   203,302,031

975   **1980**   **1985**   **1990**   **1995**

975
Vietnam War ends.

1978
Camp David Accords signed by Egypt & Israel.

1979
Iran seizes U.S. hostages.

1981
Sandra Day O'Connor becomes first woman on Supreme Court.

1981
U.S. hostages returned from Iran after 444 days.

1983
Sally Ride becomes first U.S. woman in space.

1986
Challenger spacecraft explodes, killing entire crew.

1989
Berlin Wall is torn down.

1991
Persian Gulf War begins.

1991
Restructuring of Soviet Union occurs.

1994
Nelson Mandela elected president of South Africa.

1994
NATO expands to include Eastern European countries.

1999
People prepare against "Y2K Millennium Bug."

975
VCRs introduced for home use.

1977
Apple Computers produces first personal computer.

1979
Three Mile Island nuclear power plant accident.

1981
Scientists identify AIDS.

1983
Pioneer 10 space probe passes Neptune and leaves solar system.

1984
Compact disks (CDs) developed.

1988
NASA reports greenhouse effect is caused by destruction of forests.

1991
World Wide Web is launched.

1991
Environmental Protection Agency cites growing danger of hole in Earth's ozone layer.

1993
Apple introduces laptop computer.

1995
U.S. and Russian spacecraft link up for first time.

1997
First adult sheep is cloned.

1999
Scientists map the first chromosome.

976
Alex Haley's *Roots* is published.

976
U.S. Bicentennial celebrated.

1977
Star Wars becomes one of the highest-grossing movies of all time.

1979
Yellow ribbons symbolize support for return of U.S. hostages in Iran.

1980
CNN introduces 24-hour news programming.

1986
Martin Luther King Day proclaimed national holiday.

1988
Widespread use of computers begins in schools.

1989
Amy Tan's *Joy Luck Club* is published.

1995
California bans smoking in all public places.

1998
Mark McGwire sets major league record with 70 home runs.

1999
World population reaches 6 billion.

1999
The U.S. women's soccer team wins the World Cup.

226,542,203   **248,709,873**

Index

A

A lot, 523
Abbreviations, 513–514
  Capitalization of, 509.3
  Common, 514
  Correspondence, 513.2
  Internet, 352
  Punctuation of, 487.2
  State, 513.2
Absolute phrase, 553
Abstract noun, 533.4
Academic writing,
    173–231
  Assessment rubric, 182,
    206, 231
Accept/except, 523
Acronyms, 515.1
ACT tests, 437–451
Action verbs, 539.3
Active voice, 541
Ad script, 159
Adapt/adopt, 523
Address,
  Abbreviations, 513–514
  Envelope, 327
  Inside, 322
  Punctuation of, 327,
    492.2
Adjective, 545
  Clause, 553.2
  Comma with, 489.2
  Compound, 497.3
  Forms, 545.2
  Predicate, 545.2
  Proper, 507.1, 545.1
  Specific, 117
Admit slips, 418
Adverb, 546
  Clause, 553.2
  Conjunctive, 95, 494.1
  Specific, 117
Affect/effect, 523
Agreement,
  Antecedent-pronoun, 81,
    535.2, 560
  Subject-verb, 81, 558–
    559
Aisle/isle, 523
Allegory, 253
Alliteration, 170
All right, 523
Allusion, 124, 253, 463
Allusion/illusion, 523
Already/all ready, 524
Altogether/all together, 524

Ambiguous wording, 89
Among/between, 524
Amount/number, 524
Analogy, 124, 253, 463
Analyses, 104, 247
Analysis, literary, 245–
    261
Analyzing information,
    474
Anapestic foot, 170
Anecdote, 103, 113, 124,
    175
*Annual/semiannual/
    biannual/perennial*,
    524
Antagonist, 253
Antecedent, 81, 535.2,
    560
Antithesis, 124, 256, 463
Antonym, 362, 387
Anyway, 524

APA documentation style,
    272, 309–319
  In-text citations,
    311–312
  Paper format, 310
  Reference entries,
    313–319

Apostrophe, 81, 498–499
Appeals, emotional, 202,
    477
Appendix, 365
Application, letter of, 326
Applying information, 473
Appositive,
  Phrase, 553
  Punctuation, 490.2
  Sentence combining, 95
Archaic words, 254
Argumentation,
  Definition, 127
  Essay of, 217–220
  Logical thinking, 477–
    478
Arrangement,
  Definition, 127
  Of details, 105–108
  Sentence, 555.1
Ascent/assent, 524

Assessment rubrics,
  Book review, 244
  Business writing, 328
  Descriptive writing, 138
  Expository essay, 182
  Fiction writing, 162
  Personal narrative and
    essay, 149
  Persuasive essay, 206
  Position paper, 231
  Research writing, 308

Assignments, completing,
    406
Assonance, 170
Atlases, 359
Audience, 127
Audience appeal strategy,
    46
Autobiography, 253
Auxiliary verbs, 539.2

B

Bad/badly, 524
Balance, 127
Balanced sentence, 555.1
Ballad, 170
Bandwagoning, 202, 477
Bar graphs, 369
Base/bass, 525
Base words, 389
"Be" verbs, 558.4
Beside/besides, 525
Between/among, 524
Biannual/biennial, 524
Bibliography, 268, 365
Bill of Rights, 605
Biographical dictionary,
    359
Biography, 253
Blank verse, 170
Board/bored, 525
Body, 100, 127, 322
Book,
  Parts of, 365
  Punctuation of titles,
    495.3, 502.2
  Reference, 359, 362–365
  Works-cited entries,
    287–290, 314–315
Book review, 239–244
  Assessment rubric, 244
  Mini-reviews, 243
  Sample, fiction, 241
  Sample, nonfiction, 242

Borrow/lend, 528
Brackets, 506
Brainstorming, 127
Brake/break, 525
Bring/take, 525
Broad generalization, 477
Brochures, 334–335

Business writing, 321–328
  Assessment rubric, 328
  Brochures, 334–335
  E-mail, 332–333
  Letters, 321–327
  Memos, 330–331
  Résumés, 336–337

C

Caesura, 170
Calendar, 6-year, 570
Call number, 357–358
Camera view, 259
Can/may, 525
Canto, 170
Capital/capitol, 525
Capitalization, 362,
  507–509
Card catalog, 356–358
  Computer, 354–355
Caricature, 253
Case,
  Nouns, 534.3
  Pronouns, 538.1
Case study, 127
Cause and effect,
  Essay, 188–190
  Organized by, 52, 108
  Organizer, 48, 379
  Pattern, 379
Cent/sent/scent, 525
Central idea, 127
Cereal/serial, 525
Character sketch, 254
Characterization, 254
Chart,
  5 W's, 49
  Sensory, 49
  Thinking guide, 122
Chat rooms, 351
Checklists,
  Editing and
    proofreading, 83
  Effective writing, 26
  Position statement, 223
  Revising, 72
  Thesis, 267
  Essentials of life, 44

Choice, pattern of fiction,
  153
Chord/cord, 525
Chose/choose, 526
Chronological order, 376
  Organized by, 52, 106
Circular reasoning, 202,
  478
Cite/sight/site, 531
Citing sources,
  APA style, 309–319
  MLA style, 281–298
Clarity, 66, 493.4
Classification, organized
  by, 52, 105
Classify, 424
Classroom skills, 401–406
Clauses, 553
  Dependent, 553.1–553.2
  Independent, 489.1,
    493.5, 553.1
  Introductory, 95, 491.1
  Nonrestrictive, 491.2
  Punctuation of, 489.1,
    493.5
  Restrictive, 491.2
Cliche, 92
Climax, 142, 254, 259
  Organized by, 52, 107
Closing paragraphs, 58,
  68, 178
Closing sentence, 100, 127
Clustering, 10, 43, 46, 265
Coarse/course, 526
Coherence, 127
Collecting strategies,
  details, 46–47
Collective noun, 511.5,
  533.5, 559.1
Colloquialism, 124, 254
Colon, 494.3–495.3, 500.3,
  508.3
Combining sentences, 95
Comedy, 254
Comma, 81, 489.1–493.4,
  500.3
  Splice, 81, 88
Commentary, personal,
  212–213
Commercials,
  Watching, 484
Common noun, 533.2
Comparative form,
  Adjectives, 545.2
  Adverbs, 546.2
Compare, 424
Compare-contrast, 52
  Essay, 191–193
  Pattern, 377

Comparisons, 104
  Incomplete, 89
  Metaphor, 114, 125, 256
  Organized by, 108
  Simile, 126, 256
Complement/compliment,
  526
Completeness, 66
Complex sentence, 554.2
Complimentary closing,
  322
Compound,
  Adjective, 497.3
  Noun, 499.1, 511.4
  Sentence, 81, 554.2
  Subject, 558.2
  Words, 495.4
Compound-complex
  sentence, 554.2
Computer,
  Catalog, 354–355
  E-mail, 332–333
  Publishing online, 38–39
  Terms, 577–580
  Writing with a, 27–32
Concessions, 201
Concluding paragraph, 58
Concrete noun, 533.3
Conditional sentence,
  118, 554.1
Conflict, 142, 159, 254
Conjunction, 548
Conjunctive adverb, 95,
  494.1
Connotation, 117
Consonance, 170
Constitution, U.S.,
  604–606
Construction, sentence,
  Shifts in, 94
  Unparallel, 94
Context, 254, 386, 387–388
Continual/continuous, 526
Contractions, 498.1
Contrast, 424
  Organized by, 52
Contrasted elements,
  489.3
Conventions, 22, 25, 83
Conversion tables, 574
Cooperating, group skills,
  403
Coordinating,
  conjunctions, 548.1
Copyright page, 365
Cord/chord, 525
Correction symbols,
  inside back cover

Correlative conjunctions, 95, 548.2
Counsel/council, 526
Couplet, 170
Course/coarse, 526
Creative
Thinking, 469–478
Writing, 151–171
Cumulative sentence, 97, 555.1
Cycle diagram, 49

D

Dactylic foot, 170
Dangling modifiers, 90
Dash, 504
Deadwood, 91
Decimal/fraction table, 582
Decimal point, 487.3
Declarative sentence, 554.1
Deductive reasoning, 127
Organized by, 107
Define, 424
Definition, 104
Diagram, 49
Essay of, 186–187
Delayed subject, 551.1, 558.3
Demonstrative pronoun, 535, 536.5
Denotation, 117
Denouement, 254, 259
Dependent clause, 553.1–553.2
Describe, 424
Description, 375
Definition, 127
Of a place, 137
Descriptive
Paragraph, 101
Topics, 123
Writing, 137
Desert/dessert, 526
Designing a page, 30

Details, 127
Arranging, 105–108
Collecting, 46–47
Connecting, 109
Five W's, 46
Levels of, 65, 176
Organizing, 52
Sensory, 49, 126
Understanding, 103–104

Dewey decimal system, 357
Diagonal, 503.3–503.4
Diagram, 371
Definition, 49
Line, 49, 176, 371
Picture, 371
Process, 49
Venn, 49, 377
Diagram (key word), 424
Diagramming sentences, 556–557
Dialogue, 254, 418
In plays, 159
Journals, 133
Punctuation of, 492.3
Response to literature, 236
Diary, 132
Diction, 254
Dictionary, using a, 362, 386
Sample page, 363
Didactic literature, 255
Die/dye, 526
Different from/different than, 526
Direct address, 493.2
Direct object, 86, 540.1
Direct question, 488.1
Direct quotation,
Punctuation of, 495.1, 500.3, 501
Using, 103, 175, 247, 278, 280
Directed dialoguing, 46
Directed writing, 46
Directories, 359
Discuss, 425
Distance table, 370
District or state writing tests, 433–436, 445–451
Division table, 582
Documentation in
research paper, 271
APA style, 309–319
MLA style, 281–298
Online sources, 294–296, 318
Double negative, 93
Drafting, 5, 12–13, 53–58
Drama, 158–161, 255
Dramatic
Irony, 257
Monologue, 159, 255
Scenarios, 418

E

Editing, 6, 18–19, 79–83
Checklist, 83
Definition, 127
Editorial, 210–211
Correction, 506.3
Effect/affect, 523
Effective writing, traits of, 21–26
Either/or thinking, 202, 478
Electronic source documentation,
APA style, 318
MLA style, 294–296
Elements, periodic table of, 575
Ellipsis, 505
E-mail, 332–333
Emigrate/immigrate, 527
Empathy, 255
Emphasis, 127, 493.4, 494.5, 504.5
English language, history of, 566–567
Enjambment, 170
Ensure/insure, 528
Entrance and exit exams, 437–451
Envelopes, addressing, 327
Epic, 255
Epigram, 255
Epigraph, 365
Epiphany, 255
Epitaph, 255
Epithet, 255

Essay,
Argumentation, 217–220
Cause and effect, 188–190
Comparison-contrast, 191–193
Definition, 127, 186–187, 255
Descriptive, 135–138
Expository, 173–181
Opposing ideas, 194–196
Personal, 147–148
Persuasive, 197–205
Pet peeve, 208–209
Problem-solution, 190, 214–216
Process, 184–185
Response to, 237
Strategies, 119

Essay test, taking, 424–428
Essentials of life checklist, 44, 134
Etymology, 362, 386
Euphemism, 92
Evaluate, 425
Information, 476
Evaluation collection grid, 48
Evidence, using, 477–478
Exaggeration, 124, 255
Examples, 103
Except/accept, 523
Exclamation point, 488.4, 500.3, 503.1
Exclamatory sentence, 118, 488.4, 554.1
Exit slips, 418
Exit and entrance exams, 437–451
Expanding sentences, 97
Explain, 425
Explanations, 104
Exposition, 255, 259
Paragraph, 101
Topics, 123
Writing, 127
Expository essay, 173–196
Extended definition, 127
Personal narrative, 145–146

F

Fable, 255
Facts, 103, 175
Fair language, 561–563
Fallacies of thinking, 202, 477–478
Falling action, 255, 259
Farce, 255
Farther/further, 526
Feminine gender, 534.2, 538.2, 560.2, 562.1
Fewer/less, 527
Fiction,
Assessment rubric, 162
Book, review of, 241
Creative process, 151–171
Fictionalized journal, 157
Patterns of, 153
Play, 158–161
Reading, 382–383
Short story, 152–156
Fictionalized journal entry, 157

Figurative language, 127, 255
Figure of speech, 256
First draft, 5, 12–13, 53–58
First thoughts, 418
First words, 508.1
Five W's, 46, 49
Flair/flare, 527
Flashback, 124, 257
Flowery language, 91
Focus, 65–66, 127
Foil, 257
Foot (poetic), 170
Footnote, 365
Foreshadowing, 125, 257
Formal English, 70
Forms,
Adjectives, 545.2
Adverbs, 546.2
Forms of writing, survey, 129
Fraction/decimal table, 582
Fraction, punctuation, 496.1
Fragment sentence, 87
Free verse, 166, 170
Freewriting, 43, 46, 127
Tips, 45
Further/farther, 526
Future perfect tense, 543
Future tense, 542.3

G

Gender, 534.2, 538.2, 560.2
Gender references, 562–563
Generalization, 127, 202, 477
Genre, 257
Geography, 589–602
Gerund, 540.2
Gerund phrase, 552.1
Glossary, 365
Good/well, 527
Gothic novel, 257
Government, 603–608
Grammar, 127
Graphic organizers, 48–49, 375–379
Graphs, 368–369
Group advising strategies, 76–77
Group skills, 73–78, 402–404
Writing, 74

Guidelines for writing,
Book reviews, 240
Business letters, 324
Definition, 186
Descriptive, 136
Expository, 174–179, 184, 186, 188, 191, 194
Literary analysis, 246
Personal essay, 147
Personal narrative, 140–142
Persuasive, 198–203, 208, 210, 212, 214, 217–218
Play, 158
Poetry, 164–165
Position paper, 222–227
Research paper, 265–272
Response to literature, 234
Story, 152
Writing and thinking, 470
Workplace, 330, 332, 334, 336

H

Haiku, 170
Half-truths, 202, 478
Heal/heel, 527
Healthful/healthy, 527
Hear/here, 527
Heard/herd, 527
Historical time line, 609–620

History, writing in,
Cause-and-effect paragraph, 379
Comparison/contrast, 377
E-mail, 333
Expository essay, 55, 376
Expository paragraph, 472, 473, 474, 476
Memo, 331
Narrative paragraph, 475
Research report, 31–32
Response to literature, 450
Summary, 104

Hole/whole, 527
How-to writing, 418
Hyperbole, 125, 256
Hyphen, 495.4–497.3

I

Iambic foot, 170
Ideas (writing trait), 22, 23, 65–66
Idiom, 127
Idle/idol, 527
Illusion/allusion, 523
Illustrate, 425
Illustration, 127, 362
  Organized by, 52, 107
Imagery, 257
Imaginary dialogue, 159, 236, 418
Immigrate/emigrate, 527
Imperative mood, 544.1
Imperative sentence, 118, 487.1, 554.1
Imply/infer, 527
Impressionism, 257
Incomplete comparison, 89
Indefinite pronouns, 499.2, 535, 536.3, 559.2
Indefinite reference, 89
Independent clause, 553.1
  Punctuation of, 489.1, 493.5
Index, 365, 621–631
Indicative mood, 544.1
Indirect object, 86, 540.1
Indirect question, 488.1
Inductive reasoning, 107, 127, *see also* Climax
Inferences, 247
Infinitive, 540.3
Infinitive phrase, 552.1
Informal English, 70
Information,
  Evaluating, 341
  Interviews, 346
  Packages, 342
  Places, 343
  Primary sources, 269, 297–298, 340
  Secondary sources, 340
  Surveys, 344–345
  Types of, 175, 345
Informative letter, 325
Initialisms, 515.2–515.3
Initials, punctuation of, 487.2, 493.3
Initiation, pattern of fiction, 153
Insecurity, 120
Inside address, 322
Instant versions, 418
Insure/ensure, 528

Intensive pronoun, 535
Interactive report, 467
Interjection, 548
  Punctuation of, 492.4
Internet, using the, 347–352, 485
  Citing sources, 294–296
  Navigation tips, 351
  Publishing, 38–39
  Terms, 577–580
Interpretation 247
Interrogative
  Pronoun, 535, 536.4
  Sentence, 118, 554.1
Interruptions,
  punctuation of, 492.5, 504.4
Interviews, conducting, 47, 346
In-text citations, 282–285, 311–312
Intransitive verb, 539.3
Introduction,
  Book, 365
  Speech, 456
Introductory clause, 95, 491.1
Introductory phrase, 81, 95, 490.4, 504.2
Inverted sentence, 86, 127
Irony, 125, 257, 464
Irregular plurals, 511.1
Irregular verbs, 543
I-Search paper, 264
Isle/aisle, 523
Italics, 502
It's/its, 81, 528

J

Jargon, 70, 91, 254

Journal,
  Definition, 128
  Dialogue, 133
  Diary, 132
  Fictionalized entry, 157
  Learning logs, 133, 416–417
  Responding to literature, 237–238
  Response, 133
  Travel log, 133

Journal writing, 43, 131–134
Justify, 425
Juxtaposition, 118, 125

K

Key word, 95
  In essay tests, 424–425
Keyword searching, 355

L

Language,
  Nonstandard, 93
  Parts of speech, 533–549
  Sign, 565
  Slanted, 202, 478
  Usage, 550–563
Later/latter, 528
Lay/lie, 528
Lead/led, 528
Learn/teach, 528
Learning logs, 133, 416–417
Leave/let, 528
Lend/borrow, 528
Less/fewer, 527
Letters,
  Business, 321–328
  To an author, 234–235
  Unsent, 134, 419
Letters, as letters, 509.1, 511.2
  Italic, 502.3
  Plural, 498.2
Library, using the, 353–365
  Card catalog, 356–358
  Computer catalog, 354–355
  Dictionary, 362–363
  Readers' Guide, 360–361
  Reference works, 359
  Thesaurus, 364
Like/as, 528
Limiting the subject, 128
Line break, 170
Line diagram, 49, 176, 371
Line graph, 368
Linking verb, 86, 539.1
Listening skills, 74, 402, 408–409
Listing, 43, 119, 495.2
Literal, 128
Literary analysis, 245–261
Literary terms, 253–261
Literature, personal response to, 233–238
Local color, 125, 257
Location, order of, organized by, 52, 105
Logic, 128

Logical fallacies, 202, 477–478
Loose sentence, 555.1
Lyric, 171

M

Malapropism, 258
Manual alphabet, 565
Manuscript speech, 460–461
Mapping, reading strategy, 375
Maps, 372, 589–602
Margins, 30
Masculine gender, 534.2, 538.2, 560.2, 562.1
Matching test, 429
Mathematics, 581–588
   Metrics, 573–574
   Multiplication/division table, 582
   Symbols, 581
   Terms, 583–588
   Weights/measures, 571–572
May/can, 525
Measures/weights, 571–572
Mechanics of writing, 507–522
Medal/meddle, 528
Melodrama, 258
Memoir, 258
Memos, writing, 330–331
Message boards, 351
Metal/medal, 529
Metaphor, 125, 256
   Using, 114
Meter, 171
Metonymy, 256
Metric system, 573–574
Miner/minor, 529
Middle paragraphs, 56–58
Misplaced modifier, 90

MLA research paper, 299–307
   Documentation style, 272, 281–298
   Parenthetical references, 282–285
   Works-cited list, 286–298

Modeling sentences, 96
Modifier, 128

Modifiers,
   Dangling, 90
   Misplaced, 90
Money, 512.4
Mood, 258
   Grammar, 544.1
Moral, 258
Moral/morale, 529
Motif, 258
Multimedia reports,
   Interactive report, 467
   Presentation, 466
   Storyboard, 468
Multimedia sources, citing, 297–298
Multiple-choice test, 429, 438–444
Multiplication/division table, 582
Myth, 258

N

Narration, 128, 258
Narrative,
   Paragraph, 102
   Personal, 128, 139–149
   Topics, 123
Narrator, 258
Naturalism, 258
Negative definition, 464
Negative, double, 93
Netiquette, 352
Neuter gender, 534.2, 538.2, 560.2
News, television, watching, 480–481
Nominative case,
   Noun, 534.3
   Pronoun, 538.1
Nonfiction
   Book, review of, 242
   Patterns of, 375–379
   Reading strategies, 380–381
Nonrestrictive phrase/clause, 81, 491.2
Nonstandard language, 93
Note card, 268
Note taking, 410–414
   Guide, 412–413
   Quick guide, 414
   Paraphrasing, 420
   Reading, 375–379, 412
   Research paper, 47, 268
   Shorthand system, 414
   Skills, 410–411

Noun, 533–534
   Abstract, 533.4
   Case, 534.3
   Clause, 553.2
   Collective, 511.5, 533.5, 559.1
   Common, 533.2
   Compound, 499.1, 511.4
   Concrete, 533.3
   Gender, 534.2
   Number of, 534.1
   Plural, 510–511
   Possessive, 498.3–498.4
   Proper, 507.1, 533.1
   Specific, 116
Noun clause, 553.2
Novel, 258
   Literary analysis of, 248–250
   Response to, 237
Novella, 258
Number,
   Agreement in, 560.1
   Noun, 534.1
   Pronoun, 537.1
   Shift in, 94
   Verb, 542.1
Number/amount, 524
Numbers, 512
   Compound, 496.1
   Punctuation of, 493.1, 494.4, 496.1, 496.3, 498.2, 502.3
   Use of, 512
Numerical prefixes, 391
Nutshelling, 418

O

OAQS strategy, 77
Object,
   Complement, 86
   Of preposition, 534.3, 538.1, 547
   Of verb, 86, 534.3, 538.1, 540.1
   Verbals, 540.2–540.4
Objective, 128
Objective case, 534.3
Objective tests, 429
Observation, 128
Online publishing, 38–39
Online sources, 348–350
   Research paper entries, 294–296, 318
Onomatopoeia, 171
Open-ended sentences, 134
Openings, 55, 67

Opinion statement, 199
Opposing ideas, essay of, 194–196
Order of location, 52, 105
Organization, methods of, 52, 105–108
Organization (writing trait), 22, 23, 67–68
Organizations, capitalization of, 509.1–509.2
Organizers, graphic, 48–49, 375–379
Outline (key word), 425
Outlines,
Note taking, 412
Picture, 419
Position paper, 225
Sentence, 177
Speeches, 458
Topic, 177
Oversimplification, 202, 478
Overstatement, 125
Overview, 128
Oxymoron, 125, 258

P

Page design, on computer, 30
Parable, 258
Paradox, 126, 258

Paragraph,
Closing, 58, 68, 178
Details, 103–104
Methods of organizing details, 52, 105–108
Middle, 56–58
Opening, 55, 67, 178
Parts of, 100
Strategies, 119
Topic sentence, 100, 119
Transitions in, 109
Types of, 101–102
Writing, 99–109
Paragraph types,
Descriptive, 101
Expository, 101
Narrative, 102
Persuasive, 102

Parallel structure, 94, 464
Parallelism, 126
Paraphrase, 175, 230, 247, 420
Parentheses, 503.1–503.2, 508.2

Parenthetical
Elements, 490.1, 504.3
References, *see* In-text citations
Parliamentary procedure, 569
Parody, 258
Participial phrase, 95, 552.1
Participle, 540.4
Parts of speech, 533–549
In dictionary, 362–363
Passive voice, 120, 541.1
Past/passed, 529
Past perfect tense, 543
Past tense, 542.3
Pathetic fallacy, 258
Pathos, 259
Patterns
Of fiction, 153
Of nonfiction, 375–379
Pause, 505.3
Peace/piece, 529
Peak/peek/pique, 529
Pedal/peddle/petal, 529
Peer response sheet, 78
Perennial/annual, 524
Period, 487, 500.3
Periodic sentence, 555.1
Periodic table of elements, 575
Periodicals,
Readers' Guide, 360–361
Works-cited entries, 291–293, 316–317
Person,
Of pronoun, 537.2
Of verb, 542.2
Personal
Commentary, 212–213
Essay, 147–148
Narrative, 128, 139–148
Sources, 298
Personal/personnel, 529
Personal pronouns, 535, 536.1
Personification, 126, 256
Persuasion, 128
Persuasive
Essay, 197–205
Paragraph, 102
Topics, 123
Writing, 197–220
Pet peeve, 208–209
Phrases, 81, 95, 552–553
Punctuation of 490.4, 491.2
Picaresque novel, 259
Picture diagram, 371
Picture outlines, 419

Pie graph, 368
Piece/peace, 539
Plagiarism, 230, 275–277
Plain/plane, 529
Planets, 576
Planning skills, 405
Play, response to, 237
Playwriting, 158–161
Plot, 142, 259
Plot line, 259
Plurals,
Letter, number, sign, word, 498.2, 511.2
Nouns, 510–511
Pronouns, 537.1
Spelling, 510–511
Verbs, 542.1
Poem,
Free-verse, 166
Prose, 167
Rap, 169
Tanka, 167
Tercet, 168
Poetic
Justice, 259
License, 128
Poetry,
Punctuation of, 503.4
Reading, 384
Terms, 170–171
Writing, 163–171
Point of view, 128, 259
Pointed questions, 419
Pore/pour/poor, 530
Portfolio, 35
Position paper, 221–231
Positive form,
Adjectives, 545.2
Adverbs, 546.2
Possessive case, 534.3, 538.1
Possessives, forming, 498.3–498.4
Précis, *see* Summary
Predicate adjective, 86, 545.1
Predicate noun, 86
Predicate of a sentence, 551.2–551.3
Predicting, 419
Preface, 365
Prefixes, 389, 390–391, 497.1–497.2
Premise, 128
Preposition, 547
Prepositional phrase, 547.1, 553
Present perfect tense, 543
Present tense, 542.3

Presentation,
multimedia, 465–468
Presidents, United States,
607–608
Prewriting, 5, 10–11,
41–52, 136, 140, 164,
174, 184, 186, 188,
191, 194, 198, 208,
210, 212, 214, 217,
222, 234, 240, 246,
265–269
Primary sources, 269,
297–298, 340
Principal/principle, 530
Problem-solution
Essay, 190, 214–216
Organized by, 52
Web, 48
Process, 128
Diagram, 49
Explaining a, 106,
184–185
Process of writing, 3–20
Profanity, 254
Profile, 128
Prompts, writing, 435–
436, 445–451
Pronoun, 535–538
Antecedent, 81, 535.2,
560
Case, 538.1
Classes, 535
Demonstrative, 536.5
Gender, 538.2
Indefinite, 499.2, 536.3,
559.2
Intensive, 535
Interrogative, 536.4
Number, 537.1
Person, 537.2
Personal, 536.1
Reflexive, 535
Relative, 95, 535, 536.2,
559.3
Types, 535.1
Proofreader's Guide,
487–563
Proofreading and editing,
6, 18–19, 79–83
Checklist, 83
Proper adjective, 507.1,
545.1
Proper noun, 507.1, 533.1
Prose, 128
Prose poem, 167
Protagonist, 259
Prove, 425
Pseudonym, 260
Publishing, 6, 20, 33–39

Pun, 126
Punctuation, 487–506
Marks, 506
Purpose, 128
Pyrrhic foot, 170

Q

Qualifiers, 199
Quest pattern of fiction,
153, 260
Question mark, 488.1–
488.3, 500.3, 503.1
Questioning, 47

Quick guides,
Building your
vocabulary, 386
Drafting, 54
Editing and
proofreading, 80
Marking quoted
material, 501
Note-taking shorthand,
414
Parts of speech, 549
Prewriting, 42
Revising, 60
Spelling rules, 516
Traits of writing, 22
Using an ellipsis, 505

Quiet/quit/quite, 530
Quotation marks, 500–501
Quotation, punctuation of,
495.1
Quotations, use of, 58,
103, 175, 247, 278,
280, 464
Quote/quotation, 530

R

Rap poem, 169
Readers' Guide, 360
Sample page, 361
Reading,
Context clues, 387–388
Diagrams, 371
Fiction, 382–383
Graphics, 367–372
Maps, 372
Nonfiction, 375–381
Poetry, 384
Prefix, suffix, root,
389–399
Schedules, tables, 370
SQ3R, 380
Strategies, 374
Real/very/really, 530

Realism, 260
Reasoning,
Circular, 202
Deductive, 107
Inductive, 107
Recalling information, 471
Redundancy, 70
Reference books, 359–365
Reference, indefinite, 89
Reference list, 310,
313–319
Reflective writing, *see*
Persuasive writing
Reflexive pronoun, 535
Refrain, 171
Relative pronoun, 95, 535,
536.2, 559.3
Religious words, 508.5
Reminiscence, 128, *see*
also Personal
Renaissance, 260
Repetition, 70, 115, 171,
see also Parallel
structure
Report, 128
Multimedia, 465–468

Research paper, 263–319
APA style, 309–319
Assessment rubric, 308
Giving credit, 273–280
MLA style, 281–298
Sample, 299–307
Thesis statement,
266–267
Writing the, 263–272

Researching on the
Internet, 348–350
Resolution, 142, 259, 260
Responding in a group,
404
Response journal, 133
Restrictive phrase/
clause, 491.2
Résumé writing, 336–337
Review, 425
Book, 239–244
Video, 482–483

Revising, 6, 14–17, 59–72
Checklist, 72
For ideas, 65–66
For organization, 67–68
For sentence fluency, 71
For voice, 69
For word choice, 70
Guidelines, 61
Quick guide, 60

Revision, 128, *see also*
Proofreader's Guide
Rhetorical question, 464
Rhyme, 171
Rhythm, 171
Right/write/wright/rite,
530
Ring/wring, 530
Rising action, 259, 260
Role-playing, 419
Romanticism, 260
Roots of words, 389, 393
Rubrics, see
Assessment rubrics

S

Salutation, 322, 494.3
Sarcasm, 260
SAT tests, 437–451
Satire, 261
Scene/seen, 530

Science, writing in,
Cause-and-effect
organization, 108
Description, 375
Essay exam, 442
Explaining a process,
106
Expository essay, 9–20,
276
Graphics, 368–372
Illustration, 107
Learning log, 417
MLA research paper,
301–307
Personal summary, 419
Process essay, 185
Summary, 422
Test taking, 426
Viewing skills, 483

Seam/seem, 530
Search
Engine, 348, 349
Keyword, 355
Secondary sources, 340
Selecting a subject, 43–45
Sample topics, 44, 123
Semiannual/biannual, 524
Semicolon, 95, 493.5–
494.2, 500.3
Sensory details, 126
Chart, 49
Sent/scent/cent, 525

Sentence,
Arrangement, 555.1
Closing, 100, 127
Combining, 95
Diagramming, 556–557
Expanding, 97
Fragments, 87
Inverted, 86, 127
Kinds, 554.1
Modeling, 96
Open-ended, 134
Parts of, 86, 550–553
Patterns, 86
Punctuation of, 487.1,
488
Run-ons, 88
Strategies, 118
Topic, 100
Types, 554.2
Variety, 554–555
Writing clear, 89–90
Writing tips, 98
Sentence fluency (writing
trait), 22, 25, 71
Sentence outline, 177
Sentence problems,
87–94
Serial/cereal, 525
Series, 81, 95, 490.3,
496.2, 504.2
Set/sit, 530
Setting, 142, 261, 387
Sexism, avoiding, 562.1
Shared possession, 499.4
Shift in construction, 94
Short story, 261
Response to, 237
Sample, 154–156
Writing, 152–153
Showing versus telling,
113
Sight/cite/site, 531
Sign language, 565
Signs, plural of, 498.2
Simile, 126, 256
Simple sentence, 554.2
Singular, *see* Number *and*
Plurals
Singular subject, 558.1
Sit/set, 530
Slang, 126, 254
Slanted language, 202,
478
Slash (diagonal), 503.3–
503.4
Slice of life, 261

Social studies, writing in,
Brochure, 335
Cause-and-effect essay,
189–190
Classification, 105
Editorial, 211
Essay of comparison, 192
Essay of opposing ideas,
195–196
Expository essay, 180
Expository paragraph,
101
Extended personal
narrative, 145–148
Narrative paragraph,
102
Persuasive essay, 204–
205
Persuasive paragraph,
102
Position paper, 228–230
Problem/solution essay,
215–216

Solar system, 576
Sole/soul, 531
Soliloquy, 261
Sonnet, 171
Sources, 274
Avoiding plagiarism,
230, 275–277
Citing, 282–298, 309–
319
Electronic documenting,
294–296, 318–319,
Forms of documenting,
282–298, 311–319
Internet, 264, 294–296,
318, 348–350, 361
Paraphrases, 278–279
Primary, 269, 297, 340
Secondary, 340
Specific word choice,
116–117
Speech skills, 453–464
Copy-marking symbols,
462
Delivery, 462
Manuscript, 460–461
Outline, 458
Planning, 454–455
Preparing the script,
458–459
Rehearsing, 462
Speech sample, 460–461
Style, 463–464
Writing a, 456–457

Spelling,
Commonly misspelled words, 517–521
Dictionary, 362–363
Numbers, 512
Plurals of words, 510–511
Rules, 516
Study guide, 522
Spondaic foot, 170
SQ3R, 380
Stacked bar graph, 369
Stage directions, 159
Standardized tests, 431–432
Stanza, 171
State (key word), 425
State or district writing tests, 433–436, 445–451
States, abbreviations, 513.2
Stationary/stationery, 531
Statistics, 175
Steal/steel, 531
Stereotype, 261
Stop 'n' write, 419
Story starters, 134
Story writing, 152–157
Storyboard, 468
Strategies,
Collecting, 46–47
Essay, 119
Group-advising, 76–77
Listening, 408–409
Paragraph, 119
Reading, 374
Selecting, 43–45
Sentence, 118
Stream of consciousness, 261
Study guidelines,
Listening skills, 408–409
Note-taking skills, 410–414
Taking a test, 423–436
Writing groups, 73–78
Study skills, 410–414
Style, 261
Ailments, 120
Checking for, 16–17
In speeches, 463–464
Key reminders, 112
Writing with, 111–120
Subject,
Limiting, 128
Selecting, 43–45

Subject of a sentence, 86, 550.1
Delayed, 551.1
Understood, 551.3
Subject-verb agreement, 81, 558–559
Subjective, 128
Subjunctive mood, 544.1
Submitting a manuscript, 36–38
Subordinating conjunction, 548.3
Substandard language, *see* Nonstandard language
Suffixes, 389, 392, 497.1–497.2
Summarize (key word), 425
Summary, 104, 278
Personal, 419
Writing a, 421–422
Superlative form,
Adjectives, 545.2
Adverbs, 546.2
Support, in essays, 224
Supporting your thesis, 56
Surveys, conducting, 344–345
Syllabication, 362, 496.4
Symbol, 126, 261
Symbols,
Correction, inside cover
Math, 581
Plurals of, 498.2, 511.2
Synecdoche, 126
Synonym, 362, 387
Syntax, 128
Synthesizing information, 475

T

Table of contents, iv–ix, 365
Table of elements, 575
Table organizer, 378
Tables, reading, 370
Take/bring, 525
Teach/learn, 528
Television, viewing 480–484
Tense of verbs, 542.3, 543
Tercet, 168

Test taking, 423–451
District/state writing tests, 433–436, 445–451
Essay, 424–428
Exit and entrance exams, 437–451
Objective, 429
Standardized, 431–432
Tips, 430, 432
Writing, 433–436, 445–451

Testimonial, 202, 478
Than/then, 531
That/which, 491.2, 532
Their/there/they're, 531
Theme, 128, 261
Thesaurus, 364, 386
Thesis statement, 128
Forming, 11, 51
Supporting, 56
Tips for writing, 266–267
Thinking,
And writing guidelines, 470
And writing moves, 122
Circular, 478
Fallacies of, 202, 477–478
Types of, 471
Threw/through, 531
Time,
Management, 405
Organized by, 52, 106
Punctuation of, 494.4, 499.3, 512.4
Time line, 48, 140, 376
Historical, 609–620
Timed writings, 434–436
Revising, 61
Title page, 365
Titles,
Capitalization, 508.6, 509.4, 509.5
Punctuation, 495.3, 500.1, 502.2
To/too/two, 531
Tone, 128, 261, 387
Topic outline, 177
Topic sentence, 100, 119
Topics,
Sample, 123
Selecting, 43–45
Total effect, 261
Traffic signs, 568
Tragedy, 261

Traits of effective writing, 21–26
Transcendentalism, 261
Transitions, 109, 128
Transitive verb, 539.3, 540.1
Trite expression, 91
Trochaic, 170
True/false test, 429

U

Underlining, as italics, 502
Understanding information, 472
Understatement, 126, 256
Understood subject and predicate, 551.3
Union, pattern of fiction, 153
Unity, 128
Universal, 128
Unparallel construction, 94
Unsent letters, 134, 419
Usage, 128
Using the handbook, iii
Using the right word, 523–532

V

Vain/vane/vein, 531
Variety of sentence structure, 554–555
Vary/very, 532
Venn diagram, 49, 377
Verb, 86, 539–544
  Action, 539.3
  Auxiliary, 539.2
  Intransitive, 539.3
  Irregular, 543
  Linking, 86, 539.1
  Mood of, 544
  Number of, 542.1
  Person of, 542.2
  Phrase, 552.1
  Tense of, 542.3
  Transitive, 539.3, 540.1
  Understood, 551.3
  Vivid, 116
  Voice of, 541.1
Verbal irony, 257
Verbals, 540.2–540.4, 552.1
Verse, 171
Very/real/really, 530

Vial/vile, 532
Viewing skills, 479–485
  Commercials, 484
  Television news, 480
  Video review, 482–483
  Web sites, 485
Vivid
  Details, 128
  Verbs, 116
Vocabulary skills, 385–399
Voice, 128
  Active, 541
  Passive, 541
Voice (writing trait), 22, 24, 69
Vulgarity, 254

W

Waist/waste, 532
Wait/weight, 532
Ware/wear/where, 532
Way/weigh, 532
Weather/whether, 532
Web
  Browser, 348, 350, 351
  Page, 39, 350
  Sites, viewing, 348, 485
Weights and measures, 571–572
Well/good, 527
Which/that, 491.2, 532
Who/whom, 532
Whole/hole, 527
Who's/whose, 532
Word choice (writing trait), 22, 24, 26
Word parts, 389–399
Wordiness, 92
Workplace writing, 129, 321–337
  Brochures, 334–335
  Business letters, 321–328
  E-mail, 332–333
  Memos, 330–331
  Résumés, 336–337
Works-cited list, MLA, 286, 307
  Entries, 287–298
Wring/ring, 530
Write Source web site, iii, 38
Write/wright/right/rite, 530
Writer's resource, 121–129

Writing
  A cause-effect essay, 188–190
  A comparison-contrast essay, 191–193
  A definition essay, 186–187
  A position paper, 221–231
  A summary, 421–422
  About a place, 135–138
  About literature, 129, 234–261
  An explanation, 129
  Essays, 173–196
  Paragraphs, 99–109
  Plays, 158–162
  Poetry, 163–171
  Research papers, 263–319
  Sentences, 85–98
  Stories, 152–157
  Techniques, 124–126
  Terms, 127–128
  To explain, 129
  To learn, 415–422
  To persuade, 129, 197–231
  Topics, 123
  With a computer, 27–32

Writing process, 3–20
  Drafting, 5, 12, 53
  Editing and proofreading, 6, 18, 79
  Group advising, 73–78
  Prewriting, 5, 10–11, 41–52
  Publishing, 6, 20, 33–39
  Revising, 6, 14–17, 59–72
  Selecting strategies, 43
Writing prompts, 424, 435–436, 445–451
Writing tests, 433, 445
  Assessing, 435
  Timed writing, 61, 434
  Writing prompts, 435–436, 445–451
Writing to learn, 415–422
  Activities, 418–419
  Learning log, 133, 416
  Paraphrase, 420
  Summary, 421–422

Y

Your/you're, 532